WITNESS TO AMERICA

Also by Douglas Brinkley

The Wilderness Warrior: Theodore Roosevelt and the Crusade for America
The Reagan Diaries (editor)
The Great Deluge: Hurricane Katrina, New Orleans,
 and the Mississippi Gulf Coast
The Boys of Pointe du Hoc: Ronald Reagan, D-Day,
 and the U.S. Army 2nd Ranger Battalion
Tour of Duty: John Kerry and the Vietnam War
Windblown World: The Journals of Jack Kerouac, 1947–1954 (editor)
Wheels for the World: Henry Ford, His Company,
 and a Century of Progress, 1903–2003
The Mississippi and the Making of a Nation (with Stephen E. Ambrose)
American Heritage History of the United States
The Western Paradox: Bernard DeVoto Conservation Reader
 (editor, with Patricia Nelson Limerick)
Rosa Parks
The Unfinished Presidency: Jimmy Carter's Journey Beyond the White House
John F. Kennedy and Europe (editor)
Rise to Globalism: American Foreign Policy since 1939, Eighth Edition
 (with Stephen E. Ambrose)
The Majic Bus: An American Odyssey
Dean Acheson: The Cold War Years, 1953–1971
Driven Patriot: The Life and Times of James Forrestal
 (with Townsend Hoopes)
FDR and the Creation of the U.N.

WITNESS TO AMERICA

A Documentary History of the United States

EDITED BY

DOUGLAS BRINKLEY

Based on the text originally edited by
Henry Steele Commager and Allan Nevins
and revised with Stephen Ambrose

HARPER

An Imprint of HarperCollinsPublishers
www.harpercollins.com
A Lou Reda Book

In memory of three great American historians—
Henry Steele Commager, Allan Nevins, and Stephen Ambrose,
whose work is timeless.

HarperCollins books may be purchased for educational, business, or sales promotional use. For information, please write: Special Markets Department, HarperCollins Publishers, 10 East 53rd Street, New York, NY 10022.

Endpapers: *Declaration of Independence,* c. 1817 (oil on canvas) by John Trumbull (1756–1843); United States Capitol Rotunda; photo © Boltin Picture Library/The Bridgeman Art Library.

Library of Congress Cataloging-in-Publication Data

Witness to America: a documentary history of the United States from
the Revolution to today / edited by Douglas Brinkley; based on the text originally edited by
Henry Steele Commager and Allan Nevins and revised with Stephen Ambrose.
p.   cm.
Summary: "A classic collection of primary source accounts covering the history
of the United States, now in a new format, abridged, and brought up
to the present day"—Provided by publisher.
ISBN 978-0-06-199028-1
1. United States—History—Sources.
2. United States—History—Pictorial works.   I. Brinkley, Douglas.
E173.W78   2010
973—dc22   2010015342

10   11   12   13   14   DIX/RRD   10   9   8   7   6   5   4   3   2   1

Contents

Introduction

to the 2010 edition

The United States has to move very fast to even stand still.
   —JOHN F. KENNEDY, JULY 21, 1963

    In the eleven years since the first edition of *Witness to America,* our country has faced many challenges—the tragedy of 9/11, the wars in Iraq and Afghanistan, Hurricane Katrina, the economic collapse of 2008, high rates of unemployment. In such times it is perhaps more valuable than ever to reflect on our nation's past, as told in our predecessors' words. It is my hope that this newly updated edition of *Witness to America* will give readers a deeper understanding of where our nation has been, to help us face our own path with the perspective only history can impart, as we strive toward America's future.

    Americans are instinctively looking forward, so it is not surprising that many are unaware of just how broad and variegated our country's history truly is, how filled with adventure, drama, and color. At its best, history pulses with hope and despair, ardor and endurance, and the joy and sorrow of ordinary people everywhere. *Witness to America* is intended to contribute to an understanding of the variety, the vitality, and the fascination of that immense part of our historical literature that flows from the pens of the men and women who helped to make history. These include countless vivid, enlightened, candid narratives penned by settlers, soldiers, traders, boatmen, gold seekers, runaway slaves, fur trappers, railroad builders, merchants, educators, preachers, civil rights activists, computer wizards, and politicians. The writers range from pioneers to presidents, from nurses to nabobs, from admirals to aviators, from engineers to environmentalists.

    Dr. Samuel Johnson once remarked that "a man will turn over half a library to make one book." This bit of poetic license became a reality in the making of *Witness to America.* Between 1939 and 1949 distinguished historians Henry Steele Commager and Allan Nevins first compiled an anthology of first-person narratives titled *Heritage to America.* Commager and Nevins wanted American history to ring with the voices of history's eyewitnesses. The original 1999 edition of *Witness to America,* edited by Stephen Ambrose and me, was modeled on that pioneering effort, with all the articles from the Boston Tea Party to World War II selected by Commager and Nevins; we made the selections from the *Enola Gay* to 1999. For this new edition I've abridged these existing selections to take out some of the less crucial and have also brought the collection up to the present day.

On its face, there is nothing radical about the documentary approach to history. After all, generations of dedicated scholars have relied on the same narratives excerpted in *Witness to America* as primary sources: diaries, letters, newspapers, court records, travel journals, memoirs, popular broadsides, sermons, speeches, and random jottings people leave behind, in one printed form or another, for posterity to ponder. But instead of synthesizing these historical nuggets into a single narrative, the documentary approach serves them up raw. It allows people to feel what life was like when Patrick Henry burst into a classic bit of tidewater eloquence or when the horseless carriage was a dubious contraption in Henry Ford's Dearborn garage. "We go forth all to seek America," Waldo Frank wrote in his largely forgotten 1919 classic *Our America.* "And in the seeking we create her. In the quality of our search shall be the nature of the America we created."

Of course, no single volume can embrace the totality of America—this book has always been intended simply as a fairly comprehensive harvest, representing what its editors have found the most illuminating and delightful, chosen to capture the interest and awaken the imagination of a broad swathe of readers. The principal criterion, used by me and the previous editors as well, besides our insistence upon a reasonable accuracy and authenticity, has always been that of broad human interest. The volume is not for specialists, nor does not it fall into, or even approximate, the category of "collected documents" or "source books," of which large numbers already exist. I hope that this new edition will afford instruction to students as well as pleasure to general readers.

No collection of personal writings, no matter how extensive, can provide a connected narrative of America's history. Many personal narratives are tangential rivulets. Reflecting more or less unique experiences, they lie somewhat apart from the general stream of affairs, or traverse it from an angle. To supply some coherence, context, and integration, the book is divided into sections, each representing a different phase or era of American life. Editorial additions (the headnotes opening each section) provide background and offer a measure of continuity.

The guiding principle in dealing with original texts has been to serve the general reader and the ordinary student, not to minister to the needs of scholars. The selections have verbatim accuracy, but spelling and punctuation have been conformed to modern usage. In most cases ellipses have also been omitted in the interests of readability. At the end of the book is a full bibliography so that those who wish to obtain the text of any selection in its original form may do so. Of course, it should be understood that the views expressed by the various writers included are not necessarily my own or those of the previous editors. Indeed, we have tried to obtain a wide variety of views, by no means excluding those of an extreme or eccentric character.

There is no question that America is the prime star of this endeavor, and many narratives will make the reader swell with patriotic pride. Whether it's Mark Twain's tale of becoming a Mississippi River pilot, George Washington's bidding farewell to his nation, Neil Armstrong's report of walking on the moon, or Barak Obama's stirring speech on race, the steady march of American dynamism is intoxicating. But *Witness to America* is hardly a compendium of breast-beating jingoism; it is a humbling record that illuminates that all our forebears, regardless of origin, race, or religion, possessed a common heritage. As Martin Luther King Jr. once noted, all Americans, no matter what their ethnicity, are woven together into "a single garment of destiny." It is also somehow comforting to see set down in black-and-white what we should instinctively know: Our ancestors harbored the same hopes and fears we do today. "The Founding Fathers proclaimed to all the world the revolutionary doctrine of the divine rights of the common man," Dwight D. Eisenhower declared in a May 1954 speech at Columbia University. "That doctrine has ever since been the heart of the American faith." *Witness to America* is a testimony to how our ancestors persevered, with faith in their hearts, to achieve remarkable goals—great and small—and so will we.

DOUGLAS BRINKLEY
April 2010

1

Mohawks Spill Tea in Boston Harbor

George III insisted upon a duty on tea imported by Americans. The revenue was trifling, but he regarded this tax as a matter of principle. When the colonists smuggled the commodity in from Holland, the king and his ministers took steps to cheapen English tea to such a level that Americans would find it lower priced, even with the duty added, than the smuggled substitute. They believed that the colonists would then buy the English tea. But the Americans were as firm upon a question of principle as the king. Popular wrath was aroused, and committees representing Boston and five other towns resolved in November 1773 to allow none of the tea to be landed. Under the leadership of Sam Adams, Boston merchants and shopkeepers took matters into their own hands. Conservatives were scandalized by the destruction of property, but John Adams wrote, "This is the most magnificent movement of all."

The tea destroyed was contained in three ships, lying near each other, at what was called at that time Griffin's Wharf and were surrounded by armed ships of war; the commanders of which had publicly declared that if the rebels, as they were pleased to style the Bostonians, should not withdraw their opposition to the landing of the tea before a certain day, the 17th day of December, 1773, they should on that day force it on shore, under the cover of their cannon's mouth. On the day preceding the seventeenth, there was a meeting of the citizens of the county of Suffolk, convened at one of the churches in Boston, for the purpose of consulting on what measures might be considered expedient to prevent the landing of the tea or secure the people from the collection of the duty. At that meeting a committee was appointed to wait on Governor Hutchinson and request him to inform them whether he would take any measures to satisfy the people on the object of the meeting. To the first application of this committee, the Governor told them he would give them a definite answer by five o'clock in the afternoon. At the hour appointed, the committee again repaired to the Governor's house and on inquiry found he had gone to his country seat at Milton, a distance of about six miles. When the committee returned and informed the meeting of the absence of the Governor, there was a confused murmur among the members, and the meeting was immediately dissolved, many of them crying out, "Let every man do his duty, and be true to his country," and there was a general huzzah from Griffin's Wharf. It was now evening, and I immediately dressed myself in the costume of an Indian, equipped with a small hatchet, which I and my associates denominated the tomahawk, with which, and a club, after having painted my face and hands with coal dust in the shop of a blacksmith, I repaired to Griffin's Wharf, where the ships lay that contained the tea. When I first appeared in the street, after being thus disguised, I fell in with many who were dressed, equipped, and painted as I was and who fell in with me and marched in order to the place of our destination. When we arrived at the wharf, there were three of our number who assumed an authority to direct our operations, to which we readily submitted. They divided us into three parties, for the purpose of boarding the three ships which contained the tea at the same time. The name of him who commanded the division to which I was assigned was Leonard Pitt. The names of the other commanders I never knew. We were immediately ordered by the respective commanders to board all the ships at the same time, which we promptly obeyed. The commander of the division to which I belonged, as soon as we were on board the ship, appointed me boatswain and ordered me to go to the captain and demand of him the keys to the hatches and a dozen candles. I made the demand accordingly, and the captain promptly replied and delivered the articles but requested me at the same time to do no damage to the ship or rigging. We then were ordered by our commander to open the hatches and take out all the chests of tea and throw them overboard, and we immediately proceeded to execute his orders, first cutting and splitting the chests with our tomahawks, so as thoroughly to expose them to the effects of the water. In about three hours from the time we went on board, we had thus broken and thrown overboard every tea chest to be found in the ship, while those in the other ships were disposing of the tea in the same way, at the same time. We were surrounded by British armed ships, but no attempt was made to resist us. We then quietly retired to our several places of residence, without having any conversation with each other or taking any measures to discover who were our associates; nor do I recollect of our having had the knowledge of the name of a single individual concerned in that affair, except that of Leonard Pitt, the commander of my division, whom I have mentioned. There appeared to be an understanding that each individual should volunteer his services, keep his own secret, and risk the consequences for himself. No disorder took place during that transaction, and it was observed at that time that the stillest night ensued that Boston had enjoyed for many months.

During the time we were throwing the tea overboard, there were several attempts made by some of the citizens of Boston and its vicinity to carry off small quantities of it for their family use. To effect that object, they would watch their opportunity to snatch up a handful from the deck, where it became plentifully scattered, and put it into their pockets. One Captain

O'Connor, whom I well knew, came on board for that purpose, and when he supposed he was not noticed filled his pockets and also the lining of his coat. But I had detected him and gave information to the captain of what he was doing. We were ordered to take him into custody, and just as he was stepping from the vessel, I seized him by the skirt of his coat, and in attempting to pull him back, I tore it off, but springing forward, by a rapid effort, he made his escape. He had, however, to run a gauntlet through the crowd upon the wharf, each one, as he passed, giving him a kick or a stroke.

Another attempt was made to save a little tea from the ruins of the cargo by a tall, aged man who wore a large cocked hat and white wig, which was fashionable at that time. He had sleightly slipped a little into his pocket, but being detected, they seized him and, taking his hat and wig from his head, threw them, together with the tea, of which they had emptied his pockets, into the water. In consideration of his advanced age, he was permitted to escape, with now and then a slight kick.

The next morning, after we had cleared the ships of the tea, it was discovered that very considerable quantities of it were floating upon the surface of the water, and to prevent the possibility of any of its being saved for use, a number of small boats were manned by sailors and citizens, who rowed them into those parts of the harbor wherever the tea was visible, and by beating it with oars and paddles, so thoroughly drenched it as to render its entire destruction inevitable.

GEORGE HEWES
A Retrospect of the Boston Tea-Party with a Memoir of George R. T. Hewes

2

John Adams Journeys to the Continental Congress

The punitive acts of Parliament against the province of Massachusetts that followed the destruction of the tea resulted in the adoption by the colonies of a plan for a general congress. Delegates were chosen by all the colonies except Georgia and met in Philadelphia in September of 1774. John Adams, who had graduated from Harvard almost twenty years earlier, was one of the leading attorneys of Boston. He and Josiah Quincy Jr. had defended the British soldiers arrested after the "Boston Massacre," obtaining the acquittal of all but two, and he had been prominent in the Massachusetts Legislature. A man of positive views, with a stiff, cold personality and a rather suspicious temper, he took a radical attitude toward the issues between the colonies and the British government. His diary shows how little New Englanders were acquainted with New York and Pennsylvania, and how curious they were as to life therein.

Boston. August 10, 1774. Wednesday.—

The Committee for the Congress took their departure from Boston, from Mr. Cushing's house, and rode to Coolidge's, where they dined in company with a large number of gentlemen, who went out and prepared an entertainment for them at that place. A most kindly and affectionate meeting we had, and about four in the afternoon we took our leave of them, amidst the kind wishes and fervent prayers of every man in the company for our health and success. This scene was truly affecting, beyond all description affecting. I lodged at Colonel Buck's.

16. Tuesday.—

At four we made for New Haven. Seven miles out of town, at a tavern, we met a great number of carriages and of horsemen who had come out to meet us. The sheriff of the county and constable of the town and the justices of peace were in the train. As we were coming, we met others to the amount of I know not what number, but a very great one. As we came into the town, all the bells in town were set to ringing, and the people, men, women, and children, were crowding at the doors and windows as if it was to see a coronation. At nine o'clock the cannon were fired, about a dozen guns, I think.

These expressions of respect to us are intended as demonstrations of the sympathy of this people with the Massachusetts Bay and its capital, and to show their expectations from the Congress and their determination to carry into execution whatever shall be agreed upon. No governor of a province nor general of an army was ever treated with so much ceremony and assiduity as we have been throughout the whole colony of Connecticut hitherto, but especially all the way from Hartford to New Haven inclusively.

20. Saturday.—

We breakfasted at Day's and arrived in the city of New York at ten o'clock, at Hull's, a tavern, the sign the Bunch of Grapes. We rode by several very elegant country seats before we came to the city. This city will be a subject of much speculation to me.

The streets of this town are vastly more regular and elegant than those of Boston, and the houses are more grand, as well as neat. They are almost all painted, brick buildings and all. In our walks they showed us the house of Mr. William Smith, one of their Council, and the famous lawyer, Mr. Thomas Smith, etc., Mr. Rivington's store, etc.

22. MONDAY.—

This morning we took Mr. McDougall into our coach and rode three miles out of town to Mr. Morin Scott's to breakfast—a very pleasant ride. Mr. Scott has an elegant seat there, with Hudson's River just behind his house and a rural prospect all around him. Mr. Scott, his lady, and daughter, and her husband, Mr. Litchfield, were dressed to receive us. We sat in a fine airy entry till called into a front room to breakfast. A more elegant breakfast I never saw— rich place, a very large silver coffeepot, a very large silver teapot, napkins of the very finest materials, toast, and bread and butter in great perfection. After breakfast a plate of beautiful peaches, another of pears, and another of plums, and a muskmelon were placed on the table.

Mr. Scott, Mr. William Smith, and Mr. William Livingston are the triumvirate who figured away in younger life against the Church of England, who wrote the *Independent Reflector,* the *Watch Tower,* and other papers. They are all of them children of Yale College. Scott and Livingston are said to be lazy; Smith improves every moment of his time. Livingston is lately removed into New Jersey and is one of the delegates for that province.

23. TUESDAY.—

The way we have been in, of breakfasting, dining, drinking coffee, etc., about the city, is very disagreeable on some accounts. Although it introduces us to the acquaintance of many respectable people here, yet it hinders us from seeing the college, the churches, the printers' offices and booksellers' shops, and many other things which we should choose to see.

With all the opulence and splendor of this city, there is very little good breeding to be found. We have been treated with an assiduous respect, but I have not seen one real gentleman, one well-bred man, since I came to town. At their entertainments there is no conversation that is agreeable; there is no modesty, no attention to one another. They talk very loud, very fast, and all together. If they ask you a question, before you can utter three words of your answer, they will break out upon you again and talk away.

29. MONDAY.—

We crossed the ferry over Delaware River to the province of Pennsylvania. . . . After dinner we stopped at Frankfort, about five miles out of town. A number of carriages and gentlemen came out of Philadelphia to meet us—Mr. Thomas Mifflin, Mr. McKean, of the lower counties, one of their delegates, Mr. Rutledge of Carolina, and a number of gentlemen from Philadelphia, Mr. Folsom and Mr. Sullivan, the New Hampshire delegates. We were introduced to all these gentlemen and most cordially welcomed to Philadelphia. We then rode into town, and dirty, dusty, and fatigued as we were, we could not resist the importunity to go to the tavern, the most genteel one in America. Here we had a fresh welcome to the city of Philadelphia, and after some time spent in conversation, a curtain was drawn, and in the other half of the chamber a supper appeared as elegant as ever was laid upon a table. About eleven o'clock we retired.

31. WEDNESDAY.—

Made a visit to Governor Ward of Rhode Island at his lodgings. There we were introduced to several gentlemen. Mr. Dickinson, the farmer, of Pennsylvania, came in his coach with four beautiful horses to Mr. Ward's lodgings to see us. He was introduced to us and very politely said he was exceedingly glad to have the pleasure of seeing these gentlemen; made some inquiry after the health of his brother and sister, who are now in Boston; gave us some account of his late ill health and his present gout. This was the first time of his getting out. Mr. Dickinson has been subject to hectic complaints. He is a shadow, tall but slender as a reed, pale as ashes; one would think at first sight that he could not live a month, yet upon a more attentive inspection, he looks as if the springs of life were strong enough to last many years. We dined with Mr. Lynch, his lady, and daughter, at their lodgings, Mrs. McKenzie's, and a very agreeable dinner and afternoon we had, notwithstanding the violent heat. We were all vastly pleased with Mr. Lynch. He is a solid, firm, judicious man. He told us that Colonel Washington made the most eloquent speech at the Virginia Convention that ever was made. Says he, "I will raise one thousand men, subsist them at my own expense, and march myself at their head for the relief of Boston."

The Diary of John Adams

3

"Give Me Liberty or Give Me Death!"

Patrick Henry, prominent as a radical in opposing the measures of the British government, had sat in the First Continental Congress. As a member in 1775 of the revolutionary convention of Virginia, he believed war inevitable and offered resolutions for arming the militia. Conservatives opposed this measure as premature. Henry then burst into this classic bit of eloquence. It was not written out or reported at the time, and the form undoubtedly owes something to Henry's biographer, William Wirt, but the substance and much of the phraseology is his own.

Mr. President: It is natural for man to indulge in the illusions of hope. We are apt to shut our eyes against a painful truth and listen to the song of that siren till she transforms us into beasts. Is this the part of wise men, engaged in a great and arduous struggle for liberty? Are we disposed to be of the number of those who, having eyes, see not, and having ears, hear not, the things which so nearly concern their temporal salvation? For my part, whatever anguish of spirit it may cost, I am willing to know the whole truth—to know the worst and to provide for it.

I have but one lamp by which my feet are guided, and that is the lamp of experience. I know of no way of judging of the future but by the past. And judging by the past, I wish to know what there has been in the conduct of the British ministry for the last ten years to justify those hopes with which the gentlemen have been pleased to solace themselves and the House. Is it that insidious smile with which our petition has been lately received? Trust it not, sir; it will prove a snare to your feet. Suffer not yourselves to be betrayed with a kiss. Ask yourselves how this gracious reception of our petition comports with those warlike preparations which cover our waters and darken our land. Are fleets and armies necessary to a work of love and reconciliation? Have we shown ourselves so unwilling to be reconciled that force must be called in to win back our love? Let us not deceive ourselves, sir. These are the implements of war and subjugation, the last arguments to which kings resort.

I ask the gentlemen, sir, what means this martial array, if its purpose be not to force us to submission? Can the gentlemen assign any other possible motive for it? Has Great Britain any enemy in this quarter of the world, to call for all this accumulation of navies and armies? No, sir, she has none. They are meant for us; they can be meant for no other. They are sent over to bind and rivet upon us those chains which the British ministry have been so long forging. And what have we to oppose to them? Shall we try argument? Sir, we have been trying that for the last ten years. Have we anything new to offer upon the subject? Nothing. We have held the subject up in every light of which it is capable, but it has been all in vain.

Shall we resort to entreaty and humble supplication? What terms shall we find which have not been already exhausted? Let us not, I beseech you, sir, deceive ourselves longer. Sir, we have done everything that could be done, to avert the storm which is now coming on. We have petitioned, we have remonstrated, we have supplicated; we have prostrated ourselves before the throne and have implored its interposition to arrest the tyrannical hands of the ministry and Parliament. Our petitions have been slighted; our remonstrances have produced additional violence and insult; our supplications have been disregarded; and we have been spurned, with contempt, from the foot of the throne. In vain, after these things, may we indulge the fond hope of peace and reconciliation. There is no longer any room for hope.

If we wish to be free, if we mean to preserve inviolate those inestimable privileges for which we have been so long contending, if we mean not basely to abandon the noble struggle in which we have been so long engaged, and which we have pledged ourselves never to abandon until the glorious object of our contest shall be obtained—we must fight! I repeat it, sir, we must fight! An appeal to arms, and to the God of hosts, is all that is left us.

They tell us, sir, that we are weak—unable to cope with so formidable an adversary. But when shall we be stronger? Will it be the next week or the next year? Will it be when we are totally disarmed, and when a British guard shall be stationed in every house? Shall we gather strength by irresolution and inaction? Shall we acquire the means of effectual resistance by lying supinely on our backs and hugging the delusive phantom of hope until our enemies shall have bound us hand and foot? Sir, we are not weak, if we make a proper use of those means which the God of nature hath placed in our power. Three millions of people, armed in the holy cause of Liberty, and in such a country as that which we possess, are invincible by any force which our enemy can send against us.

Besides, sir, we shall not fight our battles alone. There is a just God, who presides over the destinies of nations, and who will raise up friends to fight our battles for us. The battle, sir, is not to the strong alone; it is to the vigilant, the active, the brave. Besides, sir, we have no election. If we were base enough to desire it, it is now too late to retire from the contest. There is no retreat but in submission and slavery! Our chains are forged. Their clanking may be heard on the plains of Boston! The war is inevitable—and let it come! I repeat it, sir, let it come!

It is vain, sir, to extenuate the matter. The gentlemen may cry, Peace, peace! but there is no peace. The war has actually begun! The next gale that sweeps from the north will bring to our ears the clash of resounding arms! Our brethren are already in the field! Why stand we here idle? What is it that the gentlemen wish? What would they have? Is life so dear or peace so sweet as to be purchased at the price of chains and slavery? Forbid it, Almighty God. I know not what course others may take, but as for me, give me liberty or give me death!

WILLIAM WIRT
Sketches of the Life and Character of Patrick Henry

4

Adams Nominates Washington Commander in Chief

John Adams, only less than his second cousin, Sam Adams, was from the beginning impatient for separation from England. He had great influence in the Continental Congress. Realizing that sectional harmony was indispensable, and that union of the colonies would be promoted if the commander of troops fighting on New England soil were a Virginian, he took the leading part in the presentation of Washington—whose superiority in experience over other aspirants was manifest—as commander in chief. This was in June 1775, a full year before Adams seconded Richard Henry Lee's famous resolution that "these colonies are, and of right ought to be, free and independent States."

In several conversations, I found more than one very cool about the appointment of Washington, and particularly Mr. Pendleton was very clear and full against it. Full of anxieties concerning these confusions, and apprehending daily that we should hear very distressing news from Boston, I walked with Mr. Samuel Adams in the State House yard, for a little exercise and fresh air, before the hour of Congress, and there represented to him the various dangers that surrounded us. He agreed to them all but said, "What shall we do?" I answered him that he knew I had taken great pains to get our colleagues to agree upon some plan that we might be unanimous, but he knew that they would pledge themselves to nothing—but I was determined to take a step which should compel them and all the other members of Congress to declare themselves for or against something. "I am determined this morning to make a direct motion that Congress should adopt the army before Boston and appoint Colonel Washington commander of it." Mr. Adams seemed to think very seriously of it but said nothing.

Accordingly, when Congress had assembled, I rose in my place and, in as short a speech as the subject would admit, represented the state of the Colonies, the uncertainty in the minds of the people, their great expectation and anxiety, the distresses of the army, the danger of its dissolution, the difficulty of collecting another, and the probability that the British army would take advantage of our delays, march out of Boston, and spread desolation as far as they could go. I concluded with a motion, in form, that Congress would adopt the army at Cambridge and appoint a general; that though this was not the proper time to nominate a general, yet, as I had reason to believe this was a point of the greatest difficulty, I had no hesitation to declare that I had but one gentleman in my mind for that important command, and that was a gentleman from Virginia who was among us and very well known to all of us, a gentleman whose skill and experience as an officer, whose independent fortune, great talents, and excellent universal character, would command the approbation of all America and unite the cordial exertions of all the colonies better than any other person in the Union. Mr. Washington, who happened to sit near the door, as soon as he heard me allude to him, from his usual modesty, darted into the library room. Mr. Hancock—who was our president, which gave me an opportunity to observe his countenance while I was speaking on the state of the Colonies, the army at Cambridge, and the enemy—heard me with visible pleasure, but when I came to describe Washington for the commander, I never remarked a more sudden and striking change of countenance. Mortification and resentment were expressed as forcibly as his face could exhibit them. Mr. Samuel Adams seconded the motion, and that did not soften the president's physiognomy at all. The subject came under debate, and several gentlemen declared themselves against the appointment of Mr. Washington, not on account of any personal objection against him, but because the army were all from New England, had a general of their own, appeared to be satisfied with him, and had proved themselves able to imprison the British army in Boston, which was all they expected or desired at that time. Mr. Pendleton, of Virginia, [and] Mr. Sherman, of Connecticut, were very explicit in declaring this opinion; Mr. Cushing and several others more faintly expressed their opposition and their fears of discontents in the army and in New England. Mr. Paine expressed a great opinion of General Ward and a strong friendship for him, having been his classmate at college or at least his contemporary, but gave no opinion upon the question. The subject was postponed to a future day. In the meantime, pains were taken out-of-doors to obtain a unanimity, and the voices were generally so clearly in favor of Washington that the dissentient members were persuaded to withdraw their opposition, and Mr. Washington was nominated, I believe by Mr. Thomas Johnson of Maryland, unanimously elected, and the army adopted.

The Diary of John Adams

5

A Shot Is Fired That Is Heard
Around the World

Wʜat a glorious morning is this!" exclaimed the exultant Sam Adams as he listened to the rattle of musketry on April 19, 1775. He realized that the events of that day made independence almost inevitable. Hostilities had almost begun in February, when General Thomas Gage sent a force by water to Salem to search for powder. On April 19 he hurried a force at dawn to Concord, twenty miles from Boston, to destroy the military stores which had been collected there. This narrative from a British pen places the blame for the first shots squarely on the colonists; but the latter had witnesses who declared that the British had fired first.

On the evening of the 18th, about nine o'clock, I learned there was a large detachment going from this garrison, on which I immediately resolved to go with them, and meeting a few men in the street full accoutered, I followed them and embarked at the Magazine Guard and landed near Cambridge, where I joined Major Pitcairn, who I understood was to command next to Colonel Smith. Here we remained for two hours, partly waiting for the rest of the detachment and for provisions. About half an hour after two in the morning, on the 19th, we marched, Major Pitcairn commanding in front the light infantry. The tide being in, we were up to our middles before we got into the road. Continued for three miles without meeting with any person, when I heard Lieutenant Adair of the marines, who was a little before me in front, call out, "Here are two fellows galloping express to alarm the country," on which I immediately ran up to them, seized one of them and our guide the other, dismounted them, and by Major Pitcairn's directions, gave them in charge to the men. A little after, we were joined by Lieutenant Grant of the Royal Artillery, who told us the country, he was afraid, was alarmed, of which we had little reason to doubt as we heard several shots, being then between three and four in the morning (a very unusual time for firing), when we were joined by Major Mitchell, Captain Cochrane, Captain Lumm, and several other gentlemen who told us the whole country was alarmed and had galloped for their lives, or words to that purpose—that they had taken Paul [Revere] but were obliged to let him go after cutting his girths and stirrups. A little after, a fellow came out of a crossroad galloping. Mr. Adair and I called to him to stop, but he galloped off as hard as he could, upon which Mr. Simms, surgeon's mate of the Forty-third Regiment, who was on horseback, pursued him and took him a great way in front. A little after, I met a very genteel man riding in a carriage they call a sulky, who assured me there were six hundred men assembled at Lexington with a view of opposing us. I think I should know the man again if I saw him, as I took very particular notice of his features and dress. I waited with him till Major Pitcairn came up with the division, to whom he repeated much the same as he did to me. Then going on in front again, I met, coming out of a crossroad, another fellow galloping. However, hearing him some time before, I placed myself so that I got hold of the bridle of his horse and dismounted him. Our guide seemed to think that this was a very material fellow and said something as if he had been a member of the provincial Congress. A little after this I mounted a horse I had, and Mr. Adair went into a chaise. It began now to be daylight, and we met some men with a wagon of wood, who told us there were odds of a thousand men in arms at Lexington and added that they would fight us. Here we waited for some time, but seeing nothing of the divisions, I rode to the left about half a mile to see if I could fall in with them, but could see nothing of them. However, saw a vast number of the country militia going over the hill with their arms, to Lexington, and met one of them in the teeth whom I obliged to give up his firelock and bayonet, which I believe he would not have done so easily but from Mr. Adair's coming up. On this, we turned back the road we came and found the division who had halted in consequence of the intelligence the man in the sulky gave them, in order to make a disposition by advancing men in front and on the flanks to prevent a surprise. I went on with the front party, which consisted of a sergeant and six or eight men. I shall observe here that the road before you go into Lexington is level for about a thousand yards. Here we saw shots fired to the right and left of us, but as we heard no whizzing of balls, I conclude they were to alarm the body that was there of our approach. On coming within gunshot of the village of Lexington, a fellow from the corner of the road, on the right hand, cocked his piece at me, burnt priming [flashed in the pan]. I immediately called to Mr. Adair and the party to observe this circumstance, which they did, and I acquainted Major Pitcairn of it immediately.

We still went on farther when three shot more were fired at us, which we did not return, and this is sacred truth as I hope for mercy. These three shot were fired from a corner of a large house to the right of the church. When we came up to the main body, which appeared to me to exceed four hundred in and about the village, who were drawn up in a plain opposite to the church, several officers called out, "Throw down your arms and you shall come to no harm," or words to that effect. Which, they refusing to do, instantaneously the gentlemen who were on horseback rode in amongst them, of which I was one, at which instant I heard Major Pitcairn's voice call out, "Soldiers, don't fire; keep your ranks; form and surround them." Instantly some of the villains, who got over the hedge, fired at us, which our men for the first time returned, which set my horse a-going, who galloped with me down a road above six hundred yards among the middle of them before I turned him. And in returning, a vast number who were in a wood at the right of the grenadiers fired at me, but the distance was so great that I only heard the whistling of the balls but saw a great number of people in the wood. In consequence of their discovering themselves by firing, our grenadiers gave them a smart fire.

WILLIAM SUTHERLAND
Letter
April 27, 1775

6

Jefferson Writes the Declaration of Independence

Although Jefferson can be said never to have made a real speech, he held a pen which gave him an enormous influence from young manhood to old age. He wrote elaborate resolutions for the first revolutionary convention of Virginia in 1774, later publishing them as a pamphlet under the title *A Summary View of the Rights of America.* This work, of which numerous editions were printed in England, gave Jefferson a place among the most influential of American leaders. A little later he drafted Virginia's reply to the conciliatory proposals of Lord North and followed this by writing the reply of Congress to the same proffer. The fame won by these documents pointed him out as the logical man to draft an explanation and defense of the action of the colonies in separating from England. As John Adams says, most of the ideas were old. In fact, some of the most essential were drawn from the writings of John Locke. But the immortal phraseology of the preamble was strictly Jefferson's.

You inquire why so young a man as Mr. Jefferson was placed at the head of the committee for preparing a Declaration of Independence? I answer: It was the Frankfort advice, to place Virginia at the head of everything. Mr. Richard Henry Lee might be gone to Virginia, to his sick family, for aught I know, but that was not the reason of Mr. Jefferson's appointment. There were three committees appointed at the same time, one for the Declaration of Independence, another for preparing articles of confederation, and another for preparing a treaty to be proposed to France. Mr. Lee was chosen for the Committee of Confederation, and it was not thought convenient that the same person should be upon both. Mr. Jefferson came into Congress in June 1775 and brought with him a reputation for literature, science, and a happy talent of composition. Writings of his were handed about, remarkable for the peculiar felicity of expression. Though a silent member in Congress, he was so prompt, frank, explicit, and decisive upon committees and in conversation—not even Samuel Adams was more so—that he soon seized upon my heart; and upon this occasion I gave him my vote and did all in my power to procure the votes of others. I think he had one more vote than any other, and that placed him at the head of the committee. I had the next highest number, and that placed me the second. The committee met, discussed the subject, and then appointed Mr. Jefferson and me to make the draft, I suppose because we were the two first on the list.

The subcommittee met. Jefferson proposed to me to make the draft. I said, "I will not." "You should do it." "Oh! no." "Why will you not? You ought to do it." "I will not." "Why?" "Reasons enough." "What can be your reasons?" "Reason first, you are a Virginian, and a Virginian ought to appear at the head of this business. Reason second, I am obnoxious, suspected, and unpopular. You are very much otherwise. Reason third, you can write ten times better than I can." "Well," said Jefferson, "if you are decided, I will do as well as I can." "Very well. When you have drawn it up, we will have a meeting."

A meeting we accordingly had and conned the paper over. I was delighted with its high tone and the flights of oratory with which it abounded, especially that concerning Negro slavery, which, though I knew his Southern brethren would never suffer to pass in Congress, I certainly never would oppose. There were other expressions which I would not have inserted if I had drawn it up, particularly that which called the King tyrant. I thought this too personal, for I never believed George to be a tyrant in disposition and in nature; I always believed him to be deceived by his courtiers on both sides of the Atlantic, and in his official capacity, only, cruel. I thought the expression too passionate and too much like scolding for so grave and solemn a document, but as Franklin and Sherman were to inspect it afterwards, I thought it would not become me to strike it out. I consented to report it and do not now remember that I made or suggested a single alteration.

We reported it to the committee of five. It was read, and I do not remember that Franklin or Sherman criticized anything. We were all in haste. Congress was impatient, and the instrument was reported, as I believe, in Jefferson's handwriting, as he first drew it. Congress cut off about a quarter of it, as I expected they would, but they obliterated some of the best of it and left all that was exceptionable, if anything in it was. I have long wondered that the original draft had not been published. I suppose the reason is the vehement philippic against Negro slavery.

As you justly observe, there is not an idea in it but what had been hackneyed in Congress for two years before. The substance of it is contained in the declaration of rights and the violation of those rights in the Journals of Congress in 1774. Indeed, the essence of it is contained in a pamphlet, voted and printed by the town of Boston, before the first Congress met, composed by James Otis, as I suppose, in one of his lucid intervals, and pruned and polished by Samuel Adams.

JOHN ADAMS
Letter to Timothy Pickering
August 6, 1822

7

Ethan Allen Captures Fort Ticonderoga

The embattled colonists needed cannon and stores; also they wished to seize the gateway to Canada. To encompass these two objects, hardy fighters from Connecticut, Massachusetts, and what shortly became Vermont joined in a spring march on Ticonderoga, key fortress of northern New York. Their leader was the Vermonter Ethan Allen, who tells the story spiritedly.

Ever since I arrived at the state of manhood and acquainted myself with the general history of mankind, I have felt a sincere passion for liberty. The history of nations doomed to perpetual slavery in consequence of yielding up to tyrants their natural-born liberties, I read with a sort of philosophical horror, so that the first systematical and bloody attempt, at Lexington, to enslave America, thoroughly electrified my mind and fully determined me to take part with my country. And while I was wishing for an opportunity to signalize myself in its behalf, directions were privately sent to me from the then colony (now State) of Connecticut to raise the Green Mountain Boys and, if possible, with them to surprise and take the fortress of Ticonderoga. This enterprise I cheerfully undertook and, after first guarding all the several passes that led thither, to cut off all intelligence between the garrison and the country, made a forced march from Bennington and arrived at the lake opposite to Ticonderoga, on the evening of the 9th day of May, 1775, with two hundred and thirty valiant Green Mountain Boys, and it was with the utmost difficulty that I procured boats to cross the lake. However, I landed eighty-three men near the garrison and sent the boats back for the rear guard, commanded by Colonel Seth Warner, but the day began to dawn, and I found myself under the necessity to attack the fort, before the rear could cross the lake, and as it was viewed hazardous, I harangued the officers and soldiers in the manner following:

"Friends and fellow soldiers, you have, for a number of years past, been a scourge and terror to arbitrary power. Your valor has been famed abroad and acknowledged, as appears by the advice and orders to me from the General Assembly of Connecticut to surprise and take the garrison now before us. I now propose to advance before you and, in person, conduct you through the wicket gate; for we must this morning either quit our pretensions to valor or possess ourselves of this fortress in a few minutes, and inasmuch as it is a desperate attempt, which none but the bravest of men dare undertake, I do not urge it on any contrary to his will. You that will undertake voluntarily, poise your firelocks."

The men being, at this time, drawn up in three ranks, each poised his firelock. I ordered them to face to the right and, at the head of the center file, marched them immediately to the wicket gate aforesaid, where I found a sentry posted, who instantly snapped his fusee at me; I ran immediately toward him, and he retreated through the covered way into the parade within the garrison, gave a halloo, and ran under a bombproof. My party, who followed me into the fort, I formed on the parade in such a manner as to face the two barracks which faced each other.

The garrison being asleep, except the sentries, we gave three huzzahs, which greatly surprised them. One of the sentries made a pass at one of my officers with a charged bayonet and slightly wounded him. My first thought was to kill him with my sword, but in an instant, I altered the design and fury of the blow to a slight cut on the side of the head, upon which he dropped his gun and asked quarter, which I readily granted him and demanded of him the place where the commanding officer kept; he showed me a pair of stairs in the front of a barrack, on the west part of the garrison, which led up to a second story in said barrack, to which I immediately repaired and ordered the commander, Captain de la Place, to come forth instantly or I would sacrifice the whole garrison, at which the Captain came immediately to the door, with his breeches in his hand, when I ordered him to deliver me the fort instantly; he asked me by what authority I demanded it. I answered him, *"In the name of the great Jehovah and the Continental Congress."* The authority of the Congress being very little known at that time, he began to speak again, but I interrupted him and, with my drawn sword over his head, again demanded an immediate surrender of the garrison, with which he then complied and ordered his men to be forthwith paraded without arms, as he had given up the garrison. In the meantime some of my officers had given orders, and in consequence thereof, sundry of the barrack doors were beat down, and about one-third of the garrison imprisoned, which consisted of the said commander, a Lieutenant Feltham, a conductor of artillery, a gunner, two sergeants, and forty-four rank and file, about one hundred pieces of cannon, one thirteen-inch mortar, and a number of swivels. This surprise was carried into execution in the gray of the morning of the 10th of May, 1775. The sun seemed to rise that morning with a superior luster, and Ticonderoga and its dependencies smiled to its conquerors, who tossed about the flowing bowl and wished success to Congress and the liberty and freedom of America.

ETHAN ALLEN
Ethan Allen Captures Fort Ticonderoga

8

The American Army Suffers
at Valley Forge

Washington's army, defeated by Howe at the battle of Brandywine on September 11, 1777, was compelled to retire beyond Philadelphia while the British entered that city. The Continental Congress fled first to Lancaster and then to York in Pennsylvania. Meanwhile the British fleet held Delaware Bay and captured Forts Mercer and Mifflin. All the maritime areas of Rhode Island, New York, Delaware, and Pennsylvania were thus in the hands of the royal forces. For the darkest winter of the war, Washington settled down with his fragmentary army at Valley Forge. But somehow the army got through that winter and emerged stronger and better disciplined than it had ever been.

Sand and forest, forest and sand, formed the whole way from Williamsburg to the camp at Valley Forge. I do not remember how many days I took to accomplish this difficult journey. Being badly fed, as a natural consequence I walked badly and passed at least six nights under the trees through not meeting with any habitation. Not knowing the language, I often strayed from the right road, which was so much time and labor lost. At last, early in November [1777], I arrived at Valley Forge.

The American army was then encamped three or four leagues from Philadelphia, which city was then occupied by the British, who were rapidly fulfilling the prophecy of Dr. Franklin.

That celebrated man—an ambassador who amused himself with science, which he adroitly made to assist him in his diplomatic work—said, when some friends came to Passy to condole with him on the fall of Philadelphia: "You are mistaken; it is not the British army that has taken Philadelphia, but Philadelphia that has taken the British army." The cunning old diplomatist was right. The capital of Pennsylvania had already done for the British what Capua did in a few months for the soldiers of Hannibal. The Americans— the "insurgents" as they were called—camped at Valley Forge; the British officers, who were in the city, gave themselves up to pleasure; there were continual balls and other amusements; the troops were idle and enervated by inaction, and the generals undertook nothing all the winter.

Soon I came in sight of the camp. My imagination had pictured an army with uniforms, the glitter of arms, standards, etc., in short, military pomp of all sorts. Instead of the imposing spectacle I expected, I saw, grouped together or standing alone, a few militiamen, poorly clad, and for the most part without shoes—many of them badly armed, but all well supplied with provisions, and I noticed that tea and sugar formed part of their rations. I did not then know that this was not unusual, and I laughed, for it made me think of the recruiting sergeants on the Quai de la Ferraille at Paris, who say to the yokels, "You will want for nothing when you are in the regiment, but if bread should run short you must not mind eating cakes." Here the soldiers had tea and sugar. In passing through the camp I also noticed soldiers wearing cotton nightcaps under their hats, and some having for cloaks or great-coats coarse woolen blankets, exactly like those provided for the patients in our French hospitals. I learned afterwards that these were the officers and generals.

Such, in strict truth, was, at the time I came amongst them, the appearance of this armed mob, the leader of whom was the man who has rendered the name of Washington famous; such were the colonists—unskilled warriors who learned in a few years how to conquer the finest troops that England could send against them. Such also, at the beginning of the War of Independence, was the state of want in the insurgent army, and such was the scarcity of money, and the poverty of that government, now so rich, powerful, and prosperous, that its notes, called Continental paper money, were nearly valueless.

THE CHEVALIER DE PONTGIBAUD
A French Volunteer of the War of Independence

9

The World Turned Upside Down at Yorktown

For a brief period before the British commander Rodney annihilated a French fleet in the West Indies, the French navy held the upper hand on the American coast. When Cornwallis in the summer of 1781 placed his small army at the end of the Virginia peninsula, Washington's quick eye saw the opportunity. By rapid movements the French and American land forces were united before Yorktown, while De Grasse with the French navy closed the Chesapeake. The capitulation of Cornwallis meant the downfall of Lord North's ministry, and the end of the war.

OCTOBER 18, 1781.—

It is now ascertained that Lord Cornwallis, to avoid the necessity of a surrender, has determined on the bold attempt to make his escape in the night of the 16th, with a part of his army, into the country. His plan was to leave sick and baggage behind and to cross with his effective force over to Gloucester Point, there to destroy the French legion and other troops, and to mount his infantry on their horses and such others as might be procured and thus push their way to New York by land. A more preposterous and desperate attempt can scarcely be imagined. Boats were secretly prepared, arrangements made, and a large proportion of his troops actually embarked and landed on Gloucester Point, when from a moderate and calm evening, a most violent storm of wind and rain ensued. The boats with the remaining troops were all driven down the river, and it was not till the next day that his troops could be returned to the garrison at York.

At an early hour this forenoon General Washington communicated to Lord Cornwallis the general basis of the terms of capitulation, which he deemed admissible, and allowed two hours for his reply. Commissioners were soon afterward appointed to prepare the particular terms of agreement. The gentlemen appointed by General Washington are Colonel Laurens, one of his aide-de-camps, and Viscount Noailles of the French army. They have this day held an interview with the two British officers on the part of Lord Cornwallis; the terms of capitulation are settled, and being confirmed by the commanders of both armies, the royal troops are to march out tomorrow and surrender their arms.

19TH.—

This is to us a most glorious day, but to the English, one of bitter chagrin and disappointment. Preparations are now making to receive as captives that vindictive, haughty commander and that vanquished army who, by their robberies and murders, have so long been a scourge to our brethren of the Southern states. Being on horseback, I anticipate a full share of satisfaction in viewing the various movements in the interesting scene. The stipulated terms of capitulation are similar to those granted to General Lincoln at Charleston the last year. The captive troops are to march out with shouldered arms, colors cased, and drums beating a British or German march, and to ground their arms at a place assigned for the purpose. The officers are allowed their side arms and private property, and the generals and such officers as desire it are to go on parole to England or New York. The marines and seamen of the King's ships are prisoners of war to the navy of France, and the land forces to the United States. All military and artillery stores to be delivered up unimpaired. The royal prisoners to be sent into the interior of Virginia, Maryland, and Pennsylvania in regiments, to have rations allowed them equal to the American soldiers, and to have their officers near them, Lord Cornwallis to man and dispatch the *Bonetta* sloop of war with dispatches to Sir Henry Clinton at New York without being searched, the vessel to be returned and the hands accounted for.

At about twelve o'clock, the combined army was arranged and drawn up in two lines extending more than a mile in length. The Americans were drawn up in a line on the right side of the road, and the French occupied the left. At the head of the former, the great American commander, mounted on his noble courser, took his station, attended by his aides. At the head of the latter was posted the excellent Count Rochambeau and his suite. The French troops, in complete uniform, displayed a martial and noble appearance; their band of music, of which the timbrel formed a part, is a delightful novelty and produced while marching to the ground a most enchanting effect. The Americans, though not all in uniform nor their dress so neat, yet exhibited an erect, soldierly air, and every countenance beamed with satisfaction and joy. The concourse of spectators from the country was prodigious, in point of numbers was probably equal to the military, but universal silence and order prevailed. It was about two o'clock when the captive army advanced through the line formed for their reception. Every eye was prepared to gaze on Lord Cornwallis, the object of peculiar interest and solicitude, but he disappointed our anxious expectations; pretending indisposition, he made General O'Hara his substitute as the leader of his army. This officer was followed by the conquered troops in a slow and solemn step, with shouldered arms, colors cased, and drums beating a British march. Having arrived at the head of the line, General O'Hara, elegantly mounted, advanced to his Excellency the Commander-in-Chief, taking off his hat, and apologized for the nonappearance of Earl Cornwallis. With his usual dignity and politeness, his Excellency pointed to Major General Lincoln for directions, by whom the British army was conducted into a spacious field, where it was intended they should ground their arms. The royal troops, while marching through the line formed by the allied army, exhibited a decent and neat appearance, as respects arms and clothing, for their commander opened his store and directed every soldier to be furnished with a new suit complete, prior to the capitulation. But in their line of march we remarked a disorderly and unsoldierly conduct; their step was irregular, and their ranks frequently broken. But it was in the field, when they came to the last act of the drama, that the spirit and pride of the British soldier was put to the severest test: here their mortification could not be concealed. Some of the platoon officers appeared to be exceedingly chagrined when giving the word, "Ground arms," and I am a witness that they performed this duty in a very unofficer-like manner and that many of the soldiers manifested a *sullen temper,* throwing their arms on the pile with violence, as if determined to render them useless. This irregularity, however, was checked by the authority of General Lincoln. After having grounded their arms and divested themselves of their accouterments, the captive troops were conducted back to Yorktown and guarded by our troops till they could be removed to the place of their destination.

JAMES THACHER
Military Journal During the American Revolutionary War,
from 1775 to 1783

PART III

CONFEDERATION, CONSTITUTION, AND LAUNCHING THE NEW GOVERNMENT

10

The Thirteen States Establish a Confederation

John Dickinson was head of a committee of the Continental Congress that on July 12, 1776, reported the draft of some "Articles of Confederation." They were not formally adopted until more than a year later, were not signed for almost another year, and were not ratified by all the States until 1781. But they were a long first step toward a true Union.

The style of this confederacy shall be "The United States of America."

Each state retains its sovereignty, freedom, and independence, and every power, jurisdiction, and right, which is not by this confederation expressly delegated to the United States in Congress assembled.

The said states hereby severally enter into a firm league of friendship with each other, for their common defense, the security of their liberties, and their mutual and general welfare, binding themselves to assist each other against all force offered to, or attacks made upon them, or any of them, on account of religion, sovereignty, trade, or any other pretense whatever. . . .

Every state shall abide by the determinations of the United States in Congress assembled, on all questions which by this confederation are submitted to them. And the articles of this confederation shall be inviolably observed by every state, and the union shall be perpetual; nor shall any alteration at any time hereafter be made in any of them; unless such alteration be agreed to in a Congress of the United States, and be afterwards confirmed by the legislature of every state.

And whereas it hath pleased the Great Governor of the World to incline the hearts of the legislatures we respectively represent in Congress, to approve of, and to authorize us to ratify the said articles of confederation and perpetual union, know ye that we the undersigned delegates . . . do by these presents . . . fully and entirely ratify and confirm each and every of the said articles of confederation and perpetual union, and all and singular the matters and things therein contained. And we do further solemnly plight and engage the faith of our respective constituents, that they shall abide by the determinations of the United States in Congress assembled, on all questions, which by the said confederation are submitted to them. And that the articles thereof shall be inviolably observed by the states we respectively represent, and that the union shall be perpetual.

The Articles of Confederation
1781

11

"A Rising, Not a Setting Sun"

While George III still ruled the American colonies, Franklin had tried to bring them into a confederation within the British Empire. He was the principal author of the Albany Plan of Union in 1754. Twenty-two years later he had signed the Declaration of Independence. Eleven years later still, he joyfully signed the new Constitution and uttered the hopeful prophecy that James Madison—one of the leading framers of the great document—here records. More than once the convention had seemed on the point of breaking up amid bitter quarrels, but at last it had finished its colossal work, which went to the thirteen states for ratification.

The engrossed Constitution being read [September 17, 1787], Dr. Franklin rose with a speech in his hand, which he had reduced to writing for his own convenience and which Mr. Wilson read in the words following:

"Mr. President: I confess that there are several parts of this Constitution which I do not at present approve, but I am not sure I shall never approve them. For, having lived long, I have experienced many instances of being obliged, by better information or fuller consideration, to change opinions, even on important subjects, which I once thought right but found to be otherwise. It is therefore that, the older I grow, the more apt I am to doubt my own judgment and to pay more respect to the judgment of others. Most men, indeed, as well as most sects in religion, think themselves in possession of all truth and that wherever others differ from them it is so far error. Steele, a Protestant, in a dedication, tells the Pope that the only difference between our churches in their opinions of the certainty of their doctrines is 'the Church of Rome is infallible and the Church of England is never in the wrong.' But though many private persons think almost as highly of their own infallibility as of that of their sect, few express it so naturally as a certain French lady, who, in a dispute with her sister, said, 'I don't know how it happens, sister, but I meet with nobody but myself that is always in the right—*il n'y a que moi qui a toujours raison.*'

"In these sentiments, sir, I agree to this Constitution, with all its faults, if they are such, because I think a general government necessary for us, and there is no form of government but what may be a blessing to the people if well administered, and believe further that this is likely to be well administered for a course of years and can only end in despotism, as other forms have done before it, when the people shall become so corrupted as to need despotic government, being incapable of any other. I doubt, too, whether any other convention we can obtain may be able to make a better constitution. For when you assemble a number of men to have the advantage of their joint wisdom, you inevitably assemble with those men all their prejudices, their passions, their errors of opinion, their local interests, and their selfish views. From such an assembly can a perfect production be expected? It therefore astonishes me, sir, to find this system approaching so near to perfection as it does, and I think it will astonish our enemies, who are waiting with confidence to hear that our councils are confounded, like those of the builders of Babel, and that our States are on the point of separation, only to meet hereafter for the purpose of cutting one another's throats. Thus I consent, sir, to this Constitution, because I expect no better, and because I am not sure that it is not the best. The opinions I have had of its errors I sacrifice to the public good. I have never whispered a syllable of them abroad. Within these walls they were born, and here they shall die. If every one of us, in returning to our constituents, were to report the objections he has had to it and endeavor to gain partisans in support of them, we might prevent its being generally received and thereby lose all the salutary effects and great advantages resulting naturally in our favor among foreign nations, as well as among ourselves, from our real or apparent unanimity. Much of the strength and efficiency of any government, in procuring and securing happiness to the people, depends on opinion—on the general opinion of the goodness of the government, as well as of the wisdom and integrity of its governors. I hope, therefore, that for our own sakes, as a part of the people, and for the sake of posterity, we shall act heartily and unanimously in recommending this Constitution (if approved by Congress and confirmed by the conventions) wherever our influence may extend and turn our future thoughts and endeavors to the means of having it well administered.

"On the whole, sir, I cannot help expressing a wish that every member of the Convention, who may still have objections to it, would with me, on this occasion, doubt a little of his own infallibility and, to make manifest our unanimity, put his name to this instrument." He then moved that the Constitution be signed by the members and offered the following as a convenient form, viz.: "Done in Convention by the unanimous consent of *the States* present, the 17th of September, etc. In witness whereof, we have hereunto subscribed our names."

This ambiguous form had been drawn up by Mr. Gouverneur Morris in order to gain the dissenting members and put into the hands of Dr. Franklin that it might have the better chance of success. . . .

On the question to agree to the Constitution, enrolled, in order to be signed, it was agreed to, all the States answering aye.

Mr. Randolph then rose and, with an allusion to the observations of Dr. Franklin, apologized for his refusing to sign the Constitution, notwithstanding the vast majority and venerable names that would give sanction to its wisdom and its worth. He said, however, that he did not mean by this refusal to decide that he should oppose the Constitution withoutdoors. He meant only to keep himself free to be governed by his duty, as it should be prescribed by his future judgment. He refused to sign, because he thought the object of the Convention would be frustrated by the alternative which it presented to the people. Nine states will fail to ratify the plan, and confusion must ensue. With such a view of the subject he ought not, he could not, by pledging himself to support the plan, restrain himself from taking such steps as might appear to him most consistent with the public good.

Mr. Gouverneur Morris said that he too had objections, but considering the present plan as the best that was to be attained, he should take it with all its faults. The majority had determined in its favor, and by that determination he should abide. The moment this plan goes forth, all other considerations will be laid aside, and the great question will be, shall there be a national government or not? and this must take place, or a general anarchy will be the alternative. He remarked that the signing, in the form proposed, related only to the fact that the States present were unanimous.

Mr. Williamson suggested that the signing should be confined to the letter accompanying the Constitution to Congress, which might perhaps do nearly as well and would be found satisfactory to some members who disliked the Constitution. For himself, he did not think a better plan was to be expected and had no scruples against putting his name to it.

Mr. Hamilton expressed his anxiety that every member should sign. A few characters of consequence, by opposing or even refusing to sign the Constitution, might do infinite mischief, by kindling the latent sparks that lurk under an enthusiasm in favor of the Convention which may soon subside. No man's ideas were more remote from the plan than his own were known to be, but is it possible to deliberate between anarchy and convulsion on one side and the chance of good to be expected from the plan on the other?. . .

Whilst the last members were signing, Dr. Franklin, looking towards the president's chair at the back of which a rising sun happened to be painted, observed to a few members near him that painters had found it difficult to distinguish, in their art, a rising from a setting sun. "I have," said he, "often and often, in the course of the session and the vicissitudes of my hopes and fears as to its issue, looked at that behind the president without being able to tell whether it was rising or setting, but now, at length, I have the happiness to know that it is a rising, and not a setting sun."

JAMES MADISON
Debates in the Federal Convention

12

Washington Is Inaugurated President

Even before the early ratifications of the Constitution, Washington had been designated by public opinion for the first president. He modestly tried to refuse the honor. Fifty-six years old, he declared that he had no "wish but that of living and dying an honest man on my own farm." But the nation insisted, and borrowing some money for traveling expenses, he set out for the temporary capital, New York. He was to take the oath of office April 30, 1789. One of the leading Federalists in New Jersey, Elias Boudinot, helped conduct him to his new duties and set down an animated narrative of the scenes they encountered.

My Dearest Wife:

If it was in my power, I could wish to give you an adequate account of the proceedings of the citizens of this metropolis on the approach and at the reception of our President when he arrived here yesterday *New York, April 24, 1789.*

When we drew near to the mouth of the Kills, a number of boats with various flags came up with us and dropped in our wake. Soon after we opened the bay, General Knox and several generals in a large barge presented themselves with their splendid colors. Boat after boat and sloop after sloop added to our train, gaily dressed in all their naval ornaments, made a most splendid appearance. Before we got to Bedloe Island, a large sloop came with full sail on our starboard bow, when there stood up about twenty gentlemen and ladies and with most excellent voices sang an elegant ode prepared for the purpose, to the tune of "God Save the King," welcoming their great chief to the seat of government. On the conclusion we gave them our hats, and then they with the surrounding boats gave us three cheers. Soon after, another boat came under our stern and presented us with a number of copies of another ode, and immediately about a dozen gentlemen began to sing it in parts as we passed along. Our worthy President was greatly affected with these tokens of profound respect.

As we approached the harbor, our train increased, and the huzzahing and shouts of joy seemed to add life to this lively scene. At this moment a number of porpoises came playing amongst us, as if they had risen up to know what was the cause of all this joy. We now discovered the shores covered with thousands of people—men, women, and children—nay, I may venture to say tens of thousands. From the fort to the place of landing although near half a mile, you could see little else along the shores—in the streets and on board every vessel—but heads standing as thick as ears of corn before the harvest. The vessels in the harbor made a most superb appearance indeed, dressed in all the pomp of attire. The Spanish packet in a moment, on a signal given, discovered twenty-seven or twenty-eight different colors of all nations on every part of the rigging and paid us the compliment of thirteen guns, with her yards all manned, as did another vessel in the harbor, displaying colors in the same manner. I have omitted the like compliment from the battery of eighteen-pounders.

We soon arrived at the ferry stairs, where there were many thousands of the citizens waiting with all the eagerness of expectation to welcome our excellent patriot to that shore, which he had regained from a powerful enemy by his valor and good conduct. We found the stairs covered with carpeting and the rails hung with crimson. The President, being preceded by the committee, was received by the Governor and the citizens in the most brilliant manner. Here he was met on the wharf by many of his old and faithful officers and fellow patriots who had borne the heat and burden of the day with him, and who, like him, had experienced every reverse of fortune with fortitude and patience, and who now joined the universal chorus of welcoming their great deliverer (under Providence) from their fears.

It was with difficulty a passage could be made by the troops through the pressing crowds, who seemed to be incapable of being satisfied by gazing at this man of the people. You will see the particulars of the procession, from the wharf to the house appointed for his residence, in the newspapers. The streets were lined with the inhabitants as thick as the people could stand, and it required all the exertions of a numerous train of city officers, with their staffs, to make a passage for the company. The houses were filled with gentlemen and ladies, the whole distance being half a mile, and the windows to the highest stories were illuminated by the sparkling eyes of innumerable companies of ladies, who seemed to vie with each other to show their joy on this great occasion.

It was half an hour before we could finish our commission and convey the President to the house prepared for his residence. As soon as this was done, notwithstanding his great fatigue of both body and mind, he had to receive all the gentlemen and officers to a very large amount who wished to show their respect in the most affectionate manner. When this was finished and the people dispersed, we went, undressed, and dined with his Excellency Governor Clinton, who had provided an elegant dinner for the purpose. Thus ended our commission.

The evening, though very wet, was spent by all ranks in visiting the city, street after street being illuminated in a superb manner. I cannot help stating now how highly we were favored in the weather, the whole procession having been completely finished and we had repaired to the Governor's before it began to rain. When the President was on the wharf, an officer came up and, addressing the President, said he had the honor to command his guard, and it was ready to obey his orders. The President answered that as to the present arrangement he should proceed as was directed, but that after that was over, he hoped he would give himself no further trouble, as the affections of his fellow citizens (turning to the crowd) was all the guard he wanted.

Good night. May God bless you.

ELIAS BOUDINOT
Letter to His Wife

13

Jefferson and Hamilton Strike a Bargain

The new federal government was no sooner set up than it became plain that Jefferson and Hamilton held divergent views of its proper functions and were certain to quarrel. Parties sprang up about them. Jefferson, who was secretary of state, trusted the people and feared a strong government; Hamilton, the secretary of the treasury, trusted in a strong government and feared the people. In order to make the nation more powerful, Hamilton wished the Treasury to assume all the state debts, so that holders of government paper would support it. Jefferson opposed this program, but it was carried by an ingenious bargain which Jefferson later came to regret.

This game was over, and another was on the carpet at the moment of my arrival, and to this I was most ignorantly and innocently made to hold the candle. This fiscal maneuver is well known by the name of the Assumption [1790]. Independently of the debts of Congress, the States had during the war contracted separate and heavy debts; . . . the more debt Hamilton could rake up, the more plunder for his mercenaries. This money, whether wisely or foolishly spent, was pretended to have been spent for general purposes and ought, therefore, to be paid from the general purse. But it was objected that nobody knew what these debts were, what their amount or what their proofs. No matter; we will guess them to be twenty millions. But of these twenty millions, we do not know how much should be reimbursed to one State or how much to another. No matter; we will guess. And so another scramble was set on foot among the several States, and some got much, some little, some nothing. But the main object was obtained; the phalanx of the Treasury was reinforced by additional recruits. This measure produced the most bitter and angry contest ever known in Congress before or since the Union of the States. I arrived in the midst of it. But a stranger to the ground, a stranger to the actors on it, so long consent as to have lost all familiarity with the subject, and as yet unaware of its object, I took no concern in it.

The great and trying question, however, was lost in the House of Representatives. So high were the feuds excited by this subject, that on its rejection, business was suspended. Congress met and adjourned from day to day without doing anything, the parties being too much out of temper to do business together. The Eastern members, particularly, who, with Smith from South Carolina, were the principal gamblers in these scenes, threatened a secession and dissolution. Hamilton was in despair. As I was going to the President's one day, I met him in the street. He walked me backwards and forwards before the President's door for half an hour. He painted pathetically the temper into which the legislature had been wrought, the disgust of those who were called the creditor States, the danger of the secession of their members, and the separation of the States. He observed that the members of the administration ought to act in concert; that though this question was not of my department, yet a common duty should make it a common concern; that the President was the center on which all administrative questions ultimately rested, and that all of us should rally around him and support with joint efforts measures approved by him; and that the question having been lost by a small majority only, it was probable that an appeal from me to the judgment and discretion of some of my friends might effect a change in the vote, and the machine of government, now suspended, might be again set into motion. I told him that I was really a stranger to the whole subject; that not having yet informed myself of the system of finances adopted, I knew not how far this was a necessary sequence; that undoubtedly if its rejection endangered a dissolution of our Union at this incipient stage, I should deem that the most unfortunate of all consequences, to avert which all partial and temporary evils should be yielded. I proposed to him, however, to dine with me the next day, and I would invite another friend or two, bring them into conference together, and I thought it impossible that reasonable men, consulting together coolly, could fail, by some mutual sacrifices of opinion, to form a compromise which was to save the Union.

The discussion took place. I could take no part in it but an exhortatory one, because I was a stranger to the circumstances which should govern it. But it was finally agreed that whatever importance had been attached to the rejection of this proposition, the preservation of the Union and of concord among the States was more important, and that therefore it would be better that the vote of rejection should be rescinded, to effect which some members should change their votes. But it was observed that this pill would be peculiarly bitter to the Southern States, and that some concomitant measure should be adopted to sweeten it a little to them. There had before been propositions to fix the seat of government either at Philadelphia or at Georgetown on the Potomac, and it was thought that by giving it to Philadelphia for ten years and to Georgetown permanently afterwards, this might, as an anodyne, calm in some degree the ferment which might be excited by the other measure alone. So two of the Potomac members (White and Leem, but White with a revulsion of stomach almost convulsive) agreed to change their votes, and Hamilton undertook to carry the other point. In doing this, the influence he had established over the Eastern members with the agency of Robert Morris with those of the Middle States effected his side of the engagement, and so the Assumption was passed, and twenty millions of stock divided among favored States and thrown in as pabulum to the stock-jobbing herd. This added to the number of votaries in the Treasury and made its chief the master of every vote in the legislature, which might give to the government the direction suited to his political views.

THOMAS JEFFERSON
The Anas

14

Washington Bids Farewell to His Countrymen

Washington's Farewell Address, long and carefully prepared with the aid of Hamilton's pen, was published in September 1796, six months before he left office. In it he explained the course he had taken as president, set forth some political precepts that he believed the country should follow, and insisted upon the duty of patriotism. "Be united," he said, "be Americans."

Friends and fellow citizens: The period for a new election of a citizen to administer the executive government of the United States being not far distant, and the time actually arrived when your thoughts must be employed in designating the person who is to be clothed with that important trust, it appears to me proper, especially as it may conduce to a more distinct expression of the public voice, that I should now apprise you of the resolution I have formed to decline being considered among the number of those out of whom a choice is to be made. . . .

Here, perhaps, I ought to stop. But a solicitude for your welfare which cannot end with my life, and the apprehension of danger natural to that solicitude, urge me on an occasion like the present to offer to your solemn contemplation and to recommend to your frequent review some sentiments which are the result of much reflection, of no inconsiderable observation, and which appear to me all-important to the permanency of your felicity as a people. . . .

Interwoven as is the love of liberty with every ligament of your hearts, no recommendation of mine is necessary to fortify or confirm the attachment.

The unity of government which constitutes you one people is also now dear to you. It is justly so, for it is a main pillar in the edifice of your real independence, the support of your tranquillity at home, your peace abroad, of your safety, of your prosperity, of that very liberty which you so highly prize. But as it is easy to foresee that from different causes and from different quarters much pains will be taken, many artifices employed, to weaken in your minds the conviction of this truth, as this is the point in your political fortress against which the batteries of internal and external enemies will be most constantly and actively (though often covertly and insidiously) directed, it is of infinite moment that you should properly estimate the immense value of your national union to your collective and individual happiness; that you should cherish a cordial, habitual, and immovable attachment to it; accustoming yourselves to think and speak of it as of the palladium of your political safety and prosperity; watching for its preservation with jealous anxiety; discountenancing whatever may suggest even a suspicion that it can in any event be abandoned; and indignantly frowning upon the first dawning of every attempt to alienate any portion of our country from the rest or to enfeeble the sacred ties which now link together the various parts. . . .

Is there a doubt whether a common government can embrace so large a sphere? Let experience solve it. To listen to mere speculation in such a case were criminal. It is well worth a fair and full experiment. With such powerful and obvious motives to union affecting all parts of our country, while experience shall not have demonstrated its impracticability, there will always be reason to distrust the patriotism of those who in any quarter may endeavor to weaken its bands. . . .

This Government, the offspring of our own choice, uninfluenced and unawed, adopted upon full investigation and mature deliberation, completely free in its principles, in the distribution of its powers, uniting security with energy, and containing within itself a provision for its own amendment, has a just claim to your confidence and your support. Respect for its authority, compliance with its laws, acquiescence in its measures, are duties enjoined by the fundamental maxims of true liberty. The basis of our political systems is the right of the people to make and to alter their constitutions of government. But the constitution which at any time exists, till changed by an explicit and authentic act of the whole people, is sacredly obligatory upon all. The very idea of the power and the right of the people to establish government presupposes the duty of every individual to obey the established government. . . .

I have already intimated to you the danger of parties in the State, with particular reference to the founding of them on geographical discriminations. Let me now take a more comprehensive view, and warn you in the most solemn manner against the baneful effects of the spirit of party generally. . . .

It is important, likewise, that the habits of thinking in a free country should inspire caution in those entrusted with its administration to confine themselves within their respective constitutional spheres, avoiding in the exercise of the powers of one department to encroach upon another. The spirit of encroachment tends to consolidate the powers of all the departments in one, and thus to create, whatever the form of government, a real despotism. . . .

Of all the dispositions and habits which lead to political prosperity, religion and morality are indispensable supports. . . . And let us with caution indulge the supposition that morality can be maintained without religion. Whatever may be conceded to the influence of refined education on minds of peculiar structure, reason and experience both forbid us to expect that national morality can prevail in exclusion of religious principle.

It is substantially true that virtue or morality is a necessary spring of popular government. The rule indeed extends with more or less force to every species of free government. Who that is a sincere friend to it can look with indifference upon attempts to shake the foundation of the fabric? Promote, then, as an object of primary importance, institutions for the general diffusion of knowledge. In proportion as the structure of a government gives force to public opinion, it is essential that public opinion should be enlightened. . . .

Observe good faith and justice toward all nations. Cultivate peace and harmony with all. . . .

In the execution of such a plan nothing is more essential than that permanent, inveterate antipathies against particular nations and passionate attachments for others should be excluded, and that in place of them just and amicable feelings toward all should be cultivated. . . .

So, likewise, a passionate attachment of one nation for another produces a variety of evils. Sympathy for the favorite nation, facilitating the illusion of an imaginary common interest in cases where no real common interest exists, and infusing into one the enmities of the other betrays the former into a participation in the quarrels and wars of the latter without adequate inducement or justification. . . .

Against the insidious wiles of foreign influence (I conjure you to believe me, fellow citizens) the jealousy of a free people ought to be *constantly* awake, since history and experience prove that foreign influence is one of the most baneful foes of republican government. . . .

The great rule of conduct for us in regard to foreign nations is, in extending our commercial relations, to have with them as little *political* connection as possible. So far as we have already formed engagements let them be fulfilled with perfect good faith. Here let us stop.

Europe has a set of primary interests which to us have none or a very remote relation. Hence she must be engaged in frequent controversies, the causes of which are essentially foreign to our concerns. Hence, therefore, it must be unwise in us to implicate ourselves by artificial ties in the ordinary vicissitudes of her politics or the ordinary combinations and collisions of her friendships or enmities.

Our detached and distant situation invites and enables us to pursue a different course. If we remain one people, under an efficient government, the period is not far off when we may defy material injury from external annoyance; when we may take such an attitude as will cause the neutrality we may at any time resolve upon to be scrupulously respected; when belligerent nations, under the impossibility of making acquisitions upon us, will not lightly hazard the giving us provocation; when we may choose peace or war, as our interest, guided by justice, shall counsel.

Why forego the advantages of so peculiar a situation? Why quit our own to stand upon foreign ground? Why, by interweaving our destiny with that of any part of Europe, entangle our peace and prosperity in the toils of European ambition, rivalship, interest, humor, or caprice?

It is our true policy to steer clear of permanent alliances with any portion of the foreign world, so far, I mean, as we are now at liberty to do it; for let me not be understood as capable of patronizing infidelity to existing engagements. I hold the maxim no less applicable to public than to private affairs that honesty is always the best policy. I repeat, therefore, let those engagements be observed in their genuine sense. But in my opinion it is unnecessary and would be unwise to extend them. . . .

Though in reviewing the incidents of my Administration I am unconscious of intentional error, I am nevertheless too sensible of my defects not to think it probable that I may have committed many errors. Whatever they may be, I fervently beseech the Almighty to avert or mitigate the evils to which they may tend. I shall also carry with me the hope that my country will never cease to view them with indulgence, and that, after forty-five years of my life dedicated to its service with upright zeal, the faults of incompetent abilities will be consigned to oblivion, as myself must soon be to the mansions of rest.

Relying on its kindness in this as in other things, and actuated by that fervent love toward it which is so natural to a man who views it in the native soil of himself and his progenitors for several generations, I anticipate with pleasing expectation that retreat in which I promise myself to realize without alloy the sweet enjoyment of partaking in the midst of my fellow citizens the benign influence of good laws under a free government—the ever-favorite object of my heart, and the happy reward, as I trust, of our mutual cares, labors, and dangers.

GEORGE WASHINGTON
Farewell Address
1796

15

How Jefferson Lived in the White House

Jefferson was a widower when he began his eight years in the White House in 1801. Tall, loosely built, rather carelessly dressed, informal of manner, full of endless frank, entertaining, shrewd talk, he impressed many observers as lacking in dignity. But his unaffected simplicity was actually one of the virtues of as true a gentleman as ever occupied the presidential chair. One of his intimate friends was Mrs. Harrison Smith, long a leader in Washington society.

When he took up his residence in the President's House, he [Jefferson] found it scantily furnished with articles brought from Philadelphia and which had been used by General Washington. These, though worn and faded, he retained from respect to their former possessor. His drawing room was fitted up with the same crimson damask furniture that had been used for the same purpose in Philadelphia. The additional furniture necessary for the more spacious mansion provided by the government was plain and simple to excess. The large East Room was unfinished and therefore unused. The apartment in which he took most interest was his cabinet; this he had arranged according to his own taste and convenience. It was a spacious room.

In the center was a long table, with drawers on each side, in which were deposited not only articles appropriate to the place, but a set of carpenter's tools in one and small garden implements in another, from the use of which he derived much amusement. Around the walls were maps, globes, charts, books, etc. In the window recesses were stands for the flowers and plants which it was his delight to attend, and among his roses and geraniums was suspended the cage of his favorite mockingbird, which he cherished with peculiar fondness, not only for its melodious powers, but for its uncommon intelligence and affectionate disposition, of which qualities he gave surprising instances. It was the constant companion of his solitary and studious hours. Whenever he was alone, he opened the cage and let the bird fly about the room. After flitting for a while from one object to another, it would alight on his table and regale him with its sweetest notes, or perch on his shoulder and take its food from his lips. Often when he retired to his chamber it would hop up the stairs after him and, while he took his siesta, would sit on his couch and pour forth its melodious strains. How he loved this bird! How he loved his flowers! He could not live without something to love, and in the absence of his darling grandchildren, his bird and his flowers became objects of tender care. In a man of such dispositions, such tastes, who would recognize the rude, unpolished democrat which foreigners and political enemies described him to be? If his dress was plain, unstudied, and sometimes old-fashioned in its form, it was always of the finest materials; in his personal habits he was fastidiously neat; and if in his manners he was simple, affable, and unceremonious, it was not because he was ignorant of but because he despised the conventional and artificial usages of courts and fashionable life. His simplicity never degenerated into vulgarity, nor his affability into familiarity. On the contrary, there was a natural and quiet dignity in his demeanor that often produced a degree of restraint in those who conversed with him, unfavorable to that free interchange of thoughts and feelings which constitute the greatest charm of social life. His residence in foreign courts never imparted that polish to his manners which courts require, and though possessed of ease they were deficient in grace. His external appearance had no pretensions to elegance, but it was neither coarse nor awkward, and it must be owned his greatest personal attraction was a countenance beaming with benevolence and intelligence.

He was called, even by his friends, a national man, full of odd fancies in little things, and it must be confessed that his local and domestic arrangements were full of contrivances or *conveniences,* as he called them, peculiarly his own and never met with in other houses. Too often the practical was sacrificed to the fanciful, as was evident to the most superficial observer in the location and structure of his house at Monticello.

The same fanciful disposition characterized all his architectural plans and domestic arrangements, and even in the President's House were introduced some of these favorite contrivances, many of them really useful and convenient. Among these, there was in his dining room an invention for introducing and removing the dinner without the opening and shutting of doors. A set of circular shelves were so contrived in the wall that on touching a spring they turned into the room loaded with the dishes placed on them by the servants without the wall, and by the same process the removed dishes were conveyed out of the room. When he had any persons dining with him with whom he wished to enjoy a free and unrestricted flow of conversation, the number of persons at table never exceeded four, and by each individual was placed a *dumbwaiter* containing everything necessary for the progress of the dinner from beginning to end so as to make the attendance of servants entirely unnecessary, believing, as he did, that much of the domestic and even public discord was produced by the mutilated and misconstructed repetition of free conversation at dinner tables by these mute but not inattentive listeners. William McClure and Caleb Lowndes, both distinguished and well-known citizens of Philadelphia, were invited together to one of these dinners. Mr. McClure, who had traveled over a great part of Europe and after a long residence in Paris had just returned to the United States, could of course impart a great deal of important and interesting information with an accuracy and fullness unattainable through the medium of letters. Interesting as were the topics of his discourse, Mr. Jefferson gave him his whole attention, but closely as he listened, Mr. McClure spoke so low that although seated by his side, the President scarcely heard half that was said. "You need not speak so low," said Mr. Jefferson, smiling; "you see we are alone and *our walls have no ears.*" "I have so long been living in Paris, where the walls have ears," replied Mr. McClure, "that I have contracted this habit of speaking in an undertone." He then described the system of espionage established throughout France, whose vigilance pervaded the most private circles and retired families, among whose servants one was sure to be in the employment of the police.

At his usual dinner parties the company seldom if ever exceeded fourteen, including himself and his secretary. The invitations were not given promiscuously, or as has been done of late years, alphabetically, but his guests were generally selected in reference to their tastes, habits, and suitability in all respects, which attention had a wonderful effect in making his parties more agreeable than dinner parties usually are; this limited number prevented the company's forming little knots and carrying on in undertones separate conversations, a custom so common and almost unavoidable in a large party. At Mr. Jefferson's table the conversation was general; every guest was entertained and interested in whatever topic was discussed. To each an opportunity was offered for the exercise of his colloquial powers, and the stream of conversation, thus enriched by such various contributions, flowed on, full, free, and animated. Of course he took the lead and gave the tone with a tact so true and discriminating that he seldom missed his aim, which was to draw forth the talents and information of each and all of his guests and to place everyone in an advantageous light, and by being pleased with themselves, be enabled to please others. Did he perceive any one individual silent and unattended to, he would make him the object of his peculiar attention and in a manner apparently the most undesigning would draw him into notice and make him a participator in the general conversation. One instance will be given which will better illustrate this trait in Mr. Jefferson's manners of presiding at his table than any verbal description. On an occasion when the company was composed of several distinguished persons and the conversation was eager and animated, one individual remained silent and unnoticed; he had just arrived from Europe, where he had so long been a resident that on his return he felt himself a stranger in his own country and was totally unknown to the present company. After having, seemingly without design, led the conversation to the desired point, Mr. Jefferson, turning to this individual, said, "To you, Mr. C., we are indebted to this benefit; no one more deserves the gratitude of his country." Every eye was turned on the hitherto unobserved guest, who honestly looked as much astonished as anyone in the company. The President continued, "Yes, sir, the upland rice which you sent from Algiers and which thus far succeeds will, when generally adopted by the planters, prove an inestimable blessing to our Southern States." At once Mr. C., who had been a mere cipher in this intelligent circle, became a person of importance and took a large share in the conversation that ensued. . . .

Mr. Jefferson was known in Europe as much, if not more, as a philosopher than as a politician. Mr. Jefferson's acquaintance in this wide and distinguished circle in Paris made him well known throughout Europe, and when he became President his reputation as a philosopher and man of letters brought many literary and scientific foreigners to our country. Among others, Baron Humboldt one day, in answer to some inquiries addressed to this celebrated traveler, replied, "I have come not to see your great rivers and mountains, but to become acquainted with your great men." Of these, he held Mr. Jefferson in the highest estimation. Soon after the Baron's arrival on our shores, he hastened to Washington and, during his visit to our city, passed many hours of every day with Mr. Jefferson. Baron Humboldt formed not his estimate of men and manners by their habiliments and conventionalisms, and refined as were his tastes and polished as were his manners, he was neither shocked nor disgusted, as was the case with the British minister (Mr. Foster), by the old-fashioned form, ill-chosen colors, or simple material of the President's dress. Neither did he remark the deficiency of elegance in his person or of polish in his manners, but indifferent to these external and extrinsic circumstances, he easily discerned and most highly appreciated the intrinsic qualities of the philosophic statesman through even the homely costume which had concealed them from the ken of the fastidious diplomat.

His visits at the President's House were unshackled by mere ceremony and not limited to any particular hour. One evening he called about twilight, and being shown into the drawing room without being announced, he found Mr. Jefferson seated on the floor, surrounded by half a dozen of his little grandchildren, so eagerly and noisily engaged in a game of romps that for some moments his entrance was not perceived. When his presence was discovered, Mr. Jefferson rose up and shaking hands with him said, "You have found me playing the fool, Baron, but I am *sure* to you I need make no apology."

Another time he called of a morning and was taken into the cabinet. As he sat by the table, among the newspapers that were scattered about, he perceived one that was always filled with the most virulent abuse of Mr. Jefferson, calumnies the most offensive, personal as well as political. "Why are these libels allowed?" asked the Baron, taking up the paper. "Why is not this libelous journal suppressed, or its editor at least fined and imprisoned?"

Mr. Jefferson smiled, saying: "Put that paper in your pocket, Baron, and should you hear the reality of our liberty, the freedom of our press, questioned, show this paper and tell where you found it."

Mrs. Samuel Harrison Smith
The First Forty Years of Washington Society

16

Tecumseh Pledges Support to the British

The Shawnee chief Tecumseh felt outraged by what he considered American aggressions upon the lands of his tribe, and he willingly joined with the British to halt them. General William Henry Harrison met Tecumseh and his braves at the battle of Tippecanoe, November 1811, and destroyed the Indian confederacy. Two years later Tecumseh was killed at the battle of the Thames.

Father, listen to your children! You have them now all before you. The war before this, our British father gave the hatchet to his red children, when old chiefs were alive. They are now dead. In that war our father was thrown on his back by the Americans, and our father took them by the hand without our knowledge, and we are afraid that our father will do so again at this time.

Summer before last, when I came forward with my red brethren and was ready to take up the hatchet in favor of our British father, we were told not to be in a hurry, that he had not yet determined to fight the Americans.

Listen! When war was declared, our father stood up and gave us the tomahawk and told us that he was ready to strike the Americans; that he wanted our assistance; and that he would certainly get us our lands back, which the Americans had taken from us.

Listen! You told us, at that time, to bring forward our families to this place, and we did so—and you promised to take care of them, and that they should want for nothing, while the men would go and fight the enemy; that we need not trouble ourselves about the enemy's garrisons; that we knew nothing about them; and that our father would attend to that part of the business. You also told your red children that you would take good care of your garrison here, which made our hearts glad.

Listen! When we were last at the Rapids, it is true we gave you little assistance. It is hard to fight people who live like groundhogs.

Father, listen! Our fleet has gone out; we know they have fought; we have heard the great guns, but know nothing of what has happened to our father with one arm. Our ships have gone one way, and we are much astonished to see our father tying up everything and preparing to run away the other, without letting his red children know what his intentions are. You always told us to remain here and take care of our lands. It made our hearts glad to hear that was your wish. Our great father, the King, is the head, and you represent him. You always told us that you would never draw your foot off British ground; but now, Father, we see you are drawing back, and we are sorry to see our father doing so without seeing the enemy. We must compare our father's conduct to a fat animal that carries its tail upon its back, but when affrighted, it drops it between its legs and runs off.

Listen, Father! The Americans have not yet defeated us by land; neither are we sure that they have done so by water—we therefore wish to remain here and fight our enemy, should they make their appearance. If they defeat us, we will then retreat with our father.

At the battle of the Rapids, last war, the Americans certainly defeated us, and when we retreated to our father's fort in that place, the gates were shut against us. We were afraid that it would now be the case, but instead of that, we now see our British father preparing to march out of his garrison.

Father! You have got the arms and ammunition which our great father sent for his red children. If you have an idea of going away, give them to us, and you may go and welcome, for us. Our lives are in the hands of the Great Spirit. We are determined to defend our lands, and if it is His will, we wish to leave our bones upon them.

FRANK MOORE
American Eloquence

17

Andrew Jackson Routs the Redcoats at New Orleans

The British force which had taken Washington soon left to join the army of Sir Edward Pakenham, a relative of Wellington who had been sent to capture New Orleans. The military situation of the Americans at the mouth of the Mississippi was very weak. But the government did the one thing needed to save Louisiana when it placed the tall, lanky, hot-tempered, and singularly effective Andrew Jackson in command there. He arrived on the second of December, 1814, and set every man within reach to work throwing up earthworks and mounting guns. Our British officer tells what happened when the battle of New Orleans was fought the following month—eleven days after peace had been signed at Ghent. When Britons and Americans met again on a battlefield just over a century later, it was as comrades facing a common enemy.

The morning of the 1st of January [1815] chanced to be peculiarly gloomy. A thick haze obscured for a long time the rays of the sun, nor could objects be discerned with any accuracy till a late hour.

But, at length, the mist gave way, and the American camp was fully exposed to view. Being at this time only three hundred yards distant, we could perceive all that was going forward with great exactness. The different regiments were upon parade and, being dressed in holiday suits, presented really a fine appearance. Mounted officers were riding backwards and forwards through the ranks, bands were playing, and colors floating in the air; in a word, all seemed jollity and gala, when suddenly our batteries opened, and the face of affairs was instantly changed. The ranks were broken; the different corps, dispersing, fled in all directions, while the utmost terror and disorder appeared to prevail. Instead of nicely dressed lines, nothing but confused crowds could now be observed; nor was it without much difficulty that order was finally restored.

While this consternation prevailed among the infantry, their artillery remained silent, but as soon as the former rallied, they also recovered confidence and answered our salute with great rapidity and precision. A heavy cannonade therefore commenced on both sides and continued during the whole of the day, till towards evening our ammunition began to fail, and our fire in consequence to slacken. The fire of the Americans, on the other hand, was redoubled; landing a number of guns from the flotilla, they increased their artillery to a prodigious amount, and directing at the same time the whole force of their cannon on the opposite bank, against the flank of our batteries, they soon convinced us that all endeavors to surpass them in this mode of fighting would be useless. Once more, therefore, were we obliged to retire, leaving our heavy guns to their fate, but as no attempt was made by the Americans to secure them, working parties were again sent out after dark, and such as had not been destroyed were removed.

All our plans had as yet proved abortive; even this, upon which so much reliance had been placed, was found to be of no avail, and it must be confessed that something like murmuring began to be heard through the camp. And, in truth, if ever an army might be permitted to murmur, it was this. In landing they had borne great hardships, not only without repining but with cheerfulness; their hopes had been excited by false reports as to the practicability of the attempt in which they were embarked, and now they found themselves entangled amidst difficulties from which there appeared to be no escape except by victory. In their attempts upon the enemy's line, however, they had been twice foiled; in artillery they perceived themselves so greatly overmatched that their own could hardly assist them; their provisions, being derived wholly from the fleet, were both scanty and coarse; and their rest was continually broken. For not only did the cannon and mortars from the main of the enemy's position play unremittingly upon them both day and night, but they were likewise exposed to a deadly fire from the opposite bank of the river, where no less than eighteen pieces of artillery were now mounted and swept the entire line of our encampment. Besides all this, to undertake the duty of a picket was as dangerous as to go into action. Parties of American sharpshooters harassed and disturbed those appointed to that service, from the time they took possession of their post till they were relieved, while to light fires at night was impossible because they served but as certain marks for the enemy's gunners.

It was determined to divide the army, to send part across the river, who should seize the enemy's guns and turn them on themselves, while the remainder should at the same time make a general assault along the whole entrenchment. But before this plan could be put into execution, it would be necessary to cut a canal across the entire neck of land from the Bayou de Catiline to the river, of sufficient width and depth to admit of boats being brought up from the lake. Upon this arduous undertaking were the troops immediately employed.

While these things were going on and men's minds were anxiously turned towards approaching events, fresh spirit was given to the army by the unexpected arrival of Major General Lambert with the Seventh and Forty-third— two fine battalions, mustering each eight hundred effective men. By this reinforcement together with the addition of a body of sailors and marines from the fleet, our numbers amounted now to little short of eight thousand men, a force which in almost any other quarter of America would have been irresistible.

According to the preconcerted plan, Colonel Thornton's detachment was to cross the river immediately after dark. They were to push forward so as to carry all the batteries and point the guns before daylight, when on the throwing up of a rocket, they were to commence firing upon the enemy's line, which at the same moment was to be attacked by the main of our army.

Thus were all things arranged on the night of the 7th, for the 8th was fixed upon as the day decisive of the fate of New Orleans. . . .

But unfortunately, the loss of time nothing could repair. Instead of reaching the opposite bank, at latest by midnight, dawn was beginning to appear before the boats quitted the canal. It was in vain that they rowed on in perfect silence, and with oars muffled, gaining the point of debarkation without being perceived. It was in vain that they made good their landing and formed upon the beach without opposition or alarm. Day had already broke, and the signal rocket was seen in the air while they were yet four miles from the batteries, which ought hours ago to have been taken.

In the meantime, the main body armed and moved forward some way in front of the pickets. There they stood waiting for daylight and listening with the greatest anxiety for the firing which ought now to be heard on the opposite bank. But this attention was exerted in vain, and day dawned upon them long before they desired its appearance. Nor was Sir Edward Pakenham disappointed in this part of his plan alone. Instead of perceiving everything in readiness for the assault, he saw his troops in battle array, indeed, but not a ladder or fascine upon the field. The Forty-fourth, which was appointed to carry them, had either misunderstood or neglected their orders and now headed the column of attack, without any means being provided for crossing the enemy's ditch or scaling his rampart.

The indignation of poor Pakenham on this occasion may be imagined, but cannot be described. Galloping towards Colonel Mullens, who led the Forty-fourth, he commanded him instantly to return with his regiment for the ladders, but the opportunity of planting them was lost, and though they were brought up, it was only to be scattered over the field by the frightened bearers. For our troops were by this time visible to the enemy. A dreadful fire was accordingly opened upon them, and they were mowed down by hundreds, while they stood waiting for orders.

Seeing that all his well-laid plans were frustrated, Pakenham gave the word to advance, and the other regiments, leaving the Forty-fourth with the ladders and fascines behind them, rushed on to the assault. On the left, a detachment of the Ninety-fifth, Twenty-first, and Fourth stormed a three-gun battery and took it. Here they remained for some time in the expectation of support, but none arriving, and a strong column of the enemy forming for its recovery, they determined to anticipate the attack and pushed on. The battery which they had taken was in advance of the body of the works, being cut off from it by a ditch, across which only a single plank was thrown. Along this plank did these brave men attempt to pass, but being opposed by overpowering numbers, they were repulsed, and the Americans, in turn, forcing their way into the battery, at length succeeded in recapturing it with immense slaughter. On the right, again, the Twenty-first and Fourth being almost cut to pieces and thrown into some confusion by the enemy's fire, the Ninety-third pushed on and took the lead. Hastening forward, our troops soon reached the ditch, but to scale the parapet without ladders was impossible. Some few, indeed, by mounting one upon another's shoulders, succeeded in entering the works, but these were instantly overpowered, most of them killed and the rest taken, while as many as stood without were exposed to a sweeping fire, which cut them down by whole companies. It was in vain that the most obstinate courage was displayed. They fell by the hands of men whom they absolutely did not see, for the Americans, without so much as lifting their faces above the rampart, swung their firelocks by one arm over the wall and discharged them directly upon their heads. The whole of the guns,

likewise, from the opposite bank kept up a well-directed and deadly cannonade upon their flank, and thus were they destroyed without an opportunity
being given of displaying their valor or obtaining so much as revenge.

Poor Pakenham saw how things were going and did all that a general
could do to rally his broken troops. Riding towards the Forty-fourth, which
had returned to the ground but in great disorder, he called out for Colonel
Mullens to advance, but that officer had disappeared and was not to be found.
He, therefore, prepared to lead them on himself and had put himself at their
head for that purpose, when he received a slight wound in the knee from a
musket ball, which killed his horse. Mounting another, he again headed the
Forty-fourth, when a second ball took effect more fatally, and he dropped
lifeless into the arms of his aide-de-camp.

GEORGE ROBERT GLEIG
A Narrative of the Campaigns of the British Army
at Washington and New Orleans

18

"Old America Is Moving Westward"

After the War of 1812 the westward current ran broad and fast; Indiana was admitted to the Union in 1816, Illinois in 1818. A liberal-minded English observer who became greatly interested in Illinois settlement pictures this pioneering advance as he saw it in Pennsylvania, where the great highways to the West converged on the Ohio River.

McConnel's Town. May 23, 1817.—

The road we have been traveling terminates at this place, where it strikes the great turnpike from Philadelphia to Pittsburgh, and with the road ends the line of stages by which we have been traveling, a circumstance of which we knew nothing until our arrival here, having entered ourselves passengers at George Town for Pittsburgh, by the Pittsburgh stage, as it professed to be.

So here we are, nine in number, one hundred and thirty miles of mountain country between us and Pittsburgh. We learn that the stages which pass daily from Philadelphia and Baltimore are generally full and that there are now many persons at Baltimore waiting for places. No vehicles of any kind are to be hired, and here we must either stay or *walk* off. The latter we prefer, and separating each our bundle from the little that we have of traveling stores, we are about to undertake our mountain pilgrimage—accepting the alternative most cheerfully after the dreadful shaking of the last hundred miles by stage. . . .

We have now fairly turned our backs on the old world and find ourselves in the very stream of emigration. Old America seems to be breaking up and moving westward. We are seldom out of sight, as we travel on this grand track towards the Ohio, of family groups, behind and before us, some with a view to a particular spot, close to a brother, perhaps, or a friend who has gone before and reported well of the country. Many, like ourselves, when they arrive in the wilderness, will find no lodge prepared for them.

A small wagon (so light that you might almost carry it, yet strong enough to bear a good load of bedding, utensils and provisions, and a swarm of young citizens, and to sustain marvelous shocks in its passage over these rocky heights) with two small horses, sometimes a cow or two, comprises their all, excepting a little store of hard-earned cash for the land office of the district, where they may obtain a title for as many acres as they possess half-dollars, being one-fourth of the purchase money. The wagon has a tilt, or cover, made of a sheet or perhaps a blanket. The family are seen before, behind, or within the vehicle, according to the road or weather or perhaps the spirits of the party.

The New Englanders, they say, may be known by the cheerful air of the women advancing in front of the vehicle, the Jersey people by their being fixed steadily within it, whilst the Pennsylvanians creep lingering behind, as though regretting the homes they have left. A cart and single horse frequently afford the means of transfer, sometimes a horse and packsaddle. Often the back of the poor pilgrim bears all his effects, and his wife follows, naked-footed, bending under the hopes of the family. . . .

A blacksmith here earns twenty dollars per month and board, and he lives in a cabin of one room, for which, with a garden, he pays twenty dollars a year. Firewood is two dollars per cord—the price is merely the labor, as is, in fact, a great part of what you pay for everything. Thus, nothing but land is cheap in this country, excepting British goods, and they are not cheap to the consumer, because the storekeeper sells his own labor at a dear rate. Land will long be at a low price, but as produce hardly keeps pace with the population, the latter is proportionally dear. Therefore, agriculture is and will be a safe and profitable occupation. As to manufactures, they will rise as they are wanted, and if they rise spontaneously, they will flourish without extraneous aid.

MAY 26.—

We have completed our third day's march to general satisfaction. We proceed nearly as fast as our fellow travelers in carriages, and much more pleasantly.

This is a land of plenty, and we are proceeding to a land of *abundance,* as is proved by the noble droves of oxen we meet on their way from the western country to the city of Philadelphia. They are kindly, well-formed, and well-fed animals, averaging about six hundredweight.

A flock of sheep, properly speaking, has not met my eyes in America, nor a tract of good sheep pasture. Twenty or thirty half-starved creatures are seen now and then straggling about in much wretchedness. These supply a little wool for domestic use. Cattle are good and plentiful, and horses excellent.

MAY 28.—

The condition of the people of America is so different from aught that we in Europe have an opportunity of observing that it would be difficult to convey an adequate notion of their character. They are great travelers and, in general, better acquainted with the vast expanse of country spreading over their eighteen states than the English with their little island. They are also a migrating people and even when in prosperous circumstances can contemplate a change of situation which, under our old establishments and fixed habits, none but the most enterprising would venture upon when urged by adversity.

To give an idea of the internal movements of this vast hive, about twelve thousand wagons passed between Baltimore and Philadelphia in the last year, with from four to six horses, carrying from thirty-five to forty hundred-weight. The cost of carriage is about seven dollars per hundredweight from Philadelphia to Pittsburgh, and the money paid for the conveyance of goods on this road exceeds three hundred thousand pounds sterling. Add to these the numerous stages, loaded to the utmost, and the innumerable travelers on horseback, on foot, and in light wagons, and you have before you a scene of bustle and business, extending over a space of three hundred miles, which is truly wonderful.

MORRIS BIRKBECK
Notes on a Journey in America from the Coast of Virginia
to the Territory of Illinois

19

Timothy Flint Appraises
the Frontiersmen

Not all accounts of the frontier were exuberantly favorable. Some observers drew harsh pictures of its squalor, hardships, and uncouthness. A balanced description was offered by Timothy Flint, a Harvard graduate and missionary who spent a decade, beginning in 1816, in church work in the Mississippi Valley. He said much about the crudeness, drudgery, and disappointments of life in pioneer communities, but as the following pages show, he thought these difficulties an excellent school for character.

The people in the Atlantic states have not yet recovered from the horror inspired by the term "backwoodsman." This prejudice is particularly strong in New England and is more or less felt from Maine to Georgia. When I first visited this country, I had my full share, and my family by far too much for their comfort. In approaching the country, I heard a thousand stories of gougings and robberies and shooting down with the rifle. I have traveled in these regions thousands of miles under all circumstances of exposure and danger. I have traveled alone or in company only with such as needed protection, instead of being able to impart it, and this too, in many instances, where I was not known as a minister or where such knowledge would have had no influence in protecting me. I never have carried the slightest weapon of defense. I scarcely remember to have experienced anything that resembled insult or to have felt myself in danger from the people. I have often seen men that had lost an eye. Instances of murder, numerous and horrible in their circumstances, have occurred in my vicinity. But they were such lawless rencounters as terminate in murder everywhere, and in which the drunkenness, brutality, and violence were mutual. They were catastrophes in which quiet and sober men would be in no danger of being involved. When we look round these immense regions and consider that I have been in settlements three hundred miles from any court of justice, when we look at the position of the men and the state of things, the wonder is that so few outrages and murders occur. The gentlemen of the towns, even here [Louisiana], speak often with a certain contempt and horror of the backwoodsmen. It is true there are worthless people here; it is true there are gamblers and gougers and outlaws, but there are fewer of them than, from the nature of things and the character of the age and the world, we ought to expect. But the backwoodsman of the west, as I have seen him, is generally an amiable and virtuous man. His general motive for coming here is to be a freeholder, to have plenty of rich land, and to be able to settle his children about him. It is a most virtuous motive. And I fully believe that nine in ten of the emigrants have come here with no other motive. You find, in truth, that he has vices and barbarisms peculiar to his situation. His manners are rough. He wears, it may be, a long beard. He has a great quantity of bear- or deerskins wrought into his household establishment, his furniture and dress. He carries a knife or a dirk in his bosom, and when in the woods has a rifle on his back and a pack of dogs at his heels. An Atlantic stranger, transferred directly from one of our cities to his door, would recoil from a rencounter with him. But remember that his rifle and his dogs are among his chief means of support and profit. Remember that all his first days here were passed in dread of the savages. Remember that he still encounters them, still meets bears and panthers. Enter his door and tell him you are benighted and wish the shelter of his cabin for the night. The welcome is indeed seemingly ungracious: "I reckon you can stay" or "I suppose we must let you stay." But this apparent ungraciousness is the harbinger of every kindness that he can bestow and every comfort that his cabin can afford. Good coffee, cornbread and butter, venison, pork, wild and tame fowls, are set before you. His wife, timid, silent, reserved, but constantly attentive to your comfort, does not sit at the table with you, but like the wives of the patriarchs, stands and attends on you. You are shown to the best bed which the house can afford. When this kind of hospitality has been afforded you as long as you choose to stay, and when you depart and speak about your bill, you are most commonly told with some slight mark of resentment that they do not keep tavern. Even the flaxen-headed urchins will turn away from your money.

In all my extensive intercourse with these people, I do not recollect but one instance of positive rudeness and inhospitality. . . .

I have found the backwoodsmen to be such as I have described—a hardy, adventurous, hospitable, rough, but sincere and upright race of people. I have received so many kindnesses from them that it becomes me always to preserve a grateful and affectionate remembrance of them. If we were to try them by the standard of New England customs and opinions, that is to say, the customs of a people under entirely different circumstances, there would be many things in the picture that would strike us offensively. They care little about ministers and think less about paying them. They are averse to all, even the most necessary, restraints. They are destitute of the forms and observances of society and religion, but they are sincere and kind without professions and have a coarse but substantial morality, which is often rendered more striking by the immediate contrast of the graceful bows, civility, and professions of their French Catholic neighbors, who have the observances of society and the forms of worship with often but a scanty modicum of the blunt truth and uprightness of their unpolished neighbors.

I have spoken of the movable part of the community, and unfortunately for the western country, it constitutes too great a proportion of the whole community. The general inclination here is too much like that of the Tartars. Next to hunting, Indian wars, and the wonderful exuberance of Kentucky, the favorite topic is new countries. They only make such improvements as they can leave without reluctance and without loss. I have everywhere noted the operation of this impediment in the way of those permanent and noble improvements which grow out of a love for that appropriated spot where we were born and where we expect to die.

Timothy Flint
Recollections of the Last Ten Years
1826

20

William Howells Remembers
Neighborliness in Ohio

William Cooper Howells—father of the novelist William Dean Howells—was one of the notable editors of Ohio in the generation before the Civil War; migrating from town to town, editing one small journal after another, he upheld Whig principles and the antislavery cause. His recollections were later edited by his more famous son, who himself in some of his novels turned to the scenes here described.

I can hardly realize how greatly things have changed since that period and what a primitive and simple kind of life prevailed. Particularly remarkable was the general equality and the general dependence of all upon the neighborly kindness and good offices of others. Their houses and barns were built of logs and were raised by the collection of many neighbors together on one day, whose united strength was necessary to the handling of the logs. As every man was ready with the ax and understood this work, all came together within the circle where the raising was to be done, and all worked together with about equal skill. The best axmen were given charge of the placing of the logs on the wall, and someone of experience took the general direction. The logs of the width and length of the house were usually of different lengths. Those intended for the two sides were placed in a convenient place, some distance from the foundation; those for the ends, in another place. The first two side logs were put in place at the back and front; then the end logs were notched down in their places; then two side logs would be rolled up on skids and notched in their places. At the corners, the top of the log, as soon as it was put in place, would be dressed up by the cornerman, and when the next logs were rolled up, they would be notched, which notch would be turned downwards upon the saddle made to receive it, when the cornerman would saddle that log ready for the next. This kept the logs in their places like a dovetail and brought them together so as to form a closer wall. The ends of the skids would be raised on each new log as it was laid down to make a way for the next. The logs on these skids would be rolled as long as the men could handle them from the ground, but when the wall got too high, then they would use forks, made by cutting a young notched tree, with which the logs would be pushed up. By using a fork at each end of the log, it could be pushed up with ease and safety. The men understood handling timber, and accidents seldom happened, unless the logs were icy or wet or the whisky had gone round too often. I was often at these raisings, because we had raisings of the kind to do, and it was the custom always to send one from a family to help, so that you could claim like assistance in return. At the raisings I would take the position of cornerman, if the building was not too heavy, as it was a post of honor, and my head was steady when high up from the ground. In chopping on the corners we always stood up straight, and it required a good balance.

This kind of mutual help of the neighbors was extended to many kinds of work, such as rolling up the logs in a clearing, grubbing out the underbrush, splitting rails, cutting logs for a house, and the like. When a gathering of men for such a purpose took place, there was commonly some sort of mutual job laid out for women, such as quilting, sewing, or spinning up a lot of thread for some poor neighbor. This would bring together a mixed party, and it was usually arranged that after supper there should be a dance or at least plays, which would occupy a good part of the night and wind up with the young fellows seeing the girls home in the short hours or, if they went home early, sitting with them by the fire in that kind of interesting chat known as sparking.

The flax crops required a good deal of handling, in weeding, pulling, and dressing, and each of these processes was made the occasion of a joint gathering of boys and girls and a good time. As I look back now upon those times, I am puzzled to think how they managed to make such small and crowded houses serve for large parties, and how they found room to dance in an apartment of perhaps eighteen feet square, in which there would be two large beds and a trundle bed, besides the furniture, which though not of great quantity took some room. And then, if these were small houses, they often contained large families. I have often seen three or four little heads peeping out from that part of a trundle bed that was not pushed entirely under the big bed, to get their share of the fun going on among the older ones while the big beds were used to receive the hats and bonnets and perhaps a baby or two, stowed away till the mothers were ready to go home.

One of the gatherings for joint work which has totally disappeared from the agriculture of modern times, and one that was always a jolly kind of affair, was the cornhusking. It was a sort of harvest home in its department, and it was the more jolly because it was a gathering with very little respect to persons, and embraced in the invitation men and big boys, with the understanding that no one would be unwelcome. There was always a good supper served at the husking, and as certainly a good appetite to eat it with. It came at a plentiful season, when the turkeys and chickens were fat, and a fat pig was at hand, to be flanked on the table with good bread in various forms, turnips and potatoes from the autumn stores, apple and pumpkin pies, good coffee, and the like. And the cooking was always well done, and all in such bountiful abundance that no one feared to eat, while many a poor fellow was certain of a square meal by being present at a husking. You were sure to see the laboring men of the vicinity out, and the wives of a goodly number of farmhands would be on hand to help in the cooking and serving at the table. The cornhusking has been discontinued because the farmers found out that it was less trouble to husk it in the field, direct from the stalk, than to gather in the husk and go over it again. But in that day they did not know that much and therefore took the original method of managing their corn crop, which was this: As soon as the grain began to harden they would cut the stalks off just above the ears and save these tops for fodder, and if they had time they stripped all the blades off the stalks below the ears, which made very nice though costly feed. Then, as barn room was not usually over-plenty, they made a kind of frame of poles, as for a tent, and thatched it, sides and top, with the corn tops placed with the tassel downward, so as to shed the rain and snow. This was called the fodder house and was built in the barnyard. Inside they would store the blades in bundles, the husks, and the pumpkins that were saved for use in the winter. The fodder house was commonly made ten feet high and as long as was necessary, and it was used up through the winter by feeding the fodder to the cattle, beginning at the back, which would be temporarily closed by a few bundles of the tops. It would thus serve as a protection for what might be stored in it till all was used up. The fodder house was, of all things, a favorite place for the children to hide in and play. When the season for gathering the corn came, the farmers went through the fields and pulled off the ears and husks together, throwing them upon the ground in heaps, whence they were hauled into the barnyard and there piled up in a neat pile of convenient length, according to the crop, and say four or five feet high, rising to a sharp peak from a base of about six feet. Care was taken to make this pile of equal width and height from end to end so that it would be easily and fairly divided in the middle by a rail laid upon it.

When the husking party had assembled they were all called out into line, and two fellows, mostly ambitious boys, were chosen captains. These then chose their men, each calling out one of the crowd alternately, till all were chosen. Then the heap was divided, by two judicious chaps walking solemnly along the ridge of the heap of corn and deciding where the dividing rail was to be laid, and as this had to be done by starlight or moonlight at best, it took considerable deliberation, as the comparative solidity of the ends of the heap and the evenness of it had to be taken into account. This done, the captains placed a good steady man at each side of the rail, who made it a point to work through and cut the heap in two as soon as possible, and then the two parties fell to husking, all standing with the heap in front of them and throwing the husked corn onto a clear space over the heap, and the husks behind them. From the time they began till the corn was all husked at one end, there would be steady work, each man husking all the corn he could, never stopping except to take a pull at the stone jug of inspiration that passed occasionally along the line; weak lovers of the stuff were sometimes overcome, though it was held to be a disgraceful thing to take too much. The captains would go up and down their lines and rally their men as if in a battle, and the whole was an exciting affair. As soon as one party got done, they raised a shout, and hoisting their captain on their shoulders, carried him over to the other side with general cheering. Then would come a little bantering talk and explanation why the defeated party lost, and all would turn to and husk up the remnants of the heap. All hands would then join to carry the husks into the fodder house. The shout at hoisting the captain was the signal for bringing the supper on the table, and the huskers and the supper met soon after. These gatherings often embraced forty or fifty men. If the farmhouse was small it would be crowded, and the supper would be managed by repeated sittings at the table. At a large house there was less crowding and more fun, and if, as was often the case, some occasion had been given for an assemblage of the girls of the neighborhood, and particularly if the man that played the fiddle should attend, after the older men had gone there was very apt to be a good time. There was a tradition that the boys who accidentally husked a red ear and saved it would be entitled to a kiss from somebody. But I never knew it to be necessary to produce a red ear to secure a kiss where there was a disposition to give or take one.

WILLIAM COOPER HOWELLS
Recollections of Life in Ohio from 1813 to 1840

21

The First Lowering

Even before the Revolution, the skill and courage of the American whalemen were famous abroad and elicited a glowing tribute from Edmund Burke. Whaling reached its height in the period from 1840 to 1860, when never fewer than 500 and in one year as many as 735 American vessels put out to obtain sperm oil, whale oil, and whalebone. The rugged tars of New Bedford gained a salt-sprayed renown throughout the seven seas. Most famous of all their sailing hands was Herman Melville, who shipped on the *Acushnet* in 1841. When he could no longer endure the hardships of whaling life, he deserted at the Marquesas Islands; his voyage thus gave him the material for both *Moby-Dick* and *Typee*.

To a landsman, no whale, nor any sign of a herring, would have been visible at that moment; nothing but a troubled bit of greenish white water, and thin scattered puffs of vapor hovering over it and suffusingly blowing off to leeward, like the confused scud from white rolling billows. The air around suddenly vibrated—and tingled, as it were—like the air over intensely heated plates of iron. Beneath this atmospheric waving and curling, and partially beneath a thin layer of water, also, the whales were swimming. Seen in advance of all the other indications, the puffs of vapor they spouted seemed their forerunning couriers and detached flying outriders.

All four boats were now in keen pursuit of that one spot of troubled water and air. But it bade fair to outstrip them; it flew on and on, as a mass of interblending bubbles borne down a rapid stream from the hills.

"Pull, pull, my good boys," said Starbuck, in the lowest possible but intensest concentrated whisper to his men; while the sharp fixed glance from his eyes, darted straight ahead of the bow, almost seemed as two visible needles in two unerring binnacle compasses. He did not say much to his crew, though, nor did his crew say anything to him; only the silence of the boat was at intervals startlingly pierced by one of his peculiar whispers, now harsh with command, now soft with entreaty.

How different the loud little King Post. "Sing out and say something, my hearties. Roar and pull, my thunderbolts! Beach me, beach me on their black backs, boys; only do that for me, and I'll sign over to you my Martha's Vineyard plantation, boys; including wife, and children, boys. Lay me on—lay me on! O Lord, Lord! but I shall go stark, staring mad! See! see that white water!" And so shouting, he pulled his hat from his head, and stamped up and down on it; then picking it up, flirted it far off upon the sea; and finally fell to rearing and plunging in the boat's stern like a crazed colt from the prairie. . . .

Meanwhile, all the boats tore on. The repeated specific allusions of Flask to "that whale," as he called the fictitious monster which he declared to be incessantly tantalizing his boat's bow with his tail—these allusions of his were at times so vivid and lifelike that they would cause some one or two of his men to snatch a fearful look over the shoulder. But this was against all rule, for the oarsmen must put out their eyes and ram a skewer through their necks, usage pronouncing that they must have no organs but ears, and no limbs but arms, in these critical moments.

It was a sight full of quick wonder and awe! The vast swells of the omnipotent sea; the surging, hollow roar they made, as they rolled along the eight gunwales, like gigantic bowls in a boundless bowling green; the brief suspended agony of the boat, as it would tip for an instant on the knifelike edge of the sharper waves that almost seemed threatening to cut it in two; the sudden profound dip into the watery glens and hollows; the keen spurrings and goadings to gain the top of the opposite hill; the headlong, sledlike slide down its other side—all these, with the cries of the headsmen and harpooners, and the shuddering gasps of the oarsmen, with the wondrous sight of the ivory *Pequod* bearing down upon her boats with outstretched sails, like a wild hen after her screaming brood; all this was thrilling. Not the raw recruit, marching from the bosom of his wife into the fever heat of his first battle; not the dead man's ghost encountering the first unknown phantom in the other world—neither of these can feel stranger and stronger emotions than that man does, who for the first time finds himself pulling into the charmed, churned circle of the hunted sperm whale.

The dancing white water made by the chase was now becoming more and more visible, owing to the increasing darkness of the dun cloud shadows flung upon the sea. The jets of vapor no longer blended, but tilted everywhere to right and left; the whales seemed separating their wakes. The boats were pulled more apart, Starbuck giving chase to three whales running dead to leeward. Our sail was now set, and with the still rising wind, we rushed along, the boat going with such madness through the water that the lee oars could scarcely be worked rapidly enough to escape being torn from the rowlocks.

Soon we were running through a suffusing wide veil of mist, neither ship nor boat to be seen.

"Give way, men," whispered Starbuck, drawing still farther aft the sheet of his sail; "there is time to kill fish yet before the squall comes. There's white water again!—close to! Spring!"

Soon after, two cries in quick succession on each side of us denoted that the other boats had got fast; but hardly were they overheard, when with a lightninglike hurtling whisper Starbuck said, "Stand up!" and Queequeg, harpoon in hand, sprang to his feet.

Though not one of the oarsmen was then facing the life-and-death peril so close to them ahead, yet with their eyes on the intense countenance of the mate in the stern of the boat, they knew that the imminent instant had come; they heard, too, an enormous wallowing sound as of fifty elephants stirring in their litter. Meanwhile the boat was still booming through the mist, the waves curling and hissing around us like the erected crests of enraged serpents.

"That's his hump. *There, there,* give it to him!" whispered Starbuck.

A short rushing sound leaped out of the boat; it was the darted iron of Queequeg. Then all in one welded commotion came an invisible push from astern, while forward the boat seemed striking on a ledge; the sail collapsed and exploded; a gush of scalding vapor shot up nearby; something rolled and tumbled like an earthquake beneath us. The whole crew were half suffocated as they were tossed helter-skelter into the white curdling cream of the squall. Squall, whale, and harpoon had all blended together, and the whale, merely grazed by the iron, escaped.

Though completely swamped, the boat was nearly unharmed. Swimming round it, we picked up the floating oars, and lashing them across the gunwale, tumbled back to our places. There we sat up to our knees in the sea, the water covering every rib and plank, so that to our downward-gazing eyes the suspended craft seemed a coral boat grown up to us from the bottom of the ocean.

The wind increased to a howl; the waves dashed their bucklers together; the whole squall roared, forked, and crackled around us like a white fire upon the prairie, in which, unconsumed, we were burning, immortal in these jaws of death! In vain we hailed the other boats; as well roar to the live coals down the chimney of a flaming furnace as hail those boats in that storm. Meanwhile the driving scud, rack, and mist grew darker with the shadows of night; no sign of the ship could be seen. The rising sea forbade all attempts to bale out the boat. The oars were useless as propellers, performing now the office of life preservers. So cutting the lashing of the waterproof match keg, after many failures Starbuck contrived to ignite the lamp in the lantern; then stretching it on a waif pole, handed it to Queequeg as the standard-bearer of this forlorn hope. There, then, he sat, holding up that imbecile candle in the heart of that almighty forlornness. There, then, he sat, the sign and symbol of a man without faith, hopelessly holding up hope in the midst of despair.

Wet, drenched through, and shivering cold, despairing of ship or boat, we lifted up our eyes as the dawn came on. The mist still spread over the sea, the empty lantern lay crushed in the bottom of the boat. Suddenly Queequeg started to his feet, hollowing his hand to his ear. We all heard a faint creaking, as of ropes and yards hitherto muffled by the storm. The sound came nearer and nearer; the thick mists were dimly parted by a huge, vague form. Affrighted, we all sprang into the sea as the ship at last loomed into view, bearing right down upon us within distance of not much more than its length.

Floating on the waves we saw the abandoned boat, as for one instant it tossed and gaped beneath the ship's bows like a chip at the base of a cataract; and then the vast hull rolled over it, and it was seen no more till it came up weltering astern. Again we swam for it, were dashed against it by the seas, and were at last taken up and safely landed on board. Ere the squall came close to, the other boats had cut loose from their fish and returned to the ship in good time. The ship had given us up, but was still cruising, if haply it might light upon some token of our perishing, an oar or a lance pole.

Herman Melville
Moby-Dick

22

Launching the First Steamboat on Western Waters

After Robert Fulton proved his Hudson River steamboat an unquestioned success in 1807, the use of such vessels on western waters was only a question of time. As a result of a conference that Fulton and Robert R. Livingston held in 1810 with Governor Claiborne of Louisiana, the legislature of Louisiana Territory early in 1811 passed a law giving the first-named men the sole privilege of using steamboats on the lower Mississippi. As soon as news of this law came, Fulton went to Pittsburgh, and there his able assistant, Nicholas Roosevelt, directed the building and launching of the *New Orleans,* the first steamboat to navigate any stream of the interior. She weighed only about a hundred tons and had two masts as well as a stern-wheel. Roosevelt himself was an inventor, claiming to have originated the vertical paddle wheel.

Prior to the introduction of steamboats on the western waters, the means of transportation thereon consisted of keelboats, barges, and flatboats. Keelboats and barges ascended as well as descended the stream. The flatboat was an unwieldy box and was broken up, for the lumber it contained, on its arrival at the place of destination. The keelboat was long and slender, sharp fore and aft, with a narrow gangway just within the gunwale for the boatmen as they poled or warped up the stream when not aided by the eddies that made their oars available. When the keelboat was covered with a low house lengthwise between the gangways, it was dignified with the name of barge. Keelboats, barges, and flatboats had prodigious steering oars, and oars of the same dimensions were hung on fixed pivots on the sides of the last named, by which the shapeless and cumbrous contrivance was in some sort managed. Ignorant of anything better, the people of the West were satisfied with these appliances of trade in 1810.

Whether steam could be employed on the western rivers was a question that its success between New York and Albany was not regarded as having entirely solved, and after the idea had been suggested of building a boat at Pittsburgh to ply between Natchez and New Orleans, it was considered necessary that investigations should be made as to the current of the rivers to be navigated, in regard to the new system. These investigations Mr. Roosevelt undertook, with the understanding that if his report were favorable, Chancellor Livingston, Mr. Fulton, and himself were to be equally interested in the undertaking. The Chancellor and Fulton were to supply the capital, and Roosevelt was to superintend the building of the boat and engine.

The first thing to be done was to obtain the timber to build the boat, and for this purpose men were sent into the forest, there to find the necessary ribs and knees and beams, transport them to the Monongahela, and raft them to the shipyard. White pine was the only material for planking that could be obtained without a delay that was inadmissible. The sawing that was required was done in the old-fashioned and now long-forgotten saw pits of 1811. Boatbuilders, accustomed to construct the barges of that day, could be obtained in Pittsburgh, but a shipbuilder and the mechanics required in the machinery department had to be brought from New York. Under these circumstances Mr. Roosevelt began the work. . . .

At length all difficulties were overcome by steady perseverance, and the boat was launched—and called, from the place of her ultimate destination, the *New Orleans*. It cost in the neighborhood of thirty-eight thousand dollars.

As the *New Orleans* approached completion and when it came to be known that Mrs. Roosevelt intended to accompany her husband on the voyage, the numerous friends she had made in Pittsburgh united in endeavoring to dissuade her from what they regarded as utter folly, if not absolute madness. Her husband was appealed to. The criticisms that had been freely applied to the boat by the crowds of visitors to the shipyard were now transferred to the conduct of the builder. He was told that he had no right to peril his wife's life, however reckless he might be of his own. . . . But the wife believed in her husband, and in the latter part of September 1811, the *New Orleans,* after a short experimental trip up the Monongahela, commenced her voyage.

There were two cabins, one aft for ladies and a larger one forward for gentlemen. In the former there were four berths. It was comfortably furnished. Of this, Mrs. Roosevelt took possession. Mr. Roosevelt and herself were the only passengers. There was a captain, an engineer named Baker, Andrew Jack, the pilot, six hands, two female servants, a man waiter, a cook, and an immense Newfoundland dog named Tiger. Thus equipped, the *New Orleans* began the voyage which changed the relations of the West—which may almost be said to have changed its destiny.

The people of Pittsburgh turned out in mass and lined the banks of the Monongahela to witness the departure of the steamboat, and shout after shout rent the air, and handkerchiefs were waved and hats thrown up by way of Godspeed to the voyagers as the anchor was raised, and heading upstream for a short distance, a wide circuit brought the *New Orleans* on her proper course, and steam and current aiding, she disappeared behind the first headlands on the right bank of the Ohio.

Too much excited to sleep, Mr. Roosevelt and his wife passed the greater part of the first night on deck and watched the shore, covered then with an almost unbroken forest, as reach after reach and bend after bend were passed at a speed of from eight to ten miles an hour. The regular working of the engine, the ample supply of steam, the uniformity of the speed, inspired at last a confidence that quieted the nervous apprehension of the travelers. Mr. Jack, the pilot, delighted with the facility with which the vessel was steered and at a speed to which he was so little accustomed, ceased to express misgivings and became as sanguine as Mr. Roosevelt himself in regard to the success of the voyage. The very crew of unimaginative men were excited with the novelty of the situation, and when the following morning assembled all hands on deck to return the cheers of a village whose inhabitants had seen the boat approaching down a long reach in the river and turned out to greet her as she sped by, it probably shone upon as jolly a set as ever floated on the Ohio.

On the second day after leaving Pittsburgh, the *New Orleans* rounded to opposite Cincinnati and cast anchor in the stream. Levees and wharf boats were things unknown in 1811. Here, as at Pittsburgh, the whole town seemed to have assembled on the bank, and many acquaintances came off in small boats. . . .

Morning after morning, the rise in the river during the night was reported, and finally, in the last week in November, it was ascertained that the depth of water in the shallowest portion of the falls exceeded by five inches the draught of the boat. It was a narrow margin. But the rise had ceased; there was no telegraph in those days to tell hourly what was the weather in the country drained by the Ohio, and Mr. Roosevelt, assuring himself personally of the condition of the falls, determined to take the responsibility and go over them if he could. It was an anxious time. All hands were on deck. Mrs. Roosevelt, whom her husband would willingly have left behind to join him below the falls, refused to remain on shore and stood near the stern. The two pilots, for an extra one had been engaged for the passage through the rapids, took their places in the bow. The anchor was weighed. To get into the Indiana channel, which was the best, a wide circuit had to be made, bringing her head downstream, completing which, the *New Orleans* began the descent. Steerageway depended upon her speed exceeding that of the current. The faster she could be made to go, the easier would it be to guide her. All the steam the boiler would bear was put upon her. The safety valve shrieked; the wheels revolved faster than they had ever done before; and the vessel, speaking figuratively, fairly flew away from the crowds collected to witness her departure from Louisville. Instinctively each one on board now grasped the nearest object and with bated breath awaited the result. Black ledges of rock appeared, only to disappear as the *New Orleans* flashed by them. The waters whirled and eddied and threw their spray upon the deck as a more rapid descent caused the vessel to pitch forward to what at times seemed inevitable destruction. Not a word was spoken. The pilots directed the men at the helm by motions of their hands. Even the great Newfoundland dog seemed affected by the apprehension of danger and came and crouched at Mrs. Roosevelt's feet. The tension on the nervous system was too great to be long sustained. Fortunately the passage was soon made, and with feelings of profound gratitude to the Almighty at the successful issue of the adventure on the part of both Mr. Roosevelt and his wife, the *New Orleans* rounded to in safety below the falls.

J.H.B. Latrobe
The First Steamboat on the Western Waters

23

Mark Twain Learns to Be a Pilot

In 1857 Mark Twain, a restless youth who, as an itinerant printer, had wandered from Missouri as far east as Philadelphia and New York, got himself apprenticed to a Mississippi River pilot. For a year and a half he was learning his craft—a very precise and expert calling—for two years and a half he practiced it as a licensed pilot. Then the Civil War closed the river and that chapter of his career. But it was this experience that gave him material for some of his best books—notably the two from which selections are here taken, and *Tom Sawyer* and *Huckleberry Finn*.

The *Paul Jones* was now bound for St. Louis. I planned a siege against my pilot, and at the end of three hard days he surrendered. He agreed to teach me the Mississippi River from New Orleans to St. Louis for five hundred dollars, payable out of the first wages I should receive after graduating. I entered upon the small enterprise of "learning" twelve or thirteen hundred miles of the great Mississippi River with the easy confidence of my time of life. If I had really known what I was about to require of my faculties, I should not have had the courage to begin. I supposed that all a pilot had to do was to keep his boat in the river, and I did not consider that that could be much of a trick, since it was so wide.

The boat backed out from New Orleans at four in the afternoon, and it was "our watch" until eight. Mr. B—, my chief, "straightened her up," plowed her along past the sterns of the other boats that lay at the levee, and then said, "Here, take her; shave those steamships as close as you'd peel an apple." I took the wheel, and my heart went down into my boots; for it seemed to me that we were about to scrape the side off every ship in the line, we were so close. I held my breath and began to claw the boat away from the danger, and I had my own opinion of the pilot who had known no better than to get us into such peril, but I was too wise to express it. In half a minute I had a wide margin of safety intervening between the *Paul Jones* and the ships, and within ten seconds more I was set aside in disgrace, and Mr. B— was going into danger again and flaying me alive with abuse of my cowardice. I was stung, but I was obliged to admire the easy confidence with which my chief loafed from side to side of his wheel and trimmed the ships so closely that disaster seemed ceaselessly imminent. When he had cooled a little he told me that the easy water was close ashore and the current outside, and therefore we must hug the bank, upstream, to get the benefit of the former, and stay well out, downstream, to take advantage of the latter. In my own mind I resolved to be a downstream pilot and leave the upstreaming to people dead to prudence.

Now and then Mr. B— called my attention to certain things. Said he, "This is Six-Mile Point." I assented. It was pleasant enough information, but I could not see the bearing of it. I was not conscious that it was a matter of any interest to me. Another time he said, "This is Nine-Mile Point." Later he said, "This is Twelve-Mile Point." They were all about level with the water's edge; they all looked about alike to me; they were monotonously unpicturesque. I hoped Mr. B— would change the subject. But no; he would crowd up around a point, hugging the shore with affection, and then say, "The slack water ends here, abreast this bunch of China trees; now we cross over." So he crossed over. He gave me the wheel once or twice, but I had no luck. I either came near chipping off the edge of a sugar plantation, or else I yawed too far from shore, and so I dropped back into disgrace and got abused again.

The watch was ended at last, and we took supper and went to bed. At midnight the glare of a lantern shone in my eyes, and the night watchman said: "Come! turn out!"

And then he left. I could not understand this extraordinary procedure; so I presently gave up trying to, and dozed off to sleep. Pretty soon the watchman was back again, and this time he was gruff. I was annoyed. I said:

"What do you want to come bothering around here in the middle of the night for? Now as like as not I'll not get to sleep again tonight."

The watchman said, "Well, if this an't good, I'm blest."

The "off watch" was just turning in, and I heard some brutal laughter from them and such remarks as "Hello, watchman! an't the new cub turned out yet? He's delicate, likely. Give him some sugar in a rag and send for the chambermaid to sing rockabye-baby to him."

About this time Mr. B— appeared on the scene. Something like a minute later I was climbing the pilothouse steps with some of my clothes on and the rest in my arms. Mr. B— was close behind, commenting. Here was something fresh—this thing of getting up in the middle of the night to go to work. It was a detail in piloting that had never occurred to me at all. I knew that boats ran all night, but somehow I had never happened to reflect that somebody had to get up out of a warm bed to run them. I began to fear that piloting was not quite so romantic as I had imagined it was; there was something very real and worklike about this new phase of it.

It was a rather dingy night, although a fair number of stars were out. The big mate was at the wheel, and he had the old tub pointed at a star and was holding her straight up the middle of the river. The shores on either hand were not much more than a mile apart, but they seemed wonderfully far away and ever so vague and indistinct. . . .

Mr. B— made for the shore and soon was scraping it, just the same as if it had been daylight. And not only that, but singing "Father in heaven the day is declining," etc. It seemed to me that I had put my life in the keeping of a peculiarly reckless outcast. Presently he turned on me and said:

"What's the name of the first point above New Orleans?"

I was gratified to be able to answer promptly, and I did. I said I didn't know.

"Don't *know*?"

This manner jolted me. I was down at the foot again, in a moment. But I had to say just what I had said before.

"Well, you're a smart one," said Mr. B—. "What's the name of the *next* point?"

Once more I didn't know.

"Well, this beats anything. Tell me the name of *any* point or place I told you."

I studied awhile and decided that I couldn't.

"Look-a-here! What do you start out from, above Twelve-Mile Point, to cross over?"

"I—I—don't know."

"You—you—don't know?" mimicking my drawling manner of speech. "What *do* you know?"

"I—I—nothing, for certain."

"By the great Caesar's ghost I believe you! You're the stupidest dunder-head I ever saw or ever heard of, so help me Moses! The idea of *you* being a pilot—*you!* Why, you don't know enough to pilot a cow down a lane."

Oh, but his wrath was up! He was a nervous man, and he shuffled from one side of his wheel to the other as if the floor was hot. He would boil awhile to himself and then overflow and scald me again.

"Look-a-here! What do you suppose I told you the names of those points for?"

I tremblingly considered a moment, and then the devil of temptation provoked me to say:

"Well—to—to—be entertaining, I thought."

This was a red rag to the bull. He raged and stormed so (he was crossing the river at the time) that I judge it made him blind, because he ran over the steering oar of a trading scow. Of course the traders sent up a volley of red-hot profanity. Never was a man so grateful as Mr. B— was, because he was brimful, and here were subjects who would *talk back*. He threw open a window, thrust his head out, and such an eruption followed as I never had heard before. The fainter and farther away the scowmen's curses drifted, the higher Mr. B— lifted his voice and the weightier his adjectives grew. When he closed the window he was empty. You could have drawn a seine through his system and not caught curses enough to disturb your mother with. Presently he said to me in the gentlest way:

"My boy, you must get a little memorandum book, and every time I tell you a thing, put it down right away. There's only one way to be a pilot, and that is to get this entire river by heart. You have to know it just like ABC."

That was a dismal revelation to me, for my memory was never loaded with anything but blank cartridges. However, I did not feel discouraged long. I judged that it was best to make some allowances, for doubtless Mr. B— was "stretching." Presently he pulled a rope and struck a few strokes on the big bell. The stars were all gone, now, and the night was as black as ink. I could hear the wheels churn along the bank, but I was not entirely certain that I could see the shore. The voice of the invisible watchman called up from the hurricane deck:

"What's this, sir?"

"Jones's plantation."

I said to myself, I wish I might venture to offer a small bet that it isn't. But I did not chirp. I only waited to see. Mr. B— handled the engine bells, and in due time, the boat's nose came to the land, a torch glowed from the forecastle, a man skipped ashore, a darky's voice on the bank said, "Gimme de carpet-bag, Mars' Jones," and the next moment we were standing up the river again, all serene. I reflected deeply awhile and then said—but not aloud—Well, the finding of that plantation was the luckiest accident that ever happened, but it couldn't happen again in a hundred years. And I fully believed it *was* an accident, too.

By the time we had gone seven or eight hundred miles up the river, I had learned to be a tolerably plucky upstream steersman, in daylight, and before we reached St. Louis, I had made a trifle of progress in night work, but only a trifle. I had a notebook that fairly bristled with the names of towns, "points," bars, islands, bends, reaches, etc., but the information was to be found only in the notebook—none of it was in my head. It made my heart ache to think I had only got half of the river set down; for as our watch was four hours off and four hours on, day and night, there was a long four-hour gap in my book for every time I had slept since the voyage began.

My chief was presently hired to go on a big New Orleans boat, and I packed my satchel and went with him. She was a grand affair. When I stood in her pilothouse I was so far above the water that I seemed perched on a mountain, and her decks stretched so far away, fore and aft, below me that I wondered how I could ever have considered the little *Paul Jones* a large craft. There were other differences, too. The *Paul Jones'* pilothouse was a cheap, dingy, battered rattletrap, cramped for room, but here was a sumptuous glass temple; room enough to have a dance in; showy red and gold window curtains; an imposing sofa; leather cushions and a back to the high bench where visiting pilots sit, to spin yarns and "look at the river"; bright, fanciful cuspidors instead of a broad wooden box filled with sawdust; nice new oilcloth on the floor; a hospitable big stove for winter; a wheel as high as my head, costly with inlaid work; a wire tiller rope; bright brass knobs for the bells; and a tidy, white-aproned, black "texas tender" to bring up tarts and ices and coffee during midwatch, day and night. Now this was "something like," and so I began to take heart once more to believe that piloting was a romantic sort of occupation after all. The moment we were under way I began to prowl about the great steamer and fill myself with joy. She was as clean and as dainty as a drawing room; when I looked down her long, gilded saloon, it was like gazing through a splendid tunnel; she had an oil picture, by some gifted sign painter, on every stateroom door; she glittered with no end of prism-fringed chandeliers; the clerk's office was elegant, the bar was marvelous, and the barkeeper had been barbered and upholstered at incredible cost. The boiler deck (i.e., the second story of the boat, so to speak) was as spacious as a church, it seemed to me; so with the forecastle; and there was no pitiful handful of deckhands, firemen, and roustabouts down there, but a whole battalion of men. The fires were fiercely glaring from a long row of furnaces, and over them were eight huge boilers! This was unutterable pomp. The mighty engines—but enough of this. I had never felt so fine before. And when I found that the regiment of natty servants respectfully sirred me, my satisfaction was complete. When I returned to the pilothouse St. Louis was gone and I was lost. Here was a piece of river which was all down in my book, but I could make neither head nor tail of it: you understand, it was turned around. I had seen it, when coming upstream, but I had never faced about to see how it looked when it was behind me. My heart broke again, for it was plain that I had got to learn this troublesome river *both ways*.

The pilothouse was full of pilots, going down to "look at the river.". . .

We had a fine company of these river inspectors along, this trip. There were eight or ten, and there was abundance of room for them in our great pilothouse. Two or three of them wore polished silk hats, elaborate shirt fronts, diamond breastpins, kid gloves, and patent-leather boots. They were choice in their English and bore themselves with a dignity proper to men of solid means and prodigious reputation as pilots. The others were more or less loosely clad and wore upon their heads tall felt cones that were suggestive of the days of the Commonwealth.

I was a cipher in this august company and felt subdued, not to say torpid. I was not even of sufficient consequence to assist at the wheel when it was necessary to put the tiller hard down in a hurry; the guest that stood nearest did that when occasion required—and this was pretty much all the time, because of the crookedness of the channel and the scant water. I stood in a corner, and the talk I listened to took the hope all out of me. One visitor said to another:

"Jim, how did you run Plum Point, coming up?"

"It was in the night, there, and I ran it the way one of the boys on the *Diana* told me; started out about fifty yards above the woodpile on the false point and held on the cabin under Plum Point till I raised the reef—quarter less twain—then straightened up for the middle bar till I got well abreast the old one-limbed cottonwood in the bend, then got my stern on the cottonwood and head on the low place above the point, and came through a-booming—nine and a half."

"Pretty square crossing, an't it?"

"Yes, but the upper bar's working down fast."

Another pilot spoke up and said:

"I had better water than that, and ran it lower down; started out from the false point—mark twain—raised the second reef abreast the big snag in the bend and had quarter less twain."

One of the gorgeous ones remarked: "I don't want to find fault with your leadsmen, but that's a good deal of water for Plum Point, it seems to me."

There was an approving nod all around as this quiet snub dropped on the boaster and settled him. And so they went on talk-talk-talking. Meantime, the thing that was running in my mind was: "Now if my ears hear aright, I have not only to get the names of all the towns and islands and bends, and so on, by heart, but I must even get up a warm personal acquaintanceship with every old snag and one-limbed cottonwood and obscure woodpile that ornaments the banks of this river for twelve hundred miles, and more than that, I must actually know where these things are in the dark, unless these guests are gifted with eyes that can pierce through two miles of solid blackness; I wish the piloting business was in Jericho and I had never thought of it."

At dusk Mr. B— tapped the big bell three times (the signal to land), and the captain emerged from his drawing room in the forward end of the texas and looked up inquiringly. Mr. B— said:

"We will lay up here all night, Captain."

"Very well, sir."

That was all. The boat came to shore and was tied up for the night. It seemed to me a fine thing that the pilot could do as he pleased without asking so grand a captain's permission. I took my supper and went immediately to bed, discouraged by my day's observations and experiences. My late voyage's notebooking was but a confusion of meaningless names. It had tangled me all up in a knot every time I had looked at it in the daytime. I now hoped for respite in sleep, but no, it reveled all through my head till sunrise again, a frantic and tireless nightmare.

Next morning I felt pretty rusty and low-spirited. We went booming along, taking a good many chances, for we were anxious to get out of the river (as getting out to Cairo was called) before night should overtake us. But Mr. B—'s partner, the other pilot, presently grounded the boat, and we lost so much time getting her off that it was plain the darkness would overtake us a good long way above the mouth. This was a great misfortune especially to certain of our visiting pilots, whose boats would have to wait for their return, no matter how long that might be. It sobered the pilothouse talk a good deal. Coming upstream, pilots did not mind low water or any kind of darkness; nothing stopped them but fog. But downstream work was different; a boat was too nearly helpless, with a stiff current pushing behind her, so it was not customary to run downstream at night in low water.

There seemed to be one small hope, however: If we could get through the intricate and dangerous Hat Island crossing before night, we could venture the rest, for we would have plainer sailing and better water. But it would be insanity to attempt Hat Island at night. So there was a deal of looking at watches all the rest of the day and a constant ciphering upon the speed we were making; Hat Island was the eternal subject; sometimes hope was high, and sometimes we were delayed in a bad crossing, and down it went again. For hours all hands lay under the burden of this suppressed excitement; it was even communicated to me, and I got to feeling so solicitous about Hat Island, and under such an awful pressure of responsibility, that I wished I might have five minutes on shore to draw a good, full, relieving breath and start over again. We were standing no regular watches. Each of our pilots ran such portions of the river as he had run when coming upstream, because of his greater familiarity with it, but both remained in the pilothouse constantly.

An hour before sunset, Mr. B— took the wheel and Mr. W—stepped aside. For the next thirty minutes every man held his watch in his hand and was restless, silent, and uneasy. At last somebody said, with a doomful sigh, "Well, yonder's Hat Island—and we can't make it."

All the watches closed with a snap, everybody sighed and muttered something about its being "too bad, too bad—ah, if we could *only* have got here half an hour sooner!" and the place was thick with the atmosphere of disappointment. Some started to go out, but loitered, hearing no bell-tap to land. The sun dipped behind the horizon; the boat went on. Inquiring looks passed from one guest to another, and one who had his hand on the doorknob and had turned it waited, then presently took away his hand and let the knob turn back again. We bore steadily down the bend. More looks were exchanged, and nods of surprised admiration—but no words. Insensibly the men drew together behind Mr. B— as the sky darkened and one or two dim stars came out. The dead silence and sense of waiting became oppressive. Mr. B— pulled the cord, and two deep, mellow notes from the big bell floated off on the night. Then a pause, and one more note was struck. The watchman's voice followed, from the hurricane deck:

"Labboard lead, there! Stabboard lead!"

The cries of the leadsmen began to rise out of the distance and were gruffly repeated by the word-passers on the hurricane deck.

"M-a-r-k three! M-a-r-k three! Quarter-less-three! Half twain! quarter twain! M-a-r-k twain! Quarter-less—"

Mr. B— pulled two bell ropes and was answered by faint jinglings far below in the engine room, and our speed slackened. The steam began to whistle through the gauge cocks. The cries of the leadsmen went on—and it is a weird sound, always, in the night. Every pilot in the lot was watching, now, with fixed eyes, and talking under his breath. Nobody was calm and easy but Mr. B—. He would put his wheel down and stand on a spoke, and as the steamer swung into her (to me) utterly invisible marks—for we seemed to be in the midst of a wide and gloomy sea—he would meet and fasten her there. Talk was going on, now, in low voices.

"There, she's over the first reef all right!"

After a pause, another subdued voice:

"Her stern's coming down just *exactly* right, by *George!* Now she's in the marks; over she goes!"

Somebody else muttered:

"Oh, it was done beautiful—*beautiful!*"

Now the engines were stopped altogether, and we drifted with the current. Not that I could see the boat drift, for I could not, the stars being all gone by this time. This drifting was the dismalest work; it held one's heart still. Presently I discovered a blacker gloom than that which surrounded us. It was the head of the island. We were closing right down upon it. We entered its deeper shadow, and so imminent seemed the peril that I was likely to suffocate, and I had the strongest impulse to do *something,* anything, to save the vessel. But still Mr. B— stood by his wheel, silent, intent as a cat, and all the pilots stood shoulder to shoulder at his back.

"She'll not make it!" somebody whispered.

The water grew shoaler and shoaler by the leadsmen's cries, till it was down to—

"Eight-and-a-half! E-i-g-h-t feet! E-i-g-h-t feet! Seven-and—"

Mr. B— said warningly through his speaking tube to the engineer:

"Stand by, now!"

"Aye, aye, sir."

"Seven-and-a-half! Seven feet! *Six*-and—"

We touched bottom! Instantly Mr. B— set a lot of bells ringing, shouted through the tube, *"Now* let her have it—every ounce you've got!" then to his partner, "Put her hard down! snatch her! snatch her!" The boat rasped and ground her way through the sand, hung upon the apex of disaster a single tremendous instant, and then over she went! And such a shout as went up at Mr. B—'s back never loosened the roof of a pilothouse before!

There was no more trouble after that; Mr. B— was a hero that night, and it was some little time, too, before his exploit ceased to be talked about by rivermen.

Fully to realize the marvelous precision required in laying the great steamer in her marks in that murky waste of water, one should know that not only must she pick her intricate way through snags and blind reefs and then shave the head of the island so closely as to brush the overhanging foliage with her stern, but at one place she must pass almost within arm's reach of a sunken and invisible wreck that would snatch the hull timbers from under her if she should strike it, and destroy a quarter of a million dollars' worth of steamboat and cargo in five minutes, and maybe a hundred and fifty human lives into the bargain.

The last remark I heard that night was a compliment to Mr. B—, uttered in soliloquy and with unction by one of our guests. He said:

"By the shadow of Death, but he's a lightning pilot!"

MARK TWAIN
"Old Times on the Mississippi"

24

Harriet Martineau Finds a
Working Girls' Paradise

The Industrial Revolution had its brutal side in America as in England. But the factories built by Francis Cabot Lowell and other liberal-minded New Englanders made the towns of Lowell, Waltham, and Lynn seem model communities to visiting foreigners. They were placed in attractive surroundings; family life was encouraged; morals protected; the wage scale encouraged thrift; and favorable surroundings attracted a high quality of labor. An eminent Englishwoman here joins in the chorus of praise.

I visited [in 1834] the corporate factory establishment at Waltham, within a few miles of Boston. The Waltham Mills were at work before those of Lowell were set up. The establishment is for the spinning and weaving of cotton alone, and the construction of the requisite machinery. Five hundred persons were employed at the time of my visit. The girls earn two, and sometimes three, dollars a week, besides their board. The little children earn one dollar a week. Most of the girls live in the houses provided by the corporation, which accommodate from six to eight each. When sisters come to the mill, it is a common practice for them to bring their mother to keep house for them and some of their companions, in a dwelling built by their own earnings. In this case, they save enough out of their board to clothe themselves and have their two or three dollars a week to spare. Some have thus cleared off mortgages from their fathers' farms; others have educated the hope of the family at college; and many are rapidly accumulating an independence. I saw a whole street of houses built with the earnings of the girls, some with piazzas and green Venetian blinds, and all neat and sufficiently spacious.

The factory people built the church, which stands conspicuous on the green in the midst of the place. The minister's salary (eight hundred dollars last year) is raised by a tax on the pews. The corporation gave them a building for a lyceum, which they have furnished with a good library, and where they have lectures every winter—the best that money can procure. The girls have, in many instances, private libraries of some merit and value.

The managers of the various factory establishments keep the wages as nearly equal as possible and then let the girls freely shift about from one to another. When a girl comes to the overseer to inform him of her intention of working at the mill, he welcomes her and asks how long she means to stay. It may be six months or a year or five years, or for life. She declares what she considers herself fit for and sets to work accordingly. If she finds that she cannot work so as to keep up with the companion appointed to her, or to please her employer or herself, she comes to the overseer and volunteers to pick cotton or sweep the rooms or undertake some other service that she can perform.

The people work about seventy hours per week, on the average. The time of work varies with the length of the days, the wages continuing the same. All look like well-dressed young ladies. The health is good, or rather (as this is too much to be said about health anywhere in the United States) it is no worse than it is elsewhere.

These facts speak for themselves. There is no need to enlarge on the pleasure of an acquaintance with the operative classes of the United States.

The shoemaking at Lynn is carried on almost entirely in private dwellings, from the circumstance that the people who do it are almost all farmers or fishermen likewise. A stranger who has not been enlightened upon the ways of the place would be astonished at the number of small square erections, like miniature schoolhouses, standing each as an appendage to a dwelling house. These are the shoeshops, where the father of the family and his boys work, while the women within are employed in binding and trimming. Thirty or more of these shoeshops may be counted in a walk of half a mile. When a Lynn shoe manufacturer receives an order, he issues the tidings. The leather is cut out by men on his premises, and then the work is given to those who apply for it—if possible, in small quantities, for the sake of dispatch. The shoes are brought home on Friday night, packed off on Saturday, and in a fortnight or three weeks are on the feet of dwellers in all parts of the Union. The whole family works upon shoes during the winter, and in the summer the father and sons turn out into the fields or go fishing. I know of an instance where a little boy and girl maintained the whole family, while the earnings of the rest went to build a house. I saw very few shabby houses. Quakers are numerous in Lynn. The place is unboundedly prosperous, through the temperance and industry of the people. The deposits in the Lynn Savings Bank in 1834 were about thirty-four thousand dollars, the population of the town being then four thousand. Since that time, both the population and the prosperity have much increased. It must be remembered too that the mechanics of America have more uses for their money than are open to the operatives of England. They build houses, buy land, and educate their sons and daughters.

It is probably true that the pleasures and pains of life are pretty equally distributed among its various vocations and positions, but it is difficult to keep clear of the impression which outward circumstances occasion, that some are eminently desirable. The mechanics of these Northern States appear to me the most favored class I have ever known. In England, I believe the highest order of mechanics to be, as a class, the wisest and best men of the community. They have the fewest base and narrow interests; they are brought into sufficient contact with the realities of existence without being hardened by excess of toil and care; and the knowledge they have the opportunity of gaining is of the best kind for the health of the mind. To them, if to any, we may look for public and private virtue. The mechanics of America have nearly all the same advantages, and some others. They have better means of living; their labors are perhaps more honored; and they are republicans, enjoying the powers and prospects of perfectly equal citizenship. The only respect in which their condition falls below that of English artisans of the highest order is that the knowledge which they have commonly the means of obtaining is not of equal value. The facilities are great; schools, lyceums, libraries, are open to them; but the instruction imparted there is not so good as they deserve. Whenever they have this, it will be difficult to imagine a mode of life more favorable to virtue and happiness than theirs.

There seems to be no doubt among those who know both England and America that the mechanics of the New World work harder than those of the Old. They have much to do besides their daily handicraft business. They are up and at work early about this, and when it is done, they read till late or attend lectures or perhaps have their houses to build or repair or other care to take of their property. They live in a state and period of society where every man is answerable for his own fortunes and where there is therefore stimulus to the exercise of every power.

What a state of society it is when a dozen artisans of one town—Salem— are seen rearing each a comfortable one-story (or, as the Americans would say, two-story) house, in the place with which they have grown up! when a man who began with laying bricks criticizes, and sometimes corrects, his lawyer's composition; when a poor errand boy becomes the proprietor of a flourishing store before he is thirty, pays off the capital advanced by his friends at the rate of two thousand dollars per month, and bids fair to be one of the most substantial citizens of the place! Such are the outward fortunes of the mechanics of America.

HARRIET MARTINEAU
Society in America

25

Edward Everett Hale Recalls a New England Boyhood

Growing up in Boston during the 1820s, Edward Everett Hale describes his boyhood with an engaging narrative flair for detail. He reminisces about hectic days on Charles Street and the South End Wharfs, the Jamaica Pond aqueduct and the Fire Club in Worcester. Young Hale was born in 1822; his recollections were penned almost three-quarters of a century later.

So far as I remember the houses themselves and the life in them, everything was quite as elegant and finished as it is now. Furniture was stately, solid, and expensive. I use chairs, tables, and a sideboard in my house today which are exactly as good now as they were then. Carpets, then of English make, covered the whole floor and were of what we should now call perfect quality. In summer, by the way, in all houses of which I knew anything, these carpets were always taken up, and India mattings substituted in the living rooms. Observe that very few houses were closed in summer. Dress was certainly as elegant and costly as it is now; so were porcelain, glass, table linen, and all table furniture. In the earlier days of which I write, a decanter of wine would invariably have stood on a sideboard in every parlor, so that a glass of wine could readily be offered at any moment to any guest. All through my boyhood it would have been a matter of remark if, when a visitor made an evening call, something to eat or drink was not produced at nine o'clock. It might be crackers and cheese, it might be mince pie, it might be oysters or cold chicken. But something would appear as certainly as there would be a fire on the hearth in winter. Every house, by the way, was warmed by open fires, and in every kitchen cooking was done by an open fire. I doubt if I ever saw a stove in my boyhood except in a school or an office. Anthracite coal was first tried in Boston in 1824. Gas appeared about the same time. I was taken, as a little boy, to see it burning in the shops in Washington Street, and to wonder at an elephant, a tortoise, and a cow, which spouted burning gas in one window. Gas was not introduced into dwelling houses until Pemberton Square was built by the Lowells, Jacksons, and their friends, in the years 1835, 1836, and later. It was a surprise to everyone when Papanti introduced it in his new Papanti's Hall. To prepare for that occasion the ground-glass shades had a little rouge shaken about in the interior, that the white gaslight might not be too unfavorable to the complexion of the beauties below.

Whether this device is still thought necessary in ballrooms I do not know, but I suggest it as a hint to the wise.

A handsome parlor then differed from a handsome parlor now mostly in the minor matters of decoration. The pictures on the walls were few and were mostly portraits. For the rest, mirrors were large and handsome. You would see some copies from well-known paintings in European galleries, and anyone who had an Allston would be glad to show it. But I mean that most walls were bare. In good houses, if modern, the walls of the parlors would invariably be painted of one neutral tint, but in older houses there would be paper hangings, perhaps of landscape patterns. The furniture of a parlor would generally be twelve decorous heavy chairs, probably hair-seated, with their backs against the walls; a sofa which matched them, also with its back against the wall; and a heavy, perhaps marble-topped center table. There might be a rocking chair in the room also, but so far as I remember, other easy chairs, scattered as one chose about a room, were unknown.

As the snow melted, and the elms blossomed, and the grass came, the Common opened itself to every sort of game. We played marbles in holes in the malls. We flew kites everywhere, not troubled, as boys would be now, by trees on the cross paths, for there were no such trees. The old elm and a large willow by the Frog Pond were the only trees within the pentagon made by the malls and the burial ground. Kite-flying was, as it is, a science, and on a fine summer day, with southwest winds, a line of boys would be camped in groups, watching or tending their favorite kites as they hung in the air over Park Street. Occasionally a string would break. It was a matter of honor to save your twine. I remember following my falling kite, with no clew but the direction in which I saw it last, till I found that the twine was lying across a narrow court which opened where the Albion Hotel is now. There were two rows of three-story houses, which made the court, and my twine festooned it, supported by the ridgepoles of the roofs on either side. I rang a doorbell, stated my case, and ran up, almost without permission, into the attic. Here I climbed out of the attic window, ran up the roof, and drew in the coveted twine. For the pecuniary value of the twine we cared little, but it would have been, in a fashion, disgraceful to lose it.

Boats on the Frog Pond were much what they are now. The bottom of the pond was not paved until 1848. There were no frogs, so far as I know, but some small horned pout were left there, for which boys fished occasionally. The curb around the pond was laid in Mr. Quincy's day, in 1823; I mean when he was mayor. To provide the stone the last of the boulders on the Common were blasted. In old days, as appears from Sewall, they were plenty; he blasted enough for the foundations of a barn. I think the old Hancock House was built from such boulders. Among those destroyed was the Wishing Stone. This stood, or so Dr. Shurtleff told me, where two paths now join, a little east of the foot of Walnut Street. If you went round it backward nine times and repeated the Lord's Prayer backward, whatever you wished would come to pass. I once proposed to the mayor and aldermen to go round the Frog Pond nine times backward and wish that the city debt might be reduced fifty percent. But they have never had the faith to try. Mr. Quincy proposed that the Frog Pond should be called Crescent Lake. But nobody ever really called it so. I have seen the name on maps, I think, but it is now forgotten.

Charles Street was new in those days, and the handsome elms which shade the Charles Street mall were young trees, just planted, in 1825. By the building of the milldam, about that time, the water was shut out from the southern side of Charles Street. There existed a superstition among the boys that law did not extend to the flat, because it was below high-water mark. On holidays, therefore, there would be shaking of props and other games of mild gambling there, which "Old Reed" [the authorities] did not permit on the upland. This was, of course, a ridiculous boyish superstition. In those days, however, we had a large number of seafaring men, who brought with them foreign customs. Among others was the use of "props," a gambling game which the boys had introduced perfectly innocently as an element in playing marbles. I dare say people played props for money on the dried surface of the Back Bay.

The boys were in touch with the large public in their unauthorized and unrecognized connection with the fire department. Boston was still a wooden town, and the danger of fire was, as it is in all American cities, constantly present. There hung in our front entry two leather buckets; in each of them was certain apparatus which a person might need if he were in a burning house. Strange to say, there was a bedkey, that he might take down a bedstead if it were necessary. These were relics of a time when my father had been a member of one of the private fire companies. In those associations each man was bound to attend at any fire where the property of other members of the association was in danger, and there were traditions of Father's having been present at the great Court Street fire, for instance. But these fire clubs either died out or became social institutions, as the Fire Club in Worcester exists to this day, and nothing was left but the bucket as a sort of memorial of a former existence.

Before our day the volunteer fire department system of Boston had been created, and there were similar systems in all large cities. Of course we boys supposed that ours was the best in the world; each boy in Boston supposed that the engine nearest his house was the best engine in the world, and that, on occasion, it could throw water higher than any other engine. It could likewise, on occasion, pump dry any engine that was in line with it. I need not say that these notions of the boys were simply superstitions, wholly unfounded in fact. Our engine was the *New York*. The engine house was one of a curious mass of public buildings that occupied the place where Franklin's statue now stands, in front of what was the courthouse of that day. There was no electric fire alarm in those early days. The moment a fire broke out everybody who had any lungs ran up the street or down the street, or both ways, crying "Fire!" and as soon as the churches could be opened, all the bells in Boston began to ring. Then the company which was to drag the *New York* to the fire began to assemble at its house, and naturally there was great pride in seeing that your engine was first in place. You learned where the fire was, not by any signal, but by the rumor of the street. It was at the North End or at the South End or on the wharves or on Nigger Hill. As soon as boys and men, of whatever connection, arrived, sufficient to drag the engine, it started, under the direction of such officer of the company as might be present. The members of the company had no uniforms, so far as I remember; they joined the lines as quickly as they could, but there were always enough people to pull. As I have intimated, it was everybody's business to attend at the fire.

When you arrived at the spot there would be a general caucus as to the method of attack, yet I think there were people in command. Afterwards a gentleman named Amory, highly respected by all of us, was chief engineer. Whatever the caucus directed was done, with as much efficiency as was possible under such democratic institutions. But, in the first place, the probability was that there was no water near. The Jamaica Pond aqueduct carried water in log pipes to the lower levels of the city, but for fully half the city there was no such supply and wells had to be relied upon. Every engine, therefore, which was good for anything was a suction engine, as it was called; that is, it was able to pump from a well, as well as able to throw water to an indefinite height. The engine that arrived first repaired to the well best known in that neighborhood, or if the occasion were fortunate, to the sea, and began to pump. The engine that arrived next took station next to this and pumped from it through a long line of hose, and so successive engines carried the water to the place where some foreman directed it upon the flames. It was thus that the different engines attained their celebrity, as one pumped the tub of another dry, while the unfortunate members were "working the brakes" to their best to keep it full.

The buckets of which I have spoken were the remains of a yet earlier period, when people formed themselves in line to the well or to the sea and passed buckets backward and forward—full if they were going toward the fire, empty if they were going away—and the water was thus thrown upon such flames as chose to wait for it.

I need hardly say that the old method interested to the full every boy in town. If his father and mother would let him, he attended the fire, where he could at least scream "Fire!" if he could not do anything else. If a boy were big enough he was permitted almost to kill himself by working at the brakes. This was the most exhausting method for the application of human power that has been contrived, but there was power enough to be wasted, and until the introduction of steam, it was everywhere used. It is still used on board ships which have no steam power. Every enterprising boy regarded it as the one wish of his life that he might be eighteen years old so that he could join the company in his particular neighborhood, and even if he had not attained that age, he attached himself to the company as a sort of volunteer aid and, as I say, was permitted, as a favor, to assist in running through the streets, dragging at the long rope which drew the engine.

EDWARD EVERETT HALE
A New England Boyhood

26

Samuel Morse Invents the Telegraph

Few Americans have been as versatile as the brilliant, impetuous, stalwart Samuel Finley Breese Morse, painter, photographer, inventor, politician, and public figure. In 1836 (when president of the National Academy of Design, and Native American candidate for mayor of New York) he was far advanced with his telegraphic apparatus at the University of the City of New York, where he was a professor. In the next half-dozen years, with the aid of Joseph Henry and other scientists, he steadily developed his ideas. He was certain of success—but meanwhile he met poverty and even hunger.

So ended the year 1842, a decade since the first conception of the telegraph, and it found the inventor making his last stand for recognition from that government to which he had been so loyal and upon which he wished to bestow a priceless gift. With the dawn of the new year, a year destined to mark an epoch in the history of civilization, his flagging spirits were revived, and he entered with zest on what proved to be his final and successful struggle.

It passes belief that, with so many ocular demonstrations of the practicability of the Morse telegraph and with the reports of the success of other telegraphs abroad, the popular mind, as reflected in its representatives in Congress, should have remained so incredulous. Morse had been led to hope that his bill was going to pass by acclamation, but in this he was rudely disappointed.

The alternating moods of hope and despair through which the inventor passed during the next few weeks are best pictured forth by himself in brief extracts from letters to his brother Sidney.

JANUARY 6, 1843.—

I sent you a copy of the report on the telegraph a day or two since. I was in hopes of having it called up today, but the House refused to go into committee of the whole on the state of the Union, so it is deferred. The first time they go into committee of the whole on the state of the Union it will probably be called up and be decided upon.

Everything looks favorable, but I do not suffer myself to be sanguine, for I do not know what may be doing secretly against it. I shall believe it passed when the signature of the President is affixed to it, and not before.

JANUARY 16.—

I snatch the moments of waiting for company in the Committee Room of Commerce to write a few lines. Patience is a virtue much needed and much tried here. So far as opinion goes everything is favorable to my bill. I hear of no opposition but should not be surprised if it met with some. The great difficulty is to get it up before the House; there are so many who must *define their position,* as the term is, so many who must say something "Buncombe," that a great deal of the people's time is wasted in mere idle, unprofitable speechifying. I hope something may be done this week that shall be decisive, so that I may know what to do. This waiting at so much risk makes me question myself: Am I in the path of duty? When I think that the little money I brought with me is nearly gone, that if nothing should be done by Congress I shall be in a destitute state, that perhaps I shall have again to be a burden to friends until I know to what to turn my hands, I feel low-spirited. I am only relieved by naked trust in God, and it is right that this should be so.

JANUARY 20.—

My patience is still tried in waiting for the action of Congress on my bill. With so much at stake you may easily conceive how tantalizing is this state of suspense. . . . At times, after waiting all day and day after day, in the hope that my bill may be called up, and in vain, I feel heartsick, and finding nothing accomplished, that no progress is made, that *precious time* flies, I am depressed and begin to question whether I am in the way of duty. But when I feel that I have done all in my power, and that this delay may be designed by the wise Disposer of all events for a trial of patience, I find relief and a disposition quietly to wait such issue as He shall direct, knowing that, if I sincerely have put my trust in Him, He will not lead me astray, and my way will, in any event, be made plain.

JANUARY 25.—

I am still *waiting, waiting*. I know not what the issue will be and wish to be prepared, and have you all prepared, for the worst in regard to the bill. Although I learn of no opposition, yet I have seen enough of the modes of business in the House to know that everything there is more than in ordinary matters uncertain.

FEBRUARY 21.—

I think the clouds begin to break away, and a little sunlight begins to cheer me. The House in committee of the whole on the state of the Union have just passed my bill through committee to report to the House. There was an attempt made to cast ridicule upon it by a very few headed by Mr. Cave Johnson, who proposed an amendment that half the sum should be appropriated to mesmeric experiments. Only twenty-six supported him, and it was laid aside to be reported to the House without amendment and without division.

I was immediately surrounded by my friends in the House, congratulating me and telling me that the crisis is passed and that the bill will pass the House by a large majority. Mr. Kennedy, chairman of the Committee on Commerce, has put the bill on the Speaker's calendar for Thursday morning, when the final vote in the House will be taken. It then has to go to the Senate, where I have reason to believe it will meet with a favorable reception. Then to the President, and if signed by him, I shall return with renovated spirits, for I assure you I have for some time been at the lowest ebb, and can now scarcely realize that a turn has occurred in my favor.

Writing to Alfred Vail, he says after telling of the passage of the bill:

You can have but a faint idea of the sacrifices and trials I have had in getting the telegraph thus far before the country and the world. I cannot detail them here; I can only say that for two years I have labored all my time and at my own expense, without assistance from the other proprietors (except in obtaining the iron of the magnets for the last instruments obtained of you), to forward our enterprise. My means to defray my expenses, to meet which every cent I owned in the world was collected, are nearly all gone, and if by any means the bill should fail in the Senate, I shall return to New York with the *fraction of a dollar* in my pocket.

And now the final struggle which meant success or failure was on. Only eight days of the session remained, and the calendar was, as usual, crowded. The inventor, his nerves stretched to the breaking point, hoped and yet feared. He had every reason to believe that the Senate would show more broadminded enlightenment than the House, and yet he had been told that his bill would pass the House by acclamation, while the event proved that it had barely squeezed through by a beggarly majority of six. He heard disquieting rumors of a determination on the part of some of the House members to procure the defeat of the bill in the Senate. Would they succeed, would the victory, almost won, be snatched from him at the last moment, or would his faith in an overruling Providence and in his own mission as an instrument of that Providence be justified at last?

Every day of that fateful week saw him in his place in the gallery of the Senate chamber, and all day long he sat there, listening, as we can well imagine, with growing impatience to the senatorial oratory on the merits or demerits of bills which to him were of such minor importance, however heavily freighted with the destinies of the nation they may have been. And every night he returned to his room with the sad reflection that one more of the precious days had passed and his bill had not been reached. And then came the last day, March 3.

He thus describes the events of that fateful night and of the next morning:

The last days of the last session of that Congress were about to close. A bill appropriating thirty thousand dollars for my purpose had passed the House and was before the Senate for concurrence. On the last day of the session I had spent the whole day and part of the evening in the Senate chamber, anxiously watching the progress of the passing of the various bills, of which there were, in the morning of that day, over one hundred and forty to be acted upon before the one in which I was interested would be reached; and a resolution had a few days before been passed to proceed with the bills on the calendar in their regular order, forbidding any bill to be taken up out of its regular place.

As evening approached there seemed to be but little chance that the telegraph bill would be reached before the adjournment and consequently I had the prospect of the delay of another year, with the loss of time, and all my means already expended. In my anxiety I consulted with two of my senatorial friends—Senator Huntington, of Connecticut, and Senator Wright, of New York—asking their opinion of the probability of reaching the bill before the close of the session. Their answers were discouraging, and their advice was to prepare myself for disappointment. In this state of mind I retired to my chamber and made all my arrangements for leaving Washington the next day.

In the morning, as I had just gone into the breakfast room, the servant called me out, announcing that a young lady was in the parlor wishing to speak with me. I was at once greeted with the smiling face of my young friend, the daughter of my old and valued friend and classmate, the Honorable H.L. Ellsworth, the Commissioner of Patents. On my expressing surprise at so early a call, she said:

"I have come to congratulate you."

"Indeed, for what?"

"On the passage of your bill."

"Oh! no, my young friend, you are mistaken; I was in the Senate chamber till after the lamps were lighted, and my senatorial friends assured me there was no chance for me."

"But," she replied, "it is you that are mistaken. Father was there at the adjournment at midnight and saw the President put his name to your bill, and I asked Father if I might come and tell you, and he gave me leave. Am I the first to tell you?"

The news was so unexpected that for some moments I could not speak. At length I replied:

"Yes, Annie, you are the first to inform me, and now I am going to make you a promise; the first dispatch on the completed line from Washington to Baltimore shall be yours."

"Well," said she, "I shall hold you to your promise.". . .

And now at last the supreme moment had arrived. The line from Washington to Baltimore was completed, and on the 24th day of May, 1844, the company invited by the inventor assembled in the chamber of the United States Supreme Court to witness his triumph. True to his promise to Miss Annie Ellsworth, he had asked her to indite the first public message which should be flashed over the completed line, and she, in consultation with her good mother, chose the now historic words from the twenty-third verse of the twenty-third chapter of Numbers, "What hath God wrought!". . . Calmly he seated himself at the instrument and ticked off the inspired words in the dots and dashes of the Morse alphabet. Alfred Vail, at the other end of the line in Baltimore, received the message without an error and immediately flashed it back again, and the electromagnet telegraph was no longer the wild dream of a visionary, but an accomplished fact.

SAMUEL F. B. MORSE
His Letters and Journals

27

"A Fertility of Projects for the Salvation of the World"

The brilliant Transcendentalist Ralph Waldo Emerson represented the eager skepticism, the intellectual emancipation, the social and religious radicalism, of a large group of New England leaders. Unitarianism early in the nineteenth century broke down the religious dogmatism of the Bostonians and opened their minds while Republicanism cleared the way for new social and political ideas. The romanticism of the English poets Coleridge and Wordsworth, the deeper thought of Carlyle, and the idealism of Goethe and other German thinkers all laid a mark on the New England intellect. As Unitarianism thrived, as Transcendentalism reached its height, and as the Abolition agitation began, New England seemed full of yeasty aspirations, of heady ideas, of new causes. Emerson has described the appetite for novelty and "isms," often running to wild extremes.

What fertility of projects for the salvation of the world! One apostle thought all men should go to farming, and another that no man should buy or sell, that the use of money was the cardinal evil; another that the mischief was in our diet, that we eat and drink damnation. These made unleavened bread and were foes to the death to fermentation. It was in vain urged by the housewife that God made yeast as well as dough and loves fermentation just as dearly as he loves vegetation, that fermentation develops the saccharine element in the grain and makes it more palatable and more digestible. No, they wish the pure wheat and will die but it shall not ferment. Stop, dear Nature, these incessant advances of thine; let us scotch these ever-rolling wheels! Others attacked the system of agriculture, the use of animal manures in farming, and the tyranny of man over brute nature; these abuses polluted his food. The ox must be taken from the plow and the horse from the cart, the hundred acres of the farm must be spaded, and the man must walk, wherever boats and locomotives will not carry him. Even the insect world was to be defended—that had been too long neglected, and a society for the protection of ground worms, slugs, and mosquitoes was to be incorporated without delay. With these appeared the adepts of homeopathy, of hydropathy, of mesmerism, of phrenology, and their wonderful theories of the Christian miracles! Others assailed particular vocations, as that of the lawyer, that of the merchant, of the manufacturer, of the clergyman, of the scholar. Others attacked the institution of marriage as the fountain of social evils. Others devoted themselves to the worrying of churches and meetings for public worship, and the fertile forms of antinomianism among the elder puritans seemed to have their match in the plenty of the new harvest of reform.

With this din of opinion and debate there was a keener scrutiny of institutions and domestic life than any we had known; there was sincere protesting against existing evils, and there were changes of employment dictated by conscience.

There was in all the practical activities of New England for the last quarter of a century [1815–1840] a gradual withdrawal of tender consciences from the social organizations. There is observable throughout, the contest between mechanical and spiritual methods, but with a steady tendency of the thoughtful and virtuous to a deeper belief and reliance on spiritual facts.

In politics, for example, it is easy to see the progress of dissent. The country is full of rebellion; the country is full of kings. Hands off! let there be no control and no interference in the administration of the affairs of this kingdom of me. Hence the growth of the doctrine and of the party of free trade and the willingness to try that experiment in the face of what appear incontestable facts. I confess the motto of the *Globe* newspaper is so attractive to me that I can seldom find much appetite to read what is below it in its columns: "The world is governed too much." So the country is frequently affording solitary examples of resistance to the government, solitary nullifiers who throw themselves on their reserved rights, nay, who have reserved all their rights, who reply to the assessor and to the clerk of court that they do not know the State, and embarrass the courts of law by nonjuring and the commander-in-chief of the militia by nonresistance.

The same disposition to scrutiny and dissent appeared in civil, festive, neighborly, and domestic society. A restless, prying, conscientious criticism broke out in unexpected quarters. Who gave me the money with which I bought my coat? Why should professional labor and that of the counting-house be paid so disproportionately to the labor of the porter and wood sawyer? This whole business of trade gives me to pause and think, as it constitutes false relations between men, inasmuch as I am prone to count myself relieved of any responsibility to behave well and nobly to that person whom I pay with money; whereas if I had not that commodity, I should be put on my good behavior in all companies, and man would be a benefactor to man, as being himself his only certificate that he had a right to those aids and services which each asked of the other. Am I not too protected a person? Is there not a wide disparity between the lot of me and the lot of thee, my poor brother, my poor sister? Am I not defrauded of my best culture in the loss of those gymnastics which manual labor and the emergencies of poverty constitute? I find nothing healthful or exalting in the smooth conventions of society; I do not like the close air of saloons. I begin to suspect myself to be a prisoner, though treated with all this courtesy and luxury. I pay a destructive tax in my conformity.

The same insatiable criticism may be traced in the efforts for the reform of education. The popular education has been taxed with a want of truth and nature. It was complained that an education to things was not given. We are students of words; we are shut up in schools and colleges and recitation rooms for ten or fifteen years, and come out at last with a bag of wind, a memory of words, and do not know a thing. We cannot use our hands or our legs or our eyes or our arms. We do not know an edible root in the woods; we cannot tell our course by the stars, nor the hour of the day by the sun. It is well if we can swim and skate. We are afraid of a horse, of a cow, of a dog, of a snake, of a spider. The Roman rule was to teach a boy nothing that he could not learn standing. The old English rule was, "All summer in the field, and all winter in the study." And it seems as if a man should learn to plant or to fish or to hunt, that he might secure his subsistence at all events and not be painful to his friends and fellowmen. The lessons of science should be experimental also. The sight of a planet through a telescope is worth all the course on astronomy; the shock of the electric spark in the elbow outvalues all the theories; the taste of the nitrous oxide, the firing of an artificial volcano, are better than volumes of chemistry.

Ralph Waldo Emerson
"The New England Reformers"

28

The Lunatic Fringe of Reform

An American libertarian of New Hampshire origin, Thomas Low Nichols was able to write of the intellectual fads of his day from full knowledge. While he was a student at Dartmouth he adopted the food-reform principles of Sylvester Graham, who invented graham flour. A little later he became a follower of Fourier and of John Humphrey Noyes, the founder of the Oneida Community. He married a woman who specialized in the water cure or hydropathy, and the two began crusading for mesmerism, vegetarianism, and women's rights. Ultimately they turned to the Catholic Church and found England a pleasanter home than America.

When Doctor Spurzheim, the associate of Gall in the elaboration of the system of phrenology, came to America about 1834, he was received with enthusiasm. Phrenology became the rage. Plaster casts of heads and lithographs marked with the organs were sold by thousands. There was a universal feeling of heads. Lecturers went from town to town, explaining the new science and giving public and private examinations. Periodicals were published to promulgate the new philosophy, and a library of phrenological books was rapidly published. I have no doubt that in five years after the event of Doctor Spurzheim there were more believers of phrenology in the United States than in all the world beside.

Mesmerism trod closely on the heels of phrenology. Monsieur Poyen, a French Creole, from one of the West India islands, came to Boston and introduced the new science to the American public. His lectures were succeeded by experiments. At one of the hospitals a patient selected for the experiment was so thoroughly mesmerized that she remained asleep forty-eight hours, though suffering from an acute disease of the heart that usually deprived her of rest. During the trance she appeared placid and free from pain, but it was impossible to awaken her. At the end of the forty-eight hours she awoke of herself, much refreshed, and said she felt better than she had for months. The publication of this and a few similar cases, of course, set a great many people to mesmerizing each other. There were medical mesmerists and clairvoyants everywhere. Distinguished surgeons performed operations on patients who were insensible to pain during the magnetic sleep. Clairvoyants professed to inspect the internal organs of patients, describe their diseases, and prescribe remedies, which were not more varied or dangerous than those given by the regular and irregular faculty.

There were psychometrists, who could tell the lives, characters, fortunes, and diseases of people they had never seen, by holding a sealed letter, scrap of writing, lock of hair, or other connecting relic in their hands. There was one who, when a fossil of some remote geological era was placed in contact with her forehead, would give an animated description of the appearance of the planet at that period.

Mesmerism vulgarly culminated in an exhibition of what was called, absurdly enough, "psychology" or "biology," a process of hallucination by which a number of susceptible persons selected by a lecturer from his audience were made to believe and do the most ridiculous things—to fancy they were swimming or flying or drinking, at the will of the operator, and to dance, sing, declaim, and do many things they never thought of doing in their normal condition.

The vegetarian system of dietetics was taken up with great zeal and promulgated with singular ability by Sylvester Graham, Doctor Alcott, Professor Muzzy, and other sanitary reformers. The English talk a good deal about roast beef, but there are ten persons in England who do not taste flesh meat of any kind oftener than once a week, to one in America. Irish emigrants, who, perhaps, never ate meat a dozen times a year at home, think they must eat it three times a day in America. Some thousands of Americans abandoned the use of flesh entirely, and many never returned to it. These believe that most of the diseases and evils of life are caused by eating flesh and that with its disuse would come health, purity, and happiness.

The spread of hydropathy was another example of the readiness of Americans to accept anything new. The system had scarcely been heard of before several large water-cure establishments were opened in America, and in a few years five or six water-cure journals were published, medical schools of hydropathy opened, and numerous practitioners, male and female, were dispensing packs and douches, with much desirable cleanliness, and much sanitary improvement also, to the American public.

The advocacy of women's rights did not begin in America. Mary Wollstonecraft was an Englishwoman, and so was Frances Wright, who lectured thirty years ago in America on politics, socialism, and deism with considerable success, which, however, did not outlast the novelty of an accomplished woman giving public addresses on such subjects. But many American women have aspired to places in the learned professions of law, physic, and divinity. Women have practiced law, been settled as preachers, but this is scarcely a novelty, since female preachers have long been common among the Friends or Quakers and women have founded several denominations.

The attempt on the part of certain American women to assume masculine or semi-masculine habiliments—a movement which received the name of Bloomerism from one of its prominent American advocates—was a bold and energetic one, but not successful. Some thousands of American women adopted what they thought a convenient and healthful costume and were brave to heroism and persevering to fanaticism, but the attempted reform was a failure. America could rebel against a foreign government; she may revolutionize her own; but America is not strong enough to war upon the fashions of civilization. A woman in New York may make a political speech to three or four thousand people, but to wear a Bloomer dress down Broadway is another affair, and a far greater difficulty would be to get others to follow her example.

The land reformers were at one period a pretty formidable organization and had some influence on local and even on national politics. That the earth is the property of its inhabitants, that the land of every country belongs to the people of that country, that no individual can have a right to monopolize great tracts of country and compel others to pay him rent or starve, many

Americans believe. Land, said the land reformers, should be as free as air or water. Land is a necessary of life, and all men have an equal right to life and what is necessary to preserve it. A man cannot bottle up the atmosphere. Why claim exclusive possession of square leagues of territory? Who gives any man an exclusive right to earth and sunshine and the food they produce? "Land for the landless!" "No land monopoly!" "Vote yourself a farm."

THOMAS LOW NICHOLS
Forty Years of American Life, 1821–1861

29

A Woman's Declaration
of Independence

When Elizabeth Cady, of a well-known New York family, was married in 1840 to Henry B. Stanton, she was already sufficiently interested in women's rights to insist that the word "obey" be left out of the ceremony. Going to a frontier community, Seneca Falls, to live, she had the hardships and injustices of women's lot more forcibly impressed upon her. Together with Lucretia Mott, who had been from an antislavery convention because of her sex, she called a women's rights convention in the Methodist Church in Seneca Falls in the summer of 1848. Mrs. Mott protested when Mrs. Stanton offered a woman-suffrage plank. "Why, Lizzy, thee will make us ridiculous!" she exclaimed. But Mrs. Stanton stuck by her demand.

When, in the course of human events, it becomes necessary for one portion of the family of man to assume among the people of the earth a position different from that which they have hitherto occupied, but one to which the laws of nature and of nature's God entitle them, a decent respect to the opinions of mankind requires that they should declare the causes that impel them to such a course.

We hold these truths to be self-evident: that all men and women are created equal; that they are endowed by their Creator with certain inalienable rights; that among these are life, liberty, and the pursuit of happiness; that to secure these rights governments are instituted, deriving their just powers from the consent of the governed. Whenever any form of government becomes destructive of these ends, it is the right of those who suffer from it to refuse allegiance to it, and to insist upon the institution of a new government, laying its foundation on such principles, and organizing its powers in such form, as to them shall seem most likely to effect their safety and happiness. Prudence, indeed, will dictate that governments long established should not be changed for light and transient causes; and accordingly all experience hath shown that mankind are more disposed to suffer while evils are sufferable, than to right themselves by abolishing the forms to which they are accustomed. But when a long train of abuses and usurpations, pursuing invariably the same object, evinces a design to reduce them under absolute despotism, it is their duty to throw off such government, and to provide new guards for their future security. Such has been the patient sufferance of the women under this government, and such is now the necessity which constrains them to demand the equal station to which they are entitled.

The history of mankind is a history of repeated injuries and usurpations on the part of man toward woman, having in direct object the establishment of an absolute tyranny over her. To prove this, let facts be submitted to a candid world. . . .

Now, in view of this entire disfranchisement of one-half the people of this country, their social and religious degradation—in view of the unjust laws above mentioned, and because women do feel themselves aggrieved, oppressed, and fraudulently deprived of their most sacred rights, we insist that they have immediate admission to all the rights and privileges which belong to them as citizens of the United States.

In entering upon the great work before us, we anticipate no small amount of misconception, misrepresentation, and ridicule, but we shall use every instrumentality within our power to effect our object. We shall employ agents, circulate tracts, petition the state and national legislatures, and endeavor to enlist the pulpit and the press in our behalf. We hope this convention will be followed by a series of conventions embracing every part of the country.

RESOLUTIONS

Resolved, That all laws which prevent woman from occupying such a station in society as her conscience shall dictate, or which place her in a position inferior to that of man, are contrary to the great precept of nature, and therefore of no force or authority.

Resolved, That woman is man's equal—was intended to be so by the Creator, and the highest good of the race demands that she should be recognized as such. . . .

Resolved, That it is the duty of the women of this country to secure to themselves their sacred right to the elective franchise. . . .

Resolved, That the speedy success of our cause depends upon the zealous and untiring efforts of both men and women for the overthrow of the monopoly of the pulpit and for the securing to women an equal participation with men in the various trades, professions, and commerce.

Resolved, therefore, That, being invested by the Creator with the same capabilities and the same consciousness of responsibility for their exercise, it is demonstrably the right and duty of woman, equally with man, to promote every righteous cause by every righteous means; and especially in regard to the great subjects of morals and religion, it is self-evidently her right to participate with her brother in teaching them, both in private and in public, by writing and by speaking, by any instrumentalities proper to be used, and in any assemblies proper to be held; and this being a self-evident truth growing out of the divinely implanted principles of human nature, any custom or authority adverse to it, whether modern or wearing the hoary sanction of antiquity, is to be regarded as a self-evident falsehood, and at war with mankind.

Seneca Falls Declaration of Sentiments
July 19, 1848

30

Henry Thoreau Builds a Cabin at Walden Pond

To illustrate his doctrine of the simplification of life, to gain leisure to write a book, *A Week on the Concord and Merrimac,* and find material for another, and to test some of his theories both of economics and philosophy, Henry David Thoreau spent a little more than two years in his hut on Walden Pond near the village of Concord, Massachusetts. It was the most important episode in the life of a man whose stature in American letters has steadily grown and is still growing.

Near the end of March, 1845, I borrowed an ax and went down to the woods by Walden Pond, the nearest to where I intended to build my house, and began to cut down some tall arrowy white pines, still in their youth, for timber. It is difficult to begin without borrowing, but perhaps it is the most generous course thus to permit your fellow men to have an interest in your enterprise. The owner of the ax, as he released his hold on it, said that it was the apple of his eye, but I returned it sharper than I received it. It was a pleasant hillside where I worked, covered with pine woods through which I looked out on the pond, and a small open field in the woods where pines and hickories were springing up. The ice in the pond was not yet dissolved, though there were some open spaces, and it was all dark-colored and saturated with water. There were some slight flurries of snow during the day that I worked there, but for the most part when I came out on to the railroad on my way home, its yellow sand heap stretched away gleaming in the hazy atmosphere, and the rails shone in the spring sun, and I heard the lark and peewee and other birds already come to commence another year with us. They were pleasant spring days in which the winter of man's discontent was thawing as well as the earth, and the life that had lain torpid began to stretch itself. One day when my ax had come off and I had cut a green hickory for a wedge, driving it with a stone, and had placed the whole to soak in a pond hole in order to swell the wood, I saw a striped snake run into the water, and he lay on the bottom, apparently without inconvenience, as long as I stayed there, or more than a quarter of an hour, perhaps because he had not yet fairly come out of the torpid state. It appeared to me that for a like reason men remain in their low and primitive condition, but if they should feel the influence of the spring of springs arousing them, they would of necessity rise to a higher and more ethereal life. I had previously seen the snakes in frosty mornings in my path with portions of their bodies still numb and inflexible, waiting for the sun to thaw them. On the first of April it rained and melted the ice, and in the early part of the day, which was very foggy, I heard a stray goose groping about over the pond and cackling as if lost, or like the spirit of the fog.

So I went on for some days cutting and hewing timber, and also studs and rafters, all with my narrow ax, not having many communicable or scholarlike thoughts, singing to myself—

> *Men say they know many things;*
> *But lo! they have taken wings—*
> *The arts and sciences,*
> *And a thousand appliances;*
> *The wind that blows*
> *Is all that anybody knows.*

I hewed the main timbers six inches square, most of the studs on two sides only, and the rafters and floor timbers on one side, leaving the rest of the bark on, so that they were just as straight and much stronger than sawed ones. Each stick was carefully mortised or tenoned by its stump, for I had borrowed other tools by this time. My days in the woods were not very long ones, yet I usually carried my dinner of bread and butter and read the newspaper in which it was wrapped at noon, sitting amid the green boughs which I had cut off, and to my bread was imparted some of their fragrance, for my hands were covered with a thick coat of pitch. Before I had done, I was more the friend than the foe of the pine tree, though I had cut down some of them, having become better acquainted with it. Sometimes a rambler in the wood was attracted by the sound of my ax, and we chatted pleasantly over the chips which I made.

Before I finished my house, wishing to earn ten or twelve dollars by some honest and agreeable method, in order to meet my unusual expenses, I planted about two acres and a half of light sandy soil near it chiefly with beans, but also a small part with potatoes, corn, peas, and turnips. The whole lot contains eleven acres, mostly growing up to pines and hickories, and was sold the preceding season for eight dollars and eight cents an acre. One farmer said that it was "good for nothing but to raise cheeping squirrels on." I put no manure whatever on this land, not being the owner, but merely a squatter, and not expecting to cultivate so much again, and I did not quite hoe it all once. I got out several cords of stumps in plowing, which supplied me with fuel for a long time, and left small circles of virgin mold, easily distinguishable through the summer by the greater luxuriance of the beans there. The dead and for the most part unmerchantable wood behind my house and the driftwood from the pond have supplied the remainder of my fuel. I was obliged to hire a team and a man for the plowing, though I held the plow myself. My farm outgoes for the first season were: for implements, seed, work, etc., $14.72½. The seed corn was given me. This never costs anything to speak of, unless you plant more than enough. I got twelve bushels of beans and eighteen bushels of potatoes, besides some peas and sweet corn. The yellow corn and turnips were too late to come to anything. My whole income from the farm was

$23.44

Deducting the outgoes 14.72½

There are left $8.71½

beside produce consumed and on hand at the time this estimate was made of the value of $4.50—the amount on hand much more than balancing a little grass which I did not raise. All things considered, that is, considering the importance of a man's soul and of today, notwithstanding the short time occupied by my experiment, nay, partly even because of its transient character, I believe that that was doing better than any farmer in Concord did that year.

The next year I did better still, for I spaded up all the land which I required, about a third of an acre, and I learned from the experience of both years, not being in the least awed by many celebrated works on husbandry, Arthur Young among the rest, that if one would live simply and eat only the crop which he raised, and raise no more than he ate, and not exchange it for an insufficient quantity of more luxurious and expensive things, he would need to cultivate only a few rods of ground, and that it would be cheaper to spade that up than to use oxen to plow it, and to select a fresh spot from time to time than to manure the old, and he could do all his necessary farm work, as it were, with his left hand at odd hours in the summer; and thus he would not be tied to an ox or horse or cow or pig, as at present. I desire to speak impartially on this point, and as one not interested in the success or failure of the present economical and social arrangements. I was more independent than any farmer in Concord, for I was not anchored to a house or farm, but could follow the bent of my genius, which is a very crooked one, every moment. Beside being better off than they already, if my house had been burned or my crops had failed, I should have been nearly as well off as before.

I am wont to think that men are not so much the keepers of herds as herds are the keepers of men, the former are so much the freer. Men and oxen exchange work, but if we consider necessary work only, the oxen will be seen to have greatly the advantage, their farm is so much the larger. Man does some of his part of the exchange work in his six weeks of haying, and it is no boy's play. Certainly, no nation that lived simply in all respects—that is, no nation of philosophers—would commit so great a blunder as to use the labor of animals. True, there never was and is not likely soon to be a nation of philosophers, nor am I certain it is desirable that there should be. However, *I* should never have broken a horse or bull and taken him to board for any work he might do for me, for fear I should become a horse-man or a herdsman merely; and if society seems to be the gainer by so doing, are we certain that what is one man's gain is not another's loss, and that the stable boy has equal cause with his master to be satisfied? Granted that some public works would not have been constructed without this aid, and let man share the glory of such with the ox and horse; does it follow that he could not have accomplished works yet more worthy of himself in that case? When men begin to do, not merely unnecessary or artistic but luxurious and idle work with their assistance, it is inevitable that a few do all the exchange work with the oxen, or in other words, become the slaves of the strongest. Man thus not only works for the animal within him, but for a symbol of this, he works for the animal without him. Though we have many substantial houses of brick or stone, the prosperity of the farmer is still measured by the degree to which the barn overshadows the house. This town is said to have the largest houses for oxen, cows, and horses hereabouts, and it is not behindhand in its public buildings, but there are very few halls for free worship or free speech in this county.

For more than five years I maintained myself thus solely by the labor of my hands, and I found that by working about six weeks in a year, I could meet all the expenses of living. The whole of my winters, as well as most of my summers, I had free and clear for study. I have thoroughly tried school-keeping and found that my expenses were in proportion, or rather out of proportion, to my income, for I was obliged to dress and train, not to say think and believe, accordingly, and I lost my time into the bargain. As I did not teach for the good of my fellow men, but simply for a livelihood, this was a failure. I have tried trade, but I found that it would take ten years to get under way in that, and that then I should probably be on my way to the devil. I was actually afraid that I might by that time be doing what is called a good business. When formerly I was looking about to see what I could do for a living, some sad experience in conforming to the wishes of friends being fresh in my mind to tax my ingenuity, I thought often and seriously of picking huckleberries; that surely I could do, and its small prof-its might suffice—for my greatest skill has been to want but little—so little capital it required, so little distraction from my wonted moods, I foolishly thought. While my acquaintances went unhesitatingly into trade or the professions, I contemplated this occupation as most like theirs: ranging the hills all day to pick the berries which came in my way, and thereafter care-lessly dispose of them; so, to keep the flocks of Admetus. I also dreamed that I might gather the wild herbs, or carry evergreens to such villagers as loved to be reminded of the woods, even to the city, by haycart loads. But I have since learned that trade curses everything it handles, and though you trade in messages from heaven, the whole curse of trade attaches to the business.

As I preferred some things to others, and especially valued my free-dom, as I could fare hard and yet succeed well, I did not wish to spend my time in earning rich carpets or other fine furniture, or delicate cookery, or a house in the Grecian or the Gothic style just yet. If there are any to whom it is no interruption to acquire these things and who know how to use them when acquired, I relinquish to them the pursuit. Some are "in-dustrious" and appear to love labor for its own sake, or perhaps because it keeps them out of worse mischief; to such I have at present nothing to say. Those who would not know what to do with more leisure than they now enjoy, I might advise to work twice as hard as they do—work till they pay for themselves, and get their free papers. For myself I found that the oc-cupation of a day laborer was the most independent of any, especially as it required only thirty or forty days in a year to support one. The laborer's day ends with the going down of the sun, and he is then free to devote himself to his chosen pursuit, independent of his labor; but his employer, who specu-lates from month to month, has no respite from one end of the year to the other.

In short, I am convinced both by faith and experience that to maintain one's self on this earth is not a hardship but a pastime, if we will live simply and wisely, as the pursuits of the simpler nations are still the sports of the more artificial. It is not necessary that a man should earn his living by the sweat of his brow unless he sweats easier than I do.

Henry David Thoreau
Walden, or Life in the Woods

31

A Connecticut Yankee
Invents the Cotton Gin

A Massachusetts farmer boy by origin, Eli Whitney worked his way through Yale in the class of 1792. Then, going to Savannah with the intention of teaching school, he was disappointed in not finding a position. But he went to stay on the plantation of Mrs. Nathanael Greene, widow of the general, and the result was one of the most important of American inventions.

I went from N. York with the family of the late Major General Greene to Georgia. I went immediately with the family to their plantation about twelve miles from Savannah with an expectation of spending four or five days and then proceed into Carolina to take the school. During this time I heard much said of the extreme difficulty of ginning cotton, that is, separating it from its seeds. There were a number of very respectable gentlemen at Mrs. Greene's, who all agreed that if a machine could be invented which would clean the cotton with expedition, it would be a great thing both to the country and to the inventor. I involuntarily happened to be thinking on the subject and struck out a plan of a machine in my mind, which I communicated to Miller (who is agent to the executors of General Greene and resides in the family, a man of respectability and property); he was pleased with the plan and said if I would pursue it and try an experiment to see if it would answer, he would be at the whole expense; I should lose nothing but my time, and if I succeeded we would share the profits. Previous to this I found I was like to be disappointed in my school; that is, instead of a hundred, I found I could get only fifty guineas a year. I, however, held the refusal of the school until I tried some experiments. In about ten days I made a little model for which I was offered, if I would give up all right and title to it, a hundred guineas. I concluded to relinquish my school and turn my attention to perfecting the machine. I made one, before I came away, which required the labor of one man to turn it and with which one man will clean ten times as much cotton as he can in any other way before known and also cleanse it much better than in the usual mode. This machine may be turned by water or with a horse, with the greatest ease, and one man and a horse will do more than fifty men with the old machines. It makes the labor fifty times less, without throwing any class of people out of the business.

I returned to the northward for the purpose of having a machine made on a large scale and obtaining a patent for the invention. I went to Philadelphia soon after I arrived, made myself acquainted with the steps necessary to obtain a patent, took several of the steps, and the Secretary of State, Mr. Jefferson, agreed to send the patent to me as soon as it could be made out—so that I apprehended no difficulty in obtaining the patent. . . . I have employed several workmen in making machines . . . I am certain I can obtain a patent in England. As soon as I have got a patent in America I shall go with the machine which I am now making to Georgia, where I shall stay a few weeks to see it at work. From thence I expect to go to England, where I shall probably continue two or three years. How advantageous this business will eventually prove to me, I cannot say. It is generally said by those who know anything about it that I shall make a fortune by it. I have no expectation that I shall make an independent fortune by it but think I had better pursue it than any other business into which I can enter. Something which cannot be foreseen may frustrate my expectations and defeat my plan, but I am now so sure of success that ten thousand dollars, if I saw the money counted out to me, would not tempt me to give up my right and relinquish the object. I wish you, sir, not to show this letter nor communicate anything of its contents to anybody except my brother and sister, enjoining it on them to keep the whole a *profound secret.*

ELI WHITNEY
September 11, 1793

32

Luxury Among the Planters of Louisiana

To an observant traveler like Timothy Flint, the Mississippi Valley offered striking contrasts. In the upper valley were the poor but democratic frontiersmen whom he has elsewhere described. In Louisiana, however, and especially at New Orleans, he found an opulence, extravagance, and sophistication that was unique in the United States of the 1820s.

The opulent planters of this state have many amiable traits of character. They are high-minded and hospitable in an eminent degree. I have sojourned much among them and have never experienced a more frank, dignified, and easy hospitality. It is taken for granted that the guest is a gentleman and that he will not make an improper use of the great latitude that is allowed him. If he do not pass over the limits which just observance prescribes, the more liberties he takes and the more ease he feels within those limits, the more satisfaction he will give to his host. You enter without ceremony, call for what you wish, and intimate your wishes to the servants. In short, you are made to feel yourself at home. This simple and noble hospitality seems to be a general trait among these planters, for I have not yet called at a single house where it has not been exercised toward me. Suppose the traveler to be a gentleman, to speak French, and to have letters to one respectable planter, it becomes an introduction to the settlement, and he will have no occasion for a tavern.

It results in some way from their condition, from their ample income, or perhaps, as they would say, from the influence of slavery, that they are liberal in their feelings, as it respects expenditure, and are more reckless of the value of money than any people that I have seen. The ladies no doubt have their tea-table or rather their coffee-table scandal. But I confess that I have seen less of that prying curiosity to look into the affairs of neighbors and have heard less scandal here than in other parts of the United States.

The luxury of the table is carried to a great extent among them. They are ample in their supply of wines, though claret is generally drunk. Every family is provided with claret, as we at the North are with cider. I have scarcely seen an instance of intoxication among the respectable planters. In drinking, the guests universally raise their glasses and touch them together instead of a health. In the morning, before you rise, a cup of strong coffee is offered you. After the dessert at dinner you are offered another. It is but very recently that the ladies have begun to drink tea. During the warm months, before you retire, it is the custom in many places for a black girl to take off your stockings and perform the ancient ceremonial of washing the feet.

They are easy and amiable in their intercourse with one another and excessively attached to balls and parties. They certainly live more in sensation than in reflection. The past and the future are seasons with which they seem little concerned. The present is their day, and "a short life and a merry one" their motto. Their feelings are easily excited. Tears flow. The excitement passes away, and another train of sensations is started. In the pulpit they expect an ardor, an appeal to the feelings, which the calmer and more reflecting manner of the North would hardly tolerate.

An intelligent and instructed planter's family is certainly a delightful family in which to make a short sojourn, and they have many of the lesser virtues, exercised in a way so peculiar and appropriate to their modes of existence as to impress you with all the freshness of novelty. Unhappily, as appertains to all earthly things, there is a dark ground to the picture. The men are "sudden and quick in quarrel." The dirk or the pistol is always at hand. Fatal duels frequently occur. They are profane and excessively addicted to gambling. This horrible vice, so intimately associated with so many others, prevails like an epidemic. Money got easily and without labor is easily lost. Betting and horse racing are amusements eagerly pursued, and oftentimes to the ruin of the parties. A Louisianian will forego any pleasure to witness and bet at a horse race. Even the ladies visit these amusements and bet with the gentlemen.

It is true that there are opulent French planters, reared in the simplicity of the early periods of Louisiana, who can neither read nor write. I have visited more than one such. But it is also true that the improving spirit of the age, the rapid communication by steamboats, which brings all the luxuries, comforts, and instructions of society immediately to their doors, is diffusing among the planters a thirst for information, an earnest desire that their children should have all the advantages of the improved modes of present instruction. They have, in many instances, fine collections of books. A piano is seen in every good house. Their ear, taste, and voice and their excitability of character fit the ladies for excellence in music. In common with those in other parts of the Union, great and too much stress is laid upon accomplishments merely external, and there is not attached sufficient importance to that part of education which fits for rational conversation and usefulness. It is asserted here, even to a proverb, and so far as my observation extends, with great truth, that the Creole ladies are, after marriage, extremely domestic, quiet, affectionate, and exemplary wives and mothers.

TIMOTHY FLINT
Recollections of the Last Ten Years
1826

33

The Reverend Mr. Walsh
Inspects a Slave Ship

England forbade her subjects to engage in the slave trade by a law of 1807, and in the United States a similar prohibition became effective in 1808. Nevertheless, citizens of other lands (as well as some lawless Americans and Britons) continued the detestable traffic. Cuba and Brazil especially received large numbers of slaves. Both British and American warships were vigilant in trying to intercept slave ships. By an agreement in 1842, the two nations provided for the joint support of squadrons to patrol the west coast of Africa. A clergyman here describes a typical capture.

On Friday, May 22 [1829], we were talking of this pirate at breakfast and the probability of meeting her in this place, when in the midst of our conversation a midshipman entered the cabin and said in a hurried manner that a sail was visible to the northwest on the larboard quarter. We immediately all rushed on deck, glasses were called for and set, and we distinctly saw a large ship of three masts, apparently crossing our course. It was the general opinion that she was either a large slaver or a pirate, or probably both, and Captain Arabin was strongly inclined to believe it was his friend the Spaniard from the coast of Africa, for whom we had been looking out.

All night we were pointing our glasses in the direction in which she lay and caught occasional glimpses of her, and when morning dawned, we saw her like a speck on the horizon, standing due north. We followed in the same track; the breeze soon increased our way to eight knots, and we had the pleasure to find we were every moment gaining on her. We again sent a long shot after her, but she only crowded the more sail to escape.

We could now discern her whole equipment; her gun streak was distinctly seen along the water, with eight ports of a side; and it was the general opinion that she was a French pirate and slaver, notorious for her depredations. At twelve o'clock we were entirely within gunshot, and one of our long bow guns was again fired at her. It struck the water alongside, and then, for the first time, she showed a disposition to stop. While we were preparing a second she hove to, and in a short time we were alongside her, after a most interesting chase of thirty hours, during which we ran three hundred miles.

The first object that struck us was an enormous gun, turning on a swivel, on deck (the constant appendage of a pirate), and the next were large kettles for cooking, on the bows (the usual apparatus of a slaver). Our boat was now hoisted out, and I went on board with the officers. When we mounted her decks we found her full of slaves. She was called the *Veloz,* commanded by Captain José Barbosa, bound to Bahia. She was a very broad-decked ship, with a mainmast, schooner rigged, and behind her foremast was that large, formidable gun, which turned on a broad circle of iron, on deck, and which enabled her to act as a pirate if her slaving speculation failed. She had taken in, on the coast of Africa, 336 males and 226 females, making in all 562, and had been out seventeen days, during which she had thrown overboard 55. The slaves were all enclosed under grated hatchways between decks. The space was so low that they sat between each other's legs and [were] stowed so close together that there was no possibility of their lying down or at all changing their position by night or day. As they belonged to and were shipped on account of different individuals, they were all branded like sheep with the owner's marks of different forms. These were impressed under their breasts or on their arms and, as the mate informed me with perfect indifference, "burnt with the red-hot iron." Over the hatchway stood a ferocious-looking fellow with a scourge of many twisted thongs in his hand, who was the slave driver of the ship, and whenever he heard the slightest noise below, he shook it over them and seemed eager to exercise it. I was quite pleased to take this hateful badge out of his hand, and I have kept it ever since as a horrid memorial of reality, should I ever be disposed to forget the scene I witnessed.

As soon as the poor creatures saw us looking down at them, their dark and melancholy visages brightened up. They perceived something of sympathy and kindness in our looks which they had not been accustomed to, and feeling instinctively that we were friends, they immediately began to shout and clap their hands. One or two had picked up a few Portuguese words and cried out, *"Viva! Viva!"* The women were particularly excited. They all held up their arms, and when we bent down and shook hands with them, they could not contain their delight; they endeavored to scramble up on their knees, stretching up to kiss our hands, and we understood that they knew we were come to liberate them. Some, however, hung down their heads in apparently hopeless dejection; some were greatly emaciated, and some, particularly children, seemed dying.

But the circumstance which struck us most forcibly was how it was possible for such a number of human beings to exist, packed up and wedged together as tight as they could cram, in low cells three feet high, the greater part of which, except that immediately under the grated hatchways, was shut out from light or air, and this when the thermometer, exposed to the open sky, was standing in the shade, on our deck, at 89°. The space between decks was divided into two compartments 3 feet 3 inches high; the size of one was 16 feet by 18 and of the other 40 by 21; into the first were crammed the women and girls, into the second the men and boys: 226 fellow creatures were thus thrust into one space 288 feet square and 336 into another space 800 feet square, giving to the whole an average of 23 inches and to each of the women not more than 13 inches. We also found manacles and fetters of different kinds, but it appears that they had all been taken off before we boarded.

The heat of these horrid places was so great and the odor so offensive that it was quite impossible to enter them, even had there been room. They were measured as above when the slaves had left them. The officers insisted that the poor suffering creatures should be admitted on deck to get air and water. This was opposed by the mate of the slaver, who, from a feeling that they deserved it, declared they would murder them all. The officers, however, persisted, and the poor beings were all turned up together. It is impossible to conceive the effect of this eruption—517 fellow creatures of all ages and sexes, some children, some adults, some old men and women, all in a state of total nudity, scrambling out together to taste the luxury of a little fresh air and water. They came swarming up like bees from the aperture of a hive till the whole deck was crowded to suffocation from stem to stern, so that it was impossible to imagine where they could all have come from or how they could have been stowed away. On looking into the places where they had been crammed, there were found some children next the sides of the ship, in the places most remote from light and air; they were lying nearly in a torpid state after the rest had turned out. The little creatures seemed indifferent as to life or death, and when they were carried on deck, many of them could not stand.

After enjoying for a short time the unusual luxury of air, some water was brought; it was then that the extent of their sufferings was exposed in a fearful manner. They all rushed like maniacs towards it. No entreaties or threats or blows could restrain them; they shrieked and struggled and fought with one another for a drop of this precious liquid, as if they grew rabid at the sight of it.

It was not surprising that they should have endured much sickness and loss of life in their short passage. They had sailed from the coast of Africa on the 7th of May and had been out but seventeen days, and they had thrown overboard no less than fifty-five, who had died of dysentery and other complaints in that space of time, though they had left the coast in good health. Indeed, many of the survivors were seen lying about the decks in the last stage of emaciation and in a state of filth and misery not to be looked at. Evenhanded justice had visited the effects of this unholy traffic on the crew who were engaged in it. Eight or nine had died, and at that moment six were in hammocks on board, in different stages of fever. This mortality did not arise from want of medicine. There was a large stock ostentatiously displayed in the cabin, with a manuscript book containing directions as to the quantities, but the only medical man on board to prescribe it was a black, who was as ignorant as his patients.

While expressing my horror at what I saw and exclaiming against the state of this vessel for conveying human beings, I was informed by my friends, who had passed so long a time on the coast of Africa and visited so many ships, that this was one of the best they had seen. The height sometimes between decks was only eighteen inches, so that the unfortunate beings could not turn round or even on their sides, the elevation being less than the breadth of their shoulders; and here they are usually chained to the decks by the neck and legs. In such a place the sense of misery and suffocation is so great that the Negroes, like the English in the Black Hole at Calcutta, are driven to a frenzy. They had on one occasion taken a slave vessel in the river Bonny; the slaves were stowed in the narrow space between decks and chained together. They heard a horrible din and tumult among them and could not imagine from what cause it proceeded. They opened the hatches and turned them up on deck. They were manacled together in twos and threes. Their horror may be well conceived when they found a number of them in different stages of

suffocation; many of them were foaming at the mouth and in the last agonies—many were dead. A living man was sometimes dragged up, and his
companion was a dead body; sometimes of the three attached to the same
chain, one was dying and another dead. The tumult they had heard was the
frenzy of those suffocating wretches in the last stage of fury and desperation,
struggling to extricate themselves. When they were all dragged up, nineteen
were irrecoverably dead. Many destroyed one another in the hopes of procuring room to breathe; men strangled those next them, and women drove nails
into each other's brains. Many unfortunate creatures on other occasions took
the first opportunity of leaping overboard and getting rid, in this way, of an
intolerable life.

REVEREND R. WALSH
Notices of Brazil

34

Social Classes Among the Slaves

Social gradations among the slaves were as numerous and as nicely drawn
as among English servants. The social status of the slave depended in part upon
the particular work that he performed and in part upon the social position of his
master. These distinctions were of course far more elaborate on the great plantations of the Tidewater and in the Natchez region than in the less aristocratic
areas. This description by Joseph Holt Ingraham coincides with other Northern
observations of the peculiar institution.

There are properly three distinct classes of slaves in the South. The first
and most intelligent class is composed of the domestic slaves or servants, as
they are properly termed, of the planters. Some of these both read and write
and possess a great degree of intelligence, and as the Negro, of all the varie-
ties of the human species, is the most imitative, they soon learn the language
and readily adopt the manners of the family to which they are attached.

In the more fashionable families Negroes feel it their duty—to show their
aristocratic breeding—to ape manners and to use language to which the common herd cannot aspire. An aristocratic Negro, full of his master's wealth
and importance, which he feels to be reflected upon himself, is the most aristocratic personage in existence. He supports his own dignity and that of his
own master, or "family" as he phrases it, which he deems inseparable, by a

course of conduct befitting colored gentlemen. Always about the persons of their masters or mistresses, the domestic slaves obtain a better knowledge of the modes of civilized life than they could do in the field, where Negroes can rise but little above their original African state. So identified are they with the families in which they have been "raised," and so accurate, but rough, are the copies which they individually present of their masters, that were all the domestic slaves of several planters' families transferred to Liberia or Haiti, they would there constitute [an] African society whose model would be found in Mississippi. Each family would be a faithful copy of that with which it was once connected, and should their former owners visit them in their new home, they would smile at the resemblance to the original.

The second class is composed of town slaves, which not only includes domestic slaves, in the families of the citizens, but also all Negro mechanics, draymen, hostlers, laborers, hucksters, and washwomen, and the heterogeneous multitude of every other occupation who fill the streets of a busy city—for slaves are trained to every kind of manual labor. The blacksmith, cabinetmaker, carpenter, builder, wheelwright—all have one or more slaves laboring at their trades. The Negro is a third arm to every workingman who can possibly save money enough to purchase one. He is emphatically the "right-hand man" of every man. Even free Negroes cannot do without them; some of them own several, to whom they are the severest masters.

"To whom do you belong?" I once inquired of a Negro whom I had employed. "There's my master," he replied, pointing to a steady old Negro, who had purchased himself, then his wife, and subsequently his three children by his own manual exertions and persevering industry. He was now the owner of a comfortable house, a piece of land, and two or three slaves, to whom he could add one every three years. It is worthy of remark and serves to illustrate one of the many singularities characteristic of the race that the free Negro, who "buys his wife's freedom," as they term it, from her master, by paying him her full value, ever afterward considers her in the light of property.

Many of the Negroes who swarm in the cities are what are called "hired servants." They belong to planters or others who, finding them qualified for some occupation in which they cannot afford to employ them, hire them to citizens, as mechanics, cooks, waiters, nurses, etc., and receive the monthly wages for their services. Some steady slaves are permitted to "hire their own time"—that is, to go into town and earn what they can as porters, laborers, gardeners, or in other ways and pay a stipulated sum weekly to their owners, which will be regulated according to the supposed value of the slave's labor. Masters, however, who are sufficiently indulgent to allow them to "hire their time" are seldom rigorous in rating their labor very high. But whether the slave earns less or more than the specified sum, he must always pay that and neither more nor less than that to his master at the close of each week as the condition of this privilege. Few fail in making up the sum, and generally they earn more, if industrious, which is expended in little luxuries or laid by in an old rag among the rafters of their houses till a sufficient sum is thus accumulated to purchase their freedom. This they are seldom refused, and if a small amount is wanting to reach their value, the master makes it up out of his own purse, or rather, takes no notice of the deficiency. I have never known a planter refuse to aid, by peculiar indulgences, any of his steady and well-disposed slaves who desired to purchase their freedom. On the contrary, they often endeavor to excite emulation in them to the attainment of this end. This custom of allowing slaves to "hire their time," insuring the master a certain sum weekly and the slave a small surplus, is mutually advantageous to both.

The third and lowest class consists of those slaves who are termed field hands. They are, and by necessity always will be, an inferior class to the two former.

It is now popular to treat slaves with kindness, and those planters who are known to be inhumanly rigorous to their slaves are scarcely countenanced by the more intelligent and humane portion of the community. Such instances, however, are very rare, but there are unprincipled men everywhere who will give vent to their ill feelings and bad passions, not with less goodwill upon the back of an indented apprentice than upon that of a purchased slave. Private chapels are now introduced upon most of the plantations of the more wealthy which are far from any church; Sabbath schools are instituted for the black children and Bible classes for the parents, which are superintended by the planter, a chaplain, or some of the female members of the family. But with all these aids they are still, as I have remarked, the most degraded class of slaves, and they are not only regarded as such by the whites but by the two other classes, who look upon them as infinitely beneath themselves. It is a difficult matter to impress upon their minds moral or religious truths. They generally get hold of some undefined ideas, but they can go no further. Their minds seem to want the capacity to receive intellectual impressions, nor are they capable of reasoning from the simplest principles or of associating ideas. A native planter, who has had the management of between two and three hundred slaves since he commenced planting, recently informed me that if he conveyed an order to any of his field hands which contained two ideas, he was sure it would not be followed correctly.

Joseph Holt Ingraham
The South-West by a Yankee
1835

35

Garrison Is Mobbed by the
Boston Conservatives

Though by no means the first abolitionist in America, William Lloyd Garrison was the most eloquent and the most famous, as well as the best-hated. After a brief experience with editing an abolitionist sheet in Baltimore, Garrison moved to Boston and there founded the *Liberator*. He soon discovered, however, that the respectable citizens of Boston were no less hostile to antislavery agitation than were Southerners. Mr. Nichols here describes the memorable effort of the Bostonians to mob Garrison and his English abolitionist-friend George Thompson.

It was, I think, in 1834. George Thompson had been sent to America to preach abolition. He had given lectures in and around Boston, and the newspapers of the South were beginning to protest against an agitation which was increased by the addresses of this emissary of a foreign society. The merchants of Boston were aroused to the dangers of such an agitation, which, it was then believed by many, would eventually cause a dissolution of the Union.

Mr. Garrison, who published the *Liberator* in an office in the lower end of Washington Street, did not care much for that. He said, in his mild way, the "Constitution was an agreement with Death and a covenant with Hell" and that all slaveholders were thieves, robbers, murderers, and other disreputable things too numerous to mention. He wished to abolish slavery, and failing that, to turn the Southern states out of the Union.

The merchants of Boston, whose fathers had, like the merchants of Liverpool and Bristol, made fortunes by the slave trade—the merchants who were then making fortunes by Southern trade and the manufacture of cotton—were opposed to the agitation. They were indignant that the English should send emissaries to stir up sectional strife, perhaps civil war, between the states of the Union.

At that day the abolitionists in Boston and in New England were few and far between. Garrison's most earnest supporters were a few women— Mrs. Child, Mrs. Chapman, and others—good, pious souls, who formed a female Anti-Slavery Society and held prayer meetings for the slaves.

The merchants and bankers of Boston, assembled on 'Change in State Street, got into a great excitement one day about Mr. George Thompson and believing him to be at the office of Garrison's *Liberator*, they gathered tumultuously and came around from State Street into Washington Street, determined to put a stop to the eloquence of the English abolitionist.

I do not remember how it happened, but I was in the editorial office of Mr. Garrison when the crowd began to gather in the street below. It was a wonderful spectacle. There were hundreds—then thousands. It was a mob of people dressed in black broadcloth, a mob of gentlemen—capitalists, merchants, bankers, a mob of the Stock Exchange and of the first people in Boston, which considered itself the nicest of cities and intellectually the "hub of the universe."

I looked down upon this mob from the front window of the second floor, while the street became black with a dense crowd of people shouting "Thompson! Thompson!" and very evidently intending mischief to that gentleman had they found him. Mr. Garrison was writing at his desk. He was very calm about it; he had been in a state of chronic martyrdom for several years and did not seem to mind a slight exacerbation. He came to the window, however, poked his shining bald head out for a moment, and looked down on the howling mob below, and then advised me not to expose myself to observation, lest the crowd might mistake me for the object of their search.

It happened that some of the ladies I have mentioned were holding a meeting in a room of the building that afternoon. They were interrupted and ordered out. They passed through the crowd, which politely made way for them, content with expressing its feelings by a few groans and hisses.

Meantime the authorities began to bestir themselves. The city marshal made a speech, begging his fellow citizens to quietly disperse and not disgrace their great and noble city. They informed him that the man they wished to see was George Thompson. He told them he would ascertain if he was in the building and went to Mr. Garrison, who assured him that Mr. Thompson was not in town; he had fortunately left in the morning to visit a friend in the country. The officer reported to the mob and was answered by a howl of disappointed rage and then a cry for Garrison! The whole fury of the crowd—of all Boston there concentrated and represented—seemed in one instant to turn upon the editor of the *Liberator*. Had they all been constant readers of his paper, they could not have been more violent.

The marshal interposed in vain. A more powerful municipal officer now made his appearance—the mayor. He was a Boston merchant—a merchant prince. How well I remember his tall, handsome form, his noble features, his silvery voice and graceful elocution. I have always thought him a man of men. True, he did not read the riot act; he did not bring up the police—there were none to bring. The watchmen were at home asleep, and the constables were serving writs on unwilling debtors. There was no time to call out the militia, and I have a suspicion that the flower of that force was on the spot and foremost in the mischief.

The eloquence of the mayor was of no avail. At best he only gained a little time. At every pause in his speech the cry arose louder and fiercer for Garrison. The mob would have searched the building or torn it down had not the mayor given his pledge that if Garrison was in it he should be forthcoming, but he had the moment before sent the marshal to get him out by a back way and if possible secure his escape, and when Garrison had unwillingly consented to escape the threatened martyrdom, the mayor announced that he was not in the building.

There was a great howl of rage, but a moment after, it became a yell of triumph. Garrison had been seen to go from the building into a narrow lane behind it. Pursued, he took refuge in a carpenter's shop, only to be dragged out and carried into the midst of the mob, where it seemed for a moment that he would be torn in pieces. I saw him, his hat off, his bald head shining, his scanty locks flying, his face pale, his clothes torn and dusty, with a rope around his neck.

"To the Common!" shouted the mob. "To the Common!" The first thought of the whole vast crowd, all maddened as one man is mad, was to drag the poor man to Boston Common, a beautiful park in front of the State House, there to hang him upon the great elm, the "Tree of Liberty," on which Quakers had been hanged in the early Puritan days and under which Tories had been tarred and feathered before the Revolution—to hang him upon the sacred tree, or at least to give him the traditional coat of tar and feathers. So the whole mob moved toward the Common.

But to get there they had to pass by the City Hall, in which was the mayor's office, at the head of State Street. At the moment Garrison was brought opposite that point, the mayor, with a dozen or so of strong fellows to back him, dashed into the crowd, opened it like a wedge, striking right and left, gallantly seized Garrison, and carried him triumphantly into the mayor's office. The mob surged round the building with cries of rage. The mayor came out upon a balcony, looking nobler and handsomer than ever after his exploit, and told his respected fellow citizens, when they demanded Garrison, that he would shed the last drop of his blood before a hair of his head should be injured; not that he cared for him or his cause—they knew well that he sympathized with neither—but for the honor of Boston and the office he held. Then two coaches drove up to the doors of the building. The crowd was divided. A cry was raised to draw the crowd on one side while Garrison was taken out on the other, shoved into the carriage, and the coachman lashed his horses into the crowd. They grasped the wheels to turn the carriage over, but as they seized both sides at once they only lifted it from the ground. They took out knives to cut the traces. The driver knocked them down with the loaded handle of his whip. The spirited horses dashed forward; the mob opened and then ran yelling after the carriage. It was too fast for them. Up Court Street, down Leverett Street. Ponderous gates swung open—the carriage dashed in. The gates closed with a bang, and Garrison was safe in Leverett Street jail, where he could hear the howling of the pack of human wolves that had pursued him.

THOMAS LOW NICHOLS
Forty Years of American Life, 1821–1861

36

John Brown Makes a Speech
at Harpers Ferry

John Brown of Osawatomie" made his famous raid on Harpers Ferry, Virginia— hoping to free the African Americans there and begin a general slave insurrec- tion—in October 1859. When marines and militia arrived under Colonel Robert E. Lee, he was soon captured. During his trial, and at his execution on December 2, the grim, fanatical Brown gave an impressive exhibition of fortitude.

I have, may it please the Court, a few words to say.

In the first place, I deny everything but what I have all along admitted— the design on my part to free the slaves. I intended certainly to have made a clean thing of that matter, as I did last winter [1858], when I went into Missouri and there took slaves without the snapping of a gun on either side, moved them through the country, and finally left them in Canada. I designed to have done the same thing again, on a larger scale. That was all I intended. I never did intend murder or treason or the destruction of property, or to excite or incite slaves to rebellion, or to make insurrection.

I have another objection, and that is, it is unjust that I should suffer such a penalty. Had I interfered in the manner which I admit, and which I admit has been fairly proved . . . had I so interfered in behalf of the rich, the power- ful, the intelligent, the so-called great, or in behalf of any of their friends— either father, mother, brother, sister, wife, or children, or any of that class—and suffered and sacrificed what I have in this interference, it would have been all right, and every man in this court would have deemed it an act worthy of reward rather than punishment.

This court acknowledges, as I suppose, the validity of the law of God. I see a book kissed here, which I suppose to be the Bible, or at least the New Testa- ment. That teaches me that all things whatsoever I would that men should do to me, I should do even so to them. It teaches me, further, to "remember them that are in bonds, as bound with them." I endeavored to act up to that instruction. I say, I am yet too young to understand that God is any respecter of persons. I believe that to have interfered as I have done—as I have always freely admitted I have done—in behalf of His despised poor, was not wrong but right. Now if it is deemed necessary that I should forfeit my life for the furtherance of the ends of justice and mingle my blood further with the blood of my children and with the blood of millions in this slave country whose rights are disregarded by wicked, cruel, and unjust enactments—I submit, so let it be done!

Let me say one word further.

I feel entirely satisfied with the treatment I have received on my trial. Considering all the circumstances, it has been more generous than I expected. But I feel no consciousness of guilt. I have stated from the first what was my intention and what was not. I never had any design against the life of any person, nor any disposition to commit treason or excite slaves to rebel, or make any general insurrection. I never encouraged any man to do so, but always discouraged any idea of that kind.

Let me say also a word in regard to the statements made by some of those connected with me. I hear it has been stated by some of them that I have induced them to join me. But the contrary is true. I do not say this to injure them, but as regretting their weakness. There is not one of them but joined me of his own accord, and the greater part of them at their own expense. A number of them I never saw and never had a word of conversation with till the day they came to me, and that was for the purpose I have stated.

Now I have done.

JAMES REDPATH
The Public Life of Captain John Brown

37

Trading Furs on the Northwest Coast

When the British explorer Captain Cook visited Nootka Sound in the Pacific Northwest in 1778, he found the Indians there eager to sell his men beautiful furs—wolf, bear, marten, fox, sea otter, beaver, and many others—for bits of iron and brass. His two ships took aboard many pelts. Then when Captain Cook's men reached China; they found the Chinese willing to pay enormous prices for even defective skins. Out of this situation grew a great trade in Northwestern furs. British captains were first on the scene, but soon after the Revolution, Boston skippers appeared. One of these Americans was Richard Jeffry Cleveland, who was born in Salem, Massachusetts, in 1773, who became a full-fledged captain at twenty-four, and who beginning in 1797 carried out a series of daring and profitable voyages. An intrepid, able, and honest mariner, he remained at sea with brief intermissions until 1822, making and losing several fortunes. Here he tells of barter with the Northwestern Indians.

Early in the morning of the 30th of March [1799], we saw the usual indications of land—driftwood, kelp, and gulls—and at ten o'clock perceived the snow-capped hills of the American coast twelve leagues distant. We immediately set all hands to work in bending our cables and getting up a bulwark, which we had been preparing of hides sewed together. These were attached to stanchions of about six feet and completely screened us from being seen by the natives, whom it was important to our safety to keep in ignorance of our numbers. Towards evening we anchored in a snug harbor at Norfolk Sound, in latitude fifty-seven degrees ten minutes north. Here the smoothness of the water, the feeling of safety, and the silent tranquillity which reigned all round us, formed a striking contrast to the scenes with which we had been familiar since leaving Canton and would have afforded positive enjoyment, had I possessed a crew on whose fidelity I could depend.

The following day was very clear and pleasant. At the first dawn of the morning we discharged a cannon to apprise any natives who might be near of our arrival. We then loaded the cannon and a number of muskets and pistols, which were placed where they could be most readily laid hold of. The only accessible part of the vessel was the stern, and this was exclusively used (while it was necessary to keep up the bulwark) as the gangway. As it was over the stern that we meant to trade, I had mounted there two four-pound cannon and on the tafferel a pair of blunderbusses on swivels, which were also loaded. Soon after the discharge of our cannon several Indians came to us, and before dark some hundreds had arrived, who encamped on the beach near which the vessel was anchored. As we observed them to be loaded with skins, we supposed that we were the first who had arrived this season.

With a view to our own security as well as convenience, I directed my interpreter to explain to the chiefs, and through them to the tribe, that after dark no canoe would be allowed to come near the vessel, and that if I perceived anyone approaching I should fire at it; that only three or four canoes must come at a time to trade, and that they must always appear under the stern, avoiding the sides of the vessel. With my own men I neglected no precaution to make escape impossible but at the imminent risk of life. While at anchor they were divided into three watches. One of these I took charge of and, stationing them in such parts of the vessel that no movement could be made undiscovered, obliged them to strike the gong every half hour throughout the night and to call out from each end of the vessel and amidships, "All's well." This practice so amused the Indians that they imitated it by striking a tin kettle and repeating the words as near as they were able.

But a more hideous set of beings in the form of men and women I had never before seen. The fantastic manner in which many of the faces of the men were painted was probably intended to give them a ferocious appearance, and some groups looked really as if they had escaped from the dominions of Satan himself. One had a perpendicular line dividing the two sides of the face, one side of which was painted red, the other black, with the head daubed with grease and red ocher and filled with the white down of birds. Another had the face divided with a horizontal line in the middle and painted black and white. The visage of a third was painted in checkers, etc. Most of them had little mirrors, before the acquisition of which they must have been dependent on each other for those correct touches of the pencil which are so much in vogue and which daily require more time than the toilet of a Parisian belle.

The women made, if possible, a still more frightful appearance. The ornament of wood which they wear to extend an incision made beneath the upper lip so distorts the face as to take from it almost the resemblance to the human, yet the privilege of wearing this ornament is not extended to the female slaves, who are prisoners taken in war. Hence it would seem that distinctive badges have their origin in the most rude state of society. It is difficult, however, for the imagination to conceive of more disgusting and filthy beings than these patrician dames.

It was quite noon before we could agree upon the rate of barter, but when once arranged with one of the chiefs and the exchange made, they all hurried to dispose of their skins at the same rate, and before night we had purchased upwards of a hundred, at the rate of two yards of blue broadcloth each. The Indians assured us that a vessel with three masts had been there a month before, from which they had received four yards of cloth for a skin, but this story was rendered improbable by the number they had on hand, and I considered it as a maneuver to raise the price. As soon as it became dark they retired in an orderly manner to their encampment, abreast the vessel, and some of them appeared to be on the watch all night, as we never proclaimed the hour on board without hearing a repetition of it on shore.

The following morning the natives came off soon after daylight and began without hesitation to dispose of their furs to us at the price fixed upon the day before, and such was their activity in trading that, by night, we had purchased of them more than two hundred sea-otter skins, besides one hundred and twenty tails. Our barter consisted of blue cloth, greatcoats, blankets, Chinese trunks, with beads, China cash, and knives as presents. Canoes were arriving occasionally throughout the day, so that at night there was a very perceptible augmentation of their numbers.

Having observed on the 4th and 5th that their store of furs was nearly exhausted, we weighed anchor the next morning and, parting on good terms with the natives, steered up a narrow passage in an easterly direction till we arrived in that extensive sound which Vancouver has called Chatham's Straits. . . . Several women came off and told us there were no skins in the village; that the men were gone in pursuit of them; and that, if we came there again in twice ten days, they should have plenty. Here we passed a day in filling up our empty water casks and getting a supply of wood.

In the afternoon of the 9th we put out of the snug cover in which we were lying, having been informed by the Indians that there was a ship in sight. This we found to be true, as on opening the sound we saw her not more than a mile distant from us. Soon after, we were boarded by Captain Rowan of ship *Eliza,* of Boston, who had arrived on the coast at least a month before us, and who, having been very successful, was now on his way to the southward to complete his cargo and then to leave the coast. He mentioned that ten vessels would probably be dispatched from Boston for the coast this season.

RICHARD JEFFRY CLEVELAND
A Narrative of Voyages and Commercial Enterprises

38

John C. Frémont Conquers
the Sierras in Midwinter

Probably the greatest of all the American-born explorers, John C. Frémont had one of the most romantic careers in the nation's history. After some initial training as an explorer in the country between the Mississippi and the Missouri, he led five great exploring expeditions into the wild west; he took a prominent part in the American conquest of California in 1846; he owned for a time the richest of American gold mines; he was senator from California; the Republican Party nominated him as its first candidate for the presidency; and he commanded two departments in the Civil War. One of the most striking of his feats was the passage of the high Sierras in midwinter, an exploit that would be full of peril even today.

FEBRUARY 4TH, 1844.—

I went ahead early with two or three men, each with a lead horse to break the road. We were obliged to abandon the hollow entirely and work along the mountainside, which was very steep and the snow covered with an icy crust. We cut a footing as we advanced and trampled a road through for the animals, but occasionally one plunged outside the trail and slid along the field to the bottom, a hundred yards below.

Toward a pass which the guide indicated here, we attempted in the afternoon to force a road, but after a laborious plunging through two or three hundred yards our best horses gave out, entirely refusing to make any further effort, and for the time we were brought to a stand. The guide informed us that we were entering the deep snow, and here began the difficulties of the mountain, and to him, and almost to all, our enterprise seemed hopeless.

Tonight we had no shelter, but we made a large fire around the trunk of one of the huge pines and, covering the snow with small boughs, on which we spread our blankets, soon made ourselves comfortable. The night was very bright and clear, though the thermometer was only at ten degrees. Strong wind, which sprang up at sundown, made it intensely cold, and this was one of the bitterest nights during the journey.

Two Indians joined our party here, and one of them, an old man, immediately began to harangue us, saying that ourselves and animals would perish in the snow, and that if we would go back, he would show us another and a better way across the mountain. He spoke in a very loud voice, and there was a singular repetition of phrases and arrangement of words, which rendered his speech striking and not unmusical.

We had now begun to understand some words and with the aid of signs easily comprehended the old man's simple ideas.

"Rock upon rock—rock upon rock—snow upon snow," said he; "even if you get over the snow, you will not be able to get down from the mountains." He made us the sign of precipices and showed us how the feet of the horses would slip and throw them off from the narrow trails that led along their sides. Our Chinook, who comprehended even more readily than ourselves and believed our situation hopeless, covered his head with his blanket and began to weep and lament. "I wanted to see the whites," said he. "I came away from my own people to see the whites, and I wouldn't care to die among them, but here"—and he looked around into the cold night and gloomy forest and, drawing his blanket over his head, began again to lament.

Seated around the tree, the fire illuminating the rocks and the tall bolls of the pines round about and the old Indian haranguing, we presented a group of very serious faces.

5TH.—

The night had been too cold to sleep, and we were up very early. Our guide was standing by the fire with all his finery on, and seeing him shiver in the cold, I threw on his shoulders one of my blankets. We missed him a few minutes afterwards and never saw him again. He had deserted. His bad faith and treachery were in perfect keeping with the estimate of Indian character which a long intercourse with this people had gradually forced upon my mind.

While a portion of the camp were occupied in bringing up the baggage to this point, the remainder were busy making sledges and snowshoes. I had determined to explore the mountain ahead, and the sledges were to be used in transporting the baggage.

6TH.—

Accompanied by Mr. Fitzpatrick, I set out today with a reconnoitering party on snowshoes. We marched all in single file, trampling the snow as heavily as we could. Crossing the open basin, in a march of about ten miles, we reached the top of one of the peaks to the left of the pass indicated by our guide. Far below us, dimmed by the distance, was a large snowless valley, bounded on the western side, at the distance of about a hundred miles, by a low range of mountains, which Carson recognized with delight as the mountains bordering the coast. "There," said he, "is the little mountain—it is fifteen years since I saw it, but I am just as sure as if I had seen it yesterday." Between us, then, and this low coast range, was the valley of the Sacramento, and no one who had not accompanied us through the incidents of our life for the last few months could realize the delight with which at last we looked down upon it.

All our energies are now directed to getting our animals across the snow, and it was supposed that after all the baggage had been drawn with the sleighs over the trail we had made, it would be sufficiently hard to bear our animals. At several points between this point and the ridge we had discovered some grassy spots where the wind and sun had dispersed the snow from the sides of the hills, and these were to form resting places to support the animals for a night in their passage across. On our way across we had set on fire several broken stumps and dried trees to melt holes in the snow for the camps. Its general depth was five feet, but we passed over places where it was twenty feet deep, as shown by the trees.

With one party drawing sleighs loaded with baggage, I advanced to-day about four miles along the trail and encamped at the first grassy spot, where we expected to bring our horses. Mr. Fitzpatrick, with another party, remained behind, to form an intermediate station between us and the animals.

9TH.—

During the night the weather changed, the wind rising to a gale, and commencing to snow before daylight; before morning the trail was covered. We remained quiet in camp all day, in the course of which the weather improved. Four sleighs arrived toward evening, with the bedding of the men. We suffer much from the want of salt, and all the men are becoming weak from insufficient food.

10TH.—

The elevation of the camp, by the boiling point, is 8,050 feet. We are now 1,000 feet above the level of the South Pass in the Rocky Mountains, and still we are not done ascending. The top of a flat ridge near was bare of snow and very well sprinkled with bunch grass, sufficient to pasture the animals two or three days, and this was to be their main support.

11TH.—

In the evening I received a message from Mr. Fitzpatrick, acquainting me with the utter failure of his attempt to get our mules and horses over the snow—the half-hidden trail had proved entirely too slight to support them, and they had broken through and were plunging about or lying half buried in the snow. He was occupied in endeavoring to get them back to his camp and in the meantime sent to me for further instructions. I wrote to him to send the animals immediately back to their old pastures and, after having made mauls and shovels, turn in all the strength of his party to open and beat a road through the snow, strengthening it with branches and boughs of the pines.

13TH.—

We continued to labor on the road and in the course of the day had the satisfaction to see the people working down the face of the opposite hill, about three miles distant. During the morning we had the pleasure of a visit from Mr. Fitzpatrick, with the information that all was going on well. A party of Indians had passed on snowshoes, who said they were going to the western side of the mountain after fish. This was an indication that the salmon were coming up the streams, and we could hardly restrain our impatience as we thought of them and worked with increased vigor.

The meat train did not arrive this evening, and I gave Godey leave to kill our little dog (Tlamath), which he prepared in Indian fashion, scorching off the hair and washing the skin with soap and snow and then cutting it up into pieces, which were laid on the snow. Shortly afterward the sleigh arrived with a supply of horse meat, and we had tonight an extraordinary dinner— pea soup, mule, and dog.

16TH.—

We had succeeded in getting our animals safely to the first grassy hill, and this morning I started with Jacob on a reconnoitering expedition beyond the mountain. We traveled along the crests of narrow ridges extending down from the mountain in the direction of the valley from which the snow was fast melting away. On the open spots was tolerably good grass, and I judged we should succeed in getting the camp down by way of these. Toward sundown we discovered some icy spots in a deep hollow, and descending the mountain, we encamped on the headwater of a little creek, where at last the water found its way to the Pacific.

The night was clear and very long. We heard the cries of some wild animals, which had been attracted by our fire, and a flock of geese passed over during the night. Even these strange sounds had something pleasant to our senses in this region of silence and desolation.

We started again early in the morning. The creek acquired a regular breadth of about twenty feet, and we soon began to hear the rushing of water below the icy surface over which we traveled to avoid the snow; a few miles below we broke through where the water was several feet deep, and halted to make a fire and dry our clothes. We continued a few miles farther, walking being very laborious without snowshoes.

I was now perfectly satisfied that we had struck the stream on which Mr. Sutter lived and, turning about, made a hard push and reached the camp at dark. Here we had the pleasure to find all the remaining animals, fifty-seven in number, safely arrived at the grassy hill near the camp. . . .

On the 19th the people were occupied in making a road and bringing up the baggage, and on the afternoon of the next day, February 20, 1844, we encamped with the animals and all the *matériel* of the camp on the summit of the Pass in the dividing ridge, 1,000 miles by our traveled road from the Dalles to the Columbia.

J.C. FRÉMONT
The Exploring Expedition to the Rocky Mountains,
Oregon and California

39

Starvation and Death at Donner Lake

About five hundred American settlers entered California in 1846, the year that explorers John C. Frémont, Robert Field Stockton, and Stephen Watts Kearny conquered it for the United States. But one party that had set out for the Pacific Coast never reached its goal. This party originated in a group formed at Springfield, Illinois, by George and Jacob Donner and James F. Reed. They were delayed in transit and did not reach the Sierras until snow was falling and winter was coming on. The deep drifts stopped them at Truckee Lake (since called Donner Lake), their food gave out, and as members died, some of the survivors turned to cannibalism. Of the original force of eighty-seven, only forty-eight reached California alive.

Snow was already falling, although it was only the last week in October [1846]. Winter had set in a month earlier than usual. All trails and roads were covered, and our only guide was the summit, which it seemed we would never reach. Despair drove many nearly frantic. Each family tried to cross the mountains but found it impossible. When it was seen that the wagons could not be dragged through the snow, their goods and provisions were packed on oxen and another start was made, men and women walking in snow up to their waists, carrying their children in their arms and trying to drive their cattle. The Indians said they could find no road, so a halt was called, and Stanton went ahead with the guides and came back and reported that we could get across if we kept right on, but that it would be impossible if snow fell. He was in favor of a forced march until the other side of the summit should be reached, but some of our party were so tired and exhausted with the day's labor that they declared they could not take another step, so the few who knew the danger that the night might bring yielded to the many, and we camped within three miles of the summit.

That night came the dreaded snow. Around the campfires under the trees great feathery flakes came whirling down. The air was so full of them that one could see objects only a few feet away. The Indians knew we were doomed, and one of them wrapped his blanket about him and stood all night under a tree. We children slept soundly on our cold bed of snow with a soft white mantle falling over us so thickly that every few moments my mother would have to shake the shawl—our only covering—to keep us from being buried alive. In the morning the snow lay deep on mountain and valley. With heavy hearts we turned back to a cabin that had been built by the Murphy-Schallenberger party two years before. We built more cabins and prepared as best we could for the winter. That camp, which proved the camp of death to many in our company, was made on the shore of a lake, since known as Donner Lake. The Donners were camped in Alder Creek Valley below the lake and were, if possible, in a worse condition than ourselves. The snow came on so suddenly that they had no time to build cabins, but hastily put up brush sheds, covering them with pine boughs.

Three double cabins were built at Donner Lake, which were known as the Breen Cabin, the Murphy Cabin, and the Reed-Graves Cabin. The cattle were all killed, and the meat was placed in snow for preservation. My mother had no cattle to kill, but she made arrangements for some, promising to give two for one in California. Stanton and the Indians made their home in my mother's cabin.

Many attempts were made to cross the mountains, but all who tried were driven back by the pitiless storms. Finally a party was organized, since known as the Forlorn Hope. They made snowshoes, and fifteen started—ten men and five women—but only seven lived to reach California; eight men perished. They were over a month on the way, and the horrors endured by that Forlorn Hope no pen can describe nor imagination conceive. The noble Stanton was one of the party and perished the sixth day out, thus sacrificing his life for strangers. I can find no words in which to express a fitting tribute to the memory of Stanton.

The misery endured during those four months at Donner Lake in our little dark cabins under the snow would fill pages and make the coldest heart ache. Christmas was near, but to the starving its memory gave no comfort. It came and passed without observance, but my mother had determined weeks before that her children should have a treat on this one day. She had laid away a few dried apples, some beans, a bit of tripe, and a small piece of bacon. When this hoarded store was brought out, the delight of the little ones knew no bounds. The cooking was watched carefully, and when we sat down to our Christmas dinner, Mother said, "Children, eat slowly, for this one day you can have all you wish." So bitter was the misery relieved by that one bright day that I have never since sat down to a Christmas dinner without my thoughts going back to Donner Lake.

The storms would often last ten days at a time, and we would have to cut chips from the logs inside which formed our cabins in order to start a fire. We could scarcely walk, and the men had hardly strength to procure wood. We would drag ourselves through the snow from one cabin to another, and some mornings snow would have to be shoveled out of the fireplace before a fire could be made. Poor little children were crying with hunger, and mothers were crying because they had so little to give their children. We seldom thought of bread, we had been without it so long. Four months of such suffering would fill the bravest hearts with despair. . . .

Time dragged slowly along till we were no longer on short allowance but were simply starving. My mother determined to make an effort to cross the mountains. She could not see her children die without trying to get them food. It was hard to leave them, but she felt that it must be done. She told them she would bring them bread, so they were willing to stay, and with no guide but a compass we started—my mother, Eliza, Milt Elliott, and myself. Milt wore snowshoes, and we followed in his tracks. We were five days in the mountains; Eliza gave out the first day and had to return, but we kept on and climbed one high mountain after another only to see others higher still ahead. Often I would have to crawl up the mountains, being too tired to walk. The nights were made hideous by the screams of wild beasts heard in the distance. Again, we would be lulled to sleep by the moan of the pine trees, which seemed to sympathize with our loneliness. One morning we awoke to find ourselves in a well of snow. During the night, while in the deep sleep of exhaustion, the heat of the fire had melted the snow and our little camp had gradually sunk many feet below the surface until we were literally buried in a well of snow. The danger was that any attempt to get out might bring an avalanche upon us, but finally steps were carefully made and we reached the surface. My foot was badly frozen, so we were compelled to return, and just in time, for that night a storm came on, the most fearful of the winter, and we should have perished had we not been in the cabins.

We now had nothing to eat but raw hides, and they were on the roof of the cabin to keep out the snow; when prepared for cooking and boiled they were simply a pot of glue. When the hides were taken off our cabin and we were left without shelter, Mr. Breen gave us a home with his family, and Mrs. Breen prolonged my life by slipping me little bits of meat now and then when she discovered that I could not eat the hide. Death had already claimed many in our party, and it seemed as though relief never would reach us. Baylis Williams, who had been in delicate health before we left Springfield, was the first to die; he passed away before starvation had really set in. . . .

On his arrival at Sutter's Fort my father made known the situation of the emigrants, and Captain Sutter offered at once to do everything possible for their relief. He furnished horses and provisions, and my father and Mr. Mc-Clutchen started for the mountains, coming as far as possible with horses and then with packs on their backs proceeding on foot; but they were finally compelled to return. Captain Sutter was not surprised at their defeat. He stated that there were no able-bodied men in that vicinity, all having gone down the country with Frémont to fight the Mexicans. He advised my father to go to Yerba Buena, now San Francisco, and make his case known to the naval officer in command. My father was in fact conducting parties there—when the seven members of the Forlorn Hope arrived from across the mountains. Their famished faces told the story. Cattle were killed and men were up all night, drying beef and making flour by hand mills, nearly two hundred pounds being made in one night, and a party of seven, commanded by Captain Reasen P. Tucker, were sent to our relief by Captain Sutter and the alcalde, Mr. Sinclair. On the evening of February 19, 1847, they reached our cabins, where all were starving. They shouted to attract attention. Mr. Breen clambered up the icy steps from our cabin, and soon we heard the blessed words, "Relief, thank God, relief!" There was joy at Donner Lake that night, for we did not know the fate of the Forlorn Hope, and we were told that relief parties would come and go until all were across the mountains. But with the joy sorrow was strangely blended. There were tears in other eyes than those of children; strong men sat down and wept. For the dead were lying about on the snow, some even unburied, since the living had not had strength to bury their dead. When Milt Elliott died—our faithful friend who seemed so like a brother—my mother and I dragged him up out of the cabin and covered him with snow. Commencing at his feet, I patted the pure white snow down softly until I reached his face. Poor Milt! it was hard to cover that face from sight forever, for with his death our best friend was gone.

On the 22nd of February the first relief started with a party of twenty-three—men, women, and children. My mother and her family were among the number. It was a bright, sunny morning, and we felt happy, but we had not gone far when Patty and Tommy gave out. They were not able to stand the fatigue, and it was not thought safe to allow them to proceed, so Mr. Glover informed Mama that they would have to be sent back to the cabins to await the next expedition. What language can express our feelings? My mother said that she would go back with her children—that we would all go back together. This the relief party would not permit, and Mr. Glover promised Mama that as soon as they reached Bear Valley he himself would return for her children. . . . Mr. Glover returned with the children and, providing them with food, left them in the care of Mr. Breen.

With sorrowful hearts we traveled on, walking through the snow in single file. The men wearing snowshoes broke the way, and we followed in their tracks. At night we lay down on the snow to sleep, to awake to find our clothing all frozen, even to our shoestrings. At break of day we were again on the road, owing to the fact that we could make better time over the frozen snow. The sunshine, which it would seem would have been welcome, only added to our misery. The dazzling reflection of the snow was very trying to the eyes, while its heat melted our frozen clothing, making [it] cling to our bodies. My brother was too small to step in the tracks made by the men, and in order to travel he had to place his knee on the little hill of snow after each step and climb over. Mother coaxed him along, telling him that every step he took he was getting nearer Papa and nearer something to eat. He was the youngest child that walked over the Sierra Nevada. On our second day's journey John Denton gave out and declared it would be impossible for him to travel, but he begged his companions to continue their journey. A fire was built and he was left lying on a bed of freshly cut pine boughs, peacefully smoking. He looked so comfortable that my little brother wanted to stay with him, but when the second relief party reached him, poor Denton was past waking. His last thoughts seemed to have gone back to his childhood's home, as a little poem was found by his side, the pencil apparently just dropped from his hand.

Captain Tucker's party on their way to the cabins had lightened their packs of a sufficient quantity of provisions to supply the sufferers on their way out. But when we reached the place where the cache had been made by hanging the food on a tree, we were horrified to find that wild animals had destroyed it, and again starvation stared us in the face. But my father was hurrying over the mountains and met us in our hour of need with his hands full of bread. He had expected to meet us on this day and had stayed up all night, baking bread to give us. He brought with him fourteen men. Some of his party were ahead, and when they saw us coming they called out: "Is Mrs. Reed with you? If she is, tell her Mr. Reed is here." We heard the call; Mother knelt on the snow, while I tried to run to meet Papa.

When my father learned that two of his children were still at the cabins, he hurried on, so fearful was he that they might perish before he reached them. He seemed to fly over the snow and made in two days the distance we had been five in traveling and was overjoyed to find Patty and Tommy alive. He reached Donner Lake on the 1st of March, and what a sight met his gaze! The famished little children and the deathlike look of all made his heart ache. He filled Patty's apron with biscuits, which she carried around, giving one to each person. He had soup made for the infirm and rendered every assistance possible to the sufferers. Leaving them with about seven days' provisions, he started out with a party of seventeen, all that were able to travel. Three of his men were left at the cabins to procure wood and assist the helpless. My father's party (the second relief) had not traveled many miles when a storm broke upon them. With the snow came a perfect hurricane. The crying of half-frozen children, the lamenting of the mothers, and the suffering of the whole party was heartrending; and above all could be heard the shrieking of the storm king. One who has never witnessed a blizzard in the Sierra can form no idea of the situation. All night my father and his men worked unceasingly through the raging storm, trying to erect shelter for the dying women and children. At times the hurricane would burst forth with such violence that he felt alarmed on account of the tall timber surrounding the camp. The party were destitute of food, all supplies that could be spared having been left with those at the cabins. The relief party had cached provisions on their way over to the cabins, and my father had sent three of the men forward for food before the storm set in, but they could not return. Thus, again, death stared all in the face. At one time the fire was nearly gone; had it been lost, all would have perished. Three days and nights they were exposed to the fury of the elements. Finally my father became snow-blind and could do no more, and he would have died but for the exertions of William McClutchen and Hiram Miller, who worked over him all night. From this time forward the toil and responsibility rested upon McClutchen and Miller.

The storm at last ceased, and these two determined to set out over the snow and send back relief to those not able to travel. Hiram Miller picked up Tommy and started. Patty thought she could walk, but gradually everything faded from her sight, and she too seemed to be dying. All other sufferings were now forgotten, and everything was done to revive the child. My father found some crumbs in the thumb of his woolen mitten; warming and moistening them between his own lips, he gave them to her and thus saved her life, and afterward she was carried along by different ones in the company. Patty was not alone in her travels. Hidden away in her bosom was a tiny doll, which she had carried day and night through all of our trials. Sitting before a nice, bright fire at Woodworth's Camp, she took dolly out to have a talk and told her of all her new happiness.

VIRGINIA REED MURPHY
"Across the Plains in the Donner Party"

40

The Pony Express

The most famous mail route in American history, the Pony Express, was planned by William M. Gwin, senator from California. Beginning in 1854 he unsuccessfully tried to induce Congress to provide for a line of fast mail riders across the plains to California. When the government refused to risk the venture, the firm of Russell, Majors and Waddell undertook it. The first runs were made between Saint

Joseph, Missouri, and Sacramento, in April 1860. At the height of its fame, the Pony Express used 420 horses, 400 station men and helpers, and 125 riders. It was natural for Mark Twain, going west in 1861 to Carson City, where his brother was secretary to the territorial governor of Nevada, to study this famous system with keen interest. Each rider spanned from 75 to 125 miles, changing horses at relay stations scattered 10 or 15 miles apart.

In a little while all interest was taken up in stretching our necks and watching for the "pony rider"—the fleet messenger who sped across the continent from St. Joe to Sacramento, carrying letters nineteen hundred miles in eight days [1860]! Think of that for perishable horse and human flesh and blood to do! The pony rider was usually a little bit of a man, brimful of spirit and endurance. No matter what time of the day or night his watch came on and no matter whether it was winter or summer, raining, snowing, hailing, or sleeting, or whether his beat was a level straight road or a crazy trail over mountain crags and precipices, or whether it led through peaceful regions or regions that swarmed with hostile Indians, he must be always ready to leap into the saddle and be off like the wind! There was no idling time for a pony rider on duty. He rode fifty miles without stopping, by daylight, moonlight, starlight, or through the blackness of darkness—just as it happened. He rode a splendid horse that was born for a racer and fed and lodged like a gentleman; kept him at his utmost speed for ten miles, and then, as he came crashing up to the station where stood two men holding fast a fresh, impatient steed, the transfer of rider and mailbag was made in the twinkling of an eye and away flew the eager pair and were out of sight before the spectator could get hardly the ghost of a look. Both rider and horse went "flying light." The rider's dress was thin and fitted close; he wore a roundabout and a skullcap and tucked his pantaloons into his boot tops like a race rider. He carried no arms—he carried nothing that was not absolutely necessary, for even the postage on his literary freight was worth *five dollars a letter.* He got but little frivolous correspondence to carry—his bag had business letters in it mostly. His horse was stripped of all unnecessary weight too. He wore light shoes or none at all. The little flat mail pockets strapped under the rider's thighs would each hold about the bulk of a child's primer. They held many and many an important business chapter and newspaper letter, but these were written on paper as airy and thin as gold leaf, nearly, and thus bulk and weight were economized. The stagecoach traveled about a hundred to a hundred and twenty-five miles a day (twenty-four hours), the pony rider about two hundred and fifty. There were about eighty pony riders in the saddle all the time, night and day, stretching in a long, scattering procession from Missouri to California, forty flying eastward and forty toward the west, and among them making four hundred gallant horses earn a stirring livelihood and see a deal of scenery every single day in the year.

We had had a consuming desire, from the beginning, to see a pony rider, but somehow or other all that passed us and all that met us managed to streak by in the night, and so we heard only a whiz and a hail, and the swift phantom of the desert was gone before we could get our heads out of the windows. But now we were expecting one along every moment and would see him in broad daylight. Presently the driver exclaims:

"Here he comes!"

Every neck is stretched farther and every eye strained wider. Away across the endless dead level of the prairie a black speck appears against the sky, and it is plain that it moves. Well, I should think so! In a second or two it becomes a horse and rider, rising and falling, rising and falling—sweeping toward us nearer and nearer—growing more and more distinct, more and more sharply defined—nearer and still nearer, and the flutter of the hoofs comes faintly to the ear—another instant a whoop and a hurrah from our upper deck, a wave of the rider's hand, but no reply, and man and horse burst past our excited faces and go swinging away like a belated fragment of a storm!

So sudden is it all and so like a flash of unreal fancy that, but for the flake of white foam left quivering and perishing on a mail sack after the vision had flashed by and disappeared, we might have doubted whether we had seen any actual horse and man at all, maybe.

MARK TWAIN
Roughing It

41

Sarah Royce Braves the Desert
and the Mountains

The parents of the philosopher Josiah Royce were among the host of emigrants who braved fatigue, hunger, thirst, disease, and Indians in their quest for California gold. Both were of English birth, and Mrs. Sarah Royce, from whose reminiscences the following narrative is taken, had been born in Stratford-on-Avon. She and her husband, joining an emigrant train and taking with them a two-year-old daughter, encountered many hardships even before they reached Salt Lake City. From that point onward they traveled with but three men as companions and with only the manuscript diary of a Mormon who had gone to California and back in 1848 as a guide. In the Carson Valley, they were opportunely met by a detachment from a military relief party, which had been sent out to bring in the last of the year's emigrants.

We were traveling parallel with a placid river on our right, beyond which were trees, and from us to the water's edge the ground sloped so gently it appeared absurd not to turn aside to its brink and refresh ourselves and our oxen.

But as day dawned these beautiful sights disappeared, and we began to look anxiously for the depression in the ground and the holes dug which we were told would mark the Sink of the Humboldt. But it was nearly noonday before we came to them. There was still some passable water in the holes but not fit to drink clear, so we contrived to gather enough sticks of sage to boil some, made a little coffee, ate our lunch, and thus refreshed, we hastened to find the forking road. Our director had told us that within about two or three miles beyond the Sink we might look for the road, to the left, and we did look and kept looking and going on drearily till the sun got lower and lower and night was fast approaching. Then the conviction which had long been gaining ground in my mind took possession of the whole party. We had passed the forks of the road before daylight that morning and were now miles out on the desert without a mouthful of food for the cattle and only two or three quarts of water in a little cask.

What could be done? Halt we must, for the oxen were nearly worn out and night was coming on. The animals must at least rest, if they could not be fed, and that they might rest, they were chained securely to the wagon, for hungry and thirsty as they were, they would, if loose, start off frantically in search of water and food and soon drop down exhausted. Having fastened them in such a way that they could lie down, we took a few mouthfuls of food and then, we in our wagon and the men not far off upon the sand, fell wearily to sleep—a forlorn little company wrecked upon the desert.

The first question in the morning was, "How can the oxen be kept from starving?" A happy thought occurred. We had thus far on our journey managed to keep something in the shape of a bed to sleep on. It was a mattress tick, and just before leaving Salt Lake we had put into it some fresh hay—not very much, for our load must be as light as possible, but the old gentleman traveling with us had also a small straw mattress; the two together might keep the poor things from starving for a few hours. At once a small portion was dealt out to them, and for the present they were saved. For ourselves we had food which we believed would about last us till we reached the gold mines if we could go right on; if we were much delayed anywhere, it was doubtful. The two or three quarts of water in our little cask would last only a few hours, to give moderate drinks to each of the party. For myself I inwardly determined I should scarcely take any of it, as I had found throughout the journey that I could do with less drink than most land travelers. Some of the men, however, easily suffered with thirst, and as to my little girl, it is well known a child cannot do long without either water or milk. Everything looked rather dark and dubious.

Should we try to go on? But there were miles of desert before us, in which we knew neither grass or water could be found. . . . Here we were without water and with only a few mouthfuls of poor feed, while our animals were already tired out and very hungry and thirsty. No, it would be madness to go farther out in the desert under such conditions. Should we then turn back and try to reach the meadows with their wells? But as near as we could calculate, it could not be less than twelve or fifteen miles to them. Would it be possible for our poor cattle to reach there? Their only food would be that pitiful mess still left in our mattresses. It might be divided into two portions, giving them each a few mouthfuls more at noon, and then if they kept on their feet long enough to reach the holes at the Sink, we might possibly find enough water to give them each a little drink, which with the remainder of the fodder might keep them up till the meadows were reached. It was a forlorn hope, but it was all we had.

The morning was wearing away while these things were talked over. Precious time was being wasted, but the truth was the situation was so new and unexpected that it seemed for a while to confuse—almost to stupefy—most of the little party, and those least affected in this way felt so deeply the responsibility of the next move that they dared not decide upon it hastily. . . . But this would never do. So the more hopeful ones proposed that we should all eat something and as soon as the noon heat abated prepare for a move. So we took some lunch, and soon the men were lying upon the sand at short distances from each other, fast asleep. Soon some of the party awoke and after a little talk concluded that two of them would walk to a bald ridge that rose out of the flat waste about a mile and a half distant and take a view from thence in the faint hope that we might yet be mistaken and the forking road and the meadows might still be in advance. My husband said he would go, and the best of the two young men went with him, while the other two wandered listlessly off again. I made no opposition; I felt no inclination to oppose, though I knew the helplessness and loneliness of the position would thus be greatly increased. But that calm strength, that certainty of One near and all-sufficient, hushed and cheered me. Only a woman who has been alone upon a desert with her helpless child can have any adequate idea of my experience for the next hour or two. But that consciousness of an unseen Presence still sustained me.

When the explorers returned from their walk to the ridge, it was only to report no discovery, nothing to be seen on all sides but sand and scattered sagebrush interspersed with the carcasses of dead cattle. So there was nothing to be done but to turn back and try to find the meadows. Turn back! What a chill the words sent through one. *Turn back,* on a journey like that, in which every mile had been gained by most earnest labor, growing more and more intense until of late it had seemed that the certainty of *advance* with every step was all that made the next step possible. And now for miles we were to *go back.* In all that long journey no steps ever seemed so heavy, so hard to take, as those with which I turned my back to the sun that afternoon of October 4, 1849.

We had not been long on the move when we saw dust rising in the road at a distance and soon perceived we were about to meet a little caravan of wagons. Then a bright gleam of hope stole in. They had doubtless stopped at the meadows and were supplied with grass and water. Might it not be possible that they would have enough to spare for us? Then we could go on with them. My heart bounded at the thought. But the hope was short-lived. We met, and some of the men gathered round our wagon with eager inquiries, while those who could not leave their teams stood looking with wonder at a solitary wagon headed the wrong way.

Our story was soon told. It turned out that they were camping in the meadows at the very time we passed the forking road without seeing it, the morning we so ambitiously started soon after midnight. Ah, we certainly got up too early that day! If we had only seen that road and taken it, we might now have been with this company, provided for the desert, and no longer alone. But when the question was asked whether they could spare sufficient grass and water to get our team over the desert, they shook their heads and unanimously agreed that it was out of the question. Their own cattle, they

said, were weak from long travel and too often scant supplies. They had only
been able to load up barely enough to get to the Carson River. The season was
far advanced, and the clouds hanging of late round the mountaintops looked
threatening. It would be like throwing away their own lives without any
certainty of saving ours, for once out in the desert without food, we would all
be helpless together. One of the men had his family with him, a wife and two
or three children, and while they talked the woman was seen coming toward
us. She had not, when they first halted, understood that any but men were
with the lone wagon. As soon as she heard to the contrary and what were the
circumstances, she hastened, with countenance full of concern, to condole
with me, and I think, had the decision depended alone upon her, she would
have insisted upon our turning back with them and sharing their feed and
water to the last.

But fortunately for them, probably for us all, other counsels prevailed, and
we resumed our depressing backward march. . . .

I had now become so impressed with the danger of the cattle giving out
that I refused to ride except for occasional brief rests. So, soon after losing
sight of the dust of the envied little caravan, I left the wagon and walked the
remainder of the day. For a good while I kept near the wagon, but by and by,
being very weary, I fell behind. The sun had set before we reached the Sink,
and the light was fading fast when the wagon disappeared from my sight
behind a slight elevation, and as the others had gone on in advance some
time before, I was all alone on the barren waste. However, as I recognized the
features of the neighborhood and knew we were quite near the Sink, I felt no
particular apprehension, only a feeling that it was a weird and dreary scene,
and instinctively urged forward my lagging footsteps in hope of regaining
sight of the wagon.

The next morning we resumed our backward march after feeding out
the last mouthful of fodder. The water in the little cask was nearly used up
in making coffee for supper and breakfast, but if only each one would be
moderate in taking a share when thirst impelled him, we might yet reach the
wells before anyone suffered seriously. We had lately had but few chances for
cooking, and only a little boiled rice with dried fruit and a few bits of biscuit
remained after we had done breakfast. If we could only reach the meadows
by noon! But that we could hardly hope for; the animals were so weak and
tired. There was no alternative, however; the only thing to be done was to go
steadily on, determined to do and endure to the utmost.

I found no difficulty this morning in keeping up with the team. They
went so slowly and I was so preternaturally stimulated by anxiety to get forward that before I was aware of it I would be some rods ahead of the cattle,
straining my gaze as if expecting to see a land of promise, long before I had
any rational hope of the kind. My imagination acted intensely. I seemed to
see Hagar in the wilderness walking wearily away from her fainting child

among the dried-up bushes and seating herself in the hot sand. I seemed to become Hagar myself, and when my little one from the wagon behind me called out "Mamma, I want a drink," I stopped, gave her some, noted that there were but a few swallows left, then mechanically pressed onward again, alone, repeating over and over the words "Let me not see the death of the child."

Wearily passed the hottest noonday hour, with many an anxious look at the horned heads which seemed to me to bow lower and lower, while the poor tired hoofs almost refused to move. The two young men had been out of sight for some time when all at once we heard a shout and saw, a few hundred yards in advance, a couple of hats thrown into the air and four hands waving triumphantly. As soon as we got near enough, we heard them call out "Grass and water! Grass and water!" and shortly we were at the meadows.

On Monday morning we loaded up, but did not hurry, for the cattle had not rested any too long; another day would have been better, but we dared not linger. So, giving them time that morning thoroughly to satisfy themselves with grass and water, we once more set forward toward the formidable desert and, at that late season, with our equipment, the scarcely less formidable Sierras. The feeling that we were once more going forward instead of backward gave an animation to every step which we could never have felt but by contrast. By night we were again at the Sink, where we once more camped, but we durst not, the following morning, launch out upon the desert with the whole day before us, for though it was now the 9th of October, the sun was still powerful for some hours daily, and the arid sand doubled its heat. Not much after noon, however, we ventured out upon the sea of sand, this time to cross or die. . . .

Morning was now approaching, and we hoped, when full daylight came, to see some signs of the river. But for two or three weary hours after sunrise nothing of the kind appeared. The last of the water had been given to the cattle before daylight. When the sun was up we gave them the remainder of their hay, took a little breakfast, and pressed forward. For a long time not a word was spoken save occasionally to the cattle. I had again unconsciously got in advance, my eyes scanning the horizon to catch the first glimpse of any change, though I had no definite idea in my mind what first to expect. But now there was surely something. Was it a cloud? It was very low at first, and I feared it might evaporate as the sun warmed it. But it became rather more distinct and a little higher. I paused and stood till the team came up. Then, walking beside it, I asked my husband what he thought that low dark line could be. "I think," he said, "it must be the timber on Carson River." Again we were silent, and for a while I watched anxiously the heads of the two leading cattle. They were rather unusually fine animals, often showing considerable intelligence, and so faithful had they been, through so many trying scenes, I could not help feeling a sort of attachment to them, and I pitied them as I observed how low their heads drooped as they pressed their shoulders so resolutely and yet so wearily against the bows. Another glance at the horizon. Surely there was now visible a little unevenness in the top of that dark line, as though it might indeed be trees. "How far off do you think that is now?" I said. "About five or six miles, I guess" was the reply. At that moment the white-faced leader raised his head, stretched forward his nose, and uttered a low moo-o-oo. I was startled, fearing it was the sign for him to fall, exhausted. "What is the matter with him?" I said. "I think he smells the water" was the answer. "How can he at such a distance?" As I spoke, the other leader raised his head, stretched out his nose, and uttered the same sound. The hinder cattle seemed to catch the idea, whatever it was; they all somewhat increased their pace and from that time showed renewed animation.

But we had yet many weary steps to take, and noon had passed before we stood in the shade of those longed-for trees beside the Carson River. As soon as the yokes were removed, the oxen walked into the stream and stood a few moments, apparently enjoying its coolness, then drank as they chose, came out, and soon found feed that satisfied them for the present, though at this point it was not abundant. The remainder of that day was spent in much-needed rest. The next day we did not travel many miles, for our team showed decided signs of weakness, and the sand became deeper as we advanced, binding the wheels so as to make hauling very hard. We had conquered the desert.

But the great Sierra Nevada Mountains were still all before us, and we had many miles to make, up Carson River, before their ascent was fairly begun. If this sand continued many miles, as looked probable, when should we ever even begin the real climbing? The men began to talk among themselves about how much easier they could get on if they left the wagon, and it was not unlikely they would try starting out without us if we had to travel too slowly. But they could not do this to any real advantage unless they took with them their pack mule to carry some provisions. All they had was the bacon they found on the desert and some parched cornmeal, but they felt sanguine that they could go so much faster than the cattle with the wagon, they could easily make this last them through. But the bargain had been, when we agreed to supply them with flour, that the pack mule, and the old horse if he could be of any use, should be at our service to aid in any pinch that might occur, to the end of the journey. Having shared the perils of the way thus far, it certainly seemed unwise to divide the strength of so small a party when the mountains were to be scaled.

I wished most heartily there was some more rapid way for Mary and me to ride. But it was out of the question, for only a thoroughly trained mountain animal would do for me to ride, carrying her. Besides this, all the clothing and personal conveniences we had in the world were in our wagon, and we had neither a sufficient number of sound animals nor those of the right kind to pack them across the mountains. So the only way was to try to keep on. But it looked like rather a hopeless case when for this whole day we advanced but a few miles.

The next morning, Friday, the 12th of October, we set out once more, hoping the sand would become lighter and the road easier to travel. But instead of this the wheels sank deeper than yesterday, there was more of ascent to overcome, the sun shone out decidedly hot, and toward noon we saw that we were approaching some pretty steep hills, up which our road evidently led. It did not look as though we could ascend them, but we would at least try to reach their foot. As we neared them we saw dust rising from the road at one of the turns we could distinguish high up in the hills a few miles off. Probably it was some party ahead of us. There was no hope of our overtaking anybody, so when we lost sight of the dust we did not expect to see it again. But soon another section of the road was in sight, and again the dust appeared, this time nearer and plainly moving toward us. Conjecture now became very lively. It was probably Indians, but they could not be of the same tribes we had seen. Were they foes? How many were there? Repeatedly we saw the dust at different points but could make out no distinct figures.

We were now so near the foot of the hills that we could distinctly see a stretch of road leading down a very steep incline to where we were moving so laboriously along. Presently at the head of this steep incline appeared two horsemen clad in loose, flying garments that flapped like wings on each side of them, while their broad-brimmed hats, blown up from their foreheads, revealed hair and faces that belonged to no Indians. Their rapidity of motion and the steepness of the descent gave a strong impression of coming down from above, and the thought flashed into my mind, "They look heaven-sent." As they came nearer we saw that each of them led by a halter a fine mule, and the perfect ease with which all the animals cantered down that steep was a marvel in our eyes. My husband and myself were at the heads of the lead cattle, and our little Mary was up in the front of the wagon, looking with wonder at the approaching forms.

As they came near they smiled, and the forward one said, "Well, sir, you are the man we are after!" "How can that be?" said my husband with surprise. "Yes, sir," continued the stranger, "you and your wife and that little girl are what brought us as far as this. You see, we belong to the relief company sent out by order of the United States Government to help the late emigrants over the mountains. We were ordered only as far as Truckee Pass. When we got there we met a little company that had just got in. They'd been in a snow-storm at the summit—'most got froze to death themselves, lost some of their cattle, and just managed to get to where some of our men had fixed a relief camp. There was a woman and some children with them, and that woman set right to work at us fellows to go on over the mountains after a family she said they'd met on the desert going back for grass and water 'cause they'd missed their way. She said there was only one wagon, and there was a woman and child in it, and she knew they could never get through them canyons and over them ridges without help. We told her we had no orders to go any farther then. She said she didn't care for orders. She didn't believe anybody would blame us for doing what we were sent out to do, if we did have to go farther than ordered. And she kept at me so, I couldn't get rid of her. You see, I've got a wife and little girl of my own, so I felt just how it was, and I got this man to come with me, and here we are, to give you more to eat, if you want it, let you have these two mules, and tell you how to get right over the mountains the best and quickest way."

While he thus rapidly, in cheery though blunt fashion, explained their sudden presence with us, the thought of their being heaven-sent—that had so lightly flashed into my mind as I at first watched their rapid descent of the hill with flying garments—grew into a sweetly solemn conviction, and I stood in mute adoration, breathing in my inmost heart thanksgiving to that Providential hand which had taken hold of the conflicting movements, the provoking blunders, the contradictory plans, of our lives and those of a dozen other people who a few days before were utterly unknown to each other and many miles apart, and had from those rough, broken materials wrought out for us so unlooked-for a deliverance.

Sarah Royce
A Frontier Lady

42

Vigilante Days and Ways in Montana

Gold was discovered at Alder Gulch, Montana, in 1863, and within a few weeks thousands of fortune hunters poured over the mountains into the new El Dorado. For a time the activities of the notorious Henry Plummer and his gang of outlaws threatened the very existence of the new community, but a vigilante organization such as that which arose in California fifteen years earlier restored law and order. Nathaniel Langford, who played an active part in the vigilante movement, became the first superintendent of the Yellowstone National Park.

In May 1863, a company of miners, while returning from an unsuccessful exploring expedition, discovered the remarkable placer afterward known as

Alder Gulch. They gave the name of one of their number, Fairweather, to the district. Several of the company went immediately to Bannack, communicated the intelligence, and returned with supplies to their friends. The effect of the news was electrical. Hundreds started at once to the new placer, each striving to outstrip the other in order to secure a claim. In the hurry of departure, among many minor accidents, a man whose body, partially concealed by the willows, was mistaken for a beaver was shot by a Mr. Arnold. Discovering the fatal mistake, Arnold gave up the chase and bestowed his entire attention upon the unfortunate victim until his death a few days afterward. The great stampede with its numerous pack animals penetrated the dense alder thicket which filled the gulch a distance of eight miles to the site selected for building a town. An accidental fire occurring swept away the alders for the entire distance in a single night. In less than a week from the date of the first arrival hundreds of tents, brush wakiups, and rude log cabins extemporized for immediate occupancy were scattered at random over the spot, now for the first time trodden by white men. For a distance of twelve miles from the mouth of the gulch to its source in Bald Mountain claims were staked and occupied by the men fortunate enough first to assert an ownership. Laws were adopted, judges selected, and the new community was busy in upheaving, sluicing, drifting, and cradling the inexhaustible bed of auriferous gravel which has yielded under these various manipulations a greater amount of gold than any other placer on the continent.

The Southern sympathizers of the Territory gave the name of Varina to the new town which had sprung up in Alder Gulch, in honor of the wife of President Jefferson Davis. Dr. Bissell, one of the miners' judges of the Gulch, was an ardent Unionist. Being called upon to draw up some papers before the new name had been generally adopted and requested to date them at "Varina City," he declared with a very emphatic expletive he would not do it and wrote the name "Virginia City," by which name the place has ever since been known. . . .

No longer in fear of attack by the Indians, immigrants had been steadily pouring into the Territory over the Salt Lake route during the month of June. Many came also over the mountains from Salmon River. The opportune discovery of Alder Gulch relieved Bannack of a large and increasing population of unemployed gold-hunters, who, lured by the overdrawn reports of local richness, had exhausted all their means in a long and perilous journey, to meet only disappointment and disaster at its close. Almost simultaneously with the settlement at Virginia City, other settlements lower down and farther up the gulch were commenced. Those below were known by the respective names of Junction, Nevada, and Central; those above, Pine Grove, Highland, and Summit. As the entire gulch for a distance of twelve miles was appropriated, the intervals of two or three miles between the several nuclei were occupied by the cabins of miners, who owned or were developing the claims opposite to them, so that in less than three months after the discovery, the gulch was really one entire settlement. One long stream of active life filled the little creek, on its auriferous course from Bald Mountain, through a canyon of wild and picturesque character, until it emerged into the large and fertile valley of the Pas-sam-a-ri. *Pas-sam-a-ri* is the Shoshone word for "Stinking Water," and the latter is the name commonly given in Montana to the beautiful mountain stream which was called by Lewis and Clark in their journal "Philanthropy River." Lateral streams of great beauty pour down the sides of the mountain chain bounding the valley, across which they ran to their union with the Pas-sam-a-ri, which, twenty miles beyond, unites with the Beaverhead, one of the forming streams of the Jefferson. Gold placers were found upon these streams, and occupied soon after the settlement at Virginia City was commenced. One of these at Bivins's Gulch, in the mountains twelve miles from Virginia City, though limited in extent, was sufficiently productive to afford profitable employment to a little community of twenty or more miners. Twenty miles below Virginia City on the route to Bannack, a man by the name of Dempsey located a ranch, and built a large cabin for the accommodation of travelers. Seven miles above, and between that and Virginia City, another similar building for like purposes was owned by Peter Daly, and three miles above Daly's was another owned by Mr. Lorrain. These establishments are only important as they serve to locate occurrences connected with this history.

Of the settlements in Alder Gulch, Virginia City was the principal, though Nevada, two miles below, at one time was of nearly equal size and population. A stranger from the Eastern states entering the gulch for the first time two or three months after its discovery would be inspired by the scene and its associations with reflections of the most strange and novel character. This human hive, numbering at least ten thousand people, was the product of ninety days. Into it were crowded all the elements of a rough and active civilization. Thousands of cabins and tents and brush wakiups, thrown together in the roughest form and scattered at random along the banks and in the nooks of the hills, were seen on every hand. Every foot of the gulch, under the active manipulations of the miners, was undergoing displacement, and it was already disfigured by huge heaps of gravel which had been passed through the sluices and rifled of their glittering contents. In the gulch itself all was activity. Some were removing the superincumbent earth to reach the pay dirt; others who had accomplished that were gathering up the clay and gravel upon the surface of the bedrock, while by others still it was thrown into the sluice boxes. This exhibition of mining industry was twelve miles long. Gold was abundant, and every possible device was employed by the gamblers, the traders, the vile men and women that had come with the miners to the locality, to obtain it. Nearly every third cabin in the towns was a saloon where vile whiskey was peddled out for fifty cents a drink in gold dust. Many of these places were filled with gambling tables and gamblers, and the miner who was bold enough to enter one of them with his day's earnings in his pocket seldom left until thoroughly fleeced. Hurdy-gurdy dance houses were numerous, and there were plenty of camp beauties to patronize them. Not a day or night passed which did not yield its full fruition of fights, quarrels, wounds, or murders. The crack of the revolver was often heard above the merry notes of the violin. Street fights were frequent, and as no one knew when or where they would occur, everyone was on his guard against a random shot.

Sunday was always a gala day. The miners then left their work and gathered about the public places in the towns. The stores were all open, the auctioneers specially eloquent on every corner in praise of their wares. Thousands of people crowded the thoroughfares, ready to rush in any direction of promised excitement. Horse racing was among the most favored amusements. Prize rings were formed, and brawny men engaged at fisticuffs until their sight was lost and their bodies pummeled to a jelly, while hundreds of onlookers cheered the victor. Hacks rattled to and fro between the several towns, freighted with drunken and rowdy humanity of both sexes. Citizens of acknowledged respectability often walked, more often perhaps rode side by side on horseback, with noted courtesans in open day through the crowded streets and seemingly suffered no harm in reputation. Pistols flashed, bowie knives flourished, and braggart oaths filled the air, as often as men's passions triumphed over their reason. This was indeed the reign of unbridled license, and men who at first regarded it with disgust and terror, by constant exposure soon learned to become part of it and forget that they had ever been aught else. All classes of society were represented at this general exhibition. Judges, lawyers, doctors, even clergymen, could not claim exemption. Culture and religion afforded feeble protection where allurement and indulgence ruled the hour.

Underneath this exterior of recklessness there was in the minds and hearts of the miners and business men of this society a strong and abiding sense of justice—and that saved the Territory. While they could enjoy what they called sport even to the very borders of crime and indulge in many practices which in themselves were criminal, yet when any one was murdered, robbed, abused, or hurt, a feeling of resentment, a desire for retaliation, animated all. With the ingathering of new men fear of the roughs gradually wore away, but the desire to escape responsibility, to acquire something and leave in peace, prevented any active measures for protection, and so far as organization was concerned, the law-and-order citizens, though in the majority, were as much at sea as ever.

NATHANIEL PITT LANGFORD
Vigilante Days and Ways in Montana

43

Davy Crockett Defends the Alamo

The frontiersman Crockett had been dropped from Congress because he opposed many of Jackson's measures in the face of strong Jackson sentiment in his district. Determining to leave Tennessee, he heard of the movement for Texan independence, and his sympathy was fired. He arrived at San Antonio in February 1836, just in time to share in the gallant defense of the Alamo and to fall under a storm of bullets in the last Mexican assault. The authenticity of this autobiographical fragment is open to doubt, but its accuracy as a picture of the siege is accepted.

I write this on the nineteenth of February, 1836, at San Antonio. We are all in high spirits, though we are rather short of provisions for men who have appetites that could digest anything but oppression; but no matter, we have a prospect of soon getting our bellies full of fighting, and that is victuals and drink to a true patriot any day. We had a little sort of convivial party last evening: Just about a dozen of us set to work most patriotically to see whether we could not get rid of that curse of the land, whisky, and we made considerable progress.

This morning I saw a caravan of about fifty mules passing by Bexar and bound for Santa Fé. They were loaded with different articles to such a degree that it was astonishing how they could travel at all, and they were nearly worn out by their labors. They were without bridle or halter, and yet proceeded with perfect regularity in a single line, and the owners of the caravan rode their mustangs with their enormous spurs, weighing at least a pound apiece, with rowels an inch and a half in length, and lever bits of the harshest description, able to break the jaws of their animals under a very gentle pressure. The men were dressed in the costume of Mexicans. Colonel Travis sent out a guard to see that they were not laden with munitions of war for the enemy. I went out with the party.

Finding that the caravan contained nothing intended for the enemy, we assisted the owners to replace the heavy burdens on the backs of the patient but dejected mules and allowed them to pursue their weary and lonely way. For full two hours we could see them slowly winding along the narrow path, a faint line that ran like a thread through the extended prairie, and finally they were whittled down to the little end of nothing in the distance and were blotted out from the horizon.

FEBRUARY 22.—

The Mexicans, about sixteen hundred strong, with their president, Santa Anna, at their head, aided by Generals Almonte, Cos, Sesma, and Castrillon, are within two leagues of Bexar. General Cos, it seems, has already forgot his parole of honor and is come back to retrieve the credit he lost in this place in December last. If he is captured a second time, I don't think he can have the impudence to ask to go at large again without giving better bail than on the former occasion. Some of the scouts came in and bring reports that Santa Anna has been endeavoring to excite the Indians to hostilities against the Texans, but so far without effect. The Comanches in particular entertain such hatred for the Mexicans and at the same time hold them in such contempt that they would rather turn their tomahawks against them and drive them from the land than lend a helping hand. We are up and doing and as lively as Dutch cheese in the dog days. Two hunters left the town this afternoon for the purpose of reconnoitering.

FEBRUARY 23.—

Early this morning the enemy came in sight, marching in regular order and displaying their strength to the greatest advantage in order to strike us with terror. But that was no go; they'll find that they have to do with men who will never lay down their arms as long as they can stand on their legs. We held a short council of war, and finding that we should be completely surrounded and overwhelmed by numbers if we remained in the town, we concluded to withdraw to the fortress of Alamo and defend it to the last extremity. We accordingly filed off in good order, having some days before placed all the surplus provisions, arms, and ammunition in the fortress. We have had a large national flag made; it is composed of thirteen stripes, red and white alternately, on a blue ground with a large white star of five points in the center, and between the points the letters TEXAS. As soon as all our little band, about one hundred and fifty in number, had entered and secured the fortress in the best possible manner, we set about raising our flag on the battlements. The enemy marched into Bexar and took possession of the town, a blood-red flag flying at their head, to indicate that we need not expect quarters if we should fall into their clutches. In the afternoon a messenger was sent from the enemy to Colonel Travis, demanding an unconditional and absolute surrender of the garrison, threatening to put every man to the sword in case of refusal. The only answer he received was a cannon shot, so the messenger left us with a flea in his ear, and the Mexicans commenced firing grenades at us, but without doing any mischief. At night Colonel Travis sent an express to Colonel Fanning at Goliad, about three or four days' march from this place, to let him know that we are besieged. The old pirate volunteered to go on this expedition and accordingly left the fort after nightfall.

FEBRUARY 24.—

Very early this morning the enemy commenced a new battery on the banks of the river about three hundred and fifty yards from the fort, and by afternoon they amused themselves by firing at us from that quarter. Our Indian scout came in this evening, and with him a reinforcement of thirty men from Gonzales, who are just in the nick of time to reap a harvest of glory, but there is some prospect of sweating blood before we gather it in.

FEBRUARY 25.—

The firing commenced early this morning, but the Mexicans are poor engineers, for we haven't lost a single man, and our outworks have sustained no injury. Our sharpshooters have brought down a considerable number of stragglers at a long shot. I got up before the peep of day, hearing an occasional discharge of a rifle just over the place where I was sleeping, and I was somewhat amazed to see Thimblerig mounted alone on the battlement, no one being on duty at the time but the sentries. "What are you doing there?" says I. "Paying my debts," says he, "interest and all." "And how do you make out?" says I. "I've nearly got through," says he; "stop a moment, Colonel, and I'll close the account." He clapped his rifle to his shoulder and blazed away, then jumped down from his perch and said: "That account's settled; them chaps will let me play out my game in quiet next time." I looked over the wall and saw four Mexicans lying dead on the plain. I asked him to explain what he meant by paying his debts, and he told me that he had run the grapeshot into four rifle balls and that he had taken an early stand to have a chance of picking off stragglers. "Now, Colonel, let's go take our bitters," said he, and so we did. The enemy have been busy during the night and have thrown up two batteries on the opposite side of the river. The battalion of Matamoras is posted there, and cavalry occupy the hills to the east and on the road to Gonzales. They are determined to surround us and cut us off from reinforcement or the possibility of escape by a sortie. Well, there's one thing they cannot prevent: We'll still go ahead and sell our lives at a high price.

FEBRUARY 27.—

The cannonading began early this morning, and ten bombs were thrown into the fort, but fortunately exploded without doing any mischief. So far it has been a sort of tempest in a teapot, not unlike a pitched battle in the Hall of Congress, where the parties array their forces, make fearful demonstrations on both sides, then fire away with loud-sounding speeches, which contain about as much meaning as the report of a howitzer charged with a blank cartridge. Provisions are becoming scarce, and the enemy are endeavoring to cut off our water. If they attempt to stop our grog in that manner, let them look out, for we shall become too wrathy for our shirts to hold us. We are not prepared to submit to an excise of that nature, and they'll find it out. This discovery has created considerable excitement in the fort.

FEBRUARY 28.—

Last night our hunters brought in some corn and hogs and had a brush with a scout from the enemy beyond gunshot of the fort. They put the scout to flight and got in without injury. They bring accounts that the settlers are flying in all quarters, in dismay, leaving their possessions to the mercy of the ruthless invader, who is literally engaged in a war of extermination more brutal than the untutored savage of the desert could be guilty of. Slaughter is indiscriminate, sparing neither sex, age, nor condition. Buildings have been burnt down, farms laid waste, and Santa Anna appears determined to verify his threat and convert the blooming paradise into a howling wilderness. For just one fair crack at that rascal even at a hundred yards distance I would bargain to break my Betsey and never pull trigger again. My name's not Crockett if I wouldn't get glory enough to appease my stomach for the remainder of my life.

FEBRUARY 29.—

Before daybreak we saw General Sesma leave his camp with a large body of cavalry and infantry and move off in the direction of Goliad. We think that he must have received news of Colonel Fanning's coming to our relief. We are all in high spirits at the prospect of being able to give the rascals a fair shake on the plain. This business of being shut up makes a man wolfish.

I had a little sport this morning before breakfast. The enemy had planted a piece of ordnance within gunshot of the fort during the night, and the first thing in the morning they commenced a brisk cannonade pointblank against the spot where I was snoring. I turned out pretty smart and mounted the rampart. The gun was charged again, a fellow stepped forth to touch her off, but before he could apply the match I let him have it, and he keeled over. A second stepped up, snatched the match from the hand of the dying man, but Thimblerig, who had followed me, handed me his rifle, and the next instant the Mexican was stretched on the earth beside the first. A third came up to the cannon, my companion handed me another gun, and I fixed him off in like manner. A fourth, then a fifth, seized the match, who both met with the same fate, and then the whole party gave it up as a bad job and hurried off to the camp, leaving the cannon ready charged where they had planted it. I came down, took my bitters, and went to breakfast. Thimblerig told me that the place from which I had been firing was one of the snuggest stands in the whole fort, for he never failed picking off two or three stragglers before breakfast when perched up there. And I recollect now having seen him there, ever since he was wounded, the first thing in the morning and the last at night—and at times thoughtlessly playing at his eternal game.

MARCH 1.—

The enemy's forces have been increasing in numbers daily, notwithstanding they have already lost about three hundred men in the several assaults they have made upon us. I neglected to mention in the proper place that when the enemy came in sight we had but three bushels of corn in the garrison but have since found eighty bushels in a deserted house. Colonel Bowie's illness still continues, but he manages to crawl from his bed every day, that his comrades may see him. His presence alone is a tower of strength—the enemy becomes more daring as his numbers increase.

MARCH 2.—

This day the delegates meet in general convention at the town of Washington to frame our Declaration of Independence. That the sacred instrument may never be trampled on by the children of those who have freely shed their blood to establish it is the sincere wish of David Crockett.

MARCH 3.—

We have given over all hopes of receiving assistance from Goliad or Refugio. Colonel Travis harangued the garrison and concluded by exhorting them, in case the enemy should carry the fort, to fight to the last gasp and render their victory even more serious to them than to us. This was followed by three cheers.

MARCH 4.—

Shells have been falling into the fort like hail during the day, but without effect. About dusk in the evening, we observed a man running toward the fort, pursued by about half a dozen Mexican cavalry. The bee hunter immediately knew him to be the old pirate who had gone to Goliad, and calling to the two hunters, he sallied out of the fort to the relief of the old man, who was hard pressed. I followed close after. Before we reached the spot the Mexicans were close on the heel of the old man, who stopped suddenly, turned short upon his pursuers, discharged his rifle, and one of the enemy fell from his horse. The chase was renewed, but finding that he would be overtaken and cut to pieces, he now turned again and, to the amazement of the enemy, became the assailant in his turn. He clubbed his gun and dashed among them like a wounded tiger, and they fled like sparrows. By this time we reached the spot and in the ardor of the moment followed some distance before we saw that our retreat to the fort was cut off by another detachment of cavalry. Nothing was to be done but to fight our way through. We were all of the same mind. "Go ahead!" cried I, and they shouted, "Go ahead, Colonel!" We dashed among them, and a bloody conflict ensued. They were about twenty in number, and they stood their ground. After the fight had continued about five minutes, a detachment was seen issuing from the fort to our relief, and the Mexicans scampered off, leaving eight of their comrades upon the field. But we did not escape unscathed, for both the pirate and the bee hunter were mortally wounded, and I received a saber cut across the forehead. The old man died, without speaking, as soon as we entered the fort. We bore my young friend to his bed, dressed his wounds, and I watched beside him. He lay without complaint or manifesting pain until about midnight, when he spoke, and I asked him if he wanted anything. "Nothing," he replied, but drew a sigh that seemed to rend his heart as he added, "Poor Kate of Nacogdoches!" His eyes were filled with tears as he continued, "Her words were prophetic, Colonel," and then he sang in a low voice that resembled the sweet notes of his own devoted Kate:

> *But toom cam' the saddle, all bluidy to see,*
> *And hame cam' the steed, but hame never cam' he.*

He spoke no more and, a few minutes after, died. Poor Kate, who will tell this to thee!

MARCH 5.—

Pop, pop, pop! Bom, bom, bom! throughout the day. No time for memorandums now. Go ahead! Liberty and independence forever!

[Here ends Colonel Crockett's manuscript.]

Colonel Crockett's Exploits and Adventures in Texas . . .

44

Sam Houston Whips the Mexicans at San Jacinto

After various reverses to the American cause in Texas, Sam Houston took active command. He retreated before the Mexicans to the San Jacinto River, and then turning suddenly, he struck a blow that crushed Santa Anna's army and ended the war. Already a declaration of independence had been adopted, and before autumn of 1836, Houston had been elected the first president of the new republic.

HEADQUARTERS OF THE ARMY, SAN JACINTO. APRIL 25, 1836.—
To His Excellency, David G. Burnet, President of the Republic of Texas.

Sir: I regret extremely that my situation, since the battle of the 21st, has been such as to prevent my rendering you my official report of the same previous to this time.

I have the honor to inform you that on the evening of the 18th instant, after a forced march of fifty-five miles, the army arrived opposite Harrisburg. That evening a courier of the enemy was taken, from whom I learned that General Santa Anna with one division of choice troops had marched in the direction of Lynch's Ferry on the San Jacinto, burning Harrisburg as he passed down.

The army was ordered to be in readiness to march early on the next morning. The main body effected a crossing over Buffalo Bayou, below Harrisburg, on the morning of the 19th, having left the baggage, the sick, and a sufficient camp guard in the rear. We continued the march throughout the night, making but one halt in the prairie for a short time, and without refreshments. At daylight we resumed the line of march. In a short distance our scouts encountered those of the enemy, and we received information that General Santa Anna was at New Washington and would that day take up the line of march for Anahuac, crossing at Lynch's Ferry. The Texan army halted within half a mile of the ferry in some timber and were engaged in slaughtering beeves when the army of Santa Anna was discovered approaching in battle array.

About nine o'clock on the morning of the 21st the enemy were reinforced by five hundred choice troops under the command of General Cos, increasing their effective force to upward of fifteen hundred men, whilst our aggregate force for the field numbered seven hundred and eighty-three.

At half past three o'clock in the evening I ordered the officers of the Texan army to parade their respective commands, having in the meantime ordered the bridge on the only road communicating with the Brazos, distant eight miles from our encampment, to be destroyed, thus cutting off all possibility of escape. Our troops paraded down with alacrity and spirit and were anxious for the contest. The conscious disparity in numbers seemed only to increase their enthusiasm and confidence and heighten their anxiety for the conflict.

Our cavalry was first dispatched to the front of the enemy's left for the purpose of attracting notice, whilst an extensive island of timber afforded us an opportunity of concentrating our forces and deploying from that point. Every evolution was performed with alacrity, the whole advancing rapidly in line and through an open prairie, without any protection whatever for our men. The artillery advanced and took station within two hundred yards of the enemy's breastwork and commenced an effective fire with grape and canister.

Colonel Sherman with his regiment having commenced the action upon our left wing, the whole line, advancing in double-quick time, rung the war cry "Remember the Alamo!" received the enemy's fire, and advanced within pointblank shot before a piece was discharged from our lines.

The conflict lasted about eighteen minutes from the time of close action until we were in possession of the enemy's encampment. We took one piece of cannon (loaded), four stands of colors, all their camp equipage, stores, and baggage. Our cavalry had charged and routed that of the enemy upon the right and given pursuit to the fugitives, which did not cease until they arrived at the bridge which I have mentioned. Captain Karnes, always the foremost in danger, commanded the pursuers. The conflict in the breastwork lasted but a few moments. Many of the troops encountered hand to hand, and not having the advantage of bayonets on our side, our riflemen used their pieces as war clubs, breaking many of them off at the breech.

The rout commenced at half past four, and the pursuit by the main army continued until twilight. A guard was then left in charge of the enemy's encampment, and our army returned with their killed and wounded. In the battle our loss was two killed and twenty-three wounded, six of them mortally. The enemy's loss was six hundred and thirty killed; wounded, two hundred and eight; prisoners, seven hundred and thirty.

About six hundred muskets, three hundred sabers, and two hundred pistols have been collected since the action. Several hundred mules and horses were taken and near twelve thousand dollars in specie. For several days previous to the action our troops were engaged in forced marches, exposed to excessive rains and the additional inconvenience of extremely bad roads, ill supplied with rations and clothing; yet amid every difficulty, they bore up with cheerfulness and fortitude and performed their marches with spirit and alacrity. There was no murmuring.

For the commanding general to attempt discrimination as to the conduct of those who commanded in the action or those who were commanded would be impossible. Our success in the action is conclusive proof of such daring intrepidity and courage. Every officer and man proved himself worthy of the cause in which he battled, while the triumph received a luster from the humanity, which characterized their conduct after victory. Nor should we withhold the tribute of our grateful thanks from that Being who rules the destinies of nations and has in the time of greatest need enabled us to arrest a powerful invader whilst devastating our country.

I have the honor to be, with highest consideration,

Your obedient servant,
Sam Houston, Commander-in-Chief
Official Report

45

General Winfield Scott
Captures Mexico City

The annexation of Texas in 1845 made war between the United States and Mexico almost certain. The Mexican press and government felt outraged by the act and quickly broke off diplomatic relations. The American government, in June 1845, ordered Zachary Taylor to western Texas, later informing him that he should consider the Rio Grande the American boundary. When hostilities began, Taylor hastened to invade Mexico from the north, while in March 1847, Winfield Scott landed an expeditionary force at Vera Cruz to march upon Mexico City.

HEADQUARTERS OF THE ARMY, SEPTEMBER 18, 1847.—

At the end of another series of arduous and brilliant operations, of more than forty-eight hours' continuance, this glorious army hoisted, on the morning of the 14th, the colors of the United States on the walls of [the National Palace of Mexico].

The first step in the new movement was to carry Chapultepec, a natural and isolated mound of great elevation, strongly fortified at its base [and] on its acclivities and heights. Besides a numerous garrison, here was the military college of the Republic, with a large number of sublieutenants and other students. Those works were within direct gunshot of the village of Tacubaya, and until carried, we could not approach the city on the west without making a circuit too wide and too hazardous.

In the course of the same night (that of the 11th), heavy batteries within easy ranges were established. . . .

To prepare for an assault, it was foreseen that the play of the batteries might run into the second day, but recent captures had not only trebled our siege pieces but also our ammunition, and we knew that we should greatly augment both by carrying the place. I was, therefore, in no haste in ordering an assault before the works were well crippled by our missiles.

The bombardment and cannonade, under the direction of Captain Huger, were commenced early in the morning of the 12th. Before nightfall, which necessarily stopped our batteries, we had perceived that a good impression had been made on the castle and its outworks and that a large body of the enemy had remained outside, toward the city, from an early hour, to avoid our fire, but to be at hand on its cessation in order to reinforce the garrison against an assault. The same outside force was discovered the next morning after our batteries had reopened upon the castle, by which we again reduced its garrison to the minimum needed for the guns.

The signal I had appointed for the attack was the momentary cessation of fire on the part of our heavy batteries. About eight o'clock in the morning of the 13th, judging that the time had arrived by the effect of the missiles we had thrown, I sent an aide-de-camp to Pillow and another to Quitman with notice that the concerted signal was about to be given. Both columns now advanced with an alacrity that gave assurance of prompt success. The batteries, seizing opportunities, threw shots and shells upon the enemy over the heads of our men, with good effect, particularly at every attempt to reinforce the works from without to meet our assault.

Major General Pillow's approach on the west side lay through an open grove filled with sharpshooters who were speedily dislodged; when, being up with the front of the attack and emerging into open space at the foot of a rocky acclivity, that gallant leader was struck down by an agonizing wound.

The broken acclivity was still to be ascended and a strong redoubt midway to be carried before reaching the castle on the heights. The advance of our brave men, led by brave officers, though necessarily slow, was unwavering, over rocks, chasms, and mines, and under the hottest fire of cannon and musketry. The redoubt now yielded to resistless valor, and the shouts that followed announced to the castle the fate that impended. The enemy were steadily driven from shelter to shelter. The retreat allowed not time to fire a single mine without the certainty of blowing up friend and foe. Those who at a distance attempted to apply matches to the long trains were shot down by our men. There was death below- as well as aboveground.

At length the ditch and wall of the main work were reached; the scaling ladders were brought up and planted by the storming parties; some of the daring spirits, first in the assault, were cast down—killed or wounded— but a lodgment was soon made; streams of heroes followed; all opposition was overcome and several of our regimental colors flung out from the upper walls, amidst long-continued shouts and cheers, which sent dismay into the capital. No scene could have been more animating or glorious.

Major General Quitman, nobly supported by Brigadier Generals Shields and P.F. Smith, his other officers and men, was up with the part assigned him. Simultaneously with the movement on the west he had gallantly approached the southeast of the same works over a causeway with cuts and batteries and defended by an army strongly posted outside to the east of the works. Those formidable obstacles Quitman had to face with but little shelter for his troops or space for maneuvering. Deep ditches flanking the causeway made it difficult to cross on either side into the adjoining meadows, and these again were intersected by other ditches. Smith and his brigade had been early thrown out to make a sweep to the right, in order to present a front against the enemy's line (outside) and to turn two intervening batteries near the foot of Chapultepec.

Having turned the forest on the west and arriving opposite to the north center of Chapultepec, Worth came up with the troops in the road under Colonel Trousdale and aided, by a flank movement of a part of Garland's brigade, in taking the one-gun breastwork, then under the fire of Lieutenant Jackson's section of Captain Magruder's field battery. Continuing to advance, this division passed Chapultepec, attacking the right of the enemy's line resting on that road, about the moment of the general retreat consequent upon the capture of the formidable castle and its outworks.

Worth and Quitman were prompt in pursuing the retreating enemy, the former by the San Cosme aqueduct and the latter along that of Belén. Each had now advanced some hundred yards. . . .

I proceeded to join the advance of Worth within the suburb and beyond the turn at the junction of the aqueduct with the great highway from the west to the gate of San Cosme.

At this junction of roads we first passed one of those formidable systems of city defenses spoken of above, and it had not a gun!—a strong proof (1) that the enemy had expected us to fail in the attack upon Chapultepec, even if we meant anything more than a feint; (2) that, in either case, we designed, in his belief, to return and double our forces against the southern gates, a delusion kept up by the active demonstrations of Twiggs with the forces posted on that side; and (3) that advancing rapidly from the reduction of Chapultepec, the enemy had not time to shift guns—our previous captures had left him, comparatively, but few—from the southern gates.

Within those disgarnished works I found our troops engaged in a street fight against the enemy posted in gardens, at windows, and on housetops—all flat, with parapets. Worth ordered forward the mountain howitzers of Cadwalader's brigade, preceded by skirmishers and pioneers, with pickaxes and crowbars, to force windows and doors or to burrow through walls. The assailants were soon on an equality of position fatal to the enemy. By eight o'clock in the evening Worth had carried two batteries in this suburb. There was but one more obstacle, the San Cosme gate (customhouse), between him and the great square in front of the cathedral and palace—the heart of the city—and that barrier, it was known, could not by daylight resist our siege guns thirty minutes. . . .

Quitman within the city, adding several new defenses to the position he had won and sheltering his corps as well as practicable, now awaited the return of daylight under the guns of the formidable citadel yet to be subdued.

At about four o'clock next morning (September 14) a deputation of the *ayuntamiento* [city council] waited upon me to report that the federal government and the army of Mexico had fled from the capital some three hours before and to demand terms of capitulation in favor of the church, the citizens, and the municipal authorities. I promptly replied that I would sign no capitulation, that the city had been virtually in our possession from the time of the lodgments effected by Worth and Quitman the day before, that I regretted the silent escape of the Mexican army, that I should levy upon the city a moderate contribution for special purposes, and that the American army should come under no terms not *self*-imposed—such only as its own honor, the dignity of the United States, and the spirit of the age should, in my opinion, imperiously demand and impose.

The Memoirs of Lieutenant-General Scott

46

Andrew Jackson Is Inaugurated President

A new era in American political history began when Jackson was sworn in as president on March 4, 1829. He had refused to pay the customary courtesy call on the retiring executive, John Quincy Adams, for he could not forget that a newspaper believed to be Adams' personal organ had attacked Mrs. Jackson's reputation. With Jackson, there came to the capital a horde of westerners and southerners typical of the new Jacksonian Democracy. "The backwoods had boiled over and spilled into Washington." Lean, roughly dressed, profane back-woodsmen filled the city. Tobacco-chewing patriots from beyond the mountains, with muddy boots, homespun clothes, and fur caps, jostled the Tammany men from New York and the more polished Democrats from Virginia and Maryland. They stormed the inaugural reception at the White House in a way that horrified aristocratic observers.

WASHINGTON, MARCH 11 [1829], SUNDAY.—

The inauguration was not a thing of detail or a succession of small incidents. No, it was one grand whole, an imposing and majestic spectacle, and to a reflective mind one of moral sublimity. Thousands and thousands of people, without distinction of rank, collected in an immense mass round the Capitol, silent, orderly, and tranquil, with their eyes fixed on the front of that edifice, waiting the appearance of the President in the portico. The door from the rotunda opens; preceded by the marshals, surrounded by the judges of the Supreme Court, the old man with his gray locks, that crown of glory, advances, bows to the people who greet him with a shout that rends the air. The cannons from the heights around, from Alexandria and Fort Warburton, proclaim the oath he has taken, and all the hills reverberate the sound. It was grand—it was sublime! An almost breathless silence succeeded, and the multitude was still, listening to catch the sound of his voice, though it was so low as to be heard only by those nearest to him. After reading his speech the oath was administered to him by the Chief Justice. Then Marshall presented the Bible. The President took it from his hands, pressed his lips to it, laid it reverently down, then bowed again to the people—yes, to the people in all their majesty. And had the spectacle closed here, even Europeans must have acknowledged that a free people, collected in their might, silent and tranquil, restrained solely by a moral power, without a shadow around of military force, was majesty rising to sublimity and far surpassing the majesty of kings and princes surrounded with armies and glittering in gold. But I will not anticipate, but will give you an account of the inauguration in more detail. The whole of the preceding day immense crowds were coming into the city from all parts, lodgings could not be obtained, and the newcomers had to go to Georgetown, which soon overflowed, and others had to go to Alexandria. I was told the avenue and adjoining streets were so crowded on Tuesday afternoon that it was difficult to pass.

A national salute was fired early in the morning and ushered in the 4th of March. By ten o'clock the avenue was crowded with carriages of every description, from the splendid coach down to wagons and carts, filled with women and children, some in finery and some in rags, for it was the people's President, and all would see him; the men all walked. Julia, Anna Maria, and I (the other girls would not adventure), accompanied by Mr. Wood, set off before eleven and followed the living stream that was pouring along to the Capitol. The terraces, the balconies, the porticoes, seemed, as we approached, already filled. We rode round the whole square, taking a view of the animated scene. Then, leaving the carriage outside the palisades, we entered the inclosed grounds, where we were soon joined by John Cranet and another gentleman, which offered each of us a protector. We walked round the terrace several times, every turn meeting groups of ladies and gentlemen whom we knew—all with smiling faces. The day was warm and delightful. From the south terrace we had a view of Pennsylvania and Louisiana Avenues, crowded with people hurrying toward the Capitol. It was a most exhilarating scene! Most of the ladies preferred being inside of the Capitol, and the eastern portico, damp and cold as it was, had been filled from nine in the morning by ladies who wished to be near the General when he spoke. Every room was filled and the windows crowded. But as so confined a situation allowed no general view, we would not coop ourselves up and certainly enjoyed a much finer view of the spectacle, both in its whole and in its details, than those within the walls. We stood on the south steps of the terrace; when the appointed hour came, saw the General and his company advancing up the Avenue, slow, very slow, so impeded was his march by the crowds thronging around him. Even from a distance he could be discerned from those who accompanied him, for he only was uncovered (the servant in presence of his sovereign, the people). The south side of the Capitol Hill was literally alive with the multitude who stood ready to receive the hero and the multitude who attended him. "There, there, that is he," exclaimed different voices. "Which?" asked others. "He with the white head" was the reply. "Ah," exclaimed others, "there is the old man and his gray hair, there is the old veteran, there is Jackson." At last he enters the gate at the foot of the hill and turns to the road that leads round to the front of the Capitol. In a moment everyone who until then had stood like statues gazing on the scene below them rushed onward, to right, to left, to be ready to receive him in the front. Our party, of course, were more deliberate. We waited until the multitude had rushed past us and then left the terrace and walked round to the farthest side of the square, where there were no carriages to impede us, and entered it by the gate fronting the Capitol. Here was a clear space, and stationing ourselves on the central gravel walk, we stood so as to have a clear, full view of the whole scene—the Capitol in all its grandeur and beauty. The portico and grand steps leading to it were filled with ladies. Scarlet, purple, blue, yellow, white draperies and waving plumes of every kind and color among the white pillars had a fine effect. In the center of the portico was a table covered with scarlet; behind it, the closed door leading into the rotunda; below the Capitol and all around, a mass of living beings, not a ragged mob but well dressed and well behaved, respectable and worthy citizens. Mr. Frank Key, whose arm I had, and an old and frequent witness of great spectacles, often exclaimed, as well as myself, a mere novice, "It is beautiful, it is sublime!" The sun had been obscured through the morning by a mist or haziness. But the concussion in the air, produced by the discharge of the cannon, dispersed it, and the sun shone forth in all his brightness. At the moment the General entered the portico and advanced to the table, the shout that rent the air still resounds in my ears. When the speech was over and the President made his parting bow, the barrier that had separated the people from him was broken down, and they rushed up the steps, all eager to shake hands with him. It was with difficulty he made his way through the Capitol and down the hill to the gateway that opens on the Avenue. Here for a moment he was stopped. The living mass was impenetrable. After a while a passage was opened, and he mounted his horse, which had been provided for his return (for he had walked to the Capitol). Then such a cortege as followed him! Country men, farmers, gentlemen, mounted and dismounted, boys, women, and children, black and white. Carriages, wagons, and carts all pursuing him to the President's house. This I only heard of, for our party went out at the opposite side of the square and went to Colonel Benton's lodgings to visit Mrs. Benton and Mrs. Gilmore. Here was a perfect levee, at least a hundred ladies and gentlemen, all happy and rejoicing—wine and cake was handed in profusion. We sat with this company and stopped on the summit of the hill until the avenue was comparatively clear, though at any other time we should have thought it terribly crowded, streams of people on foot and in carriages of all kinds still pouring toward the President's house. We went home; found your papa and sisters at the bank, standing at the upper windows, where they had been seen by the President, who took off his hat to them, which they insisted was better than all we had seen. From the bank to the President's house, for a long while, the crowd rendered a passage for us impossible. Some went into the cashier's parlor, where we found a number of ladies and gentlemen and had cake and wine in abundance. In about an hour the pavement was clear enough for us to walk. Your father, Mr. Wood, Mr. Ward, Mr. Lyon, with us, we set off to the President's house, but on a nearer approach found an entrance impossible; the yard and avenue was compact with living matter. The day was delightful, the scene animating, so we walked backward and forward, at every turn meeting some new acquaintance and stopping to talk and shake hands. Among others we met Zavr. Dickinson with Mr. Frelinghuysen and Doctor Elmendorf, and Mr. Samuel Bradford. We continued promenading here until near three, returned home unable to stand, and threw ourselves on the sofa. Someone came and informed us the crowd before the President's house was so far lessened that they thought we might enter. This time we effected our purpose. But what a scene did we witness! *The majesty of the people* had disappeared, and a rabble, a mob, of boys, Negroes, women, children, scrambling, fighting, romping. What a pity, what a pity! No arrangements had been made, no police officers placed on duty, and the whole house had been inundated by the rabble mob. We came too late. The President, after having been *literally* nearly pressed to death and almost suffocated and torn to pieces by the people in their eagerness to shake hands with Old Hickory, had retreated through the back way or south front and had escaped to his lodgings at Gadsby's. Cut glass and china to the amount of several thousand dollars had been broken in the struggle to get the refreshments. Punch and other articles had been carried out in tubs and buckets, but had it been in hogsheads it would have been insufficient; ice creams and cake and lemonade for twenty thousand people, for it is said that number were there, though I think the estimate exaggerated. Ladies fainted, men were seen with bloody noses, and such a scene of confusion took place as is impossible to describe—those who got in could not get out by the door again but had to scramble out of windows. At one time the President, who had retreated and retreated until he was pressed against the wall, could only be secured by a number of gentlemen forming round him and making a kind of barrier of their own bodies, and the pressure was so great that Colonel Bomford, who was one, said that at one time he was afraid they should have been pushed down or on the President. It was then the windows were thrown open and the torrent found an outlet, which otherwise might have proved fatal.

This concourse had not been anticipated and therefore not provided against. Ladies and gentlemen only had been expected at this levee, not the people en masse. But it was the people's day, and the people's President, and the people would rule. God grant that one day or other the people do not put down all rule and rulers. I fear, enlightened freemen as they are, they will be found, as they have been found in all ages and countries where they get the power in their hands, that of all tyrants, they are the most ferocious, cruel, and despotic. The noisy and disorderly rabble in the President's house brought to my mind descriptions I had read of the mobs in Tuileries and at Versailles. I expect to hear the carpets and furniture are ruined; the streets were muddy, and these guests all went thither on foot.

MRS. SAMUEL HARRISON SMITH
The First Forty Years of Washington Society

47

"John Quincy Adams Is No More"

John Quincy Adams retired from the presidency, in 1829, a defeated and discouraged man, but with characteristic willingness to serve his people, he accepted a seat in the lower house of Congress, which his constituency tendered him, and served there for seventeen years. The most venerable figure in the House, he was likewise the ablest and most feared debater, and in his seventieth year he fought and won a memorable fight for the right of petition. His death, at his post of duty, was a fitting end to a long and useful life.

FEBRUARY 24, 1848.—

Death of Mr. Adams. John Quincy Adams is no more. Full of age and honors, the termination of his eventful career accorded with the character of its progress. He died, as he must have wished to die, breathing his last in the Capitol, stricken down by the angel of death on the field of his civil glory— employed in the service of the people, in the people's senate house, standing by the Constitution at the side of its altar, and administering in the temple of liberty the rites which he had assisted in establishing.

At twenty minutes past one o'clock on Monday, the 21st, Mr. Adams, being in his seat in the House of Representatives (from which he was never absent during its session), attempted to rise (as was supposed, to speak) but sank back upon his seat and fell upon his side. Those nearest caught him in their arms. Mr. Grinnell bathed his temples with ice water, when he rallied for an instant. The House immediately adjourned in the utmost consternation, as did the Senate, when informed of the melancholy event. His last words were characterized by that concise eloquence for which he was remarkable: *"This is the last of earth; I am content."* Dr. Fries of Ohio, a member, raised him in his arms and bore him to the Speaker's room, where he lay, with occasional indications of consciousness, until last evening, a few minutes before seven o'clock, when he breathed his last. The intelligence of his death came to Albany by the telegraph.

Thus has "a great man fallen in Israel"—in many respects the most wonderful man of the age; certainly the greatest in the United States—perfect in knowledge, but deficient in practical results. As a statesman, he was pure and incorruptible, but too irascible to lead men's judgment. They admired him, and all voices were hushed when he arose to speak, because they were sure of being instructed by the words he was about to utter, but he made no converts to his opinions, and when President his desire to avoid party influence lost him all the favor of all parties. In matters of history, tradition, statistics, authorities, and practice he was the oracle of the House, of which he was at the time of his decease a member. With an unfailing memory, rendered stronger by cultivation, he was never mistaken; none disputed his authority. Every circumstance of his long life was "penned down" at the moment of its occurrence; every written communication, even to the minute of a dinner invitation, was carefully preserved, and nothing passed uncopied from his pen. He "talked like a book" on all subjects. Equal to the highest, the planetary system was not above his grasp. Familiar with the lowest, he could explain the mysteries of a mousetrap.

I listened once, at my own table, with a delight which I shall never forget, to his dissertation on the writings of Shakespeare and an analysis of the character of Hamlet—the most beautiful creation (he called it) of the human imagination. At my request he afterward sent me a synopsis of the latter part of this delightful conversation, a paper which has always been a treasure to me and which will be more precious now that its illustrious author is no more. I listened once, with Mr. Webster, for an hour, at Mr. Adams' breakfast table in Washington, to a disquisition on the subject of *dancing girls;* from those who danced before the ark and the daughter of Jairus, whose premature appearance caused so melancholy a termination to her graceful movements in the dance, through the fascinating exhibition of the odalisques of the harem down to the present times of Fanny Ellsler and Taglioni. He was ignorant on no subject and could enlighten and instruct on all; he loved to talk and was pleased with good listeners—vain, no doubt, and not entirely free from prejudices, but preserving his mental faculties to the last. His sudden death, even at the advanced age of eighty years, to which he arrived in July last, will be acutely felt and deeply deplored by those who have habitually enjoyed the refreshing streams which flowed from the copious fountains of his diversified knowledge.

Mr. Adams' name will be recorded on the brightest page of American history, as statesman, diplomatist, philosopher, orator, author, and, above all, Christian.

The Diary of Philip Hone

48

William Herndon Remembers Abraham Lincoln

In 1844 William Henry Herndon, who was nearly ten years younger than Lincoln and greatly admired him, accepted his invitation to become junior law partner. That partnership was broken only by Lincoln's death, for on leaving for Washington, Lincoln requested him to keep the old "shingle" standing. Herndon, who was a great reader and strongly opposed to slavery, influenced Lincoln's thinking on many questions, while he labored with unselfish devotion to promote Lincoln's political fortunes. No man knew Lincoln better. .

Part I

SPRINGFIELD, ILL., NOVEMBER 13, 1885.—
Friend Weik:
There were three noted storytellers, jokers, jesters, in the central part of this state especially from 1840 to 1853: Lincoln of Sangamon County, William Engle of Menard, and James Murray of Logan. They were all men of mark, each in his own way; they were alike in the line of joking, storytelling, jesting. I knew the men for years. From 1840 to 1853 this section was not known for a very high standard of taste, the love for the beautiful or the good. We had not many newspapers; people in all of these counties would attend court at the respective county seats. Lincoln, Engle, and Murray would travel around from county to county with the court, and those who loved fun and sport, loved jokes, tales, stories, jests, would go with the court, too, from county to county. People had not much to do at the time, and the class of people that then lived here are gone, perished. It was a curious state of affairs indeed. As compared with now it was rough, semibarbarous. In the evening, after the court business of the day was over and book and pen had been laid [down] by the lawyers, judges, jurymen, witnesses, etc., the people generally would meet at some barroom, "gentlemen's parlor," and have a good time in storytelling, joking, jesting, etc. The barroom windows, halls, and all passageways would be filled to suffocation by the people, eager to see the "big ones" and to hear their stories told by them. Lincoln would tell his story in his very best style. The people, all present, including Lincoln, would burst out in a loud laugh and a hurrah at the story. The listeners, so soon as the laugh and the hurrah had passed and silence had come in for its turn, would cry out, "Now, Uncle Billy (William Engle), you must beat that or go home." Engle

would clear his throat and say, "Boys, the story just told by Lincoln puts me in mind of a story I heard when a boy." He would tell it and tell it well. The people would clap their hands, stamp their feet, hurrah, yell, shout, get up, hold their aching sides. Things would soon calm down. There was politeness and etiquette in it. Each must have his turn, by comity, in which to tell his story. The good people would, as soon as quiet reigned, cry out: "Now is your time; come, Murray, do your level best or never come here again to tell your stories." Murray would prepare himself with his best. At first he would be a little nervous, but he would soon gather confidence, rise up, walk about, telling his tale as he moved in harmony with his story; he would tell it well, grandly, and the people would sometimes before the story was ended catch the point and raise such a laugh and a yell that the village rang with the yells, laughs, and hurrahs, etc. Lincoln and Engle now were nervous and anxious for their turns to come around. Lincoln would tell his story, and then followed Engle, and then came Murray, and thus this storytelling, joking, jesting, would be kept up till one or two o'clock in the night, and thus night after night till the court adjourned for that term. In the morning we would all be sore all through from excessive laughing—the judge, the lawyers, jurymen, witnesses, and all. Our sides and back would ache. This was a gay time, and I'll never see it again. This is or was the way we old Westerners passed away our time. We loved fun and sport—anything for amusement. We had no learning but had good common sense with a liberal broad view of things, were generous and as brave as Caesar. When court had adjourned in Sangamon County, we went to Menard and then to Logan County. This storytelling was kept up faithfully from county to county and from term to term and from year to year.

Your friend,
W.H. Herndon

Part II

SPRINGFIELD, ILL., JULY 19, 1887.—
Mr. Bartlett. My dear sir:
Mr. Lincoln was six feet and four inches high in his sock feet; he was consumptive by build and hence more or less stoop-shouldered. He was very tall, thin, and gaunt. When he rose to speak to the jury or to crowds of people, he stood inclined forward, was awkward, angular, ungainly, odd, and being a very sensitive man, I think that it added to his awkwardness; he was a diffident man, somewhat, and a sensitive one, and both of these added to his oddity, awkwardness, etc., as it seemed to me. Lincoln had confidence, full and complete confidence in himself, self-thoughtful, self-helping, and self-supporting, relying on no man. Lincoln's voice was, when he first began speaking, shrill, squeaking, piping, unpleasant; his general look, his form,

his pose, the color of his flesh, wrinkled and dry, his sensitiveness, and his momentary diffidence, everything seemed to be against him, but he soon recovered. I can see him now, in my mind distinct. On rising to address the jury or the crowd he quite generally placed his hands behind him, the back part of his left hand resting in the palm of his right hand. As he proceeded and grew warmer, he moved his hands to the front of his person, generally interlocking his fingers and running one thumb around the other. Sometimes his hands, for a short while, would hang by his side. In still growing warmer, as he proceeded in his address, he used his hands—especially and generally his right hand—in his gestures; he used his head a great deal in speaking, throwing or jerking or moving it now here and now there, now in this position and now in that, in order to be more emphatic, to drive the idea home. Mr. Lincoln never beat the air, never sawed space with his hands, never acted for stage effect; was cool, careful, earnest, sincere, truthful, fair, self-possessed, not insulting, not dictatorial; was pleasing, good-natured; had great strong naturalness of look, pose, and act; was clear in his ideas, simple in his words, strong, terse, and demonstrative; he spoke and acted to convince individuals and masses; he used in his gestures his right hand, sometimes shooting out that long bony forefinger of his to dot an idea or to express a thought, resting his thumb on his middle finger. Bear in mind that he did not gesticulate much, and *yet it is true* that every organ of his body was in motion and acted with ease, elegance, and grace; so it all looked to *me*.

As Mr. Lincoln proceeded further along with his oration, if time, place, subject, and occasion admitted of it, he gently and gradually warmed up; his shrill, squeaking, piping voice became harmonious, melodious, musical, if you please, with face somewhat aglow; his form dilated, swelled out, and he rose up a splendid form, erect, straight, and dignified; he stood square on his feet with both legs up and down, toe even with toe—that is, he did not put one foot before another; he kept his feet parallel and close to and not far from each other. When Mr. Lincoln rose up to speak, he rose slowly, steadily, firmly; he never moved much about on the stand or platform when speaking, trusting no desk, table, railing; he ran his eyes slowly over the crowd, giving them time to be at ease and to completely recover himself, *as I suppose*. He frequently took hold with his left hand, his left thumb erect, of the left lapel of his coat, keeping his right hand free to gesture in order to drive home and to clinch an idea. In his greatest inspiration he held both of his hands out above his head at an angle of about fifty degrees, hands open or clenched according to his feelings and his ideas. If he was moved in some indignant and half-mad moment against slavery or wrong in any direction and seemed to want to tear it down, trample it beneath his feet, and to eternally crush it, thus he would extend his arms out, at about the above degree angle, with clenched big, bony, strong hands on them.

If he was defending the right, if he was defending liberty, eulogizing the

Declaration of Independence, then he extended out his arms, palms of his hands upward somewhat at about the above degree, angle, as if appealing to some superior power for assistance and support, or that he might embrace the spirit of that which he so dearly loved. It was at such moments that he seemed inspired, fresh from the hands of his Creator. Lincoln's gray eyes would flash fire when speaking against slavery or spoke volumes of hope and love when speaking of liberty, justice, and the progress of mankind. Such was this great man *to me,* and I think, I know, such he was to thousands, if not to millions of others.

Your friend,
W.H. Herndon

EMANUEL HERTE
The Hidden Lincoln

49

Abraham Lincoln Is Nominated in the Wigwam

Lincoln's name began to be widely mentioned for the Republican presidential nomination after his seven joint debates with Douglas in 1858 attracted national attention. It was as a presidential possibility that he went to New York in February 1860 and produced a remarkable impression by the logical power of his Cooper Union address. The principal aspirant for the nomination was William H. Seward of New York, but he had many enemies, including the powerful Horace Greeley, and great numbers of Republicans regarded him as too radical. Salmon P. Chase failed to gain the full support of his own state, Ohio, while Edward Bates of Missouri was disliked by the German voters. Lincoln therefore had a good chance from the outset for winning the nomination, and it was increased by the fact that the Republican convention was held in Chicago, and by the skill with which his Illinois supporters set to work. David Davis took charge of the Lincoln forces at Chicago and labored indefatigably and effectively. Here a journalist of the day tells the story.

THIRD DAY [MAY 18, 1860].—

After adjournment on Thursday (the second day) there were few men in Chicago who believed it possible to prevent the nomination of Seward. His friends had played their game to admiration and had been victorious on every preliminary skirmish. When the platform had been adopted, inclusive of the Declaration of Independence, they felt themselves already exalted upon the pinnacle of victory. They rejoiced exceedingly and, full of confidence, cried in triumphant tones, "Call the roll of states." But it was otherwise ordered. The opponents of Mr. Seward left the wigwam that evening thoroughly disheartened. Greeley was, as has been widely reported, absolutely "terrified." The nomination of Seward in defiance of his influence would have been a cruel blow. He gave up the ship. . . .

The New Yorkers were exultant. Their bands were playing and the champagne flowing at their headquarters as after a victory.

But there was much done after midnight and before the convention assembled on Friday morning. There were hundreds of Pennsylvanians, Indianians, and Illinoisians who never closed their eyes that night. I saw Henry S. Lane at one o'clock, pale and haggard, with cane under his arm, walking as if for a wager, from one caucus room to another, at the Tremont House. He had been toiling with desperation to bring the Indiana delegation to go as a unit for Lincoln. And then in connection with others, he had been operating to bring the Vermonters and Virginians to the point of deserting Seward.

The Seward men generally abounded in confidence Friday morning. The air was full of rumors of the caucusing the night before, but the opposition of the doubtful states to Seward was an old story, and after the distress of Pennsylvania, Indiana, and Company on the subject of Seward's availability had been so freely and ineffectually expressed from the start, it was not imagined their protests would suddenly become effective. The Sewardites marched as usual from their headquarters at the Richmond House after their magnificent band, which was brilliantly uniformed—epaulets shining on their shoulders and white and scarlet feathers waving from their caps—marched under the orders of recognized leaders, in a style that would have done credit to many volunteer military companies. They were about a thousand strong and, protracting their march a little too far, were not all able to get into the wigwam. This was their first misfortune. They were not where they could scream with the best effect in responding to the mention of the name of William H. Seward.

When the convention was called to order, breathless attention was given the proceedings. There was not a space a foot square in the wigwam unoccupied. There were tens of thousands still outside, and torrents of men had rushed in at the three broad doors until not another one could squeeze in.

Everybody was now impatient to begin the work. Mr. Evarts of New York nominated Mr. Seward. Mr. Judd of Illinois nominated Mr. Lincoln.

Everybody felt that the fight was between them and yelled accordingly.

The applause when Mr. Evarts named Seward was enthusiastic. When Mr. Judd named Lincoln, the response was prodigious, rising and raging far beyond the Seward shriek. Presently, upon Caleb B. Smith seconding the nomination of Lincoln, the response was absolutely terrific. It now became the Seward men to make another effort, and when Blair of Michigan seconded his nomination,

> *At once there rose so wild a yell,*
> *Within that dark and narrow dell;*
> *As all the fiends from heaven that fell*
> *Had pealed the banner cry of hell.*

The effect was startling. Hundreds of persons stopped their ears in pain. The shouting was absolutely frantic, shrill, and wild. No Comanches, no panthers, ever struck a higher note or gave screams with more infernal intensity. Looking from the stage over the vast amphitheater, nothing was to be seen below but thousands of hats—a black, mighty swarm of hats—flying with the velocity of hornets over a mass of human heads, most of the mouths of which were open. Above, all around the galleries, hats and handkerchiefs were flying in the tempest together. The wonder of the thing was that the Seward outside pressure should, so far from New York, be so powerful.

Now the Lincoln men had to try it again, and as Mr. Delano of Ohio on behalf "of a portion of the delegation of that state" seconded the nomination of Lincoln, the uproar was beyond description. Imagine all the hogs ever slaughtered in Cincinnati giving their death squeals together, a score of big steam whistles going (steam at a hundred and sixty pounds per inch), and you conceive something of the same nature. I thought the Seward yell could not be surpassed, but the Lincoln boys were clearly ahead and, feeling their victory, as there was a lull in the storm, took deep breaths all round and gave a concentrated shriek that was positively awful, and accompanied it with stamping that made every plank and pillar in the building quiver.

Henry S. Lane of Indiana leaped upon a table and, swinging hat and cane, performed like an acrobat. The presumption is he shrieked with the rest, as his mouth was desperately wide open, but no one will ever be able to testify that he has positive knowledge of the fact that he made a particle of noise. His individual voice was lost in the aggregate hurricane.

The New York, Michigan, and Wisconsin delegations sat together and were in this tempest very quiet. Many of their faces whitened as the Lincoln *yawp* swelled into a wild hosanna of victory.

The convention now proceeded to business. The most significant vote was that of Virginia, which had been expected solid for Seward, and which now gave him but eight and gave Lincoln fourteen. The New Yorkers looked significantly at each other as this was announced. Then Indiana gave her twenty-six votes for Lincoln. This solid vote was a startler. The division of the first vote caused a fall in Seward stock. It was seen that Lincoln, Cameron, and Bates had the strength to defeat Seward, and it was known that the greater part of the Chase vote would go for Lincoln.

The convention proceeded to a second ballot. Every man was fiercely enlisted in the struggle. The partisans of the various candidates were strung up to such a pitch of excitement as to render them incapable of patience, and the cries of "Call the roll" were fairly hissed through their teeth. The first gain for Lincoln was in New Hampshire. The Chase and the Frémont vote from that state were given him. His next gain was the whole vote of Vermont. This was a blighting blow upon the Seward interest. The New Yorkers started as if an Orsini bomb had exploded. And presently the Cameron vote of Pennsylvania was thrown for Lincoln, increasing his strength forty-four votes. The fate of the day was now determined. New York saw "checkmate" next move and sullenly proceeded with the game, assuming unconsciousness of her inevitable doom. On this ballot Lincoln gained seventy-nine votes. Seward had one hundred and eighty-four and a half votes, Lincoln one hundred and eighty-one. . . .

While this [the third] ballot was taken amid excitement that tested the nerves, the fatal defection from Seward in New England still further appeared, four votes going over from Seward to Lincoln in Massachusetts. The latter received four additional votes from Pennsylvania and fifteen additional votes from Ohio. It was whispered about: "Lincoln's the coming man—will be nominated this ballot." When the roll of states and territories had been called, I had ceased to give attention to any votes but those for Lincoln and had his vote added up as it was given. The number of votes necessary to a choice were two hundred and thirty-three, and I saw under my pencil as the Lincoln column was completed the figures 231½—one vote and a half to give him the nomination. In a moment the fact was whispered about. A hundred pencils had told the same story. The news went over the house wonderfully, and there was a pause. There are always men anxious to distinguish themselves on such occasions. There is nothing that politicians like better than a crisis. I looked up to see who would be the man to give the decisive vote. In about ten ticks of a watch, Cartter of Ohio was up. I had imagined Ohio would be slippery enough for the crisis. And sure enough! Every eye was on Cartter, and everybody who understood the matter at all knew what he was about to do. He said: "I rise (eh), Mr. Chairman (eh), to announce the change of four votes of Ohio from Mr. Chase to Mr. Lincoln." The deed was done. There was a moment's silence. The nerves of the thousands, which through the hours of suspense had been subjected to terrible tension, relaxed, and as deep breaths of relief were taken, there was a noise in the wigwam like the rush of a great wind in the van of a storm—and in another breath, the storm was there. There were thousands cheering with the energy of insanity.

A man who had been on the roof and was engaged in communicating the results of the ballotings to the mighty mass of outsiders now demanded, by gestures at the skylight over the stage, to know what had happened. One of the secretaries, with a tally sheet in his hands, shouted: "Fire the salute! Abe Lincoln is nominated!"

The city was wild with delight. The "Old Abe" men formed processions and bore rails through the streets. Torrents of liquor were poured down the hoarse throats of the multitude. A hundred guns were fired from the top of the Tremont House.

I left the city on the night train on the Fort Wayne and Chicago road. The train consisted of eleven cars, every seat full and people standing in the aisles and corners. I never before saw a company of persons so prostrated by continued excitement. The Lincoln men were not able to respond to the cheers which went up along the road for "Old Abe." They had not only done their duty in that respect, but exhausted their capacity. At every station where there was a village, until after two o'clock, there were tar barrels burning, drums beating, boys carrying rails, and guns, great and small, banging away. The weary passengers were allowed no rest, but plagued by the thundering jar of cannon, the clamor of drums, the glare of bonfires, and the whooping of the boys, who were delighted with the idea of a candidate for the Presidency who thirty years ago split rails on the Sangamon River—classic stream now and forevermore—and whose neighbors named him "honest."

MURAT HALSTEAD
Caucuses of 1860

50

Nathaniel Hawthorne
Sees President Lincoln

The novelist Hawthorne, now near his grave, visited Washington in the spring of 1862 for amusement and health. He saw both Lincoln and General McClellan; was disgusted by some of the politicians and lobbyists he found hanging about the Capitol; and wrote a frank and caustic article upon his observations, which the *Atlantic Monthly* published.

Nine o'clock had been appointed as the time for receiving the deputation, and we were punctual to the moment; but not so the President, who sent us word that he was eating his breakfast and would come as soon as he could. His appetite, we were glad to think, must have been a pretty fair one, for we waited about half an hour in one of the antechambers and then were ushered into a reception room, in one corner of which sat the Secretaries of War and of the Treasury, expecting, like ourselves, the termination of the presidential breakfast. During this interval there were several new additions to our group, one or two of whom were in a working garb, so that we formed a very miscellaneous collection of people, mostly unknown to each other, and without any common sponsor, but all with an equal right to look our head servant in the face.

By and by there was a little stir on the staircase and in the passageway, and in lounged a tall, loose-jointed figure, of an exaggerated Yankee port and demeanor, whom (as being about the homeliest man I ever saw, yet by no means repulsive or disagreeable) it was impossible not to recognize as Uncle Abe.

Unquestionably, Western man though he be and Kentuckian by birth, President Lincoln is the essential representative of all Yankees and the veritable specimen, physically, of what the world seems determined to regard as our characteristic qualities. It is the strangest and yet the fittest thing in the jumble of human vicissitudes that he, out of so many millions, unlooked for, unselected by any intelligible process that could be based upon his genuine qualities, unknown to those who chose him, and unsuspected of what endowments may adapt him for his tremendous responsibility, should have found the way open for him to fling his lank personality into the chair of state—where, I presume, it was his first impulse to throw his legs on the council table and tell the cabinet ministers a story. There is no describing his lengthy awkwardness nor the uncouthness of his movement, and yet it seemed as if I had been in the habit of seeing him daily and had shaken hands with him a thousand times in some village street, so true was he to the aspect of the pattern American, though with a certain extravagance which, possibly, I exaggerated still further by the delighted eagerness with which I took it in. If put to guess his calling and livelihood, I should have taken him for a country schoolmaster as soon as anything else. He was dressed in a rusty black frock coat and pantaloons, unbrushed, and worn so faithfully that the suit had adapted itself to the curves and angularities of his figure and had grown to be an outer skin of the man. He had shabby slippers on his feet. His hair was black, still unmixed with gray, stiff, somewhat bushy, and had apparently been acquainted with neither brush nor comb that morning, after the disarrangement of the pillow, and as to a nightcap, Uncle Abe probably knows nothing of such effeminacies. His complexion is dark and sallow, betokening, I fear, an insalubrious atmosphere around the White House; he has thick black eyebrows and an impending brow; his nose is large, and the lines about his mouth are very strongly defined.

The whole physiognomy is as coarse a one as you would meet anywhere in the length and breadth of the states, but withal it is redeemed, illuminated, softened, and brightened by a kindly though serious look out of his eyes and an expression of homely sagacity that seems weighted with rich results of village experience. A great deal of native sense; no bookish cultivation, no refinement; honest at heart, and thoroughly so, and yet, in some sort, sly—at least, endowed with a sort of tact and wisdom that are akin to craft, and would impel him, I think, to take an antagonist in flank, rather than to make a bull run at him right in front. But, on the whole, I like this sallow, queer, sagacious visage, with the homely human sympathies that warmed it and, for my small share in the matter, would as lief have Uncle Abe for a ruler as any man whom it would have been practicable to put in his place.

Immediately on his entrance the President accosted our member of Congress, who had us in charge, and with a comical twist of his face made some jocular remark about the length of his breakfast. He then greeted us all round, not waiting for an introduction, but shaking and squeezing everybody's hand with the utmost cordiality, whether the individual's name was announced to him or not. His manner toward us was wholly without pretense, but yet had a kind of natural dignity, quite sufficient to keep the forwardest of us from clapping him on the shoulder and asking him for a story.

NATHANIEL HAWTHORNE
Tales, Sketches, and Other Papers

51

Lincoln Reads the Emancipation Proclamation

From the very beginning of the war, radical antislavery men urged Lincoln to take immediate steps to liberate the slaves. But conservative opinion was averse to hasty measures. Moreover, Lincoln was afraid of offending the loyal border states of Missouri, Kentucky, Maryland, and Delaware, where many good Union men still held slaves. Not until public opinion had fairly ripened for the step did he issue his famous Emancipation Proclamation on September 22, 1862. Effective January 1, 1863, it declared free all the slaves within any state or part of a state then in rebellion. F.B. Carpenter was an artist who painted the reading of the proclamation to the Cabinet, and to whom Lincoln confided.

The appointed hour found me at the well-remembered door of the official chamber—that door watched daily, with so many conflicting emotions of hope and fear, by the anxious throng regularly gathered there. The President had preceded me and was already deep in Acts of Congress, with which the writing desk was strewed, awaiting his signature. He received me pleasantly, giving me a seat near his own armchair; and after having read Mr. Lovejoy's note, he took off his spectacles and said, "Well, Mr. Carpenter, we will turn you loose in here and try to give you a good chance to work out your idea." Then, without paying much attention to the enthusiastic expression of my ambitious desire and purpose, he proceeded to give me a detailed account of the history and issue of the great proclamation.

"It had got to be," said he, "midsummer, 1862. Things had gone on from bad to worse, until I felt that we had reached the end of our rope on the plan of operations we had been pursuing, that we had about played our last card and must change our tactics or lose the game! I now determined upon the adoption of the emancipation policy, and without consultation with or the knowledge of the cabinet, I prepared the original draft of the proclamation and, after much anxious thought, called a cabinet meeting upon the subject. This was the last of July or the first part of the month of August 1862." (The exact date he did not remember.) "This cabinet meeting took place, I think, upon a Saturday. All were present, excepting Mr. Blair, the postmaster general, who was absent at the opening of the discussion, but came in subsequently. I said to the cabinet that I had resolved upon this step and had not called them together to ask their advice but to lay the subject matter of a proclamation before them, suggestions as to which would be in order after they had heard it read. . . . Various suggestions were offered. Secretary Chase wished the language stronger in reference to the arming of the blacks. Mr. Blair, after he came in, deprecated the policy on the ground that it would cost the administration the fall elections. Nothing, however, was offered that I had not already fully anticipated and settled in my own mind until Secretary Seward spoke. He said in substance: 'Mr. President, I approve of the proclamation, but I question the expediency of its issue at this juncture. The depression of the public mind, consequent upon our repeated reverses, is so great that I fear the effect of so important a step. It may be viewed as the last measure of an exhausted government, a cry for help, the government stretching forth its hand to Ethiopia instead of Ethiopia stretching forth her hands to the government.' His idea," said the President, "was that it would be considered our last *shriek,* on the retreat." (This was his precise expression.) "'Now,' continued Mr. Seward, 'while I approve the measure, I suggest, sir, that you postpone its issue until you can give it to the country supported by military success, instead of issuing it, as would be the case now, upon the greatest disasters of the war!'"

Mr. Lincoln continued: "The wisdom of the view of the Secretary of State struck me with very great force. It was an aspect of the case that, in all my thought upon the subject, I had entirely overlooked. The result was that I put the draft of the proclamation aside, as you do your sketch for a picture, waiting for a victory. From time to time I added or changed a line, touching it up here and there, anxiously watching the progress of events. Well, the next news we had was of Pope's disaster at Bull Run. Things looked darker than ever. Finally came the week of the battle of Antietam. I determined to wait no longer. The news came, I think, on Wednesday, that the advantage was on our side. I was then staying at the Soldiers' Home [three miles out of Washington]. Here I finished writing the second draft of the preliminary proclamation, came up on Saturday, called the cabinet together to hear it, and it was published the following Monday."

F.B. CARPENTER
Six Months at the White House with Abraham Lincoln

52

Lincoln Frees the Slaves

Though accomplishing little at the moment (for it applied mainly to slaves within the Confederate lines), the Emancipation Proclamation did show that freedom would be granted to the bondsmen as rapidly as the Union armies advanced, and it made a profound impression upon public opinion in the North and in Europe.

Whereas on the 22nd day of September, A.D. 1862, a proclamation was issued by the President of the United States, containing, among other things, the following, to wit:

That on the 1st day of January, A.D. 1863, all persons held as slaves within any state or designated part of a state the people whereof shall then be in rebellion against the United States shall be then, thenceforward, and forever free; and the executive government of the United States, including the military and naval authority thereof, will recognize and maintain the freedom of such persons and will do no act or acts to repress such persons, or any of them, in any efforts they may make for their actual freedom.

That the executive will on the 1st day of January aforesaid, by proclamation, designate the states and parts of states, if any, in which the people thereof, respectively, shall then be in rebellion against the United States; and the fact that any state or the people thereof shall on that day be in good faith represented in the Congress of the United States by members chosen thereto at elections wherein a majority of the qualified voters of such states shall have participated shall, in the absence of strong countervailing testimony, be deemed conclusive evidence that such state and the people thereof are not then in rebellion against the United States.

Now, therefore, I, Abraham Lincoln, . . . do, on this 1st day of January, A.D. 1863, . . . order and designate . . . the states and parts of states wherein the people thereof, respectively, are this day in rebellion against the United States. . . .

And by virtue of the power and for the purpose aforesaid, I do order and declare that all persons held as slaves within said designated states and parts of states are, and henceforward shall be, free; and that the executive government of the United States, including the military and naval authorities thereof, will recognize and maintain the freedom of said persons.

And I hereby enjoin upon the people so declared to be free to abstain from all violence, unless in necessary self-defense; and I recommend to them that, in all cases when allowed, they labor faithfully for reasonable wages.

And I further declare and make known that such persons of suitable condition will be received into the armed service of the United States to garrison forts, positions, stations, and other places, and to man vessels of all sorts in said service.

And upon this act, sincerely believed to be an act of justice, warranted by the Constitution upon military necessity, I invoke the considerate judgment of mankind and the gracious favor of Almighty God.

The Emancipation Proclamation

53

President Lincoln Is Assassinated

President Lincoln had entered Richmond the day after its surrender and had then returned to Washington in time to make a public address on April 11, 1865. On the evening of the fourteenth he went to Ford's Theater to see Laura Keene in an English comedy. John Wilkes Booth, of a famous family of actors, had concocted a plot to assassinate all the principal officers of the government; a Southern sympathizer, he was sufficiently crazed to believe that this might undo the work of the Union armies. Stealthily entering Lincoln's box, he sent a pistol ball into the president's brain. Gideon Welles was Lincoln's secretary of the navy.

I had retired to bed about half past ten on the evening of the 14th of April [1865] and was just getting asleep when Mrs. Welles, my wife, said someone was at our door. Sitting up in bed, I heard a voice twice call to John, my son, whose sleeping room was on the second floor directly over the front entrance. I arose at once and raised a window, when my messenger, James Smith, called to me that Mr. Lincoln, the President, had been shot and said Secretary Seward and his son, Assistant Secretary Frederick Seward, were assassinated. James was much alarmed and excited. I told him his story was very incoherent and improbable, that he was associating men who were not together and liable to attack at the same time. "Where," I inquired, "was the

President when shot?" James said he was at Ford's Theater on Tenth Street. "Well," said I, "Secretary Seward is an invalid in bed in his house yonder on Fifteenth Street." James said he had been there, stopped in at the house to make inquiry before alarming me.

I immediately dressed myself and, against the earnest remonstrance and appeals of my wife, went directly to Mr. Seward's, whose residence was on the east side of the square, mine being on the north. . . .

As we descended the stairs, I asked Stanton what he had heard in regard to the President that was reliable. He said the President was shot at Ford's Theater, that he had seen a man who was present and witnessed the occurrence. I said I would go immediately to the White House. Stanton told me the President was not there but was at the theater. "Then," said I, "let us go immediately there." He said that was his intention and asked me, if I had not a carriage, to go with him. In the lower hall we met General Meigs, whom he requested to take charge of the house and to clear out all who did not belong there. General Meigs begged Stanton not to go down to Tenth Street; others also remonstrated against our going. Stanton, I thought, hesitated. Hurrying forward, I remarked that I should go immediately; and I thought it his duty also. He said he should certainly go, but the remonstrants increased and gathered around him. I said we were wasting time and, pressing through the crowd, entered the carriage and urged Stanton, who was detained by others after he had placed his foot on the step. Meigs called to some soldiers to go with us, and there was one on each side of the carriage. The streets were full of people. Not only the sidewalks but the carriageway was to some extent occupied, all or nearly all hurrying toward Tenth Street. When we entered that street we found it pretty closely packed.

The President had been carried across the street from the theater to the house of a Mr. Peterson. We entered by ascending a flight of steps above the basement and passing through a long hall to the rear, where the President lay extended on a bed, breathing heavily. Several surgeons were present, at least six, I should think more. Among them I was glad to observe Doctor Hall, who, however, soon left. I inquired of Doctor Hall, as I entered, the true condition of the President. He replied the President was dead to all intents, although he might live three hours or perhaps longer.

The giant sufferer lay extended diagonally across the bed, which was not long enough for him. He had been stripped of his clothes. His large arms, which were occasionally exposed, were of a size which one would scarce have expected from his spare appearance. His slow, full respiration lifted the clothes with each breath that he took. His features were calm and striking. I had never seen them appear to better advantage than for the first hour, perhaps, that I was there. After that his right eye began to swell and that part of his face became discolored.

Senator Sumner was there, I think, when I entered. If not he came in soon after, as did Speaker Colfax, Mr. Secretary McCulloch, and the other members of the cabinet, with the exception of Mr. Seward. A double guard was stationed at the door and on the sidewalk to repress the crowd, which was of course highly excited and anxious. The room was small and overcrowded. The surgeons and members of the cabinet were as many as should have been in the room, but there were many more, and the hall and other rooms in the front or main house were full. One of these rooms was occupied by Mrs. Lincoln and her attendants, with Miss Harris. Mrs. Dixon and Mrs. Kinney came to her about twelve o'clock. About once an hour Mrs. Lincoln would repair to the bedside of her dying husband and with lamentation and tears remain until overcome by emotion.

A door which opened upon a porch or gallery, and also the windows, were kept open for fresh air. The night was dark, cloudy, and damp, and about six it began to rain. I remained in the room until then without sitting or leaving it, when, there being a vacant chair which someone left at the foot of the bed, I occupied it for nearly two hours, listening to the heavy groans and witnessing the wasting life of the good and great man who was expiring before me.

About 6 A.M. I experienced a feeling of faintness, and for the first time after entering the room a little past eleven I left it and the house and took a short walk in the open air. It was a dark and gloomy morning, and rain set in before I returned to the house some fifteen minutes later. Large groups of people were gathered every few rods, all anxious and solicitous. Some one or more from each group stepped forward as I passed to inquire into the condition of the President and to ask if there was no hope. Intense grief was on every countenance when I replied that the President could survive but a short time. The colored people especially—and there were at this time more of them, perhaps, than of whites—were overwhelmed with grief.

A little before seven I went into the room where the dying President was rapidly drawing near the closing moments. His wife soon after made her last visit to him. The death struggle had begun. Robert, his son, stood with several others at the head of the bed. He bore himself well but on two occasions gave way to overpowering grief and sobbed aloud, turning his head and leaning on the shoulder of Senator Sumner. The respiration of the President became suspended at intervals and at last entirely ceased at twenty-two minutes past seven. . . .

I went after breakfast to the Executive Mansion. There was a cheerless, cold rain, and everything seemed gloomy. On the Avenue in front of the White House were several hundred colored people, mostly women and children, weeping and wailing their loss. This crowd did not appear to diminish through the whole of that cold, wet day; they seemed not to know what was to be their fate since their great benefactor was dead, and their hopeless grief affected me more than almost anything else, though strong and brave men wept when I met them.

The Diary of Gideon Welles

54

Writing "The Battle Hymn
of the Republic"

The daughter of a New York banker and the wife of a well-known New England reformer, Julia Ward Howe early made a name for herself in Boston circles by her essays and poems. She was prominent also as an abolitionist, and she became one of the leaders of the woman-suffrage movement. In her early forties, while at the front, she wrote her most famous poem and the most memorable poem of the war.

Part I

I distinctly remember that a feeling of discouragement came over me as I drew near the city of Washington. I thought of the women of my acquaintance whose sons or husbands were fighting our great battle, the women themselves serving in the hospitals or busying themselves with the work of the Sanitary Commission. My husband was beyond the age of military service, my eldest son but a stripling; my youngest was a child of not more than two years. I could not leave my nursery to follow the march of our armies; neither had I the practical deftness which the preparing and packing of sanitary stores demanded. Something seemed to say to me, "You would be glad to serve, but you cannot help anyone; you have nothing to give, and there is nothing for you to do." Yet, because of my sincere desire, a word was given me to say, which did strengthen the hearts of those who fought in the field and of those who languished in the prison.

We were invited one day to attend a review of troops at some distance from the town. While we were engaged in watching the maneuvers, a sudden movement of the enemy necessitated immediate action. The review was discontinued, and we saw a detachment of soldiers gallop to the assistance of a small body of our men who were in imminent danger of being surrounded and cut off from retreat. The regiments remaining on the field were ordered to march to their cantonments. We returned to the city very slowly, of necessity, for the troops nearly filled the road. My dear minister was in the carriage with me, as were several other friends. To beguile the rather tedious drive, we sang from time to time snatches of the army songs so popular at that time, concluding, I think, with:

> *John Brown's body lies a-moldering in the*
> *ground;*
> *His soul is marching on.*

The soldiers seemed to like this and answered back, "Good for you!" Mr. Clarke said, "Mrs. Howe, why do you not write some good words for that stirring tune?" I replied that I had often wished to do this but had not as yet found in my mind any leading toward it.

I went to bed that night as usual and slept, according to my wont, quite soundly. I awoke in the gray of the morning twilight, and as I lay waiting for the dawn, the long lines of the desired poem began to twine themselves in my mind. Having thought out all the stanzas, I said to myself, "I must get up and write these verses down, lest I fall asleep again and forget them." So with a sudden effort I sprang out of bed and found in the dimness an old stump of a pen which I remembered to have used the day before. I scrawled the verses almost without looking at the paper. I had learned to do this when, on previous occasions, attacks of versification had visited me in the night and I feared to have recourse to a light lest I should wake the baby, who slept near me. I was always obliged to decipher my scrawl before another night should intervene, as it was only legible while the matter was fresh in my mind. At this time, having completed my writing, I returned to bed and fell asleep, saying to myself, "I like this better than most things that I have written."

The poem, which was soon after published in the *Atlantic Monthly* [February 1862], was somewhat praised on its appearance, but the vicissitudes of the war so engrossed public attention that small heed was taken of literary matters. I knew and was content to know that the poem soon found its way to the camps, as I heard from time to time of its being sung in chorus by the soldiers.

Reminiscences of Julia Ward Howe, 1819–1899

Part II

> *Mine eyes have seen the glory of the coming of the Lord:*
> *He is trampling out the vintage where the grapes of wrath are stored;*
> *He hath loosed the fateful lightning of his terrible swift sword:*
> *His truth is marching on.*
>
> *I have seen Him in the watch fires of a hundred circling camps;*
> *They have builded Him an altar in the evening dews and damps;*
> *I can read His righteous sentence by the dim and flaring lamps.*
> *His day is marching on.*
>
> *I have read a fiery gospel writ in burnished rows of steel:*
> *"As ye deal with my contemners, so with you my grace shall deal;*

Let the Hero, born of woman, crush the serpent with his heel,
Since God is marching on."

He has sounded forth the trumpet that shall never call retreat;
He is sifting out the hearts of men before his judgment seat:
Oh! be swift, my soul, to answer Him! be jubilant, my feet!
Our God is marching on.

In the beauty of the lilies Christ was born across the sea,
With a glory in His bosom that transfigures you and me:
As He died to make men holy, let us die to make men free,
While God is marching on.

55

Anna Dickinson Sees Draft Riots in New York City

The Confederate government early resorted to a sweeping conscription, which finally applied to able-bodied men between seventeen and fifty-five years of age. In 1863 the Federal government also turned to conscription. The first efforts to enforce the new law encountered resistance in various parts of the North. The worst disturbances were the great "draft riots" in New York City in July, caused partly by the draft, partly by general political discontent, and partly by the resentment that Irish laborers felt over the new competition offered by refugee African Americans. Many African Americans lost their lives before troops restored order. Anna Dickinson, who describes these shocking outbreaks, was at the time a young woman but already widely known as a writer and lecturer on antislavery and temperance themes. She was of Pennsylvania Quaker stock.

On the morning of Monday, the thirteenth of July [1863], began this outbreak, unparalleled in atrocities by anything in American history and equaled only by the horrors of the worst days of the French Revolution. Gangs of men and boys, composed of railroad employees, workers in machine shops, and a vast crowd of those who lived by preying upon others, thieves, pimps, professional ruffians, the scum of the city, jailbirds, or those who were running with swift feet to enter the prison doors, began to gather on the corners and in streets and alleys where they lived; from thence issuing forth, they visited the great establishments on the line of their advance, commanding their instant close and the companionship of the workmen—many of them peaceful and orderly men—on pain of the destruction of one and a murderous assault upon the other, did not their orders meet with instant compliance.

A body of these, five or six hundred strong, gathered about one of the enrolling offices in the upper part of the city, where the draft was quietly proceeding, and opened the assault upon it by a shower of clubs, bricks, and paving stones torn from the streets, following it up by a furious rush into the office. Lists, records, books, the drafting wheel, every article of furniture or work in the room, was rent in pieces and strewn about the floor or flung into the streets, while the law officers, the newspaper reporters—who are expected to be everywhere—and the few peaceable spectators were compelled to make a hasty retreat through an opportune rear exit, accelerated by the curses and blows of the assailants.

A safe in the room, which contained some of the hated records, was fallen upon by the men, who strove to wrench open its impregnable lock with their naked hands and, baffled, beat them on its iron doors and sides till they were stained with blood, in a mad frenzy of senseless hate and fury. And then, finding every portable article destroyed —their thirst for ruin growing by the little drink it had had—and believing, or rather hoping, that the officers had taken refuge in the upper rooms, set fire to the house, and stood watching the slow and steady lift of flames, filling the air with demoniac shrieks and yells, while they waited for the prey to escape from some door or window, from the merciless fire to their merciless hands. One of these, who was on the other side of the street, courageously stepped forward and, telling them that they had utterly demolished all they came to seek, informed them that helpless women and little children were in the house and besought them to extinguish the flames and leave the ruined premises—to disperse or at least to seek some other scene.

By his dress recognizing in him a government official, so far from hearing or heeding his humane appeal, they set upon him with sticks and clubs and beat him till his eyes were blind with blood, and he, bruised and mangled, succeeded in escaping to the handful of police who stood helpless before this howling crew, now increased to thousands. With difficulty and pain the inoffensive tenants escaped from the rapidly-spreading fire, which, having devoured the house originally lighted, swept across the neighboring buildings till the whole block stood a mass of burning flames. The firemen came up tardily and reluctantly, many of them of the same class as the miscreants who surrounded them and who cheered at their approach, but either made no attempt to perform their duty or so feeble and farcical a one as to bring disgrace upon a service they so generally honor and ennoble.

At last, when there was here nothing more to accomplish, the mob, swollen to a frightful size, including myriad of wretched, drunken women and the half-grown vagabond boys of the pavements, rushed through the intervening streets, stopping cars and insulting peaceable citizens on their way, to an armory where were manufactured and stored carbines and guns for the government. In anticipation of the attack, this, earlier in the day, had been fortified by a police squad capable of coping with an ordinary crowd of ruffians, but as chaff before fire in the presence of these murderous thousands. Here, as before, the attack was begun by a rain of missiles gathered from the streets, less fatal, doubtless, than more civilized arms, but frightful in the ghastly wounds and injuries they inflicted. Of this no notice was taken by those who were stationed within. It was repeated. At last, finding they were treated with contemptuous silence and that no sign of surrender was offered, the crowd swayed back, then forward, in a combined attempt to force the wide entrance doors. Heavy hammers and sledges, which had been brought from forges and workshops, caught up hastily as they gathered the mechanics into their ranks, were used with frightful violence to beat them in at last successfully. The foremost assailants began to climb the stairs but were checked and for the moment driven back by the fire of the officers, who at last had been commanded to resort to their revolvers. A half-score fell wounded, and one who had been acting in some sort as their leader—a big, brutal Irish ruffian—dropped dead.

The pause was but for an instant. As the smoke cleared away there was a general and ferocious onslaught upon the armory; curses, oaths, revilings, hideous and obscene blasphemy, with terrible yells and cries, filled the air in every accent of the English tongue save that spoken by a native American. Such were there mingled with the sea of sound, but they were so few and weak as to be unnoticeable in the roar of voices. The paving stones flew like hail until the street was torn into gaps and ruts and every windowpane and sash and doorway was smashed or broken. Meanwhile divers attempts were made to fire the building but failed through haste or ineffectual materials or the vigilant watchfulness of the besieged. In the midst of this gallant defense word was brought to the defenders from headquarters that nothing could be done for their support and that if they would save their lives they must make a quick and orderly retreat. Fortunately there was a side passage with which the mob was unacquainted, and one by one they succeeded in gaining this and vanishing.

The work was begun, continued, gathering in force and fury as the day wore on. Police stations, enrolling offices, rooms or buildings used in any way by government authority or obnoxious as representing the dignity of law, were gutted, destroyed, then left to the mercy of the flames. Newspaper offices, whose issues had been a fire in the rear of the nation's armies by extenuating and defending treason and through violent and incendiary appeals stirring up "lewd fellows of the baser sort" to this very carnival of ruin and blood, were cheered as the crowd went by. Those that had been faithful to loyalty and law were hooted, stoned, and even stormed by the army of miscreants, who were only driven off by the gallant and determined charge of the police and in one place by the equally gallant and certainly unique defense which came from turning the boiling water from the engines upon the howling wretches, who, unprepared for any such warm reception as this, beat a precipitate and general retreat. Before night fell it was no longer one vast crowd collected in a single section, but great numbers of gatherings, scattered over the whole length and breadth of the city, some of them engaged in actual work of demolition and ruin, others, with clubs and weapons in their hands, prowling round apparently with no definite atrocity to perpetrate, but ready for any iniquity that might offer, and by way of pastime, chasing every stray police officer or solitary soldier or inoffensive Negro who crossed the line of their vision; these three objects—the badge of a defender of the law, the uniform of the Union army, the skin of a helpless and outraged race— acted upon these madmen as water acts upon a rabid dog.

Late in the afternoon a crowd, which could have numbered not less than ten thousand, the majority of whom were ragged, frowzy, drunken women, gathered about the Orphan Asylum for Colored Children—a large and beautiful building and one of the most admirable and noble charities of the city. When it became evident from the menacing cries and groans of the multitude that danger, if not destruction, was meditated to the harmless and inoffensive inmates, a flag of truce appeared, and an appeal was made in their behalf, by the principal, to every sentiment of humanity which these beings might possess—a vain appeal! Whatever human feeling had ever, if ever, filled these souls was utterly drowned and washed away in the tide of rapine and blood in which they had been steeping themselves. The few officers who stood guard over the doors and manfully faced these demoniac legions were beaten down and flung to one side, helpless and stunned, whilst the vast crowd rushed in. All the articles upon which they could seize—beds, bedding, carpets, furniture, the very garments of the fleeing inmates, some of these torn from their persons as they sped by—were carried into the streets and hurried off by the women and children who stood ready to receive the goods which their husbands, sons, and fathers flung to their care. The little ones, many of them assailed and beaten—all, orphans and caretakers, exposed to every indignity and every danger—driven on to the street, the building was fired. This had been attempted whilst the helpless children, some of them scarce more than babies, were still in their rooms, but this devilish consummation was prevented by the heroism of one man. He, the chief of the fire department, strove by voice and arm to stay the endeavor, and when, overcome by superior numbers, the brands had been lit and piled, with naked hands and in the face of threatened death he tore asunder the glowing embers and trod them underfoot. Again the effort was made and again failed through the determined and heroic opposition of this solitary soul. Then on the front steps, in the midst of these drunken and infuriated thousands, he stood up and besought them, if they cared nothing for themselves nor for those hapless orphans, that they would not bring lasting disgrace upon the city by destroying one of its noblest charities, which had for its object nothing but good.

He was answered on all sides by yells and execrations and frenzied shrieks of "Down with the nagurs!" coupled with every oath and every curse that malignant hate of the blacks could devise and drunken Irish tongues could speak. It had been decreed that this building was to be razed to the ground. The house was fired in a thousand places, and in less than two hours the walls crashed in, a mass of smoking, blackened ruins, whilst the children wandered through the streets, a prey to beings who were wild beasts in everything save the superior ingenuity of man to agonize and torture his victims.

Frightful as the day had been, the night was yet more hideous, since to the horrors which were seen was added the greater horror of deeds which might be committed in the darkness—or, if they were seen, it was by the lurid glare of burning buildings, the red flames of which, flung upon the stained and brutal faces, the torn and tattered garments, of men and women who danced and howled around the scene of ruin they had caused, made the whole aspect of affairs seem more like a gathering of fiends rejoicing in pandemonium than aught with which creatures of flesh and blood had to do. . . .

The next morning's sun rose on a city which was ruled by a reign of terror. Had the police possessed the heads of Hydra and the arms of Briareus and had these heads all seen, these arms all fought, they would have been powerless against the multitude of opposers. Outbreaks were made, crowds gathered, houses burned, streets barricaded, fights enacted, in a score of places at once. Where the officers appeared they were irretrievably beaten and overcome, their stand, were it ever so short, but inflaming the passions of the mob to fresh deeds of violence. Stores were closed, the business portion of the city deserted, the large works and factories emptied of men, who had been sent home by their employers or were swept into the ranks of the marauding bands. The city cars, omnibuses, hacks, were unable to run and remained under shelter. Every telegraph wire was cut, the posts torn up, the operators driven from their offices. The mayor, seeing that civil power was helpless to stem this tide, desired to call the military to his aid and place the city under martial law, but was opposed by the Governor—a governor who, but a few days before, had pronounced the war a failure and not only predicted but encouraged this mob rule, which was now crushing everything beneath its heavy and ensanguined feet. This man, through almost two days of these awful scenes, remained at a quiet seaside retreat but a few miles from the city. Coming to it on the afternoon of the second day, instead of ordering cannon planted in the streets, giving these creatures opportunity to retire to their homes, and in the event of refusal, blowing them there by powder and ball, he first went to the point where was collected the chiefest mob and proceeded to address them. Before him stood incendiaries, thieves, and murderers, who even then were sacking dwelling houses and butchering powerless and inoffensive beings. These wretches he apostrophized as "my friends," repeating the title again and again in the course of his harangue, assuring them that he was there as a proof of his friendship, which he had demonstrated by "sending his adjutant general to Washington to have the draft stopped," begging them to "wait for his return," "to separate now as good citizens," with the promise that they "might assemble again whenever they wished to so do"; meanwhile he would "take care of their rights." This model speech was incessantly interrupted by tremendous cheering and frantic demonstrations of delight, one great fellow almost crushing the Governor in his enthusiastic embrace.

His allies in newspaper offices attempted to throw the blame upon the loyal press and portion of the community. This was but a repetition of the cry raised by traitors in arms that the government, struggling for life in their deadly hold, was responsible for the war: "If thou wouldst but consent to be murdered peaceably, there could be no strife."

It was absurd and futile to characterize this new reign of terror as anything but an effort on the part of Northern rebels to help Southern ones at the most critical moment of the war, with the state militia and available troops absent in a neighboring commonwealth and the loyal people unprepared. These editors and their coadjutors, men of brains and ability, were of that most poisonous growth—traitors to the government and the flag of their country—renegade Americans.

Anna Elizabeth Dickinson
What Answer?

56

Suffering in Andersonville Prison

Both Northern and Southern prisons during the Civil War were horrible spots— there being less to choose between them than Northerners liked to think. At Andersonville in southwestern Georgia was one of the largest of the Confederate prison camps. The first captured Northerners arrived there early in 1863. By midsummer more than 32,000 prisoners were huddled inside a stockade that enclosed an area of only some twenty-six acres. The men lived in little huts improvised out of bits of lumber, in tents made of blankets, or in pits dug in the ground. Their food was insufficient in quantity and bad in quality; their water became polluted. Before the war ended about 50,000 prisoners in all had been received at Andersonville, and 13,000 had died. After peace arrived, the superintendent, Henry Wirz, was tried and hanged.

JANUARY 25, 1865.—
    While going our rounds in the morning we found a very important person in Peter Louis, a paroled Yankee prisoner, in the employ of Captain Bonham. The captain keeps him out of the stockade, feeds and clothes him, and in return reaps the benefit of his skill. Peter is a French Yankee, a shoemaker by trade, and makes as beautiful shoes as I ever saw imported from France. My heart quite softened toward him when I saw his handiwork, and little Mrs. Sims was so overcome that she gave him a huge slice of her Confederate fruitcake. I talked French with him, which pleased him greatly, and Mett and I engaged him to make us each a pair of shoes. I will feel like a lady once more with good shoes on my feet. I expect the poor Yank is glad to get away from Anderson on any terms. Although matters have improved somewhat with the cool weather, the tales that are told of the condition of things there last summer are appalling. Mrs. Brisbane heard all about it from Father Hamilton, a Roman Catholic priest from Macon, who has been working like a good Samaritan in those dens of filth and misery. It is a shame to us Protestants that we have let a Roman Catholic get so far ahead of us in this work of charity and mercy. Mrs. Brisbane says Father Hamilton told her that during the summer the wretched prisoners burrowed in the ground like moles to protect themselves from the sun. It was not safe to give them material to build shanties as they might use it for clubs to overcome the guard. These underground huts, he said, were alive with vermin and stank like charnel houses. Many of the prisoners were stark naked, having not so much as a shirt to their backs. He told a pitiful story of a Pole who had no garment but a shirt, and to make it cover him better, he put his legs into the sleeves and tied the tail around his neck. The others guyed him so on his appearance and the poor wretch was so disheartened by suffering that one day he deliberately stepped over the deadline and stood there till the guard was forced to shoot him. But what I can't understand is that a Pole, of all people in the world, should come over here and try to take away our liberty when his own country is in the hands of oppressors. One would think that the Poles, of all nations in the world, ought to sympathize with a people fighting for their liberties. Father Hamilton said that at one time the prisoners died at the rate of a hundred and fifty a day, and he saw some of them die on the ground without a rag to lie on or a garment to cover them. Dysentery was the most fatal disease, and as they lay on the ground in their own excrements, the smell was so horrible that the good father says he was often obliged to rush from their presence to get a breath of pure air. It is dreadful. My heart aches for the poor wretches, Yankees

though they are, and I am afraid God will suffer some terrible retribution to fall upon us for letting such things happen. If the Yankees ever should come to southwest Georgia and go to Anderson and see the graves there, God have mercy on the land! And yet what can we do? The Yankees themselves are really more to blame than we, for they won't exchange these prisoners, and our poor, hard-pressed Confederacy has not the means to provide for them when our own soldiers are starving in the field. Oh, what a horrible thing war is when stripped of all its pomp and circumstance!

ELIZA FRANCES ANDREWS
The War-Time Journal of a Georgia Girl

57

The Disintegration of the Confederate Army

The Confederate armies had reached a total strength of almost, if not quite, 700,000 men at the beginning of 1863. But after the defeats at Gettysburg and Vicksburg, discouragement spread steadily, and during 1864 desertions became a steady stream. By March 1865, when the Union armies were stronger than ever, there were probably not more than 200,000 men in the Confederate forces. The final scenes in the disbandment of the defeated but heroic Southern units are here described by Eliza Frances Andrews, a Georgia woman who, twenty-five years old the year of Appomattox, soon became well known as an educator and author.

APRIL 24, 1865. MONDAY.—

The shattered remains of Lee's army are beginning to arrive. There is an endless stream passing between the transportation office and the depot, and trains are going and coming at all hours. The soldiers bring all sorts of rumors and keep us stirred up in a state of never-ending excitement. Our avenue leads from the principal street on which they pass, and great numbers stop to rest in the grove. Emily is kept busy cooking rations for them, and pinched as we are ourselves for supplies, it is impossible to refuse anything to the men that have been fighting for us. Even when they don't ask for anything the poor fellows look so tired and hungry that we feel tempted to give them everything we have. Two nice-looking officers came to the kitchen door this afternoon while I was in there making some sorghum cakes to send to General Elzey's camp. They then walked slowly through the backyard and seemed reluctant to tear themselves away from such a sweet, beautiful place. Nearly everybody that passes the street gate stops and looks up the avenue, and I know they can't help thinking what a beautiful place it is. The Cherokee rose hedge is white with blooms. It is glorious. A great many of the soldiers camp in the grove, though Colonel Weems (the Confederate commandant of the post) has located a public camping ground for them farther out of town. The officers often ask for a night's lodging, but our house is always so full of friends who have a nearer claim that a great many have to be refused. It hurts my conscience ever to turn off a Confederate soldier on any account, but we are so overwhelmed with company—friends and people bringing letters of introduction—that the house, big as it is, will hardly hold us all, and members of the family have to pack together like sardines. Captain John Nightingale's servant came in this afternoon—the "little Johnny Nightingale" I used to play with down on the old Tallasee plantation—but reports that he does not know where his master is. He says the Yankees captured him (the Negro) and took away his master's horse that he was tending, but as soon as night came on he made his escape on another horse that he took from them, and put out for home. He says he don't like the Yankees because they "didn't show no respec' for his feelin's." He talks with a strong saltwater brogue and they laughed at him, which he thought very ill-mannered. Father sent him round to the Negro quarters to wait till his master turns up.

May 1st. Monday.—

The conduct of a Texas regiment in the streets this afternoon gave us a sample of the chaos and general demoralization that may be expected to follow the breaking up of our government. They raised a riot about their rations, in which they were joined by all the disorderly elements among both soldiers and citizens. First they plundered the commissary department and then turned loose on the quartermaster's stores. Paper, pens, buttons, tape, cloth—everything in the building—was seized and strewn about on the ground. Negroes and children joined the mob and grabbed what they could of the plunder. Colonel Weems' provost guard refused to interfere, saying they were too good soldiers to fire on their comrades, and so the plundering went on unopposed. Nobody seemed to care much, as we all know the Yankees will get it in the end, anyway, if our men don't. I was at Miss Maria Randolph's when the disturbance began, but by keeping to the back streets I avoided the worst of the row, though I encountered a number of stragglers running away with their booty. The soldiers were very generous with their "confiscated" goods, giving away paper, pens, tape, etc., to anybody they happened to meet. One of them poked a handful of pen staves at me; another, staggering under an armful of stationery, threw me a ream of paper, saying,

"There, take that and write to your sweetheart on it." I took no notice of any of them but hurried on home as fast as I could, all the way meeting Negroes, children, and men loaded with plunder. When I reached home I found some of our own servants with their arms full of thread, paper, and pens, which they offered to sell me, and one of them gave me several reams of paper. I carried them to Father, and he collected all the other booty he could find, intending to return it to headquarters, but he was told that there is no one to receive it, no place to send it to—in fact, there seemed to be no longer any headquarters nor any other semblance of authority. Father saved one box of bacon for Colonel Weems by hauling it away in his wagon and concealing it in his smokehouse. All of Johnston's army and the greater portion of Lee's are still to pass through, and since the rioters have destroyed so much of the forage and provisions intended for their use, there will be great difficulty in feeding them. They did not stop at food but helped themselves to all the horses and mules they needed. A band of them made a raid on General El-zey's camp and took nine of his mules. They excused themselves by saying that all government stores will be seized by the Yankees in a few days, any-way, if left alone, and our own soldiers might as well get the good of them while they can. This would be true if there were not so many others yet to come who ought to have their share.

Our backyard and kitchen have been filled all day, as usual, with soldiers waiting to have their rations cooked. One of them, who had a wounded arm, came into the house to have it dressed and said that he was at Salisbury when Garnett was shot and saw him fall. He told some miraculous stories about the valorous deeds of "the Colonel," and although they were so exaggerated that I set them down as apocryphal, I gave him a piece of cake, notwithstanding, to pay him for telling them.

TUESDAY.—

The disorders begun by the Texans yesterday were continued today, every fresh band that arrived from the front falling into the way of their predecessors. They have been pillaging the ordnance stores at the depot, in which they were followed by Negroes, boys, and mean white men. I don't see what people are thinking about to let ammunition fall into the hands of the Negroes, but everybody is demoralized and reckless and nobody seems to care about anything anymore. A number of paroled men came into our grove, where they sat under the trees to empty the cartridges they had seized. Confederate money is of no more use now than so much wastepaper, but by filling their canteens with powder they can trade it off along the road for provisions. They scattered lead and cartridges all over the ground. Marshall went out after they left and picked up enough to last him for years. The balls do not fit his gun, but he can remold them and draw the powder out of the cartridges to shoot with. I am uneasy at having so much explosive material in the house, especially when I consider the careless manner in which we have to live. There is so much company and so much to do that even the servants hardly have time to eat. I never lived in such excitement and confusion in my life. Thousands of people pass through Washington [Georgia] every day, and our house is like a free hotel; Father welcomes everybody as long as there is a square foot of vacant space under his roof. Meeting all these pleasant people is the one compensation of this dismal time, and I don't know how I shall exist when they have all gone their ways and we settle down in the mournful quiet of subjugation. Besides the old friends that are turning up every day, there is a continual stream of new faces crossing my path, and I make some pleasant acquaintance or form some new friendship every day. The sad part of it is that the most of them I will probably never meet again, and if I should, where and how? What will they be? What will I be? These are portentous questions in such a time as this.

It seems as if all the people I ever heard of, or never heard of, either, for that matter, are passing through Washington. Some of our friends pass on without stopping to see us because they say they are too ragged and dirty to show themselves. Poor fellows! if they only knew how honorable rags and dirt are now, in our eyes, when endured in the service of their country, they would not be ashamed of them. The son of the richest man in New Orleans trudged through the other day with no coat to his back, no shoes on his feet. The town is full of celebrities, and many poor fugitives whose necks are in danger meet here to concert plans for escape, and I put it in my prayers every night that they may be successful. General Wigfall started for the West some days ago, but his mules were stolen, and he had to return. He is frantic, they say, with rage and disappointment. General Toombs left tonight, but old Governor Brown, it is said, has determined not to desert his post. I am glad he has done something to deserve respect and hope he may get off yet, as soon as the Yankees appoint a military governor. Clement Clay is believed to be well on his way to the Trans-Mississippi, the land of promise now, or rather the city of refuge from which it is hoped a door of escape may be found to Mexico or Cuba. The most terrible part of the war is now to come, the "bloody assizes." "Kirke's lambs," in the shape of Yankee troopers, are closing in upon us; our own disbanded armies, ragged, starving, hopeless, reckless, are roaming about without order or leaders, making their way to their far-off homes as best they can. The props that held society up are broken. Everything is in a state of disorganization and tumult. We have no currency, no law save the primitive code that might makes right. We are in a transition state from war to subjugation, and it is far worse than was the transition from peace to war. The suspense and anxiety in which we live are terrible.

ELIZA FRANCES ANDREWS
The War-Time Journal of a Georgia Girl

58

Mrs. Chesnut Watches the Attack on Fort Sumter

When President Lincoln dispatched an expedition to provision Fort Sumter, Southern leaders resolved to attack. In this spirited excerpt from a diary, the wife of one of the South Carolina senators describes the feeling in Charleston during the crisis, which culminated in the bombardment of April 12–13 and the opening of the war.

APRIL 8TH, 1861.—

Allen Green came up to speak to me at dinner in all his soldier's toggery. It sent a shiver through me. Tried to read Margaret Fuller Ossoli, but could not. The air too full of war news, and we are all so restless.

Went to see Miss Pinckney, one of the last of the old-world Pinckneys. Governor Manning walked in, bowed gravely, and seated himself by me. Again he bowed low in mock-heroic style and with a grand wave of his hand said, "Madam, your country is invaded." When I had breath to speak, I asked, "What does he mean?" He meant this: There are six men-of-war outside the bar. Talbot and Chew have come to say that hostilities are to begin. Governor Pickens and Beauregard are holding a council of war. Mr. Chesnut then came in and confirmed the story. Wigfall next entered in boisterous spirits and said, "There was a sound of revelry by night." In any stir of confusion my heart is apt to beat so painfully. Now the agony was so stifling I could hardly see or hear. The men went off almost immediately. And I crept silently to my room, where I sat down to a good cry.

Mrs. Wigfall came in, and we had it out on the subject of civil war. We solaced ourselves with dwelling on all its known horrors, and then we added what we had a right to expect with Yankees in front and Negroes in the rear. "The slaveowners must expect a servile insurrection, of course," said Mrs. Wigfall, to make sure that we were unhappy enough. Suddenly loud shouting was heard. We ran out. Cannon after cannon roared. We met Mrs. Allen Green in the passageway, with blanched cheeks and streaming eyes. Governor Means rushed out of his room in his dressing gown and begged us to be calm. "Governor Pickens," said he, "has ordered, in the pleni-tude of his wisdom, seven cannon to be fired as a signal to the Seventh Regiment. Anderson will hear as well as the Seventh Regiment. Now you go back and be quiet; fighting in the streets has not begun yet."

So we retired. Doctor Gibbes calls Mrs. Allen Green, Dame Placid. There was no placidity today, with cannon bursting and Allen on the island. No sleep for anybody last night. The streets were alive with soldiers, men shouting, marching, singing. Wigfall, the stormy petrel, is in his glory, the only thoroughly happy person I see. Today things seem to have settled down a little. One can but hope still. Lincoln or Seward has made such silly advances and then far sillier drawings back. There may be a chance for peace after all. Things are happening so fast. My husband has been made an aide-de-camp to General Beauregard.

Three hours ago we were quickly packing to go home. The convention has adjourned. Now he tells me the attack on Fort Sumter may begin tonight; depends upon Anderson and the fleet outside. . . .

Mrs. Hayne called. She had, she said, but one feeling—pity for those who are not here. Jack Preston, Willie Alston, "the take-life-easys," as they are called, with John Green, "the big brave," have gone down to the islands—volunteered as privates. Seven hundred men were sent over. Ammunition wagons were rumbling along the streets all night. Anderson is burning blue lights, signs and signals for the fleet outside, I suppose.

Today at dinner there was no allusion to things as they stand in Charleston harbor. There was an undercurrent of intense excitement. There could not have been a more brilliant circle. In addition to our usual quartet, Judge Withers, Langdon Cheves, and Trescott, our two ex-governors dined with us, Means and Manning. These men all talked so delightfully. For once in my life I listened. That over, business began in earnest. Governor Means has rummaged a sword and red sash from somewhere and brought it for Colonel Chesnut, who had gone to demand the surrender of Fort Sumter. And now, patience—we must wait.

Why did that green goose Anderson go into Fort Sumter? Then everything began to go wrong. Now they have intercepted a letter from him, urging them to let him surrender. He paints the horrors likely to ensue if they will not. He ought to have thought of all that before he put his head in the hole.

12TH.—

Anderson will not capitulate. Yesterday's was the merriest, maddest dinner we have had yet. Men were audaciously wise and witty. We had an unspoken foreboding that it was to be our last pleasant meeting. Mr. Miles dined with us today. Mrs. Henry King rushed in saying: "The news, I come for the latest news! All the men of the King family are on the island," of which fact she seemed proud.

While she was here our peace negotiator or envoy came in—that is,

Mr. Chesnut returned. His interview with Colonel Anderson had been deeply interesting, but Mr. Chesnut was not inclined to be communicative. He wanted his dinner. He felt for Anderson and had telegraphed to President Davis for instructions—what answer to give Anderson, etc. He has now gone back to Fort Sumter with additional instructions. When they were about to leave the wharf, A.H. Boykin sprang into the boat in great excitement. He thought himself ill-used, with a likelihood of fighting and he to be left behind!

I do not pretend to go to sleep. How can I? If Anderson does not accept terms at four, the orders are he shall be fired upon. I count four, St. Michael's bells chime out, and I begin to hope. At half past four the heavy booming of a cannon. I sprang out of bed, and on my knees prostrate I prayed as I never prayed before.

There was a sound of stir all over the house, pattering of feet in the corridors. All seemed hurrying one way. I put on my double gown and a shawl and went too. It was to the housetop. The shells were bursting. In the dark I heard a man say, "Waste of ammunition." I knew my husband was rowing a boat somewhere in that dark bay. If Anderson was obstinate, Colonel Chestnut was to order the fort on one side to open fire. Certainly fire had begun. The regular roar of the cannon, there it was. And who could tell what each volley accomplished of death and destruction?

The women were wild there on the housetop. Prayers came from the women and imprecations from the men. And then a shell would light up the scene. Tonight they say the forces are to attempt to land. We watched up there, and everybody wondered that Fort Sumter did not fire a shot. . . .

We hear nothing, can listen to nothing; boom, boom, goes the cannon all the time. The nervous strain is awful, alone in this darkened room. "Richmond and Washington ablaze," say the papers—blazing with excitement. Why not? To us these last days' events seem frightfully great. We were all women on that iron balcony. Men are only seen at a distance now. Stark Means was leaning over and looking with tearful eyes, when an unknown creature asked, "Why did he take his hat off?" Mrs. Means stood straight up and said, "He did that in honor of his mother; he saw me." She is a proud mother and at the same time most unhappy. Her lovely daughter Emma is dying in there, before her eyes, of consumption. At that moment I am sure Mrs. Means had a spasm of the heart.

13TH.—

Nobody has been hurt after all. How gay we were last night! Reaction after the dread of all the slaughter we thought those dreadful cannon were making. Not even a battery the worse for wear. Fort Sumter has been on fire. Anderson has not yet silenced any of our guns. So the aides, still with swords and red sashes by way of uniform, tell us. But the sound of those guns makes regular meals impossible. None of us goes to table. Tea trays pervade the corridors, going everywhere. Some of the anxious hearts lie on their beds and moan in solitary misery. Mrs. Wigfall and I solace ourselves with tea in my room. These women have all a satisfying faith. "God is on our side," they say. When we are shut in Mrs. Wigfall and I ask, "Why?" "Of course, He hates the Yankees," we are told. "You'll think that well of Him."

Not by one word or look can we detect any change in the demeanor of these Negro servants. Lawrence sits at our door, sleepy and respectful, and profoundly indifferent. So are they all, but they carry it too far. You could not tell that they even heard the awful roar going on in the bay, though it has been dinning in their ears night and day. People talk before them as if they were chairs and tables. They make no sign. Are they stolidly stupid? or wiser than we are; silent and strong, biding their time?

15TH.—

I did not know that one could live such days of excitement. Some one called: "Come out! There is a crowd coming." A mob it was, indeed, but it was headed by Colonels Chesnut and Manning. The crowd was shouting and showing these two as messengers of good news. They were escorted to Beauregard's headquarters. Fort Sumter had surrendered! Those upon the housetops shouted to us, "The fort is on fire." That had been the story once or twice before.

When we had calmed down, Colonel Chesnut, who had taken it all quietly enough, if anything more unruffled than usual in his serenity, told us how the surrender came about. Wigfall was with them on Morris Island when they saw the fire in the fort; he jumped in a little boat and, with his handkerchief as a white flag, rowed over. Wigfall went in through a porthole. When Colonel Chesnut arrived shortly after and was received at the regular entrance, Colonel Anderson told him he had need to pick his way warily, for the place was all mined. As far as I can make out the fort surrendered to Wigfall. But it is all confusion. Our flag is flying there. Fire engines have been sent for to put out the fire. Everybody tells you half of something and then rushes off to tell something else or to hear the last news.

In the afternoon Mrs. Preston, Mrs. Joe Heyward, and I drove out around the battery. We were in an open carriage. What a changed scene—the very liveliest crowd I think I ever saw, everybody talking at once. All glasses were still turned on the grim old fort.

MARY BOYKIN CHESNUT
A Diary from Dixie

59

Abner Doubleday Defends Fort Sumter

A New Yorker by birth and a West Point graduate who had fought in the Mexican War, Abner Doubleday was second in command at Fort Sumter when it was captured by the Confederates in 1861. He served gallantly throughout the rest of the war, fighting at Antietam, at Fredericksburg, at Chancellorsville, and at Gettysburg. His other claim to fame is as the "father" of baseball.

About 4 A.M. on the 12th I was awakened by someone groping about my room in the dark and calling out my name. It proved to be Anderson, who came to announce to me that he had just received a dispatch from Beauregard, dated 3:20 A.M., to the effect that he should open fire upon us in an hour. Finding it was determined not to return the fire until after breakfast, I remained in bed. As we had no lights, we could in fact do nothing before that time except to wander around in the darkness and fire without an accurate view of the enemy's works.

As soon as the outline of our fort could be distinguished, the enemy carried out their program. It had been arranged, as a special compliment to the venerable Edmund Ruffin, who might almost be called the father of secession, that he should fire the first shot against us from the Stevens battery on Cummings Point. Almost immediately afterward a ball from Cummings Point lodged in the magazine wall and by the sound seemed to bury itself in the masonry about a foot from my head, in very unpleasant proximity to my right ear. This is the one that probably came with Mr. Ruffin's compliments. In a moment the firing burst forth in one continuous roar, and large patches of both the exterior and interior masonry began to crumble and fall in all directions. The place where I was had been used for the manufacture of cartridges, and there was still a good deal of powder there, some packed and some loose. A shell soon struck near the ventilator, and a puff of dense smoke entered the room, giving me a strong impression that there would be an immediate explosion. Fortunately, no sparks had penetrated inside.

Nineteen batteries were now hammering at us, and the balls and shells from the ten-inch columbiads, accompanied by shells from the thirteen-inch mortars, which constantly bombarded us, made us feel as if the war had commenced in earnest.

When it was broad daylight, I went down to breakfast. I found the officers already assembled at one of the long tables in the mess hall. Our party were calm and even somewhat merry. We had retained one colored man to wait on us. He was a spruce-looking mulatto from Charleston, very active and efficient on ordinary occasions, but now completely demoralized by the thunder of the guns and crashing of the shot around us. He leaned back against the wall, almost white with fear, his eyes closed, and his whole expression one of perfect despair. Our meal was not very sumptuous. It consisted of pork and water, but Doctor Crawford triumphantly brought forth a little farina, which he had found in a corner of the hospital.

When this frugal repast was over, my company was told off in three details for firing purposes, to be relieved afterward by Seymour's company. As I was the ranking officer, I took the first detachment and marched them to the casemates which looked out upon the powerful ironclad battery of Cummings Point.

In aiming the first gun fired against the rebellion I had no feeling of self-reproach, for I fully believed that the contest was inevitable and was not of our seeking. . . .

Our firing now became regular and was answered from the rebel guns, which encircled us on the four sides of the pentagon upon which the fort was built. The other side faced the open sea. Showers of balls from ten-inch columbiads and forty-two-pounders and shells from thirteen-inch mortars poured into the fort in one incessant stream, causing great flakes of masonry to fall in all directions. When the immense mortar shells, after sailing high in the air, came down in a vertical direction and buried themselves in the parade ground, their explosion shook the fort like an earthquake.

The firing continued all day without any special incident of importance and without our making much impression on the enemy's works. They had a great advantage over us as their fire was concentrated on the fort, which was in the center of the circle, while ours was diffused over the circumference. Their missiles were exceedingly destructive to the upper exposed portion of the work, but no essential injury was done to the lower casemates which sheltered us.

From 4 to 6:30 A.M. the enemy's fire was very spirited. From 7 to 8 A.M. a rainstorm came on, and there was a lull in the cannonading. About 8 A.M. the officers' quarters were ignited by one of Ripley's incendiary shells or by shot heated in the furnaces at Fort Moultrie. The fire was put out, but at 10 A.M. a mortar shell passed through the roof and lodged in the flooring of the second story, where it burst and started the flames afresh. This too was extinguished, but the hot shot soon followed each other so rapidly that it was impossible for us to contend with them any longer. It became evident that the entire block, being built with wooden partitions, floors, and roofing, must be consumed, and that the magazine, containing three hundred barrels of powder, would be endangered; for even after closing the metallic door sparks might penetrate through the ventilator. The floor was covered with loose powder where a detail of men had been at work manufacturing cartridge bags out of old shirts, woolen blankets, etc.

While the officers exerted themselves with axes to tear down and cut away all the woodwork in the vicinity, the soldiers were rolling barrels of powder out to more sheltered spots and were covering them with wet blankets. The labor was accelerated by the shells which were bursting around us, for Ripley had redoubled his activity at the first signs of a conflagration. We only succeeded in getting out some ninety-six barrels of powder, and then we were obliged to close the massive copper door and await the result. A shot soon after passed through the intervening shield, struck the door, and bent the lock in such a way that it could not be opened again. We were thus cut off from our supply of ammunition but still had some piled up in the vicinity of the guns. Anderson officially reported only four barrels and three cartridges as on hand when we left.

By 11 A.M. the conflagration was terrible and disastrous. One fifth of the fort was on fire, and the wind drove the smoke in dense masses into the angle where we had all taken refuge. It seemed impossible to escape suffocation. Some lay down close to the ground, with handkerchiefs over their mouths, and others posted themselves near the embrasures, where the smoke was somewhat lessened by the draught of air. Everyone suffered severely. I crawled out of one of these openings and sat on the outer edge, but Ripley made it lively for me there with his case shot, which spattered all around. Had not a slight change of wind taken place, the result might have been fatal to most of us.

Our firing having ceased and the enemy being very jubilant, I thought it would be as well to show them that we were not all dead yet and ordered the gunners to fire a few rounds more. I heard afterward that the enemy loudly cheered Anderson for his persistency under such adverse circumstances.

The scene at this time was really terrific. The roaring and crackling of the flames, the dense masses of whirling smoke, the bursting of the enemy's shells and our own, which were exploding in the burning rooms, the crashing of the shot, and the sound of masonry falling in every direction made the fort a pandemonium. When at last nothing was left of the building but the blackened walls and smoldering embers, it became painfully evident that an immense amount of damage had been done. There was a tower at each angle of the fort. One of these, containing great quantities of shells upon which we had relied, was almost completely shattered by successive explosions. The massive wooden gates studded with iron nails were burned, and the wall built behind them was now a mere heap of debris, so that the main entrance was wide open for an assaulting party. The sally ports were in a similar condition, and the numerous windows on the gorge side which had been planked up had now become all open entrances.

About 12:48 P.M. the end of the flagstaff was shot down and the flag fell. . . .

About 2 P.M. Senator Wigfall, in company with W. Gourdin Young, of Charleston, unexpectedly made his appearance at one of the embrasures, having crossed over from Morris Island in a small boat rowed by Negroes. He had seen the flag come down and supposed that we had surrendered in consequence of the burning of the quarters. An artilleryman serving his gun was very much astonished to see a man's face at the entrance and asked him what he was doing there. Wigfall replied that he wished to see Major Anderson. The man, however, refused to allow him to enter until he had surrendered himself as a prisoner and given up his sword. . . . Wigfall, in Beauregard's name, offered Anderson his own terms, which were the evacuation of the fort, with permission to salute our flag and to march out with the honors of war with our arms and private baggage, leaving all other war material behind. As soon as this matter was arranged, Wigfall returned to Cummings Point.

All of the preliminaries having been duly adjusted, it was decided that the evacuation should take place the next morning. Our arrangements were few and simple, but the rebels made extensive preparations for the event in order to give it the greatest éclat and gain from it as much prestige as possible. The population of the surrounding country poured into Charleston in vast multitudes to witness the humiliation of the United States flag. We slept soundly that night for the first time, after all the fatigue and excitement of the two preceding days.

The next morning, Sunday, the 14th, we were up early, packing our baggage in readiness to go on board the transport. The time having arrived, I made preparations, by order of Major Anderson, to fire a national salute to the flag.

The salute being over, the Confederate troops marched in to occupy the fort. The Palmetto Guard, Captain Cuthbert's company, detailed by Colonel De Saussure, and Captain Hollinquist's Company B, of the regulars, detailed by Colonel Ripley, constituted the new garrison under Ripley. Anderson directed me to form the men on the parade ground, assume command, and march them on board the transport. I told him I should prefer to leave the fort with the flag flying and the drums beating "Yankee Doodle," and he authorized me to do so. As soon as our tattered flag came down and the silken banner made by the ladies of Charleston was run up, tremendous shouts of applause were heard from the vast multitude of spectators, and all the vessels and steamers, with one accord, made for the fort.

Abner Doubleday
Reminiscences of Forts Sumter and Moultrie

60

"Bull Run" Russell Reports the Rout of the Federals

The English journalist William Howard Russell arrived in America in 1861 with a great and well-merited reputation as a war correspondent. He had distinguished himself by his shrewd, careful, and courageous articles on the Crimean War, in which he had exposed the mismanagement of affairs at the front. From America he began sending the (London) *Times* equally honest and outspoken accounts of American affairs. He visited both the Federal and Confederate capitals and drew vivid pictures of Jefferson Davis and Lincoln. Then, having watched the battle of Bull Run, he told just how badly many of the Northern troops had behaved. His account aroused intense criticism, but on the whole it was just and fair.

JULY 20TH, 1861.—

The great battle which is to arrest rebellion or to make it a power in the land is no longer distant or doubtful. McDowell has completed his reconnaissance of the country in front of the enemy, and General Scott anticipates that he will be in possession of Manassas tomorrow night.

Some senators and many congressmen have already gone to join McDowell's army or to follow in its wake in the hope of seeing the Lord deliver the Philistines into his hands. Every carriage, gig, wagon, and hack has been engaged by people going out to see the fight. The price is enhanced by mysterious communications respecting the horrible slaughter in the skirmishes at Bull Run. The French cooks and hotelkeepers, by some occult process of reasoning, have arrived at the conclusion that they must treble the prices of their wines and of the hampers of provisions which the Washington people are ordering to comfort themselves at their bloody Derby. . . .

It was a strange scene before us. From the hill a densely wooded country, dotted at intervals with green fields and cleared lands, spread five or six miles in front, bounded by a line of blue and purple ridges, terminating abruptly in escarpments toward the left front and swelling gradually towards the right into the lower spines of an offshoot from the Blue Ridge Mountains. On our left the view was circumscribed by a forest which clothed the side of the ridge on which we stood and covered its shoulder far down into the plain. A gap in the nearest chain of the hills in our front was pointed out by the bystanders as the Pass of Manassas by which the railway from the west is carried into the plain, and still nearer at hand before us is the junction of that rail with the line from Alexandria and with the railway leading southward to Richmond. The intervening space was not a dead level; undulating lines of forest marked the course of the streams which intersected it and gave by their variety of color and shading an additional charm to the landscape, which, enclosed in a framework of blue and purple hills, softened into violet in the extreme distance, presented one of the most agreeable displays of simple pastoral woodland scenery that could be conceived.

But the sounds which came upon the breeze and the sights which met our eyes were in terrible variance with the tranquil character of the landscape. The woods far and near echoed to the roar of cannon, and thin, frayed lines of blue smoke marked the spots whence came the muttering sound of rolling musketry; the white puffs of smoke burst high above the treetops, and the gunners' rings from shell and howitzer marked the fire of the artillery.

Clouds of dust shifted and moved through the forest, and through the wavering mists of light blue smoke and the thicker masses which rose commingling from the feet of men and the mouths of cannon, I could see the gleam of arms and the twinkling of bayonets.

On the hill beside me there was a crowd of civilians on horseback and in all sorts of vehicles, with a few of the fairer, if not gentler, sex. A few officers and some soldiers, who had straggled from the regiments in reserve, moved about among the spectators and pretended to explain the movements of the troops below, of which they were profoundly ignorant.

The spectators were all excited, and a lady with an opera glass who was near me was quite beside herself when an unusually heavy discharge roused the current of her blood—"That is splendid. Oh, my! Is not that first-rate? I guess we will be in Richmond this time tomorrow." These, mingled with coarser exclamations, burst from the politicians who had come out to see the triumph of the Union arms.

Loud cheers suddenly burst from the spectators as a man dressed in the uniform of an officer, whom I had seen riding violently across the plain in an open space below, galloped along the front, waving his cap and shouting at the top of his voice. He was brought up, by the press of people round his horse, close to where I stood. "We've whipped them on all points," he cried. "We have taken all their batteries. They are retreating as fast as they can, and we are after them." Such cheers as rent the welkin! The congressmen shook hands with each other and cried out: "Bully for us! Bravo! Didn't I tell you so?" The Germans uttered their martial cheers, and the Irish hurrahed wildly. At this moment my horse was brought up the hill and I mounted and turned toward the road to the front . . .

I had ridden between three and a half and four miles, as well as I could judge, when I was obliged to turn for the third and fourth time into the road by a considerable stream which was spanned by a bridge, toward which I was threading my way, when my attention was attracted by loud shouts in advance and I perceived several wagons coming from the direction of the battlefield, the drivers of which were endeavoring to force their horses past the ammunition carts going in the contrary direction near the bridge; a thick cloud of dust rose behind them, and running by the side of the wagons were a number of men in uniform whom I supposed to be the guard. My first impression was that the wagons were returning for fresh supplies of ammunition. But every moment the crowd increased; drivers and men cried out with the most vehement gestures: "Turn back! Turn back! We are whipped." They seized the heads of the horses and swore at the opposing drivers. Emerging from the crowd, a breathless man in the uniform of an officer, with an empty scabbard dangling by his side, was cut off by getting between my horse and a cart for a moment. "What is the matter, sir? What is all this about?" "Why, it means we are pretty badly whipped, that's the truth," he gasped, and continued.

By this time the confusion had been communicating itself through the line of wagons toward the rear, and the drivers endeavored to turn round their vehicles in the narrow road, which caused the usual amount of imprecations from the men and plunging and kicking from the horses.

The crowd from the front continually increased, the heat, the uproar, and the dust were beyond description, and these were augmented when some cavalry soldiers, flourishing their sabers and preceded by an officer, who cried out, "Make way there—make way there for the General," attempted to force a covered wagon, in which was seated a man with a bloody handkerchief round his head, through the press.

I had succeeded in getting across the bridge, with great difficulty, before the wagon came up, and I saw the crowd on the road was still gathering thicker and thicker. Again I asked an officer, who was on foot with his sword under his arm, "What is all this for?" "We are whipped, sir. We are all in retreat. You are all to go back." "Can you tell me where I can find General McDowell?" "No! nor can anyone else."

In a few seconds a crowd of men rushed out of the wood down toward the guns, and the artillerymen near me seized the trail of a piece and were wheeling it round to fire when an officer or sergeant called out: "Stop! stop! They are our own men"; and in two or three minutes the whole battalion came sweeping past the guns at the double and in the utmost disorder. Some of the artillerymen dragged the horses out of the tumbrels, and for a moment the confusion was so great I could not understand what had taken place, but a soldier whom I stopped said, "We are pursued by their cavalry; they have cut us all to pieces."

Murat himself would not have dared to move a squadron on such ground. However, it could not be doubted that something serious was taking place, and at that moment a shell burst in front of the house, scattering the soldiers near it, which was followed by another that bounded along the road, and in a few minutes more out came another regiment from the wood, almost as broken as the first. The scene on the road had now assumed an aspect which has not a parallel in any description I have ever read. Infantry soldiers on mules and draft horses with the harness clinging to their heels, as much frightened as their riders; Negro servants on their masters' chargers; ambulances crowded with unwounded soldiers; wagons swarming with men who threw out the contents in the road to make room, grinding through a shouting, screaming mass of men on foot who were literally yelling with rage at every halt and shrieking out: "Here are the cavalry! Will you get on?" This portion of the force was evidently in discord.

There was nothing left for it but to go with the current one could not stem. I turned round my horse . . . I was unwillingly approaching Centerville in the midst of heat, dust, confusion, imprecations inconceivable. On arriving at the place where a small rivulet crossed the road the throng increased still more. The ground over which I had passed going out was now covered with arms, clothing of all kinds, accouterments thrown off and left to be trampled in the dust under the hoofs of men and horses. The runaways ran alongside the wagons, striving to force themselves in among the occupants, who resisted tooth and nail. The drivers spurred and whipped and urged the horses to the utmost of their bent. I felt an inclination to laugh, which was overcome by disgust and by that vague sense of something extraordinary taking place which is experienced when a man sees a number of people acting as if driven by some unknown terror. As I rode in the crowd, with men clinging to the stirrup leathers or holding on by anything they could lay hands on, so that I had some apprehension of being pulled off, I spoke to the men and asked them over and over again not to be in such a hurry. "There's no enemy to pursue you. All the cavalry in the world could not get at you." But I might as well have talked to the stones.

It never occurred to me that this was a grand debacle. All along I believed the mass of the army was not broken and that all I saw around was the result of confusion created in a crude organization by a forced retreat, and knowing the reserves were at Centerville and beyond, I said to myself, "Let us see how this will be when we get to the hill."

I was trotting quietly down the hill road beyond Centerville when suddenly the guns on the other side or from a battery very near opened fire, and a fresh outburst of artillery sounded through the woods. In an instant the mass of vehicles and retreating soldiers, teamsters, and civilians, as if agonized by an electric shock, quivered throughout the tortuous line. With dreadful shouts and cursings the drivers lashed their maddened horses and, leaping from the carts, left them to their fate and ran on foot. Artillerymen and foot soldiers and Negroes, mounted on gun horses with the chain traces and loose trappings trailing in the dust, spurred and flogged their steeds down the road or by the side paths. The firing continued and seemed to approach the hill, and at every report the agitated body of horsemen and wagons was seized, as it were, with a fresh convulsion.

Once more the dreaded cry: "The cavalry! cavalry are coming!" rang through the crowd, and looking back to Centerville, I perceived coming down the hill, between me and the sky, a number of mounted men who might at a hasty glance be taken for horsemen in the act of sabering the fugitives. In reality they were soldiers and civilians, with, I regret to say, some officers among them, who were whipping and striking their horses with sticks or whatever else they could lay hands on. I called out to the men who were frantic with terror beside me, "They are not cavalry at all; they're your own men"—but they did not heed me. A fellow who was shouting out, "Run! run!" as loud as he could beside me, seemed to take delight in creating alarm, and as he was perfectly collected as far as I could judge, I said: "What on earth are you running for? What are you afraid of?" He was in the roadside below me and, at once turning on me and exclaiming, "I'm not afraid of you," presented his piece and pulled the trigger so instantaneously that had it gone off I could not have swerved from the ball. As the scoundrel deliberately drew up to examine the nipple, I judged it best not to give him another chance and spurred on through the crowd, where any man could have shot as many as he pleased without interruption. The only conclusion I came to was that he was mad or drunken. When I was passing by the line of the bivouacs a battalion of men came tumbling down the bank from the field into the road with fixed bayonets, and as some fell in the road and others tumbled on top of them, there must have been a few ingloriously wounded.

22ND.—

I awoke from a deep sleep this morning about six o'clock. The rain was falling in torrents and beat with a dull, thudding sound on the leads outside my window; but louder than all came a strange sound as if of the tread of men, a confused tramp and splashing and a murmuring of voices. I got up and ran to the front room, the windows of which looked on the street, and there, to my intense surprise, I saw a steady stream of men covered with mud, soaked through with rain, who were pouring irregularly, without any semblance of order, up Pennsylvania Avenue toward the Capitol. A dense stream of vapor rose from the multitude, but looking closely at the men, I perceived they belonged to different regiments, New Yorkers, Michiganders, Rhode Islanders, Massachusetters, Minnesotans, mingled pell-mell together. Many of them were without knapsacks, crossbelts, and firelocks. Some had neither greatcoats nor shoes; others were covered with blankets. Hastily putting on my clothes, I ran downstairs and asked an officer who was passing by, a pale young man who looked exhausted to death and who had lost his sword, for the empty sheath dangled at his side, where the men were coming from. "Where from? Well, sir, I guess we're all coming out of

Virginny as far as we can, and pretty well whipped too." "What! the whole army, sir?" "That's more than I know. They may stay that like. I know I'm going home. I've had enough of fighting to last my lifetime."

The news seemed incredible. But there before my eyes were the jaded, dispirited, broken remnants of regiments passing onward, where and for what I knew not, and it was evident enough that the mass of the grand army of the Potomac was placing that river between it and the enemy as rapidly as possible. "Is there any pursuit?" I asked of several men. Some were too surly to reply; others said, "They're coming as fast as they can after us"; others, "I guess they've stopped it now—the rain is too much for them." A few said they did not know and looked as if they did not care.

The rain has abated a little, and the pavements are densely packed with men in uniforms, some with, others without, arms, on whom the shopkeepers are looking with evident alarm. They seem to be in possession of all the spirit houses. Now and then shots are heard down the street or in the distance, and cries and shouting, as if a scuffle or a difficulty were occurring. Willard's is turned into a barrack for officers and presents such a scene in the hall as could only be witnessed in a city occupied by a demoralized army. There is no provost guard, no patrol, no authority visible in the streets. General Scott is quite overwhelmed by the affair and is unable to stir. General McDowell has not yet arrived. The Secretary of War knows not what to do, Mr. Lincoln is equally helpless, and Mr. Seward, who retains some calmness, is, notwithstanding his military rank and militia experience, without resource or expedient. There are a good many troops hanging on about the camps and forts on the other side of the river, it is said; but they are thoroughly disorganized and will run away if the enemy comes in sight without a shot, and then the capital must fall at once. Why Beauregard does not come I know not, nor can I well guess. I have been expecting every hour since noon to hear his cannon. Here is a golden opportunity. If the Confederates do not grasp that which will never come again on such terms, it stamps them with mediocrity.

WILLIAM HOWARD RUSSELL
My Diary North and South

61

The *Monitor* and the *Merrimac*

When reports reached the North that the Confederates were converting the ship *Merrimac,* captured at Norfolk, into an ironclad, the Navy Department asked for bids for the building of armored vessels. The well-known naval engineer John Ericsson, who had been born in Sweden, was among those who replied. His small armored ship the *Monitor* was launched on January 30, 1862, just in time to meet the *Merrimac* when she finally came out to attack the Union fleet. The great duel of March 9, 1862, between these two craft is one of the most famous naval encounters in modern history.

U.S. Steamer *Monitor*, Hampton Roads, Va.—

At 4 P.M. [March 8, 1862] we passed Cape Henry and heard heavy firing in the direction of Fortress Monroe. As we approached, it increased, and we immediately cleared ship for action. When about halfway between Fortress Monroe and Cape Henry we spoke [to] the pilot boat. He told us the *Cumberland* was sunk and the *Congress* was on fire and had surrendered to the *Merrimac.* We could not credit it at first, but as we approached Hampton Roads, we could see the fine old *Congress* burning brightly, and we knew it must be true. Sad indeed did we feel to think those two fine old vessels had gone to their last homes with so many of their brave crews. Our hearts were very full, and we vowed vengeance on the *Merrimac* if it should be our lot to fall in with her. At 9 P.M. we anchored near the frigate *Roanoke,* the flagship, *Captain Marston.* Captain Worden immediately went on board and received orders to proceed to Newport News and protect the *Minnesota* (then aground) from the *Merrimac.*

We got under way and arrived at the *Minnesota* at 11 P.M. I went on board in our cutter and asked the captain what his prospects were of getting off. He said he should try to get afloat at 2 A.M., when it was high water. I asked him if we could render him any assistance, to which he replied, "No!" I then told him we should do all in our power to protect him from the *Merrimac.* He thanked me kindly and wished us success. Just as I arrived back to the *Monitor* the *Congress* blew up, and certainly a grander sight was never seen, but it went straight to the marrow of our bones. Not a word was said, but deeply did each man think and wish we were by the side of the *Merrimac.* At 1 A.M. we anchored near the *Minnesota.* The captain and myself remained on deck, waiting for the appearance of the *Merrimac.* At 3 A.M. we thought the *Minnesota* was afloat and coming down on us, so we got under way as soon as possible and stood out of the channel. After backing and filling about for an hour, we found we were mistaken and anchored again. At daylight we discovered the *Merrimac* at anchor with several vessels under Sewall's Point. We immediately made every preparation for battle. At 8 A.M. on Sunday the *Merrimac* got under way, accompanied by several steamers, and started direct for the *Minnesota*. When a mile distant she fired two guns at her. By this time our anchor was up, the men at quarters, the guns loaded, and everything ready for action. As the *Merrimac* came close, the captain passed the word to commence firing. I triced up the port, ran out the gun, and fired the *first* gun, and thus commenced the great battle between the *Monitor* and the *Merrimac*.

Now mark the condition our men and officers were in. Since Friday morning, forty-eight hours, they had had no rest and very little food, as we could not conveniently cook. They had been hard at work all night, and nothing to eat for breakfast except hard bread, and were thoroughly worn out. As for myself, I had not slept a wink for fifty-one hours and had been on my feet almost constantly. But after the first gun was fired we forgot all fatigues, hard work, and everything else and fought as hard as men ever fought. We loaded and fired as fast as we could. I pointed and fired the guns myself. Every shot I would ask the captain the effect, and the majority of them were encouraging. The captain was in the pilothouse, directing the movements of the vessel; Acting Master Stodder was stationed at the wheel which turns the tower but, as he could not manage it, was relieved by Steiners. The speaking trumpet from the tower to the pilothouse was broken, so we passed the word from the captain to myself on the berth deck by Paymaster Keeler and Captain's Clerk Toffey. Five times during the engagement we touched each other, and each time I fired a gun at her, and I will vouch the hundred and sixty-eight pounds penetrated her sides. Once she tried to run us down with her iron prow but did no damage whatever. After fighting for two hours we hauled off for half an hour to hoist shot in the tower. At it we went again as hard as we could, the shot, shell, grape, canister, musket, and rifle balls flying in every direction but doing no damage. Our tower was struck several times, and though the noise was pretty loud it did not affect us any. Stodder and one of the men were carelessly leaning against the tower when a shot struck it exactly opposite them and disabled them for an hour or two. At about 11:30 A.M. the captain sent for me. I went forward, and there stood as noble a man as lives, at the foot of the ladder to the pilothouse, his face perfectly black with powder and iron, and apparently perfectly blind. I asked him what was the matter. He said a shot had struck the pilothouse exactly opposite his eyes and blinded him, and he thought the pilothouse was damaged. He told me to take charge of the ship and use my own discretion. I led him to his room, laid him on the sofa, and then took his position. On examining the pilothouse I found the iron hatch on top, on the forward side, was completely cracked through. We still continued firing, the tower being under the direction of Steiners. We were between two fires, the *Minnesota* on one side and the *Mer*-

rimac on the other. The latter was retreating to Sewall's Point, and the *Minnesota* had struck us twice on the tower. I knew if another shot should strike our pilothouse in the same place, our steering apparatus would be disabled, and we should be at the mercy of the batteries on Sewall's Point. We had *strict* orders to act on the defensive and protect the *Minnesota*. We had evidently finished the *Merrimac* as far as the *Minnesota* was concerned. Our pilothouse was damaged, and we had orders *not* to follow the *Merrimac* up; therefore, after the *Merrimac* had retreated, I went to the *Minnesota* and remained by her until she was afloat. General Wool and Secretary Fox both commended me for acting as I did and said it was the strict military plan to follow. This is the reason we did not sink the *Merrimac,* and everyone here capable of judging says we acted perfectly right.

JOHN ERICSSON
Soldiers' Letters from Camp, Battle-field, and Prison

62

Eating Mules at Port Hudson

When General N.P. Banks led the Union forces from New Orleans up the Mississippi toward Vicksburg, he found his way blocked by heavy fortifications at Port Hudson (135 miles above New Orleans), with a garrison that was soon increased to 6,000 men. Flanking movements failed, and there was nothing to do but lay siege to the place. The investment was completed on May 26, 1863, and during all of June the Union forces hemmed in the Confederates along a front of seven miles. Both sides suffered severely, the Federal troops from sickness, the Confederates from increasing hunger. By the beginning of July the garrison was literally starving. Here one of the officers describes their straits.

The last quarter ration of beef had been given out to the troops on the 29th of June [1863]. On the 1st of July, at the request of many officers, a wounded mule was killed and cut up for experimental eating. All those who partook of it spoke highly of the dish. The flesh of mules is of a darker color than beef, of a finer grain, quite tender and juicy, and has a flavor something between that of beef and venison. There was an immediate demand for this kind of food, and the number of mules killed by the commissariat daily increased. Some horses were also slaughtered, and their flesh was found to be very good eating, but not equal to mule. Rats, of which there were plenty about the deserted camps, were also caught by many officers and men and were found to be quite a luxury—superior, in the opinion of those who eat them, to spring chicken, and if a philosopher of the Celestial Empire could have visited Port Hudson at the time, he would have marveled at the progress of the barbarians there toward the refinements of his own people.

Mule meat was regularly served out in rations to the troops from and after the 4th of July, and there were very few among the garrison whose natural prejudices were so strong as to prevent them from cooking and eating their share. The stock of corn was getting very low, and besides that nothing was left but peas, sugar, and molasses. These peas were the most indigestible and unwholesome articles that were ever given to soldiers to eat, and that such a large quantity was left on hand was probably accounted for by the fact that most of the troops would not have them on any consideration. To save corn they were issued out to horses and mules and killed a great many of these animals. All of the horses and mules which were not needed for hauling or other imperative duties had been turned out to graze, where numbers of them were killed or disabled by the enemy's cannonade and rain of Minié balls and the rest nearly starved to death.

The sugar and molasses were put to good use by the troops in making a weak description of beer, which was constantly kept at the lines by the barrelful and drunk by the soldiers in preference to the miserable water with which they were generally supplied. This was a very pleasant and healthful beverage and went far to recompense the men for the lack of almost every other comfort or luxury. In the same way, after the stock of tobacco had given out, they substituted sumac leaves, which grew wild in the woods. It had always been smoked by the Indians under the name of killickinnic and when properly prepared for the pipe is a tolerably good substitute for tobacco.

There was a small proportion of the garrison who could not, however, reconcile themselves so easily to the hardships and dangers of the siege. Some one hundred and fifty or more men, almost entirely foreigners of a low class or ignorant conscripts from western Louisiana, men who were troubled with none of that common feeling usually styled patriotism, deserted us for the better-provided commissariats of the enemy, slinking away by couples and squads during the nighttime. Their loss was not wept over, nor could the information they carried with them concerning our position enable the enemy to capture it.

HOWARD C. WRIGHT
Port Hudson—Its History from an Interior Point of View,
as Sketched from the Diary of an Officer

63

General Lee Invades Pennsylvania

After his victories at Fredericksburg and Chancellorsville, General Lee resolved to invade the North. He felt confident in the superior fighting ability of his troops and overestimated the effect of successive defeats on the morale of the Northern armies. While he knew that Grant was likely soon to capture Vicksburg, he rejected Longstreet's proposal that he try to save the situation in the West by advancing against Cincinnati. Before the middle of June his army was on the march. On the twenty-fourth and twenty-fifth Longstreet and Hill crossed the Potomac and pushed toward the heart of Pennsylvania. Before the month ended, Lee's troops had captured Chambersburg and York and were menacing Harrisburg, but the Union army under Meade was coming up rapidly.

CAMP NEAR GREENWOOD, PA., JUNE 28, 1863.—
My own darling wife:

You can see by the date of this that we are now in Pennsylvania. We crossed the line day before yesterday and are resting today near a little one-horse town on the road to Gettysburg, which we will reach tomorrow. We are paying back these people for some of the damage they have done us, though we are not doing them half as bad as they done us. We are getting up all the horses, etc., and feeding our army with their beef and flour, etc., but there are strict orders about the interruption of any private property by individual soldiers.

Though with these orders, fowls and pigs and eatables don't stand much chance. I felt when I first came here that I would like to revenge myself upon these people for the desolation they have brought upon our own beautiful home, that home where we could have lived so happy and that we loved so much, from which their vandalism has driven you and my helpless little ones. But though I had such severe wrongs and grievances to redress and such great cause for revenge, yet when I got among these people I could not find it in my heart to molest them. They looked so dreadfully scared and talked so humble that I have invariably endeavored to protect their property and have prevented soldiers from taking chickens, even in the main road; yet there is a good deal of plundering going on, confined principally to the taking of provisions. No houses were searched and robbed, like our houses were done by the Yankees. Pigs, chickens, geese, etc., are finding their way into our camp; it can't be prevented, and I can't think it ought to be. We must show them something of war. I have sent out today to get a good horse; I have no scruples about that, as they have taken mine. We took a lot of Negroes yesterday. I was offered my choice, but as I could not get them back home I would not take them. In fact my humanity revolted at taking the poor devils away from their homes. They were so scared that I turned them all loose.

I dined yesterday with two old maids. They treated me very well and seemed greatly in favor of peace. I have had a great deal of fun since I have been here. The country that we have passed through is beautiful, and everything in the greatest abundance. You never saw such a land of plenty. We could live here mighty well for the next twelve months, but I suppose old Hooker will try to put a stop to us pretty soon. Of course we will have to fight here, and when it comes it will be the biggest on record. Our men feel that there is to be no back-out. A defeat here would be ruinous. This army has never done such fighting as it will do now, and if we can whip the armies that are now gathering to oppose us, we will have everything in our own hands. We must conquer a peace. If we can come out of this country triumphant and victorious, having established a peace, we will bring back to our own land the greatest joy that ever crowned a people. We will show the Yankees this time how we can fight.

Be of good cheer, and write often to your fondly attached husband.

William S. Christian
The Rebellion Record

64

High Tide at Gettysburg

The culminating event of the three-day battle of Gettysburg was the assault of 15,000 Confederate troops under General George Pickett upon the Union lines strongly posted along Cemetery Ridge. The thrust was preceded by a three-hour bombardment by 115 Confederate guns, to which 80 Federal guns replied. At two o'clock in the afternoon the great charge began. Pickett's men had nearly a mile to go; they moved at a walk, keeping their lines as precisely as on parade; and as they came under a withering Union fire the slaughter was terrific. "A thousand fell where Kemper led, a thousand died where Garnett bled." The Confederate battle flags were planted at one point on the crest of the ridge—but they were kept there only a few minutes. Here the story is told by an English observer, and by one of Lee's most gifted but most stubborn generals.

Part I

JULY 2, 1863 (THURSDAY).—

I arrived at 5 A.M. at the same commanding position we were on yesterday, and I climbed up a tree in company with Captain Schreibert of the Prussian army. Just below us were seated Generals Lee, Hill, Longstreet, and Hood in consultation, the two latter assisting their deliberations by the truly American custom of whittling sticks. General Heth was also present; he was wounded in the head yesterday, and although not allowed to command his brigade, he insists upon coming to the field.

At 7 A.M. I rode over part of the ground with General Longstreet and saw him disposing of McLaws' division for today's fight. The enemy occupied a series of high ridges, the tops of which were covered with trees, but the intervening valleys between their ridges and ours were mostly open and partly under cultivation. The cemetery was on their right, and their left appeared to rest upon a high rocky hill. The enemy's forces, which were now supposed to comprise nearly the whole Potomac army, were concentrated into a space apparently not more than a couple of miles in length. The Confederates enclosed them in a sort of semicircle, and the extreme extent of our position must have been from five to six miles at least. The enemy was evidently entrenched, but the Southerns had not broken ground at all. A dead silence reigned till 4:45 P.M., and no one would have imagined that such masses of men and such a powerful artillery were about to commence the work of destruction at that hour.

At that time, however, Longstreet suddenly commenced a heavy cannonade on the right. Ewell immediately took it up on the left. The enemy replied with at least equal fury, and in a few moments the firing along the whole line was as heavy as it is possible to conceive. A dense smoke arose for six miles, there was little wind to drive it away, and the air seemed full of shells. Every now and then a caisson would blow up; if a Federal one, a Confederate yell would immediately follow. The Southern troops, when charging or to express their delight, always yell in a manner peculiar to themselves. The Yankee cheer is much more like ours, but the Confederate officers declare that the rebel yell has a particular merit and always produces a salutary and useful effect upon their adversaries. A corps is sometimes spoken of as a good yelling regiment.

So soon as the firing began, General Lee joined Hill just below our tree, and he remained there nearly all the time, looking through his field glass, sometimes talking to Hill and sometimes to Colonel Long of his staff. But generally he sat quite alone on the stump of a tree. What I remarked especially was that during the whole time the firing continued he sent only one message and only received one report. It is evidently his system to arrange the plan thoroughly with the three corps commanders and then leave to them the duty of modifying and carrying it out to the best of their abilities.

When the cannonade was at its height, a Confederate band of music, between the cemetery and ourselves, began to play polkas and waltzes, which sounded very curious, accompanied by the hissing and bursting of shells.

At five-forty-five all became comparatively quiet on our left and in the cemetery, but volleys of musketry on the right told us that Longstreet's infantry were advancing, and the onward progress of the smoke showed that he was progressing favorably. But about six-thirty there seemed to be a check and even a slight retrograde movement. Soon after seven, General Lee got a report by signal from Longstreet to say "we are doing well."

A little before dark the firing dropped off in every direction and soon ceased altogether.

3RD.—

The distance between the Confederate guns and the Yankee position— i.e., between the woods crowning the opposite ridges—was at least a mile, quite open, gently undulating, and exposed to artillery the whole distance. This was the ground which had to be crossed in today's attack. Pickett's division, which had just come up, was to bear the brunt in Longstreet's attack, together with Heth and Pettigrew in Hill's corps. Pickett's division was a weak one (under five thousand), owing to the absence of two brigades.

At noon all Longstreet's dispositions were made; his troops for attack were deployed into line and lying down in the woods; his batteries were ready to open. The General then dismounted and went to sleep for a short time.

Finding that to see the actual fighting it was absolutely necessary to go into the thick of the thing, I determined to make my way to General Longstreet. It was then about two-thirty. After passing General Lee and his staff, I rode on through the woods in the direction in which I had left Longstreet. I soon began to meet many wounded men returning from the front; many of them asked in piteous tones the way to a doctor or an ambulance. The farther I got, the greater became the number of the wounded. At last I came to a perfect stream of them flocking through the woods in numbers as great as the crowd in Oxford Street in the middle of the day. Some were walking alone on crutches composed of two rifles, others supported by men less badly wounded than themselves, and others were carried on stretchers by the ambulance corps, but in no case did I see a sound man helping the wounded to the rear unless he carried the red badge of the ambulance corps. They were still under a heavy fire; the shells were continually bringing down great limbs of trees and carrying further destruction amongst this melancholy procession. I saw all this in much less time than it takes to write it, and although astonished to meet such vast numbers of wounded, I had not seen enough to give me any idea of the real extent of the mischief.

When I got close up to General Longstreet, I saw one of his regiments advancing through the woods in good order, so thinking I was just in time to see the attack, I remarked to the General that "I wouldn't have missed this for anything." Longstreet was seated at the top of a snake fence at the edge of the wood and looking perfectly calm and unperturbed. He replied, laughing: "The devil you wouldn't! I would like to have missed it very much; we've attacked and been repulsed; look there!"

For the first time I then had a view of the open space between the two positions and saw it covered with Confederates, slowly and sulkily returning toward us in small broken parties, under a heavy fire of artillery. But the fire where we were was not so bad as farther to the rear, for although the air seemed alive with shell, yet the greater number burst behind us. The General told me that Pickett's division had succeeded in carrying the enemy's position and capturing his guns, but after remaining there twenty minutes, it had been forced to retire, on the retreat of Heth and Pettigrew on its left. . . .

Soon afterward I joined General Lee, who had in the meanwhile come to the front on becoming aware of the disaster. If Longstreet's conduct was admirable, that of Lee was perfectly sublime. He was engaged in rallying and in encouraging the broken troops and was raiding about a little in front of the wood, quite alone, the whole of his staff being engaged in a similar manner farther to the rear. His face, which is always placid and cheerful, did not show signs of the slightest disappointment, care, or annoyance, and he was addressing to every soldier he met a few words of encouragement, such as: "All this will come right in the end; we'll talk it over afterwards, but in the meantime, all good men must rally. We want all good and true men just now," etc. He spoke to all the wounded men that passed him, and the slightly wounded he exhorted to "bind up their hurts and take up a musket" in this emergency. Very few failed to answer his appeal, and I saw many badly wounded men take off their hats and cheer him.

He said to me, "This has been a sad day for us, Colonel—a sad day, but we can't expect always to gain victories." I saw General Willcox come up to him and explain, almost crying, the state of his brigade. General Lee immediately shook hands with him and said cheerfully: "Never mind, General, all this has been *my* fault—it is I that have lost this fight, and you must help me out of it in the best way you can."

In this way I saw General Lee encourage and reanimate his somewhat dispirited troops and magnanimously take upon his own shoulders the whole weight of the repulse. It was impossible to look at him or to listen to him without feeling the strongest admiration.

ARTHUR J.L. FREMANTLE
"The Battle of Gettysburg and the Campaign in Pennsylvania"

Part II

The signal guns broke the silence, the blaze of the second gun mingling in the smoke of the first, and salvoes rolled to the left and repeated themselves, the enemy's fine metal spreading its fire to the converging lines, plowing the trembling ground, plunging through the line of batteries, and clouding the heavy air. The two or three hundred guns seemed proud of their undivided honors and organized confusion. The Confederates had the benefit of converging fire into the enemy's massed position, but the superior metal of the enemy neutralized the advantage of position. The brave and steady work progressed. . . .

General Pickett rode to confer with Alexander, then to the ground upon which I was resting, where he was soon handed a slip of paper. After reading it he handed it to me. It read:

If you are coming at all, come at once, or I cannot give you proper support, but the enemy's fire has not slackened at all. At least eighteen guns are still firing from the cemetery itself.

—Alexander

Pickett said, "General, shall I advance?"

The effort to speak the order failed, and I could only indicate it by an affirmative bow. He accepted the duty, with seeming confidence of success, leaped on his horse, and rode gaily to his command. I mounted and spurred for Alexander's post. He reported that the batteries he had reserved for the charge with the infantry had been spirited away by General Lee's chief of artillery, that the ammunition of the batteries of position was so reduced that he could not use them in proper support of the infantry. He was ordered to stop the march at once and fill up his ammunition chests. But, alas! there was no more ammunition to be had.

The order was imperative. The Confederate commander had fixed his heart upon the work. Just then a number of the enemy's batteries hitched up and hauled off, which gave a glimpse of unexpected hope. Encouraging messages were sent for the columns to hurry on—and they were then on elastic springing step. The officers saluted as they passed, their stern smiles expressing confidence. General Pickett, a graceful horseman, sat lightly in the saddle, his brown locks flowing quite over his shoulders. Pettigrew's division spread their steps and quickly rectified the alignment, and the grand march moved bravely on. As soon as the leading columns opened the way, the supports sprang to their alignments. General Trimble mounted, adjusting his seat and reins with an air and grace as if setting out on a pleasant afternoon ride. When aligned to their places solid march was made down the slope and past our batteries of position.

Confederate batteries put their fire over the heads of the men as they moved down the slope and continued to draw the fire of the enemy until the smoke lifted and drifted to the rear, when every gun was turned upon the infantry columns. The batteries that had been drawn off were replaced by others that were fresh. Soldiers and officers began to fall, some to rise no more, others to find their way to the hospital tents. Single files were cut here and there; then the gaps increased, and an occasional shot tore wider openings, but, closing the gaps as quickly as made, the march moved on. . . .

Colonel Latrobe was sent to General Trimble to have his men fill the line of the broken brigades, and bravely they repaired the damage. The enemy moved out against the supporting brigade in Pickett's rear. Colonel Sorrel was sent to have that move guarded, and Pickett was drawn back to that contention. McLaws was ordered to press his left forward, but the direct line of infantry and cross fire of artillery was telling fearfully on the front. Colonel Fremantle ran up to offer congratulations on the apparent success, but the big gaps in the ranks grew until the lines were reduced to half their length. I called his attention to the broken, struggling ranks. Trimble mended the battle of the left in handsome style, but on the right the massing of the enemy grew stronger and stronger. Brigadier Garnett was killed; Kemper and Trimble were desperately wounded; Generals Hancock and Gibbon were wounded. General Lane succeeded Trimble and with Pettigrew held the battle of the left in steady ranks.

Pickett's lines being nearer, the impact was heaviest upon them. Most of the field officers were killed or wounded. Colonel Whittle, of Armistead's brigade, who had been shot through the right leg at Williamsburg and lost his left arm at Malvern Hill, was shot through the right arm, then brought down by a shot through his left leg.

General Armistead, of the second line, spread his steps to supply the places of fallen comrades. His colors cut down, with a volley against the bristling line of bayonets, he put his cap on his sword to guide the storm. The enemy's massing, enveloping numbers held the struggle until the noble Armistead fell beside the wheels of the enemy's battery. Pettigrew was wounded but held his command.

General Pickett, finding the battle broken while the enemy was still reinforcing, called the troops off. There was no indication of panic. The broken files marched back in steady step. The effort was nobly made and failed from blows that could not be fended.

JAMES LONGSTREET
From Manassas to Appomattox

65

General Sherman Marches
from Atlanta to the Sea

When in the spring of 1864 Grant went east to take command of all the Union armies, he left William Tecumseh Sherman in charge in the West. The plan of campaign that summer called for an attack in the East upon Lee's forces in front of Richmond and an attack in the West upon General Johnston's forces in front of Atlanta. Sherman, with about 100,000 men at his back, commenced operations on May 5. On September 2 he captured Atlanta. Six weeks later he set out, with some 62,000 men, to march from Atlanta through the heart of Georgia to Savannah. Living on the country as he went, and destroying munitions, public buildings, and railroads, he made the capture of Savannah a Christmas present to the nation.

About 7 A.M. of November 16th [1864] we rode out of Atlanta by the Decatur road, filled by the marching troops and wagons of the Fourteenth Corps, and reaching the hill, just outside of the old rebel works, we naturally paused to look back upon the scenes of our past battles. We stood upon the very ground whereon was fought the bloody battle of July 22nd and could see the copse of wood where McPherson fell. Behind us lay Atlanta, smoldering and in ruins, the black smoke rising high in air and hanging like a pall over the ruined city. Away off in the distance, on the McDonough road, was the rear of Howard's column, the gun barrels glistening in the sun, the white-topped wagons stretching away to the south, and right before us the Fourteenth Corps, marching steadily and rapidly with a cheery look and swinging pace that made light of the thousand miles that lay between us and Richmond. Some band by accident struck up the anthem of "John Brown's soul goes marching on"; the men caught up the strain, and never before or since have I heard the chorus of "Glory, glory, hallelujah!" done with more spirit or in better harmony of time and place.

Then we turned our horses' heads to the east; Atlanta was soon lost behind the screen of trees and became a thing of the past. Around it clings many a thought of desperate battle, of hope and fear, that now seem like the memory of a dream, and I have never seen the place since. The day was extremely beautiful, clear sunlight, with bracing air, and an unusual feeling of exhilaration seemed to pervade all minds—a feeling of something to come, vague and undefined, still full of venture and intense interest. Even the common soldiers caught the inspiration, and many a group called out to me as

I worked my way past them, "Uncle Billy, I guess Grant is waiting for us at Richmond!" Indeed, the general sentiment was that we were marching for Richmond and that there we should end the war, but how and when they seemed to care not; nor did they measure the distance or count the cost in life or bother their brains about the great rivers to be crossed and the food, required for man and beast, that had to be gathered by the way. There was a devil-may-care feeling pervading officers and men that made me feel the full load of responsibility, for success would be accepted as a matter of course, whereas should we fail, this march would be adjudged the wild adventure of a crazy fool.

I had no purpose to march direct for Richmond by way of Augusta and Charlotte but always designed to reach the seacoast first at Savannah or Port Royal, South Carolina, and even kept in mind the alternative of Pensacola.

The first night out we camped by the roadside near Lithonia. Stone Mountain, a mass of granite, was in plain view, cut out in clear outline against the blue sky; the whole horizon was lurid with the bonfires of rail ties, and groups of men all night were carrying the heated rails to the nearest trees and bending them around the trunks. Colonel Poe had provided tools for ripping up the rails and twisting them when hot, but the best and easiest way is . . . heating the middle of the iron rails on bonfires made of the cross ties and then winding them around a telegraph pole or the trunk of some convenient sapling. I attached much importance to this destruction of the railroad, gave it my personal attention, and made reiterated orders to others on the subject.

The next day we passed through the handsome town of Covington, the soldiers closing up their ranks, the color-bearers unfurling their flags, and the band striking up patriotic airs. The white people came out of their houses to behold the sight, spite of their deep hatred of the invaders, and the Negroes were simply frantic with joy. Whenever they heard my name, they clustered about my horse, shouted and prayed in their peculiar style, which had a natural eloquence that would have moved a stone. I have witnessed hundreds, if not thousands, of such scenes and can now see a poor girl, in the very ecstasy of the Methodist "shout," hugging the banner of one of the regiments and jumping up to the "feet of Jesus."

I remember, when riding around by a bystreet in Covington to avoid the crowd that followed the marching column, that someone brought me an invitation to dine with a sister of Samuel Anderson, who was a cadet at West Point with me, but the messenger reached me after we had passed the main part of the town. I asked to be excused and rode on to a place designated for camp, at the crossing of the Ulcofauhachee River, about four miles to the east of the town. Here we made our bivouac, and I walked up to a plantation house close by, where were assembled many Negroes, among them an old gray-haired man, of as fine a head as I ever saw. I asked him if he understood about the war and its progress. He said he did, that he had been looking for the "angel of the Lord" ever since he was knee-high, and though we professed to be fighting for the Union, he supposed that slavery was the cause and that our success was to be his freedom. I asked him if all the Negro slaves comprehended this fact, and he said they surely did. I then explained to him that we wanted the slaves to remain where they were and not to load us down with useless mouths, which would eat up the food needed for our fighting men, that our success was their assured freedom, that we could receive a few of their young, hearty men as pioneers, but that if they followed us in swarms of old and young, feeble and helpless, it would simply load us down and cripple us in our great task. I think Major Henry Hitchcock was with me on that occasion and made a note of the conversation, and I believe that old man spread this message to the slaves, which was carried from mouth to mouth to the very end of our journey, and that it in part saved us from the great danger we incurred of swelling our numbers so that famine would have attended our progress.

It was at this very plantation that a soldier passed me with a ham on his musket, a jug of sorghum molasses under his arm, and a big piece of honey in his hand, from which he was eating, and catching my eye, he remarked *sotto voce* and carelessly to a comrade, "Forage liberally on the country," quoting from my general orders. On this occasion, as on many others that fell under my personal observation, I reproved the man, explained that foraging must be limited to the regular parties properly detailed and that all provisions thus obtained must be delivered to the regular commissaries to be fairly distributed to the men who kept their ranks.

From Covington the Fourteenth Corps [Davis'], with which I was traveling, turned to the right for Milledgeville via Shady Dale. General Slocum was ahead at Madison with the Twentieth Corps, having torn up the railroad as far as that place, and thence had sent Geary's division on to the Oconee to burn the bridges across that stream when this corps turned south by Eatonton for Milledgeville, the common objective for the first stage of the march. We found abundance of corn, molasses, meal, bacon, and sweet potatoes. We also took a good many cows and oxen and a large number of mules. In all these the country was quite rich, never before having been visited by a hostile army; the recent crop had been excellent, had been just gathered and laid by for the winter. As a rule, we destroyed none but kept our wagons full and fed our teams bountifully.

The skill and success of the men in collecting forage was one of the features of this march. Each brigade commander had authority to detail a company of foragers, usually about fifty men, with one or two commissioned officers selected for their boldness and enterprise. This party would be dispatched before daylight with a knowledge of the intended day's march and camp, would proceed on foot five or six miles from the route traveled by their brigade, and then visit every plantation and farm within range. They would usually procure a wagon or family carriage, load it with bacon, cornmeal, turkeys, chickens, ducks, and everything that could be used as food or forage, and would then regain the main road, usually in advance of their train. When this came up, they would deliver to the brigade commissary the supplies thus gathered by the way. Often would I pass these foraging parties at the roadside, waiting for their wagons to come up, and was amused at their strange collections—mules, horses, even cattle, packed with old saddles and loaded with hams, bacon, bags of cornmeal, and poultry of every character and description. Although this foraging was attended with great danger and hard work, there seemed to be a charm about it that attracted the soldiers, and it was a privilege to be detailed on such a party. Daily they returned mounted on all sorts of beasts, which were at once taken from them and appropriated to the general use, but the next day they would start out again on foot, only to repeat the experience of the day before. No doubt, many acts of pillage, robbery, and violence were committed by these parties of foragers, usually called bummers, for I have since heard of jewelry taken from women and the plunder of articles that never reached the commissary, but these acts were exceptional and incidental. I never heard of any cases of murder or rape, and no army could have carried along sufficient food and forage for a march of three hundred miles, so that foraging in some shape was necessary. The country was sparsely settled, with no magistrates or civil authorities who could respond to requisitions, as is done in all the wars of Europe, so that this system of foraging was simply indispensable to our success. By it our men were well supplied with all the essentials of life and health, while the wagons retained enough in case of unexpected delay, and our animals were well fed. Indeed, when we reached Savannah, the trains were pronounced by experts to be the finest in flesh and appearance ever seen with any army.

The Memoirs of General William T. Sherman

66

General Lee Surrenders at Appomattox

By March 1865, the Confederate forces under Lee in front of Petersburg and Richmond were reduced to about 50,000 men, while Grant had 124,000, far better fed and equipped. On April 2, by a series of fierce attacks, Grant finally broke the Confederate lines before Petersburg. That night Lee, abandoning the capital, began to march his army toward Danville and the mountainous country of western Virginia. But Sheridan cut off his retreat and Grant brought him to bay at Appomattox. The story of the surrender is here told by Grant himself.

When the white flag was put out by Lee I was moving toward Appomattox Courthouse and consequently could not be communicated with immediately and be informed of what Lee had done. Lee, therefore, sent a flag to the rear to advise Meade and one to the front to Sheridan, saying that he had sent a message to me for the purpose of having a meeting to consult about the surrender of his army, and asked for a suspension of hostilities until I could be communicated with. As they had heard nothing of this until the fighting had got to be severe and all going against Lee, both of these commanders hesitated very considerably about suspending hostilities at all. They were afraid it was not in good faith, and we had the Army of Northern Virginia where it could not escape except by some deception. They, however, finally consented to a suspension of hostilities for two hours to give an opportunity of communicating with me in that time, if possible. It was found that, from the route I had taken, they would probably not be able to communicate with me and get an answer back within the time fixed unless the messenger should pass through the rebel lines.

Lee, therefore, sent an escort with the officer bearing this message through his lines to me.

April 9, 1865

General:
I received your note of this morning on the picket line, whither I had come to meet you and ascertain definitely what terms were embraced in your proposal of yesterday with reference to the surrender of this army. I now request an interview in accordance with the offer contained in your letter of yesterday for that purpose.

R.E. Lee, General
Lieutenant General U.S. Grant,
Commanding U.S. Armies

When the officer reached me I was still suffering with the sick headache, but the instant I saw the contents of the note I was cured. I wrote the following note in reply and hastened on:

April 9, 1865

General R.E. Lee, Commanding C.S. Armies:
Your note of this date is but this moment (11:50 A.M.) received, in consequence of my having passed from the Richmond and Lynchburg road to the Farmville and Lynchburg road. I am at this writing about four miles west

of Walker's Church and will push forward to the front for the purpose of
meeting you. Notice sent to me on this road where you wish the interview
to take place will meet me.

U.S. Grant, Lieutenant General

I was conducted at once to where Sheridan was located with his troops
drawn up in line of battle facing the Confederate army nearby. They were
very much excited and expressed their view that this was all a ruse employed
to enable the Confederates to get away. They said they believed that Johnston
was marching up from North Carolina now, and Lee was moving to join
him, and they would whip the rebels where they now were in five minutes if
I would only let them go in. But I had no doubt about the good faith of Lee
and pretty soon was conducted to where he was. I found him at the house of
a Mr. McLean, at Appomattox Courthouse, with Colonel Marshall, one of his
staff officers, awaiting my arrival. The head of his column was occupying a
hill, on a portion of which was an apple orchard, beyond a little valley which
separated it from that on the crest of which Sheridan's forces were drawn up
in line of battle to the south. . . .

I had known General Lee in the old army and had served with him in the
Mexican War but did not suppose, owing to the difference in our age and
rank, that he would remember me, while I would more naturally remember
him distinctly, because he was the chief of staff of General Scott in the Mexican War.

When I had left camp that morning I had not expected so soon the result
that was then taking place and consequently was in rough garb. I was without a sword, as I usually was when on horseback on the field, and wore a
soldier's blouse for a coat, with the shoulder straps of my rank to indicate to
the army who I was. When I went into the house I found General Lee. We
greeted each other and, after shaking hands, took our seats. I had my staff
with me, a good portion of whom were in the room during the whole of the
interview.

What General Lee's feelings were I do not know. As he was a man of
much dignity, with an impassible face, it was impossible to say whether he
felt inwardly glad that the end had finally come or felt sad over the result and
was too manly to show it. Whatever his feelings, they were entirely concealed
from my observation, but my own feelings, which had been quite jubilant on
the receipt of his letter, were sad and depressed. I felt like anything rather
than rejoicing at the downfall of a foe who had fought so long and valiantly
and had suffered so much for a cause, though that cause was, I believe, one
of the worst for which a people ever fought and one for which there was the
least excuse. I do not question, however, the sincerity of the great mass of
those who were opposed to us.

General Lee was dressed in a full uniform, which was entirely new, and was wearing a sword of considerable value, very likely the sword which had been presented by the State of Virginia; at all events, it was an entirely different sword from the one that would ordinarily be worn in the field. In my rough traveling suit, the uniform of a private with the straps of a lieutenant general, I must have contrasted very strangely with a man so handsomely dressed, six feet high, and of faultless form. But this was not a matter that I thought of until afterward.

We soon fell into a conversation about old army times. He remarked that he remembered me very well in the old army, and I told him that as a matter of course I remembered him perfectly, but from the difference in our rank and years (there being about sixteen years' difference in our ages), I had thought it very likely that I had not attracted his attention sufficiently to be remembered by him after such a long interval. Our conversation grew so pleasant that I almost forgot the object of our meeting. After the conversation had run on in this style for some time, General Lee called my attention to the object of our meeting and said that he had asked for this interview for the purpose of getting from me the terms I proposed to give his army. I said that I meant merely that his army should lay down their arms, not to take them up again during the continuance of the war unless duly and properly exchanged. He said that he had so understood my letter.

Then we gradually fell off again into conversation about matters foreign to the subject which had brought us together. This continued for some little time, when General Lee again interrupted the course of the conversation by suggesting that the terms I proposed to give his army ought to be written out. I called to General Parker, secretary on my staff, for writing materials, and commenced writing out the following terms:

Appomattox Courthouse, Va.
April 9th, 1865
General R.E. Lee, Comd'g C.S.A.

General:

In accordance with the substance of my letter to you of the 8th instant, I propose to receive the surrender of the Army of Northern Virginia on the following terms, to wit: Rolls of all the officers and men to be made in duplicate. One copy to be given to an officer designated by me, the other to be retained by such officer or officers as you may designate. The officers to give their individual paroles not to take up arms against the Government of the United States until properly exchanged, and each company or regimental commander sign a like parole for the men of their commands. The arms, artillery, and public property to be parked and stacked and turned over to the officer appointed by me to receive them. This will not embrace the sidearms of the officers nor their private horses or baggage. This done, each officer and man will be allowed to return to their homes, not to be disturbed by United States authority so long as they observe their paroles and the laws in force where they may reside.

Very respectfully,
U.S. Grant, Lieutenant General

When I put my pen to the paper I did not know the first word that I should make use of in writing the terms. I only knew what was in my mind, and I wished to express it clearly, so that there could be no mistaking it. As I wrote on, the thought occurred to me that the officers had their own private horses and effects, which were important to them but of no value to us; also that it would be an unnecessary humiliation to call upon them to deliver their sidearms.

No conversation, not one word, passed between General Lee and myself, either about private property, sidearms, or kindred subjects. He appeared to have no objections to the terms first proposed, or if he had a point to make against them he wished to wait until they were in writing to make it. When he read over that part of the terms about sidearms, horses, and private property of the officers, he remarked, with some feeling, I thought, that this would have a happy effect upon his army.

Then, after a little further conversation, General Lee remarked to me again that their army was organized a little differently from the army of the United States (still maintaining by implication that we were two countries), that in their army the cavalrymen and artillerists owned their own horses; and he asked if he was to understand that the men who so owned their horses were to be permitted to retain them. I told him that as the terms were written they would not, that only the officers were permitted to take their private property. He then, after reading over the terms a second time, remarked that that was clear.

I then said to him that I thought this would be about the last battle of the war—I sincerely hoped so—and I said further I took it that most of the men in the ranks were small farmers. The whole country had been so raided by the two armies that it was doubtful whether they would be able to put in a crop to carry themselves and their families through the next winter without the aid of the horses they were then riding. The United States did not want them, and I would, therefore, instruct the officers I left behind to receive the paroles of his troops to let every man in the Confederate army who claimed to own a horse or mule take the animal to his home. Lee remarked again that this would have a happy effect.

He then sat down and wrote out the following letter:

Headquarters, Army of Northern Virginia
April 9, 1865

General:

I received your letter of this date containing the terms of the surrender of the Army of Northern Virginia as proposed by you. As they are substantially the same as those expressed in your letter of the 8th instant, they are accepted. I will proceed to designate the proper officers to carry the stipulations into effect.

R.E. Lee, General
Lieutenant General U.S. Grant

    While duplicates of the two letters were being made, the Union generals present were severally presented to General Lee.

    The much-talked-of surrendering of Lee's sword and my handing it back, this and much more that has been said about it is the purest romance. The word *sword* or *sidearms* was not mentioned by either of us until I wrote it in the terms. There was no premeditation, and it did not occur to me until the moment I wrote it down. If I had happened to omit it and General Lee had called my attention to it, I should have put it in the terms precisely as I acceded to the provision about the soldiers retaining their horses.

    General Lee, after all was completed and before taking his leave, remarked that his army was in a very bad condition for want of food and that they were without forage, that his men had been living for some days on parched corn exclusively, and that he would have to ask me for rations and forage. I told him "certainly" and asked for how many men he wanted rations. His answer was about twenty-five thousand, and I authorized him to send his own commissary and quartermaster to Appomattox station, two or three miles away, where he could have, out of the trains we had stopped, all the provisions wanted. As for forage, we had ourselves depended almost entirely upon the country for that.

Personal Memoirs of U.S. Grant

67

Sidney Andrews Views the War-Torn South

Much of the South at the close of the war was a shocking scene of confusion and ruin. With buildings destroyed, railroads torn up, farms devastated, and bridges down, with no capital to repair their losses, and with their labor system suddenly revolutionized, the Southern people faced a gloomier future than any considerable body of Americans had ever before known. Sidney Andrews, who here gives us a glimpse of their losses, was a New England journalist who visited the Carolinas and Georgia in the autumn of 1865 and sent his impressions to Boston and Chicago newspapers.

Part I

CHARLESTON, S.C. SEPTEMBER 4, 1865.—

A city of ruins, of desolation, of vacant houses, of widowed women, of rotting wharves, of deserted warehouses, of weed-wild gardens, of miles of grass-grown streets, of acres of pitiful and voiceful barrenness—that is Charleston, wherein Rebellion loftily reared its head five years ago, on whose beautiful promenade the fairest of cultured women gathered with passionate hearts to applaud the assault of ten thousand upon the little garrison of Fort Sumter!

Who kindled the greedy fire of December 1861, whereby a third of the city was destroyed? No one yet knows. "It was de good Jesus Hisself," said an old Negro to me when I asked him the question—"it was de Almighty Hand workin' fru de man's hand." Certain it is that the people were never able to discover the agency of the fire, though, so far as I can learn, no one doubts that it was the work of an incendiary, "some man," say the ex-Rebels, "who wanted to do you Federals a good turn."

We never again can have the Charleston of the decade previous to the war. The beauty and pride of the city are as dead as the glories of Athens. Five millions of dollars could not restore the ruin of these four past years, and that sum is so far beyond the command of the city as to seem the boundless measure of immeasurable wealth. Yet, after all, Charleston was Charleston because of the hearts of its people. St. Michael's Church, they held, was the center of the universe, and the aristocracy of the city were the very elect of God's children on earth. One marks now how few young men there are, how generally the young women are dressed in black. The flower of their proud aristocracy is buried on scores of battlefields. If it were possible to restore the broad acres of crumbling ruins to their foretime style and uses, there would even then be but the dead body of Charleston.

The Charleston of 1875 will doubtless be proud in wealth and intellect and rich in grace and culture. Let favoring years bring forward such fruitage! Yet the place has not in itself recuperative power for such a result. The material on which to build that fair structure does not here exist and, as I am told by dozens, cannot be found in the state. If Northern capital and Northern energy do not come here, the ruin, they say, must remain a ruin.

Business is reviving slowly, though perhaps the more surely. The resident merchants are mostly at the bottom of the ladder of prosperity. They have idled away the summer in vain regrets for vanished hopes, and most of them are only just now beginning to wake to the new life. Some have already been north for goods, but more are preparing to go, not heeding that, while they vacillate with laggard time, Northern men are springing in with hands swift to catch opportunity. It pains me to see the apathy and indifference that so generally prevail, but the worst feature of the situation is that so many young men are not only idle but give no promise of being otherwise in the immediate future.

Many of the stores were more or less injured by the shelling. A few of these have been already repaired and are now occupied, very likely by Northern men. A couple of dozen, great and small, are now in process of repair, and scores stand with closed shutters or gaping doors and windows. The doubt as to the title of property and the wise caution of the President in granting pardons unquestionably has something to do with the stagnation so painfully apparent, but very much of it is due to the hesitating shiftlessness of even the Southern merchant, who forever lets *I dare not* wait upon *I would.* Rents of eligible storerooms are at least from one-fourth to one-third higher than before the war, and resident business men say only Northern men who intend staying but a short time can afford to pay present prices. I'm sure I can't see how anyone can afford to pay them, but I know the demand is greater than the supply.

I queried of the returning merchants on the steamship how they were received in the North. An Augusta man complained that he could get no credit and that there was a disposition to be grinding and exacting. One Charleston man said he asked for sixty days and got it without a word of objection. Another told me that he asked for four months, was given three, and treated like a gentleman everywhere.

It would seem that it is not clearly understood how thoroughly Sherman's army destroyed everything in its line of march—destroyed it without questioning who suffered by the action. That this wholesale destruction was often without orders and often against most positive orders does not change the fact of destruction. The rebel leaders were, too, in their way, even more wanton and just as thorough as our army in destroying property. They did not burn houses and barns and fences as we did, but during the last three months of the war they burned immense quantities of cotton and rosin.

The action of the two armies put it out of the power of men to pay their debts. The values and the bases of value were nearly all destroyed. Money lost about everything it had saved. Thousands of men who were honest in purpose have lost everything but honor. The cotton with which they meant to pay their debts has been burned, and they are without other means. What is the part of wisdom in respect to such men? It certainly cannot be to strip them of the last remnant. Many of them will pay in whole or in part if proper consideration be shown them. It is no question of favor to anyone as a favor, but a pure question of business—how shall the commercial relations of the two sections be reestablished? In determining it, the actual and exceptional condition of the state with respect to property should be constantly borne in mind.

The city is under thorough military rule, but the iron hand rests very lightly. Soldiers do police duty, and there is some nine-o'clock regulation, but so far as I can learn, anybody goes anywhere at all hours of the night without molestation. "There never was such good order here before," said an old colored man to me. The main street is swept twice a week, and all garbage is removed at sunrise. "If the Yankees was to stay here always and keep the city so clean, I don't reckon we'd have yellow jack here any more" was a remark I overheard on the street. "Now is de fust time sence I can 'mem'er when brack men was safe in de street af'er nightfall," stated the Negro tailor in whose shop I sat an hour yesterday.

On the surface Charleston is quiet and well behaved, and I do not doubt that the more intelligent citizens are wholly sincere in their expressions of a desire for peace and reunion. The city has been humbled as no other city has been, and I can't see how any man, after spending a few days here, can desire that it be further humiliated merely for revenge. Whether it has been humiliated enough for health is another thing. Said one of the Charlestonians on the boat: "You won't see the real sentiment of our people, for we are under military rule; we are whipped, and we are going to make the best of things, but we hate Massachusetts as much as we ever did." This idea of making the best of things is one I have heard from scores of persons. I find very few who hesitate to frankly own that the South has been beaten. "We made the best fight we could, but you were too strong for us, and now we are only anxious to get back into the old Union and live as happily as we can," said a large cotton factor. I find very few who make any special profession of Unionism, but they are almost unanimous in declaring that they have no desire but to live as good and quiet citizens under the laws.

For the first two months of our occupancy of the city scarcely a white woman but those of the poorer classes was seen on the street, and very few were even seen at the windows and doors of the residences. That order of things is now happily changed. There doesn't yet appear to be as much freedom of appearance as would be natural, but very many of what are called the first ladies are to be seen shopping in the morning and promenading in the evening. They, much more than the men, have contemptuous motions for the Negro soldiers, and scorn for Northern men is frequently apparent in the swing of their skirts when passing on the sidewalk.

One doesn't observe so much pleasantness and cheerfulness as would be agreeable, but the general demeanor is quite consonant with the general mourning costume. A stroller at sunset sees not a few pale and pensive-faced young women of exquisite beauty, and a rambler during the evening not infrequently hears a strain of touching melody from the darkened parlor of some roomy old mansion, with now and then one of the ringing, passionate airs with which the Southern heart has been fired during the war.

Part II

ATLANTA, GA. NOVEMBER 23, 1865.—

Coming here has dispelled two illusions under which I rested: first, that Atlanta was a small place, and second, that it was wholly destroyed. It was a city of about fourteen thousand inhabitants two years ago, and it was not more than half burned last fall. The entire business portion, excepting the Masonic Hall building and one block of six stores and a hotel, was laid in ruins, and not a few of the larger residences in all parts of the city were also burned. But the City Hall and the Medical College, and all the churches, and many of the handsomest and more stylish private dwellings, and nearly all the houses of the middling and poorer classes, were spared, and on the first of last June there was ample shelter here for at least six or eight thousand persons. Of course, however, when the entire business portion of the place had disappeared, the city had been practically put out of the way for the time being, even if nothing be said of the fact that it was depopulated by military orders.

The marks of the conflict are everywhere strikingly apparent. The ruin is not so massive and impressive as that of Columbia and Charleston, but as far as it extends it is more complete and of less value. The city always had a mushroom character, and the fire king must have laughed in glee when it was given over into his keeping. There is yet abundant evidence of his energy, not so much in crumbling walls and solitary chimneys as in thousands of masses of brick and mortar, thousands of pieces of charred timber, thousands of half-burned boards, thousands of scraps of tin roofing, thousands of car and engine bolts and bars, thousands of ruined articles of hardware, thousands upon thousands of tons of debris of all sorts and shapes. Moreover, there are plenty of cannonballs and long shot lying about the streets, with not a few shell-struck houses in some sections, and from the courthouse square can be seen a dozen or more forts and many a hillside from which the timber was cut so that the enemy might not come upon the city unawares.

From all this ruin and devastation a new city is springing up with marvelous rapidity. The narrow and irregular and numerous streets are alive from morning till night with drays and carts and hand barrows and wagons, with hauling teams and shouting men, with loads of lumber and loads of brick and loads of sand, with piles of furniture and hundreds of packed boxes, with mortar makers and hod carriers, with carpenters and masons, with rubbish removers and house builders, with a never-ending throng of pushing and crowding and scrambling and eager and excited and enterprising men, all bent on building and trading and swift fortune-making.

Chicago in her busiest days could scarcely show such a sight as clamors for observation here. Every horse and mule and wagon is in active use. The four railroads centering here groan with the freight and passenger traffic and yet are unable to meet the demand of the nervous and palpitating city. Men rush about the streets with little regard for comfort or pleasure and yet find the days all too short and too few for the work in hand. The sound of the saw and plane and hammer rings out from daylight to dark, and yet master builders are worried with offered contracts which they cannot take. Rents are so high that they would seem fabulous on Lake Street, and yet there is the most urgent cry for storeroom and office room. Four thousand mechanics are at work, and yet five thousand more could get immediate employment if brick and lumber were to be had at any price. There are already over two hundred stores, so called, and yet every day brings some trader who is restless and fretful till he secures a place in which to display another stock of goods.

Where all this eagerness and excitement will end, no one seems to care to inquire. The one sole idea first in every man's mind is to make money. That this apparent prosperity is real, no outsider can believe. That business is planted on sure foundations, no merchant pretends. That there will come a pause and then a crash, a few prudent men prophesy.

Meantime Atlanta is doing more than Macon and Augusta combined. The railroad from here to Chattanooga clears over one hundred thousand dollars per month and could add fifty thousand more to that enormous sum if it had plenty of engines and rolling stock. The trade of the city is already thirty per cent greater than it was before the war, and it is limited only by the accommodations afforded and has even now spread its wings far out on streets heretofore sacred to the privacy of home.

Part III

COLUMBIA, S.C. SEPTEMBER 12, 1865.—

Columbia is in the heart of Destruction. Being outside of it, you can only get in through one of the roads built by Ruin. Being in it, you can only get out over one of the roads walled by Desolation. You go north thirty-two miles and find the end of one railroad; southeast thirty miles and find the end of another; south forty-five miles and find the end of a third; southwest fifty miles and meet a fourth; and northwest twenty-nine miles and find the end of still another. Sherman came in here, the papers used to say, to break up the railroad system of the seaboard states of the Confederacy. He did his work so thoroughly that half a dozen years will nothing more than begin to repair the damage, even in this regard.

Certain bent rails are the first thing one sees to indicate the advent of his army. They are at Branchville. I looked at them with curious interest. "It passes my comprehension to tell what became of our railroads," said a traveling acquaintance. "One week we had passably good roads, on which we could reach almost any part of the state, and the next week they were all gone—not simply broken up, but gone; some of the material was burned, I know, but miles and miles of iron have actually disappeared, gone out of existence." Branchville, as I have already said, was flanked, and the army did not take it in the line of march, but some of the boys paid it a visit.

At Orangeburg there is ample proof that the army passed that way. About one third of the town was burned. I found much dispute as to the origin of the fire, and while certain fellows of the baser sort loudly assert that it was the work of the Yankee, others of the better class express the belief that it originated with a resident who was angry at the Confederate officers. Thereabouts one finds plenty of railroad iron so bent and twisted that it can never again be used. The genius which our soldiers displayed in destroying railroads seems remarkable. How effectually they did it, when they undertook the work in earnest, no pen can make plain. "We could do something in that line, we thought," said an ex-Confederate captain, "but we were ashamed of ourselves when we saw how your men could do it."

We rode over the road where the army marched. Now and then we found solitary chimneys, but on the whole comparatively few houses were burned, and some of those were fired, it is believed, by persons from the Rebel army or from the neighboring locality. The fences did not escape so well, and most of the planters have had these to build during the summer. This was particularly the case near Columbia. Scarcely a tenth of that destroyed appears to have been rebuilt, and thousands of acres of land of much richness lie open as a common.

There is a great scarcity of stock of all kinds. What was left by the Rebel conscription officers was freely appropriated by Sherman's army, and the people really find considerable difficulty, not less in living than in traveling. Milk, formerly an article much in use, can only be had now in limited quantities; even at the hotels we have more meals without than with it. There are more mules than horses, apparently, and the animals, whether mules or horses, are all in ill condition and give evidence of severe overwork.

Columbia was doubtless once the gem of the state. It is as regularly laid out as a checkerboard—the squares being of uniform length and breadth and the streets of uniform width. What with its broad streets, beautiful shade trees, handsome lawns, extensive gardens, luxuriant shrubbery, and wealth of flowers, I can easily see that it must have been a delightful place of residence. No South Carolinian with whom I have spoken hesitates an instant in declaring that it was the most beautiful city on the continent, and as already mentioned, they charge its destruction directly to General Sherman.

It is now a wilderness of ruins. Its heart is but a mass of blackened chimneys and crumbling walls. Two thirds of the buildings in the place were burned, including, without exception, everything in the business portion. Not a store, office, or shop escaped, and for a distance of three fourths of a mile on each of twelve streets there was not a building left. . . .

Every public building was destroyed, except the new and unfinished statehouse. This is situated on the summit of tableland whereon the city is built, and commands an extensive view of the surrounding country and must have been the first building seen by the victorious and on-marching Union army. From the summit of the ridge, on the opposite side of the river, a mile and a half away, a few shells were thrown at it, apparently by way of reminder, three or four of which struck it, without doing any particular damage. With this exception, it was unharmed, though the workshops, in which were stored many of the architraves, caps, sills, etc., were burned—the fire, of course, destroying or seriously damaging their contents. The poverty of this people is so deep that there is no probability that it can be finished, according to the original design, during this generation at least.

The ruin here is neither half so eloquent nor touching as that at Charleston. This is but the work of flame and might have mostly been brought about in time of peace. Those ghostly and crumbling walls and those long-deserted and grass-grown streets show the prostration of a community—such prostration as only war could bring.

Sidney Andrews
The South Since the War

68

J. S. Pike Attends a Black
Parliament in South Carolina

No one could accuse James S. Pike of being biased in favor of the Southern whites. Born in Maine, he had given many years of service as Washington correspondent and editorial writer to Horace Greeley's *New York Tribune*. He was an uncompromising antislavery man, and Lincoln rewarded him for his work in behalf of the Republican Party by appointment in 1861 as minister to Holland. In the midst of Reconstruction he made a trip to South Carolina to view the workings of the "black and tan" government there, and in his famous book *The Prostrate State* he showed vividly and eloquently the tyranny under which the carpetbag regime had placed the Southern whites.

Yesterday, about 4 P.M., the assembled wisdom of the state, whose achievements are illustrated on that theater, issued forth from the statehouse. About three-quarters of the crowd belonged to the African race. They were of every hue, from the light octoroon to the deep black. They were such a looking body of men as might pour out of a market house or a courthouse at random in any Southern state. Every Negro type and physiognomy was here to be seen, from the genteel serving man to the roughhewn customer from the rice or cotton field. Their dress was as varied as their countenances. There was the secondhand black frock coat of infirm gentility, glossy and threadbare. There was the stovepipe hat of many ironings and departed styles. There was also to be seen a total disregard of the proprieties of costume in the coarse and dirty garments of the field, the stub jackets and slouch hats of soiling labor. In some instances rough woolen comforters embraced the neck and hid the absence of linen. Heavy brogans and short, torn trousers it was impossible to hide. The dusky tide flowed out into the littered and barren grounds and, issuing through the coarse wooden fence of the enclosure, melted away into the street beyond. These were the legislators of South Carolina.

We will enter the House of Representatives. Here sit one hundred and twenty-four members. Of these, twenty-three are white men, representing the remains of the old civilization. These are good-looking, substantial citizens. They are men of weight and standing in the communities they represent. They are all from the hill country. The frosts of sixty and seventy winters whiten the heads of some among them. There they sit, grim and silent. They feel themselves to be but loose stones, thrown in to partially obstruct a current they are powerless to resist. They say little and do little as the days go by. They simply watch the rising tide and mark the progressive steps of the inundation. They hold their places reluctantly. They feel themselves to be in some sort martyrs, bound stoically to suffer in behalf of that still great element in the state whose prostrate fortunes are becoming the sport of an unpitying fate. Grouped in a corner of the commodious and well-furnished chamber, they stolidly survey the noisy riot that goes on in the great black Left and Center, where the business and debates of the House are conducted and where sit the strange and extraordinary guides of the fortunes of a once proud and haughty state. In this crucial trial of his pride, his manhood, his prejudices, his spirit, it must be said of the Southern Bourbon of the Legislature that he comports himself with a dignity, a reserve, and a decorum that command admiration. He feels that the iron hand of destiny is upon him. He is gloomy, disconsolate, hopeless. The gray heads of this generation openly profess that they look for no relief. They see no way of escape. The recovery of influence, of position, of control in the state, is felt by them to be impossible. They accept their position with a stoicism that promises no reward here or hereafter. They are the types of a conquered race. They staked all and lost all. Their lives remain; their property and their children do not. War, emancipation, and grinding taxation have consumed them. Their struggle now is against complete confiscation. They endure, and wait for the night.

This dense Negro crowd they confront do the debating, the squabbling, the lawmaking, and create all the clamor and disorder of the body. These twenty-three white men are but the observers, the enforced auditors, of the dull and clumsy imitation of a deliberative body whose appearance in their present capacity is at once a wonder and a shame to modern civilization.

Deducting the twenty-three members referred to, who comprise the entire strength of the opposition, we find one hundred and one remaining. Of this one hundred and one, ninety-four are colored, and seven are their white allies. . . .

One of the things that first strike a casual observer in this Negro assembly is the fluency of debate, if the endless chatter that goes on there can be dignified with this term. The leading topics of discussion are all well understood by the members, as they are of a practical character and appeal directly to the personal interests of every legislator as well as to those of his constituents. When an appropriation bill is up to raise money to catch and punish the Ku Klux, they know exactly what it means. They feel it in their bones. So too with educational measures. The free school comes right home to them; then the business of arming and drilling the black militia—they are eager on this point. Sambo can talk on these topics and those of a kindred character and their endless ramifications day in and day out. There is no end to his gush and babble. The intellectual level is that of a bevy of fresh converts at a Negro camp meeting. Of course this kind of talk can be extended indefinitely. It is the doggerel of debate and not beyond the reach of the lowest parts. Then the Negro is imitative in the extreme. He can copy like a parrot or a monkey, and he is always ready for a trial of his skill. He believes he can do anything and never loses a chance to try and is just as ready to be laughed at for his failure as applauded for his success. He is more vivacious than the white, and being more volatile and good-natured, he is correspondingly more irrepressible. His misuse of language in his imitations is at times ludicrous beyond measure. He notoriously loves a joke or an anecdote and will burst into a broad guffaw on the smallest provocation. He breaks out into an incoherent harangue on the floor just as easily, and being without practice, discipline, or experience and wholly oblivious of Lindley Murray or any other restraint on composition, he will go on repeating himself, dancing as it were to the music of his own voice, forever. He will speak half a dozen times on one question and every time say the same things without knowing it. He answers completely to the description of a stupid speaker in Parliament given by Lord Derby on one occasion; it was said of him that he did not know what he was going to say when he got up, he did not know what he was saying while he was speaking, and he did not know what he had said when he sat down.

But the old stagers admit that the colored brethren have a wonderful aptness at legislative proceedings. They are quick as lightning at detecting points of order, and they certainly make incessant and extraordinary use of their knowledge. No one is allowed to talk five minutes without interruption, and one interruption is the signal for another and another until the original speaker is smothered under an avalanche of them. Forty questions of privilege will be raised in a day. At times nothing goes on but alternating questions of order and of privilege. The inefficient colored friend who sits in the Speaker's chair cannot suppress this extraordinary element of the debate. Some of the blackest members exhibit a pertinacity of intrusion in raising these points of order and questions of privilege that few white men can equal. Their struggles to get the floor, their bellowings and physical contortions, baffle description. The Speaker's hammer plays a perpetual tattoo, all to no purpose. The talking and the interruptions from all quarters go on with the utmost license. Every one esteems himself as good as his neighbor and puts in his oar, apparently as often for love of riot and confusion as for anything else. It is easy to imagine what are his ideas of propriety and dignity among a crowd of his own color, and these are illustrated without reserve. The Speaker orders a member whom he has discovered to be particularly unruly to take his seat. The member obeys and, with the same motion that he sits down, throws his feet on to his desk, hiding himself from the Speaker by the soles of his boots. In an instant he appears again on the floor. After a few experiences of this sort, the Speaker threatens, in a laugh, to call "the gemman" to order. This is considered a capital joke, and a guffaw follows. The laugh goes round, and then the peanuts are cracked and munched faster than ever, one hand being employed in fortifying the inner man with this nutriment of universal use while the other enforces the views of the orator. This laughing propensity of the sable crowd is a great cause of disorder. They laugh as hens cackle—one begins and all follow.

But underneath all this shocking burlesque upon legislative proceedings, we must not forget that there is something very real to this uncouth and un-tutored multitude. It is not all sham nor all burlesque. They have a genuine interest and a genuine earnestness in the business of the assembly, which we are bound to recognize and respect unless we would be accounted shallow critics. They have an earnest purpose, born of a conviction that their posi-tion and condition are not fully assured, which lends a sort of dignity to their proceedings. The barbarous, animated jargon in which they so often indulge is on occasion seen to be so transparently sincere and weighty in their own minds that sympathy supplants disgust. The whole thing is a wonderful nov-elty to them as well as to observers. Seven years ago these men were raising corn and cotton under the whip of the overseer. Today they are raising points of order and questions of privilege. They find they can raise one as well as the other. They prefer the latter. It is easier and better paid. Then, it is the evidence of an accomplished result. It means escape and defense from old oppressors. It means liberty. It means the destruction of prison walls only too real to them. It is the sunshine of their lives. It is their day of jubilee. It is their long-promised vision of the Lord God Almighty.

James Shepherd Pike
The Prostrate State

69

The Ku Klux Klan Rides

The insecurity of the Southern whites in Reconstruction days, and their desire to shake off the domination of the blacks and the carpetbaggers who had come down from the North, led to a rapid growth of secret organizations. The most powerful of these bodies, the Ku Klux Klan, was founded in Tennessee in 1865 and quickly spread throughout most of the section. At the head of this "In-visible Empire" was a grand wizard, while under him each State or "Realm" was ruled by a grand dragon. It is said that nearly all the Southern whites (except the "Scalawags," who helped the carpetbaggers gain power) aided the Klan in some way. In general, the society tried to intimidate the blacks and their white allies by threats and demonstrations, and a good deal of violence was used.

Blacks and carpetbag politicians were whipped, and some were murdered. Stern federal action finally broke up the last vestiges of the Klan, but not before it had accomplished most of its purposes.

It was a chill, dreary night. A dry, harsh wind blew from the north. The moon was at the full and shone clear and cold in the blue vault.

There was one shrill whistle, some noise of quietly moving horses; and those who looked from their windows saw a black-gowned and grimly masked horseman sitting upon a draped horse at every corner of the streets and before each house—grim, silent, threatening. Those who saw dared not move or give any alarm. Instinctively they knew that the enemy they had feared had come, had them in his clutches, and would work his will of them, whether they resisted or not. So, with the instinct of self-preservation, all were silent—all simulated sleep.

Five, ten, fifteen minutes the silent watch continued. A half hour passed, and there had been no sound. Each masked sentry sat his horse as if horse and rider were only some magic statuary with which the bleak night cheated the affrighted eye. Then a whistle sounded on the road toward Verdenton. The masked horsemen turned their horses' heads in that direction and slowly and silently moved away. Gathering in twos, they fell into ranks with the regularity and ease of a practiced soldiery and, as they filed on toward Verdenton, showed a cavalcade of several hundred strong, and upon one of the foremost horses rode one with a strange figure lashed securely to him.

When the few who were awake in the little village found courage to inquire as to what the silent enemy had done, they rushed from house to house with chattering teeth and trembling limbs, only to find that all were safe within, until they came to the house where old Uncle Jerry Hunt had been dwelling alone since the death of his wife six months before. The door was open.

The house was empty. The straw mattress had been thrown from the bed, and the hempen cord on which it rested had been removed.

The Sabbath morrow was well advanced when the Fool was first apprised of the raid. He at once rode into the town, arriving there just as the morning services closed, and met the people coming along the streets to their homes. Upon the limb of a low-branching oak not more than forty steps from the Temple of Justice hung the lifeless body of old Jerry. The wind turned it slowly to and fro. The snowy hair and beard contrasted strangely with the dusky pallor of the peaceful face, which seemed even in death to proffer a benison to the people of God who passed to and fro from the house of prayer, unmindful both of the peace which lighted the dead face and of the rifled temple of the Holy Ghost which appealed to them for sepulture. Over all pulsed the sacred echo of the Sabbath bells. The sun shone brightly. The wind rustled the autumn leaves. A few idlers sat upon the steps of the courthouse and gazed carelessly at the ghastly burden on the oak. The brightly dressed churchgoers enlivened the streets. Not a colored man was to be seen. All except the brown cadaver on the tree spoke of peace and prayer—a holy day among a godly people, with whom rested the benison of peace.

The Fool asked of some trusty friends the story of the night before. With trembling lips one told it to him:

"I heard the noise of horses—quiet and orderly, but many. Looking from the window in the clear moonlight, I saw horsemen passing down the street, taking their stations here and there like guards who have been told off for duty at specific points. Two stopped before my house, two opposite Mr. Haskin's, and two or three upon the corner below. They seemed to have been sent on before as a sort of picket guard for the main body, which soon came in. I should say there were from a hundred to a hundred and fifty still in line. They were all masked and wore black robes. The horses were disguised, too, by drapings. There were only a few mules in the whole company. They were good horses, though; one could tell that by their movements. Oh, it was a respectable crowd! No doubt about that, sir. Beggars don't ride in this country. I don't know when I have seen so many good horses together since the Yankee cavalry left here after the surrender. They were well drilled too. Plenty of old soldiers in that crowd. Why, everything went just like clockwork. Not a word was said—just a few whistles given. They came like a dream and went away like a mist. I thought we should have to fight for our lives, but they did not disturb anyone here. They gathered down by the courthouse. I could not see precisely what they were at but from my back upper window saw them down about the tree. After a while a signal was given, and just at that time a match was struck, and I saw a dark body swing down under the limb. I knew then they had hanged somebody, but had no idea who it was. To tell the truth, I had a notion it was you, Colonel. I saw several citizens go out and speak to these men on the horses. There were lights in some of the offices about the courthouse and in several of the houses about town. Everything was as still as the grave—no shouting or loud talking and no excitement or stir about town. It was evident that a great many of the citizens expected the movement and were prepared to cooperate with it by manifesting no curiosity or otherwise endangering its success. I am inclined to think a good many from this town were in it. I never felt so powerless in my life. Here the town was in the hands of two or three hundred armed and disciplined men, hidden from the eye of the law, and having friends and co-workers in almost every house. I knew that resistance was useless."

"But why," asked the Fool, "has not the body been removed?"

"We have been thinking about it" was the reply, "but the truth is, it don't seem like a very safe business. And after what we saw last night, no one feels like being the first to do what may be held an affront by those men. I tell you, Colonel, I went through the war and saw as much danger as most men in it, but I would rather charge up the heights of Gettysburg again than be the object of a raid by that crowd."

After some parley, however, some colored men were found and a little party made up who went out and saw the body of Uncle Jerry cut down and laid upon a box to await the coming of the coroner, who had already been notified. The inquest developed only these facts, and the sworn jurors solemnly and honestly found the cause of death unknown. One of the colored men who had watched the proceedings gave utterance to the prevailing opinion when he said: "It don't do fer niggers to know *too much!* Dat's what ail Uncle Jerry!"

And indeed it did seem as if his case was one in which ignorance might have been bliss.

Albion Tourgée
A Fool's Errand

70

George Julian Regrets the Johnson Impeachment

Andrew Johnson, favoring the same mild policy of Reconstruction that Lincoln had preached, soon quarreled with the vindictive members of Congress who wished to punish the Southerners. The quarrel became bitter, involving important constitutional questions. One of President Johnson's opponents was George Julian of Indiana, a lawyer and an abolitionist, who had been elected to Congress in 1860. He favored suffrage for blacks and the seizure of the lands of all the Confederate leaders. In 1867 he was one of the committee of seven members of the House of Representatives who prepared the formal impeachment of Johnson. But within a few years Julian broke with his party and in 1872 joined the Liberal Republicans who opposed Grant's reelection. He repented his hostility to Johnson and makes this plain in his *Political Recollections.*

On the 24th of February, 1868, the House, by a vote of one hundred and twenty-six to forty-seven, declared in favor of impeachment. The crowds in the galleries, in the lobbies, and on the floor were unprecedented and the excitement at high tide. The fifty-seven who had voted for impeachment in December were now happy. They felt at last that the country was safe. The whole land seemed to be electrified, as they believed it would have been at any previous time if the House had had the nerve to go forward, and they rejoiced that the madness of Johnson had at last compelled Congress to face the great duty. A committee of seven was appointed by the Speaker to prepare articles of impeachment, of whom Thaddeus Stevens was chairman. He was now rapidly failing in strength and every morning had to be carried upstairs to his seat in the House, but his humor never failed him, and on one of these occasions he said to the young men who had him in charge, "I wonder, boys, who will carry me when you are dead and gone." He was very thin, pale, and haggard. His eye was bright, but his face was "scarred by the crooked autograph of pain." He was a constant sufferer and during the sessions of the committee kept himself stimulated by sipping a little wine or brandy, but he was its ruling spirit and greatly speeded its work by the clearness of his perceptions and the strength of his will. His mental force seemed to defy the power of disease. The articles of impeachment were ready for submission in a few days and adopted by the House on the second of March by a majority of considerably more than two thirds, when the case was transferred to the Senate.

The popular feeling against the President was now rapidly nearing its climax and becoming a sort of frenzy. Andrew Johnson was no longer merely a "wrongheaded and obstinate man" but a "genius in depravity," whose hoarded malignity and passion were unfathomable. He was not simply "an irresolute mule," as General Schenck had styled him, but was devil-bent upon the ruin of his country, and his trial connected itself with all the memories of the war and involved the nation in a new and final struggle for its life. Even so sober and unimaginative a man as Mr. Boutwell, one of the managers of the impeachment in the Senate, lost his wits and completely surrendered himself to the passions of the hour.

No extravagance of speech or explosion of wrath was deemed out of order during this strange dispensation in our politics.

The trial proceeded with unabated interest, and on the afternoon of the eleventh of May the excitement reached its highest point. Reports came from the Senate, then in secret session, that Grimes, Fessenden, and Henderson were certainly for acquittal, and that other senators were to follow them. An indescribable gloom now prevailed among the friends of impeachment, which increased during the afternoon and at night when the Senate was again in session. At the adjournment there was some hope of conviction, but it was generally considered very doubtful. On meeting my old antislavery friend, Doctor Brisbane, he told me he felt as if he were sitting up with a sick friend who was expected to die. His face was the picture of despair. To such men it seemed that all the trials of the war were merged in this grand issue and that it involved the existence of free government on this continent.

The final vote was postponed till the sixteenth, owing to Senator Howard's illness, and on the morning of that day the friends of impeachment felt more confident. The vote was first taken on the eleventh article. The galleries were packed, and an indescribable anxiety was written on every face. Some of the members of the House near me grew pale and sick under the burden of suspense. Such stillness prevailed that the breathing in the galleries could be heard at the announcement of each senator's vote. This was quite noticeable when any of the doubtful senators voted, the people holding their breath as the words "guilty" or "not guilty" were pronounced and then giving it simultaneous vent. Every heart throbbed more anxiously as the name of Senator Fowler was reached and the Chief Justice propounded to him the prescribed question: "How say you, is the respondent, Andrew Johnson, President of the United States, guilty or not guilty of a high misdemeanor, as charged in this article of impeachment?" The senator, in evident excitement, inadvertently answered "guilty" and thus lent a momentary relief to the friends of impeachment, but this was immediately dissipated by correcting his vote on the statement of the Chief Justice that he did not understand the Senator's response to the question. Nearly all hope of conviction fled when Senator Ross of Kansas voted "not guilty," and a long breathing of disappointment and despair followed the like vote of Van Winkle, which settled the case in favor of the President.

It is impossible now to realize how perfectly overmastering was the excitement of these days. The exercise of calm judgment was simply out of the question. As I have already stated, passion ruled the hour and constantly strengthened the tendency to one-sidedness and exaggeration. The attempt to impeach the President was undoubtedly inspired mainly by patriotic motives, but the spirit of intolerance among Republicans toward those who differed with them in opinion set all moderation and common sense at defiance. Patriotism and party animosity were so inextricably mingled and confounded that the real merits of the controversy could only be seen after the heat and turmoil of the strife had passed away. Time has made this manifest. Andrew Johnson was not the devil incarnate he was then painted, nor did he monopolize entirely the wrong-headedness of the times. No one will now dispute that the popular estimate of his character did him very great injustice. It is equally certain that great injustice was done to Trumbull, Fessenden, Grimes, and other senators who voted to acquit the President and gave proof of their honesty and independence by facing the wrath and scorn of the party with which they had so long been identified. The idea of making the question of impeachment a matter of party discipline was utterly indefensible and preposterous.

GEORGE W. JULIAN
Political Recollections, 1840–1872

71

Walt Whitman Scans Democratic Vistas

The Grant administrations, 1869–1877, were filled with political corruption. Scandals were so numerous and so shocking that by the centennial year, 1876, all patriotic Americans hung their heads in shame. Thomas Carlyle had recently indicted democracy in his essay "Shooting Niagara." Walt Whitman in his pamphlet *Democratic Vistas,* published just as the unhappy Grant era was fully opening, indicated a clear understanding of the weaknesses of and perils to democracy, but sturdily defended it nonetheless.

For my part, I would alarm and caution even the political and business reader, and to the utmost extent, against the prevailing delusion that the establishment of free political institutions, and plentiful intellectual smartness, with general good order, physical plenty, industry, etc. (desirable and precious advantages as they all are), do of themselves determine and yield to our experiment of democracy the fruitage of success. With such advantages at present fully, or almost fully, possessed—the Union just issued victorious from the struggle with the only foes it need ever fear (namely, those within itself, the interior ones), and with unprecedented materialistic advancement— society in these states is cankered, crude, superstitious, and rotten. Political or law-made society is, and private or voluntary society is also. In any vigor, the element of the moral conscience, the most important, the vertebra to state or man, seems to me either entirely lacking or seriously enfeebled or ungrown.

I say we had best look our times and lands searchingly in the face, like a physician diagnosing some deep disease. Never was there, perhaps, more hollowness at heart than at present and here in the United States. Genuine belief seems to have left us. The underlying principles of the states are not honestly believed in (for all this hectic glow and these melodramatic screamings), nor is humanity itself believed in. What penetrating eye does not everywhere see through the mask? The spectacle is appalling. We live in an atmosphere of hypocrisy throughout. The men believe not in the women, nor the women in the men. A scornful superciliousness rules in literature. The aim of all the *littérateurs* is to find something to make fun of. A lot of churches, sects, etc., the most dismal phantasms I know, usurp the name of religion. Conversation is a mass of badinage. From deceit in the spirit, the mother of all false deeds, the offspring is already incalculable. An acute and candid person in the revenue department in Washington, who is led by the course of his employment to regularly visit the cities, north, south, and west, to investigate frauds, has talked much with me about his discoveries. The depravity of the business classes of our country is not less than has been supposed but infinitely greater. The official services of America, national, state, and municipal, in all their branches and departments except the judiciary, are saturated in corruption, bribery, falsehood, maladministration; and the judiciary is tainted. The great cities reek with respectable as much as nonrespectable robbery and scoundrelism. In fashionable life, flippancy, tepid amours, weak infidelism, small aims, or no aims at all, only to kill time. In business (this all-devouring modern word, *business*) the one sole object is, by any means, pecuniary gain. The magician's serpent in the fable ate up all the other serpents, and moneymaking is our magician's serpent, remaining today sole master of the field. The best class we show is but a mob of fashionably dressed speculators and vulgarians. True, indeed, behind this fantastic farce, enacted on the visible stage of society, solid things and stupendous labors are to be discovered, existing crudely and going on in the background, to advance and tell themselves in time. Yet the truths are none the less terrible. I say that our New World democracy, however great a success in uplifting the masses out of their sloughs, in materialistic development, products, and in a certain highly deceptive superficial popular intellectuality, is so far an almost complete failure in its social aspects and in really grand religious, moral, literary, and esthetic results. In vain do we march with unprecedented strides to empire so colossal, outvying the antique, beyond Alexander's, beyond the proudest sway of Rome. In vain have we annexed Texas, California, Alaska, and reach north for Canada and south for Cuba. It is as if we were somehow being endowed with a vast and more and more thoroughly appointed body and then left with little or no soul.

WALT WHITMAN
Democratic Vistas
1871

72

General Dodge Builds the Union Pacific

The Pacific Railway Act of 1862 provided for the construction of a transcontinental railroad to be undertaken by the Central Pacific and Union Pacific Railway companies, the first building eastward from the California line, the second westward from Council Bluffs, Iowa. General Grenville M. Dodge, who had proved his talents as Sherman's engineer in the Atlanta campaign, was made chief engineer of the Union Pacific and was largely responsible for the rapidity and efficiency with which the road was constructed. The juncture of the Union Pacific with the Central Pacific at Promontory Point, Utah, was an event of national importance.

The organization for work on the plains away from civilization was as follows: Each of our surveying parties consisted of a chief who was an experienced engineer, two assistants, also civil engineers, rodmen, flagmen, and chainmen, generally graduated civil engineers but without personal experience in the field, besides ax men, teamsters, and herders. When the party was expected to live upon the game of the country, a hunter was added. Each party would thus consist of from eighteen to twenty-two men, all armed. When operating in a hostile Indian country they were regularly drilled, though after the Civil War this was unnecessary, as most of them had been in the army. Each party entering a country occupied by hostile Indians was generally furnished with a military escort of from ten men to a company under a competent officer. The duty of this escort was to protect the party when in camp. In the field the escort usually occupied prominent hills commanding the territory in which the work was to be done, so as to head off sudden attacks by the Indians. Notwithstanding this protection the parties were often attacked, their chief or some of their men killed or wounded, and their stock run off. . . .

The location part in our work on the Union Pacific was followed by the construction corps, grading generally a hundred miles at a time. That distance was graded in about thirty days on the plains, as a rule, but in the mountains we sometimes had to open our grading several hundred miles ahead of our track in order to complete the grading by the time the track should reach it. All the supplies for this work had to be hauled from the end of the track, and the wagon transportation was enormous. At one time we were using at least ten thousand animals, and most of the time from eight to ten thousand laborers. The bridge gangs always worked from five to twenty miles ahead of the track, and it was seldom that the track waited for a bridge. To supply one mile of track with material and supplies required about forty cars, as on the plains everything—rails, ties, bridging, fastenings, all railway supplies, fuel for locomotives and trains, and supplies for men and animals on the entire work—had to be transported from the Missouri River. Therefore, as we moved westward, every hundred miles added vastly to our transportation. Yet the work was so systematically planned and executed that I do not remember an instance in all the construction of the line of the work being delayed a single week for want of material. Each winter we planned the work for the next season. By the opening of spring, about April 1st, every part of the machinery was in working order, and in no year did we fail to accomplish our work. After 1866 the reports will show what we started out to do each year and what we accomplished.

Our Indian troubles commenced in 1864 and lasted until the tracks joined at Promontory. We lost most of our men and stock while building from Fort Kearney to Bitter Creek. At that time every mile of road had to be surveyed, graded, tied, and bridged under military protection. The order to every surveying corps, grading, bridging, and tie outfit was never to run when attacked. All were required to be armed, and I do not know that the order was disobeyed in a single instance, nor did I ever hear that the Indians had driven a party permanently from its work. I remember one occasion when they swooped down on a grading outfit in sight of the temporary fort of the military some five miles away and right in sight of the end of the track. The government commission to examine that section of the completed road had just arrived, and the commissioners witnessed the fight. The graders had their arms stacked on the cut. The Indians leaped from the ravines and, springing upon the workmen before they could reach their arms, cut loose the stock and caused a panic. General Frank P. Blair, General Simpson, and Doctor White were the commissioners, and they showed their grit by running to my car for arms to aid in the fight. We did not fail to benefit from this experience, for on returning to the East the commission dwelt earnestly on the necessity of our being protected.

The Union Pacific and Central Pacific were allowed to build, one east and the other west, until they met. The building of five hundred miles of road during the summers of 1866 and 1867, hardly twelve months' actual work, had aroused great interest in the country and much excitement, in which the government took a part. We were pressed to as speedy a completion of the road as possible, although ten years had been allowed by Congress. The officers of the Union Pacific had become imbued with this spirit, and they urged me to plan to build as much road as possible in 1868. . . . The reaching of the summit of the first range of the Rocky Mountains, which I named

Sherman, in honor of my old commander, in 1867, placed us comparatively near good timber for ties and bridges which, after cutting, could be floated down the mountain streams at some points to our crossing and at others within twenty-five or thirty miles of our work. This afforded great relief to the transportation.

We made our plans to build to Salt Lake, four hundred and eighty miles, in 1868, and to endeavor to meet the Central Pacific at Humboldt Wells, two hundred and nineteen miles west of Ogden, in the spring of 1869. I had extended our surveys during the years 1867 and 1868 to the California state line and laid my plans before the company, and the necessary preparations were made to commence work as soon as frost was out of the ground, say about April 1st. Material had been collected in sufficient quantities at the end of the track to prevent any delay. During the winter, ties and bridge material had been cut and prepared in the mountains to bring to the line at convenient points, and the engineering forces were started to their positions before cold weather was over, that they might be ready to begin their work as soon as the temperature would permit. I remember that the parties going to Salt Lake crossed the Wasatch Mountains on sledges and that the snow covered the tops of the telegraph poles. We all knew and appreciated that the task we had laid out would require the greatest energy on the part of all hands. About April 1st, therefore, I went on to the plains myself and started our construction forces, remaining the whole summer between Laramie and the Humboldt Mountains. I was surprised at the rapidity with which the work was carried forward. Winter caught us in the Wasatch Mountains, but we kept on grading our road and laying our track in the snow and ice, at a tremendous cost. I estimated for the company that the extra cost of thus forcing the work during that summer and winter was over ten million dollars, but the instructions I received were to go on, no matter what the cost. Spring found us with the track at Ogden, and by May 1st we had reached Promontory, five hundred and thirty-four miles west of our starting point twelve months before. Work on our line was opened to Humboldt Wells, making in the year a grading of seven hundred and fifty-four miles of line.

The Central Pacific had made wonderful progress coming east, and we abandoned the work from Promontory to Humboldt Wells, bending all our efforts to meet them at Promontory. Between Ogden and Promontory each company graded a line, running side by side, and in some places one line was right above the other. The laborers upon the Central Pacific were Chinamen, while ours were Irishmen, and there was much ill feeling between them. Our Irishmen were in the habit of firing their blasts in the cuts without giving warning to the Chinamen on the Central Pacific working right above them. From this cause several Chinamen were severely hurt. Complaint was made to me by the Central Pacific people, and I endeavored to have the contractors bring all hostilities to a close, but for some reason or other they failed to do so. One day the Chinamen, appreciating the situation, put in what is called a "grave" on their work and, when the Irishmen right under them were all at work, let go their blast and buried several of our men. This brought about a truce at once. From that time the Irish laborers showed due respect for the Chinamen, and there was no further trouble.

When the two roads approached in May, 1869, we agreed to connect at the summit of Promontory Point, and the day was fixed so that trains could reach us from New York and California. We laid the rails to the junction point a day or two before the final closing. . . . The two trains pulled up facing each other, each crowded with workmen who sought advantageous positions to witness the ceremonies and literally covered the cars. The officers and invited guests formed on each side of the track, leaving it open to the south. The telegraph lines had been brought to that point, so that in the final spiking as each blow was struck the telegraph recorded it at each connected office from the Atlantic to the Pacific. Prayer was offered; a number of spikes were driven in the two adjoining rails, each one of the prominent persons present taking a hand, but very few hitting the spikes, to the great amusement of the crowd. When the last spike was placed, light taps were given upon it by several officials, and it was finally driven home by the chief engineer of the Union Pacific Railway. The engineers ran up their locomotives until they touched, the engineer upon each engine breaking a bottle of champagne upon the other one, and thus the two roads were wedded into one great trunk line from the Atlantic to the Pacific. Spikes of silver and gold were brought specially for the occasion and later were manufactured into miniature spikes as mementos of the occasion. It was a bright but cold day. After a few speeches we all took refuge in the Central Pacific cars, where wine flowed freely and many speeches were made.

GRENVILLE M. DODGE
"How We Built the Union Pacific Railway,
and Other Railway Papers and Addresses"

73

Robert Louis Stevenson
Travels Across the Plains

The journey which Stevenson here chronicles marked the opening of the second period in his adventurous life. He had left his home in Edinburgh with very slender means in his pocket, and under the disadvantage of very bad health, to marry a lady of whom he believed his parents would disapprove. This was a Mrs. Osbourne, whom he intended to join in San Francisco. He sailed from the Clyde in August 1879 and within twenty-four hours of his arrival in New York was on his way west as an emigrant. The trip across the continent required almost two weeks, under conditions of the greatest discomfort, and when Stevenson reached the Pacific he "looked like a man at death's door." Indeed, at Monterey, where he went to recuperate, he promptly broke down. But his history of the journey makes light of its hardships. Emigrants who did not know the language, who were not acquainted with Anglo-Saxon ways, and who lacked his cheeriness and breadth of sympathy would have suffered far more.

It was about two in the afternoon of Friday that I found myself in front of the Emigrant House [Council Bluffs, Iowa], with more than a hundred others, to be sorted and boxed for the journey. A white-haired official with a stick under one arm and a list in the other hand stood apart in front of us and called name after name in the tone of a command. At each name you would see a family gather up its brats and bundles and run for the hindmost of the three cars that stood awaiting us, and I soon concluded that this was to be set apart for the women and children. The second or central car, it turned out, was devoted to men traveling alone, and the third to Chinese. The official was easily moved to anger at the least delay, but the emigrants were both quick at answering their names and speedy in getting themselves and their effects on board.

The families once housed, we men carried the second car without ceremony by simultaneous assault. I suppose the reader has some notion of an American railroad car, that long, narrow wooden box like a flat-roofed Noah's ark, with a stove and a convenience, one at either end, a passage down the middle, and transverse benches upon either hand. Those destined for emigrants on the Union Pacific are only remarkable for their extreme plainness, nothing but wood entering in any part into their constitution, and for the usual inefficacy of the lamps, which often went out and shed but a dying glimmer even while they burned. The benches are too short for anything but a young child. Where there is scarce elbowroom for two to sit, there will not be space enough for one to lie. Hence the company, or rather, as it appears from certain bills about the transfer station, the company's servants, have conceived a plan for the better accommodation of travelers. They prevail on every two to chum together. To each of the chums they sell a board and three square cushions stuffed with straw and covered with thin cotton. The benches can be made to face each other in pairs, for the backs are reversible. On the approach of night the boards are laid from bench to bench, making a couch wide enough for two and long enough for a man of the middle height, and the chums lie down side by side upon the cushions with the head to the conductor's van and the feet to the engine. When the train is full, of course this plan is impossible, for there must not be more than one to every bench; neither can it be carried out unless the chums agree. It was to bring about this last condition that our white-haired official now bestirred himself. He made a most active master of ceremonies, introducing likely couples and even guaranteeing the amiability and honesty of each. The greater the number of happy couples the better for his pocket, for it was he who sold the raw material of the beds. His price for one board and three straw cushions began with two dollars and a half, but before the train left and, I am sorry to say, long after I had purchased mine, it had fallen to one dollar and a half.

The day faded; the lamps were lit; a party of wild young men, who got off next evening at North Platte, stood together on the stern platform, singing "The Sweet By-and-By" with very tuneful voices; the chums began to put up their beds; and it seemed as if the business of the day were at an end. But it was not so, for, the train stopping at some station, the cars were instantly thronged with the natives, wives and fathers, young men and maidens, some of them in a little more than night gear, some with stable lanterns, and all offering beds for sale. Their charge began with twenty-five cents a cushion but fell, before the train went on again, to fifteen, with the bed board gratis, or less than one-fifth of what I had paid for mine at the transfer. This is my contribution to the economy of future emigrants.

A great personage on an American train is the newsboy. He sells books (such books!), papers, fruit, lollipops, and cigars, and on emigrant journeys soap, towels, tin washing dishes, tin coffee pitchers, coffee, tea, sugar, and tinned eatables, mostly hash or beans and bacon. Early next morning the newsboy went around the cars, and chumming on a more extended principle became the order of the hour. It requires but a copartnery of two to manage beds, but washing and eating can be carried on most economically by a syndicate of three. I myself entered a little after sunrise into articles of agreement and became one of the firm of Pennsylvania, Shakespeare, and Dubuque. Shakespeare was my own nickname on the cars, Pennsylvania that of my bedfellow, and Dubuque, the name of a place in the state of Iowa, that of an amiable young fellow going west to cure an asthma and retarding his recovery by incessantly chewing or smoking and sometimes chewing and smoking together. Shakespeare bought a tin washing dish, Dubuque a towel, and Pennsylvania a brick of soap. The partners used these instruments, one after another, according to the order of their first awaking, and when the firm had finished there was no want of borrowers. Each filled the tin dish at the water filter opposite the stove and retired with the whole stock in trade to the platform of the car. There he knelt down, supporting himself by a shoulder against the woodwork or one elbow crooked about the railing, and made shift to wash his face and neck and hands—a cold, an insufficient, and, if the train is moving rapidly, a somewhat dangerous toilet.

On a similar division of expense, the firm of Pennsylvania, Shakespeare, and Dubuque supplied themselves with coffee, sugar, and necessary vessels; and their operations are a type of what went on through all the cars. Before the sun was up the stove would be brightly burning; at the first station the natives would come on board with milk and eggs and coffee cakes, and soon from end to end the car would be filled with little parties breakfasting upon the bed boards. It was the pleasantest hour of the day. . . .

Many conductors, again, will hold no communication with an emigrant. As you are thus cut off from the superior authorities, a great deal of your comfort depends on the character of the newsboy. He has it in his power indefinitely to better and brighten the emigrant's lot. The newsboy with whom we started from the transfer was a dark, bullying, contemptuous, insolent scoundrel, who treated us like dogs. On the other hand, the lad who rode with us in this capacity from Ogden to Sacramento made himself the friend of all and helped us with information, attention, assistance, and a kind countenance. He told us where and when we should have our meals and how long the train would stop, kept seats at table for those who were delayed, and watched that we should neither be left behind nor yet unnecessarily hurried. You who live at home at ease can hardly realize the greatness of this service, even had it stood alone. When I think of that lad coming and going, train after train, with his bright face and civil words, I see how easily a good man may become the benefactor of his kind. Perhaps he is discontented with himself, perhaps troubled with ambitions; why, if he but knew it, he is a hero of the old Greek stamp; and while he thinks he is only earning a profit of a few cents, and that perhaps exorbitant, he is doing a man's work and bettering the world. . . .

I had been suffering in my health a good deal all the way, and at last, whether I was exhausted by my complaint or poisoned in some wayside eating house, the evening we left Laramie, I fell sick outright. That was a night which I shall not readily forget. The lamps did not go out; each made a faint shining in its own neighborhood, and the shadows were confounded together in the long, hollow box of the car. The sleepers lay in uneasy attitudes—here two chums alongside, flat upon their backs like dead folk, there a man sprawling on the floor with his face upon his arm, there another half seated, with his head and shoulders on the bench. The most passive were continually and roughly shaken by the movement of the train; others stirred, turned, or stretched out their arms like children; it was surprising how many groaned and murmured in their sleep; and as I passed to and fro, stepping across the prostrate, and caught now a snore, now a gasp, now a half-formed word, it gave me a measure of the worthlessness of rest in that unresting vehicle. Although it was chill, I was obliged to open my window, for the degradation of the air soon became intolerable to one who was awake and using the full supply of life. Outside, in a glimmering night, I saw the black, amorphous hills shoot by unweariedly into our wake. They that long for morning have never longed for it more earnestly than I.

And yet when day came, it was to shine upon the same broken and unsightly quarter of the world. Mile upon mile, and not a tree, a bird, or a river. Only down the long, sterile canyons the train shot hooting and awoke the resting echo. That train was the one piece of life in all the deadly land; it was the one actor, the one spectacle fit to be observed in this paralysis of man and nature. And when I think how the railroad has been pushed through this unwatered wilderness and haunt of savage tribes and now will bear an emigrant for some twelve pounds from the Atlantic to the Golden Gates; how at each stage of the construction roaring, impromptu cities, full of gold and lust and death, sprang up and then died away again, and are now but wayside stations in the desert; how in these uncouth places pigtailed Chinese pirates worked side by side with border ruffians and broken men from Europe, talking together in a mixed dialect, mostly oaths, gambling, drinking, quarreling, and murdering like wolves; how the plumed hereditary lord of all America heard, in this last fastness, the scream of the "bad medicine wagon" charioting his foes; and then when I go on to remember that all this epical turmoil was conducted by gentlemen in frock coats and with a view to nothing more extraordinary than a fortune and a subsequent visit to Paris, it seems to me, I own, as if this railway were the one typical achievement of the age in which we live, as if it brought together into one plot all the ends of the world and all the degrees of social rank, and offered to some great writer the busiest, the most extended, and the most varied subject for an enduring literary work. If it be romance, if it be contrast, if it be heroism that we require, what was Troy town to this?

At Ogden we changed cars from the Union Pacific to the Central Pacific line of railroad.

The cars on the Central Pacific were nearly twice as high, and so proportionally airier; they were freshly varnished, which gave us all a sense of cleanliness as though we had bathed; the seats drew out and joined in the center, so that there was no more need for bed boards; and there was an upper tier of berths which could be closed by day and opened at night.

I had by this time some opportunity of seeing the people whom I was among. They were in rather marked contrast to the emigrants I had met on board ship while crossing the Atlantic. They were mostly lumpish fellows, silent and noisy, a common combination, somewhat sad, I should say, with an extraordinary poor taste in humor, and little interest in their fellow creatures beyond that of a cheap and merely external curiosity.

There were no emigrants direct from Europe save one German family and a knot of Cornish miners who kept grimly by themselves, one reading the New Testament all day long through steel spectacles, the rest discussing privately the secrets of their old-world, mysterious race.

The rest were all American born, but they came from almost every quarter of that continent. All the states of the North had sent out a fugitive to cross the plains with me. From Virginia, from Pennsylvania, from New York, from far western Iowa and Kansas, from Maine that borders on the Canadas, and from the Canadas themselves—some one or two were fleeing in quest of a better land and better wages. The talk in the train, like the talk I heard on the steamer, ran upon hard times, short-commons, and hope that moves ever westward. I thought of my shipful from Great Britain with a feeling of despair. They had come three thousand miles, and yet not far enough. Hard times bowed them out of the Clyde and stood to welcome them at Sandy Hook. Where were they to go? Pennsylvania, Maine, Iowa, Kansas? These were not places for immigration, but for emigration, it appeared—not one of them, but I knew a man who had lifted up his heel and left it for an ungrateful country. And it was still westward that they ran. Hunger, you would have thought, came out of the east like the sun, and the evening was made of edible gold. And meantime, in the car in front of me, were there not half a hundred emigrants from the opposite quarter? Hungry Europe and hungry China, each pouring from their gates in search of provender, had here come face to face. The two waves had met; east and west had alike failed; the whole round world had been prospected and condemned; there was no El Dorado anywhere; and till one could emigrate to the moon, it seemed as well to stay patiently at home. Nor was there wanting another sign, at once more picturesque and more disheartening; for as we continued to steam westward toward the land of gold, we were continually passing other emigrant trains upon the journey east; and these were as crowded as our own. Had all these return voyagers made a fortune in the mines? Were they all bound for Paris and to be in Rome by Easter? It would seem not, for whenever we met them, the passengers ran on the platform and cried to us through the windows, in a kind of wailing chorus, to "come back." On the plains of Nebraska, in the mountains of Wyoming, it was still the same cry and dismal to my heart:

"Come back!" That was what we heard by the way "about the good country we were going to." And at that very hour the sand lot of San Francisco was crowded with the unemployed and the echo from the other side of Market Street was repeating the rant of demagogues.

ROBERT LOUIS STEVENSON
Across the Plains, with Other Memories and Essays

74

Andy Adams Herds Texas
Cattle on the Long Drive

For generations cattle had grazed wild on the plains of the Southwest, too far distant from market to have any value. In 1867 the Kansas Pacific Railway began to reach out into the Plains, and in that year J.G. McCoy established the first of the cow towns, Abilene, Kansas, from which live cattle could be shipped to the stock markets of the East. Then began the "long drive" northward along the Goodnight or the Chisholm or other trails to one of the roaring cattle towns on the Kansas Pacific or the Union Pacific railroads. Andy Adams, one of the greatest of the Texas cattlemen, here describes some of the perils of the "long drive."

The next morning by daybreak the cattle were thrown off the bed ground and started grazing before the sun could dry out what little moisture the grass had absorbed during the night. The heat of the past week had been very oppressive, and in order to avoid it as much as possible, we made late and early drives. Before the wagon passed the herd during the morning drive, what few canteens we had were filled with water for the men. The *remuda* was kept with the herd, and four changes of mounts were made during the day, in order not to exhaust any one horse. Several times, for an hour or more, the herd was allowed to lie down and rest; but by the middle of the afternoon thirst made them impatient and restless, and the point men were compelled to ride steadily in the lead in order to hold the cattle to a walk. A number of times during the afternoon we attempted to graze them, but not until the twilight of evening was it possible. . . .

We were handling the cattle as humanely as possible under the circumstances. The guards for the night were doubled, six men on the first half and the same on the latter, Bob Blades being detailed to assist Honeyman in night-herding the saddle horses. If any of us got more than an hour's sleep that night, he was lucky. Flood, McCann, and the horse wranglers did not even try to rest. To those of us who could find time to eat, our cook kept open house. Our foreman knew that a well-fed man can stand an incredible amount of hardship and appreciated the fact that on the trail a good cook is a valuable asset. Our outfit, therefore, was cheerful to a man, and jokes and songs helped to while away the weary hours of the night.

The second guard, under Flood, pushed the cattle off their beds an hour before dawn, and before they were relieved had urged the herd more than five miles on the third day's drive over this waterless mesa. In spite of our economy of water, after breakfast on this third morning there was scarcely enough left to fill the canteens for the day. In view of this, we could promise ourselves no midday meal—except a can of tomatoes to the man—so the wagon was ordered to drive through to the expected water ahead, while the saddle horses were held available as on the day before for frequent changing of mounts. The day turned out to be one of torrid heat, and before the middle of the forenoon, the cattle lolled their tongues in despair, while their sullen lowing surged through from rear to lead and back again in piteous yet ominous appeal. The only relief we could offer was to travel them slowly, as they spurned every opportunity offered them either to graze or to lie down.

It was nearly noon when we reached the last divide and sighted the scattering timber of the expected watercourse. The enforced order of the day before—to hold the herd in a walk and prevent exertion and heating—now required four men in the lead, while the rear followed over a mile behind, dogged and sullen. Near the middle of the afternoon McCann returned on one of his mules with the word that it was a question if there was water enough to water even the horse stock. The preceding outfit, so he reported, had dug a shallow well in the bed of the creek, from which he had filled his kegs, but the stock water was a mere loblolly. On receipt of this news, we changed mounts for the fifth time that day, and Flood, taking Forrest, the cook, and the horse wrangler, pushed on ahead with the *remuda* to the waterless stream.

The outlook was anything but encouraging. Flood and Forrest scouted the creek up and down for ten miles in a fruitless search for water. The outfit held the herd back until the twilight of evening, when Flood returned and confirmed McCann's report. It was twenty miles yet to the next water ahead, and if the horse stock could only be watered thoroughly, Flood was determined to make the attempt to nurse the herd through to water. McCann was digging an extra well, and he expressed the belief that by hollowing out a number of holes, enough water could be secured for the saddle stock. Honeyman had corralled the horses and was letting only a few go to the water at a time, while the night horses were being thoroughly watered as fast as the water rose in the well.

Holding the herd this third night required all hands. Only a few men at a time were allowed to go into camp and eat, for the herd refused even to lie down. What few cattle attempted to rest were prevented by the more restless ones. By spells they would mill, until riders were sent through the herd at a breakneck pace to break up the groups. During these milling efforts of the herd, we drifted over a mile from camp, but by the light of moon and stars and the number of riders, scattering was prevented. As the horses were loose for the night, we could not start them on the trail until daybreak gave us a change of mounts, so we lost the early start of the morning before.

Good cloudy weather would have saved us, but in its stead was a sultry morning without a breath of air, which bespoke another day of sizzling heat. We had not been on the trail over two hours before the heat became almost unbearable to man and beast. Had it not been for the condition of the herd, all might yet have gone well, but over three days had now elapsed without water for the cattle, and they became feverish and ungovernable. The lead cattle turned back several times, wandering aimlessly in any direction, and it was with considerable difficulty that the herd could be held on the trail. The rear overtook the lead, and the cattle gradually lost all semblance of a trail herd. Our horses were fresh, however, and after about two hours' work, we once more got the herd strung out in trailing fashion; but before a mile had been covered, the leaders again turned, and the cattle congregated into a mass of unmanageable animals, milling and lowing in their fever and thirst. The milling only intensified their sufferings from the heat, and the outfit split and quartered them again and again, in the hope that this unfortunate outbreak might be checked. No sooner was the milling stopped than they would surge hither and yon, sometimes half a mile, as ungovernable as the waves of an ocean. After wasting several hours in this manner, they finally turned back over the trail, and the utmost efforts of every man in the outfit failed to check them. We threw our ropes in their faces, and when this failed, we resorted to shooting, but in defiance of the fusillade and the smoke they walked sullenly through the line of horsemen across their front. Six-shooters were discharged so close to the leaders' faces as to singe their hair; yet under a noonday sun they disregarded this and every other device to turn them and passed wholly out of our control. In a number of instances wild steers deliberately walked against our horses, and then for the first time a fact dawned on us that chilled the marrow in our bones—*the herd was going blind.*

The bones of men and animals that lie bleaching along the trails abundantly testify that this was not the first instance in which the plain had baffled the determination of man. It was now evident that nothing short of water would stop the herd, and we rode aside and let them pass. As the outfit turned back to the wagon, our foreman seemed dazed by the sudden and unexpected turn of affairs but rallied and met the emergency.

"There's but one thing left to do," said he, as we rode along, "and that is to hurry the outfit back to Indian Lakes. The herd will travel day and night, and instinct can be depended on to carry them to the only water they know. It's too late to be of any use now, but it's plain why those last two herds turned off at the lakes; someone had gone back and warned them of the very thing we've met. We must beat them to the lakes, for water is the only thing that will check them now. It's a good thing that they are strong, and five or six days without water will hardly kill any. It was no vague statement of the man who said if he owned hell and Texas, he'd rent Texas and live in hell, for if this isn't Billy hell, I'd like to know what you call it."

We spent an hour watering the horses from the wells of our camp of the night before, and about two o'clock started back over the trail for Indian Lakes. We overtook the abandoned herd during the afternoon. They were strung out nearly five miles in length and were walking about a three-mile gait. Four men were given two extra horses apiece and left to throw in the stragglers in the rear, with instructions to follow them well into the night, and again in the morning as long as their canteens lasted. The remainder of the outfit pushed on without a halt except to change mounts and reached the lakes shortly after midnight. There we secured the first good sleep of any consequence for three days.

It was fortunate for us that there were no range cattle at these lakes, and we had only to cover a front of about six miles to catch the drifting herd. It was nearly noon the next day before the cattle began to arrive at the water holes in squads of from twenty to fifty. Pitiful objects as they were, it was a novelty to see them reach the water and slack their thirst. Wading out into the lakes until their sides were half covered, they would stand and low in a soft moaning voice, often for half an hour before attempting to drink. Contrary to our expectation, they drank very little at first, but stood in the water for hours. After coming out, they would lie down and rest for hours longer and then drink again before attempting to graze, their thirst overpowering hunger. That they were blind there was no question, but with the causes that produced it once removed, it was probable their eyesight would gradually return.

ANDY ADAMS
The Log of a Cowboy

75

The Grasshopper Plague
Hits the High Plains

The region of the High Plains—roughly from the one hundredth meridian to the Rocky Mountains—suffered from insufficient rainfall and from recurrent insect plagues, which made farming highly hazardous. Dry farming and irrigation in part solved the problem of aridity, but no method was known of dealing with the grasshopper plagues. When the locusts came, they denuded a field in a few moments, and the farmers stood by helpless as they watched the labor of a year wasted.

In 1874 came a gigantic calamity in the form of a raid of grasshoppers, which ate up every bit of green vegetation from the Rocky Mountains to and beyond the Missouri River. I recall that when coming home late one afternoon for supper I stepped back surprised to see what became known as Rocky Mountain locusts covering the side of the house. Already inside, they feasted on the curtains. Clouds of them promptly settled down on the whole country—everywhere, unavoidable. People set about killing them to save gardens, but this soon proved ridiculous. Specially contrived machines, pushed by horses, scooped up the hoppers in grain fields by the barrelful to burn them. This, too, was then nonsensical. Vast hordes, myriad. In a week grain fields, gardens, shrubs, vines, had been eaten down to the ground or to the bark. Nothing could be done. You sat by and saw everything go.

When autumn came with the country devastated, the population despaired again when seeing the insects remaining for the winter with the apparent plan of being on hand for the next season. It seemed that they could be counted on as a curse for all time, since the Rocky Mountain locusts, as the name indicates, appeared new to science, to the civilized world. No one, accordingly, knew of their habits. And their ingenuity confounded close observers. As if intending to stay permanently on the plains, they bored holes only in hard ground, in roads and other firm places, for their winter occupancy. Intelligently did they avoid soft ground, since tenancy there would be more easily, more apt to be, disturbed. . . .

To add to the terror of the locust invasion was the general accompaniment of weather tending always to be dry. Kansans—"people of the south wind." This poetic Indian meaning might bear a still more distinctive signification if it ran "people of the hot southwest wind." For continental western Kansas, lying in the exact center of the United States, turned out to be subject in summer to burning south or southwest winds untempered by cooling salt breezes creeping up from the Gulf of Mexico or cooling zephyrs descending from Canada. The middle area often missed the relief that either the southern or northern areas might experience. And a steady hot current of air, though mild in velocity, brought the dreaded dry times.

How one hated to see the heavens seal their cisterns and the plains to be sear! A few showers would dash upon the ground and run to cover in the creek and river beds, not stopping to penetrate to roots. Matters seemed, indeed, to be made worse by these spurts of moisture, the blazing sun promptly coming out afterward, baking the earth harder.

Almost hilarious, many of the old-timers during such months! They underwent the stark privations in very fair style, having been shown to be prophets with honor in their own land.

"Hee-hee! Didn't I tell you so? This ain't no farmin' country. Too droughty. Lucky fer cattle if lucky fer anything. An' these 'ere Easterners ruinin' the buffalo grass by plowin' it up! Spilin' everything. Yaps that want to farm better stay back East where there ain't anything better to do. They have driv' out the Texas cattle trade. What have they got left? Mighty little, by cracky!"

People still often considered the plains fit at best for very light spring crops. If these shrank up just before harvest, there would be left after June nothing to fall back upon during the rest of the year. The small corn areas along the streams then resembled patches of sticks. The local livestock in 1874 had to be disposed of, fodder lacking. Pitiful little vegetable gardens shriveled. The few flower plots planted by housewives were at first bravely watered. Like tiny, ghastly totem poles did the scarred stalks afterward look.

In a hot droughty summer most of the wells and springs gave out early. Water in creeks trickled so shallowly that dogs lay panting in them while hardly able to immerse more than their paws. Then the burning spell! The southwest wind blew at frequent intervals out of its Sahara ovens, sweeping the land with a flinty dust. You thought of it as a finely textured burial shroud. People told the old joke: "We'd have had to soak our pigs overnight so that they could hold swill." The nights proved as debilitating as the days, since humanity couldn't sleep for the heat. This was the worst of it—they couldn't sleep. No part of each twenty-four hours furnished forgetfulness of the nightmare of failure.

In that country of poor farming and upon a population heedless about laying by supplies for a scarce period, the disaster of 1874 doubled its effect. One conceded: Of what use to work? Farmers, of course, stood out of a job. They loafed in town from midsummer on. For many said they could hardly have plowed or broken prairie. The lumps of sod needed to be knocked up by axes. Seven months before there would be a thing to do. Locusts and scanty rainfall together!

One watched the office men in towns lounging day after day at their doors or hanging out of their windows, with nothing on hand. Business collapsed. It looked like an idiotic insult to ask anyone for what he owed. Tillers of soil could not be counted on to pay anyhow till after harvest, once a year, and now, in 1874, no harvest. The merchants, townsmen in general, were expected to cash up from month to month. They stared blankly at the streets, trying to figure how they could get through the winter with their money and credit mostly gone up the spout. The sight of farmers dawdling in stores and saloons added to the dismalness. What if *next* year brought a blank? Too awful to contemplate! Meanwhile—it looked like sheer unavoidable starvation.

Moral stamina? One knew how the women slouched around red-hot cookstoves three times a day for the regular if skimpy meals. Some strength *must* be kept up, some flesh *must* be kept on bones. Even wives who had had a little pardonable vanity left quit trying to save their complexions. They let their tresses go dry and stick out any way. Hair got crinkly, few bothering much about brushes and combs. Hollow-eyed, fagged out, the fair sex came to care little how they looked, what they wore. The story was told of seeing on a street a woman in a garment she had sewed together from the halves of different flour sacks without taking the pains to remove their brands, the result being shocking. Men swore and played poker no more. Fathers dreaded to face their children, who grew raggeder. As for their dirtiness, who, you might almost ask, hardly dared spare water to wash them? Husbands hated to go home to meals, for they must meet the appeals of their wives to climb on wagons and strike out for back home.

"Sell for what you can get, John—give it away—leave it—only let's get out. I don't have to ride on a railroad. A schooner headed east looks awful good to me.". . .

Prayer meetings being held, a few of the men who had not gone to church dropped in and sat before pulpits, heads bowed, humbled in respect. They wondered now if there might be some virtue in supplication. At least they risked no money nor chances by attending meeting. Anything, even prayer, to see mud puddles drowning out the hoppers! But the believers in the great god luck—the majority—stood, in the main, by their guns. They didn't think petitions by four-hundred-dollar-a-year ministers had enough breeze behind them to be shot clear up to Heaven so that the yelpings could be heard there. Wouldn't luck bring a favorable year next time, since this one could be called a ripper? Herein lay the dependable thing about luck: It always changes. . . .

What with federal and other public aid and a steady immigration with money in larger sums, the population lived through the great grasshopper year mainly from necessity as well as pluck. It was a close call. But the locusts or a drought or both the next year would practically wipe out this early folk. A mighty and unsuspected blessing, however, intervened. Since low and moister regions than the Rocky Mountains cause its grasshopper progeny to die before maturity, one raid will not continue elsewhere its severest damage into the following years. This is what took place on the plains in the spring of 1875, though it could not have been foreseen by the disheartened people. In that year and the year or two afterward this insect did not cause the harm suffered in 1874.

Also the seed grain supplied by Eastern charity made good, and the fortunate season in 1875 brought ample crops to meet good prices. Buoyant faith at once reestablished itself. . . . The god luck had again veered. The plains now reigned in prosperity and was freely wagered on in terms of a wet, though glowing, future.

STUART HENRY
Conquering Our Great American Plains

76

Horace White Sees
the Great Chicago Fire

The spectacularly rapid growth of Chicago had involved the almost universal use of wood for construction purposes and made it peculiarly vulnerable to fire. Older cities, to be sure, like Boston, had been swept by fires, but the Great Chicago Fire of 1871 was the most catastrophic thing of its kind in nineteenth-century America. Horace White, whose report of the fire is the most vivid that we have, was editor of the *Chicago Tribune* and later of the *New York Evening Post*.

I had retired to rest, though not to sleep (Sunday, October 8, 1871), when the great bell struck the alarm, but fires had been so frequent of late and had been so speedily extinguished that I did not deem it worthwhile to get up and look at it or even to count the strokes on the bell to learn where it was. The bell paused for fifteen minutes before giving the general alarm, which distinguishes a great fire from a small one. When it sounded the general alarm I rose and looked out. There was a great light to the southwest of my residence, but no greater than I had frequently seen in that quarter, where vast piles of pine lumber have been stored all the time I have lived in Chicago, some eighteen years. But it was not pine lumber that was burning this time. It was a row of wooden tenements in the south division of the city, in which a few days ago were standing whole rows of the most costly buildings which it hath entered into the hearts of architects to conceive. I watched the increasing light for a few moments. Red tongues of light began to shoot upward; my family were all aroused by this time, and I dressed myself for the purpose of going to the *Tribune* office to write something about the catastrophe. Once out upon the street, the magnitude of the fire was suddenly disclosed to me.

The dogs of hell were upon the housetops of La Salle and Wells Streets, just south of Adams, bounding from one to another. The fire was moving northward like ocean surf on a sand beach. It had already traveled an eighth of a mile and was far beyond control. A column of flame would shoot up from a burning building, catch the force of the wind, and strike the next one, which in turn would perform the same direful office for its neighbor. It was simply indescribable in its terrible grandeur. Vice and crime had got the first scorching. The district where the fire got its first firm foothold was the Alsatia of Chicago. Fleeing before it was a crowd of blear-eyed, drunken, and diseased wretches, male and female, half naked, ghastly, with painted cheeks, cursing and uttering ribald jests as they drifted along.

I went to the *Tribune* office, ascended to the editorial rooms, took the only inflammable thing there, a kerosene lamp, and carried it to the basement, where I emptied the oil into the sewer. This was scarcely done when I perceived the flames breaking out of the roof of the courthouse, the old nucleus of which, in the center of the edifice, was not constructed of fireproof material as the new wings had been. As the flames had leaped a vacant space of nearly two hundred feet to get at this roof, it was evident that most of the business portion of the city must go down, but I did not reflect that the city waterworks, with their four great pumping engines, were in a straight line with the fire and wind. Nor did I know then that this priceless machinery was covered by a wooden roof. The flames were driving thither with demon precision.

Billows of fire were rolling over the business palaces of the city and swallowing up their contents. Walls were falling so fast that the quaking of the ground under our feet was scarcely noticed, so continuous was the reverberation. Sober men and women were hurrying through the streets from the burning quarter, some with bundles of clothes on their shoulders, others dragging trunks along the sidewalks by means of strings and ropes fastened to the handles, children trudging by their sides or borne in their arms. Now and then a sick man or woman would be observed half concealed in a mattress doubled up and borne by two men. Droves of horses were in the streets, moving by some sort of guidance to a place of safety. Vehicles of all descriptions were hurrying to and fro, some laden with trunks and bundles, others seeking similar loads and immediately finding them, the drivers making more money in one hour than they were used to see in a week or a month. Everybody in this quarter was hurrying toward the lake shore. All the streets crossing that part of Michigan Avenue which fronts on the lake (on which my own residence stood) were crowded with fugitives hastening towards the blessed water. . . .

There was still a mass of fire to the southwest, in the direction whence it originally came, but as the engines were all down there and the buildings small and low, I felt sure that the firemen would manage it. As soon as I had swallowed a cup of coffee and communicated to my family the facts that I had gathered, I started out to see the end of the battle. Reaching State Street, I glanced down to Field, Leiter and Company's store and to my surprise noticed that the streams of water which had before been showering it, as though it had been a great artificial fountain, had ceased to run. But I did not conjecture the awful reality, viz., that the great pumping engines had been disabled by a burning roof falling upon them. I thought perhaps the firemen on the store had discontinued their efforts because the danger was over. But why were men carrying out goods from the lower story? This query was soon answered by a gentleman who asked me if I had heard that the water had stopped! The awful truth was here! The pumping engines were disabled, and though we had at our feet a basin sixty miles wide by three hundred and sixty long and seven hundred feet deep, all full of clear green water, we could not lift enough to quench a cooking stove. Still the direction of the wind was such that I thought the remaining fire would not cross State Street nor reach the residences on Wabash and Michigan Avenues and the terrified people on the lake shore. I determined to go down to the black cloud of smoke which was rising away to the southwest, the course of which could not be discovered on account of the height of the intervening buildings, but thought it most prudent to go home again and tell my wife to get the family wearing apparel in readiness for moving. I found that she had already done so. I then hurried toward the black cloud, some ten squares distant, and there found the rows of wooden houses on Third and Fourth Avenues falling like ripe wheat before the reaper. At a glance I perceived that all was lost in our part of the city, and I conjectured that the *Tribune* building was doomed too, for I had noticed with consternation that the fireproof post office had been completely gutted, notwithstanding it was detached from other buildings. The *Tribune* [building] was fitted into a niche, one side of which consisted of a wholesale stationery store and the other of McVicker's Theater. But there was now no time to think of property. Life was in danger. The lives of those most dear to me depended upon their getting out of our house, out of our street, through an infernal gorge of horses, wagons, men, women, children, trunks, and plunder.

My brother was with me, and we seized the first empty wagon we could find, pinning the horse by the head. A hasty talk with the driver disclosed that we could have his establishment for one load for twenty dollars. I had not expected to get him for less than a hundred unless we should take him by force, and this was a bad time for a fight. He approved himself a muscular as well as a faithful fellow, and I shall always be glad that I avoided a personal difficulty with him. One peculiarity of the situation was that nobody could get a team without ready money. I had not thought of this when I was revolving in my mind the offer of one hundred dollars, which was more greenbacks than our whole family could have put up if our lives had depended upon the issue. This driver had divined that, as all the banks were burned, a check on the Commercial National would not carry him very far, although it might carry me to a place of safety. All the drivers had divined the same. Every man who had anything to sell perceived the same. "Pay as you go" had become the watchword of the hour. Never was there a community so hastily and so completely emancipated from the evils of the credit system.

With some little difficulty we reached our house, and in less time than we ever set out on a journey before, we dragged seven trunks, four bundles, four valises, two baskets, and one hamper of provisions into the street and piled them on the wagon. The fire was still more than a quarter of a mile distant, and the wind, which was increasing in violence, was driving it not exactly in our direction. The low wooden houses were nearly all gone, and after that the fire must make progress, if at all, against brick and stone. Several churches of massive architecture were between us and harm, and the great Palmer House had not been reached and might not be if the firemen, who had now got their hose into the lake, could work efficiently in the ever-increasing jam of fugitives.

My wife thought we should have time to take another load; my brother thought so; we all thought so. We had not given due credit either to the savage strength of the fire or the firm pack on Michigan Avenue. Leaving my brother to get the family safely out if I did not return in time and to pile the most valuable portion of my library into the drawers of bureaus and tables ready for moving, I seized a bird cage containing a talented green parrot and mounted the seat with the driver. For one square southward from the corner of Monroe Street we made pretty fair progress. The dust was so thick that we could not see the distance of a whole square ahead. It came not in clouds but in a steady storm of sand, the particles impinging against our faces like needle points. Pretty soon we came to a dead halt. We could move neither forward nor backward nor sidewise. The gorge had caught fast somewhere. Yet everybody was good-natured and polite. If I should say I didn't hear an oath all the way down Michigan Avenue, there are probably some mule drivers in Cincinnati who would say it was a lie. But I did not. The only quarrelsome person I saw was a German laborer (a noted exception to his race), who was protesting that he had lost everything and that he would not get out of the middle of the road although he was on foot. He became obstreperous on this point and commenced beating the head of my horse with his fist. My driver was preparing to knock him down with the butt end of his whip when two men seized the insolent Teuton and dragged him to the water's edge, where it is to be hoped he was ducked.

Presently the jam began to move, and we got on perhaps twenty paces and stuck fast again. By accident we had edged over to the east side of the street, and nothing but a board fence separated us from the lake park, a strip of ground a little wider than the street itself. A benevolent laborer on the park side of the fence pulled a loose post from the ground and with this for a catapult knocked off the boards and invited us to pass through. It was a hazardous undertaking, as we had to drive diagonally over a raised sidewalk, but we thought it was best to risk it. Our horse mounted and gave us a jerk which nearly threw us off the seat and sent the provision basket and one bundle of clothing whirling into the dirt. The eatables were irrecoverable. The bundle was rescued, with two or three pounds of butter plastered upon it. We started again, and here our parrot broke out with great rapidity and sharpness of utterance, "Get up, get up, get up, hurry up, hurry up, it's eight o'clock," ending with a shrill whistle. These ejaculations frightened a pair of carriage horses close to us on the other side of the fence, but the jam was so tight they couldn't run.

By getting into the park we succeeded in advancing two squares without impediment, and we might have gone farther had we not come upon an excavation which the public authorities had recently made. This drove us back to the Avenue, where another battering ram made a gap for us at the intersection of Van Buren Street, the north end of Michigan Terrace. Here the gorge seemed impassable. The difficulty proceeded from teams entering Michigan Avenue from cross streets. Extempore policemen stationed themselves at these crossings and helped as well as they could, but we were half an hour passing the terrace. From this imposing row of residences the millionaires were dragging their trunks and their bundles, and yet there was no panic, no frenzy, no boisterousness, but only the haste which the situation authorized. There was real danger to life all along this street, but nobody realized it, because the park was ample to hold all the people. None of us asked or thought what would become of those nearest the water if the smoke and cinders should drive the whole crowd down to the shore or if the vast bazaar of luggage should itself take fire, as some of it afterward did. Fortunately for those in the street, there was a limit to the number of teams available in that quarter of the city. The contributions from the cross streets grew less, and soon we began to move on a walk without interruption. Arriving at Eldridge Court, I turned into Wabash Avenue, where the crowd was thinner. Arriving at the house of a friend, who was on the windward side of the fire, I tumbled off my load and started back to get another. Halfway down Michigan Avenue, which was now perceptibly easier to move in, I perceived my family on the sidewalk with their arms full of light household effects. My wife told me that the house was already burned, that the flames burst out ready-made in the rear hall before she knew that the roof had been scorched, and that one of the servants, who had disobeyed orders in her eagerness to save some article, had got singed, though not burned, in coming out. My wife and mother and all the rest were begrimed with dirt and smoke, like blackamoors; everybody was. The "bloated aristocrats" all along the streets, who supposed they had lost both home and fortune at one swoop, were a sorry but not despairing congregation. They had saved their lives at all events, and they knew that many of their fellow creatures must have lost theirs. I saw a great many kindly acts done as we moved along. The poor helped the rich, and the rich helped the poor (if anybody could be called rich at such a time) to get on with their loads. I heard of cartmen demanding one hundred and fifty dollars (in hand, of course) for carrying a single load. Very likely it was so, but those cases did not come under my own notice. It did come under my notice that some cartmen worked for whatever the sufferers felt able to pay,

and one I knew worked with alacrity for nothing. It takes all sorts of people
to make a great fire.

Horace White
"The Great Chicago Fire"

77

Jacob Riis Discovers How
the Other Half Lives

A Danish immigrant, Jacob Riis brought to his adopted country not only intelligence and industry, but faith in the possibility of creating here a more just and
more humane social order. As a newspaper reporter he was familiar with life in
the slums and the tenements of New York, and as a reformer he was determined
to improve the lot of the poor and the underprivileged. *How the Other Half Lives*
was a powerful piece of journalism, which did more to dramatize the problem of
tenement-house reform than did anything else at that time. President Theodore
Roosevelt called Jacob Riis "the best American I ever knew."

New York's wage earners have no other place to live, more is the pity.
They are truly poor for having no better homes; waxing poorer in purse as
the exorbitant rents to which they are tied, as ever was serf to soil, keep rising. The wonder is that they are not all corrupted, and speedily, by their
surroundings. If on the contrary there be a steady working up, if not out of
the slough, the fact is a powerful argument for the optimist's belief that the
world is after all growing better not worse, and would go far toward disarm-
ing apprehension were it not for the steadier growth of the sediment of the
slums and its constant menace. Such an impulse toward better things there
certainly is. The German ragpicker of thirty years ago, quite as low in the
scale as his Italian successor, is the thrifty tradesman or prosperous farmer
of today.

The Italian scavenger of our time is fast graduating into exclusive control
of the corner fruit stands, while his black-eyed boy monopolizes the boot-
blacking industry in which a few years ago he was an intruder. The Irish hod
carrier in the second generation has become a bricklayer, if not the alderman
of his ward, while the Chinese coolie is in almost exclusive possession of the
laundry business. The reason is obvious. The poorest immigrant comes here

with the purpose and ambition to better himself and, given half a chance, might be reasonably expected to make the most of it. To the false plea that he prefers the squalid homes in which his kind are housed there could be no better answer. The truth is his half chance has too long been wanting, and for the bad result he has been unjustly blamed.

As emigration from east to west follows the latitude, so does the foreign influx in New York distribute itself along certain well-defined lines that waver and break only under the stronger pressure of a more gregarious race or the encroachments of inexorable business. A feeling of dependence upon mutual effort, natural to strangers in a strange land, unacquainted with its language and customs, sufficiently accounts for this.

The Irishman is the true cosmopolitan immigrant. All-pervading, he shares his lodging with perfect impartiality with the Italian, the Greek, and the "Dutchman," yielding only to sheer force of numbers, and objects equally to them all. A map of the city, colored to designate nationalities, would show more stripes than on the skin of a zebra and more colors than any rainbow. The city on such a map would fall into two great halves, green for the Irish prevailing in the West Side tenement districts and blue for the Germans on the East Side. But intermingled with these ground colors would be an odd variety of tints that would give the whole the appearance of an extraordinary crazy quilt. From down in the Sixth Ward, upon the site of the old Collect Pond that in the days of the fathers drained the hills which are no more, the red of the Italian would be seen forcing its way northward along the line of Mulberry Street to the quarter of the French purple on Bleecker Street and south Fifth Avenue, to lose itself and reappear, after a lapse of miles, in the Little Italy of Harlem, east of Second Avenue. Dashes of red, sharply defined, would be seen strung through the annexed district northward to the city line. On the West Side the red would be seen overrunning the old Africa of Thompson Street, pushing the black of the Negro rapidly uptown, against querulous but unavailing protests, occupying his home, his church, his trade and all, with merciless impartiality. There is a church in Mulberry Street that has stood for two generations as a sort of milestone of these migrations. Built originally for the worship of staid New Yorkers of the old stock, it was engulfed by the colored tide when the draft riots drove the Negroes out of reach of Cherry Street and the Five Points. Within the past decade the advance wave of the Italian onset reached it, and today the arms of United Italy adorn its front. The Negroes have made a stand at several points along Seventh and Eighth Avenues, but their main body, still pursued by the Italian foe, is on the march yet, and the black mark will be found overshadowing today many blocks on the East Side, with One Hundredth Street as the center, where colonies of them have settled recently.

Hardly less aggressive than the Italian, the Russian and Polish Jew, having overrun the district between Rivington and Division Streets, east of the

Bowery, to the point of suffocation, is filling the tenements of the old Seventh Ward to the river front and disputing with the Italian every foot of available space in the back alleys of Mulberry Street. The two races, differing hopelessly in much, have this in common; they carry their slums with them wherever they go, if allowed to do it. Little Italy already rivals its parent, the "Bend," in foulness. Other nationalities that begin at the bottom make a fresh start when crowded up the ladder. Happily both are manageable, the one by rabbinical, the other by the civil law. Between the dull gray of the Jew, his favorite color, and the Italian red, would be seen squeezed in on the map a sharp streak of yellow marking the narrow boundaries of Chinatown. Dovetailed in with the German population, the poor but thrifty Bohemian might be picked out by the somber hue of his life as of his philosophy, struggling against heavy odds in the big human beehives of the East Side. Colonies of his people extend northward, with long lapses of space, from below the Cooper Institute more than three miles. The Bohemian is the only foreigner with any considerable representation in the city who counts no wealthy man of his race, none who has not to work hard for a living or has got beyond the reach of the tenement.

Down near the Battery, the West Side emerald would be soiled by a dirty stain, spreading rapidly like a splash of ink on a sheet of blotting paper, headquarters of the Arab tribe that in a single year has swelled from the original dozen to twelve hundred, intent, every mother's son, on trade and barter. Dots and dashes of color here and there would show where the Finnish sailors worship their *Djumala* (God), the Greek peddlers the ancient name of their race, and the Swiss the goddess of thrift. And so on to the end of the long register, all toiling together in the galling fetters of the tenement. Were the question raised who makes the most of life thus mortgaged, who resists most stubbornly its leveling tendency—knows how to drag even the barracks upward a part of the way at least toward the ideal plane of the home—the palm must be unhesitatingly awarded the Teuton. The Italian and the poor Jew rise only by compulsion. The Chinaman does not rise at all; here, as at home, he remains stationary. The Irishman's genius runs to public affairs rather than domestic life; wherever he is mustered in force the saloon is the gorgeous center of political activity. The German struggles vainly to learn his trick; his Teutonic wit is too heavy, and the political ladder he raises from his saloon usually too short or too clumsy to reach the desired goal. The best part of his life is lived at home, and he makes himself a home independent of the surroundings, giving the lie to the saying, unhappily become a maxim of social truth, that pauperism and drunkenness naturally grow in the tenements. He makes the most of his tenement, and it should be added that whenever and as soon as he can save up money enough, he gets out and never crosses the threshold of one again.

• • •

Hamilton Street, like Water Street, is not what it was. The missions drove from the latter the worst of its dives. A sailors mission has lately made its appearance in Hamilton Street, but there are no dives there, nothing worse than the ubiquitous saloon and tough tenements.

Enough of them everywhere. Suppose we look into one, No. — Cherry Street. Be a little careful, please! The hall is dark, and you might stumble over the children pitching pennies back there. Not that it would hurt them; kicks and cuffs are their daily diet. They have little else. Here where the hall turns and dives into utter darkness is a step, and another, another. A flight of stairs. You can feel your way if you cannot see it. Close? Yes! What would you have? All the fresh air that ever enters these stairs comes from the hall door that is forever slamming and from the windows of dark bedrooms that in turn receive from the stairs their sole supply of the elements God meant to be free but man deals out with such niggardly hand. That was a woman filling her pail by the hydrant you just bumped against. The sinks are in the hallway, that all the tenants may have access—and all be poisoned alike by their summer stenches. Hear the pump squeak! It is the lullaby of tenement house babes. In summer, when a thousand thirsty throats pant for a cooling drink in this block, it is worked in vain. But the saloon, whose open door you passed in the hall, is always there. The smell of it has followed you up. Here is a door. Listen! That short, hacking cough, that tiny, helpless wail—what do they mean? They mean that the soiled bow of white you saw on the door downstairs will have another story to tell—oh! a sadly familiar story—before the day is at an end. The child is dying with measles. With half a chance it might have lived, but it had none. That dark bedroom killed it.

"It was took all of a suddint," says the mother, smoothing the throbbing little body with trembling hands. There is no unkindness in the rough voice of the man in the jumper who sits by the window grimly smoking a clay pipe, with the little life ebbing out in his sight, bitter as his words sound: "Hush, Mary! If we cannot keep the baby, need we complain—such as we?"

Such as we! What if the words ring in your ears as we grope our way up the stairs and down from floor to floor, listening to the sounds behind the closed doors—some of quarreling, some of coarse songs, more of profanity. They are true. When the summer heats come with their suffering they have meaning more terrible than words can tell. Come over here. Step carefully over this baby—it is a baby, spite of its rags and dirt—under these iron bridges called fire escapes, but loaded down, despite the incessant watchfulness of the firemen, with broken household goods, with washtubs and barrels, over which no man could climb from a fire. This gap between dingy brick walls is the yard. That strip of smoke-colored sky up there is the heaven of these people. Do you wonder the name does not attract them to the churches? That baby's parents live in the rear tenement here. She is at least as clean as the steps we are now climbing. There are plenty of houses with half a hundred such in. The tenement is much like the one in front we just left, only fouler, closer, darker—we will not say more cheerless. The word is a mockery. A hundred thousand people lived in rear tenements in New York last year. Here is a room neater than the rest. The woman, a stout matron with hard lines of care in her face, is at the washtub. "I try to keep the childer clean," she says, apologetically, but with a hopeless glance around. The spice of hot soapsuds is added to the air already tainted with the smell of boiling cabbage, of rags and uncleanliness all about. It makes an overpowering compound. It is Thursday, but patched linen is hung upon the pulley line from the window. There is no Monday cleaning in the tenements. It is washday all the week round, for a change of clothing is scarce among the poor. They are poverty's honest badge, these perennial lines of rags hung out to dry, those that are not the washerwoman's professional shingle. The true line to be drawn between pauperism and honest poverty is the clothesline. With it begins the effort to be clean that is the first and the best evidence of a desire to be honest.

What sort of an answer, think you, would come from these tenements to the question "Is life worth living?" were they heard at all in the discussion?

JACOB A. RIIS
How the Other Half Lives
1890

78

Jane Addams Establishes Hull House

Inspired by the example of Toynbee Hall in London, social workers began, around the close of the century, to establish settlement houses in the slums of the great cities. The most famous of these were the Henry Street Settlement in New York, the South End House in Boston, and Hull House in Chicago, which first opened its hospitable doors in September 1889. Jane Addams was largely responsible for its establishment and was its guide for over forty years. Her broadening activities, which eventually brought her the Nobel Peace Prize, made her by common consent the most distinguished of American social workers of her generation.

As social reformers gave themselves over to discussion of general principles, so the poor invariably accused poverty itself of their destruction. I recall a certain Mrs. Moran who was returning one rainy day from the office of the county agent with her arms full of paper bags containing beans and flour, which alone lay between her children and starvation. Although she had no money, she boarded a street car in order to save her booty from complete destruction by the rain, and as the burst bags dropped "flour on the ladies' dresses" and "beans all over the place," she was sharply reprimanded by the conductor, who was further exasperated when he discovered she had no fare. He put her off, as she had hoped he would, almost in front of Hull House. She related to us her state of mind as she stepped off the car and saw the last of her wares disappearing; she admitted she forgot the proprieties and "cursed a little," but curiously enough, she pronounced her malediction not against the rain nor the conductor, nor yet against the worthless husband who had been sent up to the city prison, but true to the Chicago spirit of the moment, went to the root of the matter and roundly "cursed poverty.". . .

I remember one family in which the father had been out of work for this same winter, most of the furniture had been pawned, and as the worn-out shoes could not be replaced the children could not go to school. The mother was ill and barely able to come for the supplies and medicines. Two years later she invited me to supper one Sunday evening in the little home which had been completely restored, and she gave as a reason for the invitation that she couldn't bear to have me remember them as they had been during that one winter, which she insisted had been unique in her twelve years of married life. She said that it was as if she had met me, not as I am ordinarily, but as I should appear misshapen with rheumatism or with a face distorted by neuralgic pain; that it was not fair to judge poor people that way. She perhaps unconsciously illustrated the difference between the relief station's relation to the poor and the Settlement's relation to its neighbors, the latter wishing to know them through all the varying conditions of life, to stand by when they are in distress, but by no means to drop intercourse with them when normal prosperity has returned, enabling the relation to become more social and free from economic disturbance.

Possibly something of the same effort has to be made within the Settlement itself to keep its own sense of proportion in regard to the relation of the crowded city quarter to the rest of the country. It was in the spring following this terrible winter, during a journey to meet lecture engagements in California, that I found myself amazed at the large stretches of open country and prosperous towns through which we passed day by day, whose existence I had quite forgotten.

In the latter part of the summer of 1895 I served as a member on a commission appointed by the mayor of Chicago to investigate conditions in the county poorhouse, public attention having become centered on it through one of those distressing stories which exaggerates the wrong in a public institution while at the same time it reveals conditions which need to be rectified. However necessary publicity is for securing reformed administration, however useful such exposures may be for political purposes, the whole is attended by such a waste of the most precious human emotions, by such a tearing of live tissue, that it can scarcely be endured. Every time I entered Hull House during the days of the investigation I would find waiting for me from twenty to thirty people whose friends and relatives were in the suspected institution, all in such acute distress of mind that to see them was to look upon the victims of deliberate torture. In most cases my visitor would state that it seemed impossible to put their invalids in any other place, but if these stories were true, something must be done. Many of the patients were taken out, only to be returned after a few days or weeks to meet the sullen hostility of their attendants and with their own attitude changed from confidence to timidity and alarm.

This piteous dependence of the poor upon the good will of public officials was made clear to us in an early experience with a peasant woman straight from the fields of Germany, whom we met during our first six months at Hull House. Her four years in America had been spent in patiently carrying water up and down two flights of stairs and in washing the heavy flannel suits of iron foundry workers. For this her pay had averaged thirty-five cents a day. Three of her daughters had fallen victims to the vice of the city. The mother was bewildered and distressed, but understood nothing. We were able to induce the betrayer of one daughter to marry her; the second, after a tedious lawsuit, supported his child; with the third we were able to do nothing. This woman is now living with her family in a little house seventeen miles from the city. She has made two payments on her land and is a lesson to all beholders as she pastures her cow up and down the railroad tracks and makes money from her ten acres. She did not need charity, for she had an immense capacity for hard work, but she sadly needed the service of the state's attorney's office, enforcing the laws designed for the protection of such girls as her daughters.

We early found ourselves spending many hours in efforts to secure support for deserted women, insurance for bewildered widows, damages for injured operators, furniture from the clutches of the installment store. The Settlement is valuable as an information and interpretation bureau. It constantly acts between the various institutions of the city and the people for whose benefit these institutions were erected. The hospitals, the county agencies, and state asylums are often but vague rumors to the people who need them most. Another function of the Settlement to its neighborhood resembles that of the big brother whose mere presence on the playground protects the little one from bullies.

We early learned to know the children of hard-driven mothers who went out to work all day, sometimes leaving the little things in the casual care of a neighbor, but often locking them into their tenement rooms. The first three crippled children we encountered in the neighborhood had all been injured while their mothers were at work; one had fallen out of a third-story window, another had been burned, and the third had a curved spine due to the fact that for three years he had been tied all day long to the leg of the kitchen table.

JANE ADDAMS
Forty Years at Hull House

79

Booker T. Washington Tours Alabama

Born a slave, Booker T. Washington became one of the greatest African-American leaders of the twentieth century. Trained at Hampton Institute, he early became convinced that blacks must achieve economic independence before attaining political equality. Idolized by his own people, he was trusted too by the whites, and the great Kentucky editor Henry Watterson said of him that "no man, since the war of sections, has exercised such beneficent influence and done such real good for the country—especially to the South."

I reached Tuskegee, as I have said, early in June 1881. The first month I spent in finding accommodations for the school and in traveling through Alabama, examining into the actual life of the people, especially in the country districts, and in getting the school advertised among the class of people that I wanted to have attend it. The most of my traveling was done over the country roads with a mule and a cart or a mule and a buggy wagon for conveyance. I ate and slept with the people in their little cabins. I saw their farms, their schools, their churches. Since in the case of the most of these visits there had been no notice given in advance that a stranger was expected, I had the advantage of seeing the real, everyday life of the people.

In the plantation districts I found that as a rule the whole family slept in one room and that in addition to the immediate family there sometimes were relatives, or others not related to the family, who slept in the same room. On more than one occasion I went outside the house to get ready for bed or to wait until the family had gone to bed. They usually contrived some kind of place for me to sleep, either on the floor or in a special part of another's bed. Rarely was there any place provided in the cabin where one could bathe even the face and hands, but usually some provision was made for this outside the house, in the yard.

The common diet of the people was fat pork and cornbread. At times I have eaten in cabins where they had only cornbread and black-eye peas cooked in plain water. The people seemed to have no other idea than to live on this fat meat and cornbread, the meat and the meal of which the bread was made having been bought at a high price at a store in town, notwithstanding the fact that the land all about the cabin homes could easily have been made to produce nearly every kind of garden vegetable that is raised anywhere in the country. Their one object seemed to be to plant nothing but cotton, and in many cases cotton was planted up to the very door of the cabin.

In these cabin homes I often found sewing machines which had been bought, or were being bought, on installments, frequently at a cost of as much as sixty dollars, or showy clocks for which the occupants of the cabins had paid twelve or fourteen dollars. I remember that on one occasion when I went into one of these cabins for dinner, when I sat down to the table for a meal with the four members of the family, I noticed that, while there were five of us at the table, there was but one fork for the five of us to use. Naturally there was an awkward pause on my part. In the opposite corner of that same cabin was an organ for which the people told me they were paying sixty dollars in monthly installments. One fork and a sixty-dollar organ! . . .

With a few exceptions I found that the crops were mortgaged in the counties where I went and that the most of the colored farmers were in debt. The state had not been able to build schoolhouses in the country districts, and as a rule the schools were taught in churches or in log cabins. More than once while on my journeys I found that there was no provision made in the house used for school purposes for heating the building during the winter, and consequently a fire had to be built in the yard and teacher and pupils passed in and out of the house as they got cold or warm. With few exceptions I found the teachers in these country schools to be miserably poor in preparation for their work and poor in moral character. The schools were in session from three to five months. There was practically no apparatus in the schoolhouses except that occasionally there was a rough blackboard. I recall that one day I went into a schoolhouse—or rather into an abandoned log cabin that was being used as a schoolhouse—and found five pupils who were studying a lesson from one book. Two of these, on the front seat, were using the book between them; behind these were two others peeping over the shoulders of the first two, and behind the four was a fifth little fellow who was peeping over the shoulders of all four.

What I have said concerning the character of the schoolhouses and teachers will also apply quite accurately as a description of the church buildings and the ministers.

Booker T. Washington
Up from Slavery

80

Herbert Quick Studies the
McGuffey Readers

It was in 1836 that William Holmes McGuffey, clergyman, lecturer, and college president, published the first of the *McGuffey Eclectic Readers;* by the end of the century something over one hundred million copies of the *Readers* had been sold. By introducing children to "selections" from the best of English and American literature, the *Readers* performed a service of immense value and helped to set the popular literary standard for a whole generation. Herbert Quick, who here recalls the *Readers* with affection, was the author of a series of novels dealing with the settlement of Iowa.

I have just looked at a copy of a twenty-year-old edition of the *McGuffey's First Reader.* It has not a single lesson that was in the one I took in my trembling hand when Maggie Livingstone called me to her to begin learning my letters. Mine had a green cover, but it was hidden by the muslin which my mother had stitched over it to save the wear on a book that cost thirty cents. It was filled with illustrations which I now know were of British origin, for all the men wore knee breeches, the girls had on fluffy pantalets and sugarscoop bonnets, and the ladies huge many-flounced skirts. One boy had a cricket bat in his hand, and the ruling passions of the youngsters seemed to be to shoot with the bow and to roll the hoop. "Can you hop, Tom? See, I can hop! Tom, hop to me." How easily does the English language lend itself to early lessons of such simplicity!

These books were intensely moral, soundly religious, and addicted to the inculcation of habits of industry, mercy, and most of the virtues. Lucy was exhorted to rise because the sun was up. "Mary was up at six," she was assured, and then was added the immortal line, "Up, up, Lucy, and go out to Mary," which scoffers perverted to "Double up, Lucy." Most of the words were of one syllable, but "How doth the little busy bee" was in it, I am certain, and "I like to see a little dog and pat him on the head." It was an easy book, and if it fell short of the power in the moral and religious fields of the more advanced volumes—why, so did its students in the practice of the vices and the need for reproof or warning.

My mastery of the *First* and *Second Readers*—just the opening of the marvels of the printed page—was a poignant delight. The reading of anything gave me a sort of ecstasy. These books did not, however, set in operation the germinant powers of actual literary treasure hunting. They did give to the mind of the writer and to the world some things of universal knowledge. We learned that George Washington could not tell a lie about the cherry tree and that his father proved to him the existence of God by the device of sowing lettuce in a trench which spelled George's name. "It might have grown so by chance," said the elder Washington in this *Second Reader* lesson, but George saw clearly that it could not have come by chance. Someone sowed those seeds in that way. And his father assured him that this world of wonderful adaptations could not have come as it has by chance. There were many fables and lessons about insects, birds, and beasts. Most of the scenes were British. Our habits, our morals, and our faith were carefully kept in mind, and we grew to know Mary's lamb by heart.

In the *Third Reader* Mr. McGuffey began to give to my young mind some tastes of real literature. It had several beautiful selections from the Bible. Croly's description of the burning of the amphitheater at Rome, which I have never run across anywhere since, was one of the lessons. There was an analysis of How a Fly Walks on the Ceiling, which gave me as much of an urge toward natural philosophy as if it had been a correct one—which it was not. One gets a glimpse into the McGuffey character from the treatment which the Indian received in these books. The author, whose father was an Indian fighter of renown and who must have sat entranced at fireside stories of Indian wars, in several lessons in these *Readers* treated the Indian with great respect. There was Logan's great speech in the *Fifth,* for instance. I can see it before my eyes still:

> *I appeal to any white man to say, if ever he entered Logan's cabin hungry, and he gave him not meat; if ever he came cold and naked and he clothed him not.*

I wonder how much of the persistent sentiment among Americans favoring justice to the Indians comes from these old *Readers.* It has not saved the race from exploitation and oppression, but it has always persisted and it has done much good.

The *Third Reader* introduced me to such writers as Croly, Irving, Woodworth, through "The Old Oaken Bucket," Scott, and others, but not by their names. In the *Fourth* we had William Wirt, Wendell Phillips, Lord Bacon, Eliphalet Nott, Addison, Samuel Rogers in his "Ginevra," Willis, Montgomery, Milton and Shakespeare, Campbell, and a variety of lesser and anonymous authors. The *Fifth Reader* carried me on to longer and more mature selections, all chosen by the same rules—the rules of gradually introducing the child to the best of English literature with no letting down of the requirements as to morality and religious sentiment. There was more of Shakespeare, some of Byron, Milton, Johnson, Bryant, Addison, more of the Bible, and much British matter now lost—to me at least. Every selection was classic English.

But the old *Fifth Reader* of 1844 we never used in our school. My brother's copy was a wonderful mine for me. The front cover was gone, and a part of the Rhetorician's Guide, which told us when to let our voices fall, when they should rise, and when the circumflex was required. I never regretted the loss. But the text consisted of some hundreds of pages of closely printed selections made by Alexander McGuffey with all the family judgment and taste. There was Pope with "Hector's Attack on the Grecian Walls," from that version of the *Iliad* of which a critic said, "A very pretty poem, Mr. Pope, but don't call it Homer!" There was "How the Water Comes Down at Lodore." There was oratory—Pitt, Burke, Fox, Barré, Otis, Adams, Webster, Hayne. I had the volume all to myself. There were months when it was my only resource in my favorite dissipation of reading.

A small ration, these *McGuffey Readers,* for an omnivorous mind, but by no means a negligible one. I did not use them with any intelligence. I simply enjoyed them. I found a tune to which I could sing Browning's "How They Brought the Good News from Ghent to Aix" and sang it at the top of my voice as I followed my cows or the plow or harrow. I shouted "Ivry" to the vastnesses of the prairie. I deepened my boyish voice to orotund on "Now godlike Hector and his troops descend" and "They tug, they sweat, but nei-ther gain nor yield, One foot, one inch, of the contested field!"

And somehow I was inoculated with a little of the virus of good litera-ture. I gained no knowledge that it was anything of the sort. I got not the slightest glimpse into the world of letters as a world. Nobody ever said a word to me about that. I read nothing about it for years and years afterward. But when I did come to read the English classics, I felt as one who meets in after years a charming person with whom he has had a chance encounter on the train. I had already met the gentlemen.

Herbert Quick
One Man's Life, an Autobiography

81

Andrew Carnegie Gets a Start in Life

Andrew Carnegie, who here recalls his first modest ventures into business, turned his great talents eventually to the manufacture of iron and steel and became, within a few years, the greatest industrialist of his generation. At the height of his power he sold his interests to the new United States Steel Corporation and retired to spend the enormous fortune that he had accumulated. It is as a philanthropist that he is probably best known. Most of his money went to public libraries, but other millions were given to the cause of peace and education.

It is a great pleasure to tell how I served my apprenticeship as a businessman. But there seems to be a question preceding this: Why did I become a businessman? I am sure that I should never have selected a business career if I had been permitted to choose.

The eldest son of parents who were themselves poor, I had, fortunately, to begin to perform some useful work in the world while still very young in order to earn an honest livelihood and was thus shown even in early boyhood that my duty was to assist my parents and, like them, become as soon as possible a breadwinner in the family. What I could get to do, not what I desired, was the question.

When I was born [1837] my father was a well-to-do master weaver in Dunfermline, Scotland. He owned no less than four damask looms and employed apprentices. This was before the days of steam factories for the manufacture of linen. A few large merchants took orders and employed master weavers such as my father to weave the cloth, the merchants supplying the materials.

As the factory system developed, hand-loom weaving naturally declined, and my father was one of the sufferers by the change. The first serious lesson of my life came to me one day when he had taken in the last of his work to the merchant and returned to our little home greatly distressed because there was no more work for him to do. I was then just about ten years of age, but the lesson burned into my heart, and I resolved then that the wolf of poverty should be driven from our door some day if I could do it.

The question of selling the old looms and starting for the United States came up in the family council, and I heard it discussed from day to day. It was finally resolved to take the plunge and join relatives already in Pittsburgh. I well remember that neither Father nor Mother thought the change would be otherwise than a great sacrifice for them, but that "it would be better for the two boys."

In afterlife, if you can look back as I do and wonder at the complete surrender of their own desires which parents make for the good of their children, you must reverence their memories with feelings akin to worship.

On arriving in Allegheny City (there were four of us: Father, Mother, my younger brother, and myself), my father entered a cotton factory. I soon followed and served as a "bobbin boy," and this is how I began my preparation for subsequent apprenticeship as a businessman. I received one dollar and twenty cents a week and was then just about twelve years old.

I cannot tell you how proud I was when I received my first week's own earnings. One dollar and twenty cents made by myself and given to me because I had been of some use in the world! No longer entirely dependent upon my parents, but at last admitted to the family partnership as a contributing member and able to help them! I think this makes a man out of a boy sooner than almost anything else, and a real man, too, if there be any germ of true manhood in him. It is everything to feel that you are useful. . . .

For a lad of twelve to rise and breakfast every morning except the blessed Sunday morning and go into the streets and find his way to the factory and begin to work while it was still dark outside, and not be released until after darkness came again in the evening, forty minutes' interval only being allowed at noon, was a terrible task.

But I was young and had my dreams, and something within always told me that this would not, could not, should not last—I should some day get into a better position. Besides this, I felt myself no longer a mere boy, but quite a little man, and this made me happy.

A change soon came, for a kind old Scotsman, who knew some of our relatives, made bobbins and took me into his factory before I was thirteen. But here for a time it was even worse than in the cotton factory, because I was set to fire a boiler in the cellar and actually to run the small steam engine which drove the machinery. The firing of the boiler was all right, for fortunately we did not use coal but the refuse wooden chips, and I always liked to work in wood. But the responsibility of keeping the water right and of running the engine and the danger of my making a mistake and blowing the whole factory to pieces caused too great a strain, and I often awoke and found myself sitting up in bed through the night, trying the steam gauges. But I never told them at home that I was having a hard tussle. No, no! everything must be bright to them.

This was a point of honor, for every member of the family was working hard, except, of course, my little brother, who was then a child, and we were telling each other only all the bright things. Besides this, no man would whine and give up—he would die first.

There was no servant in our family, and several dollars per week were earned by the mother by binding shoes after her daily work was done! Father was also hard at work in the factory. And could I complain?

My kind employer, John Hay—peace to his ashes!—soon relieved me of the undue strain, for he needed someone to make out bills and keep his accounts, and finding that I could write a plain schoolboy hand and could cipher, he made me his only clerk. But still I had to work hard upstairs in the factory, for the clerking took but little time. . . .

I come now to the third step in my apprenticeship, for I had already taken two, as you see—the cotton factory and then the bobbin factory. And with the third—the third time is the chance, you know—deliverance came. I obtained a situation as messenger boy in the telegraph office of Pittsburgh when I was fourteen. Here I entered a new world.

Amid books, newspapers, pencils, pens and ink and writing pads, and a clean office, bright windows, and the literary atmosphere, I was the happiest boy alive.

My only dread was that I should someday be dismissed because I did not know the city, for it is necessary that a messenger boy should know all the firms and addresses of men who are in the habit of receiving telegrams. But I was a stranger in Pittsburgh. However, I made up my mind that I would learn to repeat successively each business house in the principal streets and was soon able to shut my eyes and begin at one side of Wood Street and call every firm successively to the top, then pass to the other side and call every firm to the bottom. Before long I was able to do this with the business streets generally. My mind was then at rest upon that point.

Of course every ambitious messenger boy wants to become an operator, and before the operators arrive in the early mornings the boys slipped up to the instruments and practiced. This I did and was soon able to talk to the boys in the other offices along the line who were also practicing.

One morning I heard Philadelphia calling Pittsburgh and giving the signal, "Death message." Great attention was then paid to "death messages," and I thought I ought to try to take this one. I answered and did so, and went off and delivered it before the operator came. After that the operators sometimes used to ask me to work for them.

Having a sensitive ear for sound, I soon learned to take messages by the ear, which was then very uncommon—I think only two persons in the United States could then do it. Now every operator takes by ear, so easy is it to follow and do what any other boy can—if you only have to. This brought me into notice, and finally I became an operator and received the, to me, enormous recompense of twenty-five dollars per month—three hundred dollars a year!

This was a fortune—the very sum that I had fixed when I was a factory worker as the fortune I wished to possess, because the family could live on three hundred dollars a year and be almost or quite independent. Here it was at last! But I was soon to be in receipt of extra compensation for extra work.

The six newspapers of Pittsburgh received telegraphic news in common. Six copies of each dispatch were made by a gentleman who received six dollars per week for the work, and he offered me a gold dollar every week if I would do it, of which I was very glad indeed, because I always liked to work with news and scribble for newspapers.

The reporters came to a room every evening for the news which I had prepared, and this brought me into most pleasant intercourse with these clever fellows, and besides, I got a dollar a week as pocket money, for this was not considered family revenue by me.

I think this last step of doing something beyond one's task is fully entitled to be considered "business." The other revenue, you see, was just salary obtained for regular work, but here was a little business operation upon my own account, and I was very proud indeed of my gold dollar every week.

The Pennsylvania Railroad shortly after this was completed to Pittsburgh, and that genius, Thomas A. Scott, was its superintendent. He often came to the telegraph office to talk to his chief, the general superintendent, at Altoona, and I became known to him in this way.

When that great railway system put up a wire of its own, he asked me to be his clerk and operator, so I left the telegraph office—in which there is great danger that a young man may be permanently buried, as it were—and became connected with the railways.

The new appointment was accompanied by what was to me a tremendous increase of salary. It jumped from twenty-five to thirty-five dollars per month. Mr. Scott was then receiving one hundred and twenty-five dollars per month, and I used to wonder what on earth he could do with so much money.

I remained for thirteen years in the service of the Pennsylvania Railroad Company and was at last superintendent of the Pittsburgh division of the road, successor to Mr. Scott, who had in the meantime risen to the office of vice president of the company.

One day Mr. Scott, who was the kindest of men and had taken a great fancy to me, asked if I had or could find five hundred dollars to invest.

Here the business instinct came into play. I felt that as the door was opened for a business investment with my chief, it would be willful flying in the face of Providence if I did not jump at it, so I answered promptly:

"Yes, sir, I think I can."

"Very well," he said, "get it; a man has just died who owns ten shares in the Adams Express Company, which I want you to buy. It will cost you fifty dollars per share, and I can help you with a little balance if you cannot raise it all."

Here was a queer position. The available assets of the whole family were not five hundred dollars. But there was one member of the family whose ability, pluck, and resource never failed us, and I felt sure the money could be raised somehow or other by my mother.

Indeed, had Mr. Scott known our position he would have advanced it himself, but the last thing in the world the proud Scot will do is to reveal his poverty and rely upon others. The family had managed by this time to purchase a small house and pay for it in order to save rent. My recollection is that it was worth eight hundred dollars.

The matter was laid before the council of three that night, and the oracle spoke: "Must be done. Mortgage our house. I will take the steamer in the morning for Ohio and see Uncle and ask him to arrange it. I am sure he can." This was done. Of course her visit was successful—where did she ever fail?

The money was procured, paid over; ten shares of Adams Express Company stock was mine, but no one knew our little home had been mortgaged "to give our boy a start."

Adams Express stock then paid monthly dividends of one percent, and the first check for five dollars arrived. I can see it now, and I well remember the signature of "J.C. Babcock, Cashier," who wrote a big "John Hancock" hand.

The next day being Sunday, we boys—myself and my ever-constant companions—took our usual Sunday afternoon stroll in the country, and sitting down in the woods, I showed them this check, saying: "Eureka! We have found it."

Here was something new to all of us, for none of us had ever received anything but from toil. A return from capital was something strange and new.

How money could make money, how, without any attention from me, this mysterious golden visitor should come, led to much speculation upon the part of the young fellows, and I was for the first time hailed as a "capitalist."

You see, I was beginning to serve my apprenticeship as a businessman in a satisfactory manner.

A very important incident in my life occurred when one day in a train a nice, farmer-looking gentleman approached me, saying that the conductor had told him I was connected with the Pennsylvania Railroad, and he would like to show me something. He pulled from a small green bag the model of the first sleeping car. This was Mr. Woodruff, the inventor.

Its value struck me like a flash. I asked him to come to Altoona the following week, and he did so. Mr. Scott, with his usual quickness, grasped the idea. A contract was made with Mr. Woodruff to put two trial cars on the Pennsylvania Railroad. Before leaving Altoona, Mr. Woodruff came and offered me an interest in the venture, which I promptly accepted. But how I was to make my payments rather troubled me, for the cars were to be paid for in monthly installments after delivery, and my first monthly payment was to be two hundred and seventeen dollars and a half.

I had not the money, and I did not see any way of getting it. But I finally decided to visit the local banker and ask him for a loan, pledging myself to repay at the rate of fifteen dollars per month. He promptly granted it. Never shall I forget his putting his arm over my shoulder, saying, "Oh, yes, Andy, you are all right!"

I then and there signed my first note. Proud day this, and surely now no one will dispute that I was becoming a businessman. I had signed my first note, and most important of all—for any fellow can sign a note—I had found a banker willing to take it as good.

My subsequent payments were made by the receipts from the sleeping cars, and I really made my first considerable sum from this investment in the Woodruff Sleeping Car Company, which was afterward absorbed by Mr. Pullman, a remarkable man whose name is now known over all the world.

Shortly after this I was appointed superintendent of the Pittsburgh division and returned to my dear old home, smoky Pittsburgh. Wooden bridges were then used exclusively upon the railways, and the Pennsylvania Railroad was experimenting with a bridge built of cast iron. I saw that wooden bridges would not do for the future and organized a company in Pittsburgh to build iron bridges.

Here again I had recourse to the bank, because my share of the capital was twelve hundred and fifty dollars, and I had not the money, but the bank lent it to me, and we began the Keystone Bridge Works, which proved a great success. This company built the first great bridge over the Ohio River, three hundred feet span, and has built many of the most important structures since.

This was my beginning in manufacturing, and from that start all our other works have grown, the profits of one building the other. My apprenticeship as a businessman soon ended, for I resigned my position as an officer of the Pennsylvania Railroad Company to give exclusive attention to business.

I was no longer merely an official working for others upon a salary, but a full-fledged businessman working upon my own account.

And so ends the story of my apprenticeship and graduation as a businessman.

ANDREW CARNEGIE
"How I Served My Apprenticeship"

82

Henry Ford Constructs a Gasoline Buggy

Henry Ford did not invent the automobile, but it was his engineering skill and business acumen that was largely responsible for changing the automobile from a rich man's luxury to a common necessity, and the famous Model T Ford was the evidence of that change. Less than forty years after the experiments here described, the automobile industry was first in the country in the value of its products.

Even before that time [1879] I had the idea of making some kind of a light steam car that would take the place of horses—more especially, however, as a tractor to attend to the excessively hard labor of plowing. It occurred to me, as I remember somewhat vaguely, that precisely the same idea might be applied to a carriage or a wagon on the road. A horseless carriage was a common idea. People had been talking about carriages without horses for many years back—in fact, ever since the steam engine was invented—but the idea of the carriage at first did not seem so practical to me as the idea of an engine to do the harder farm work, and of all the work on the farm plowing was the hardest. Our roads were poor, and we had not the habit of getting around. One of the most remarkable features of the automobile on the farm is the way that it has broadened the farmer's life. We simply took for granted that unless the errand were urgent we would not go to town, and I think we rarely made more than a trip a week. In bad weather we did not go even that often.

Being a full-fledged machinist and with a very fair workshop on the farm, it was not difficult for me to build a steam wagon or tractor. In the building of it came the idea that perhaps it might be made for road use. I felt perfectly certain that horses, considering all the bother of attending them and the expense of feeding, did not earn their keep. The obvious thing to do was to design and build a steam engine that would be light enough to run an ordinary wagon or to pull a plow. I thought it more important first to develop the tractor. To lift farm drudgery off flesh and blood and lay it on steel and motors has been my most constant ambition. It was circumstances that took me first into the actual manufacture of road cars. I found eventually that people were more interested in something that would travel on the road than in something that would do the work on the farms. In fact, I doubt that the light farm tractor could have been introduced on the farm had not the farmer had his eyes opened slowly but surely by the automobile. But that is getting ahead of the story. I thought the farmer would be more interested in the tractor.

I built a steam car that ran. It had a kerosene-heated boiler, and it developed plenty of power and a neat control—which is so easy with a steam throttle. But the boiler was dangerous. To get the requisite power without too big and heavy a power plant required that the engine work under high pressure; sitting on a high pressure steam boiler is not altogether pleasant. To make it even reasonably safe required an excess of weight that nullified the economy of the high pressure. For two years I kept experimenting with various sorts of boilers—the engine and control problems were simple enough—and then I definitely abandoned the whole idea of running a road vehicle by steam.

A few years before—it was while I was an apprentice—I read in *The World of Science,* an English publication, of the silent gas engine, which was then coming out in England. I think it was the Otto engine. It ran with illuminating gas, had a single large cylinder, and the power impulses being thus intermittent, required an extremely heavy flywheel. As far as weight was concerned, it gave nothing like the power per pound of metal that a steam engine gave, and the use of illuminating gas seemed to dismiss it as even a possibility for road use. It was interesting to me only as all machinery was interesting. I followed in the English and American magazines which we got in the shop the development of the engine and most particularly the hints of the possible replacement of the illuminating gas fuel by a gas formed by the vaporization of gasoline. The idea of gas engines was by no means new, but this was the first time that a really serious effort had been made to put them on the market. They were received with interest rather than enthusiasm, and I do not recall anyone who thought that the internal combustion engine could ever have more than a limited use. All the wise people demonstrated conclusively that the engine could not compete with steam. They never thought that it might carve out a career for itself.

The gas engine interested me, and I followed its progress, but only from curiosity, until about 1885 or 1886, when, the steam engine being discarded as the motive power for the carriage that I intended someday to build, I had to look around for another sort of motive power. In 1885 I repaired an Otto engine at the Eagle Iron Works in Detroit. No one in town knew anything about them. There was a rumor that I did, and although I had never before been in contact with one, I undertook and carried through the job. That gave me a chance to study the new engine at firsthand, and in 1887 I built one on the Otto four-cycle model just to see if I understood the principles. "Four cycle" means that the piston traverses the cylinder four times to get one power impulse. The first stroke draws in the gas, the second compresses it, the third is the explosion or power stroke, while the fourth stroke exhausts the waste gas. The little model worked well enough; it had a one-inch bore and a three-inch stroke, operated with gasoline, and while it did not develop much power, it was slightly lighter in proportion than the engines being offered commercially. I gave it away later to a young man who wanted it for something or other and whose name I have forgotten; it was eventually destroyed. That was the beginning of the work with the internal combustion engine.

I was then on the farm to which I had returned, more because I wanted to experiment than because I wanted to farm, and now, being an all-around machinist, I had a first-class workshop to replace the toy shop of earlier days. My father offered me forty acres of timber land, provided I gave up being a machinist. I agreed in a provisional way, for cutting the timber gave me a chance to get married. I fitted out a sawmill and a portable engine and started to cut out and saw up the timber on the tract. Some of the first of that lumber went into a cottage on my new farm, and in it we began our married life. It was not a big house—thirty-one feet square and only a story and a half high—but it was a comfortable place. I added to it my workshop, and when I was not cutting timber I was working on the gas engines—learning what they were and how they acted. I read everything I could find, but the greatest knowledge came from the work. A gas engine is a mysterious sort of thing—it will not always go the way it should. You can imagine how those first engines acted!

It was in 1890 that I began on a double-cylinder engine. It was quite impractical to consider the single cylinder for transportation purposes—the flywheel had to be entirely too heavy. Between making the first four-cycle engine of the Otto type and the start on a double cylinder I had made a great many experimental engines out of tubing. I fairly knew my way about. The double cylinder, I thought, could be applied to a road vehicle, and my original idea was to put it on a bicycle with a direct connection to the crankshaft and allowing for the rear wheel of the bicycle to act as the balance wheel. The speed was going to be varied only by the throttle. I never carried out this plan because it soon became apparent that the engine, gasoline tank, and the various necessary controls would be entirely too heavy for a bicycle. The plan of the two opposed cylinders was that while one would be delivering power the other would be exhausting. This naturally would not require so heavy a flywheel to even the application of power. The work started in my shop on the farm. Then I was offered a job with the Detroit Electric Company as an engineer and machinist at forty-five dollars a month. I took it because that was more money than the farm was bringing me, and I had decided to get away from the farm life anyway. The timber had all been cut. We rented a house on Bagley Avenue, Detroit. The workshop came along, and I set it up in a brick shed at the back of the house. During the first several months I was in the night shift at the electric light plant—which gave me very little time for experimenting—but after that I was in the day shift, and every night and all of every Saturday night I worked on the new motor. I cannot say that it was hard work. No work with interest is ever hard. I always am certain of results.

They always come if you work hard enough. But it was a very great thing to have my wife even more confident than I was. She has always been that way.

I had to work from the ground up—that is, although I knew that a number of people were working on horseless carriages, I could not know what they were doing. The hardest problems to overcome were in the making and breaking of the spark and in the avoidance of excess weight. For the transmission, the steering gear, and the general construction, I could draw on my experience with the steam tractors. In 1892 I completed my first motor car, but it was not until the spring of the following year that it ran to my satisfaction. This first car had something of the appearance of a buggy. There were two cylinders, with a two-and-a-half-inch bore and a six-inch stroke, set side by side and over the rear axle. I made them out of the exhaust pipe of a steam engine that I had bought. They developed about four horsepower. The power was transmitted from the motor to the countershaft by a belt and from the countershaft to the rear wheel by a chain. The car would hold two people, the seat being suspended on posts and the body on elliptical springs. There were two speeds—one of ten and the other of twenty miles per hour—obtained by shifting the belt, which was done by a clutch lever in front of the driving seat. Thrown forward, the lever put in the high speed; thrown back, the low speed; with the lever upright the engine could run free. To start the car it was necessary to turn the motor over by hand with the clutch free. To stop the car one simply released the clutch and applied the foot brake. There was no reverse, and speeds other than those of the belt were obtained by the throttle. I bought the ironwork for the frame of the carriage and also the seat and the springs. The wheels were twenty-eight-inch wire bicycle wheels with rubber tires. The balance wheel I had cast from a pattern that I made, and all of the more delicate mechanism I made myself. One of the features that I discovered necessary was a compensating gear that permitted the same power to be applied to each of the rear wheels when turning corners. The machine altogether weighed about five hundred pounds. A tank under the seat held three gallons of gasoline, which was fed to the motor through a small pipe and a mixing valve. The ignition was by electric spark. The original machine was air-cooled—or to be more accurate, the motor simply was not cooled at all. I found that on a run of an hour or more the motor heated up, and so I very shortly put a water jacket around the cylinders and piped it to a tank in the rear of the car over the cylinders.

Nearly all of these various features had been planned in advance. That is the way I have always worked. I draw a plan and work out every detail on the plan before starting to build. For otherwise one will waste a great deal of time in makeshifts as the work goes on and the finished article will not have coherence. It will not be rightly proportioned. Many inventors fail because they do not distinguish between planning and experimenting. The largest building difficulties that I had were in obtaining the proper materials. The next were with tools. There had to be some adjustments and changes in details of the design, but what held me up most was that I had neither the time nor the money to search for the best material for each part. But in the spring of 1893 the machine was running to my partial satisfaction and giving an opportunity further to test out the design and material on the road.

My gasoline buggy was the first and for a long time the only automobile in Detroit. It was considered to be something of a nuisance, for it made a racket and it scared horses. Also it blocked traffic. For if I stopped my machine anywhere in town a crowd was around it before I could start up again. If I left it alone even for a minute some inquisitive person always tried to run it. Finally, I had to carry a chain and chain it to a lamp post whenever I left it anywhere. And then there was trouble with the police. I do not know quite why, for my impression is that there were no speed laws in those days. Anyway, I had to get a special permit from the mayor and thus for a time enjoyed the distinction of being the only licensed chauffeur in America. I ran that machine about one thousand miles through 1895 and 1896 and then sold it to Charles Ainsley of Detroit for two hundred dollars. That was my first sale. I had built the car not to sell but only to experiment with. I wanted to start another car.

HENRY FORD
My Life and Work

83

Rockefeller Founds the Standard Oil Company

It was in 1859 that oil was struck in western Pennsylvania; within a few years oil and its products were transforming American industry and transportation and profoundly influencing American social life. It was John D. Rockefeller who organized this industry—often by methods that excited the disapproval of socially minded critics—who created the greatest "trust" of our times, who accumulated the greatest fortune of his day, and who gave more to philanthropic causes than any man in history.

The story of the early history of the oil trade is too well known to bear repeating in detail. The cleansing of crude petroleum was a simple and easy process, and at first the profits were very large. Naturally, all sorts of people went into it; the butcher, the baker, and the candlestick maker began to refine oil, and it was only a short time before more of the finished product was put on the market than could possibly be consumed. The price went down and down until the trade was threatened with ruin. It seemed absolutely necessary to extend the market for oil by exporting to foreign countries, which required a long and most difficult development, and also to greatly improve the processes of refining so that oil could be made and sold cheaply, yet with a profit, and to use as by-products all of the materials which in the less efficient plants were lost or thrown away.

These were the problems which confronted us almost at the outset, and this great depression led to consultations with our neighbors and friends in the business in the effort to bring some order out of what was rapidly becoming a state of chaos. To accomplish all these tasks of enlarging the market and improving the methods of manufacture in a large way was beyond the power or ability of any concern as then constituted. It could only be done, we reasoned, by increasing our capital and availing ourselves of the best talent and experience.

It was with this idea that we proceeded to buy the largest and best refining concerns and centralize the administration of them with a view to securing greater economy and efficiency. The business grew faster than we anticipated.

This enterprise, conducted by men of application and ability working hard together, soon built up unusual facilities in manufacture, in transportation, in finance, and in extending markets. We had our troubles and setbacks; we suffered from some severe fires; and the supply of crude oil was most uncertain. Our plans were constantly changed by changed conditions. We developed great facilities in an oil center, erected storage tanks, and connected pipelines; then the oil failed and our work was thrown away. At best it was a speculative trade, and I wonder that we managed to pull through so often, but we were gradually learning how to conduct a most difficult business. . . .

I ascribe the success of the Standard Oil Company to its consistent policy of making the volume of its business large through the merit and cheapness of its products. It has spared no expense in utilizing the best and most efficient method of manufacture. It has sought for the best superintendents and workmen and paid the best wages. It has not hesitated to sacrifice old machinery and old plants for new and better ones. It has placed its manufactories at the points where they could supply markets at the least expense. It has not only sought markets for its principal products but for all possible by-products, sparing no expense in introducing them to the public in every nook and corner of the world. It has not hesitated to invest millions of dollars in methods for cheapening the gathering and distribution of oils by pipelines, special cars, tank-steamers, and tank-wagons. It has erected tank stations at railroad centers in every part of the country to cheapen the storage and delivery of oil. It has had faith in American oil and has brought together vast sums of money for the purpose of making it what it is and for holding its market against the competition of Russia and all the countries which are producers of oil and competitors against American products.

John D. Rockefeller
Random Reminiscences of Men and Events

84

Theodore Roosevelt Takes
Charge of the Navy

Influenced by Admiral Mahan, Theodore Roosevelt had for some years advocated the strengthening of the American navy and the adoption of a policy of aggressive imperialism. His enthusiastic support of McKinley in 1896 brought him the post of assistant secretary of the navy, and from this vantage point he labored to put into effect his ideas about American foreign policy and naval preparedness. When the war with Spain came, Roosevelt resigned from the Navy Department and organized a regiment of Rough Riders, which saw active service in Cuba.

FEBRUARY 25, 1898.—

These are trying times. In the evening Roosevelt, whom I had left as Acting Secretary during the afternoon, came around. He is so enthusiastic and loyal that he is in certain respects invaluable; yet I lack confidence in his good judgment and discretion. He goes off very impulsively, and if I have a good night tonight I shall feel that I ought to be back in the Department rather than take a day's vacation.

FEBRUARY 26.—

I had a splendid night last night and return to the office both because I feel so much better and because I find that Roosevelt, in his precipitate way, has come very near causing more of an explosion than happened to the *Maine*. His wife is very ill, and his little boy is just recovering from a long and dangerous illness, so his natural nervousness is so much accentuated that I really think he is hardly fit to be entrusted with the responsibility of the Department at this critical time. He is full of suggestions, many of which are of great value to me, and his spirited and forceful habit is a good tonic for one who is disposed to be as conservative and careful as I am. He seems to be thoroughly loyal, but the very devil seemed to possess him yesterday afternoon.

Having the authority for that time of Acting Secretary, he immediately began to launch peremptory orders: distributing ships; ordering ammunition, which there is no means to move, to places where there is no means to store it; sending for Captain Barker to come on about the guns of the *Vesuvius*, which is a matter that might have been arranged by correspondence; sending messages to Congress for immediate legislation authorizing the enlistment of an unlimited number of seamen; and ordering guns from the Navy Yard at Washington to New York, with a view to arming auxiliary cruisers which are now in peaceful commercial pursuit. The only effect of this last order would be.to take guns which are now carefully stored, ready for shipment any moment, and which could be shipped in ample time to be put on any vessel, and dump them in the open weather in the New York Navy Yard, where they would be only in the way and under no proper care.

He has gone at things like a bull in a china shop, and with the best purposes in the world has really taken what, if he could have thought, he would not for a moment have taken, and that is the one course which is most discourteous to me, because it suggests that there had been a lack of attention which he was supplying. It shows how the best fellow in the world—and with splendid capacities—is worse than no use if he lack a cool head and careful discretion.

JOHN DAVIS LONG
America of Yesterday

85
Admiral Dewey Wins the
Battle of Manila Bay

The war with Spain was designed, supposedly, to liberate the Cubans from Spanish misrule, and few Americans had contemplated action in the Far East. The Navy men, imperialists, and merchants, however, had long foreseen the opportunity that such a war would give for the establishment of American power in the Orient. The battle of Manila Bay proved to be one of the decisive battles of history. It effectively ended Spain's century-long dominion in the Pacific, made possible if not inevitable the American acquisition of the Philippines, and dramatized the advent of the United States to world power. Dewey's spectacular victory made him, for a short time, the great popular hero of the American people.

Before me now was the object for which we had made our arduous preparations and which indeed must ever be the supreme test of a naval officer's career. I felt confident of the outcome, though I had no thought that victory would be won at so slight a cost to our own side. Confidence was expressed in the very precision with which the dun, war-colored hulls of the squadron followed in column behind the flagship, keeping their distance excellently. All the guns were pointed constantly at the enemy, while the men were at their stations waiting the word. There was no break in the monotone of the engines save the mechanical voice of the leadsman or an occasional low-toned command by the quartermaster at the conn or the roar of a Spanish shell. The Manila batteries continued their inaccurate fire, to which we paid no attention.

The misty haze of the tropical dawn had hardly risen when at five-fifteen, at long range, the Cavite forts and Spanish squadron opened fire. Our course was not one leading directly toward the enemy, but a converging one, keeping him on our starboard bow. Our speed was eight knots, and our converging course and ever-varying position must have confused the Spanish gunners. My assumption that the Spanish fire would be hasty and inaccurate proved correct.

So far as I could see, none of our ships was suffering any damage, while in view of my limited ammunition supply it was my plan not to open fire until we were within effective range and then to fire as rapidly as possible with all of our guns.

At five-forty, when we were within a distance of five thousand yards (two and one-half miles), I turned to Captain Gridley and said: "You may fire when you are ready, Gridley."

While I remained on the bridge with Lamberton, Brumby, and Stickney, Gridley took his station in the conning tower and gave the order to the battery. The very first gun to speak was an eight-inch from the forward turret of the *Olympia,* and this was the signal for the other ships to join the action. . . .

When the flagship neared the five-fathom curve off Cavite, she turned to the westward, bringing her port batteries to bear on the enemy, and followed by the squadron, passed along the Spanish line until north of and only some fifteen hundred yards distant from the Sangley Point battery, when she again turned and headed back to the eastward, thus giving the squadron an opportunity to use their port and starboard batteries alternately and to cover with their fire all the Spanish ships as well as the Cavite and Sangley Point batteries. While I was regulating the course of the squadron, Lieutenant Calkins was verifying our position by cross bearings and by the lead.

Three runs were thus made from the eastward and two from the westward, the length of each run averaging two miles and the ships being turned each time with port helm. . . . The fifth run past the Spaniards was farther inshore than any preceding run. At the nearest point to the enemy our range was only two thousand yards.

There had been no cessation in the rapidity of fire maintained by our whole squadron, and the effect of its concentration, owing to the fact that our ships were kept so close together, was smothering, particularly upon the two largest ships, the *Reina Cristina* and *Castilla*. The *Don Juan de Austria* first and then the *Reina Cristina* made brave and desperate attempts to charge the *Olympia,* but becoming the target for all our batteries, they turned and ran back. In this sortie the *Reina Cristina* was raked by an eight-inch shell, which is said to have put out of action some twenty men and to have completely destroyed her steering gear. Another shell in her forecastle killed or wounded all the members of the crews of four rapid-fire guns; another set fire to her after orlop; another killed or disabled nine men on her poop; another carried away her mizzenmast, bringing down the ensign and the admiral's flag, both of which were replaced; another exploded in the after ammunition room; and still another exploded in the sick bay, which was already filled with wounded.

Though in the early part of the action our firing was not what I should have liked it to be, it soon steadied down, and by the time the *Reina Cristina* steamed toward us it was satisfactorily accurate. The *Castilla* fared little better than the *Reina Cristina*. All except one of her guns were disabled; she was set on fire by our shells and finally abandoned by her crew after they had sustained a loss of twenty-three killed and eighty wounded. The *Don Juan de Austria* was badly damaged and on fire, the *Isla de Luzón* had three guns dismounted, and the *Marqués del Duero* was also in a bad way. Admiral Montojo, finding his flagship no longer manageable, half her people dead or wounded, her guns useless, and the ship on fire, gave the order to abandon and sink her and transferred his flag to the *Isla de Cuba* shortly after seven o'clock.

Victory was already ours, though we did not know it. . . .

Feeling confident of the outcome, I now signaled that the crews, who had had only a cup of coffee at 4:00 A.M., should have their breakfast. The public at home, on account of this signal, to which was attributed a nonchalance that had never occurred to me, reasoned that breakfast was the real reason for our withdrawing from action. Meanwhile I improved the opportunity to have the commanding officers report on board the flagship.

There had been such a heavy flight of shells over us that each captain, when he arrived, was convinced that no other ship had had such good luck as his own in being missed by the enemy's fire and expected the others to have both casualties and damages to their ships to report. But fortune was as pronouncedly in our favor at Manila as it was later at Santiago. To my gratification not a single life had been lost, and considering that we would rather measure the importance of an action by the scale of its conduct than by the number of casualties, we were immensely happy. On the *Baltimore* two officers and six men were slightly wounded. None of our ships had been seriously hit, and every one was still ready for immediate action.

At 11:16 A.M. we stood in to complete our work. There remained to oppose us, however, only the batteries and the gallant little *Ulloa*. Both opened fire as we advanced. But the contest was too unequal to last more than a few minutes. Soon the *Ulloa,* under our concentrated fire, went down valiantly with her colors flying.

At 12:30 the *Petrel* signaled the fact of the surrender, and the firing ceased. But the Spanish vessels were not yet fully destroyed. Therefore the executive officer of the *Petrel,* Lieutenant E.M. Hughes, with a whaleboat and a crew of only seven men, boarded and set fire to the *Don Juan de Austria, Isla de Cuba, Isla de Luzón, General Lezo, Coreo,* and *Marqués del Duero,* all of which had been abandoned in shallow water and left scuttled by their deserting crews. This was a courageous undertaking, as these vessels were supposed to have been left with trains to their magazines and were not far from the shore, where there were hundreds of Spanish soldiers and sailors, all armed and greatly excited. The *Manila,* an armed transport, which was found uninjured after having been beached by the Spaniards, was therefore spared. Two days later she was easily floated and for many years did good service as a gunboat. The little *Petrel* continued her work until 5:20 P.M., when she rejoined the squadron, towing a long string of tugs and launches, to be greeted by volleys of cheers from every ship.

The order to capture or destroy the Spanish squadron had been executed to the letter. Not one of its fighting vessels remained afloat. That night I wrote in my diary: "Reached Manila at daylight. Immediately engaged the Spanish ships and batteries at Cavite. Destroyed eight of the former, including the *Reina Cristina* and *Castilla.* Anchored at noon off Manila."

The Autobiography of George Dewey

86

Frances Willard Embarks on the Temperance Crusade

The origins of the temperance crusade date back to the early years of the Republic and by the mid-nineteenth century the cause of temperance had made impressive headway. Immigration and the growth of cities, however, gave a new impetus to the liquor traffic: between 1860 and 1880 the liquor business increased sevenfold, and the temperance crusade gave way to the prohibition movement. For this change Frances Willard of Evanston, Illinois, was largely responsible. In 1874 she founded the Woman's Christian Temperance Union and thereafter devoted her life to this cause.

The first saloon I ever entered was Sheffner's, on Market Street, Pittsburgh. In fact that was the only glimpse I ever personally had of the crusade [1874]. It had lingered in this dun-colored city well nigh a year, and when I visited my old friends at the Pittsburgh Female College I spoke with enthusiasm of the crusade and of the women who were, as I judged from a morning paper, still engaged in it here. They looked upon me with astonishment when I proposed to seek out those women and go with them to the saloons, for in the two years that I had taught in Pittsburgh these friends associated me with the recitation room, the Shakespeare Club, the lecture course, the opera, indeed all the haunts open to me that a literary-minded woman would care to enter. However, they were too polite to desire to disappoint me; and so they had me piloted by some of the factotums of the place to the headquarters of the crusade, where I was warmly welcomed and soon found myself walking downstreet arm in arm with a young teacher from the public school who said she had a habit of coming in to add one to the procession when her day's duties were over. We paused in front of the saloon that I have mentioned. The ladies ranged themselves along the curbstone, for they had been forbidden in any wise to incommode the passers-by, being dealt with much more strictly than a drunken man or a heap of dry-goods boxes would be. At a signal from our gray-haired leader a sweet-voiced woman began to sing, "Jesus the water of life will give," all our voices soon blending in that sweet song. I think it was the most novel spectacle that I recall. There stood women of undoubted religious devotion and the highest character, most of them crowned with the glory of gray hairs. Along the stony pavement of that stoniest of cities rumbled the heavy wagons, many of them carriers of beer; between us and the saloon in front of which we were drawn up in line passed the motley throng, almost every man lifting his hat and even the little newsboys doing the same. It was American manhood's tribute to Christianity and to womanhood, and it was significant and full of pathos. The leader had already asked the saloonkeeper if we might enter, and he had declined; else the prayer meeting would have occurred inside his door. A sorrowful old lady whose only son had gone to ruin through that very deathtrap knelt on the cold, moist pavement and offered a brokenhearted prayer while all our heads were bowed. At a signal we moved on, and the next saloonkeeper permitted us to enter. I had no more idea of the inward appearance of a saloon than if there had been no such place on earth. I knew nothing of its high, heavily corniced bar, its barrels with the ends all pointed toward the looker-on, each barrel being furnished with a faucet; its floors thickly strewn with sawdust, and here and there a round table with chairs—nor of its abundant fumes, sickening to healthful nostrils. The tall, stately lady who led us placed her Bible on the bar and read a psalm, whether hortatory or imprecatory I do not remember, but the spirit of these crusaders was so gentle, I think it must have been the former. Then we sang "Rock of Ages" as I thought I had never heard it sung before, with a tender confidence to the height of which one does not rise in the easy-going regulation prayer meeting, and then one of the older women whispered to me softly that the leader wished to know if I would pray. It was strange, perhaps, but I felt not the least reluctance, and kneeling on that sawdust floor, with a group of earnest hearts around me, and behind them, filling every corner and extending out into the street, a crowd of unwashed, unkempt, hard-looking drinking men, I was conscious that perhaps never in my life save beside my sister Mary's dying bed had I prayed as truly as I did then. This was my crusade baptism. The next day I went on to the West and within a week had been made president of the Chicago W.C.T.U.

Frances E. Willard
Glimpses of Fifty Years, the Autobiography of an American Woman

87

Sam Jones Preaches the Golden Rule in Toledo

Golden Rule" Jones was one of a number of reform mayors who, at the turn of the twentieth century, attempted to end what Lincoln Steffens called "the shame of the cities." In this task he had the loyal support of young Brand Whitlock, who, on Jones's death, succeeded him as mayor of Toledo. Whitlock later achieved fame as a novelist, as a historian, and as minister to Belgium during the First World War.

There was in Toledo one man who could sympathize with my attitude, and that was a man whose determination to accept literally and to try to practise the fundamental philosophy of Christianity had so startled and confounded the Christians everywhere that he at once became famous throughout Christendom as Golden Rule Jones. I had known of him only as the eccentric mayor of our city, and nearly every one whom I had met since my advent in Toledo spoke of him only to say something disparaging of him. The most charitable thing they said was that he was crazy. All the newspapers were against him and all the preachers. My own opinion, of course, could have been of no consequence, but I had learned in the case of Altgeld that almost universal condemnation of a man is to be examined before it is given entire credit. I do not mean to say that there was universal condemnation of Golden Rule Jones in Toledo in those days; it was simply that the institutional voices of society, the press and the pulpit, were thundering in condemnation of him. When the people came to vote for his re-election, his majorities were overwhelming, so that he used to say that everybody was against him but the people. But that is another story.

In those days I had not met him. I might have called at his office, to be sure, but I did not care to add to his burdens.

One day suddenly, as I was working on a story in my office, in he stepped with a startling, abrupt manner, wheeled a chair up to my desk, and sat down. He was a big Welshman with a sandy complexion and great hands that had worked hard in their time, and he had an eye that looked right into the center of your skull. He wore, and all the time he was in the room continued to wear, a large cream-colored slouch hat, and he had on the flowing cravat which for some inexplicable reason artists and social reformers wear, their affinity being due, no doubt, to the fact that the reformer must be an artist of a sort; else he could not dream his dreams. I was relieved, however, to find that Jones wore his hair clipped short, and there was still about him that practical air of the very practical businessman he had been before he became mayor. He had been such a practical businessman that he was worth half a million, a fairly good fortune for our town; but he had not been in office very long before all the businessmen were down on him and saying that what the town needed was a businessman for mayor, a statement that was destined to ring in my ears for a good many years.

They disliked him, of course, because he would not do just what they told him to—that being the meaning and purpose of a businessman for mayor—but insisted that there were certain other people in the city who were entitled to some of his service and consideration; namely, the working people and the poor. The politicians and the preachers objected to him on the same grounds: the unpardonable sin being to express in any but a purely ideal and sentimental form sympathy for the workers or the poor. It seemed to be particularly exasperating that he was doing all this in the name of the Golden Rule, which was for the Sunday school; and they even went so far as to bring to town another Sam Jones, the Reverend Sam Jones, to conduct a revival and to defeat the Honorable Sam Jones. The Reverend Sam Jones had big meetings and said many clever things and many true ones, the truest among them being his epigram, "I am for the Golden Rule myself, up to a certain point, and then I want to take the shotgun and the club." I think that expression marked the difference between him and our Sam Jones, in whose philosophy there was no place at all for the shotgun or the club. The preachers were complaining that Mayor Jones was not using shotguns or at least clubs on the bad people in the town; I suppose that since their own persuasions had in a measure failed, they felt that the mayor with such instruments might have made the bad people look as if they had been converted, anyway.

It was our interest in the disowned, the outcast, the poor, and the criminal that drew us first together, that and the fact that we are gradually assuming the same attitude toward life.

He was always going down to the city prisons or to the workhouses and talking to the poor devils there quite as if he were one of them, which indeed he felt he was and as all of us are, if we only knew it. And he was working all the time to get them out of prison, and finally he and I entered into a little compact by which he paid the expenses incident to their trials—the fees for stenographers and that sort of thing—if I would look after their cases. Hard as the work was and sad as it was, and grievously as my law partners complained of the time it took and of its probable effect on business (since no one wished to be known as a criminal lawyer!), it did pay in the satisfaction there was in doing a little to comfort and console—and, what was so much more, to compel in one city, at least, a discussion of the grounds and the purpose of our institutions. For instance, if some poor girl were arrested and a jury trial were demanded for her and her case were given all the care and attention it would have received had she been some wealthy person, the police, when they found they could not convict, were apt to be a little more careful of the liberties of individuals; they began to have a little regard for human rights and for human life.

We completely broke up the old practice of arresting persons on suspicion and holding them at the will and pleasure of the police without any charge having been lodged against them; two or three trials before juries, the members of which could very easily be made to see, when it was pointed out to them a few times in the course of a three days' trial, that there is nothing more absurd than that policemen should make criminals of people merely by suspecting them and sending them to prison on that sole account, wrought a change. Jones managed to get himself fined for contempt one day, and he immediately turned the incident to his own advantage and made his point by drawing out his checkbook with a flourish, writing his check for the amount of his fine, and declaring that this proved his contention that the only crime our civilization punishes is the crime of being poor.

But he was most in his element when the police judge was absent, as he was now and then. In that exigency the law gave Jones as mayor the power to appoint the acting police judge, and when Jones did not go down and sit as magistrate himself he appointed me, and we always found some reason or other for letting all the culprits go. The foundations of society were shaken, of course, and the editorials and sermons were heavy with all the predictions of disaster. One might have supposed that the whole wonderful and beautiful fabric of civilization which man had been so long in rearing was to fall forever into the awful abyss because a few miserable outcasts had not been put in prison. But nothing happened after all; the poor *misérables* were back again in a few days and made to resume their hopeless rounds through the prison doors. But the policemen of Toledo had their clubs taken away from them, and they became human and learned to help people and not to hurt them if they could avoid it; and that police judge who once fined Jones became in time one of the leaders in our city of the new social movement that has marked the last decade in America. . . .

I regard it as Jones's supreme contribution to the thought of his time that by the mere force of his own original character and personality he compelled a discussion of fundamental principles of government. Toledo today is a community which has a wider acquaintance with all the abstract principles of social relations than any other city in the land—or in the world, since when one ventures into generalities one might as well make them as sweeping as one can.

Jones's other great contribution to the science of municipal government was that of nonpartisanship in local affairs. That is the way he used to express it; what he meant was that the issues of national politics must not be permitted to obtrude themselves into municipal campaigns and that what divisions there are should be confined to local issues. There is, of course, in our cities, as in our land or any land, only one issue, that which is presented by the conflict of the aristocratic or plutocratic spirit and the spirit of democracy.

Jones used to herald himself as a man without a party, but he was a great democrat, the most fundamental I ever knew or imagined; he summed up in himself, as no other figure in our time since Lincoln, all that the democratic spirit is and hopes to be. Perhaps in this characterization I seem to behold his figure larger than it was in relation to the whole mass, but while his work may appear at first glance local, it was really general and universal. No one can estimate the peculiar and lively forces of such a personality; certainly no one can presume to limit his influence, for such a spirit is illimitable and irresistible.

He was elected in that last campaign for the fourth time, but he did not live very long. When he died the only wounds he left in human hearts were because he was no more. They understood him at last, those who had scoffed and sneered and abused and vilified; and I who had had the immense privilege of his friendship and thought I knew him—when I stood that July afternoon, on the veranda of his home, beside his bier to speak at his funeral and looked out over the thousands who were gathered on the wide lawn before his home—I realized that I too had not wholly understood him.

I know not how many thousands were there; they were standing on the lawns in a mass that extended across the street and into the yards on the farther side. Down to the corner and into the side streets they were packed, and they stood in long lines all the way out to the cemetery. In that crowd there were all sorts of that one sort he knew as humanity without distinction—judges and women of prominence and women whom he alone would have included in humanity; there were thieves and prizefighters—and they all stood there with the tears streaming down their faces.

Brand Whitlock
Forty Years of It

88

"Crucify Mankind upon a Cross of Gold"

In 1896 the great issue before the American people was the "money question." The Republican Party had committed itself to the gold standard, but the Democrats, under the leadership of men like "Silver Dick" Bland and young William Jennings Bryan, broke away from the Cleveland leadership and endorsed free silver. The "Cross of Gold" speech, delivered before the Democratic convention at Chicago, ensured the adoption of a silver platform by that party, but it did more: it ensured the nomination of Bryan himself as the party's candidate for the presidency. The "Cross of Gold" speech is an excellent example of the eloquence for which Bryan was famous.

I would be presumptuous, indeed, to present myself against the distinguished gentlemen to whom you have listened if this were a mere measuring of abilities; but this is not a contest between persons. The humblest citizen in all the land, when clad in the armor of a righteous cause, is stronger than all the hosts of error. I come to speak to you in defense of a cause as holy as the cause of liberty—the cause of humanity. . . .

Never before in the history of this country has there been witnessed such a contest as that through which we have just passed. Never before in the history of American politics has a great issue been fought out as this issue has been, by the voters of a great party. On the fourth of March, 1893, a few Democrats, most of them members of Congress, issued an address to the Democrats of the nation, asserting that the money question was the paramount issue of the hour; declaring that a majority of the Democratic party had the right to control the action of the party on this paramount issue; and concluding with the request that the believers in the free coinage of silver in the Democratic party should organize, take charge of, and control the policy of the Democratic party. Three months later, at Memphis, an organization was perfected, and the silver Democrats went forth openly and courageously proclaiming their belief and declaring that if successful they would crystallize into a platform the declaration which they had made. Then began the struggle. With a zeal approaching the zeal which inspired the Crusaders who followed Peter the Hermit, our silver Democrats went forth from victory unto victory until they are now assembled, not to discuss, not to debate, but to enter up the judgment already rendered by the plain people of this country. In this contest brother has been arrayed against brother, father against son. The warmest ties of love, acquaintance, and association have been disregarded; old leaders have been cast aside when they have refused to give expression to the sentiments of those whom they would lead, and new leaders have sprung up to give direction to this cause of truth. Thus has the contest been waged, and we have assembled here under as binding and solemn instructions as were ever imposed upon representatives of the people. . . .

When you [turning to the gold delegates] come before us and tell us that we are about to disturb your business interests, we reply that you have disturbed our business interests by your course.

We say to you that you have made the definition of a business man too limited in its application. The man who is employed for wages is as much a business man as his employer; the attorney in a country town is as much a business man as the corporation counsel in a great metropolis; the merchant at the crossroads store is as much a business man as the merchant of New York; the farmer who goes forth in the morning and toils all day, who begins in the spring and toils all summer, and who by the application of brain and muscle to the natural resources of the country creates wealth, is as much a business man as the man who goes upon the Board of Trade and bets upon the price of grain; the miners who go down a thousand feet into the earth or climb two thousand feet upon the cliffs and bring forth from their hiding places the precious metals to be poured into the channels of trade are as much business men as the few financial magnates who, in a back room, corner the money of the world. We come to speak of this broader class of business men.

Ah, my friends, we say not one word against those who live upon the Atlantic coast, but the hardy pioneers who have braved all the dangers of the wilderness, who have made the desert to bloom as the rose—the pioneers away out there [pointing to the west] who rear their children near to Nature's heart, where they can mingle their voices with the voices of the birds—out there where they have erected schoolhouses for the education of their young, churches where they praise their Creator, and cemeteries where rest the ashes of their dead—these people, we say, are as deserving of the consideration of our party as any people in this country. It is for these that we speak. We do not come as aggressors. Our war is not a war of conquest; we are fighting in the defense of our homes, our families, and posterity. We have petitioned, and our petitions have been scorned; we have entreated, and our entreaties have been disregarded; we have begged, and they have mocked when our calamity came. We beg no longer; we entreat no more; we petition no more. We defy them! . . .

And now, my friends, let me come to the paramount issue. If they ask us why it is that we say more on the money question than we say upon the tariff question, I reply that if protection has slain its thousands the gold standard has slain its tens of thousands. If they ask us why we do not embody in our platforms all the things that we believe in, we reply that when we have restored the money of the Constitution, all other necessary reform will be possible; but that until this is done, there is no other reform that can be accomplished.

Why is it that within three months such a change has come over the country? Three months ago when it was confidently asserted that those who believed in the gold standard would frame our platform and nominate our candidates, even the advocates of the gold standard did not think that we could elect a President. And they had good reason for their doubt, because there is scarcely a state here today asking for the gold standard which is not in the absolute control of the Republican party. But note the change. Mr. McKinley was nominated at St. Louis upon a platform which declared for the maintenance of the gold standard until it can be changed into bimetallism by international agreement. Mr. McKinley was the most popular man among the Republicans, and three months ago everybody in the Republican party prophesied his election. How is it today? Why, the man who was once pleased to think that he looked like Napoleon—that man shudders today when he remembers that he was nominated on the anniversary of the battle of Waterloo.

Not only that, but as he listens he can hear with ever-increasing distinctness the sound of the waves as they beat upon the lonely shores of St. Helena.

Why this change? Ah, my friends, is not the reason for the change evident to any one who will look at the matter? No private character however pure, no personal popularity however great, can protect from the avenging wrath of an indignant people a man who will declare that he is in favor of fastening the gold standard upon this country or who is willing to surrender the right of self-government and place the legislative control of our affairs in the hands of foreign potentates and powers. . . .

You come to us and tell us that the great cities are in favor of the gold standard; we reply that the great cities rest upon our broad and fertile prairies. Burn down your cities and leave our farms, and your cities will spring up again as if by magic; but destroy our farms, and the grass will grow in the streets of every city in the country.

My friends, we declare that this nation is able to legislate for its own people on every question, without waiting for the aid or consent of any other nation on earth; and upon that issue we expect to carry every state in the Union. I shall not slander the inhabitants of the fair state of Massachusetts nor the inhabitants of the state of New York by saying that, when they are confronted with the proposition, they will declare that this nation is not able to attend to its own business. It is the issue of 1776 over again. Our ancestors when but three million in number had the courage to declare their political independence of every other nation; shall we their descendants, when we have grown to seventy millions, declare that we are less independent than our forefathers?

No, my friends, that will never be the verdict of our people. Therefore we care not upon what lines the battle is fought. If they say bimetallism is good but that we cannot have it until other nations help us, we reply that instead of having a gold standard because England has, we will restore bimetallism and then let England have bimetallism because the United States has it. If they dare to come out in the open field and defend the gold standard as a good thing, we will fight them to the uttermost. Having behind us the producing masses of this nation and the world, supported by the commercial interests, the laboring interests, and the toilers everywhere, we will answer their demand for a gold standard by saying to them: You shall not press down upon the brow of labor this crown of thorns, you shall not crucify mankind upon a cross of gold.

W.J. Bryan
Speech at the Democratic Convention
1896

89

The Roosevelts Take Over the White House

The youngest of American presidents, impetuous, temperamental, and colorful, Roosevelt, eagerly aided and abetted by his family, brought a sense of life and gusto into official Washington that had long been lacking. Ike Hoover, who describes the change, was White House usher for some forty years.

One might have expected that the Roosevelts, coming in under such tragic conditions, would have been hesitant and subdued. On the contrary, from the day of their arrival they displayed the characteristics which were to distinguish their entire administration.

To those around the White House who had a personal recollection of Mr. Roosevelt as Civil Service Commissioner and later as Assistant Secretary of the Navy, his bold step of taking up his residence in the place so soon after the funeral of Mr. McKinley was no surprise. They vividly pictured him coming in—as he had on many occasions as commissioner and as assistant secretary—and going upstairs two steps at a time, expounding his positive ideas in a manner that permitted of no contradiction. As had been expected, it was a continual two-step and spirited waltz for seven and one half years. The music varied, but the pace never ceased.

After the McKinley funeral Mr. Roosevelt himself did not appear for several days, but in the meantime Mrs. Roosevelt and her son Teddy arrived. After looking the place over they sent word to the others to join them, and in less than a week all the family were living in their new quarters. Then began the wildest scramble in the history of the White House. The children, hearty and full of spirits, immediately proceeded to cut loose.

The life of the employees who took their responsibilities too seriously was made miserable. The children left no nook or corner unexplored. From the basement to the flagpole on the roof, every channel and cubbyhole was thoroughly investigated. Places that had not seen a human being for years were now made alive with the howls and laughter of these newcomers. The house became one general playground for them and their associates. Nothing was too sacred to be used for their amusement, and no place too good for a playroom. The children seemed to be encouraged in these ideas by their elders, and it was a brave man indeed who dare say no or suggest putting a stop to these escapades.

One of the favorite stunts of the children was to crawl through the space between ceilings and floors where no living being but rats and ferrets had been for years. They took delight also in roller-skating and bicycle-riding all over the house, especially on the smooth hardwood floors. Practically every member of the family, with the exception of the President and Mrs. Roosevelt, had a pair of wooden stilts, and no stairs were too well carpeted or too steep for their climbing, no tree too high to scramble to the top, no fountain too deep to take a dip, no furniture too good or too high to use for leapfrog and horseplay, no bed was too expensive or chair too elegantly upholstered to be used as a resting place for the various pets in the household.

Giving the pony a ride in the elevator was but one of many stunts. This little fellow, spotted and handsome, had free access to any of the children's bedrooms. By means of the elevator he would be conveyed to the bedroom floor from the basement, a distance of two complete floors. As the children grew, there grew with them the idea on the part of the staff that such a situation was really necessary to the proper conduct of things. In fact it seemed as natural to the daily life of the White House as it was for an officer to arrest a crank or for the cook to prepare the meals.

These indeed were interesting days. The two smaller children, Archie and Quentin, were mere babies. Ethel and Kermit were about the same age and were inseparable, one just as daring as the other, and Ethel not willing to permit Kermit to outdo her in any respect. The escapades of these two alone would set any household agog.

Alice and Teddy completed the younger part of the household, and while both had their share of fun, it must be said they were the more subdued upon their arrival. Alice appeared more sedate than in after years. Ted seemed quiet enough, but as time wore on he too got his share in the way of sport and amusement.

But to leave the younger set and proceed to the daily life of these exciting times. Immediately upon the Roosevelts' arrival, the usual household changes were begun, only in this case they were more numerous and more radical than ever before. Instead of moving a piece of furniture here and there whole rooms were changed outright. Where one bed might have been before, two were now placed, and vice versa. The children were assigned to convenient apartments, and all settled down to enjoy the White House to the utmost. As the President was heard to remark just before finally leaving, "Perhaps others have lived longer in the place and enjoyed it quite as much, but none have ever really had more fun out of it than we have."

That describes best the everyday life of the Roosevelts. From the hour of rising in the morning plans were immediately prepared as to how best to enjoy the day. Meal hours, office hours, school hours, were all subject to change to fit in with these plans. Nothing was ever known to interfere— neither weather, company, business, nor anything else.

These pastimes took on all forms. First and foremost, of course. were the horseback rides. Every member of the family was an expert rider, and the President never seemed so happy as when either Mrs. Roosevelt or one of the children accompanied him on his ride. Next perhaps might be mentioned his lawn tennis games. It was great sport for him to figure just whom he preferred to play with in the afternoon. Of course none dared refuse the invitation, but it was well known that a poor player was never invited a second time. His favorites seemed to be Garfield, Pinchot, and Murray, but Bacon, Jusserand, and Meyer were close up, while experts like McCawley and Hurstman were only invited when he was feeling especially good. No sport seemed to be amiss in this family. Boxing, wrestling, fencing, running, and walking were among the President's favorite diversions.

Entering upon the daily routine, we found the entire family down to breakfast at eight o'clock. After breakfast the President spent an hour or so in his study, perhaps reading, while Mrs. Roosevelt arranged the details of the day's program. The President went to his office at nine-thirty or ten o'clock, and Mrs. Roosevelt for a walk or shopping, often accompanied by her secretary or one of her many friends.

All returned just about in time for lunch. Those famous lunches! Something indeed was wrong when there were not two or more guests for this meal. To prepare properly for a certain number was almost a physical impossibility, for notice was continually coming from the office that some one had been invited at the last minute, and many times the family and guests had to wait until the table was made larger before they could be seated. The place was really a transient boardinghouse, and how every one got enough to eat was the wonder of the household. Lunch being over, the rest of the afternoon was given over to sport—"exercise" as the President used to call it.

At one time it would be the famous Mike Donovan engaging in battles royal with the President and taking on one of the boys for a side issue. Then again it would be Joe Grant, the famous District champion wrestler, who would spend two or three hours at a time trying his prowess with the head of the nation and giving his points to the younger ones. Then again there would be broadsword battles with General Wood and others and games of medicine ball with Garfield and Pinchot.

Not content with these ordinary playtimes, the President took up jujitsu and put in two full seasons learning this famous art of self-defense. Upon one occasion, not knowing just which was preferable from a defensive standpoint, he decided to try out the two schemes of American wrestling and Japanese jujitsu. The most expert exponent of the Japanese art and the wrestler Grant were to test their respective merits before the President and a few especially invited guests.

On another occasion famous Chinese wrestlers gave an exhibition of their prowess in the East Room, which had been especially prepared for the occasion. These were the big fellows, and, quite different from the jujitsu people, they depended upon their strength alone. It was a very interesting affair and was witnessed by fifty or sixty guests, including cabinet members, senators, and a few others. This was a wholly Chinese contest, and while Mr. Roosevelt expressed offhandedly a wish to take on one of the big fellows, he did not try it.

So it went. Nothing seemed too absurd in the way of exercise and sport. Those employed around the house vied with each other to be the first to get the information of the day's doings.

In more serious matters great stress was laid on the fact that everything must be just right down to the smallest detail. No excuse would be accepted for the slightest error of omission or commission. Everything must be perfect. This led to a state of efficiency that was a pleasure to behold. While the demand was in a measure severe, still the thanks were so profuse that one felt amply repaid for both work and worry.

The Roosevelt family did not care a great deal about elaborate entertaining. Yet the most minute details were gone into in arranging the necessary social affairs. The formalities were so keenly observed that they were sometimes tiresome to every one rather than pleasant or brilliant.

It was more to the liking of the family to spend a quiet evening in the library, either playing cards or reading the current magazines. The whole family were fiends when it came to reading. No newspapers. Never a moment was allowed to go to waste; from the oldest to the youngest they always had a book or a magazine before them. The President, in particular, would just devour a book, and it was no uncommon thing for him to go entirely through three or four volumes in the course of an evening. Likewise we frequently saw one of the children stretched out on the floor flat on his stomach eating a piece of candy and with his face buried deep in a book. The current magazines were entirely too slow coming out, and we were kept busy trying to get them for the different members of the family the moment they appeared. And yet the Roosevelts were early birds, both in retiring and arising. Very seldom, unless something special was on hand, did they go to bed later than ten-thirty. In going out to dinner they made it a rule to make their departure promptly at ten o'clock, then home and immediately to their bedrooms.

Irwin Hood (Ike) Hoover
Forty-two Years in the White House

90

Taft and Roosevelt
Come to a Parting of Ways

Roosevelt might have had another term in 1908, but preferred to install as his successor his secretary of war, William Howard Taft. Taft, however, proved less liberal and more independent than Roosevelt had expected, and gradually the two men drifted into opposite camps. By 1912 the break was complete; Roosevelt headed a revolt, split his party, and ran for the presidency on his own Progressive platform. Archie Butt, whose letters reveal the course of the historic break, was military aide to both presidents, and was torn between his affection for Roosevelt and his loyalty to Taft.

July 6, 1910.—

The press this morning carried a report from Oyster Bay that Mr. Roosevelt had had an interview with Representative Poindexter of Washington State and had pledged him his support against Secretary Ballinger, who is an applicant for the Senate. I went for the President at nine o'clock and found him sitting on the porch. He had no sooner started to Myopia than he said to me:

"Archie, I am very distressed. I do not see how I am going to get out of having a fight with President Roosevelt."

"You refer to the Poindexter matter?" I asked.

"Yes. He seems to have thrown down the gauntlet in this matter, for what was given to the press he gave out himself. I have doubted up to the present time whether he really intended to fight my administration or not, but he sees no one but my enemies, and if by chance he sees any supporters of the administration, he does not talk intimately with any of them. Poindexter is one of the most bitter political opponents and always has been. Mr. Roosevelt's support of him seems most gratuitous and unnecessary. I confess it wounds me very deeply. I hardly think the prophet of the square deal is playing it exactly square with me now."

"Don't you think it possible that he intends to support the insurgent wing of the party up to a certain point and then unite it against the Democratic?"

"I should like to think so. But I think if he intended to do that, he would at least take into his confidence some other members of the party than those who have fought me and whom I have had to fight. But I shall do nothing. I shall let matters shape themselves in his mind and give him every chance to whip around if he sees he is making a mistake. I shall take no notice of it until it absolutely forces itself on me or the administration.". . .

I asked the President if he thought it possible that Mr. Roosevelt really contemplated forming a third party.

"I do not know. I have thought sometimes he did, and then I don't see how he can. In his mind, however, it may be the only logical way of reaching a third term. Then, too, his tour of Europe, his reception there, and the fact that every crowned head seemed to take it for granted that he would be elected to another term may have caused him to think that he should be, so as to realize the prophecies of so many people."

I felt his talk with me had had some especial significance, for as we neared Myopia he said to me:

"You may hear me say some bitter things of our old chief at times, and I fear it may distress you, but as long as I confine my criticism of him to my immediate official family you will have to put up with it, Archie, and I want you to know that it will be quite as distressing to me to break with him as it will be to you to see this break come." . . .

The view of the President at this moment is of interest and marks one more step which so many people think will end in the disruption of the old Republican party and the overthrow of the present administration.

AUGUST 25.—

The President told me yesterday that the whole trouble between him and Mr. Roosevelt started, he feared, with that letter which I carried to the ex-President when he was sailing for Europe.

"Something offended him in that letter," said the President, "but I was never certain what it was until recently when some one who was with him on the steamer told me. It seems that I said that I would never forget what he and my brother Charlie had done for me. He became very angry and said how dared I couple him with my brother, and he would teach me to compare what he had done for me with what my brother had done, at the same time using some rather objectionable terms in description of old Charlie. I was sure there was some offense taken, because, as you remember, he has never answered it, after telling you that he would do so. Of course he does not think that Charlie was a factor in my nomination, and for this very reason he does not understand my desire to recognize what my brother did."

The President is in a little better frame of mind, but he is still pretty thoughtful. Mr. Roosevelt has made no acknowledgment at all of his letter in which he stated that he was not a party to the program to humiliate him in New York. The letter was addressed to Lloyd Griscom, but it was really intended for the ex-President, and the President feels that Mr. Roosevelt might have at least sent him some word which would indicate to him that he accepted the truth of the statement.

September 20.—

It did not take long for the bomb to explode. Mr. Roosevelt is out in a statement tonight denying that he sought the interview, and both he and Griscom charge Norton and inferentially the President with giving false statements as to who asked for it and what was done there. . . .

Colonel Roosevelt, whatever his object was in coming to the conference, acted squarely and gave to the President every opportunity to get nearer to him. The conference was a great, serious thing, not only to the two men concerned, but for the party and the country. Mr. Roosevelt treated it seriously, and the President did not. That is the truth of the matter, and in consequence the two men are further apart than ever. But facts are more interesting now than comments.

The President told us just what occurred.

He said that Roosevelt was not genial and quite offish, he thought, and talked on matters of a general nature. He said they did not touch on Federal matters, but that he, in order to bring things to a head, brought up the New York matter and volunteered to help Mr. Roosevelt in his fight on bossism in that state. So, strictly speaking, Mr. Roosevelt did not ask for any assistance.

"But that was what he was there for," said the President, "and I went to the point at once, but Roosevelt said the conference was necessary to help bring the party together—that both of us owed that much to the party."

"The fact of the matter is," said the President, "if you were to remove Roosevelt's skull now, you would find written on his brain '1912.' But he is so purely an opportunist that should he find conditions changed materially in another year and you were to open his brain, you would not find there 1912, and Roosevelt would deny it was ever there."

"That makes it all the more important," said Schmidlapp, "that you say nothing which will widen the breach so that he cannot support you should you be renominated. If your administration is a success, the party will have to renominate you; if it is a failure, no Republican can be elected, and Roosevelt will be the first one to recognize this fact."

It was not a very cheerful meal.

OCTOBER 19.—

We had rather a scene at the breakfast table this morning. Mrs. Henry Taft told the President that the Troy *Times* was owned by a Mr. Francis, an old friend of hers, who had always written to her, but he had stopped writing, and she felt certain that he was attacking the administration bitterly, and she was able to account for it. Troy, I think, is her old home. She said that Francis had told her two years ago that he was to be appointed ambassador to Italy, that President Roosevelt had got the promise from Mr. Taft, who was then just elected, to send him to Rome. Later some one else had been appointed, and Francis looked upon the matter as an intentional insult both to himself and the ex-President, and he was now taking it out on the administration.

The President was indignant and proceeded to hit out right and left. He said that Mr. Roosevelt had never asked it of him as a favor but merely expressed the hope that Francis would be named to Italy. He then said:

"I meet this sort of thing everywhere. One day just after I was nominated I told Roosevelt that, should I be elected, I did not see how I could do anything else but retain all the old members of the cabinet who had been associated with me. I thought nothing more about it, but I learned later that Roosevelt had practically told every member of his cabinet that he was going to be retained should I be elected. The only one he made it a point to ask me to retain was Meyer, and I retained him. I am now placed in the attitude of breaking a promise to each of these men."

He said much more of a character to show how deeply he felt, but this gives the gist of what he said.

JANUARY 19, 1911.—

I had a conversation with the President about Colonel Roosevelt. I repeated to him what Mr. Griscom had said to me the night before at the diplomatic dinner, which had saddened me very much. I could not get out of my mind all day the picture he drew of Colonel and Mrs. Roosevelt at Oyster Bay. He and Mrs. Griscom had gone down to spend Sunday, and he said that he had found the Colonel in a most depressed state of mind; all his old buoyancy was gone, and he really seemed to him to be a changed man. Mrs. Roosevelt, he said, seemed more depressed than the Colonel, and this I realized came from the state he must be in, for if she could have her wish it would be never to hear of politics again. But if he is wounded she shows her distress just in this way. Her depression told me, better than anything else which Mr. Griscom could have said, the state of the Colonel's mind.

At any rate I told the President just what Griscom had told me, and when he got to the White House he asked me to come in, as he wanted to talk, and while I took off my things he walked ahead of me and turned on the lights in the Red Room and sat down with his overcoat on.

"Tell me again what Griscom said. It is strange he never told me any of this."

I told the President that Griscom had said he would not repeat it to any one else but myself, for he knew my interest in and love for the family.

"Archie," said the President, "I don't see what I could have done to make things different. Somehow people have convinced the Colonel that I have gone back on him, and he does not seem to be able to get that out of his mind. But it distresses me very deeply, more deeply than any one can know, to think of him sitting there at Oyster Bay alone and feeling himself deserted. I know just what he feels. It is a dreary spot in winter, and the surroundings must have a bad effect on both of them."

The President stopped talking and looked hard ahead of him. He reached up and wiped his eye. I don't know whether a tear had formed there or not, but I could see that something of a big nature was going on in his mind. He may have been reviewing all those years of intimacy and come face to face with some thought of disloyalty on his own part. I started to rise, but he waved me back, and he sat for some time longer in absolute silence. When he broke it again, it was to say:

"It may be that a break had to come. The situation was a most difficult one for both of us, but no harder for him than for me, and I don't think he ever saw my side of it. What he is undergoing now may be the thing most needed to get him back to a normal frame of mind. The American people are strange in their attitudes toward their idols. This is not the first time this sort of thing has happened. They have even led their idols on and on, to cut their legs from under them later and apparently to make their fall all the greater.

"Where I do blame Roosevelt is for allowing them to get him in this position. He should have kept aloof and not given the people an opportunity to do what they have done. But I don't know when I have had anything affect me as deeply as the picture which this conversation brings to my mind. To feel everything slipping away from him, all the popularity, the power which he loved, and above all the ability to do what he thought was of real benefit to his country, to feel it all going and then to be alone! I hope the old boy has enough philosophy left to take him through this period; that is all. If he could only fight! That is what he delights in, and that is what is denied to him now. The papers in the East have adopted a policy of ignoring him, of never mentioning him. I had heard that this was done with a view of driving home the iron. This robs him of the right to hit back, to fight, and leaves him in a way without an audience. I hear Pinchot has deserted him and that his old allies are weakening. It is all sad! Well, do you see where I could have acted differently?"

He appealed to me for comfort, for in his mind there was the still small voice saying I know not what, but enough to make the quiver in his voice genuine.

"I don't see how you could have done differently," I said.

FEBRUARY 14.—

The President and I took a long walk in the afternoon. He was most talkative all the way. He could not get Roosevelt off his mind and kept saying that if Roosevelt succeeded in defeating him for the nomination, he [Roosevelt] would be the most bitterly discredited statesman ever in American politics.

"The humiliation which will be meted out to him in November and during the campaign will cause any humiliation I may feel at the convention to seem as nothing."

He told me he felt certain that Roosevelt would become in the near future a declared candidate. He believes every story brought to him, from whatever source, and is growing more bitter every hour toward the man who nominated him before. He thinks that the Colonel has no cause for resentment at all, and it is not for me to say now that he is right, for I remember too much in the past. The clash which must follow between these two men is tragic. It is moving now from day to day with the irresistible force of the Greek drama, and I see no way for anything save divine Providence to interpose to save the reputation of either should they hurl themselves at each other. Their most intimate friends are all mutually intimate with both, and every one of us feels involved in the outcome.

21ST.—

I went walking with the President this afternoon. President Roosevelt had delivered his much-advertised speech in Columbus, Ohio, coming out for the initiative, referendum, and recall, and the reports show that he had been given an overwhelming reception. When asked if he were to be a candidate he answered:

"My hat is in the ring. I will answer all such questions Monday."

The President had long told me that Roosevelt would be a candidate, and he simply dreaded the issue. I saw that he was worried from the moment we left the White House and so said hardly a word to him. Finally as we neared Dupont Circle he said to me:

"Well, Archie, what do you think of the recall of judges as announced by the Colonel today?"

"I have always been opposed to the recall of the judiciary, Mr. President."

We took a long walk, being out nearly two hours. When we were nearly home he turned to me and stopped and said:

"Archie, I am going to say something which may surprise you, and therefore you must not say anything about it. Do you know those presentiments which sometimes come over one, even against his reasoning? Well, I have a strong presentiment that the Colonel is going to beat me in the convention. It is almost a conviction with me. I shall continue to fight to the last moment, but when you see me claiming victory or my friends claiming victory for me, remember that I feel that I am losing a battle and that I am not blind myself, no matter what my friends may put out."

"My presentiment is all the other way," I said, to show some cheerful side.

"No, that is because you want to see me win. But don't think me capable of quitting. I can fight just as well when losing as when certain of victory, and I have made up my mind to answer that speech of Theodore's and answer it in Ohio, where he dared to deliver it. He has drawn the line now, and I hope we can keep the fight from becoming personal. He has leaped far ahead of the most radical leaders of the Progressive Party, and his heart is not with them, but he deludes himself that he will be able to guide it and stem it when he gets in power. He can't do it. He has gone too far. He will either be a hopeless failure if elected or else destroy his own reputation by becoming a socialist, being swept there by force of circumstances just as the leaders of the French Revolution were swept on and on, all their individual efforts failing to stem the tide until it had run itself out."

It was a nasty and wet afternoon, and I don't know whether that had anything to do with the President's mood, but I never saw him quite so pessimistic before.

25TH.—

I was at the White House tonight when the President received the announcement of Colonel Roosevelt's candidacy. There was nothing very dramatic about it, and little to be remembered except the simple way it was received.

Job Hedges and Crawford Hill, the latter from Denver, were spending the night at the White House. Mrs. Taft ordered dinner at half past seven in order that we might be on time at the Belasco to hear Buffalo Jones describe in a ludicrous way his catching of live animals in Africa. Just as we were going in to dinner a short note was handed to the President. He read it and passed it to each one of us. It was merely an announcement of the Associated Press that it had the Colonel's letter to the governors, the gist of which was that he would accept the nomination if offered to him.

We had sat down to the table before any one made a comment, Mrs. Taft was the first to break the silence.

"I told you so four years ago, and you would not believe me."

The President laughed good-naturedly and said:

"I know you did, my dear, and I think you are perfectly happy now. You would have preferred the Colonel to come out against me than to have been wrong yourself."

"Well, she is a better guesser than I," said Jacob Hedges, "for only last week I was predicting that under no conditions would the Colonel be a declared candidate."

Conversation became general, and we tried to rattle Helen about always coming in late to dinner. She said:

"I don't see why Father and Mother don't scold me for being late, as I always am, but they take it very good-naturedly."

"One of the saddest things that can come to a parent is to see his own faults coming out in his own children," said the President.

Just at this time there was sent from the office the entire letter of Colonel Roosevelt, which was short, clear-cut, and a plain statement that the Colonel was a candidate for the nomination. The President read it aloud. Every one took a whack at it, but the President regarded it as much stronger than he had thought it would be. He explained that he had believed it would come out loaded with conditions and explanations, whereas it was a short, brief announcement and direct to the people.

"No, he could not have made it stronger," said the President. "It is characteristic of him, and it will be a rallying cry to the Progressives of the country and to the discontented, but I think you will find that in a week or ten days it will have lost much of its clarion note, and there will be a great sag in the sentiment which will at first be aroused by it."

Taft and Roosevelt: The Intimate Letters of Archie Butt, Military Aide

91

Herbert Hoover Feeds the Belgians

The German invasion of Belgium in August 1914 brought ruin and starvation to that hapless country, and in October a Commission for Relief in Belgium was organized in London with semiofficial support from the United States. Herbert Clark Hoover, a consulting engineer then living in London, was placed in charge of relief work, and within less than a month the first food ship docked at Rotterdam. Hoover's achievement as director of relief work brought him world renown as a humanitarian and an administrator, and paved the way for his subsequent political career in the United States. The author of this journal entry is Brand Whitlock, who was mayor of Toledo, Ohio, from 1905 to 1911, and later authored numerous novels, including *Uprooted* (1926) and *Narcissus* (1931).

SUNDAY, NOVEMBER 29, 1914.—

Took a walk this morning, and I have seldom worked so hard as I did in the afternoon, preparing the courier who goes out early in the morning with letters to London, and so on. Then at four arrived Shaler with Hoover, Doctor Rose, and Bicknell. Doctor Rose and Bicknell represent the Rockefeller Foundation and are here to investigate conditions in Belgium. Doctor Rose is the great hookworm specialist, and Bicknell is the Red Cross expert; Rose a little man who looks something like a preacher; Bicknell tall, fine-looking, with white hair and a sense of humor. Hoover just as Francqui described him, the type of American business man, a face somewhat *fruste,* very direct, positive, able, speaks little, but everything he says counts. I talked to him for a while and explained the situation to him here and learned what has been going on outside. The usual amount of quarreling in America between rival committees, Catholics and Protestants, and so forth. Nothing so sweet and charming and altogether lovely as to see rival religions in each other's hair over some question of sweet charity! The poor man has had many troubles but seems to surmount them all bravely.

The Rockefeller representatives, with the right by money to ask questions, cross-examined me for two hours; and for two hours I answered questions explaining the situation here and when I was through felt that I had made out my case. Hoover thought so too, and so did Shaler and so did the Rockefeller men; but I was as tired as though I had been making an argument before the Supreme Court. We had them here to dinner and still more talk. Then at ten Madame Carton de Wiart came in. Francqui had been here at noon to see me. He had known Hoover in China and admired him immensely and wished to have an hour with Hoover before Hoover saw any of the others. We discussed Heineman somewhat, but agreed that we had great need of him since he has influence with the Germans. Hoover speaks no French and Francqui pigeon English; so it is amusing to hear them.

30TH.—

I showed to Kaufmann the figures that Hoover had given me, namely twenty-seven hundred thousand pounds, which translated into German means fifty-four million marks, the amount of the value of foodstuffs already imported into Belgium from America! *"Sapristi!"* said Kaufmann.

This afternoon a long session with Hoover, Francqui, Heineman, Rose, Bicknell, and Shaler about the problem of financing the scheme. Six hundred thousand pounds furnished by the English and French governments to the Belgian government are to be turned over by the Belgian government to our committee, credited to the Comité National here, and by them distributed among the communes. The Rockefeller men are much impressed by our organization and by conditions in Belgium. They start in a day or two on a tour, to be accompanied by Gibson and probably Francqui. Tomorrow we go to see the soup kitchens; in the afternoon a session of the Comité National. The consul general was in, and I asked him to go with us.

DECEMBER 1.—

This morning Hoover, Bell, Doctor Rose, Bicknell, Francqui, Shaler, Gibson, Leval, Watts, and I drove about in the rain to see the soup kitchens, a doleful morning's business, though not without its reassurance of the goodness that still is in human nature. We went first to the Boulevard Anspach, and there in a great circular dome that was once used by an express company was a wire ring of caldrons with cooks bending over them brewing the savory soup that is sent out to the various kitchens and there served to the poor. We then drove to some of these stations, notably one in the Rue Blaes near the Boulevard du Midi, in the very heart of the Quartier des Marolles. Long lines of poor women and men crowding the sidewalks and inside the hall, once a kind of theater and café, its garish decorations full of mockery. Each poor soul entered with a ticket and there was given a bit of coffee, a bit of chicory, a loaf of bread. Each person receives enough for the day's nourishment, a noble answer to the prayer, "Give us this day our daily bread."

Each person has a card from his commune with a number. The numbers are checked off. The lines are inspected in groups by persons connected with the neighborhoods whence they come. If one is missing, the absence is instantly detected: "Where is Jeanne today? Is she sick? Or what?"

The admirable organization deeply impressed Hoover and Rose. We stayed some time there watching this line of poor march by. Each one, as he or she received his or her ration, said "Thank you," and I had to turn away to hide my tears.

I came back to the Legation, wrote letters for Hoover to take to Page, very tired and worn out by the day, and then Madame Carton de Wiart came, wishing to see the Rockefeller men, and then Hoover to bid me good-bye. He was very much moved by the sight of suffering he saw today, and very cordial and very fine. A remarkable man indeed. His last thought was to place enough money on deposit here to pay all expenses. The Belgians, he said, must not be put to a pennyworth of expense. His meeting with Francqui in this work is quite interesting. Years ago Hoover was in China managing a profitable business, a veritable king of a little province. One morning Francqui arrived and said Belgian capital had bought the control. So Hoover was displaced, though he stayed and worked with Francqui for some time. Now after all these years they meet and are friends again, working in a great cause. I was proud today to think that my country was doing this noble work amidst all this rage, this brutal and ignorant destruction, but one's thoughts are almost drowned these days, and it is difficult to express them.

The Journal of Brand Whitlock

92

Woodrow Wilson Breaks with Germany

It was German submarine warfare that caused a crisis in her relations with the United States. On May 4, 1916, Germany promised that no more merchant vessels would be sunk without warning, but nine months thereafter her condition was so desperate she found it necessary to repudiate the promise and inaugurate unrestricted submarine warfare. It was this shift in German policy that precipitated the final crisis and led directly to the rupture of relations. Robert Lansing, who tells the story of the break, had succeeded William Jennings Bryan as secretary of state.

During the forenoon of Wednesday, January 31, 1917, the German ambassador telephoned my office and arranged an interview for four o'clock that afternoon. He did not indicate his purpose, and my own idea was that he probably desired to talk over confidentially the terms on which Germany would make peace.

When he entered my room at ten minutes after four I noticed that, though he moved with his usual springy step, he did not smile with his customary assurance. After shaking hands and sitting down in the large easy chair by the side of my desk he drew forth from an envelope which he carried several papers. Selecting one, he held it out, saying that he had been instructed to deliver it to me. As I took the paper he said that for convenience he had prepared an English translation. He then handed me three documents in English consisting of a note and two accompanying memoranda.

He asked me if he should read them to me or if I would read them to myself before he said anything about them. I replied that I would read the papers, which I did slowly and carefully; for as the nature of the communication was disclosed I realized that it was of very serious import and would probably bring on the gravest crisis which this government had had to face during the war. The note announced the renewal *on the next day* of indiscriminate submarine warfare and the annulment of the assurances given this government by Germany in the note of May 4, 1916, following the *Sussex* affair.

While I had been anticipating for nearly three months this very moment in our relations with Germany and had given expression to my conviction in the public statement which I made concerning our note of December 18, for which I had been so generally criticized, I was nevertheless surprised that Germany's return to ruthless methods came at this time. I knew that all her shipyards had been working to their full capacity in constructing submarines for the past seven months and that thousands of men were being trained to handle their complex mechanism, but I assumed that on account of the difficulties of using submarines in northern waters during midwinter the campaign would not begin before March and probably not until April. It was therefore with real amazement that I read the note and memoranda handed me. I can only account for the premature announcement of indiscriminate warfare on the ground that the food situation in Germany had reached such a pass that the Imperial Government had to do something to satisfy public opinion.

As I finished my deliberate perusal of the papers, I laid them on the desk and turned toward Count von Bernstorff. "I am sorry," he said, "to have to bring about this situation, but my government could do nothing else."

I replied, "That is of course the excuse given for this sudden action, but you must know that it cannot be accepted."

"Of course, of course," he said, "I understand that. I know it is very serious, very, and I deeply regret that it is necessary."

"I believe you do regret it," I answered, "for you know what the result will be. But I am not blaming you personally."

"You should not," he said with evident feeling; "you know how constantly I have worked for peace."

"I do know it," I said. "I have never doubted your desire or failed to appreciate your efforts."

"I still hope," he said, speaking with much earnestness, "that with a full realization of Germany's situation your government will in justice decide that the notification of blockade is entirely warranted."

I answered him that I could not discuss the merits until I had thoroughly digested the documents, but I would say that the first reading had made a very bad impression and that to give only eight hours' notice without any previous warning of intention was in my opinion an unfriendly and indefensible act.

He exclaimed: "I do not think it was so intended; I am sure it was not."

"I regret that I must differ with you," I replied, "but this has come so suddenly that I am sure you will understand I do not wish to discuss the matter further."

"Of course, of course; I quite understand," he said, rising and extending his hand, which I took with a feeling almost of compassion for the man, whose eyes were suffused and who was not at all the jaunty, carefree man-of-the-world he usually was. With a ghost of a smile he bowed as I said "Good afternoon," and turning, left the room.

Immediately on his departure I called in Polk and Woolsey and read the communication which I had received. We all agreed that the only course which seemed open was to break off diplomatic relations.

I telephoned to the White House and found the President was out. I then wrote him a short letter transmitting the papers and sent it by Sweet to the White House, who between five and five-thirty left it with the usher to be put in the President's hands as soon as he returned. Through some confusion with other papers the President did not get the papers until after eight o'clock. He then telephoned me to come to the White House.

From a quarter to nine until half past ten we conferred in his study. Throughout the conference I maintained that we must pursue the course which he had declared we would pursue in our *Sussex* note of April 18, 1916, namely to break off relations with Germany if she practiced ruthless submarine warfare, that any lesser action would be impossible, and that the only question in my mind was whether we ought not to go further and declare that the actual renewal of indiscriminate submarine attack affecting our citizens or ships would be considered by us to be an act of war.

The President, though deeply incensed at Germany's insolent notice, said that he was not yet sure what course we must pursue and must think it over; that he had been more and more impressed with the idea that "white civilization" and its domination over the world rested largely on our ability to keep this country intact, as we would have to build up the nations ravaged by the war. He said that as this idea had grown upon him he had come to the feeling that he was willing to go to any lengths rather than to have the nation actually involved in the conflict.

I argued with him that if the break did not come now, it was bound to do so in a very short time and that we would be in a much stronger position before the world if we lived up to our declared purpose than if we waited until we were further humiliated. I said that if we failed to act I did not think we could hold up our heads as a great nation and that our voice in the future would be treated with contempt by both the Allies and Germany.

The President said that he was not sure of that; that, if he believed it was for the good of the world for the United States to keep out of the war in the present circumstances, he would be willing to bear all the criticism and abuse which would surely follow our failure to break with Germany; that contempt was nothing unless it impaired future usefulness; and that nothing could induce him to break off relations unless he was convinced that, viewed from every angle, it was the wisest thing to do.

I replied to this that I felt that the greatness of the part which a nation plays in the world depends largely upon its character and the high regard of other nations, that I felt that to permit Germany to do this abominable thing without firmly following out to the letter what we had proclaimed to the world we would do would be to lose our character as a great power and the esteem of all nations, and that to be considered a bluffer was an impossible position for a nation which cherished self-respect.

There was, of course, much more said during our conference. The President showed much irritation over the British disregard for neutral rights and over the British plan (asserted by Germany) to furnish British merchant ships with heavy guns. I told him that . . . proof of this we had none, but it seemed to me that Germany's declaration in any event justified such a practice. He replied that he was not certain that the argument was sound, but he did not think it worth while to discuss it now in view of the present crisis.

After some further talk it was agreed that I should prepare a note to Bernstorff setting out the breach of faith by Germany and breaking off diplomatic relations. . . .

On returning home I immediately prepared a draft in rough form, and the next morning (Thursday) I redrew it in my own handwriting, using for the quoted parts clippings from the printed correspondence. (This note, with practically no changes, was the one finally sent.)

Although many diplomats called at the Department, I denied myself to them all as I did not care to discuss the situation. However, I had to see Senator Hitchcock, who was the ranking Democrat on the Committee on Foreign Relations. He suggested that we ask the belligerents of both sides for a ten-day armistice. I asked him what good that would do. He said, "To gain time." "Well, and then what?" I asked. He had nothing to offer, and I told him that I did not think that it would get us anywhere, but that even if there were some benefit to be gained, I was sure that Germany would decline and the Allies would probably do the same. He went away in a dispirited frame of mind, saying that he saw no other way of avoiding trouble.

At noon on Thursday (the first of February) I went over to the White House and, with Colonel House, who had arrived early that morning, conferred with the President for about an hour in his study. We went over substantially the same ground which the President and I had covered the night before. The Colonel, as is customary with him, said very little, but what he did say was in support of my views.

I went further in this conference than I did in the previous one by asserting that in my opinion peace and civilization depended on the establishment of democratic institutions throughout the world and that this would be impossible if Prussian militarism after the war controlled Germany. The President said that he was not sure of this, as it might mean the disintegration of German power and the destruction of the German nation. His argument did not impress me as very genuine, and I concluded that he was in his usual careful way endeavoring to look at all sides of the question.

When I left the conference I felt convinced that the President had almost reached a decision to send Bernstorff home. It was not any particular thing which he said but rather a general impression gained from the entire conversation. At any rate I felt very much better than I had the night before, when the President's tone of indecision had depressed me. Probably I misjudged him because he did not at once fall in with my views, which were certainly radical. . . .

At two-thirty Friday afternoon the cabinet met and sat until four forty-five. The entire time was given to a discussion of the crisis with Germany. The discussion was very general, although it was chiefly confined to the subjects which the President and I had been over in our conference.

Friday was a day of extreme tension. From morning till night officials and newspaper men were fairly on tiptoe with suppressed excitement. Fully eighty of the correspondents were present at my interview in the morning, and they were swarming in the corridors when I returned to the Department at five o'clock. I slept soundly that night, feeling sure the President would act vigorously.

Saturday morning (the third), soon after I reached the Department, Polk and I discussed the situation. He was doubtful and distressed, and I assured him that I was certain the President would act that day. . . .

At ten-thirty I reached the President's study, and we conferred for half an hour. He told me that he had decided to hand Bernstorff his passports and to recall Gerard and that at two o'clock that afternoon he would address Congress, laying before them in a little more elaborate form the substance of the note which I had drafted, together with a statement that he would come before them again and ask for powers in case Germany should carry out her threats. I congratulated him on his decision, saying I was sure that he was right and that the American people almost to a man would stand behind him.

The War Memoirs of Robert Lansing

93

President Harding Helps His Friends

The nomination of Warren G. Harding by the Republican convention of 1920 was not a response to popular demand but to the demands of a group of political bosses, of whom Boies Penrose was the most notorious. Harding was well-intentioned, but he found it difficult to refuse a friend anything that was within his power to give. With Harding's election the "Ohio gang" took over national politics and for three years had things pretty much their own way. Mrs. McLean, who here describes the Hardings, was a woman of great wealth and the wife of the editor of the *Washington Post*.

The one time in our life when I thought that Ned McLean was going to be saved from a disastrous end in dissipation was when he was going around with Warren Gamaliel Harding. Good heavens! I had cause enough for hope, because that friend of my husband and of mine became the President and thus possessed not only the power but the will to confer on us some great distinction that would fully gratify the most ambitious appetite for dignity. I have the President's written word that he was alert to recognize becomingly our "valued and devoted friendship."

In that stage of the 1920 campaign when the Republican candidate was leaving his front porch from time to time to make speeches from the rear platform of his train and in auditoriums before vast gatherings of cheering people whom he addressed as his "fellow countrymen," Ned and I were with the Hardings for a while and found out that the Hardings we had known as poker-playing friends were quite unchanged. However, out-of-doors or any place where others might observe us, Mrs. Harding was clutched by a set of the strangest fears that I ever encountered; and so, to a less degree, was her husband.

I stood beside her one day as photographers prepared to take our picture in a group with several others. I was engaged at the time in what for thirty years or more has been one of the least compromising of my habits—I was smoking a cigarette. Suddenly, aware of its smoke, she whirled on me and snatched the cigarette from my lips. She was as much concerned as if its tip had been hovering over a powder barrel.

"Evalyn," she chided me a little later, "you've got to help us by being circumspect. The Lord knows *I* don't mind your cigarettes, or jewels. You know how much I think of you; but you must give a thought to what we now are doing."

"But the senator smokes cigarettes," I said.

"Not when he is having his picture taken," said Mrs. Harding grimly. "Just let me catch him light a cigarette where any hostile eye might see him! He can't play cards until the campaign is over, either."

"But does he smoke tobacco?"

"A pipe, cigars, yes; but a cigarette is something that seems to infuriate swarms of voters who have a prejudice against cigarettes. He can chew tobacco, though." When she added that bit of information Mrs. Harding grimaced with a twinkle in her cornflower-blue eyes.

I learned that golf was something else that seemed to upset the stomachs of great masses of the voters, of factory laborers, of farmers, and of others who dwelt by myriads in those states where the campaign would be won or lost. Altogether the candidate had to shape himself, or seem to, just to fit the convolutions of the voters' minds.

I began to understand how sincere Warren Harding had been when he told us one time when we played poker that he really did not want to run for President.

"I'm satisfied with being senator," he said. "I'd like to go on living here in Washington and continue to be a member of the world's most exclusive club. I'm sure I can have six years more; I may have twelve or eighteen. If I have to go on and live in the White House I won't be able to call my soul my own. I don't want to be spied on every minute of the day and night. I don't want secret-service men trailing after me." He meant it, and it is my conviction that his wife meant it, too, when she said she preferred that they should be to the end of their days Senator and Mrs. Harding. The one who nagged and coaxed them to change their course was Harry M. Daugherty.

I remembered that Mr. Cox, who owned a newspaper in Dayton, Ohio, and one or two other small city newspapers, came to see us in Washington almost before the campaign was under way. He wanted to make sure that Ned would put the *Cincinnati Enquirer* wholeheartedly on the side of the Democratic party—and Cox. The *Enquirer* always had been Democratic.

"We've got to make up our minds," said Ned. "We're for Harding, you and me, but the readers of the *Enquirer* and the *Post* may be less ready for a shift than we should like to have them."

The fact is, I suppose, that old John R. [McLean] would have walked the earth as Hamlet's father did if he had known how lightly Ned was flipping back and forth with the idea of altering overnight the political complexion of two big, money-making papers. The question was especially vital with the *Enquirer.* Always under John R.'s direction it had been devoted to the Democratic party, which was natural since he himself was a party boss out in Ohio.

Just what to do came to me clearly in the night! Harding was going to win hands down, and everybody loves a winner. I put it plainly up to Ned, and he to me; we convinced each other (and I think so still) that as between Harding and Cox for President my choice to the end of time would be Warren G. Harding. There was no open break with the party, but Ned made it clear that he wanted nothing printed that would interfere even a little with the success of the Harding campaign.

The constant adulation of people was beginning to have an effect on Senator Harding. He was more and more inclined to believe in himself. He cherished an idea that when a man was elevated to the presidency his wits by some automatic mental chemistry were increased to fit the stature of his office. We, his friends, could see him, during that vacation, as a young Aladdin testing experimentally the terrific power of the mighty engine called the presidency.

"Hey, Ed," we would hear him call in a loud tone, as a king in olden times called for a jester. He really loved Ed Scobey, and it was fun for Harding to be able to announce to him that he should become the Director of the Mint and to know that what he promised would, by reason of his great power, come to pass.

Ned, before long, was to learn that he had been made chairman of the inaugural committee, which would have full charge of all arrangements for the celebration in connection with the ceremony whereby Woodrow Wilson would relinquish power and Warren Harding take it. A few other acts of powered graciousness were revealed to us on that trip, or just a few weeks later, as, one by one, all of Harding's well-liked friends received some kind of title. Dick Crissinger, for example, had been Harding's playmate when they were barefoot country boys. He grew up to be a Democrat of consequence in Marion, but it was his old pal Harding who made him governor of the Federal Reserve Board. These were not bad appointments; as good, no doubt, as needed for the jobs; but it seems significant to me, now, that they were made as they were—because Warren Harding had received the presidency by chance, without having expected until late in life that he had even, as he might have said, a Chinaman's chance to win the office. The office of president was hardly a subject that he had studied. I think it was a thing he had merely dreamed about, as we all dream when we wish we had power to fix everything. It is my opinion that Warren Harding, if he could have looked ahead when he was young and seen a vision of the time when he would be selected to go and live in the White House, would have lived quite differently. As it happened, he was a loyal friend who was, unhappily, loyal sometimes to the wrong people.

Guns, dogs, and horses were the instruments with which my husband had much of his fun; a duck blind on a raw and foggy morning was for him a place rich with excitement, and I think he liked nothing better than to see some horse he owned racing—out in front. However, when Senator Harding was elected Ned took up golf. He was well equipped to play at poker, but not so well equipped as the President-elect at bridge. Upon deciding to become a better golfer Ned did not merely buy a book; he hired the full-time services of a first-rate professional, Freddie McLeod. When that was done we had at Friendship all the appurtenances of a splendid country club, but this was a club where none paid dues nor any other fees—except we two McLeans. We had our money's worth in providing entertainment for those who came. As for me, there was an added value in the chance I seemed to sense that Ned McLean would stir with fine ambitions as he watched our friend, President-elect Harding, wield power and change the destinies of other men.

Certainly when Harding started in to pick his cabinet some of his selections were of a kind to make other men envy him his power. Charles Evans Hughes, Herbert Hoover, John W. Weeks, were names that aroused my enthusiasm when I heard they were slated for the Harding cabinet. There was a special thrill for me in those choices, because one afternoon during his post-election vacation at Brownsville, Texas, Senator Harding talked to me about that first big job he had to do.

"I want to have a really great cabinet," he said. Saying this, he was looking out the window of our private car. His shaggy brows were knit, and under them his blue-gray eyes were tender as he let them peer beyond the flatness of the Texas landscape until he took into his mind some concept of the whole of that country of which he had become the leader. Even there and then, however, one might have seen that troubles were in store for a man so easy-going with his friends. He was himself a loyal friend and could not think that treachery could mask itself behind the eyes of those he looked upon as friends of his. Unhappily, for many persons he had become something other than a friend; he was to all of these no less a thing than Opportunity. In consequence, if he talked alone with one man for five or ten minutes some others became uncomfortable, fearful of losing an expected favor.

EVALYN WALSH McLEAN
Father Struck It Rich

94

Charles Lindbergh Flies to Paris

God never intended man to fly" was a serious conviction in 1900, but before the end of the decade the vision of Samuel P. Langley and the perseverance of the Wright brothers proved that the airplane was a practical invention. As early as 1919 two Englishmen, Alcock and Brown, made a nonstop flight from Newfoundland to Ireland, and throughout the twenties other aviators had revealed the almost limitless possibilities of aviation. But no feat of that generation caught the imagination of Americans as did Lindbergh's solo flight from New York to Paris, and the modesty with which Lindbergh received the universal acclaim further endeared him to his countrymen.

On the morning of May nineteenth, a light rain was falling and the sky was overcast. Weather reports from land stations and ships along the great circle course were unfavorable and there was apparently no prospect of taking off for Paris for several days at least. But at about six o'clock I received a special report from the New York Weather Bureau. A high pressure area was over the entire North Atlantic and the low pressure area over Nova Scotia and Newfoundland was receding. It was apparent that the prospects of the fog clearing up were as good as I might expect for some time to come. The North Atlantic should be clear with only local storms on the coast of Europe. The moon had just passed full and the percentage of days with fog over Newfoundland and the Grand Banks was increasing so that there seemed to be no advantage in waiting longer.

We went to Curtiss Field as quickly as possible and made arrangements for the barograph to be sealed and installed, and for the plane to be serviced and checked.

We decided partially to fill the fuel tanks in the hangar before towing the ship on a truck to Roosevelt Field which adjoins Curtiss on the east, where the servicing would be completed.

I left the responsibility for conditioning the plane in the hands of the men on the field while I went into the hotel for about two and one-half hours of rest; but at the hotel there were several more details which had to be completed and I was unable to get any sleep that night.

I returned to the field before daybreak on the morning of the twentieth. A light rain was falling which continued until almost dawn; consequently we did not move the ship to Roosevelt Field until much later than we had planned, and the take off was delayed from daybreak until nearly eight o'clock.

At dawn the shower had passed, although the sky was overcast, and occasionally there would be some slight precipitation. The tail of the plane was lashed to a truck and escorted by a number of motorcycle police. The slow trip from Curtiss to Roosevelt was begun.

The ship was placed at the extreme west end of the field heading along the east and west runway and the final fueling commenced.

About 7:40 A.M. the motor was started and at 7:52 I took off on the flight for Paris.

The field was a little soft due to the rain during the night and the heavily loaded plane gathered speed very slowly. After passing the halfway mark, however, it was apparent that I would be able to clear the obstructions at the end. I passed over a tractor by about fifteen feet and a telephone line by about twenty, with a fair reserve of flying speed. I believe that the ship would have taken off from a hard field with at least five hundred pounds more weight.

I turned slightly to the right to avoid some high trees on a hill directly ahead, but by the time I had gone a few hundred yards I had sufficient altitude to clear all obstructions and throttled the engine down to 1750 R.P.M. I took up a compass course at once and soon reached Long Island Sound where the Curtiss Oriole with its photographer, which had been escorting me, turned back.

The haze soon cleared and from Cape Cod through the southern half of Nova Scotia the weather and visibility were excellent. I was flying very low, sometimes as close as ten feet from the trees and water.

On the three-hundred-mile stretch of water between Cape Cod and Nova Scotia I passed within view of numerous fishing vessels.

The northern part of Nova Scotia contained a number of storm areas and several times I flew through cloudbursts.

As I neared the northern coast, snow appeared in patches on the ground and far to the eastward the coastline was covered with fog.

For many miles between Nova Scotia and Newfoundland the ocean was covered with caked ice, but as I approached the coast the ice disappeared entirely and I saw several ships in this area.

I had taken up a course for St. John's, which is south of the great circle from New York to Paris, so that there would be no question of the fact that I had passed Newfoundland in case I was forced down in the North Atlantic.

I passed over numerous icebergs after leaving St. John's, but saw no ships except near the coast.

Darkness set in about 8:15 and a thin, low fog formed over the sea through which the white bergs showed up with surprising clearness. This fog became thicker and increased in height until within two hours I was just skimming the top of storm clouds at about ten thousand feet. Even at this altitude there was a thick haze through which only the stars directly overhead could be seen.

There was no moon and it was very dark. The tops of some of the storm clouds were several thousand feet above me and at one time, when I attempted to fly through one of the larger clouds, sleet started to collect on the plane and I was forced to turn around and get back into clear air immediately and then fly around any clouds which I could not get over.

The moon appeared on the horizon after about two hours of darkness; then the flying was much less complicated.

Dawn came at about 1 A.M., New York time, and the temperature had risen until there was practically no remaining danger of sleet.

Shortly after sunrise the clouds became more broken, although some of them were far above me and it was often necessary to fly through them, navigating by instruments only.

As the sun became higher, holes appeared in the fog. Through one the open water was visible, and I dropped down until less than a hundred feet above the waves. There was a strong wind blowing from the northwest and the ocean was covered with white caps.

After a few miles of fairly clear weather the ceiling lowered to zero and for nearly two hours I flew entirely blind through the fog at an altitude of about 1500 feet. Then the fog raised and the water was visible again.

On several more occasions it was necessary to fly by instrument for short periods; then the fog broke up into patches. These patches took on forms of every description. Numerous shorelines appeared, with trees perfectly outlined against the horizon. In fact, the mirages were so natural that, had I not been in mid-Atlantic and known that no land existed along my route, I would have taken them to be actual islands.

As the fog cleared I dropped down closer to the water, sometimes flying within ten feet of the waves and seldom higher than two hundred.

There is a cushion of air close to the ground or water through which a plane flies with less effort than when at a higher altitude, and for hours at a time I took advantage of this factor.

Also it was less difficult to determine the wind drift near the water. During the entire flight the wind was strong enough to produce white caps on the waves. When one of these formed, the foam would be blown off, showing the wind's direction and approximate velocity. This foam remained on the water long enough for me to obtain a general idea of my drift.

During the day I saw a number of porpoises and a few birds but no ships, although I understand that two different boats reported me passing over.

The first indication of my approach to the European Coast was a small fishing boat which I first noticed a few miles ahead and slightly to the south of my course. There were several of these fishing boats grouped within a few miles of each other.

I flew over the first boat without seeing any signs of life. As I circled over the second, however, a man's face appeared, looking out of the cabin window.

I have carried on short conversations with people on the ground by flying low with throttled engine, and shouting a question, and receiving the answer by some signal. When I saw this fisherman I decided to try to get him to point towards land. I had no sooner made the decision than the futility of the effort became apparent. In all likelihood he could not speak English, and even if he could he would undoubtedly be far too astounded to answer. However, I circled again and closing the throttle as the plane passed within a few feet of the boat I shouted, "Which way is Ireland?" Of course the attempt was useless, and I continued on my course.

Less than an hour later a rugged and semi-mountainous coastline appeared to the northeast. I was flying less than two hundred feet from the water when I sighted it. The shore was fairly distinct and not over ten or fifteen miles away. A light haze coupled with numerous storm areas had prevented my seeing it from a long distance.

The coastline came down from the north and curved towards the east. I had very little doubt that it was the southwestern end of Ireland, but in order to make sure I changed my course towards the nearest point of land.

I located Cape Valencia and Dingle Bay, then resumed my compass course towards Paris.

After leaving Ireland I passed a number of steamers and was seldom out of sight of a ship.

In a little over two hours the coast of England appeared. My course passed over southern England and a little south of Plymouth; then across the English Channel, striking France over Cherbourg.

I was flying at about a fifteen-hundred-foot altitude over England and as I crossed the Channel and passed over Cherbourg, France, I had probably seen more of that part of Europe than many native Europeans. The visibility was good and the country could be seen for miles around.

The sun went down shortly after passing Cherbourg and soon the beacons along the Paris-London airway became visible.

I first saw the lights of Paris a little before 10 P.M., or 5 P.M., New York time, and a few minutes later I was circling the Eiffel Tower at an altitude of about four thousand feet.

The lights of Le Bourget were plainly visible, but appeared to be very close to Paris. I had understood that the field was farther from the city, so continued out to the northeast into the country for four or five miles to make sure that there was not another field farther out which might be Le Bourget. Then I returned and spiralled down closer to the lights. Presently I could make out long lines of hangars, and the roads appeared to be jammed with cars.

I flew low over the field once, then circled around into the wind and landed.

CHARLES A. LINDBERGH
We

95

Franklin D. Roosevelt Promises a New Deal

Confident of victory, the Democrats nominated Franklin D. Roosevelt at their Chicago convention of 1932 as their standard-bearer and adopted a platform calling for far-reaching reforms. Democratic confidence was justified. Roosevelt carried every state but six, and Democratic control of both houses of Congress was complete. In his inaugural address the new president promised "a new deal" to the "forgotten man"—a promise that he proceeded to carry out with breathtaking rapidity in the early months of his administration.

This is a day of national consecration, and I am certain that my fellow Americans expect that on my induction into the Presidency I will address them with a candor and a decision which the present situation of our nation impels.

This is pre-eminently the time to speak the truth, the whole truth, frankly and boldly. Nor need we shrink from honestly facing conditions in our country today. This great nation will endure as it has endured, will revive and will prosper.

So first of all let me assert my firm belief that the only thing we have to fear is fear itself—nameless, unreasoning, unjustified terror which paralyzes needed efforts to convert retreat into advance.

In every dark hour of our national life a leadership of frankness and vigor has met with that understanding and support of the people themselves which is essential to victory. I am convinced that you will again give that support to leadership in these critical days.

In such a spirit on my part and on yours we face our common difficulties. They concern, thank God, only material things. Values have shrunken to fantastic levels; taxes have risen; our ability to pay has fallen; government of all kinds is faced by serious curtailment of income; the means of exchange are frozen in the currents of trade; the withered leaves of industrial enterprise lie on every side; farmers find no markets for their produce; the savings of many years in thousands of families are gone.

More important, a host of unemployed citizens face the grim problem of existence, and an equally great number toil with little return. Only a foolish optimist can deny the dark realities of the moment.

Yet our distress comes from no failure of substance. We are stricken by no plague of locusts. Compared with the perils which our forefathers conquered because they believed and were not afraid, we have still much to be thankful for. Nature still offers her bounty and human efforts have multiplied it.

Plenty is at our doorstep, but a generous use of it languishes in the very sight of the supply.

Primarily, this is because the rulers of the exchange of mankind's goods have failed through their own stubbornness and their own incompetence, have admitted their failure and abdicated. Practices of the unscrupulous money-changers stand indicted in the court of public opinion, rejected by the hearts and minds of men.

True, they have tried, but their efforts have been cast in the pattern of an outworn tradition. Faced by failure of credit, they have proposed only the lending of more money.

Stripped of the lure of profit by which to induce our people to follow their false leadership, they have resorted to exhortations, pleading tearfully for restored confidence. They know only the rules of a generation of self-seekers.

They have no vision, and when there is no vision the people perish.

The money-changers have fled from their high seats in the temple of civilization. We may now restore that temple to the ancient truths. . . .

Restoration calls, however, not for changes in ethics alone. This nation asks for action, and action now.

Our greatest primary task is to put people to work. This is no unsolvable problem if we face it wisely and courageously.

It can be accomplished in part by direct recruiting by the government itself, treating the task as we would treat the emergency of a war, but at the same time, through this employment, accomplishing greatly needed projects to stimulate and reorganize the use of our natural resources.

Hand in hand with this, we must frankly recognize the overbalance of population in our industrial centers and, by engaging on a national scale in a redistribution, endeavor to provide a better use of the land for those best fitted for the land.

The task can be helped by definite efforts to raise the values of agricultural products and with this the power to purchase the output of our cities.

It can be helped by preventing realistically the tragedy of the growing loss, through foreclosure, of our small homes and our farms.

It can be helped by insistence that the Federal, state, and local governments act forthwith on the demand that their cost be drastically reduced.

It can be helped by the unifying of relief activities which today are often scattered, uneconomical, and unequal. It can be helped by national planning for and supervision of all forms of transportation and of communications and other utilities which have a definitely public character.

There are many ways in which it can be helped, but it can never be helped merely by talking about it. We must act, and act quickly. . . .

Action in this image and to this end is feasible under the form of government which we have inherited from our ancestors.

Our Constitution is so simple and practical that it is possible always to meet extraordinary needs by changes in emphasis and arrangement without loss of essential form.

That is why our constitutional system has proved itself the most superbly enduring political mechanism the modern world has produced. It has met every stress of vast expansion of territory, of foreign wars, of bitter internal strife, of world relations.

It is to be hoped that the normal balance of executive and legislative authority may be wholly adequate to meet the unprecedented task before us. But it may be that an unprecedented demand and need for undelayed action may call for temporary departure from that normal balance of public procedure.

I am prepared under my constitutional duty to recommend the measures that a stricken nation in the midst of a stricken world may require.

These measures, or such other measures as the Congress may build out of its experience and wisdom, I shall seek, within my constitutional authority, to bring to speedy adoption.

But in the event that the Congress shall fail to take one of these two courses, and in the event that the national emergency is still critical, I shall not evade the clear course of duty that will then confront me.

I shall ask the Congress for the one remaining instrument to meet the crisis—broad executive power to wage a war against the emergency as great as the power that would be given me if we were in fact invaded by a foreign foe.

For the trust reposed in me I will return the courage and the devotion that befit the time. I can do no less.

We face the arduous days that lie before us in the warm courage of national unity; with the clear consciousness of seeking old and precious moral values; with the clean satisfaction that comes from the stern performance of duty by old and young alike.

We aim at the assurance of a rounded and permanent national life.

We do not distrust the future of essential democracy. The people of the United States have not failed. In their need they have registered a mandate that they want direct, vigorous action.

They have asked for discipline and direction under leadership. They have made me the present instrument of their wishes. In the spirit of the gift I take it.

In this dedication of a nation we humbly ask the blessing of God. May He protect each and every one of us! May He guide me in the days to come!

FRANKLIN D. ROOSEVELT
First Inaugural Address
1933

96

David Lilienthal Describes
the Work of the TVA

One of the first acts of the New Deal was the creation of the Tennessee Valley Authority (TVA). Its primary purpose was to construct dams for hydroelectric power, but the terms of the TVA Act were broadly drawn, and the TVA early embarked upon a program of regional reconstruction. The TVA region embraces an area of some 40,000 square miles in seven states, and within this region the TVA works closely with state and local authorities on such things as public health, recreation, the improvement of agriculture, and rural electrification. The story of its accomplishments is here told by its director, David Lilienthal, who was later appointed director of the Atomic Energy Commission.

This is an entirely different region from what it was ten years ago. You can see the change almost everywhere you go. You can see it in the copper lines strung along back-country roads, in the fresh paint on the houses those electric lines were built to serve. You can see it in new electric water pumps in the farmyards, in the community refrigerators at the crossroads, in the feed grinders in the woodsheds. You can see the factories that stand today where there were worn-out cotton fields and rows of tenant shacks a few years ago. You can see new houses, by the thousands, on the edges of the towns—new houses of the men who take away as much cash from a few trips to the payroll window as they used to earn in a year.

You can see the change best of all if you have flown down the valley from time to time, as I have done so frequently during these past ten years. From five thousand feet the great change is unmistakable. There it is, stretching out before your eyes, a moving and exciting picture. You can see the undulation of neatly terraced hillsides newly contrived to make the beating rains "walk, not run, to the nearest exit"; you can see the gray bulk of the dams, stout marks across the river now deep blue, no longer red and murky with its hoard of soil washed from the eroding land. You can see the barges with their double tows of goods to be unloaded at new river terminals. And marching toward every point on the horizon you can see the steel crisscross of electric transmission towers, a twentieth-century tower standing in a cove beside an eighteenth-century mountain cabin, a symbol and a summary of the change. These are among the things you can see as you travel through the Tennessee Valley today. And on every hand you will also see the dimensions of the job yet to be done, the problem and the promise of the valley's future. . . .

The story of the change begins with the river. On the map the river's five mountain tributaries, each a considerable stream—the French Broad, the Holston, the Hiwassee, the Little Tennessee, the Clinch—are clearly set off from the broad main stem, the Tennessee itself, a major river of great volume, fed by the heaviest rainfall in eastern America. The map shows that main stem as a deep crescent, its source and eastern tip in the Appalachian Mountains, the dip of the crescent slicing off the northern third of Alabama, the western tip arching northward through the flat red lands of western Tennessee and Kentucky. The river flows not in one general direction, but in three; it moves southward first, then its middle course is westward, and its lower reaches turn back toward the north. A river that "flows up the map," as visitors to TVA almost invariably remark, seems to be water flowing perversely uphill, making its way more than 650 miles from Knoxville in Tennessee, in sight of the virgin timber in the Great Smoky Mountains, the highest peaks in eastern North America, to Paducah in the lowlands of Kentucky where across the broad Ohio you can see the fields of Illinois.

The valley through which the river flows actually lies in seven historic states of the Old South: the western part of the seacoast states of North Carolina and Virginia; the northern parts of Georgia, Alabama, and Mississippi; the western half of Kentucky from its southern jointure with Tennessee north to the Ohio River; and almost the whole of the wide reaches of the state of Tennessee. Less exactly, the region reaches from the mountains about Asheville west to the sluggish Mississippi at Memphis, and north and south from the old steamboat whistle landings on Ohio's shores to the cotton fields of Mississippi and the flambeau of the furnaces at Birmingham—an area all told about the size of England and Scotland, with a population of about 4,500,000 persons.

This is the river system that twenty-one dams of the TVA now control and have put to work for the people. To do that job sixteen new dams, several among the largest in America, were designed and constructed. Five dams already existing have been improved and modified. One of TVA's carpenters, a veteran who worked on seven of these dams, described this to me as "one hell of a big job of work." I cannot improve on that summary. It is the largest job of engineering and construction ever carried out by any single organization in all our history.

In heat and cold, in driving rain and under the blaze of the August sun, tens of thousands of men have hewed and blasted and hauled with their teams and tractors, clearing more than 175,000 acres of land, land that the surface of the lakes now covers. They have built or relocated more than 1200 miles of highway and almost 140 miles of railroad. With thousands of tons of explosives and great electric shovels they have excavated nearly 30,000,000 cubic yards of rock and earth to prepare the foundations of these dams—an excavation large enough to bury 20 Empire State buildings. To hold the river the men of the TVA have poured and placed concrete, rock fill, and earth in a total quantity of 113 million cubic yards.

To comprehend these figures requires a few comparisons. This 113 million cubic yards of material is more than twelve times the bulk of the seven great pyramids of Egypt. Of these materials, the concrete alone poured into the TVA dams is two and a half times as much as used in all the locks and structures of the Panama Canal; is four times as much as in Boulder Dam, 1,200,000 cubic yards greater than in the Grand Coulee Dam; would build more than seven dams as large as Soviet Russia's great Dnieprostroy Dam. The Grand Coulee Dam is the largest single masonry structure yet built, and Boulder Dam the second largest. Boulder was in the process of construction for five years and took the combined efforts of six of our largest private building contractor firms. Grand Coulee took eight years to build, and ten major private construction firms were engaged on it.

Thirty-five Boulder dams or ten Grand Coulee dams could have been built with the total materials required for completion of this valley's dams, the work of a single organization. The TVA's employees in 1942 were simultaneously designing and building a dozen dams and improving four others, were erecting the South's largest steam-electric plant, and building large chemical and munitions factories, with a total of 40,000 men and women at work.

The work of the builders has made of the river a highway that is carrying huge amounts of freight over its deep watercourses. In 1942 more than 161 million ton-miles of traffic moved through locks, designed in cooperation with the Army Corps of Engineers and operated by them, which raise the barges from one lake's level to another. But in 1928 only a little more than 46 million ton-miles of traffic moved on the river; in 1933 the figure was 32 million. This was mostly sand and gravel moving in short hauls between adjacent areas, and some forest products.

Today huge modern towboats, powered by great Diesel engines, move up and down the channel, pushing double columns of barges, and the cargo is no longer limited to raw materials. Billets of steel and cotton goods come from Birmingham headed north, grain from Minneapolis, millions of gallons of gasoline, oil, machinery, merchandise, automobiles, military ambulances and jeeps. It is estimated that in 1945, when the channel will be fully completed for all the year and for the river's total length, the savings to shippers will be about three and a half million dollars each year.

Quiet cotton towns of yesterday are now busy river ports. And, as always has been true of water transportation, new industries are rising along its course. Millions of dollars have been invested and thousands of jobs created as new grain elevators, flour mills, and oil terminals have been erected along the river's banks. At Decatur in Alabama, on land where a few years ago farmers were raising corn and cotton, now newly built ocean-going vessels go down the ways into "Wheeler Lake" and thence to their North Atlantic job.

And on these same lakes are thousands of new pleasure craft of every kind—costly yachts, sailboats, homemade skiffs. Nine thousand miles of shoreline—more than the total of the seacoast line of the United States on the Atlantic, the Pacific, and the Gulf of Mexico—are available for the recreation of the people. Thousands of acres along the shore are devoted to public parks, operated by the states, by counties, cities, and by the TVA. More than fifty boat docks serve the needs of fishermen from all parts of the United States. By patient scientific methods designed to give nature a chance, the number of fish has been increased fortyfold in the storage reservoirs, fifteen times in the main stream reservoirs. More than forty species of fish have been caught in these lakes—a variety comparable to that of the Great Lakes. Here is the basis of a thriving industry that in 1943 produced six million pounds of edible fish, and is expected to increase to twenty-five million pounds a year.

Before the men of the Tennessee Valley built these dams, flooding was a yearly threat to every farm and industry, every town and village and railroad on the river's banks, a barrier to progress. Today there is security from that annual danger in the Tennessee Valley. With the erection of local protective works at a few points this region will be completely safe, even against a flood bigger than anything in recorded history. A measure of protection resulting from the Tennessee's control extends even beyond this valley; for no longer will the Tennessee send her torrents at flood crest to add what might be fatal inches to top the levees and spread desolation on the lower Ohio and the Mississippi.

In others of the earth's thousand valleys people live under the shadow of fear that each year their river will bring upon them damage to their property, suffering, and death. Here the people are safe. In the winter of 1942 torrents came raging down this valley's two chief tributaries, in Tennessee and Virginia. Before the river was controlled this would have meant a severe flood; the machinery of vital war industries down the river at Chattanooga would have stopped, under several feet of water, with over a million dollars of direct damage resulting.

But in 1942 it was different. Orders went out from the TVA office of central control to every tributary dam. The message came flashing to the operator in the control room at Hiwassee Dam, deep in the mountains of North Carolina: "Hold back all the water of the Hiwassee River. Keep it out of the Tennessee." The operator pressed a button. Steel gates closed. The water of the tributary was held. To Cherokee Dam on the Holston went the message: "Keep back the flow of the Holston." To Chickamauga Dam just above the industrial danger spot at Chattanooga: "Release water to make room for the waters from above."

Day by day till the crisis was over the men at their control instruments at each dam in the system received their orders. The rate of water release from every tributary river was precisely controlled. The Tennessee was kept in hand. There was no destruction, no panic, no interruption of work. Most of the water, instead of wrecking the valley, actually produced a benefit in power, when later it was released through the turbines.

DAVID LILIENTHAL
Democracy on the March

97

Japan Strikes at Pearl Harbor

To most Americans in the closing weeks of 1941, it seemed likely that the United States would soon be in the great new world war, and most people believed the country would enter by some blow in the Atlantic area. But in the Far East, where Japan had been on an aggressive course for twenty years, the leaders in Tokyo deemed the moment ripe for decisive action. They thought that the United States could never fight a successful war on two great fronts. Even while their envoys in Washington parleyed with Secretary of State Cordell Hull, they were planning a sudden treacherous effort to put the Pacific fleet of the United States out of commission—and temporarily they almost succeeded.

Sunday morning December 7, 1941, I went to my office, as I had done almost every Sunday since I entered the State Department in 1933. I first conferred with Far Eastern experts Hornbeck, Hamilton, and Ballantine, and then had a lengthy conference with Secretaries Stimson and Knox. The faces of my visitors were grim. From all our reports it appeared that zero hour was a matter of hours, perhaps minutes.

During the morning I received a series of decoded intercepts consisting of fourteen parts of a long telegram from Foreign Minister Togo to Nomura and Kurusu. This was the answer to our proposals of November 26. There was also a short message instructing the Ambassadors to present this to our Government, if possible to me, at one o'clock that afternoon. Here then was the zero hour.

The Japanese note was little more than an insult. It said that our proposal "ignores Japan's sacrifices in the four years of the China affair, menaces the Empire's existence itself, and disparages its honor and prestige." It accused us of conspiring with Great Britain and other countries "to obstruct Japan's efforts toward the establishment of peace through the creation of a new order in East Asia." It concluded by saying that, in view of the attitude of the American Government, the Japanese Government considered it impossible to reach an agreement through further negotiations.

The note did not declare war. Neither did it break off diplomatic relations. Japan struck without such preliminaries.

Toward noon Ambassador Nomura telephoned my office to ask for an appointment with me at one o'clock for himself and Kurusu. I granted his request.

A few minutes after one, Nomura telephoned again to ask that the appointment be postponed until 1:45. I agreed.

The Japanese envoys arrived at the Department at 2:05 and went to the diplomatic waiting room. At almost that moment the President telephoned me from the White House. His voice was steady but clipped.

He said, "There's a report that the Japanese have attacked Pearl Harbor."

"Has the report been confirmed?" I asked.

He said, "No."

While each of us indicated his belief that the report was probably true, I suggested that he have it confirmed, having in mind my appointment with the Japanese Ambassadors.

With me in my office were Green H. Hackworth, Legal Adviser, and Joseph W. Ballantine, who had been with me during most of my conversations with the Japanese. I turned to them, saying:

"The President has an unconfirmed report that the Japanese have attacked Pearl Harbor. The Japanese Ambassadors are waiting to see me. I know what they want. They are going to turn us down on our note of November 26. Perhaps they want to tell us that war has been declared. I am rather inclined not to see them."

As I thought it over, however, I decided that, since the President's report had not been confirmed and there was one chance out of a hundred that it was not true, I would receive the envoys. After a brief discussion, Hackworth left the room, and Ballantine remained as I called for the Ambassadors.

Nomura and Kurusu came into my office at 2:20. I received them coldly and did not ask them to sit down.

Nomura diffidently said he had been instructed by his Government to deliver a document to me at one o'clock, but that difficulty in decoding the message had delayed him. He then handed me his Government's note.

I asked him why he had specified one o'clock in his first request for an interview.

He replied that he did not know, but that was his instruction.

I made a pretense of glancing through the note. I knew its contents already but naturally could give no indication of this fact.

After reading two or three pages, I asked Nomura whether he had presented the document under instructions from his Government.

He replied that he had.

When I finished skimming the pages, I turned to Nomura and put my eye on him.

"I must say," I said, "that in all my conversations with you during the last nine months I have never uttered one word of untruth. This is borne out absolutely by the record. In all my fifty years of public service I have never seen a document that was more crowded with infamous falsehoods and distortions—infamous falsehoods and distortions on a scale so huge that I never imagined until today that any Government on this planet was capable of uttering them."

Nomura seemed about to say something. His face was impassive, but I felt he was under great emotional strain. I stopped him with a motion of my hand. I nodded toward the door. The Ambassadors turned without a word and walked out, their heads down.

I have seen it stated that I "cussed out" the Japanese envoys in rich Tennessee mountain language, but the fact is I told them exactly what I said above. No "cussing out" could have made it any stronger.

Ballantine took notes of what I said. The moment the Ambassadors left, I called in a stenographer and dictated from memory what I had told them. This is the statement as issued to the press.

Nomura's last meeting with me was in keeping with the ineptitude that had marked his handling of the discussions from the beginning. His Government's intention, in instructing him to ask for the meeting at one o'clock, had been to give us their note a few minutes in advance of the attack at Pearl Harbor. Nomura's Embassy had bungled this by its delay in decoding. Nevertheless, knowing the importance of a deadline set for a specific hour, Nomura should have come to see me precisely at one o'clock, even though he had in his hand only the first few lines of his note, leaving instructions with the Embassy to bring him the remainder as it became ready.

It was therefore without warning that the Japanese struck at Pearl Harbor, more than an hour before Nomura and Kurusu delivered their note.

I talked with the President on the telephone shortly after the Ambassadors left my office, and repeated to him what I had told them. He said he was pleased that I had spoken so strongly. By then he had received further reports on the attack at Pearl Harbor.

Shortly after three o'clock I went to the White House, where I talked with the President and others for forty minutes. Mr. Roosevelt was very solemn in demeanor and conversation. The magnitude of the surprise achieved by the Japanese at Pearl Harbor was already becoming evident. But neither he nor any of us lost faith for a moment in the ability of the United States to cope with the danger.

We had a general discussion preparatory to a conference that the President decided to hold that evening with Stimson, Knox, myself, General Marshall, Admiral Stark, and other principal advisers. We discussed in a tentative way the many different steps that would have to be taken, when and by whom. The President early determined to go to Congress with a message asking for a declaration of a state of war with Japan.

The Memoirs of Cordell Hull

98

The Marines Cross a River
Under Fire on Guadalcanal

The Japanese, driving forward far and fast after Pearl Harbor, established themselves across a wide perimeter, reaching almost to Australia and the New Hebrides in the south, to the central archipelagoes of the middle Pacific, and to the Aleutians in the north. In 1942 and the first half of 1943 the American forces could only nibble at this defensive perimeter. But two notable attacks, on the island of Guadalcanal in the south and on Attu in the Aleutians, proved that man for man the Americans could outfight the best Japanese troops. No story of the war was more heroic than that of Guadalcanal. The author of this essay, John Hersey, served as a war correspondent and wrote both nonfiction and fiction accounts of the war. His novel *A Bell for Adano,* about the American occupation of Sicily, won the Pulitzer Prize in 1944.

When the runner returned, he reported just what Rigaud's lieutenants had guessed—that George and Easy Companies had moved up to make contact with our right, and that they were to try to help force the river. He also reported that we were only about a hundred yards from the river.

Captain Rigaud passed this whispered order: "Advance and watch out for friendly troops on the right."

The men who were carrying machine gun parts seemed to bunch up together as we moved forward this time. They wanted to be ready to assemble their guns on shortest notice.

Occasional whispering, which had been visible though not audible along the line when we moved before, now stopped.

Men picked their footsteps carefully now.

Captain Rigaud's small back and stooped shoulders hardly moved up and down at all. His knees were a little bent, like those of a cat about to leap.

We crossed and recrossed the stream very carefully but rather hurriedly: no one wanted to be caught in the water. It was much wider now, much browner and more sluggish. We were apparently quite near the Matanikau.

Up ahead, as a matter of fact, some of Rigaud's men and a few of the men of George and Easy Companies had already crossed the river. No shots had been fired. There seemed to be no opposition: there was reason to hope that Whaling had already swept around behind whatever was on the other side and cleaned it out (we had heard some firing from the other side during the morning), so that now our job would be a pushover. Maybe, if we were lucky, just a sniper or two to hunt down and kill.

The trail left the stream, turned off to the right, and climbed up onto a spur. Up there, on the spur, we could see the thinning of the trees which meant the Matanikau. In a moment we would be at the river and, if Whaling had been as successful as we hoped, across it.

The captain and I were about seventy-five feet from the river when we found out how wrong our hope was.

The signal was a single shot from a sniper.

It came from somewhere behind us, but probably not as far as the first shots we had heard. The high flat snap was easily recognizable as a Japanese sound, and immediately after it, overhead, went the sound of the bullet, like a supercharged bee.

After a couple of too quick seconds, snipers all around us opened up. There would be the snap, and the whine, and then the tuck when the bullet went into the ground. There was no way of knowing where the next was coming from. The only thing you could be certain of was that it would come soon enough to take your eye off the place where you thought you might spot the last one.

Then machine guns from across the river opened up.

But the terrible thing was that Jap mortars over there opened up, too.

The first thing a green man fixes upon in his mind is the noise of these weapons. This was the first time I had ever been surrounded this way by the tight-woven noise of war.

Its constant fabric was rifle fire; this sounded like Bucks County, Pennsylvania, on the first day of the pheasant season, only near by and not an amusement. Like a knife tearing into the fabric, every once in a while, there would be the short bursts of machine gun fire. The noise of the mortars was awful, a thump which vibrated not just your eardrums, but your entrails as well. Forward we could still hear our aviation—dive bombs fumbling into the jungle, and the laughter of strafing P–39s. And every once in a while the soft, fluttery noise of our artillery shells making a trip. The noise alone was enough to scare a new man, to say nothing of the things which were done by the things which were making the noise.

The Japs had made their calculations perfectly. There were only three or four natural crossings of the river; this was one of them. And so they had set their trap.

They had machine guns all mounted, ready to pour stuff into the jungle bottleneck at the stream's junction with the river. They had snipers scattered on both sides of the river. And they had their mortars all set to lob deadly explosions into the same area. Their plan was to hold their fire and let the enemy get well into the trap before snapping it, and this they had done with too much success.

Apparently the single sniper shot had given the command to the other snipers; when the machine gunners across the river heard all the snipers firing, they let go; and when the Jap mortar batteries farther back heard the machine gun bursts, they in turn opened up.

Had we been infantry, the trap might not have worked. Brave men with rifles and grenades could have wiped out the enemy nests. Captain Rigaud's helplessness was that he could not bring his weapons to bear. Heavy machine guns take some time to be assembled and mounted. In that narrow defile his men, as brave as any, never succeeded in getting more than two guns firing.

As soon as the firing broke out, the men with the machine gun parts rushed together, and regardless of cover put their weapons together. Then the crews felt their way along, trying to find a place where they could both have a little cover and do some harm. As they went they approach-fired, throwing out little fifty caliber exclamations, as if the guns could say: "Look out, you Japs."

But they never had a chance. The enemy had his guns in position, with nothing to do but aim and squeeze the trigger. And even if the enemy had had no machine guns, his mortar fire had Rigaud's men boxed.

The mortar fire was what was terrifying. Beside it the Japs' sniper fire and even machine gun fire, with its soprano, small-sounding report, seemed a mere botheration. It is hard to think of death as having anything but a deep bass voice. Each roar of mortar certainly seemed to be a word spoken by death.

Having seen Lou Diamond's mortar battery in action, I had a clear picture of what was happening to us. In some small clearing about a half a mile beyond the river, four little tubes, looking like stubby stove pipes, were set up at a high angle on a tripod. Somewhere behind them a Japanese officer stood. A man beside him gave him reports from a telephone or from runners. After each report he would bark out brief orders. A swarm of intelligent little animals would fuss around each tube, changing the angle a hair, turning the aim a trifle. Then the officer would shout to stand by. Some of the animals would step back, one or two at each tube would put their fingers in their ears. Then one, in the attitude of a small boy setting punk to a giant firecracker, would reach out over the mouth of each tube, holding in his hand a thing which looked very much like a miniature aerial bomb, complete with fins. At the order to fire, he would drop the thing, fins first, down the tube. As soon as it struck the bottom there would be a huge thump, and the thing was off on its uncertain flight.

Mortars send their shells in an exceedingly high toss. Consequently their aim is by guess and by God. You will understand this if you have ever seen the job an outfielder has judging a high fly, or if you are an inexpert tennis player and often have been embarrassed by trying to smash a high lob and misjudging it.

That was what made being on the receiving end of mortar fire so terrible: the next thing that those little tubes gave off might land anywhere. We would almost have felt more comfortable if something which could aim was aiming right at us.

When the first bolts of this awful thunder began to fall among Rigaud's men, we hit the ground. We were like earthy insects with some great foot being set down in our midst, and we scurried for little crannies—cavities under the roots of huge trees, little gullies, dead logs. I found a good spot to the left of the trail. It was the combination of a small embankment and a big tree; I grew very affectionate toward the spot; I embraced it. Captain Rigaud, I noticed, took little or no cover. He kept darting back and forth to see what was happening to his men.

What was happening to his men was something terrible. The mortar shells were exploding among them and bleaching some of the bravery out of them. The noise and seeing friends hurt were not things to be dismissed.

The reports were about ten seconds apart, and the shells burst erratically all around us, now fifty yards away, now twenty feet.

And all the while snipers and machine gunners wrote in their nasty punctuation. Our own guns answered from time to time with good, deep, rich sound, but not enough.

We heard one of our guns knocked out. If you have never heard a conversation between two machine guns which are trying to knock each other out, you cannot imagine what a terrible debate it is. At first they talk back and forth equally. Then, as in most human arguments, one begins to get the upper hand and finally winds up doing all the talking. That was how it was when our gun was knocked out. It sounded like this:

"Tatatatatatatatatatat," said the Jap gun, in a high Japanese voice.

"Bubububububububububub," said ours, deeply.

"Tatatatatatatatatatatatat," the Jap insisted.

"Bubububububububububub," said ours.

"Tatatatatatatatatat," the Jap said, sure of itself.

"Bubububub . . . bubub," ours said, uncertainly.

"Tatatatatatatatatatatatat," the Jap reiterated.

"Bubub." Ours seemed almost to have been convinced.

"Tatatatatatatatat," said the Jap, to clinch the matter.

"Bub," ours said, in pathetic protest.

"Tatatatatatatatat . . .

"Tatatatatatatatatatatatat."

And then silence. It was awful. (I have heard some conversations in which our guns talked theirs down. Then it is not awful; it makes you cheer.)

I don't believe that this was one of Captain Rigaud's guns. It was a gun belonging to George or Easy Company, and it was manned to the end by a brave man named Sergeant Bauer.

We could not see the enemy, either on our side of the river or the other. All this hatred was pouring out of jungle too thick to see more than twenty or thirty feet.

This was advantageous, in a way. It meant that the enemy no longer seemed animate. There was no excuse for feelings such as I had had when I picked up the head net. The firing over there was coming from the enemy as an idea, something easy to hate.

But this invisibility was also unsettling. You might have thought that the jungle itself had grown malevolent, and hated us. The trees were hurling little pellets at us; the vines were slinging great explosions.

But even if we had been able to see the enemy, we could not have done anything to him. We couldn't get our weapons to work. We were helpless. Our men were being killed and wounded. We were trapped, hopelessly trapped.

Individually the Marines in that outfit were as brave as any fighters in any army in the world, I am positive; but when fear began to be epidemic in that closed-in place, no one was immune. No one could resist it.

The first sign of flight among those men was in their eyes. At first they watched what was going on as calmly as an audience at some play. Then suddenly they were looking around for the nearest exit. They would look at Captain Rigaud's face, looking for some sign that he would order them to retire; or their eyes would dart along the trail back, as they wished they could.

I myself kept looking at Captain Rigaud, to see what he would do with us. His expression had not changed. It had the same look of desperate vigilance that it had worn all along the trail.

The next sign of the growing fear was the way the men started moving around. When a mortar shell would go off near by, they would scramble away from the vicinity to new cover, as if the thing could explode a second time.

The men began to think that it was time to get away from that whole place.

Any men who were men would have taken flight from that impossible place. Some Japanese might not have, if they had had specific orders to stay there; but they would no longer have been much use to the Emperor. I think even most Japanese would have fled. Certainly Germans would have: they are good fighters: they have the sense to live and fight more advantageously another day. I think it is safe to say that Italians would have fled.

The Marines had been deeply enough indoctrinated so that even flight did not wipe out the formulas, and soon the word came whispering back along the line:

"Withdraw."

"Withdraw."

"Withdraw. . . ."

Then they started moving back, slowly at first, then running wildly, scrambling from place of cover to momentary cover.

This was a distressing sight, and though I myself was more than eager to be away from that spot, I had a helpless desire to do something to stop the flight. It seemed wrong. One had heard so much about how the Marines kill ten Japs for every man they lose (which is true), of the callousness of the Marines (true in a way), and of our endless successes against the Japs (true in sum total). Captain Rigaud had told me that this would probably be an easy job. It sounded so. And yet here were our men running away.

I couldn't do anything about it because I was caught up in the general feeling. It is curious how this feeling communicated itself. Except for the hard knot which is inside some men, courage is largely the desire to show other men that you have it. And so, in a large group, when a majority have somehow signalled to each other a willingness to quit acting, it is very hard indeed not to quit. The only way to avoid it is to be put to shame by a small group of men to whom this acting is life itself, and who refuse to quit; or by a naturally courageous man doing a brave deed.

It was at this moment that Charles Alfred Rigaud, the boy with tired circles under his eyes, showed himself to be a good officer and grown man.

Despite snipers all around us, despite the machine guns and the mortar fire, he stood right up on his feet and shouted out: "Who in Christ's name gave that order?"

This was enough to freeze the men in their tracks. They threw themselves on the ground, in attitudes of defense; they took cover behind trees from both the enemy and the anger of their captain.

Next, by a combination of blistering sarcasm, orders and cajolery, he not only got the men back into position: he got them in a mood to fight again.

"Where do you guys think you're going?" he shouted. And: "Get back in there. . . . Take cover, you. . . . What do you guys do, just invent orders? . . . Listen, it's going to get dark and we got a job to do. . . . You guys make me ashamed. . . ."

But the most telling thing he said was: "Gosh, and they call you Marines."

JOHN HERSEY
Into the Valley

99

General Eisenhower Describes
the Great Invasion

So successful was Eisenhower's management of the African and Sicilian campaigns that he was appointed to the Supreme Command of American and British forces in the European theater. Transferring his headquarters to London, in 1943, he began preparations for the greatest of all military gambles—the cross-channel invasion of France. Although the enemy had expected the invasion for months, they miscalculated both the time and the place, and the Allies scored a strategic, though not a tactical, surprise. Only the weather surprised the Allies: just before the scheduled invasion the worst June gale in forty years struck the treacherous English Channel and threatened, for a moment, to upset all carefully laid plans. Eisenhower, however, took the responsibility of ordering the invasion to go ahead.

The final conference for determining the feasibility of attacking on the tentatively selected day, June 5, was scheduled for 4:00 A.M. on June 4. However, some of the attacking contingents had already been ordered to sea, because if the entire force was to land on June 5, then some of the important elements stationed in northern parts of the United Kingdom could not wait for final decision on the morning of June 4.

When the commanders assembled on the morning of June 4 the report we received was discouraging. Low clouds, high winds, and formidable wave action were predicted to make landing a most hazardous affair. The meteorologists said that air support would be impossible, naval gunfire would be inefficient, and even the handling of small boats would be rendered difficult. Admiral Ramsay thought that the mechanics of landing could be handled, but agreed with the estimate of the difficulty in adjusting gunfire. His position was mainly neutral. General Montgomery, properly concerned with the great disadvantages of delay, believed that we should go. Tedder disagreed.

Weighing all factors, I decided that the attack would have to be postponed. This decision necessitated the immediate dispatch of orders to the vessels and troops already at sea and created some doubt as to whether they could be ready twenty-four hours later in case the next day should prove favorable for the assault. Actually the maneuver of the ships in the Irish Sea proved most difficult by reason of the storm. That they succeeded in gaining ports, refueling, and readying themselves to resume the movement a day later represented the utmost in seamanship and in brilliant command and staff work.

The conference on the evening of June 4 presented little, if any, added brightness to the picture of the morning, and tension mounted even higher because the inescapable consequences of postponement were almost too bitter to contemplate.

At three-thirty the next morning our little camp was shaking and shuddering under a wind of almost hurricane proportions and the accompanying rain seemed to be traveling in horizontal streaks. The mile-long trip through muddy roads to the naval headquarters was anything but a cheerful one, since it seemed impossible that in such conditions there was any reason for even discussing the situation.

When the conference started the first report given us by Group Captain Stagg and the Meteorologic Staff was that the bad conditions predicted the day before for the coast of France were actually prevailing there and that if we had persisted in the attempt to land on June 5 a major disaster would almost surely have resulted. This they probably told us to inspire more confidence in their next astonishing declaration, which was that by the following morning a period of relatively good weather, heretofore completely unexpected, would ensue, lasting probably thirty-six hours. The long-term prediction was not good but they did give us assurance that this short period of good weather would intervene between the exhaustion of the storm we were then experiencing and the beginning of the next spell of really bad weather.

The prospect was not bright because of the possibility that we might land the first several waves successfully and then find later build-up impracticable, and so have to leave the isolated original attacking forces easy prey to German counteraction. However, the consequences of the delay justified great risk and I quickly announced the decision to go ahead with the attack on June 6. The time was then 4:15 A.M., June 5. No one present disagreed and there was a definite brightening of faces as, without a further word, each went off to his respective post of duty to flash out to his command the messages that would set the whole host in motion.

A number of people appealed to me for permission to go aboard the supporting naval ships in order to witness the attack. Every member of a staff can always develop a dozen arguments why he, in particular, should accompany an expedition rather than remain at the only post, the center of communications, where he can be useful. Permission was denied to all except those with specific military responsibility and, of course, the allotted quotas of press and radio representatives.

Among those who were refused permission was the Prime Minister. His request was undoubtedly inspired as much by his natural instincts as a warrior as by his impatience at the prospect of sitting quietly back in London to await reports. I argued, however, that the chance of his becoming an accidental casualty was too important from the standpoint of the whole war effort and I refused his request. He replied, with complete accuracy, that while I was in sole command of the operation by virtue of authority delegated to me by both governments, such authority did not include administrative control over the British organization. He said, "Since this is true it is not part of your responsibility, my dear General, to determine the exact composition of any ship's company in His Majesty's Fleet. This being true," he rather slyly continued, "by shipping myself as a bona fide member of a ship's complement it would be beyond your authority to prevent my going."

All of this I had ruefully to concede, but I forcefully pointed out that he was adding to my personal burdens in this thwarting of my instructions. Even, however, while I was acknowledging defeat in the matter, aid came from an unexpected source. The King had learned of the Prime Minister's intention and, while not presuming to interfere with the decision reached by Mr. Churchill, the King sent word that if the Prime Minister felt it necessary to go on the expedition he, the King, felt it to be equally his duty and privilege to participate at the head of his troops. This instantly placed a different light upon the matter and I heard no more of it.

Nevertheless, my sympathies were entirely with the Prime Minister. Again I had to endure the interminable wait that always intervenes between the final decision of the high command and the earliest possible determination of success or failure in such ventures. I spent the time visiting troops that would participate in the assault. A late evening visit on the fifth took me to the camp of the U.S. 101st Airborne Division, one of the units whose participation had been so severely questioned by the air commander. I found the men in fine fettle, many of them joshingly admonishing me that I had no cause for worry, since the 101st was on the job and everything would be taken care of in fine shape. I stayed with them until the last of them were in the air, somewhere about midnight. After a two-hour trip back to my own camp, I had only a short time to wait until the first news should come in. . . .

The first report came from the airborne units I had visited only a few hours earlier and was most encouraging in tone. As the morning wore on it became apparent that the landing was going fairly well. Montgomery took off in a destroyer to visit the beaches and to find a place in which to set up his own advanced headquarters. I promised to visit him on the following day.

Operations in the Utah area, which involved the co-ordination of the amphibious landing with the American airborne operation, proceeded satisfactorily, as did those on the extreme left flank. The day's reports, however, showed that extremely fierce fighting had developed in the Omaha sector. That was the spot, I decided, to which I would proceed the next morning.

We made the trip in a destroyer and upon arrival found that the 1st and 29th Divisions, assaulting on Omaha, had finally dislodged the enemy and were proceeding swiftly inland. Isolated centers of resistance still held out and some of them sustained a most annoying artillery fire against our beaches and landing ships. I had a chance to confer with General Bradley and found him, as always, stouthearted and confident of the result. In point of fact the resistance encountered on Omaha Beach was at about the level we had feared all along the line. The conviction of the Germans that we would not attack in the weather then prevailing was a definite factor in the degree of surprise we achieved and accounted to some extent for the low order of active opposition on most of the beaches. In the Omaha sector an alert enemy division, the 352d, which prisoners stated had been in the area on maneuvers and defense exercises, accounted for some of the intense fighting in that locality.

Dwight D. Eisenhower
Crusade in Europe

100
Ernie Pyle Describes Hedgerow Fighting in Normandy

Within five days of the original landings the Allies had landed sixteen divisions in Normandy. By June 12 Omaha and Utah beachheads had been joined by the capture of Carentan, and the Allies controlled eighty miles of the Normandy coast. Another week and they swept across the Cotentin Peninsula, seized the great port of Cherbourg, and prepared to swing inland to the heart of France and to Paris. As the fighting moved deeper into Normandy our troops met a new obstacle, the age-old hedgerows of the Normandy farms. Ernie Pyle tells how they overcame this formidable obstacle.

I want to describe to you what the weird hedgerow fighting in northwestern France was like. This type of fighting was always in small groups, so let's take as an example one company of men. Let's say they were working forward on both sides of a country lane, and the company was responsible for clearing the two fields on either side of the road as it advanced. That meant there was only about one platoon to a field, and with the company's understrength from casualties, there might be no more than twenty-five or thirty men.

The fields were usually not more than fifty yards across and a couple of hundred yards long. They might have grain in them, or apple trees, but mostly they were just pastures of green grass, full of beautiful cows. The fields were surrounded on all sides by the immense hedgerows—ancient earthen banks, waist high, all matted with roots, and out of which grew weeds, bushes, and trees up to twenty feet high. The Germans used these barriers well. They put snipers in the trees. They dug deep trenches behind the hedgerows and covered them with timber, so that it was almost impossible for artillery to get at them. Sometimes they propped up machine guns with strings attached so that they could fire over the hedge without getting out of their holes. They even cut out a section of the hedgerow and hid a big gun or a tank in it, covering it with bush. Also they tunneled under the hedgerows from the back and made the opening on the forward side just large enough to stick a machine gun through. But mostly the hedgerow pattern was this: a heavy machine gun hidden at each end of the field and infantrymen hidden all along the hedgerow with rifles and machine pistols.

We had to dig them out. It was a slow and cautious business, and there was nothing dashing about it. Our men didn't go across the open fields in dramatic charges such as you see in the movies. They did at first, but they learned better. They went in tiny groups, a squad or less, moving yards apart and sticking close to the hedgerows on either end of the field. They crept a few yards, squatted, waited, then crept again.

If you could have been right up there between the Germans and the Americans you wouldn't have seen many men at any one time—just a few here and there, always trying to keep hidden. But you would have heard an awful lot of noise. Our men were taught in training not to fire until they saw something to fire at. But the principle didn't work in that country, because there was very little to see. So the alternative was to keep shooting constantly at the hedgerows. That pinned the Germans to their holes while we sneaked up on them. The attacking squads sneaked up the sides of the hedgerows while the rest of the platoon stayed back in their own hedgerow and kept the forward hedge saturated with bullets. They shot rifle grenades too, and a mortar squad a little farther back kept lobbing mortar shells over onto the Germans. The little advance groups worked their way up to the far ends of the hedgerows at the corners of the field. They first tried to knock out the machine guns at each corner. They did this with hand grenades, rifle grenades and machine guns. . . .

Usually, when the pressure was on, the German defenders of the hedgerow started pulling back. They would take their heavier guns and most of the men back a couple of fields and start digging in for a new line. They left about two machine guns and a few riflemen scattered through the hedge to do a lot of shooting and hold up the Americans as long as they could. Our men would then sneak along the front side of the hedgerow, throwing grenades over onto the other side and spraying the hedges with their guns. The fighting was close—only a few yards apart. . . .

This hedgerow business was a series of little skirmishes like that clear across the front, thousands and thousands of little skirmishes. No single one of them was very big. Added up over the days and weeks, however, they made a man-sized war—with thousands on both sides getting killed. But that is only a general pattern of the hedgerow fighting. Actually each one was a little separate war, fought under different circumstances. For instance, the fight might be in a woods instead of an open field. The Germans would be dug in all over the woods, in little groups, and it was really tough to get them out. Often in cases like that we just went around the woods and kept going, and let later units take care of those surrounded and doomed fellows. Or we might go through a woods and clean it out, and another company, coming through a couple of hours later, would find it full of Germans again. In a war like this everything was in such confusion that I never could see how either side ever got anywhere. . . .

In a long drive an infantry company often went for a couple of days without letting up. Ammunition was carried up to it by hand, and occasionally by jeep. The soldiers sometimes ate only one K ration a day. They sometimes ran out of water. Their strength was gradually whittled down by wounds, exhaustion cases and straggling. Finally they would get an order to sit where they were and dig in. Then another company would pass through, or around them, and go on with the fighting. The relieved company might get to rest as much as a day or two. But in a big push such as the one that broke us out of the beachhead, a few hours' respite was about all they could expect.

The company I was with got its orders to rest about five o'clock one afternoon. They dug foxholes along the hedgerows, or commandeered German ones already dug. Regardless of how tired a man might be, he always dug in the first thing. Then they sent some men looking for water. They got more K rations up by jeep, and sat on the ground eating them. They hoped they would stay there all night, but they weren't counting on it too much. Shortly after supper a lieutenant came out of a farmhouse and told the sergeants to pass the word to be ready to move in ten minutes. They bundled on their packs and started just before dark. Within half an hour they had run into a new fight that lasted all night. They had had less than four hours' rest in three solid days of fighting. . . .

There in Normandy the Germans went in for sniping in a wholesale manner. There were snipers everywhere: in trees, in buildings, in piles of wreckage, in the grass. But mainly they were in the high, bushy hedgerows that form the fences of all the Norman fields and line every roadside and lane.

It was perfect sniping country. A man could hide himself in the thick fence-row shrubbery with several days' rations, and it was like hunting a needle in a haystack to find him. Every mile we advanced there were dozens of snipers left behind us. They picked off our soldiers one by one as they walked down the roads or across the fields. It wasn't safe to move into a new bivouac area until the snipers had been cleaned out. The first bivouac I moved into had shots ringing through it for a full day before all the hidden gunmen were rounded up. It gave me the same spooky feeling that I got on moving into a place I suspected of being sown with mines.

ERNIE PYLE
Brave Men

101

An American Plane Ushers
in the Atomic Age

By midsummer of 1945 Japan was reeling under repeated blows. Great cities like Tokyo and Yokohama were charred ruins; Admiral Halsey's Third Fleet cruised at will up and down the coast; submarines cut off Japanese access to the Asiatic mainland. Meeting at Potsdam, Germany, in July the Allied leaders served notice on Japan to get out of the war. But the Japanese ignored the Potsdam Declaration. On August 6 a lone B-29 flew over the great industrial city of Hiroshima and dropped a single atomic bomb. A vast explosion shattered the city, and when the smoke blew away it was seen that over half of the city had been destroyed. To the stunned Japanese President Truman gave a new ultimatum, which was once more ignored. On August 9 a second, improved and more powerful, atomic bomb was released on the city of Nagasaki. William E. Laurence, consultant to the War Department, went on the flight which dropped the bomb and here describes it for us.

We flew southward down the channel and at 11:33 crossed the coastline and headed straight for Nagasaki about 100 miles to the west. Here again we circled until we found an opening in the clouds. It was 12:01 and the goal of our mission had been reached.

We heard the prearranged signal on our radio, put on our arc-welder's glasses and watched tensely the maneuverings of the strike ship about half a mile in front of us.

"There she goes!" someone said.

Out of the belly of *The Great Artiste* what looked like a black object went downward.

Captain Bock swung around to get out of range; but even though we were turning away in the opposite direction, and despite the fact that it was broad daylight in our cabin, all of us became aware of a giant flash that broke through the dark barrier of our arc-welder's lenses and flooded our cabin with intense light.

We removed our glasses after the first flash, but the light still lingered on, a bluish-green light that illuminated the entire sky all around. A tremendous blast wave struck our ship and made it tremble from nose to tail. This was followed by four more blasts in rapid succession, each resounding like the boom of cannon fire hitting our plane from all directions.

Observers in the tail of our ship saw a giant ball of fire rise as though from the bowels of the earth, belching forth enormous white smoke rings. Next they saw a giant pillar of purple fire, 10,000 feet high, shooting skyward with enormous speed.

By the time our ship had made another turn in the direction of the atomic explosion, the pillar of purple fire had reached the level of our altitude. Only about forty-five seconds had passed. Awestruck, we watched it shoot upward like a meteor coming from the earth instead of from outer space, becoming ever more alive as it climbed skyward through the white clouds. It was no longer smoke, or dust, or even a cloud of fire. It was a living thing, a new species of being born before our incredulous eyes.

At one stage of its evolution, covering millions of years in terms of seconds, the entity assumed the form of a giant square totem pole, with its base about three miles long, tapering off to about a mile at the top. Its bottom was brown, its center was amber, its top white. But it was a living totem pole, carved with many grotesque masks grimacing at the earth.

Then, just when it appeared as if the thing had settled down into a state of permanence, there came shooting out of the top a giant mushroom that increased the height of the pillar to a total of 45,000 feet. The mushroom top was even more alive than the pillar, seething and boiling in a white fury of creamy foam, sizzling upward and then descending earthward, a thousand Old Faithful geysers rolled into one.

It kept struggling in an elemental fury, like a creature in the act of breaking the bonds that held it down. In a few seconds it had freed itself from its gigantic stem and floated upward with tremendous speed, its momentum carrying into the stratosphere to a height of about 60,000 feet.

But no sooner did this happen than another mushroom, smaller in size than the first one, began emerging out of the pillar. It was as though the decapitated monster were growing a new head.

As the first mushroom floated off into the blue, it changed its shape into a flower-like form, its giant petal curving downward, creamy white outside, rose-colored inside. It still retained that shape when we last gazed at it from a distance of about 200 miles.

WILLIAM E. LAURENCE
New York Times
September 9, 1945

102

Carl T. Rowan

Takes on Jim Crow

Carl T. Rowan, born in 1925, grew up in Tennessee in impoverished circumstances. The prospects for African Americans were bleak: only about 9 percent attended any sort of college in the early 1940s and a scant 2 percent of the men (6 percent of women) found employment in the professions. The outlook in the South was even worse in many ways, since "Jim Crow" laws there enforced a demeaning code of behavior on blacks. However, Carl Rowan managed to hoist himself out of poverty, and out of the South, too, working his way through college and graduate school, with an interruption for service in the navy. He started his career at the *Minneapolis Tribune* and became a reporter in 1950. Having successfully distanced himself from the surroundings of his youth, he chose to return to them in 1951, filing a series of articles later collected in the book *South of Freedom*. Rowan's smoldering reports distinguished him as a leading commentator on race relations, and in the 1960s he was named to several cabinet-level positions in the U.S. government. He was best known after this time as a prominent newspaper columnist.

Part I

I remember 1943 as the year of the "great rebellion." For it was in the summer of 1943 that my mind, heart, and soul rebelled and ceased being part of a green, small-town Negro youth, well-schooled in the ways of his native South. During that summer, I broke all mental ties with my home town; yet, physically, I was still very much a part of McMinnville, Tennessee, a farm-industrial community of about five thousand persons, at the foot of the Cumberland Mountains. It was a foolish and rather dangerous predicament for a young Southern Negro.

As I remember that summer, I realize how fortunate I was to get out of McMinnville. Obviously, I had lost my usefulness to that middle-Tennessee community; and I cannot remember McMinnville ever being of particular usefulness to me. I had returned to McMinnville after spending my freshman year at Tennessee Agricultural and Industrial State College in Nashville. I felt that even in those nine months of college life I had outgrown my narrow life in McMinnville. I betrayed my feelings easily, much to the irritation of whites whose lawns I had mowed, whose windows I had washed, or whose basements I had scrubbed in past years.

During my year at Tennessee State, I had passed tests given by the United States Navy and was promised the opportunity to earn a commission, something the Navy had given no Negro at the time. After being sworn in at Nashville, I had returned to McMinnville, an apprentice seaman in the Naval Reserve. I was on inactive duty, awaiting assignment to what, in effect, was to be officers' candidate school.

For nearly eighteen years, practically all my life, I had lived in McMinnville. I had mowed lawns, swept basements, unloaded boxcars of coal, dug basements, hoed bulb-grass out of lawns, and done scores of other menial tasks that fell to Negroes by default. Until 1943, I did these jobs because almost all McMinnville Negroes did such jobs; the community expected it of us. In 1943, with Negro manpower already swept away by the draft board, I could see that I was expected to handle a greater-than-normal share of such jobs. But my year outside McMinnville, and my status as a Navy man, created revulsion within me and an air of haughtiness not designed to make me popular with the white citizens of my home town.

The Navy had put me outside the jurisdiction of draft boards, so, unlike many "rebellious" Negroes of the South, I could not be railroaded into the Armed Forces as punishment for offending some staunch citizen by rejecting his dirty chores. The Navy already had me, and I would be around until the Navy decided I should move elsewhere. I felt that, for the first time in my life, I was out of reach of all McMinnville and all her twenty-five-cents-an-hour jobs.

I became self-employed. I had learned to weave cane bottoms and backs for chairs in a shopwork class at Bernard High School, where the instructor had charged chair owners a very modest amount and the pupils did the work for sticks of peppermint candy. Since Bernard no longer was doing such work, I had a corner on the market. I tripled the charges and notified the "antique furniture" set that I was in business. Soon I had enough chairs piled up at my home to keep me busy most of the summer.

Tennessee summer days were not made for work; in fact, many a resident has doubted that they were made at all, but that they sprang to life from the caldrons of hell. In any event, I dressed more like a Southern Colonel than a Southern Negro, and spent the days reading. Occasionally I strolled through town, driving town and military policemen almost crazy in their efforts to understand how an apparently able-bodied Negro male had escaped the draft board. In three months they stopped me at least thirty times, demanding to see my draft-registration card.

That I was stopped so frequently was partially attributable to my conspicuous dress. Any Negro in a small Southern town is viewed with suspicion if he wears a tie and suit on weekdays, unless he is the principal of the Negro school, or perhaps a minister. I wore suits, which, though secondhand, were new to McMinnville. I had got them at the State Tuberculosis Hospital in Nashville, where I worked the summer of 1942 to earn tuition funds. I had left McMinnville for Nashville that summer—with seventy-seven cents in my pocket, and my clothes in a cardboard box—aboard a McBroom Lines truck on which I had wangled a ride from the white driver. I remember him only as a good Joe who drove me out to the college campus because he figured I could stand to save the bus fare.

At the hospital I carried food to the patients, bussed and washed dishes, swept ward floors and screens, and did almost everything but wash the nurses' feet. But I needed the thirty dollars a month—desperately. Occasionally, a doctor would complain that he had outgrown a suit. He would pass it to me, suggesting that I find someone who could use it. That was a fairly simple assignment. These suits made me one of the best-dressed freshmen on the Tennessee State campus; and but for my Naval Reserve card would have made me one of the best-dressed McMinnvillians ever jailed on a vagrancy charge.

After loafing through the blistering days that summer in McMinnville, I worked while the community slept. I weaved cane far into the cool night-hours, when the town was so silent that the rustle of wind in the pear tree behind the house was like the echo of a thousand chorus-girls, simultaneously swishing their taffeta skirts.

Early mornings, shortly after crawling into bed, and in the daze of half-sleep, I could smell boiling coffee and fried white salt-pork, and hear the splatter of hot grease as eggs were dropped into a frying-pan. Soon my father would be off to his job, stacking lumber at a near-by mill. And the rest of my family would be up, some heading for what work they could find, and my two younger sisters off to play. I would sleep until the sun's merciless rays curled the tin roof and drove me out of bed.

But morning after morning, before I arose, one or more cars pulled up in front of the house. A voice, obviously of a white person, would ask youngsters playing near by if "Tom Rowan's boy" lived there. "Yessir, Carl Rowan lives there," some child would reply, and, without further instructions, a clattering horde of kids would stampede into the house and to my bed to say: "Some white man wants you out there."

This irked me enough; but the whites always came with a half-demand, saying: "Somebody *has got* to do this job for me," and they irritated me until I acquired a smart-aleck disposition that was not part of my true nature. I had begun to love independence, and it pleased a part of me that I could not name, or even place, to be able to say that "Tom Rowan's boy" didn't *have* to do the job.

A man named Hunter, whose lawn I had mowed scores of times in previous years, several times for ten cents an hour, had me awakened early one morning. "Boy, they (he didn't say who) tell me uptown that you ain't doin' nothing. We're going to have a lawn party, and I gotta have my grass cut." With what now strikes me as boldness verging on recklessness, I told him that I had been so busy lately that I planned to hire someone to mow my lawn. He looked at my house, which sat about two feet off the gravel street, those two feet of yard containing not one blade of grass. He gave me a stare of contempt and drove away.

With reluctant thanks to man's greediness and inclination to war, I got out of McMinnville before I so provoked the whites as to jeopardize my physical well-being. One morning in late October I was ordered to active duty. On October 30, 1943, my secondhand clothes in a borrowed suitcase, I boarded a Jim Crow train and left the past and present of a life that I had begun to abhor. I had received more than the call of the United States Navy; as it turned out, I was answering the call of opportunity, for my hello to arms was farewell to the South in which I had been born and reared.

That I was leaving by Jim Crow train meant little to me then. Jim Crow was all I had known. For all the years that I had lived in the shadow of the Cumberland Mountains, two things were always certain: racial segregation and a steady stream of moonshine liquor out of the hills. I was a small-time youngster, off to a big-time war, riding the train for the first time in my life; and except for an accidental journey into Alabama aboard a lost bus, I was leaving Tennessee for the first time. Caught in a maelstrom of excitement, I could get little disturbed about Jim Crow—even when I was refused a Pullman berth from Nashville to St. Louis, despite a Navy order. The ticket-seller told me none was available, and, even after my "great rebellion," I had not acquired the habit of challenging the word of a white man—not even after watching several whites get berths after my request was rejected. I took my first-class ticket and boarded a last-class coach, as Negroes had done for years.

I propped my head on my hand and dozed that autumn night as my dirty, smoky Jim Crow coach rolled across Kentucky and southern Illinois. I was bound for Topeka, Kansas, and a Navy V-12 unit at Washburn Municipal University. There I found that I had crossed from my world of bare black feet on red clay and white perspiration on black brows into a strange new land. I had been snatched completely from a life of segregation; I was in a unit of 335 sailors, 334 of them white.

Part II

In 1951, nearly eight years later, I returned to McMinnville. It was the opening of old wounds. It was like rolling back time. I found that Negro youths still leaned against the First National Bank Building, where I once leaned hour upon hour. We had no place to go, nothing to do except wait for a white man to come along and offer twenty-five cents an hour for whatever job had gone without white takers.

There was the colored section of town. It was the same squalor, the same unpainted dwellings huddled close to narrow, hole-filled streets, some of which town officials had named, with apparent sincerity, "African Avenue," "Egypt Alley," and "Congo Street." The same paths led through weedy backyards to smelly wooden privies.

There, on Congo Street, was the little frame house in which I had lived during my early teenage years. To the rear of it was a row of privies, and in front of it had been a junkyard. I recalled hot summer days when I sat on the rough oak front-porch with my brother and sisters. On those sultry afternoons we would watch the mountains, waiting for them to belch up the rain that we knew was coming. As the downpour rode across the distant fields like a wind-driven silver wave, we young dreamers would pretend that this was a magic puff of rain that would cleanse McMinnville of junkyards and privies, pave Congo Street and give it a new name, and transform our frame house into a stone mansion with a huge brick chimney.

Upon returning, I found the house still frame. It was partially wired for electricity and had an outdoor hydrant for city water, two improvements over my days there. I had carried water from a neighbor's house at the end of the water-supply main, more than a block away, or fought off black gnats while filling my bucket at Hughes's spring. But the privies still were there; and weeds and wild cane had hidden remnants of the junkyard in a veritable wilderness. Weeds and time had even choked out two peach trees that I once robbed with great delight. It appeared that McMinnville Negroes still were waiting for that magic rainstorm to wash away deprivation and human wretchedness.

But I did not return to *expose* McMinnville, or the South. You do not expose racial hatred and social and economic injustices any more than you expose a fresh dunghill; you tell Americans that it exists and wait until the wind blows in their direction. I returned to McMinnville, to my native Dixie, to keep a promise to a white Southern sailor who found in 1943 that he was a stranger in his native land. I was to pay a debt to this sailor who had helped to keep me from being a stranger when I so abruptly left the world of segregation.

I had reached Topeka with no idea as to the nature of my Navy unit. Although the Navy had promised me the opportunity to earn a commission, I knew that it was notorious for restricting Negroes to mess-attendant duties. I also knew that the Navy followed the segregation pattern of the South, which I had just left, so I expected segregation at Washburn.

I reached the campus and stared up a long, tree-lined driveway at the University buildings. It was a warm night, with the kind of breeze poets write of, and sailors and their girls lined the driveway like Burma Shave signs. I saw that they all were white sailors, and I wondered, as I walked toward the nearest building, where the back road was. Because of my background, I thought they must have reserved another road for Negro sailors and their girls.

I walked into a building as white sailors observed me with ill-concealed curiosity. I asked where I should report, and was directed to the Administration building. The looks on a few faces made me feel as if I had barged into a ladies' restroom. I paused under a street light and re-read my orders. Thus assured that at least I was at the correct school, I reported to the Administration building. A chief petty officer named Pappas and a Lt. Beuhler gave me an extra-warm welcome. As Pappas stepped near me to hand me a slip with my house, room, and bunk numbers on it, he whispered: "I don't think you'll be *lonely* here."

Then I sensed that I was a lone Negro in a white unit. The First National Bank Building was gone. I had nothing on which to lean. It was like losing a raft after drifting out from shore: I would either sink or swim.

But the white sailors and I found that the things we had in common far outweighed our differences. We all hated early-morning calisthenics, Friday afternoon drills, and Saturday inspections. The color of my skin became less important daily. When Charley Van Horn of Coffeyville, Kansas, learned that he was to be my roommate, he quipped: "I'll be too damned busy trying to memorize Ohm's law and pass this physics course to count the pigment in your skin." That is how it was.

For Noah Brannon, a religion student who planned to become a chaplain, it was not so simple. Brannon came from near Brownsville, Texas, where prejudices run a bit deeper, perhaps, than in Coffeyville. But Brannon loved music, and that is where we found our common ground—he at the piano and I above him, singing "My Ideal," "Star Eyes" or some other popular song. We quickly became piano pals.

But I was the first Negro whom Brannon had known on an equal basis. One day he said to me, with the startled expression of a man awakening in the darkness and feeling a stranger in bed with him: "Carl, where is that overpowering odor they told me all Negroes have?"

Laughter spread to every muscle of my face. I thought Brannon's first racial question was exceedingly funny. Then I saw the utter sincerity of his expression as he awaited my answer. I bit my lip to recall laughter and wipe the smile wrinkles off my face. I offered a serious reply:

"If I don't have such an odor, Noah, I must have lost it in the shower room. I'll bet that could happen to anybody—of any race."

Brannon shook his head as an admission of naïveté. I soon learned that he was even more misinformed about Negroes. "Until I met you, Carl, I didn't even know Negroes had last names. Honestly," he went on as I gave him a look of disbelief, "we always called them 'Aunt Susie' or 'Uncle Charlie'!"

I explained to Brannon that, for decades, the South had refused to accord to Negroes the dignity of the titles Mr. and Mrs. A large segment had refused to acknowledge the Negro as participant in the institution of a family, so in the minds of these people Negroes could have no family name. "Is it possible that you grew up in an area of such great darkness, and among people who wanted to keep you misinformed?" I asked, trying to emphasize the human and regional background of something that had struck my friend only as "peculiar" at the time.

Brannon expressed amazement when I told him that in McMinnville I could not get a drink of water in any drugstore unless the fountain clerk could find a paper cup. (I found on my return that this is still the custom; no Negro drinks out of a glass.)

One afternoon in June 1944, nearly eight months after we had met, Brannon abruptly stopped playing "I'll be Seeing You." I had been ordered to a new station, and I could see that before we parted he wanted to get something off his mind. He turned to me and said: "You plan to be a writer after the war. Some time, why don't you just sit down and tell all the little things it means to be a Negro in the South, or anyplace where being a Negro makes a difference. It all was right there before my eyes, but I'd never have known it. You probably can't get a drink of water in a Brownsville drugstore either.

"If you're a Southern white person, you see these things and you don't. You're taught not to care. It's something that exists because it exists. Don't preach, but tell it all," Brannon pleaded, "for there must be many people in the South with big hearts but so little knowledge of this thing."

I promised Noah Brannon that some day I would tell Americans of "the little things" about being a Negro in America, and seven years later I had not forgotten. Because Brannon's words kept haunting me—and because a secretary made a typing error—I was able to keep my promise.

In December 1950, I asked for a change in my days off at the Minneapolis *Morning Tribune*. The change was approved by City Editor Bower Hawthorne, but in revising the work schedule his secretary unwittingly gave me an extra day off. I knew that I was to work that extra day, but the assistant city editor who made story assignments did not, and he was somewhat surprised when I reported for work. He had assigned someone to each of the immediate news events, so I retired to the library to do research on a story for the following Sunday. As I rambled through the files of the *New York Times,* stories about Negroes and happenings in the South kept staring out of the pages at me, reminding me of my promise to Brannon. I stopped my research and wrote Hawthorne a memorandum, suggesting that I be allowed to return to the South to gather data on Negro life for my report to all of America's Noah Brannons.

There was much more to tell than I had been able to discuss with Brannon, I told Hawthorne. There was much about being a Negro in the South that I had not personally experienced. There were new things happening in my native land, things that I should be able to interpret because of my Southern birth and background. I proposed that I be allowed to write a series of articles on the South, to tell the story as it is seen by a Negro who has lived it; to tell it not in terms of the statistician or the politician or the professional ranter on either side of the fence, but in the human terms of the men, women, and children who live and are the South. I suggested that I start by revisiting McMinnville and that I go on to scores of cities, towns, and villages throughout the South and the District of Columbia.

Despite the *Tribune*'s well-earned reputation as a champion of racial justice, I feared that my three-page memorandum would be laughed off. Both the race question and the South were explosive subjects, and, with a few notable exceptions, had been given only cursory treatment in the daily American press. I took a copy of my memorandum home. When my wife and I had finished laughing at what we considered my audacity, I had built up a dread of going to work the next day. But I went to work and was surprised. Hawthorne had liked the idea, as had Managing Editor Paul Swensson. Executive Editor Gideon Seymour agreed that there was much America's Noah Brannons ought to be told. But I knew that Seymour would remember a day in August 1948, when I talked to him about a job on the *Tribune*. I was about to receive my master's degree in journalism from the University of Minnesota's School of Journalism. I had walked into the *Star* and *Tribune* personnel department and asked for a job, the way any other applicant would have done. I wanted the same kind of job that any other applicant would expect. That was how Seymour wanted it: we both agreed that the only terms on which I would work for the *Tribune* were that I be just another newsman, that I not be a specialist in so-called Negro news. Seymour did remember that day, and he mentioned it, because he figured—correctly—that there would be readers who would accuse the *Tribune* of exploiting the fact that I was a Negro. But we agreed that the project was more important than all such accusations, so he approved the assignment, with only libel laws and truthfulness to limit what I could write. His sole plea was that I try to stay out of jail. I knew then that for the first time a daily metropolitan newspaper was going to print a Negro's account of Negro life in the kingdom of Jim Crow.

So on January 11, 1951, I returned to the South, where the color of my skin counts above all things. I returned to a South that had undergone many changes since Noah Brannon and I shared torch tunes and laughed at racial myths that antedate slavery. I wondered just how much change had taken place since my childhood. Certainly, I would find the Negro better off in some big and some small ways. Aided by the federal courts, he had made much progress toward equality of educational opportunity on higher levels; yet I knew that complete equality still was far away. In other fields— employment, health, and equality at the hands of the law—progress had come at a snail's pace.

But this progress, made largely during and after World War II, had stirred Southerners proudly to proclaim a New South. They spoke of ferment within the South, and self-styled Southern liberals swore that out of this social upheaval was to emerge a new day for the Negro in Dixieland.

"Will I find a New South?" I asked myself as once again I turned my face toward the land of mint juleps, cotton rows, and peanut patches. I looked at democracy and civilization, caught in the shadows of their gloomiest hour, and I hoped that I would find a New South. I hoped that I would find the social turmoil of a white South casting off the mental shackles of belief in white supremacy; and a Negro South casting off old, uncertain fetters in preparation and demand for a new day. Together, I believed, they could lift the South out of its decades-old social and economic morass, and give American democracy a sword of unity to help cut the threads of international despair.

CARL T. ROWAN
South of Freedom

103
Jackie Robinson
Joins the Brooklyn Dodgers

Brooklyn-born sportswriter Roger Kahn wrote *The Boys of Summer* as a paean to the Brooklyn Dodgers ballplayers of the early 1950s. The Dodgers of that era played good baseball, winning their share of pennants, but they also played a role in a larger sphere by signing Jackie Robinson to play in 1947: the first African-American player in the modern-day major leagues. A native of Georgia and the son of sharecroppers, Robinson grew up in the white enclave of Pasadena, California. He enjoyed himself as a star athlete at UCLA in the late 1930s, but found he nonetheless had to fight his way into officer-candidate school in the army during World War Two. While at the school, he was court-martialed—and subsequently acquitted—for refusing to sit in the back of a camp bus. By the time he resumed his career as an athlete, he was accustomed to the struggle a black man needed to wage for respect in the white world. For Dodgers general manager Branch Rickey, Jackie Robinson's combination of self-control and fierce spirit was as important to his selection as was his ability as a second baseman. During his first few seasons with the Dodgers, Robinson held to a promise he made to Rickey to ignore racist attacks at the ballpark. However, in later seasons, as Kahn relates, Robinson answered provocation, resoundingly.

This was the man Branch Rickey hired, proud, as his mother had wanted him to be, fierce in his own nature, scarred because white America wounds its fierce proud blacks. I once asked Rickey if he was surprised by the full measure of Robinson's success and I heard him laugh deep in his chest. "Adventure. Adventure. The man is all adventure. I only wish I could have signed him five years sooner."

As surely as Robinson's genius at the game transcends his autobiography, it also transcends record books. In two seasons, 1962 and 1965, Maury Wills stole more bases than Robinson did in all of a ten-year career. Ted Williams' lifetime batting average, .344, is two points higher than Robinson's best for any season. Robinson never hit twenty home runs in a year, never batted in 125 runs. Stan Musial consistently scored more often. Having said those things, one has not said much because troops of people who were there believe that in his prime Jackie Robinson was a better ball player than any of the others. "Ya want a guy that comes to play," suggests Leo Durocher, whose personal relationship with Robinson was spiky. "This guy didn't just come to play. He come to beat ya. He come to stuff the goddamn bat right up your ass."

He moved onto the field with a pigeon-toed shuffle, Number 42 on his back. Reese wore 1. Billy Cox wore 3. Duke Snider wore 4. Carl Furillo wore 6. Dressen wore 7. Shuba wore 8. Robinson wore 42. The black man had to begin in double figures. So he remained.

After 1948 he had too much belly, and toward the end fat rolled up behind his neck. But how this lion sprang. Like a few, very few athletes, Babe Ruth, Jim Brown, Robinson did not merely play at center stage. He was center stage; and wherever he walked, center stage moved with him.

When the Dodgers needed a run and had men at first and second, it was Robinson who came to bat. Would he slap a line drive to right? Would he slug the ball to left? Or would he roll a bunt? From the stands at Ebbets Field, close to home plate, the questions rose into a din. The pitcher saw Robinson. He heard the stands. He bit his lip.

At times when the team lagged, Robinson found his way to first. Balancing evenly on the balls of both feet, he took an enormous lead. The pitcher glared. Robinson stared back. There was no action, only two men throwing hard looks. But time suspended. The cry in the grandstands rose. And Robinson hopped a half yard farther from first. The pitcher stepped off the mound, calling time-out, and when the game resumed, he walked the hitter.

Breaking, Robinson reached full speed in three strides. The pigeon-toed walk yielded to a run of graceful power. He could steal home, or advance two bases on someone else's bunt, and at the time of decision, when he slid, the big dark body became a bird in flight. Then, safe, he rose slowly, often limping, and made his pigeon-toed way to the dugout.

Once Russ Meyer, a short-tempered right-hander, pitched a fine game against the Dodgers. The score going into the eighth inning was 2 to 2, and it was an achievement to check the Brooklyn hitters in Ebbets Field. Then, somehow, Robinson reached third base. He took a long lead, threatening to steal home, and the Phillies, using a set play, caught him fifteen feet off base. A rundown developed. This is the major league version of a game children call getting into a pickle. The runner is surrounded by fielders who throw the ball back and forth, gradually closing the gap. Since a ball travels four times faster than a man's best running speed, it is only a question of time before the gap closes and the runner is tagged. Except for Robinson. The rundown was his greatest play. Robinson could start so fast and stop so short that he could elude anyone in baseball, and he could feint a start and feint a stop as well.

All the Phillies rushed to the third-base line, a shortstop named Granny Hammer and a second baseman called Mike Goliat and the first baseman, Eddie Waitkus. The third baseman, Puddin' Head Jones, and the catcher, Andy Seminick, were already there. Meyer himself joined. Among the gray uniforms Robinson in white lunged and sprinted and leaped and stopped. The Phils threw the ball back and forth, but Robinson anticipated their throws, and after forty seconds, and six throws, the gap had not closed. Then, a throw toward third went wild and Robinson made his final victorious run at home plate. Meyer dropped to his knees and threw both arms around Robinson's stout legs. Robinson bounced a hip against Meyer's head and came home running backward, saying, "What the hell are you trying to do?"

"Under the stands, Robinson," Meyer said.

"Right now," Robinson roared.

Police beat them to the proposed ring. Robinson not only won games; he won and infuriated the losers.

In Ebbets Field one spring day in 1955 Sal Maglie was humiliating the Brooklyn hitters. Not Cox or Robinson, but most of the others were clearly alarmed by Maglie's highest skill. He threw at hitters, as he said, "whenever they didn't expect it. That way I had them looking to duck all the time." The fast pitch at the chin or temple is frightening but not truly dangerous as long as the batter sees the ball. He has only to move his head a few inches to safety.

On this particular afternoon, Maglie threw a fast pitch behind Robinson's shoulders, and that is truly dangerous, a killer pitch. As a batter strides, and one strides automatically, he loses height. A normal defensive reflex is to fall backward. When a pitch is shoulder-high behind a man, he ducks directly into the baseball.

I can see Maglie, saturnine in the brightness of May, winding up and throwing. Robinson started to duck and then, with those extraordinary reflexes, hunched his shoulders and froze. The ball sailed wild behind him. He must have felt the wind. He held the hunched posture and gazed at Maglie, who began fidgeting on the mound.

A few innings later, as Maglie continued to overwhelm the Brooklyn hitters, Pee Wee Reese said, "Jack, you got to do something."

"Yeah," Robinson said.

The bat boy overheard the whispered conversation, and just before Jack stepped in to hit, he said in a voice of anxiety, "Don't you do it. Let one of the others do it. You do enough."

Robinson took his stance, bat high. He felt a certain relief. Let somebody else do it, for a change.

"Come on, Jack." Reese's voice carried from the dugout. "We're counting on you."

Robinson took a deep breath. Somebody else? What somebody else? Hodges? Snider? Damn, there wasn't anybody else.

The bunt carried accurately toward first baseman Whitey Lockman, who scooped the ball and looked to throw. That is the play. Bunt and make the pitcher cover first. Then run him down. But Maglie lingered in the safety of the mound. He would not move, and a second baseman named Davey Williams took his place. Lockman's throw reached Williams at first base. Then Robinson struck. A knee crashed into Williams' lower spine and Williams spun into the air, twisting grotesquely, and when he fell he lay in an awkward sprawl, as people do when they are seriously injured.

He was carried from the field. Two innings after that, Alvin Dark, the Giant captain, lined a two-base hit to left field. Dark did not stop at second. Instead, he continued full speed toward third base and Jackie Robinson. The throw had him beaten. Robinson put the ball into his bare right hand and decided to tag Dark between the eyes.

As Dark began to slide, Robinson faked to his right. Dark followed his fake. Robinson stepped aside and slammed the ball at Dark's brow. To his amazement, it bounced free. He had not gotten a secure grip. Dark, avenging Davey Williams, substituting for Sal Maglie, was safe at third.

Both men dusted their uniforms. Lockman was batting. Staring toward home, Robinson said through rigid lips, "This isn't the end. There'll be another day." But when the game was over, Dark asked a reporter to carry a message into the Brooklyn clubhouse. "Tell him we're even," the Giant captain said. "Tell him I don't want another day."

. . . Watching the deep-set angry eyes, I could not forget that when combat reached close quarters, it was the Southerner not the black who had backed off.

ROGER KAHN
The Boys of Summer

104

Paul Nitze Ponders the Origins of the Cold War

A hardened Cold Warrior, Paul Nitze devoted a long career in Washington to national security and the overshadowing threat from the Soviet Union. He was well-suited to his role, with an agile mind, a fountain of energy, and strong convictions. In response to these qualities, Soviet diplomats who negotiated with him in the 1980s nicknamed him "the silver fox." Paul Nitze started his career at the State Department in 1946 by joining George F. Kennan on the Policy Planning Staff: the vanguard of U.S.-Soviet relations at the time. In *From Hiroshima to Glasnost: At the Center of Decision,* he recalled the atmosphere and some of the personalities he encountered during 1949, a year during which he grew increasingly concerned over the Soviet Union's bulging arsenal. One year later, Nitze would be largely responsible for a memo, known as "NSC 68," that enlarged upon George Kennan's definition of containment of Soviet communism by calling for a drastic military buildup. NSC 68 helped ignite U.S. policy along exactly those lines and it extended Nitze's influence in the years to follow, when he was generally counted among the hard-liners.

From all outward appearances it was a routine patrol off the coast of Alaska by an Air Force WB-29 weather reconnaissance plane. Such flights were almost daily occurrences, though for this plane the mission was part of what was then a closely guarded secret. It was not in fact a typical weather plane, but a unit of the Air Force's Long Range Detection System that had been established less than a year earlier to monitor the Soviet Union's atomic energy program. Equipped with sensitive instruments using specially treated filter paper to pick up any radioactive dust that might be in the air, these planes would loiter for hours at high altitudes off the Soviet coast, downwind from where U.S. intelligence analysts suspected the Soviets' test range for atomic devices was located. The results of the flight this day—September 3, 1949—showed an abnormally high count of radioactive particles. Upon closer inspection, they confirmed what we had feared would eventually happen—that sometime the previous week the Soviets had detonated a nuclear device. With this one event, the threat posed by the Soviet Union acquired a new, more ominous and dangerous dimension.

At the time I learned about the Soviet detonation, I was just settling into a new job as deputy director of the State Department's Policy Planning Staff, or S/P as it was identified on the department's organization charts. ("S" stood for "Secretary," indicating that it was part of the secretary of state's immediate office, and "P" stood for "Policy.") As I mentioned earlier, it was created in 1947 at the direction of George Marshall as a planning and advisory body to the secretary of state. S/P had no operating responsibilities; its task was to study longer-range problems and recommend solutions which, if approved by the secretary, would then guide the department's operating divisions. In practice, of course, things were rarely this simple. But it did mean that there was a group in addition to the secretary and the under secretary that was not specialized either in a particular area, such as Europe, Asia, or the Middle East, or in a particular function like economics, and that could worry about troublesome problems that cut across the board and appeared likely to have long-range significance. In collaboration with the Joint Staff and the Joint Strategic Survey Committee in the Pentagon, S/P became a significant part of the President's politico-military advisory support mechanism.

To my mind, the success and effectiveness of this system in the late 1940s and early 1950s when I was part of it were the result of President Truman's unwavering confidence in his senior advisers, especially Secretaries Marshall and Acheson. As I look back on it, the relationship between Truman and Acheson was probably the best between a president and his secretary of state in this century. They knew each other's thoughts and, more importantly, they had the deepest respect for each other. Mr. Truman realized that he needed someone with Dean's foreign policy experience and analytical mind, while Acheson realized that he needed Mr. Truman's down-to-earth commonsense qualities. Mr. Truman never tried to hide anything from Mr. Acheson and he, in turn, never tried to hide anything from the President. They worked together as a team.

Mr. Truman was a man of strong opinions and convictions; one of the hallmarks of his presidency was that he never shirked decisions and rarely second-guessed those that he made. Had he confronted the Cuban missile crisis, I have no doubt that he would have taken a course similar to that chosen by John F. Kennedy, but with a great deal less agonizing. I remember one episode around 1952 when we were involved in a reassessment of our policy toward Spain. The Joint Chiefs deemed Spain a highly desirable location for important air and naval bases, and we on the Policy Planning Staff had accordingly initiated a review of our policy aimed at normalizing relations with Spain. At the time, Spain was under a fascist dictator, General Francisco Franco, who had leaned toward the Axis in World War II. Having completed the necessary analytical work and having secured all the necessary concurrences short of the President's, we placed our proposals before the NSC for Mr. Truman's consideration. I accompanied Acheson to the meeting. Mr. Truman came in, took a look around the room, and said, matter-of-factly, that he had a brief announcement. "I am not going to approve this proposed change of policy," he said. "Mr. Franco was an associate of Mr. Hitler and Mr. Mussolini in the last war, and I do not approve of people who once kept company with those men." And with that, he declared the meeting adjourned and left the room. Later, he changed his mind and the process of normalization began, but he gave in only with the greatest reluctance.

I confess that my initial impression of Mr. Truman, formed during World War II, was less than favorable. My first contacts with him were while I was in charge of overseas procurement for the Board of Economic Warfare. At the time, he was chairman of a Senate committee investigating fraud, waste, and abuse in the war effort. The committee's general counsel was a man named McGhee (no relation to George McGhee, later the State Department's Middle East expert), who sometimes showed up in my office to relay complaints from Mr. Truman about my procurement activities. Mr. Truman felt that we should buy as much as possible from domestic suppliers to help the people and economy in this country. This was not always possible, since the quality of some imported materials, like mica, for example, was often so far superior to what we could buy here in the United States that the domestic product was worthless. Mr. Truman's attempts to intervene in this fashion seemed to me grossly improper. When he became President I had visions of the country being turned over to political cronies of his like McGhee.

My wife Phyllis caused me to change my mind about Mr. Truman. When I came home from Europe in 1945 I found her convinced that the Trumans— Mrs. Truman, in particular—were wonderful people of great integrity. Through her wartime volunteer work she had met Mrs. Truman and had formed a favorable opinion of her and of her husband. My respect for Phyllis's invariably sound and perceptive judgment of others told me that I must have underestimated Mr. Truman; she was, of course, right. Mr. Truman had the utmost respect for the office of the presidency, and while he did keep a few cronies like General Harry Vaughan around for company, his respect for the office of the presidency kept him from letting them meddle in decisions he considered to be presidential.

After his meetings with the President, Acheson would come back and brief his immediate staff on what had transpired. Dean was easy to work for because he kept his immediate associates fully informed and up-to-date. I could go over to the Pentagon and talk to the Joint Chiefs, for example, knowing that what I said correctly reflected not only the secretary's views but those of the President. So, even though I was a senior civil servant, not a presidential appointee, I was able to speak with authority and helped take some of the burden from Acheson's shoulders.

Acheson was an exceptional individual, a commanding presence wherever he went, distinguished in appearance, well dressed and witty, and entertaining in speech. Among his greatest joys were the long walks he regularly took with his close friend Justice Felix Frankfurter; they would discuss everything from the major events of the day to the latest Washington gossip. Their common interest was, of course, the law, which Dean saw as bringing out into the open and reflecting the true values and central issues of American life. In contrast to General Marshall, his predecessor as secretary of state, a man of impeccable character, who represented the best that middle-class America can offer, Dean Acheson had the grace and bearing of an aristocrat. Both were great men, though vastly different in style, but both worked well with Mr. Truman and with each other.

PAUL H. NITZE
From Hiroshima to Glasnost

105
George F. Kennan's
Strategy of Containment

George F. Kennan had been a student of Russian life ever since boyhood, when he became fascinated by a series of articles written by one of his distant relatives on the subject of the imperial justice system. After joining the Foreign Service in 1926, Kennan was systematically educated to become an authority on the Soviet Union. Unlike some U.S. policymakers, he openly admired many cultural aspects of the lands braced within the Soviet system. However, he knew firsthand the dangers and shortcomings of Soviet rule. As Washington's spirit of camaraderie with Moscow faded in the aftermath of World War Two, Kennan sent a long telegram from Moscow, containing a sensitive analysis of the USSR's expansionist intentions. Kennan's "long telegram" was widely read and in some respects served to justify the inception of Cold War policy toward the USSR. Back in America in 1947, Kennan made his views public in an article expressing a bold belief that America had no choice but to "contain" Soviet communism. That article stirred debate on all sides, as Kennan recalled in his *Memoirs: 1925–1950*.

Among the many papers prepared in the winter of 1946–1947, there was one that was written not for delivery as a lecture and not for publication but merely for the private edification of Secretary of the Navy James Forrestal. Ever since the receipt in Washington of the long telegram of February 22, 1946, Mr. Forrestal had taken a lively personal interest in my work. It was, I suspect, due to his influence that I was assigned to the War College and later chosen by General Marshall to head the Planning Staff.

During the period of my service at the War College—in December 1946, to be exact—Mr. Forrestal sent me a paper on the subject of Marxism and Soviet power, prepared by a member of his immediate entourage, and asked me to comment on it. This I found hard to do. It was a good paper. With parts of it I could agree; other parts were simply not put the way I would have put them. The whole subject was one too close to my own experience and interests for me to discuss it in terms of someone else's language. I sent the paper back to him with the observation that rather than commenting I would prefer, if he agreed, to address myself to the same subject in my own words. This, he replied, he would like me to do.

The result was that on January 31, 1947, I sent to him, for his private and personal edification, a paper discussing the nature of Soviet power as a problem in policy for the United States. It was a literary extrapolation of the thoughts which had been maturing in my mind, and which I had been expressing in private communications and speeches, for at least two years into the past. Even the term "containment" which appeared in the course of the argument was, as we have just observed, not new.

Mr. Forrestal read the paper. He acknowledged it, on February 17, with the words: "It is extremely well-done and I am going to suggest to the Secretary that he read it."

Now I had, as it happened, spoken informally, early in January, at the Council of Foreign Relations, in New York, on the same general subject. The editor of the council's magazine *Foreign Affairs,* Mr. Hamilton Fish Armstrong (a great editor and, incidentally, one with whom this association was to be the beginning of a long and close friendship), asked me whether I did not have something in writing, along the lines of what I had said to the council, that could be published in the magazine. I had no text of what I had said on that occasion, but I thought of the paper I had prepared for Mr. Forrestal. In early March, therefore, I sought and obtained Mr. Forrestal's assurance that he had no objection to its publication. I then submitted it (March 13) to the Committee on Unofficial Publication, of the Department of State, for the usual official clearance. In doing so, I explained that it was the intention that it should be published anonymously. The committee pondered it at leisure, found in it nothing particularly remarkable or dangerous from the government's standpoint, and issued, on April 8, permission for its publication in the manner indicated. I then crossed out my own name in the signature of the article, replaced it with an "X" to assure the anonymity, sent it on to Mr. Armstrong, and thought no more about it. I knew that it would be some weeks before it would appear. I did not know how my position would be changed in the course of those weeks, or how this would affect the interpretations that would be placed upon the article when it was published.

In late June, as I recall it, the article appeared in the July issue of *Foreign Affairs,* under the title: "The Sources of Soviet Conduct." Its appearance was

followed shortly (July 8) by that of a piece in the *New York Times* from the
pen of the well-known and experienced Washington columnist Mr. Arthur
Krock, hinting at the official origin of the article and pointing to the importance that attached to it by virtue of that fact. He, I later learned, had been
shown the article by Mr. Forrestal at a time when it was no more than a
private paper lying around in Mr. Forrestal's office. His keen journalistic eye
had at once recognized it when it appeared in print; and he had put two and
two together.

It was not long, after the appearance of Mr. Krock's piece, before the au-
thorship of the article became common knowledge. Others began to write
about it, to connect it with the Truman Doctrine and Marshall Plan, to speculate on its significance. It soon became the center of a veritable whirlpool of
publicity. *Life* and *Reader's Digest* reprinted long excerpts from it. The term
"containment" was picked up and elevated, by common agreement of the
press, to the status of a "doctrine," which was then identified with the foreign
policy of the administration. In this way there was established—before our
eyes, so to speak—one of those indestructible myths that are the bane of the
historian.

Feeling like one who has inadvertently loosened a large boulder from the
top of a cliff and now helplessly witnesses its path of destruction in the valley
below, shuddering and wincing at each successive glimpse of disaster, I absorbed the bombardment of press comment that now set in. I had not meant
to do anything of this sort. General Marshall, too, was shocked. It was a firm
principle, for him, that "planners don't talk." The last thing he had expected
was to see the name of the head of his new Planning Staff bandied about
in the press as the author of a programmatical article—or an article hailed
as programmatical—on the greatest of our problems of foreign policy. He
called me in, drew my attention to this anomaly, peered at me over his glasses
with raised eyebrows (eyebrows before whose raising, I may say, better men
than I had quailed), and waited for an answer. I explained the origins of the
article, and pointed out that it had been duly cleared for publication by the
competent official committee. This satisfied him. He was, as I have already
observed, an orderly man, accustomed to require and to respect a plain delineation of responsibility. If the article had been cleared in this manner, the
responsibility was not mine. He never mentioned the matter again, nor did
he hold it officially against me. But it was long, I suspect, before he recovered from his astonishment over the strange ways of the department he now
headed.

Measured against the interpretations that were at once attached to it, and
have continued to a considerable extent to surround it ever since, the article
that appeared in *Foreign Affairs,* in June 1947, suffered, unquestionably, from
serious deficiencies. Some of these I might have corrected at the time by more

careful editing and greater forethought, had I had any idea of the way it was to be received. But I cannot lay these failures exclusively to the innocent and unsuspecting manner in which the article was written. Certain of the public reactions were ones I would not, in any event, have foreseen.

A serious deficiency of the article was the failure to mention the satellite area of Eastern Europe—the failure to discuss Soviet power, that is, *in terms* of its involvement in this area. Anyone reading the article would have thought—and would have had every reason to think—that I was talking only about Russia proper; that the weaknesses of the Soviet system to which I was drawing attention were ones that had their existence only within the national boundaries of the Soviet state; that the geographic extension that had been given to the power of the Soviet leaders, by virtue of the recent advances of Soviet armies into Eastern Europe and the political exploitation of those advances for Communist purposes, were irrelevant to the weaknesses of which I was speaking. Obviously, in mentioning the uncertainties of the Soviet situation—such things as the weariness and poor morale among the population, the fragility of the constitutional arrangements within the party, etc.—I would have had a far stronger case had I added the characteristic embarrassments of imperialism which the Soviet leaders had now taken upon themselves with their conquest of Eastern Europe, and the unlikelihood that Moscow would be permanently successful in holding this great area in subjection.

To this day, I am not sure of the reason for this omission. It had something to do, I suspect, with what I felt to be Mr. Forrestal's needs at the time when I prepared the original paper for him. I have a vague recollection of feeling that to go into the problems of the satellite area would be to open up a wholly new subject, confuse the thesis I was developing, and carry the paper beyond its intended scope. Whatever the reason, it was certainly not that I underrated the difficulties with which the Soviet leaders were faced in their attempt to exercise political dominion over Eastern Europe. It has been noted above, in Chapter 9, that even as early as V-E Day, two years before, I had expressed the view that the Russians were overextended in this area. Without Western support, I had written at that time

> *Russia would probably not be able to maintain its hold successfully for any length of time over all the territory over which it has today staked out a claim . . . The lines would have to be withdrawn somewhat.*

Similarly, in the long telegram I had sent to Washington from Moscow, in February 1946, I had pointed out that the Soviet internal system

> *will now be subjected, by virtue of recent territorial expansions, to a series of additional strains which once proved a severe tax on Tsardom.*

Had I included these appreciations in the X-Article, and added to the description of the internal weaknesses of Soviet power a mention of the strains of Moscow's new external involvement in Eastern Europe, I would have had a far stronger case for challenging the permanency of the imposing and forbidding facade which Stalin's Russia presented to the outside world in those immediate postwar years.

A second serious deficiency of the X-Article—perhaps the most serious of all—was the failure to make clear that what I was talking about when I mentioned the containment of Soviet power was not the containment by military means of a military threat, but the political containment of a political threat. Certain of the language used—such as "a long-term, patient but firm and vigilant containment of Russian expansive tendencies" or "the adroit and vigilant application of counterforce at a series of constantly shifting geographical and political points"—was at best ambiguous, and lent itself to misinterpretation in this respect.

A third great deficiency, intimately connected with the one just mentioned, was the failure to distinguish between various geographic areas, and to make clear that the "containment" of which I was speaking was not something that I thought we could, necessarily, do everywhere successfully, or even needed to do everywhere successfully, in order to serve the purpose I had in mind. Actually, as noted in connection with the Truman Doctrine above, I distinguished clearly in my own mind between areas that I thought vital to our security and ones that did not seem to me to fall into this category. My objection to the Truman Doctrine message revolved largely around its failure to draw this distinction. Repeatedly, at that time and in ensuing years, I expressed in talks and lectures the view that there were only five regions of the world—the United States, the United Kingdom, the Rhine valley with adjacent industrial areas, the Soviet Union, and Japan—where the sinews of modern military strength could be produced in quantity; I pointed out that only one of these was under Communist control; and I defined the main task of containment, accordingly, as one of seeing to it that none of the remaining ones fell under such control. Why this was not made clear in the X-Article is, again, a mystery. I suppose I thought that such considerations were subsumed under the reference to the need for confronting the Russians with unalterable counterforce *"at every point where they show signs of encroaching upon the interests of a peaceful world."*

So egregious were these errors that I must confess to responsibility for the greatest and most unfortunate of the misunderstandings to which they led. This was the one created in the mind of Mr. Walter Lippmann. It found its expression in the series of twelve pieces attacking the X-Article (later published in book form as *The Cold War, A Study in U.S. Foreign Policy,* New York: Harper and Brothers, 1947) which he published in his newspaper column in the late summer and autumn of 1947. As I read these articles over to-day (and they are well worth the effort), I find the misunderstanding almost tragic in its dimensions. Mr. Lippmann, in the first place, mistook me for the author of precisely those features of the Truman Doctrine which I had most vigorously opposed—an assumption to which, I must say, I had led squarely with my chin in the careless and indiscriminate language of the X-Article. He held up, as a deserved correction to these presumed aberrations on my part, precisely those features of General Marshall's approach, and those passages of the Harvard speech, for which I had a primary responsibility. He interpreted the concept of containment in just the military sense I had not meant to give it. And on the basis of these misimpressions he proceeded to set forth, as an alternative to what I had led him to think my views were, a concept of American policy so similar to that which I was to hold and to advance in coming years that one could only assume I was subconsciously inspired by that statement of it—as perhaps, in part, I was. He urged a concentration on the vital countries of Europe; he urged a policy directed toward a mutual withdrawal of Soviet and American (also British) forces from Europe; he pointed with farsighted penetration to the dangers involved in any attempt to make of a truncated Western Germany an ally in an anti-Soviet coalition. All these points would figure prominently in my own later writings. He saw them, for the most part, long before I did. I accept the blame for misleading him. My only consolation is that I succeeded in provoking from him so excellent and penetrating a treatise.

Nevertheless, the experience was a painful one. It was doubly painful by reason of the great respect I bore him. I can still recall the feeling of bewilderment and frustration with which—helpless now to reply publicly because of my official position—I read these columns as they appeared and found held against me so many views with which I profoundly agreed. A few months later (April 1948), lying under treatment for ulcers on the sixteenth floor of the Naval Hospital in Bethesda, very bleak in spirit from the attendant fasting and made bleaker still by the whistling of the cold spring wind in the windows of that lofty pinnacle, I wrote a long letter to Mr. Lippmann, protesting the misinterpretation of my thoughts which his articles, as it seemed to me, implied. I never sent it to him. It was probably best that I didn't. The letter had a plaintive and overdramatic tone, reflecting the discomfort of flesh and spirit in which it was written. I took a more cruel but less serious revenge a year or two later when I ran into him on a parlor car of the Pennsylvania Railroad, and wore him relentlessly down with a monologue on these same subjects that lasted most of the way from Washington to New York.

But the terms of the unsent letter still hold, as I see them, a certain interest as expressions of the way the Lippmann columns then affected me.

I began, of course, with a peal of anguish over the confusion about the

Truman Doctrine and the Marshall Plan. To be held as the author of the former, and to have the latter held up to me as the mature correction of my youthful folly, hurt more than anything else.

I also naturally went to great lengths to disclaim the view, imputed to me by implication in Mr. Lippmann's columns, that containment was a matter of stationing military forces around the Soviet borders and preventing any outbreak of Soviet military aggressiveness. I protested, as I was to do on so many other occasions over the course of the ensuing eighteen years, against the implication that the Russians were aspiring to invade other areas and that the task of American policy was to prevent them from doing so. "The Russians don't want," I insisted,

to invade anyone. It is not in their tradition. They tried it once in Finland and got their fingers burned. They don't want war of any kind. Above all, they don't want the open responsibility that official invasion brings with it. They far prefer to do the job politically with stooge forces. Note well: when I say politically, that does not mean without violence. But it means that the violence is nominally domestic, not international, violence. It is, if you will, a police violence . . . not a military violence.

The policy of containment related to the effort to encourage other peoples to resist this type of violence and to defend the internal integrity of their countries.

I tried, then, to explain (I could have done it better) that the article was in reality a plea—addressed as much to our despairing liberals as to our hotheaded right-wingers—for acceptance of the belief that, ugly as was the problem of Soviet power, war was not inevitable, nor was it a suitable answer; that the absence of war did not mean that we would lose the struggle; that there was a middle ground of political resistance on which we could stand with reasonable prospect of success. We were, in fact, already standing on that ground quite successfully. And I went ahead to point proudly (and rather unfairly, for after all, Lippmann had approved and praised the rationale of the Marshall Plan in his articles) to what had already been accomplished. I cite this passage here, not as a correction to Mr. Lippmann, to whose arguments it was not really an answer, but as a sort of epilogue to the discussion of both Marshall Plan and X-Article.

Something over a year has now gone by since General Marshall took over his present job. I would ask you to think back on the state of the world, as he faced it last spring. At that time, it was almost impossible to see how Europe could be saved. We were still caught in the fateful confusion between the "one-world" and the "two-world" concepts. The economic plight of the continent was rapidly revealing itself as far worse than anyone had dreamed, and was steadily deteriorating. Congress was in an ugly frame of mind, convinced that all foreign aid was "operation rathole." The Communists were at the throat of France. A pall of fear, of bewilderment, of discouragement, hung over the continent and paralyzed all constructive activity. Molotov sat adamant at the Moscow council table, because he saw no reason to pay us a price for things which he thought were bound to drop into his lap, like ripe fruits, through the natural course of events.

Compare that with today? Europe is admittedly not over the hump. But no fruits have dropped [into Molotov's lap]. We know what is West and what is East. Moscow was itself compelled to make that unpleasant delineation. Recovery is progressing rapidly in the West. New hope exists. People see the possibility of a better future. The Communist position in France has been deeply shaken. The Western nations have found a common political language. They are learning to lean on each other, and to help each other. Those who fancied they were neutral are beginning to realize that they are on our side. A year ago only that which was Communist had firmness and structure. Today the non-Communist world is gaining daily in rigidity and in the power of resistance. Admittedly, the issue hangs on Italy; but it hangs, in reality, on Italy alone. A year ago it hung on all of Europe and on us.

You may say: this was not the doing of US policy makers; it was others who worked this miracle.

Certainly, we did not do it alone; and I have no intention of attempting to apportion merit. But you must leave us some pride in our own legerdemain. In international affairs, the proof of the pudding is always in the eating. If the development of the past year had been in the opposite direction—if there had been a deterioration of our position as great as the actual improvement—there is not one of you who would not have placed the blame squarely on the failure of American statesmanship. Must it always, then, be "heads you win; tails I lose" for the US Government?

In the years that have passed since that time, the myth of the "doctrine of containment" has never fully lost its spell. On innumerable occasions, I have been asked to explain it, to say whether I thought it had been a success, to explain how it applied to China, to state a view as to whether it was still relevant in later situations, etc. It has been interpreted by others in a variety of ways. Pro-Soviet writers have portrayed it as the cloak for aggressive designs on the Soviet Union. Right-wing critics have assailed it precisely for its lack of aggressiveness: for its passivity, for its failure to promise anything like "victory." Serious commentators have maintained that it was all very well in 1947 but that it lost its rationale with the Korean War, or with Stalin's death, or with the decline of bipolarity.

It is hard for me to respond to all these criticisms. What I said in the X-Article was not intended as a doctrine. I am afraid that when I think about foreign policy, I do not think in terms of doctrines. I think in terms of principles.

In writing the X-Article, I had in mind a long series of what seemed to me to be concessions that we had made, during the course of the war and just after it, to Russian expansionist tendencies—concessions made in the hope and belief that they would promote collaboration between our government and the Soviet government in the postwar period. I had also in mind the fact that many people, seeing that these concessions had been unsuccessful and that we had been unable to agree with the Soviet leaders on the postwar order of Europe and Asia, were falling into despair and jumping to the panicky conclusion that this spelled the inevitability of an eventual war between the Soviet Union and the United States.

It was this last conclusion that I was attempting, in the X-Article, to dispute. I thought I knew as much as anyone in the United States about the ugliness of the problem that Stalin's Russia presented to us. I had no need to accept instruction on this point from anybody. But I saw no necessity of a Soviet-American war, nor anything to be gained by one, then or at any time. There was, I thought, another way of handling this problem—a way that offered reasonable prospects of success, at least in the sense of avoiding a new world disaster and leaving the Western community of nations no worse off than it then was. This was simply to cease at that point making fatuous unilateral concessions to the Kremlin, to do what we could to inspire and support resistance elsewhere to its efforts to expand the area of its dominant political influence, and to wait for the internal weaknesses of Soviet power, combined with frustration in the external field, to moderate Soviet ambitions and behavior. The Soviet leaders, formidable as they were, were not supermen. Like all rulers of all great countries, they had their internal contradictions and dilemmas to deal with. Stand up to them, I urged, manfully but not aggressively, and give the hand of time a chance to work.

This is all that the X-Article was meant to convey. I did not suppose, in saying all this, that the situation flowing immediately from the manner in which hostilities ended in 1945 would endure forever. It was my assumption that if and when the Soviet leaders had been brought to a point where they would talk reasonably about some of the problems flowing from the outcome of the war, we would obviously wish to pursue this possibility and to see what could be done about restoring a more normal state of affairs. I shared to the full, in particular, Walter Lippmann's view of the importance of achieving, someday, the retirement of Soviet military power from Eastern Europe, although I did not then attach quite the same political importance to such a retirement as he did. (In this he was more right than I was.)

No one was more conscious than I was of the dangers of a permanent division of the European continent. The purpose of "containment" as then conceived was not to perpetuate the status quo to which the military operations and political arrangements of World War II had led; it was to tide us over a difficult time and bring us to a point where we could discuss effectively with the Russians the drawbacks and dangers this status quo involved, and to arrange with them for its peaceful replacement by a better and sounder one.

And if the policy of containment could be said in later years to have failed, it was not a failure in the sense that it proved impossible to prevent the Russians from making mortally dangerous encroachments "upon the interests of a peaceful world" (for it did prevent that); nor was it a failure in the sense that the mellowing of Soviet power, which Walter Lippmann took me so severely to task for predicting, failed to set in (it did set in). The failure consisted in the fact that our own government, finding it difficult to understand a political threat as such and to deal with it in other than military terms, and grievously misled, in particular, by its own faulty interpretations of the significance of the Korean War, failed to take advantage of the opportunities for useful political discussion when, in later years, such opportunities began to open up, and exerted itself, in its military preoccupations, to seal and to perpetuate the very division of Europe which it should have been concerned to remove. It was not "containment" that failed; it was the intended follow-up that never occurred.

When I used the term "Soviet power" in the X-Article, I had in view, of course, the system of power organized, dominated, and inspired by Joseph Stalin. This was a monolithic power structure, reaching through the network of highly disciplined Communist parties into practically every country in the world. In these circumstances, any success of a local Communist party, any advance of Communist power anywhere, had to be regarded as an extension in reality of the political orbit, or at least the dominant influence, of the Kremlin. Precisely because Stalin maintained so jealous, so humiliating a control over foreign Communists, all of the latter had, at that time, to be regarded as the vehicles of his will, not their own. His was the only center of authority in the Communist world; and it was a vigilant, exacting, and imperious headquarters, prepared to brook no opposition.

Tito's break with Moscow, in 1948, was the first overt breach in the monolithic unity of the Moscow-dominated Communist bloc. For long, it remained the only one. It did not affect immediately and importantly the situation elsewhere in the Communist world. But when, in the period between 1957 and 1962, the differences between the Chinese and Russian Communist parties, having lain latent in earlier years, broke to the surface and assumed the form of a major conflict between the two regimes, the situation in the world Communist movement became basically different. Other Communist parties, primarily those outside Eastern Europe but partly the Eastern European ones as well, had now two poles—three, if Belgrade was included—to choose among. This very freedom of choice not only made possible for them a large degree of independence; in many instances it forced that independence upon them. Neither of the two major centers of Communist power was now in a position to try to impose upon them a complete disciplinary control, for fear of pushing them into the arms of the other. They, on the other hand, reluctant for the most part to take the risks of total identification with one or the other, had little choice but to maneuver, to think and act for themselves, to accept, in short, the responsibilities of independence. If, at the end of the 1940s, no Communist party (except the Yugoslav one) could be considered anything else than an instrument of Soviet power, by the end of the 1950s none (unless it be the Bulgarian and the Czech) could be considered to be such an instrument at all.

This development changed basically the assumptions underlying the concept of containment, as expressed in the X-Article. Seen from the standpoint upon which that article rested, the Chinese-Soviet conflict was in itself the greatest single measure of containment that could be conceived. It not only invalidated the original concept of containment, it disposed in large measure of the very problem to which it was addressed.

Efforts to enlist the original concept of containment with relation to situations that postdate the Chinese-Soviet conflict, particularly when they are described in terms that refer to some vague "communism" in general and do not specify what particular communism is envisaged, are therefore wholly misconceived. There is today no such thing as "communism" in the sense that there was in 1947; there are only a number of national regimes which cloak themselves in the verbal trappings of radical Marxism and follow domestic policies influenced to one degree or another by Marxist concepts.

If, then, I was the author in 1947 of a "doctrine" of containment, it was a doctrine that lost much of its rationale with the death of Stalin and with the development of the Soviet-Chinese conflict. I emphatically deny the paternity of any efforts to invoke that doctrine today in situations to which it has, and can have, no proper relevance.

GEORGE F. KENNAN
Memoirs: 1925–1950

106
Harry Truman Fires Douglas MacArthur

By 1951, General Douglas MacArthur had been on duty in the Pacific without a single visit back to the United States since 1935. He was out of touch in many ways, but he could still command brilliant victories in the field of battle, as he had in orchestrating the surprise attack on Inchon in South Korea in 1950. In 1951, however, he began to issue policy statements in direct contradiction to those emanating from Washington. His views took an aggressive stance, suggesting an expansion of the Korean War in order to confront communist China. In response, President Harry Truman was compelled to relieve General MacArthur of command, as of April 9, 1951: to Truman, it had nothing to do with the issues of the moment, but everything to do with his obligation to uphold the Constitution and the power of the executive branch over the military. He was careful to garner support for the decision from military leaders, including General George Marshall (then secretary of defense) and General Omar Bradley, chairman of the Joint Chiefs of Staff. Nonetheless, it was Truman's decision and it was a lonely one: according to the polls, 69 percent of the populace sided with the general, while only 29 percent supported the president. Truman described the days leading up to the dismissal in the oral history, *Plain Speaking,* compiled by Merle Miller.

APRIL 6–9, 1951, WASHINGTON, D.C.—

General Marshall was concerned about the reaction of certain Congressmen, and he wanted to think over what he felt the reaction of the troops would be. And so at the end of the meeting I asked him, I said, "General, you go over there and you read all the correspondence that's passed between MacArthur and me for the last two years. Then be in my office at nine in the morning, and if you still feel I shouldn't fire him, I won't."

I knew the general very, very well; we'd been through a lot together, and I knew how his mind worked, and there wasn't a doubt in the world in my mind that when he saw what I'd put up with, that he'd agree with me.

And the next morning at eight fifteen when I got to my office, he was out there waiting for me, which was very unusual. General Marshall was usually a punctual man, but I had never known him to be ahead of time. He worked on a very tight schedule.

But that morning he looked up at me, and he says, "I spent most of the night on that file, Mr. President, and you should have fired the son of a bitch two years ago."

And so we went right ahead, and we did it. There were a good many details to be worked out. I asked General Bradley to be sure we had the full agreement of the Joint Chiefs of Staff, which he got; they were all unanimous in saying he should be fired. And we had to arrange to turn the command over to General Ridgway.

And then, of course, we wanted to be sure that MacArthur got the news through official channels. We didn't want it to get into the newspapers first. I signed all the papers and went over to Blair House to have dinner. Some of the others stayed behind at the White House to decide on exactly how to get the word to Frank Pace [secretary of the army, then in Korea]. Pace was supposed to notify the general.

While I was still at Blair House, Joe Short [press secretary] came in to where the others were, and he said he had heard that the *Chicago Tribune* had the whole story and was going to print it the next morning.

So General Bradley came over to Blair House and told me what was up, and he says if MacArthur hears he's going to be fired before he officially is fired, before he's notified, he'd probably up and resign on me.

And I told Bradley, "The son of a bitch isn't going to resign on me, I want him fired."

Harry S. Truman
Plain Speaking

107
Dean Acheson Battles McCarthyism

The years 1947 to 1953 were hectic ones for Dean Acheson, who was named secretary of state in 1949. Within that span, he helped to originate the Marshall Plan and to launch NATO, in addition to overseeing U.S. diplomacy surrounding the Korean War. Acheson was not a career diplomat, but a lawyer who had built a thriving practice in Washington. He possessed a strong personality, naturally commanding attention in most gatherings, along with a sly sense of humor that helped him withstand difficult times, especially during the ascendency of Joseph McCarthy. A misguided freshman senator from Wisconsin, McCarthy led the nation on a self-destructive communist hunt in the early 1950s. He commonly referred to Acheson as "the Red Dean," and accused him of working secretly for Moscow. As such attacks grew, Acheson was in the ironic—and extremely trying—position of combating communism tirelessly at a complex juncture in the Cold War, even while hearing exclamations at home that he was secretly a communist.

Senator McCarthy Merges the Themes

Joseph R. McCarthy, Republican, thirty-seven years old, was elected to the United States Senate from Wisconsin in the Republican upsurge of 1946. He was not heard from until he made his debut in Wheeling, West Virginia, on February 9, 1950, as a crusader against "Communists in government." From then until December 2, 1954, when he was "condemned" by the Senate for contempt of a subcommittee, abuse of its members, and insults to the Senate, he filled the newspapers of the nation and did incalculable harm to its governance. Then he disappeared from notice as rapidly as he had attained it and died in May 1957. When asked for a comment about him, I quoted the Latin maxim, *"De mortuis nil nisi bonum."* One could have said that his name, like those of Judge Lynch and Captain Boycott, had enlarged the vocabulary.

As I have mentioned earlier, Soviet attempts to penetrate American Government and other institutions through Communist agents had been known, discussed, and feared—sometimes to the point of hysteria—long before McCarthy appeared on the political scene. The situation in 1949 was similar to that following World War I. Our concern with it here is as a means of attack on the Administration, how McCarthy came to be the instrument of attack, and the extent to which the attack affected the conduct of our foreign policy.

McCarthy's Wheeling speech was not a brilliant maiden effort in the traditional parliamentary or senatorial style. It was the rambling, ill-prepared result of his slovenly, lazy, and undisciplined habits with which we were soon to become familiar. No copy of the speech existed and newspaper reports varied. It was not until February 20, having created an interest in generalized charges of disloyalty against unnamed State Department employees, that he read in the Senate what he said was a recording of the earlier speech. In it and other speeches and interviews he charged that he had the names and records of eighty-one persons with Communist leanings who were or had been in the Department; that the President's Loyalty Board had certified to me as disloyal some two hundred employees, of whom I had discharged eighty; that there were presently fifty-seven card-carrying Communists in the Department. Interspersed with these were charges against me, Assistant Secretary of State John E. Peurifoy (in charge of administration), and the Department's Security and Loyalty Board. All of these precipitated such an uproarious exchange of denials, countercharges, speeches, and further denial that on February 20 the Committee on Foreign Relations, by direction of the Senate, set up a subcommittee under the chairmanship of Senator Millard Tydings of Maryland to investigate McCarthy's charges. The Tydings committee began its hearings on March 8. On that day I opened my press conference in this way:

With all these charges flying around I want to tell you about the meeting which was being broken up by communists so that the chairman had to send for the police. When they entered the hall they started wielding their clubs pretty vigorously. The unfortunate chairman got a crack over the head and, when he protested, the cop shouted, "You're under arrest!"

"I can't be," pleaded the chairman, "I'm an anti-communist."

"I don't give a damn," hollered the cop, "whether you're a communist, or an anti-communist, or what kind of a communist you are. You're under arrest!"

At the same press conference I was asked:

Q: Are you aware, Mr. Secretary, that Senator McCarthy saw fit to inject Mrs. Acheson's name into the proceedings?

A: I understand that he made that contribution to the gaiety of the situation.

Q: Do you have anything to say in that particular situation?

A: Well, like any husband who finds his wife injected into a controversy the first thing is to go to headquarters and find out about it. So I telephoned my wife and said, "What's this you've been up to?" And she hadn't the faintest conception nor had she ever heard of the organization which Senator McCarthy accused her of belonging to. It was something like the Women's National Congress or something of that sort. So we looked up this organization and found that it was a merger of many others, among them one called the Washington League of Women Shoppers. That rang a bell. She said that ten years or so ago she had paid two dollars (she thinks, perhaps, she paid two dollars twice which she regards as rather extravagant under the circumstances) and she was given a list of stores in Washington classified as fair or unfair to their employees. That was the extent of her recollection of the matter.

I told her that it was charged that she was a sponsor of it. She said that was interesting and asked who were the other sponsors. So I read them to her and she said that sounded rather like the Social Register and she thought her position was going up, but she couldn't recall whether she had been a sponsor or not. I think that is the extent of the information I got from her over the telephone before coming down here.

The subcommittee furnished McCarthy with a platform, loudspeaker, and full press coverage for his campaign of vilification. He made a shambles of the hearings. Far quicker than Tydings, who was a man of character but unfortunately had a short temper and a pompous manner, McCarthy maneuvered the chairman into insisting on open and public hearings and bringing out the names of alleged Communists, thus providing a feast of privileged slander. More important, however, in the course of the hearings McCarthy stumbled on the combination of themes that made him a welcome tool for the conservative Taft-led Republicans. As already pointed out, five years earlier General Patrick Hurley had charged that conspiracy in the State Department had frustrated his efforts in China. Two years after that Congressman Walter Judd had voiced the same suspicions. McCarthy now took this line. China had been lost through the machination of Soviet sympathizers and agents in the State Department. In this category he placed John Carter Vincent, John Service, Philip C. Jessup, and Dr. Owen Lattimore of the Johns Hopkins University. The last named, he charged, was "the architect of our Far Eastern policy," though Dr. Lattimore had never been connected with the Department and I did not know him.

Taft Supports McCarthy

Senator Taft, who had first regarded McCarthy as reckless, now decided to give him Republican backing and help. McCarthy, he was quoted as saying, "should keep talking and if one case doesn't work out, he should proceed with another." Senator Knowland opened up with a series of speeches during the spring linking Lattimore's views—apparently on the theory that he was an adviser of mine—with current Communist pronouncements. At the end of March, Senator Bridges announced that a group of Republicans would "go after" me in public attacks, which he inaugurated on March 27; and my old enemy, Senator Kenneth Wherry, the Nebraska undertaker, declared that I "must go" as a "bad security risk." Taft, again returning to the battle, attacked "the pro-Communist group in the State Department who surrendered to every demand of Russia at Yalta and Potsdam, and promoted at every opportunity the Communist cause in China." As William S. White, Taft's biographer, put it in discussing this "sad, worst period" in his life: "All this—the debacle of 1948 and the Eastern challenge to him again in early 1949—stirred him in most unfortunate ways. It seemed even to some of his friends and admirers that he began, if unconsciously, to adopt the notion that almost *any* way to defeat or discredit the Truman plans was acceptable. There was, in the intellectual sense, a blood-in-the-nostrils approach, and no mistake about it."

For two or three weeks after the June 25 attack on South Korea the attack of the primitives quieted down, only to burst into full fury again on July 20, when the Tydings subcommittee filed its reports. (Its membership, besides the chairman, was Brien McMahon of Connecticut and Theodore Francis Green of Rhode Island, Democrats, and Henry Cabot Lodge, Jr., of Massachusetts and Bourke B. Hickenlooper of Iowa, Republicans.) All agreed that the charges had not been substantiated. The majority report criticized McCarthy bitterly as having tried to "inflame the American people with a wave of hysteria and fear on an unbelievable scale in this free nation" and added that "fraught with falsehood from beginning to end, its reprehensible and contemptible character defies adequate condemnation." After a wild fight on the floor, the Senate adopted the report by a strictly party vote of 45 to 37. For a long time the only other articulate support in the Congress for decency came from Maine's Republican Senator, Margaret Chase Smith, and the honorable half dozen who joined her in her "Declaration of Conscience" on June 2, 1950. She criticized her own party for allowing the Senate to have been "too often . . . debased to the level of a forum of hate and character assassination sheltered by the shield of congressional immunity." The statement continued: "The nation sorely needs a Republican victory. But I do not want to see the Republican Party ride to political victory on the Four Horsemen of Calumny—fear, ignorance, bigotry and smear."

On August 7 Wherry demanded my dismissal; on the fourteenth, my resignation; and on the sixteenth he declared that "the blood of our boys in Korea is on [Acheson's] shoulders, and no one else." On the thirteenth, four of the five Republican members of the Foreign Relations Committee, followed by Senator Taft, accused President Truman and me of having invited the attack on Korea. The nadir of this shameful performance came in September during consideration of a bill to permit President Truman to appoint General Marshall, while still remaining a five-star general, as Secretary of Defense to succeed Louis Johnson, who had resigned. Senator William E. Jenner, Republican of Indiana, said of the man who, in the words of President Conant of Harvard, brooked only one comparison in our nation's history:

> *General Marshall is not only willing, he is eager to play the role of a front man, for traitors.*
> *The truth is this is no new role for him, for Gen. George C. Marshall is a living lie. . . .*
> *. . . [As a result,] this Government of ours [has been turned] into a military dictatorship, run by Communist-appeasing, Communist-protecting betrayer of America, Secretary of State Dean Acheson. . . .*
> *Unless he, himself [General Marshall], were desperate, he could not possibly agree to continue as an errand boy, a front man, a stooge, or a co-conspirator for this administration's crazy assortment of collectivist cutthroat crackpots and Communist fellow-traveling appeasers. . . .*
> *. . . How can the Senate confirm the appointment of General Marshall, and thus turn Dean Acheson into a Siamese twin, in control of two of the most important Cabinet posts in the executive branch of the Government? That is what we are asked to do.*
> *It is tragic, Mr. President, that General Marshall is not enough of a patriot to tell the American people the truth of what has happened, and the terrifying story of what lies in store for us, instead of joining bands once more with this criminal crowd of traitors and Communist appeasers who, under the continuing influence and direction of Mr. Truman and Mr. Acheson, are still selling America down the river.*

Immediately, an honorable gentleman from Massachusetts, Senator Saltonstall, followed by Senator Lucas, rose to rebuke such words as being as contemptible as any ever uttered in that place of easy standards.

The Attack Reaches Its Climax

The height of the attack on me came in December. On the fifteenth the President proclaimed a national emergency arising out of the war in Korea; on the seventeenth I left Washington for Brussels to attend the North Atlantic Treaty Council meeting, which was to create the integrated force and the united command and appoint General Eisenhower as Supreme Commander

Allied Forces Europe. As I left, the Republicans in the House and Senate caucused and asked President Truman to remove me from office. At this he blew up in typical fashion:

There have been new attacks within the past week against Secretary of State Acheson. I have been asked to remove him from office. The authors of this suggestion claim that this would be good for the country.

How our position in the world would be improved by the retirement of Dean Acheson from public life is beyond me. Mr. Acheson has helped shape and carry out our policy of resistance to communist imperialism. From the time of our sharing of arms with Greece and Turkey nearly four years ago, and coming down to the recent moment when he advised me to resist the Communist invasion of South Korea, no official in our government has been more alive to Communism's threat to freedom or more forceful in resisting it.

At this moment, he is in Brussels representing the United States in setting up mutual defenses against aggression. This has made it possible for me to designate General Eisenhower as Supreme Allied Commander in Europe.

If Communism were to prevail in the world today—as it shall not prevail— Dean Acheson would be one of the first, if not the first, to be shot by the enemies of liberty and Christianity. . . .

It is the same sort of thing that happened to Seward. President Lincoln was asked by a group of Republicans to dismiss Secretary of State Seward. He refused. So do I refuse to dismiss Secretary Acheson.

The foregoing summary of 1950's shameful and nihilistic orgy exaggerates its effect upon us. Our minds were occupied with great problems and our time with equally great efforts to meet them, with which subsequent chapters will deal. The fight with the footpads brought its own zest and evoked some generous responses from political opponents. Humor and "contempt for the contemptible," in Douglas Freeman's phrase, proved, as always, a shield and buckler against "the fiery darts of the wicked." At one of my press conferences at the height of the mid-1950 attacks on me, I replied to a question about how they affected me with the story of the poor fellow found on the prairie during the days of Indian fighting in the West and brought into a fort hospital. He was in bad shape, scalped, wounded with an arrow sticking into his back, and left for dead. As the surgeon prepared to extract the arrow, he asked, "Does it hurt very much?"

To which the wounded man gasped out, "Only when I laugh."

One of the pleasanter memories of this period concerns my extemporaneous remarks made at the end of a speech to the American Society of Newspaper Editors on April 22, 1950, which led the late Joseph Pulitzer to utter a rebel yell and shout, "Pour it on 'em, Mr. Secretary!" Some of these gentlemen, I said, reminded me of Mr. Gladstone's explanation of his efforts to reform the unfortunate "fallen women" who accosted him and of counsel's esthetic defense of pornographic art and literature. It was not the activity, but the sprinkling of holy water that one found tiresome.

In a few concluding minutes I tried to make my audience think of the Foreign Service and the State Department not as stereotypes but as people giving their whole lives to the United States, competent, courageous, devoted. Only the last week, I said, two of our missions had been bombed—bombs had been tossed in the window and had exploded. No one, fortunately, had been killed, but a lot of people had been hurt. Had any of my audience ever experienced this sort of thing? Would they stick to a job where it was an occupational hazard? It was quite likely that some of these men and women would be killed. But there was no squeak out of them. We had an officer just back from Asia who had been held prisoner by the Chinese for a year, jailed, tortured. He had applied again for foreign duty.

Scores of people, I continued, were serving in areas of hot war where bombs were dropping and bullets were flying, and others were serving where dangers to health were as great as bullets, doctors few, and mothers were nurses as well as schoolteachers. They knew their duty and did it. Some were behind the Iron Curtain, where they were treated as criminals and denied all association with the people of the countries.

Why, I asked, did the editors not try the experiment of writing an open letter in their papers to these Foreign Service officers, our first line of defense in dangerous and difficult parts of the world. explaining to them the attacks being made upon them and upon the service of which they were as proud as these editors were of their profession? "Explain that to them if you can. You will find it difficult to do."

It was not strange that efforts should be made to penetrate the Department, I continued. They had been made throughout its history. There was a right way and a wrong way to solve that problem. The right way met the evil and preserved the institution; the wrong way did not meet the evil and destroyed the institution. More than that, it destroyed the faith of the country in its Government, and of our allies in us. I explained to the editors what we were doing to protect the Department; it did not include irresponsible character assassination. What had been going on reminded me of a recent horrible episode in Camden, New Jersey. A madman had appeared on the street and begun shooting people whom he met—a woman coming out of a store, a couple in a car stopped by a traffic light, another passing motorist—no plan, no purpose. It recalled the whimsical, mad brutality of Browning's Caliban, comparing his god, Setebos, to himself watching a procession of crabs on the sand. He lets twenty go by, picks up the twenty-first, tears off a flipper and throws it down. Three more go by, a fourth he crushes with his heel to watch it wriggle.

• • •

I don't ask you for sympathy. I don't ask you for help. You are in a worse situation than I am. I and my associates are only the intended victims of this mad and vicious operation. But you, unhappily, you by reason of your calling, are participants. You are unwilling participants, disgusted participants, but, nevertheless participants, and your position is far more serious than mine.

As I leave this filthy business, and I hope never to speak of it again, I should like to leave in your minds the words of John Donne . . .

> *Any man's death diminishes me, because I am involved in mankind.*
> *And, therefore, never send to know for whom the bell tolls;*
> *It tolls for thee.*

As I sat down, it was with a hope that here and there among those rows of white, and possibly stuffed, shirt-fronts a conscience pricked.

A Few Bright Spots

Another episode I remember with gratitude and pleasure occurred at the Governors' Conference at White Sulphur Springs on June 20, 1950. I had gone there at the governors' invitation to discuss with them the State Department and the charges being made against it. This was five days before the attack from the north on Korea. Standing for four hours before them, for the most part answering a barrage of questions, I had begun to think that I had no friends—for enemies are more articulate than friends—when two men began to intervene on my behalf. They objected to loaded questions, getting them rephrased; protested against sneers and insults stated as questions, insisting that the chairman rule them out of order: and corrected misstatements of fact embedded in long-winded questions. These two governors had been the Republican candidates for President and Vice President of the United States in the election of 1948—Thomas E. Dewey of New York and Earl Warren of California. Tom Dewey and I had been friends for a good many years; I had never before had the pleasure of meeting Governor Warren. As both of these gentlemen could wield a shillelagh right lustily, my assailants grew more cautious and began to lose zest for the fray. When it ended in time for lunch, the two governors carried me off for a reviving drink and then to lunch with them in the center of the dining room, where everyone, they said, including the press, could see us and draw the obvious conclusion. My gratitude to and affection for these two great gentlemen has never wavered throughout what is now nearly twenty years.

The last episode occurred in December 1950. While his colleagues were caucusing to ask the President to remove me from office, my friend Congressman James Fulton, Republican of Pennsylvania, came to the airport with other friends, including the President, to see me off to Brussels. He brought me two presents: a pair of cuff links to help me keep my shirt on if foreigners started treating me as my fellow countrymen did, and a beautifully printed and bound edition of the Koran. Since my enemies had not taken kindly to a certain reference to Christian principles, I might find the same ideas expressed more acceptably in the Koran.

Two other acts of public support touched me in those days of harsh attack. In the early summer Harvard University conferred on me the honorary degree of Doctor of Laws. I found it an intimidating experience to appear and speak from the same platform on the same occasion upon which my illustrious predecessor three years before had made his memorable speech proposing the Marshall Plan. In the autumn of the same year Freedom House in New York gave me its award for 1950. "This evening," I said, "spent with friends who have come together to do me honor and give me heart, is a cool spring to a thirsty wayfarer."

I met McCarthy only once, when leaving the Senate office building, after one of the hearings on the removal of General MacArthur, accompanied by my guard and a pack of reporters and photographers. As we approached the elevators, the guard, a pleasant but stupid former football player, ran ahead to hold the elevator for me. As I entered, a man was already there. "Hello, Mr. Secretary," he said, and stuck out his hand. Instinctively I took it, simultaneously recognizing his much-cartooned, black-jowled face. Flashbulbs exploded as the doors slid shut. Neither of us spoke during our few seconds' ride. "What happened in the elevator?" the press asked him. "Neither of us," he replied, "turned his back on the other." It was a smart trick and, of course, got him on front pages across the country.

Concluding Thoughts

A good deal of nonsense has been written about the effect of the attack of the primitives, before and during McCarthy's reign, on the China policy of the Truman Administration. Whatever effect it had on our successors, it had little on us. The fact was that, caught between the bungling incompetence of Chiang Kai-shek's Kuomintang and the intransigence of Mao Tse-tung's Communists, our choices for policy decisions were small indeed. The Chinese clearly found the United States far more useful as an enemy than in any other relationship, and went out of their way to insure that an enemy we remained. Those who tried to establish diplomatic and friendly relations with Peking found it a useless formality. The most deluded of them all, Nehru's India, received a military attack for her pains. Our European friends found their missions contemptuously isolated and neglected.

Relations with Formosa underwent a change on June 25, 1950, with the attack on Korea. Then the President announced a policy intended to seal off Formosa from the conflict. He interposed the Seventh Fleet to prevent any attack from either Chinese side upon the other, the purpose being to quarantine the fighting within Korea, not to encourage its extension. When General

MacArthur toyed with undercutting this policy by suggesting, as some Republican senators had, using Chiang's refugee army in the Korean fighting, he was sharply rapped over the knuckles. Koreans were being trained and armed to defend their own country.

McCarthy's name has been given, as I have said, to a phenomenon broader than his own participation in it, the hysteria growing out of fear of Communist subversion that followed both world wars. His influence was purely domestic as gauleiter and leader of the mob in the last, mad massacre. The result was deplorable. The Government's foreign and civil services, universities, and China-studies programs in them took a decade to recover from this sadistic pogrom; congressional assaults on the executive branch under the leadership of McCarran and Bridges approximated those in 1919 to 1922 under Attorney General A. Mitchell Palmer. The slaughter occurred in the night of the long knives from 1950 through 1953.

McCarthy was often and erroneously compared to Hitler, but he lacked the ambition, the toughness, the demonic drive to become a villain on a grand scale. He read Hitler. My wife insisted that this must be so because of his methods; I doubted. One evening sitting beside President Nathan M. Pusey of Harvard, who had lived in Appleton, Wisconsin, when McCarthy lived there, she put the question to him. He confirmed her views, telling her that fellow boarders in the boardinghouse McCarthy lived in and patrons of the same barber shop he used had reported that McCarthy would produce *Mein Kampf* and read from it, chuckling and saying, "That's the way to do it." But he was essentially a lazy, small-town bully, without sustaining purpose, who on his own would soon have petered out. Flattered, built up and sustained by Taft, the Republican right, and their accomplice, the press, printing what was not news and not fit to print, he served their various purposes. After the election of 1952 they no longer had any use for him, but, encouraged by the fear of the timorous in high places, he was not shrewd enough to see that his day was over. For a year his own momentum carried him on. He became a nuisance; those who had used him dropped him. Finally a peppery little man from Vermont, Senator Ralph Flanders, tired of the antics of this boor in a supposed gentlemen's club, called upon the members to censure him for—of all things!—being rude in the clubhouse. This they did by just over a two-thirds majority. The very contemptuousness of his rejection broke him.

For my fifty-eighth birthday some of my friends with curious prescience had engraved, adding my name and the date April 11, 1951, an extract from a letter written by Thomas Jefferson to Judge James Sullivan on May 21, 1805. I say "curious prescience" because on that April 11 General Douglas MacArthur was relieved by President Truman of all his commands and a new torrent of abuse broke over the President and myself, chosen as chief villain by the Republican right. Mr. Jefferson had written:

You have indeed received the federal unction of lying and slandering. But who has not? Who will ever come again into eminent office, unanointed by this chrism? It seems to be fixed that falsehood and calumny are to be their ordinary engines of opposition: engines which will not be entirely without effect. The circle of characters equal to the first stations is not too large, and will be lessened by the voluntary retreat of those whose sensibilities are stronger than their confidence in the justice of public opinion. . . . Yet this effect of sensibility must not be yielded to. If we suffer ourselves to be frightened from our post by mere lying, surely the enemy will use that weapon: for what one so cheap to those of whose system of politics morality makes no part.

DEAN ACHESON
Present at the Creation

108

Rosa Parks Gets Arrested in Montgomery

Rosa Parks made history when she was arrested in Montgomery, Alabama, on December 1, 1955, for refusing to give up her seat on the Cleveland Avenue bus to a white man, touching off a 381-day boycott led by Dr. Martin Luther King Jr. In her autobiography, *My Story,* Parks recounts how she was "fed up" with being treated "less than a free person" due to Jim Crow segregation laws. While serving as NAACP secretary in the 1940s she tried three times to register to vote and was turned away each time. Her education in nonviolent resistance reached a new level during the summer of 1955 when she attended a workshop run by radical Myles Horton at the Highlander Fold School in Monteagle, Tennessee. "The school offered workshops to train future leaders so they could go back home and work for change using what they had learned at school," Parks explained. The stage was set for what is perhaps the most famous act of civil disobedience in American history, which, among other efforts, brought King, the minister of Montgomery's Dexter Baptist Church, to national prominence.

I don't think any segregation law angered black people in Montgomery more than bus segregation. And that had been so since the laws about segregation on public transportation had been passed. That was back in 1900, and black people had boycotted Montgomery streetcars until the City Council changed its ordinance so that nobody would be forced to give up a seat unless there was another seat to move to. But over the years practices had changed, although the law had not. When I was put off the bus back in 1943, the bus driver was really acting against the law. In 1945, two years after that incident, the State of Alabama passed a law requiring that all bus companies under its jurisdiction enforce segregation. But that law did not spell out what bus drivers were supposed to do in a case like mine.

Here it was, half a century after the first segregation law, and there were 50,000 African Americans in Montgomery. More of us rode the buses than Caucasians did, because more whites could afford cars. It was very humiliating having to suffer the indignity of riding segregated buses twice a day, five days a week, to go downtown and work for white people.

There were incidents all the time. Mrs. Durr says that I would tell her about them time and time again. Mr. Nixon used to try to negotiate some small changes. I know Mr. Nixon said that at some point he went to the bus company about black people having to pay at the front door and then go around to the back door to enter. They told him, "Your folks started it. They do it because they want to."

Another time he went to see about extending the route of the Day Street bus. Black people in a little community on the other side of the Day Street Bridge had to walk across the bridge, about half a mile, to get to the bus. Mr. Nixon went down to the bus company to protest. He was always going down to the bus company to protest; sometimes he went by himself, sometimes he took someone with him. He himself did not ride the buses—he had his own car; but he was acting on behalf of the community. The bus company told him that as long as the people were willing to walk the half mile and then pay to ride the rest of the way downtown, they had no need to extend the bus line.

Jo Ann Robinson was an English professor at Alabama State College. Back in 1946 she had helped found the Women's Political Council. Over the years she'd had her share of run-ins with bus drivers, but at first she couldn't get the other women in the Council to get indignant. She was from Cleveland, Ohio, and most of them were natives of Montgomery. When she complained about the rudeness of the bus drivers, they said that was a fact of life in Montgomery. She had often brought protests to the bus company on behalf of the Women's Political Council. Finally she managed to get the company to agree that the buses would stop at every corner in black neighborhoods, just as they did in the white neighborhoods. But this was a very small victory.

What galled her, and many more of us, was that blacks were over sixty-six percent of the riders. It was unfair to segregate us. But neither the bus company nor the mayor nor the city commissioners would listen. I remember having discussions about how a boycott of the city buses would really hurt the bus company in its pocketbook. But I also remember asking a few people if they would be willing to stay off the buses to make things better for us, and them saying that they had too far to go to work. So it didn't seem as if there would be much support for a boycott. The Montgomery NAACP was beginning to think about filing suit against the city of Montgomery over bus segregation. But they had to have the right plaintiff and a strong case. The best plaintiff would be a woman, because a woman would get more sympathy than a man. And the woman would have to be above reproach, have a good reputation, and have done nothing wrong but refuse to give up her seat.

Back in the spring of 1955 a teenage girl named Claudette Colvin and an elderly woman refused to give up their seats in the middle section of a bus to white people. When the driver went to get the police, the elderly woman got off the bus, but Claudette refused to leave, saying she had already paid her dime and had no reason to move. When the police came, they dragged her from the bus and arrested her. Now, her name was familiar to me, and it turned out that Claudette Colvin was the great-granddaughter of Mr. Gus Vaughn, the unmixed black man with all the children back in Pine Level who refused to work for the white man. His great-granddaughter must have inherited his sense of pride. I took a particular interest in the girl and her case.

After Claudette's arrest, a group of activists took a petition to the bus company officials and city officials. The petition asked for more courteous treatment and for no visible signs of segregation. They didn't ask for the end of the segregation, just for an understanding that whites would start sitting at the front of the bus and blacks would start sitting at the back, and wherever they met would be the dividing line. I think that petition also asked that black bus drivers be hired. The city officials and the bus company took months to answer that petition, and when they did, every request in it was turned down.

I did not go down with the others to present that petition to the bus company and the city officials, because I didn't feel anything could be accomplished. I had decided that I would not go anywhere with a piece of paper in my hand asking white folks for any favors. I had made that decision myself, as an individual.

I did meet with Claudette, along with Mr. Nixon and Jo Ann Robinson, and talked about taking her case to the federal courts. Claudette was willing, and we started making plans to raise money for her defense by having her speak in various parts of town. Everything was going along fine until Mr. Nixon discovered that Claudette was pregnant. She wasn't married, and so that was the end of that case. If the white press got hold of that information, they would have a field day. They'd call her a bad girl, and her case wouldn't have a chance. So the decision was made to wait until we had a plaintiff who was more upstanding before we went ahead and invested any more time and effort and money.

Another bus incident involving a woman occurred that summer. I didn't know much about the girl. Her name was Louise Smith, and she was about eighteen years old. They say she paid her fine and didn't protest. Hers certainly wasn't a good case for Mr. Nixon to appeal to a higher court.

I knew they needed a plaintiff who was beyond reproach, because I was in on the discussions about the possible court cases. But that is not why I refused to give up my bus seat to a white man on Thursday, December 1, 1955. I did not intend to get arrested. If I had been paying attention, I wouldn't even have gotten on that bus.

I was very busy at that particular time. I was getting an NAACP workshop together for the 3rd and 4th of December, and I was trying to get the consent of Mr. H. Council Trenholm at Alabama State to have the Saturday meeting at the college. He did give permission, but I had a hard time getting to him to get permission to use the building. I was also getting the notices in the mail for the election of officers of the Senior Branch of the NAACP, which would be the next week.

When I got off from work that evening of December 1, I went to Court Square as usual to catch the Cleveland Avenue bus home. I didn't look to see who was driving when I got on, and by the time I recognized him, I had already paid my fare. It was the same driver who had put me off the bus back in 1943, twelve years earlier. He was still tall and heavy, with red, rough-looking skin. And he was still mean-looking. I didn't know if he had been on that route before—they switched the drivers around sometimes. I do know that most of the time if I saw him on a bus, I wouldn't get on it.

I saw a vacant seat in the middle section of the bus and took it. I didn't even question why there was a vacant seat even though there were quite a few people standing in the back. If I had thought about it at all, I would probably have figured maybe someone saw me get on and did not take the seat but left it vacant for me. There was a man sitting next to the window and two women across the aisle.

The next stop was the Empire Theater, and some whites got on. They filled up the white seats, and one man was left standing. The driver looked back and noticed the man standing. Then he looked back at us. He said, "Let me have those front seats," because they were the front seats of the black section. Didn't anybody move. We just sat right where we were, the four of us. Then he spoke a second time: "Y'all better make it light on yourselves and let me have those seats."

The man in the window seat next to me stood up, and I moved to let him pass by me, and then I looked across the aisle and saw that the two women were also standing. I moved over to the window seat. I could not see how standing up was going to "make it light" for me. The more we gave in and complied, the worse they treated us.

I thought back to the time when I used to sit up all night and didn't sleep, and my grandfather would have his gun right by the fireplace, or if he had his one-horse wagon going anywhere, he always had his gun in the back of the wagon. People always say that I didn't give up my seat because I was tired, but that isn't true. I was not tired physically, or no more tired than I usually was at the end of a working day. I was not old, although some people have an image of me as being old then. I was forty-two. No, the only tired I was, was tired of giving in.

The driver of the bus saw me still sitting there, and he asked was I going to stand up. I said, "No." He said, "Well, I'm going to have you arrested." Then I said, "You may do that." These were the only words we said to each other. I didn't even know his name, which was James Blake, until we were in court together. He got out of the bus and stayed outside for a few minutes, waiting for the police.

As I sat there, I tried not to think about what might happen. I knew that anything was possible. I could be manhandled or beaten. I could be arrested. People have asked me if it occurred to me then that I could be the test case the NAACP had been looking for. I did not think about that at all. In fact if I had let myself think too deeply about what might happen to me, I might have gotten off the bus. But I chose to remain.

Meanwhile there were people getting off the bus and asking for transfers, so that began to loosen up the crowd, especially in the back of the bus. Not every one got off, but everybody was very quiet. What conversation there was, was in low tones; no one was talking out loud. It would have been quite interesting to have seen the whole bus empty out. Or if the other three had stayed where they were, because if they'd had to arrest four of us instead of one, then that would have given me a little support. But it didn't matter. I never thought hard of them at all and never even bothered to criticize them.

Eventually two policemen came. They got on the bus, and one of them asked me why I didn't stand up. I asked him, "Why do you all push us around?" He said to me, and I quote him exactly, "I don't know, but the law is the law and you're under arrest." One policeman picked up my purse, and the second one picked up my shopping bag and escorted me to the squad car. In the squad car they returned my personal belongings to me. They did not put their hands on me or force me into the car. After I was seated in the car, they went back to the driver and asked him if he wanted to swear out a warrant. He answered that he would finish his route and then come straight back to swear out the warrant. I was only in custody, not legally arrested, until the warrant was signed.

As they were driving me to the city desk, at City Hall, near Court Street, one of them asked me again, "Why didn't you stand up when the driver spoke to you?" I did not answer. I remained silent all the way to City Hall.

As we entered the building, I asked if I could have a drink of water, because my throat was real dry. There was a fountain, and I was standing right next to it. One of the policemen said yes, but by the time I bent down to drink, another policeman said, "No, you can't drink no water. You have to wait until you get to the jail." So I was denied the chance to drink a sip of water. I was not going to do anything but wet my throat. I wasn't going to drink a whole lot of water, even though I was quite thirsty. That made me angry, but I did not respond.

At the city desk they filled out the necessary forms as I answered questions such as what my name was and where I lived. I asked if I could make a telephone call and they said, "No." Since that was my first arrest, I didn't know if that was more discrimination because I was black or if it was standard practice. But it seemed to me to be more discrimination. Then they escorted me back to the squad car, and we went to the city jail on North Ripley Street.

I wasn't frightened at the jail. I was more resigned than anything else. I don't recall being real angry, not enough to have an argument. I was just prepared to accept whatever I had to face. I asked again if I could make a telephone call. I was ignored.

They told me to put my purse on the counter and to empty my pockets of personal items. The only thing I had in my pocket was a tissue. I took that out. They didn't search me or handcuff me.

I was then taken to an area where I was fingerprinted and where mug shots were taken. A white matron came to escort me to my jail cell, and I asked again if I might use the telephone. She told me that she would find out.

She took me up a flight of stairs (the cells were on the second level), through a door covered with iron mesh, and along a dimly lighted corridor. She placed me in an empty dark cell and slammed the door closed. She walked a few steps away, but then she turned around and came back. She said, "There are two girls around the other side, and if you want to go over there with them instead of being in a cell by yourself, I will take you over there." I told her that it didn't matter, but she said, "Let's go around there, and then you won't have to be in a cell alone." It was her way of being nice. It didn't make me feel any better.

As we walked to the other cell, I asked her again, "May I use the telephone?" She answered that she would check.

There were two black women in the cell that the matron took me to, as she had said. One of them spoke to me and the other didn't. One just acted as if I wasn't there. The one who spoke to me asked me what had happened to me. I told her that I was arrested on the bus.

She said, "Some of those bus drivers sure are mean. You married?"

I said, "Yes," and she said, "Your husband ain't going to let you stay in here."

She wanted to know if there was anything she could do, and I said, "If you have a cup, I could drink a little water." She had a dark metal mug hanging above the toilet, and she caught a little water from the tap, and I took two swallows of that. She then started telling me about her problems. I became interested in her story and wondered how I could assist her.

She said she had been there for fifty-five or fifty-seven days and that she was a widow, her husband had died. She'd been keeping company with another man, and he'd got angry with her and struck her. She took a hatchet and went after him, and he had her arrested.

She said she had two brothers, but she had not been able to get in touch with them. Meanwhile, after she'd been in jail for a certain length of time, the man had kind of healed up and he wanted to get her out of jail, but only providing that she would keep on going with him. But she didn't want any more to do with him. So she was in jail without any way of getting in touch with anybody who could get her out.

She had a pencil but no paper, and I didn't have any either, because they had taken my purse. By the time she got through telling me about what was going on, the matron returned and told me to come out of the cell. I did not know where I was going until we reached the telephone booth. She gave me a card and told me to write down who I was calling and the telephone number. She placed a dime in the slot, dialed the number, and stayed close by to hear what I was saying.

I called home. My husband and mother were both there. She answered the telephone. I said, "I'm in jail. See if Parks will come down here and get me out."

She wanted to know, "Did they beat you?"

I said, "No, I wasn't beaten, but I am in jail."

She handed him the telephone, and I said, "Parks, will you come get me out of jail?"

He said, "I'll be there in a few minutes." He didn't have a car, so I knew it would be longer. But while we were still on the phone, a friend came by in his car. He'd heard about my being in jail and had driven to our place on Cleveland Court to see if he could help. He said he'd drive Parks to the jail.

The matron then took me back to the cell.

As Parks' friend had indicated, the word was already out about my arrest. Mr. Nixon had been notified by his wife, who was told by a neighbor, Bertha Butler, who had seen me escorted off the bus. Mr. Nixon called the jail to find out what the charge was, but they wouldn't tell him. Then he had tried to reach Fred Gray, one of the two black lawyers in Montgomery, but he wasn't home. So finally Mr. Nixon called Clifford Durr, the white lawyer who was Mrs. Virginia Durr's husband. Mr. Durr called the jail and found out that I'd been arrested under the segregation laws. He also found out what the bail was.

Meanwhile Parks had called a white man he knew who could raise the bail. His friend took him over to the man's house to pick him up. I don't remember how much the bail was.

When I got back to the cell, the woman had found some little crumpled-up paper, and she wrote both of her brothers' names and telephone numbers on it. She said to call them early in the morning because they went to work around six A.M. I told her I would.

Just then the matron came to let me know that I was being released, and the woman hadn't given me the piece of paper. They were rushing me out, and she was right behind me. She knew she would not get through the iron-mesh door at the end of the stairs, so she threw it down the stairs and it landed right in front of me. I picked it up and put it in my pocket.

Mrs. Durr was the first person I saw as I came through the iron mesh door with matrons on either side of me. There were tears in her eyes, and she seemed shaken, probably wondering what they had done to me. As soon as they released me, she put her arms around me, and hugged and kissed me as if we were sisters.

I was real glad to see Mr. Nixon and Attorney Durr too. We went to the desk, where I picked up my personal belongings and was given a trial date. Mr. Nixon asked that the date be the following Monday, December 5, 1955, explaining that he was a Pullman porter and would be out of Montgomery until then. We left without very much conversation, but it was an emotional moment. I didn't realize how much being in jail had upset me until I got out.

As we were going down the stairs, Parks and his friends were driving up, so I got in the car with them, and Mr. Nixon followed us home.

By the time I got home, it was about nine-thirty or ten at night. My mother was glad to have me home and wanted to know what she could do to make me comfortable. I told her I was hungry (for some reason I had missed lunch that day), and she prepared some food for me. Mrs. Durr and my friend Bertha Butler were there, and they helped my mother. I was thinking about having to go to work the next day, but I knew I would not get to bed anytime soon.

Everyone was angry about what had happened to me and talking about how it should never happen again. I knew that I would never, never ride another segregated bus, even if I had to walk to work. But it still had not occurred to me that mine could be a test case against the segregated buses.

Then Mr. Nixon asked if I would be willing to make my case a test case against segregation. I told him I'd have to talk with my mother and husband. Parks was pretty angry. He thought it would be as difficult to get people to support me as a test case as it had been to develop a test case out of Claudette Colvin's experience. We discussed and debated the question for a while. In the end Parks and my mother supported the idea. They were against segregation and were willing to fight it. And I had worked on enough cases to know that a ruling could not be made without a plaintiff. So I agreed to be the plaintiff.

Rosa Parks: My Story

109
The Honky-Tonk Roots of Rock 'n' Roll

For some, it might be hard to define exactly when rock and roll started. As a musical form, it emerged somehow at the juncture of jazz, country, and rhythm & blues: a force starting to spread throughout the world by 1954. Rock and roll was uniquely able to match the postwar world's accelerating pace, accommodating and even requiring change in the form of rebellion. Rebellion was such a natural part of the music that the important question isn't when rock and roll was born in America, but when it was born within each individual who was to embrace it. Robert Palmer described his own early days as a rock and roll musician in the introduction to his book, *Rock and Roll: An Unruly History.* Working with musicians of different backgrounds, and playing for audiences of varied tastes, he came to see that rock and roll reached them all, somehow. As he makes clear, though, he didn't know he was a rebel . . . he just went where the music took him, "on the back roads of Central Arkansas, circa 1960."

The strip straddled the county line, outside town and outside the law. Few of the joints and dives strung out along the highway advertised their presence with more than a single dim beer sign, but every weekend the local Billy Bobs—long sideburns, slicked-back hair, pack of Camels rolled up in a T-shirt sleeve—and their bouffant babes flocked to cavernous dance halls like the Club 70 and smaller, darker holes like the Blue Room. So did fly-boys stationed at the nearby Jacksonville air force base, most of them Irish- and Italian-rooted inner-city kids from places like Philly and Detroit. Inevitably, a drunken flyer would make eyes at some local's girl, or worse yet, insult the Arkansas Razorbacks, the state's sainted football team. You'd hear glass bottles breaking, chairs would start to fly, and if you were in the band, you'd scurry back behind the stage to the storeroom where they kept the liquor. I read plenty of beer and whiskey labels those nights. If the cops were called, I'd have to remain in hiding until they left; I was underage, fifteen when I started lugging my saxophone out to the strip.

One night in the Blue Room, a sort of elongated shotgun shack in the middle of a field out behind the more commodious Club 70, a wild-eyed Billy Bob approached me during a band break. Peering at him through the smoke, in the minimal blue-tinged lighting that tended to give the joint's regulars a faintly embalmed look, I surmised that he was maximally wired. (The nearby Club 70's parking lot was a trucker's hangout and a widely known connection point for copping speed.) Sure enough, he pulled a pint of sour-mash bourbon and a handful of black beauties out of his jeans as he was sitting down at my table. I eyed him warily; in school, his kind usually meant trouble for kids like me. He downed the pills, chugged the pint in one long gulp, and chased it with a tall Budweiser. Then he asked to see my saxophone. Biceps bulging, veins kicking and throbbing at his temples, eyes glittery and wild, he was a formidable sight. I handed him the sax.

Billy Bob examined the beat-up old Army Band Selmer for a long time, trying to figure out where his fingers would go, how to hold the thing. Finally, he put it to his lips and blew a single, eloquent squawk. Then he handed the horn back and smiled. No words were exchanged; that joyous squawk, and the open, almost childlike, delight in his smile, said everything. Basically a suburban kid, a music freak and a loner, I now felt that I had penetrated some underground cult or secret society, one that somehow thrived in the shadows, out beyond the neat suburban plots and well-lit streets of familiar white-bread reality. Penetrated, but not like an anthropologist braving some primitive backwater. I had been accepted; whatever this new world signified, I was somehow a part of it.

Not long after that—I might have been sixteen—a rumpled old hillbilly approached the Blue Room's tinsel-decked bandstand, peered nervously over his shoulder, and muttered low, "Say, could you boys play me, oh, *any* old Hank Williams tune? It sure would sound good to a man on the run." We played "Your Cheating Heart," giving it all we had. The man broke into another of those unforgettable smiles, gulped a quick beer, and left. Half an hour later, the state troopers arrived. They ignored the almost entirely underage band and questioned everyone at the bar. A man had robbed a bank and they were hot on his trail; they felt sure he must have stopped here. Nope, swore the regulars, ain't seen nobody answering that description all night, not around here. Again, I felt I was *part of something*. I knew I'd never again be able to dismiss Hank's music, and country music in general, from the ironic distance of the suburban hipster manqué. Not when it was so real, and meant so much, for a "man on the run."

These run-ins between the law and the lawless didn't always end happily. When I was seventeen, I played a truly seedy upstairs joint called the South Main Businessmen's Club. Ninth Street, Little Rock's black entertainment strip in those days, was just around the corner, but the club's patrons were white. They were the kind of "businessmen" who wore T-shirts, tattoos, and ducktail haircuts. They were not always entirely happy to see me, the only white musician in a black band led by a middle-aged tenor saxophonist, Mose Reed.

Mose was my first real teacher. He had played bebop in Los Angeles in the wake of Charlie Parker's first mid-forties visit, and later played on r&b sessions for Memphis's Sun Records. When I met him, he was down on his luck, bitter that his teenage rhythm section "don't want to learn their chords, not even their triads." He'd praise my white guitarist friend Fred Tackett and me to the black junior-high-school students in his rhythm section, which added yet another dimension of racial tension to an already volatile situation. Then came the night I showed up early for a gig, sensed something profoundly wrong about the atmosphere in the club, and found myself leaving before I knew what I was doing. I'd paced halfway up the block in puzzlement when a fusillade of shots rang out behind me. The story was in the papers the next day: a table of bank robbers, a table of plainclothes agents, a shootout leaving several bystanders dead or injured. The club closed, Mose Reed disappeared; I never saw him again.

Risky as these scenes were, you wouldn't think they'd be amenable to *musical* risk taking and experimentation. But the way I remember it, the music in those joints did have a freedom about it, a sense of almost limitless possibilities. On the strip, we'd play Hank Williams back-to-back with John Lee Hooker. Every band had its special version of some little-known tune, whether originated by Bobby "Blue" Bland, Fats Waller, or the Valentinos. The top band on the circuit was Ronnie Hawkins's Hawks, later to find fame as Bob Dylan's backup group known only as the Band. The Hawks didn't have to play the latest hits; they had their own ingenious arrangements and were especially admired for their tough takes on the most intense black r&b of the day, from "Shout" to James Brown's "Please Please Please." The Hawks also had a reputation for pill popping, whoring, and brawling that was second to none. That's what made them heroes around the Club 70 (where they often played) and the Blue Room (where my bandmates and I assiduously copied their arrangements).

The Hawks weren't the only musicians on that scene who were going places. Fred Tackett, the school chum who'd taken lessons from black musicians along Ninth Street and took me out on my first gig when I was fifteen, went on to play guitar on hundreds of pop records, toured and recorded with Bob Dylan, and eventually joined Little Feat. That first gig with Tackett was also my first intimation of how freely inclusive this thing called "rock and roll" could be.

I'd been waiting for almost an hour, feigning sleep, when my mom glanced into my bedroom, didn't see my horn case under the pillow, and went on to bed herself. The '57 Chevy killed its motor, blinked its taillights, and coasted silently to a stop down the block. Fred and my drummer friend Killer Matthews, fellow outcasts from the high-school marching band, waited while

I quietly removed the screen from the bedroom window and slipped out. They had a can of Bud open for me and an Old Gold already lit. Killer, who was big and imposing-looking and as mild-mannered as they come, gunned the engine and headed out of town. We took a two-lane asphalt highway, turned onto a rutted local road with packed-dirt shoulders, and followed it through stands of oak and cypress and the occasional field of rice. "This is really the sticks," I noted as I popped open a second beer. "Just wait," said Fred. Killer turned onto a narrow dirt track. We seemed to be plunging into deep woods, but here and there I noticed cars, mostly old and dilapidated, parked in among the trees. The joint was at the end of the lane, a rambling, single-story frame house, built up above the soggy ground on cinder blocks. There was a Jax beer sign; the place had no name.

I'd gravitated to Fred and Killer because they seemed to be the only other kids in our (all-white) high school who bought Ray Charles and Charlie Parker records and subscribed to Cannonball Adderly's dictum (on *The Cannonball Adderly Quintet Live in San Francisco*) that "hipness isn't a state of mind, it's a fact of life." We often went to r&b package shows, where we were usually the only whites in attendance, and we'd organized a jazz band among our schoolmates. Fred and Killer played Buddy Holly songs and early surf music at school dances, and from time to time they subbed with bands in the black clubs along Ninth Street. They were vastly more experienced than I was, and seldom let me forget it.

The two guys who'd hired us were frat men/hustlers at the local community college. They played corny trumpet and trombone by ear, knew a few songs, and were paying us something in the neighborhood of ten dollars apiece to complete their "band," or more accurately, to *be* their band. Killer had filled me in on the drive out: "Last time we played for these guys, they went off and got drunk and left Fred and me there for an hour. We played everything we knew by Duane Eddy, everything by the Ventures, everything by Link Wray—not much else you can do with just guitar and drums. Then they came back in, and one of 'em staggers up to the mike and says, 'And now, Killer Matthews, one of Little Rock's most fantastic young drummers, will play a dynamic drum solo!' And I played a half-hour drum solo and we all went home."

Inside the joint, the jukebox wailed Ferlin Huskey and Sonny James. Couples were dancing in a desultory fashion around the rough plank floor, the hard-faced women in gingham thrift-store dresses, the men in overalls and work shirts, skin ruddy and creased from hard labor and hard drinking. The two frat men, spiffy in their Gant shirts and striped ties, watched silently while the three of us carried in Fred's guitar and amp and Killer's drum kit. We set up in a corner. There was no stage, and a single microphone for announcements and the occasional ill-advised vocal. When we'd huddled and come up with a few songs we thought we all knew, our stay-pressed leaders deferred to Fred, who named a key and counted off the tempo. The bartender sullenly unplugged the jukebox, right in the middle of a Marty Robbins gunslinger ballad. We got a few glares for that, but we were on.

And somehow it worked. The horns would take the lead on old pop and Dixieland tunes; we'd jazz up some Hank Williams and Lefty Frizzell; Fred and Killer would do their minimalist Ventures impersonation; and we'd start the cycle again. Forty minutes on, fifteen minutes off, all night long. Nobody seemed particularly enthusiastic about the evening's entertainment, but then, nobody seemed enthusiastic about much of anything. These folks were either dead drunk or dead on their feet, or both. They danced like the zombies in *Carnival of Souls.* But when Killer did his big drum solo, cribbed for the most part from Gene Krupa's work on "Sing Sing Sing," he actually drew a smattering of applause—the first, and last, of the evening.

"I don't think they liked us much," I mused drunkenly on the way home.

"Aw, they liked us okay," said Fred. "When they *don't* like you, they let you know. Some of these places have to string chicken wire up around the bandstand so that when people start throwing things at you, you can keep right on playing." Tales of knife fights, shootings, and other adventures filled up the time on the drive back into Little Rock. I would have my own tales soon enough. One thing we didn't talk about was what a contemporary music critic might call the astonishing eclecticism of our musical offering. There we were, stirring Dixieland and surf music, rockabilly and r&b, pseudojazz and honky-tonk country and western into a big gumbo. We had no idea we were breaking down barriers and cross-fertilizing genres. In those days, the definitions were not so firmly fixed.

ROBERT PALMER
Rock & Roll: An Unruly History

110

Edward R. Murrow on the
Meaning of Television

Edward R. Murrow, born in 1908, was the most respected journalist of his time. What made that remarkable was that he was neither a newspaperman nor a magazine writer: he made his name in the nascent fields of radio and then television journalism. It would not be going too far to add that his work established a reputation for both of those broadcast media, so respected were his reports. Murrow was born in a cabin in North Carolina, where his father was a farmer: the family did not even have indoor plumbing until Ed's teenage years. However, Murrow took advantage of educational opportunities and graduated from Washington State University with a fervent interest in radio. At the time, though, there was no such thing as a broadcast journalist—Murrow joined CBS in 1935 as a script editor, but as the network went on to develop a news-gathering organization, Murrow was at the very center of it. Assigned to cover London in the early days of World War II, he sent on-the-spot reports of the blitz and its effects that bristled with clarity and urgency. In the 1950s, Murrow turned to television, where his influential documentaries set standards still unchallenged for integrity and truthfulness. They brought CBS great respect, but also constant controversy. By the time Murrow delivered his appraisal of television's first full decade, in a speech at London's Guildhall in 1959, he was within a year of leaving television. In the end, television failed to meet Ed Murrow's standards.

. . . I am to try to talk to you about television and politics. Both professions involve curious contradictions, and when combined represent a dangerous mixture. Being without substantial credentials in either area, being without political affiliation or technical skill—knowing only that the long waves are short and the short waves are long—I take refuge in a remark of my fellow-countryman who said: "It is better to know less than to know so much that ain't so." So much that we think we know about both television and politics ain't so. My own attitude towards politicians has ranged from sympathy to affection, although as a political reporter I have found the late Vice President Barkley's advice to be sound. He counselled: "A political reporter must be agin [sic] everybody, some." . . .

Having undertaken massive research on this subject, you will excuse me for not saying that the television camera has revolutionized politics, and that it is an all-seeing X-ray eye which will make it inevitable that the voter will sort out the charlatan from the statesman. Nor shall I remind you that in my country we have more television sets than bathtubs. For candor compels me to confess that I do not know what this fascinating statistic proves. Television has been variously described as the opiate of the people, a group of midgets in a black box, and the most powerful instrument of communication yet devised. It was to "revolutionize politics" but it hasn't. I do know of one senator who was badly beaten in the last election who is entirely convinced that the major reason for his defeat was that he so far forgot himself as to correct his wife's pronunciation during a television program. He was inundated with furious letters from female viewers, and is persuaded that they voted him out of office. The moral of this story probably is that a penalty must be paid for correcting one's wife in front of a television camera or anywhere else.

There is also the case of a politician who ran for public office four times, always assisted by his wife. Three times he won; once he was defeated. In all three victorious campaigns his wife was pregnant; the occasion when he went down to defeat, she wasn't. It would seem that no general law regarding television and politics can be formulated as a result of this experience.

Probably the single most effective use of television in politics occurred in my own country during the 1952 presidential campaign. General Eisenhower was the Republican nominee, having been selected after a bitter convention battle over Senator Taft—not because he was better qualified but because leaders of the Republican Party thought he had a better chance of winning. Richard Nixon, a relatively obscure senator from California, was the vice-presidential candidate. The two men were campaigning in different parts of the country when it was disclosed that a group of California citizens had raised a special fund for Senator Nixon, and it amounted to approximately eighteen thousand dollars. This disclosure created a political storm equal to that produced in your country by the Zinoviev Letter. What came to be known as the "Nixon Fund" was to be used to pay for transportation, hotel expenses, telephone tolls, Christmas cards, advertising and general publicity. When the storm broke, excited politicians of both parties took counsel. The Democrats demanded that the Republicans jettison Nixon as their candidate. Many Republican newspapers echoed the demand. Candidate Eisenhower echoed uncertainty. Many professional Republican politicians said privately that Nixon must go or the Party would be lost. Many personal friends and political cronies urged Nixon to resign for the good of the Party. Nixon and his advisors finally decided that he should make a nation-wide television explanation. The necessary arrangements were made, and the tension and suspense mounted. Would the senator quit or try to ride out the storm? He hadn't made up his own mind until a few hours before air time. When he faced the cameras he talked from notes, made an explanation of the fund which probably would not entirely have satisfied a Royal Commission, said he didn't think he ought to quit because he wasn't a quitter, and "incidentally," said Nixon, "Pat is not a quitter." At this point the camera panned around to show Mrs. Nixon's profile. "After all," said the senator, "her name was Patricia Ryan and she was born on St. Patrick's Day, and you know the Irish never quit." Nixon admitted that he had received one gift after his election to the Senate. He spoke as follows: "It was a little cocker spaniel dog— black and white spotted—and our little girl Tricia, the six-year-old, named it Checkers. And you know, the kids love that dog, and I just want to say this right now, that regardless of what they say about it we're going to keep it." Checkers was not present in the studio.

As the clock ran out, the candidate for vice president, with tears in his eyes and voice, was saying: "Wire and write to the Republican National Committee on whether you think I should get off, and whatever their decision is, I will abide."

The result was sensational—telegrams, telephone calls, came pouring in; Eisenhower and Nixon staged a reunion, posed for pictures with arms around each other; and said Eisenhower to Nixon: "You're my boy!" No Hollywood writer would have dared write such a script, but it worked. Without question, Nixon was saved by television, although any fair-minded observer would probably have to give some of the credit to his wife, the Irish and to Checkers. Still the fact remains that the climate of opinion could not have been changed so quickly had television not been available to transmit throughout the country this amazing performance, which caused many to weep, and only a few to laugh.

Senator Joseph R. McCarthy, of Wisconsin, could not play upon the human emotions with the same skill as his friend, Richard Nixon. The trail that he left on the face of my country will not soon fade, and there may be others who will try to follow in his footsteps. His weapon was fear. He was a politically unsophisticated man with a flair for publicity; and he was powerfully aided by the silence of timid men who feared to be the subject of his unfounded accusations. He polluted the channels of communication, and every radio and television network, every newspaper and magazine publisher who did not speak out against him, contributed to his evil work and must share part of the responsibility for what he did, not only to our fellow citizens but to our self-respect. He was in a real sense the creature of the mass media. They made him. They gave nation-wide circulation to his mouthings. They defended their actions on the grounds that what he said was news, when they knew he lied. His initial appearances on television were in the role of a man whose sole desire was to oust communists from government and all responsible positions. That was his announced objective. The overwhelming majority of people undoubtedly sympathized with him. It has been said repeatedly that television caused his downfall. This is not precisely true. His prolonged exposure during the so-called Army-McCarthy Hearings certainly did something to diminish his stature. He became something of a bore. But his downfall really stemmed from the fact that he broke the rules of the club, the United States Senate, when he began attacking the integrity, the loyalty of fellow senators, he was censured by that body, and was finished. The timidity of television in dealing with this man when he was spreading fear throughout the land, is not something to which this art of communication can ever point with pride, nor should it be allowed to forget it. . . .

In a free society, politics essentially involve the resolution of conflict. It is part of television's duty to define, illuminate and illustrate the nature of the conflict—to supply the voter with the raw material upon which informed opinion may be based. Thucydides said: "We both alike know that into the discussion of human affairs the question of justice arises only where the pressure of necessity is equal; that the strong take what they can, and the weak grant what they must." The true function of television in politics is to operate a market place in which ideas may compete on an equal footing. It is true that the voter may elect to purchase the second rate, shopworn or shoddy idea. He may mistake a mobile countenance for an agile mind. He may vote for Profile rather than for Principle. An unruly lock of hair may be more effective than a disciplined mind. There is no way to guarantee that television will prevent the voter from being as wrong as he has been so often in the past. Television offers no guarantee that demagogues can be kept from political power. It merely provides them with wider and more intimate, more immediate circulation. I would suggest that the evidence so far indicates that television can retard or accelerate a trend in public opinion, but it cannot reverse it. The hope so fondly held by enthusiasts a few years ago, the hope that television would make certain that the voter would sort out the phony from the statesman, is not proved. I would doubt that under today's system of communication a Lincoln or a Jefferson could be nominated or elected. According to all reports, Jefferson had a most abrasive voice, and did not suffer fools gladly. While being interviewed on some panel program he might have told a particularly obnoxious questioner just what he thought of him, and that, of course, would have been fatal. Mr. Lincoln did not move gracefully, was not a handsome man, had a wife who was no political asset, and he was a solitary man. In our present society, he probably would have been examined at an early age by a psychiatrist, received an unfavorable report, have been told his attitude toward "togetherness" was altogether wrong, and advised to enter a trade school if he could gain admittance. On the other hand, it is conceivable that Woodrow Wilson might have won his fight for the League of Nations, and thereby changed world history, had he been able to use the tools of television and radio. He was a rather pedantic persuader, and these instruments wouldn't have changed him, but they would have given his ideas wider circulation; and the efforts of those who attempted to distort those ideas, might have had less success. It is part of the brief history of television that circulation is directly related to controversy.

But it is well to bear in mind that no large section of the public demands more information or a better presentation of it. Public affairs is a form of specialization. It is *not* recreation. The public as such does not feel the call to specialize, even in its own good. On the whole, it is unenterprising—it wants its fun. By the time most people turn on the television set, the work of the day is over. There is a welcome break in drudgery. Most people, after working hours, prefer to be called away from reality, not made to face it. There is a limit upon the attention the public is willing to devote to politics. This would be true even if television fulfilled its functions to the utmost. Television by itself does not usher in the democratic millennium, and its inability to do so is not its own peculiar failure. It is due to the unwillingness of men and women, even in the highly developed democracies of Britain and the United States, to take more trouble to govern themselves better.

Both radio and television started as novelties, not as sociological or political devices. Their social importance was not at first imagined. They cost a great deal of money to develop. The pioneers in what Americans call "the industry" were businessmen and financiers, not scholars, statesmen or politicians. They still do not put public service first, for the simple reason that in my country it must pay its way. Business success has to come first.

In a competitive society, political broadcasts must compete. Generally they don't. For example, . . . in 1957, President Eisenhower and Secretary of State Dulles delivered a half-hour report on the Summit Conference. . . . They were competing with a bunch of "good guys" and "bad guys" in a Western epic called "Wells Fargo." The gun slingers had almost precisely the same audience as the word slingers.

In 1958, President Eisenhower spoke solo for half-an-hour to a Republican gathering. A non-politico on another network—fellow named Bat Masterson, who wears a bowler hat and goes about bashing people over the head with a gold-headed cane, was viewed by more than twice the number of people who watched the president. And on the third network, a personable young singer named Patti Page attracted the attention of a few million more citizens than the president.

During the 1956 presidential campaign, the average audience for all night-time political programs was roughly sixty percent below the average audience for regular entertainment programs. . . .

The television viewer is not fascinated by political orations. This may be due in part to the absence of meaningful controversy. The voter isn't interested. One of our most distinguished jurists—Judge Learned Hand—has remarked: "Doubtless things might become uncomfortable enough to arouse them, but, given reasonable opportunity for personal favors, and not too irksome control, they are content to abdicate their sovereignty and to be fleeced, if the shepherds will only shear them in their sleep."

It may be that television magnifies all the facets of personality, the defects along with the merits. This ability of television to magnify the components of personality is not necessarily pure gain. A man's weaknesses may be brought to light, which is all to the good. But that is not all that happens, because a public leader in the age of television must be popular as well as sincere. He must have a quality not considered essential in the past, that is, simplicity. A politician to be popular must not be too complicated. He must not appear to be too subtle. He must be accessible, must be able to avoid the difficult question without appearing to do so. . . .

Simplicity communicates itself more easily than complexity in persons: and it also does when it comes to issues. And this is part of the change brought about by television. This is by no means a boon. It surely is essential to have abstruse and complex ideas simplified, so that many can understand them. But we live in an age in which intelligence may not be able to simplify truthfully. The frontiers of knowledge have been pushed back, and the more that comes to be known, the less is understood, or perhaps I should say completely understood, even by the wisest. And since politics and television, more than ever before, have to take account of much of this abstruse and complicated knowledge, the art of self-government is not going to be perfected by the process of simplification alone. Indeed, looking ahead to the time when human destinies are to be determined by the uses or abuses of new sources of almost unlimited physical power, one may well ask if democracy will be able to develop the competence to deal with these complexities. If so, it must be through a broadening of education and a use of communications not yet realized, or perhaps even conceived.

I would suggest that the art of government in the near future, if it is to improve or indeed survive, must develop along one of two approaches: either through a society in which politics—the whole art of governing—is left exclusively to the wise, or through an intellectually improved democracy. A society of the wise does not need television. Democracy, I suggest, cannot do its work well without it.

Supposing that freedom is more important than safety, then the tyranny of the wise is only less objectionable than the tyranny of the unwise. The choice we face is between a despotism of the ruthlessly ambitious, not of the wise, and of an intelligent democracy. The function of television in either kind of state is sure to be of tremendous importance. But in a free society it might almost be called supreme.

In a totalitarian state the role of television will not be to teach or facilitate self-government. It must be the opposite. Its purpose must be to make the governed content not to govern themselves. It will be to distract, and indeed to entertain. I suggest that what we are now asking from television is precisely what the totalitarian dictators will order when their countries have as many television sets per capita as we have. For people whose standard of living is rising, and who do not feel that their poverty is a sacrifice they are paying for the future, will need to be distracted if they are to be ruled by a despot.

It is surely ironic that we in the United States and Britain who ask for so much entertainment from television—so much escapism—so much insulation from harsh reality—are not having such programs imposed upon us by tyrants. We have been making the choice freely. But we have made it without any awareness of the nature, intensity and inevitability of the contest between the democracies and totalitarianism. We have reached our present prosperity and seeming security without taking much heed. But now our societies must take on a new and more conscious development, and television must rise to a more constructive task. We must rid ourselves of our allergy to unpleasant and disturbing information.

I have acknowledged the natural limits to the performance of this task. I have admitted that television of itself cannot usher in the Utopia of freedom.

I have ventured to suggest that the great drag on the growth of democracy is that people do not care to specialize in self-government, even if they know vaguely that the science of government never was as difficult as it is growing to be. Television is a tool that is not being used to finish the job of Education.

It is the duty of the politician to see to it that the controls imposed on television do not prevent it from being a medium where ideas may compete for the allegiance of the viewer. And it is the duty of those who control television to use it as a sound mirror to reflect conditions as they are. If what is reflected on the end of that tube is bigotry, poverty, discrimination or prejudice, that is good and wholesome so long as the picture be true. Where there is controversy it must be reflected. We have no alternative system so long as we are dedicated to the proposition that the voter in the polling booth is sovereign.

Television must find a little time to remind us of our inheritance, and it must find more than a little time for the dissenters, the heretics, the minority spokesmen who may be tomorrow's majority. . . .

Perhaps the most important thing to be said about television and politics is that the politicians, whoever they are, should not be permitted to control television. Let them use it; let them be as persuasive as they may be. But do not permit them to use this instrument to prevent today's minority from becoming tomorrow's majority. . . .

The relationship between television and the politician should be at arm's length; the eye of the camera should pursue the politician to the very limits of privacy and decency. When the politicians complain, as they have in several countries, that television turns their proceedings into a circus, it should be made clear that the circus was already there, and that television has merely demonstrated that not all the performers are well trained. In short, the politicians ought to leave television alone, but never at any time should television leave the politician alone, except when he seeks refuge in his home, or when he becomes so boring as to drive viewers back to radio or a good book.

I would suppose that the important thing for politicians and others who use television to remember is that the fact the voice and picture can be transmitted from one end of the country to the other does not confer upon the speaker greater wisdom, perception or effectiveness than was the case when his voice reached only from one end of the street to the other. This new instrument only gives wider circulation to the cry of "Hope!" or "Havoc!" It doesn't make either more imminent or more believable.

The information program can compete successfully for the listener's attention, but it must be good and it must be fair, and it must be fearless. Television won't save us, and probably it won't destroy us, but we should be mindful of Bernard Shaw's counsel: "We must get what we want, or we will come to want what we get."

It is a limited medium; it can amuse, entertain, and it can sell goods. It can also arouse curiosity, stimulate interest, cause the viewer to read and argue.

It can stretch the horizon of his interest. But it can't reason—and is no substitute for reading. . . .

Edward R. Murrow
Guildhall Speech
1959

111

Dwight D. Eisenhower Warns of the Industrial/Military Complex

When Dwight D. Eisenhower took office in 1953, no one could be quite sure what to expect. After rising from the rank of colonel to five-star general during World War II, Eisenhower held a series of high-profile posts without indicating any particular political priorities. In the 1952 election, he ran as a Republican, but didn't identify himself with any of the more flagrant issues or causes of the day. Eight years later, looking back on his two terms in office, Eisenhower could draw a list of accomplishments that affected the country, still without quite affecting its politics. His administration watched over a stable economy that grew by 25 percent during his two terms. He made a small start, but a determined one, in adapting and enforcing civil rights laws. He changed the pace of the country by authorizing 41,000 miles in highway construction. But for the former general, the seminal achievement of his presidency was that "Americans have lived in peace in highly troubled times." Peace was on Eisenhower's mind as he delivered his farewell address to the nation via television on January 17, 1961. Eight years of peace had cost America something, as Eisenhower detected in looking back—and also forward—in his farewell.

Good evening, my fellow Americans. . . .

Three days from now, after half a century in the service of our country, I shall lay down the responsibilities of office as, in traditional and solemn ceremony, the authority of the Presidency is vested in my successor.

This evening I come to you with a message of leavetaking and farewell, and to share a few final thoughts with you, my countrymen. . . .

I wish the new President, and all who will labor with him, Godspeed. I pray that the coming years will be blessed with peace and prosperity for all. . . .

We now stand ten years past the midpoint of a century that has witnessed four major wars among great nations—three of these involved our own country.

Despite these holocausts America is today the strongest, the most influential and most productive nation in the world. Understandably proud of this pre-eminence, we yet realize that America's leadership and prestige depend, not merely upon our unmatched material progress, riches and military strength, but on how we use our power in the interests of world peace and human betterment.

Throughout America's adventure in free government, our basic purposes have been to keep the peace; to foster progress in human achievement, and to enhance liberty, dignity and integrity among peoples and among nations.

To strive for less would be unworthy of a free and religious people.

Any failure traceable to arrogance or our lack of comprehension or readiness to sacrifice would inflict upon us grievous hurt, both at home and abroad.

Progress toward these noble goals is persistently threatened by the conflict now engulfing the world. It commands our whole attention, absorbs our very beings. . . .

Threats, new in kind or degree, constantly arise. Of these, I mention two only.

A vital element in keeping the peace is our military establishment. Our arms must be mighty, ready for instant action, so that no potential aggressor may be tempted to risk his own destruction.

Our military organization today bears little relation to that known of any of my predecessors in peacetime—or, indeed, by the fighting men of World War II or Korea.

Until the latest of our world conflicts, the United States had no armaments industry. American makers of plowshares could, with time and as required, make swords as well.

But we can no longer risk emergency improvisation of national defense. We have been compelled to create a permanent armaments industry of vast proportions. Added to this, three and a half million men and women are directly engaged in the defense establishment. We annually spend on military security alone more than the net income of all United States corporations.

Now this conjunction of an immense military establishment and a large arms industry is new in the American experience. The total influence—economic, political, even spiritual—is felt in every city, every state house, every office of the Federal Government. We recognize the imperative need for this development. Yet we must not fail to comprehend its grave implications. Our toil, resources and livelihood are all involved; so is the very structure of our society.

In the councils of Government, we must guard against the acquisition of unwarranted influence, whether sought or unsought, by the military-industrial complex. The potential for the disastrous rise of misplaced power exists and will persist.

We must never let the weight of this combination endanger our liberties or democratic processes. We should take nothing for granted. Only an alert and knowledgeable citizenry can compel the proper meshing of the huge industrial and military machinery of defense with our peaceful methods and goals, so that security and liberty may prosper together.

Akin to, and largely responsible for the sweeping changes in our industrial-military posture, has been the technological revolution during recent decades.

In this revolution research has become central. It also becomes more formalized, complex and costly. A steadily increasing share is conducted for, by, or at the direction of the Federal Government.

Today the solitary inventor, tinkering in his shop, has been overshadowed by task forces of scientists, in laboratories and testing fields. In the same fashion, the free university, historically the fountainhead of free ideas and scientific discovery, has experienced a revolution in the conduct of research. Partly because of the huge costs involved, a Government contract becomes virtually a substitute for intellectual curiosity.

For every old blackboard there are now hundreds of new electronic computers.

The prospect of domination of the nation's scholars by Federal employment, project allocations and the power of money is ever present, and is gravely to be regarded.

Yet, in holding scientific research and discovery in respect, as we should, we must also be alert to the equal and opposite danger that public policy could itself become the captive of a scientific-technological elite.

It is the task of statesmanship to mold, to balance, and to integrate these and other forces, new and old, within the principles of our democratic system ever aiming toward the supreme goals of our free society. . . .

Disarmament, with mutual honor and confidence, is a continuing imperative. Together we must learn how to compose differences—not with arms, but with intellect and decent purpose. Because this need is so sharp and apparent, I confess that I lay down my official responsibilities in this field with a definite sense of disappointment. As one who has witnessed the horror and the lingering sadness of war, as one who knows that another war could utterly destroy this civilization which has been so slowly and painfully built over thousands of years, I wish I could say tonight that a lasting peace is in sight.

Happily, I can say that war has been avoided. Steady progress toward our ultimate goal has been made. But so much remains to be done. . . .

To all the peoples of the world, I once more give expression to America's prayerful and continuing aspiration:

We pray that peoples of all faiths, all races, all nations, may have their great human needs satisfied; that those now denied opportunity shall come to enjoy it to the full; that all who yearn for freedom may experience its spiritual blessings, those who have freedom will understand, also, its heavy responsibility; that all who are insensitive to the needs of others, will learn charity, and that the sources—scourges of poverty, disease and ignorance—will be made to disappear from the earth; and that in the goodness of time, all peoples will come to live together in a peace guaranteed by the binding force of mutual respect and love. . . .

Thank you, and, good night.

> DWIGHT D. EISENHOWER
> Farewell Address
> 1961

112
John F. Kennedy Delivers
His Inaugural Address

While Dwight D. Eisenhower's farewell address seemed wary of the future, John F. Kennedy's inaugural address, delivered three days later on January 20, 1961, placed America in an eager stance: hungry for challenge on every front. Kennedy wrote the speech with Theodore Sorenson, who later said that they patterned it on Lincoln's Gettysburg Address in two respects: using shorter expressions and simpler words whenever possible. As a result, Kennedy was proud to note that it was the second-shortest inaugural address delivered up to that time. It was also one of the most memorable. With his insistent enthusiasm, Kennedy turned back the national tendency toward self-interest, sharing both the responsibility and the opportunity of the new presidency with each individual American. Filled with potent phrases, the speech was widely praised at the time. Carl Sandburg called it "a manner of summons to citizens by the new head of our Great Republic." In later years, though, especially during the Vietnam War, the speech was criticized as having led America and Americans into situations around the world in which it might have been well to be wary.

We observe today not a victory of party but a celebration of freedom—symbolizing an end as well as a beginning—signifying renewal as well as change. For I have sworn before you and Almighty God the same solemn oath our forebears prescribed nearly a century and three-quarters ago.

The world is very different now. For man holds in his mortal hands the power to abolish all forms of human poverty and all forms of human life. And yet the same revolutionary beliefs for which our forebears fought are still at issue around the globe—the belief that the rights of man come not from the generosity of the state but from the hand of God.

We dare not forget today that we are the heirs of that first revolution. Let the word go forth from this time and place, to friend and foe alike, that the torch has been passed to a new generation of Americans—born in this century, tempered by war, disciplined by a hard and bitter peace, proud of our ancient heritage—and unwilling to witness to or permit the slow undoing of those human rights to which this nation has always been committed, and to which we are committed today at home and around the world.

Let every nation know, whether it wishes us well or ill, that we shall pay any price, bear any burden, meet any hardship, support any friend, oppose any foe to assure the survival and the success of liberty.

This much we pledge—and more.

To those old allies whose cultural and spiritual origins we share, we pledge the loyalty of faithful friends. United, there is little we cannot do in a host of new cooperative ventures. Divided, there is little we can do—for we dare not meet a powerful challenge at odds and split asunder.

To those new states whom we welcome to the ranks of the free, we pledge our word that one form of colonial control shall not have passed away merely to be replaced by a far more iron tyranny. We shall not always expect to find them supporting our view. But we shall always hope to find them strongly supporting their own freedom—and to remember that, in the past, those who foolishly sought power by riding the back of the tiger ended up inside.

To those people in the huts and villages of half the globe struggling to break the bonds of mass misery, we pledge our best efforts to help them help themselves, for whatever period is required—not because the Communists may be doing it, not because we seek their votes, but because it is right. If a free society cannot help the many who are poor, it cannot save the few who are rich.

To our sister republics south of our border, we offer a special pledge—to convert our good words into good deeds—in a new alliance for progress—to assist free men and free governments in casting off the chains of poverty. But this peaceful revolution of hope cannot become the prey of hostile powers. Let all our neighbors know that we shall join with them to oppose aggression or subversion anywhere in the Americas. And let every other power know that this hemisphere intends to remain the master of its own house.

To that world assembly of sovereign states, the United Nations, our last best hope in an age where the instruments of war have far outpaced the instruments of peace, we renew our pledge of support—to prevent it from becoming merely a forum for invective—to strengthen its shield of the new and the weak—and to enlarge the area in which its writ may run.

Finally, to those nations who would make themselves our adversary, we offer not a pledge but a request: that both sides begin anew the quest for peace, before the dark powers of destruction unleashed by science engulf all humanity in planned or accidental self-destruction.

We dare not tempt them with weakness. For only when our arms are sufficient beyond doubt can we be certain beyond doubt that they will never be employed.

But neither can two great and powerful groups of nations take comfort from our present course—both sides overburdened by the cost of modern weapons, both rightly alarmed by the steady spread of the deadly atom, yet both racing to alter that uncertain balance of terror that stays the hand of mankind's final war.

So let us begin anew—remembering on both sides that civility is not a sign of weakness, and sincerity is always subject to proof. Let us never negotiate out of fear. But let us never fear to negotiate.

Let both sides explore what problems unite us instead of belaboring those problems which divide us.

Let both sides, for the first time, formulate serious and precise proposals for the inspection and control of arms—and bring the absolute power to destroy other nations under the absolute control of all nations.

Let both sides seek to invoke the wonders of science instead of its terrors. Together let us explore the stars, conquer the deserts, eradicate disease, tap the ocean depths and encourage the arts and commerce.

Let both sides unite to heed in all corners of the earth the command of Isaiah—to "undo the heavy burdens . . . [and] let the oppressed go free."

And if a beachhead of cooperation may push back the jungles of suspicion, let both sides join in creating a new endeavor—not a new balance of power, but a new world of law, where the strong are just and the weak secure and the peace preserved.

All this will not be finished in the first 100 days. Nor will it be finished in the first 1,000 days, nor in the life of this Administration, nor even perhaps in our lifetime on this planet. But let us begin.

In your hands, my fellow citizens, more than mine, will rest the final success or failure of our course. Since this country was founded, each generation of Americans has been summoned to give testimony to its national loyalty. The graves of young Americans who answered the call to service surround the globe.

Now the trumpet summons us again—not as a call to bear arms, though arms we need—not as a call to battle, though embattled we are—but a call to bear the burden of a long twilight struggle year in and year out, "rejoicing in hope, patient in tribulation"—a struggle against the common enemies of man: tyranny, poverty, disease and war itself.

Can we forge against these enemies a grand and global alliance, north and south, east and west, that can assure a more fruitful life for all mankind? Will you join in that historic effort?

In the long history of the world, only a few generations have been granted the role of defending freedom in its hour of maximum danger. I do not shrink from this responsibility—I welcome it. I do not believe that any of us would exchange places with any other people or any other generation. The energy, the faith, the devotion which we bring to this endeavor will light our country and all who serve it—and the glow from that fire can truly light the world.

And so, my fellow Americans: ask not what your country can do for you—ask what you can do for your country.

My fellow citizens of the world: ask not what America will do for you, but what together we can do for the freedom of man.

Finally, whether you are citizens of America or citizens of the world, ask of us here the same high standards of strength and sacrifice which we ask of you. With a good conscience our only sure reward, with history the final judge of our deeds, let us go forth to lead the land we love, asking His blessing and His help, but knowing that here on earth God's work must truly be our own.

JOHN F. KENNEDY
Inaugural Address
1961

113

Martin Luther King Jr.'s
Plea from the Birmingham City Jail

On April 11, 1963, Martin Luther King Jr. was preparing to lead a march the next day in Birmingham, Alabama: an act that was certain to provoke his arrest. That evening, King's lieutenants begged him to reconsider, arguing that he would be more valuable to the difficult campaign for civil rights in Birmingham if he were not in jail. King wrestled with the decision. "I think I was standing also at the center of all that my life had brought me to be," he said later. The next day, April 12, King led the march and was duly arrested. Held in solitary confinement, he wondered why he was there and why he hadn't waited for other, more amenable means to force progress on civil rights. His train of thought led him to recall an essay he had received from eight well-meaning, white clergymen, suggesting just such means in lieu of King's more pressured, more exacting campaign. Sitting alone for days in jail—and standing also at the center of his life's work—King used any scrap of paper he could find in his raw surroundings to answer the clergymen in "A Letter from the Birmingham Jail," one of his most intimate and introspective writings.

My dear Fellow Clergymen,

While confined here in the Birmingham City Jail, I came across your recent statement calling our present activities "unwise and untimely" . . . since I feel that you are men of genuine goodwill and your criticisms are sincerely set forth, I would like to answer your statement in what I hope will be patient and reasonable terms.

I think I should give the reason for my being in Birmingham, since you have been influenced by the argument of "outsiders coming in" . . . Several months ago our local affiliate here in Birmingham invited us to be on call to engage in a nonviolent direct action program if such were deemed necessary. . . . So I am here, along with several members of my staff, because we were invited here. I am here because I have basic organizational ties here.

Beyond this, I am in Birmingham because injustice is here. Just as the eighth-century prophets left their little villages and carried their "thus saith the Lord" far beyond the boundaries of their home towns; and just as the Apostle Paul left his little village of Tarsus and carried the gospel of Jesus Christ to practically every hamlet and city of the Graeco-Roman world, I too am compelled to carry the gospel of freedom beyond my particular home town. Like Paul, I must constantly respond to the Macedonian call for aid.

Moreover, I am cognizant of the interrelatedness of all communities and states. I cannot sit idly by in Atlanta and not be concerned about what happens in Birmingham. Injustice anywhere is a threat to justice everywhere. We are caught in an inescapable network of mutuality, tied in a single garment of destiny. Whatever affects one directly affects all indirectly. Never again can we afford to live with the narrow, provincial "outside agitator" idea. Anyone who lives inside the United States can never be considered an outsider anywhere in this country.

You deplore the demonstrations that are presently taking place in Birmingham. But I am sorry that your statement did not express a similar concern for the conditions that brought the demonstrations into being. I am sure that each of you would want to go beyond the superficial social analyst who looks merely at effects, and does not grapple with underlying causes. I would not hesitate to say that it is unfortunate that so-called demonstrations are taking place in Birmingham at this time, but I would say in more emphatic terms that it is even more unfortunate that the white power-structure of this city left the Negro community with no other alternative . . .

Birmingham is probably the most thoroughly segregated city in the United States. Its ugly record of police brutality is known in every section of this country. Its unjust treatment of Negroes in the courts is a notorious reality. There have been more unsolved bombings of Negro homes and churches in Birmingham than in any city in this nation. These are the hard, brutal, and unbelievable facts. On the basis of these conditions Negro leaders sought to negotiate with the city fathers. But the political leaders consistently refused to engage in good-faith negotiation. . . .

You may well ask, "Why direct action? Why sit-ins, marches, etc.? Isn't negotiation a better path?" You are exactly right in your call for negotiation. Indeed, this is the purpose of direct action. Nonviolent direct action seeks to create such a crisis and establish such creative tension that a community that has constantly refused to negotiate is forced to confront the issue. It seeks so to dramatize the issue that it can no longer be ignored. I just referred to the creation of tension as a part of the work of the nonviolent resister. This may sound rather shocking. But I must confess that I am not afraid of the word tension. I have earnestly worked and preached against violent tension, but there is a type of constructive nonviolent tension that is necessary for growth. Just as Socrates felt that it was necessary to create a tension in the mind so that individuals could rise from the bondage of myths and half-truths to the unfettered realm of creative analysis and objective appraisal, we must see the need of having nonviolent gadflies to create the kind of tension in society that will help men to rise from the dark depths of prejudice and racism to the majestic heights of understanding and brotherhood. So the purpose of the direct action is to create a situation so crisis-packed that it will inevitably open the door to negotiation. We, therefore, concur with you in your call for negotiation. Too long has our beloved Southland been bogged down in the tragic attempt to live in monologue rather than dialogue. . . .

My friends, I must say to you that we have not made a single gain in civil rights without determined legal and nonviolent pressure. History is the long and tragic story of the fact that privileged groups seldom give up their privileges voluntarily. Individuals may see the moral light and voluntarily give up their unjust posture; but as Reinhold Neibuhr has reminded us, groups are more immoral than individuals.

We know through painful experience that freedom is never voluntarily given by the oppressor; it must be demanded by the oppressed. Frankly, I have never yet engaged in a direct-action movement that was "well timed," according to the timetable of those who have not suffered unduly from the disease of segregation. For years now I have heard the word "Wait!" It rings in the ear of every Negro with a piercing familiarity. This "wait" has almost always meant "never." It has been a tranquilizing thalidomide, relieving the emotional stress for a moment, only to give birth to an ill-formed infant of frustration. We must come to see with the distinguished jurist of yesterday that "justice too long delayed is justice denied." We have waited for more than three hundred and forty years for our constitutional and God-given rights. The nations of Asia and Africa are moving with jetlike speed toward the goal of political independence, and we still creep at horse and buggy pace toward the gaining of a cup of coffee at a lunch counter. I guess it is easy for those who have never felt the stinging darts of segregation to say, "Wait." But when you have seen vicious mobs lynch your mothers and fathers at will and drown your sisters and brothers at whim; when you have seen hate-filled policemen curse, kick, brutalize, and even kill your black brothers and sisters with impunity; when you see the vast majority of your twenty million Negro brothers smothering in an airtight cage of poverty in the midst of an affluent society; when you suddenly find your tongue twisted and your speech stammering as you seek to explain to your six-year-old daughter why she can't go to the public amusement park that has just been advertised on television, and see tears welling up in her little eyes when she is told that Funtown is closed to colored children, and see the depressing clouds of inferiority begin to form in her little mental sky, and see her begin to distort her little personality by unconsciously developing a bitterness toward white people; when you have to concoct an answer for a five-year-old son asking in agonizing pathos: "Daddy, why do white people treat colored people so mean?"; when you take a cross-country drive and find it necessary to sleep night after night in the uncomfortable corners of your automobile because no motel will accept you; when you are humiliated day in and day out by nagging signs reading "white" and "colored"; when your first name becomes "nigger" and your middle name becomes "boy" (however old you are) and your last name becomes "John," and when your wife and mother are never given the respected title "Mrs."; when you are harried by day and haunted at night by the fact that you are a Negro, living constantly at tip-toe stance never quite knowing what to expect next, and plagued with inner fears and outer resentments; when you are forever fighting a degenerating sense of "nobodiness"; then you will understand why we find it difficult to wait. There comes a time when the cup of endurance runs over, and men are no longer willing to be plunged into an abyss of injustice where they experience the blackness of corroding despair. I hope, sirs, you can understand our legitimate and unavoidable impatience.

You express a great deal of anxiety over our willingness to break laws. This is certainly a legitimate concern. Since we so diligently urge people to obey the Supreme Court's decision of 1954 outlawing segregation in the public schools, it is rather strange and paradoxical to find us consciously breaking laws. One may well ask, "How can you advocate breaking some laws and obeying others?" The answer is found in the fact that there are two types of laws: There are *just* and there are *unjust* laws. I would agree with Saint Augustine that "an unjust law is no law at all."

Now what is the difference between the two? How does one determine when a law is just or unjust? A just law is a manmade code that squares with the moral law or the law of God. An unjust law is a code that is out of harmony with the moral law. To put it in the terms of Saint Thomas Aquinas, an unjust law is a human law that is not rooted in eternal and natural law. Any law that uplifts human personality is just. Any law that degrades human personality is unjust. All segregation statutes are unjust because segregation distorts the soul and damages the personality. It gives the segregator a false sense of superiority, and the segregated a false sense of inferiority. To use the words of Martin Buber, the great Jewish philosopher, segregation substitutes an "I-it" relationship for the "I-thou" relationship, and ends up relegating persons to the status of things. So segregation is not only politically, economically, and sociologically unsound, but it is morally wrong and sinful. Paul Tillich has said that sin is separation. Isn't segregation an existential expression of man's tragic separation, an expression of his awful estrangement, his terrible sinfulness? So I can urge men to disobey segregation ordinances because they are morally wrong. . . .

There are some instances when a law is just on its face and unjust in its application. For instance, I was arrested Friday on a charge of parading without a permit. Now there is nothing wrong with an ordinance which requires a permit for a parade, but when the ordinance is used to preserve segregation and to deny citizens the First Amendment privilege of peaceful assembly and peaceful protest, then it becomes unjust.

I hope you can see the distinction I am trying to point out. In no sense do I advocate evading or defying the law as the rabid segregationist would do. This would lead to anarchy. One who breaks an unjust law must do it *openly, lovingly* (not hatefully as the white mothers did in New Orleans when they were seen on television screaming "nigger, nigger, nigger"), and with a willingness to accept the penalty. I submit that an individual who breaks a law that conscience tells him is unjust, and willingly accepts the penalty by staying in jail to arouse the conscience of the community over its injustice, is in reality expressing the very highest respect for law.

Of course, there is nothing new about this kind of civil disobedience. It was seen sublimely in the refusal of Shadrach, Meshach, and Abednego to obey the laws of Nebuchadnezzar because a higher moral law was involved. It was practiced superbly by the early Christians who were willing to face hungry lions and the excruciating pain of chopping blocks, before submitting to certain unjust laws of the Roman empire. To a degree academic freedom is a reality today because Socrates practiced civil disobedience.

We can never forget that everything Hitler did in German was "legal" and everything the Hungarian freedom fighters did in Hungary was "illegal." It was "illegal" to aid and comfort a Jew in Hitler's Germany. But I am sure that if I had lived in Germany during that time, I would have aided and comforted my Jewish brothers even though it was illegal. If I lived in a Communist country today, where certain principles dear to the Christian faith are suppressed, I believe I would openly advocate disobeying these anti-religious laws. I must make two honest confessions to you, my Christian and Jewish brothers. First I must confess that over the last few years I have been gravely disappointed with the white moderate. I have almost reached the regrettable conclusion that the Negro's great stumbling block in the stride toward freedom is not the White Citizen's Council-er or the Ku Klux Klanner, but the white moderate who is more devoted to "order" than to justice; who prefers a negative peace which is the absence of tension to a positive peace which is the presence of justice; who constantly says "I agree with you in the goal you seek, but I can't agree with your methods of direct action"; who paternalistically feels that he can set the timetable for another man's freedom; who lives by the myth of time and who constantly advises the Negro to wait until a "more convenient season." Shallow understanding from people of goodwill is more frustrating than absolute misunderstanding from people of ill will. Lukewarm acceptance is much more bewildering than outright rejection.

I had hoped that the white moderate would understand that law and order exist for the purpose of establishing justice, and that when they fail to do this they become dangerously structured dams that block the flow of social progress. I had hoped that the white moderate would understand that the present tension in the South is merely a necessary phase of the transition from an obnoxious negative peace, where the Negro passively accepted his unjust plight, to a substance-filled positive peace, where all men will respect the dignity and worth of human personality. Actually, we who engage in nonviolent direct action are not the creators of tension. We merely bring to the surface the hidden tension that is already alive. We bring it out in the open where it can be seen and dealt with. Like a boil that can never be cured as long as it is covered up but must be opened with all its pus-flowing ugliness to the natural medicines of air and light, injustice must likewise be exposed, with all of the tension its exposing creates, to the light of human conscience and the air of national opinion before it can be cured.

In your statement you asserted that our actions, even though peaceful, must be condemned because they precipitate violence. But can this assertion be logically made? Isn't this like condemning the robbed man because his possession of money precipitated the evil act of robbery? Isn't this like condemning Socrates because his unswerving commitment to truth and his philosophical delvings precipitated the misguided popular mind to make him drink the hemlock? Isn't this like condemning Jesus because His unique God-Consciousness and never-ceasing devotion to His will precipitated the evil act of cruciflxion? We must come to see, as federal courts have consistently affirmed, that it is immoral to urge an individual to withdraw his efforts to gain his basic constitutional rights because the quest precipitates violence. Society must protect the robbed and punish the robber.

I had also hoped that the white moderate would reject the myth of time. I received a letter this morning from a white brother in Texas which said: "All Christians know that the colored people will receive equal rights eventually, but it is possible that you are in too great of a religious hurry. It has taken Christianity almost two thousand years to accomplish what it has. The teachings of Christ take time to come to earth." All that is said here grows out of a tragic misconception of time. It is the strangely irrational notion that there is something in the very flow of time that will inevitably cure all ills. Actually time is neutral. It can be used either destructively or constructively. I am coming to feel that the people of ill-will have used time much more effectively than the people of good will. We will have to repent in this generation not merely for the vitriolic words and actions of the bad people, but for the appalling silence of good people. We must come to see that human progress never rolls in on wheels of inevitability. It comes through the tireless efforts and persistent work of men willing to be coworkers with God, and without this hard work time itself becomes an ally of the forces of social stagnation. We must use time creatively, and forever realize that the time is always ripe to do right. Now is the time to make real the promise of democracy, and transform our pending national elegy into a creative psalm of brotherhood. Now is the time to lift our national policy from the quicksand of racial injustice to the solid rock of human dignity. . . .

. . . I stand in the middle of two opposing forces in the Negro community. One is a force of complacency made up of Negroes who, as a result of long years of oppression, have been so completely drained of self-respect and a sense of "somebodiness" that they have adjusted to segregation, and of a few Negroes in the middle class who, because of a degree of academic and economic security, and because at points they profit by segregation, have unconsciously become insensitive to the problems of the masses. The other force is one of bitterness and hatred, and comes perilously close to advocating violence. It is expressed in the various black-nationalist groups that are springing up over the nation, the largest and best known being Elijah Muhammad's Muslim movement. This movement is nourished by the contemporary frustration over the continued existence of racial discrimination. It is made up of people who have lost faith in America, who have absolutely repudiated Christianity, and who have concluded that the white man is an incurable "devil." I have tried to stand between these two forces, saying that we need not follow the "do-nothingism" of the complacent or the hatred and despair of the black nationalist. There is the more excellent way of love and nonviolent protest. I'm grateful to God that, through the Negro church, the dimension of nonviolence entered our struggle. If this philosophy had not emerged, I am convinced that by now many streets of the South would be flowing with floods of blood. And I am further convinced that if our white brothers dismiss as "rabble-rousers" and "outside agitators" those of us who are working through the channels of nonviolent direct action and refuse to support our nonviolent efforts, millions of Negroes, out of frustration and despair, will seek solace and security in black-nationalist ideologies, a development that will lead inevitably to a frightening racial nightmare.

Oppressed people cannot remain oppressed forever. The urge for freedom will eventually come. This is what happened to the American Negro. Something within has reminded him of his birthright of freedom; something without has reminded him that he can gain it. Consciously and unconsciously, he has been swept in by what the Germans call the *Zeitgeist,* and with his black brothers of Africa, and his brown and yellow brothers of Asia, South America, and the Caribbean, he is moving with a sense of cosmic urgency toward the promised land of racial justice. Recognizing this vital urge that has engulfed the Negro community, one should readily understand public demonstrations. The Negro has many pent-up resentments and latent frustrations. He has to get them out. So let him march sometime; let him have his prayer pilgrimages to the city hall; understand why he must have sit-ins and freedom rides. If his repressed emotions do not come out in these nonviolent ways, they will come out in ominous expressions of violence. This is not a threat; it is a fact of history. So I have not said to my people "get rid of your discontent." But I have tried to say that this normal and healthy discontent can be channelized through the creative outlet of nonviolent direct action. Now this approach is being dismissed as extremist. I must admit that I was initially disappointed in being so categorized.

But as I continued to think about the matter I gradually gained a bit of satisfaction from being considered an extremist. Was not Jesus an extremist in love—"Love your enemies, bless them that curse you, pray for them that despitefully use you." Was not Amos an extremist for justice—"Let justice roll down like waters and righteousness like a mighty stream." Was not Paul an extremist for the gospel of Jesus Christ—"I bear in my body the marks of the Lord Jesus." Was not Martin Luther an extremist—"Here I stand; I can do none other so help me God." Was not John Bunyan an extremist—"I will stay in jail to the end of my days before I make a butchery of my conscience." Was not Abraham Lincoln an extremist—"This nation cannot survive half slave and half free." Was not Thomas Jefferson an extremist—"We hold these truths to be self-evident, that all men are created equal." So the question is not whether we will be extremist but what kind of extremist will we be. Will we be extremists for hate or will we be extremists for love? Will we be extremists for the preservation of injustice—or will we be extremists for the cause of justice? In that dramatic scene on Calvary's hill, three men were crucified. We must not forget that all three were crucified for the same crime—the crime of extremism. Two were extremists for immorality, and thusly fell below their environment. The other, Jesus Christ, was an extremist for love, truth, and goodness, and thereby rose above his environment. So, after all, maybe the South, the nation, and the world are in dire need of creative extremists. . . .

I hope the church as a whole will meet the challenge of this decisive hour. But even if the church does not come to the aid of justice, I have no despair about the future. I have no fear about the outcome of our struggle in Birmingham, even if our motives are presently misunderstood. We will reach the goal of freedom in Birmingham and all over the nation, because the goal of America is freedom. Abused and scorned though we may be, our destiny is tied up with the destiny of America. Before the pilgrims landed at Plymouth we were here. Before the pen of Jefferson etched across the pages of history the majestic words of the Declaration of Independence, we were here. For more than two centuries our fore-parents labored in this country without wages; they made cotton king, and they built the homes of their masters in the midst of brutal injustice and shameful humiliation—and yet out of a bottomless vitality they continued to thrive and develop. If the inexpressible cruelties of slavery could not stop us, the opposition we now face will surely fail. We will win our freedom because the sacred heritage of our nation and the eternal will of God are embodied in our echoing demands.

Yours for the cause of Peace and Brotherhood
Martin Luther King Jr.
1963

114

The March on Washington

On the afternoon of August 28, 1963, over two hundred thousand people attended a rally in Washington, D.C., to demand passage of a civil rights bill. The March on Washington had been organized by A. Philip Randolph, a longtime activist for African-American rights, and it was a success even beyond his fondest expectations. Tears filled his eyes—and those of many others—as the energy of a newly charged electorate filled the open space before the Lincoln Monument. However, it was a hot day and a few people were moving off the grounds as the last speaker, Dr. Martin Luther King, was introduced. King's speech had been carefully written out, but after reading a few paragraphs of it, he left the text and developed a different theme, one that captured the moment and connected it to all Americans. Dr. King's "I Have a Dream" speech, as it has come to be known, lifted up that day in his passionate baritone and moved the crowd "almost off the earth," in the words of one marcher. The words lingered over the era that followed, placing the country within reach of a new American dream, as King set it forth.

In the summer of 1963 a great shout for freedom reverberated across the land. It was a shout from the hearts of a people who had been too patient, too long. It was a shout which arose from the North and from the South. It was a shout which reached the ears of a President and stirred him to unprecedented statesmanship. It was a shout which reached the halls of Congress and brought back to the legislative chambers a re-sumption of the Great Debate. It was a shout which awoke the consciences of millions of white Americans and caused them to examine themselves and to consider the plight of twenty million black disinherited brothers. It was a shout which brought men of God down out of their pulpits, where they had been preaching only a Sunday kind of love, out into the streets to practice a Monday kind of militancy. Twenty million strong, militant, marching blacks, flanked by legions of white allies, were volunteers in an army which had a will and a purpose—the realization of a new and glorious freedom.

The shout burst into the open in Birmingham. The contagion of the will to be free, the spreading virus of the victory which was proven possible when black people stood and marched together with love in their hearts instead of hate, faith instead of fear—that virus spread from Birmingham across the land and a summer of blazing discontent gave promise of a glorious autumn of racial justice. The Negro revolution was at hand.

Birmingham had made it clear that the fight of the Negro could be won if he moved that fight out to the sidewalks and the streets, down to the city halls and the city jails and—if necessary—into the martyred heroism of a Medgar Evers. The Negro revolution in the South had come of age. It was mature. It was courageous. It was epic—and it was in the American tradition, a much delayed salute to the Bill of Rights, the Declaration of Independence, the Constitution, and the Emancipation Proclamation.

The Negro in the North came to the shocking realization that the subtle and hidden discrimination of the North was as humiliating and vicious as the obvious and overt sins of the South. In the South, the shout was being heard for public rights—nondiscrimination in hotels, motels, schools, parks. In the North, the shout was raised for private advancement—the elimination of de facto school segregation, the wiping out of housing and job discrimination. In Chicago, Illinois, intensified situations involving residential bias came to the fore.

Seen in perspective, the summer of 1963 was historic because it witnessed the first offensive in history launched by Negroes along a broad front. The heroic but spasmodic and isolated slave revolts of the antebellum South had fused, more than a century later, into a simultaneous, massive assault against segregation. And the virtues so long regarded as the exclusive property of the white South—gallantry, loyalty, and pride—had passed to the Negro demonstrators in the heat of the summer's battles.

In assessing the summer's events, some observers have tended to diminish the achievement by treating the demonstrations as an end in themselves. The heroism of the march, the drama of the confrontation, became in their minds the total accomplishment. It is true that these elements have meaning, but to ignore the concrete and specific gains in dismantling the structure of segregation is like noticing the beauty of the rain, but failing to see that it has enriched the soil. A social movement that only moves people is merely a revolt. A movement that changes both people and institutions is a revolution.

The summer of 1963 was a revolution because it changed the face of America. Freedom was contagious. Its fever boiled in nearly one thousand cities, and by the time it had passed its peak, many thousands of lunch counters, hotels, parks, and other places of public accommodation had become integrated.

The sound of the explosion in Birmingham reached all the way to Washington, where the Kennedy administration, which had firmly declared that civil rights legislation would have to be shelved for 1963, hastily reorganized its priorities and placed a strong civil rights bill at the top of the Congressional calendar.

"Free in '63"

The thundering events of the summer required an appropriate climax. The dean of Negro leaders, A. Philip Randolph, whose gifts of imagination and tireless militancy had for decades dramatized the civil rights struggle, once again provided the uniquely suitable answer. He proposed a March on Washington to unite in one luminous action all of the forces along the far-flung front.

It took daring and boldness to embrace the idea. The Negro community was firmly united in demanding a redress of grievances, but it was divided on tactics. It had demonstrated its ability to organize skillfully in single communities, but there was no precedent for a convocation of national scope and gargantuan size. Complicating the situation were innumerable prophets of doom who feared that the slightest incidence of violence would alienate Congress and destroy all hope of legislation. Even without disturbances, they were afraid that inadequate support by Negroes would reveal weaknesses that were better concealed.

The debate on the proposal neatly polarized positions. Those with faith in the Negro's abilities, endurance, and discipline welcomed the challenge. On the other side were the timid, confused, and uncertain friends, along with those who had never believed in the Negro's capacity to organize anything of significance. The conclusion was never really in doubt, because the powerful momentum of the revolutionary summer had swept aside all opposition.

The shout had roared across America. It reached Washington, the nation's capital, on August 28 when more than two hundred thousand people, black and white, people of all faiths, people of every condition of life, stood together before the stone memorial to Abraham Lincoln. The enemies of racial justice had not wanted us to come. The enemies of civil rights legislation had warned us not to come. There were dire predictions of mass rioting and dark Southern hints of retaliation.

Even some friends of our cause had honest fears about our coming. The President of the United States publicly worried about the wisdom of such a project, and congressmen from states in which liberality supposedly prevailed broadly hinted that such a march would have no effect on their deliberative process. The sense of purpose which pervaded preparations for the march had an infectious quality that made liberal whites and leaders of great religious organizations realize that the oncoming march could not be stopped. Like some swelling chorus promising to burst into glorious song, the endorsement and pledges of participation began.

Just as Birmingham had caused President Kennedy to completely reverse his priorities with regard to seeking legislation, so the spirit behind the ensuing march caused him to become a strong ally on its execution. The President's reversal was characterized by a generous and handsome new interest not only in seeing the march take place but in the hope that it would have a solid impact on the Congress.

Washington is a city of spectacles. Every four years imposing Presidential inaugurations attract the great and the mighty. Kings, prime ministers, heroes, and celebrities of every description have been feted there for more than 150 years. But in its entire glittering history, Washington had never seen a spectacle of the size and grandeur that assembled there on August 28, 1963. Among the nearly 250,000 people who journeyed that day to the capital, there were many dignitaries and many celebrities, but the stirring emotion came from the mass of ordinary people who stood in majestic dignity as witnesses to their single-minded determination to achieve democracy in their time.

They came from almost every state in the union; they came in every form of transportation; they gave up from one to three days' pay plus the cost of transportation, which for many was a heavy financial sacrifice. They were good-humored and relaxed, yet disciplined and thoughtful. They applauded their leaders generously, but the leaders, in their own hearts, applauded their audience. Many a Negro speaker that day had his respect for his own people deepened as he felt the strength of their dedication. The enormous multitude was the living, beating heart of an indefinitely noble movement. It was an army without guns, but not without strength. It was an army into which no one had to be drafted. It was white, and Negro, and of all ages. It had adherents of every faith, members of every class, every profession, every political party, united by a single ideal. It was a fighting army, but no one could mistake that its most powerful weapon was love.

One significant element of the march was the participation of white churches. Never before had they been so fully, so enthusiastically, so directly involved. One writer observed that the march "brought the country's three major religious faiths closer than any other issue in the nation's peacetime history." I venture to say that no single factor which emerged in the summer of 1963 gave so much momentum to the on-rushing revolution and to its aim of touching the conscience of the nation as the decision of the religious leaders of this country to defy tradition and become an integral part of the quest of the Negro for his rights.

In unhappy contrast, the National Council of the AFL-CIO declined to support the march and adopted a position of neutrality. A number of international unions, however, independently declared their support, and were present in substantial numbers. In addition, hundreds of local unions threw their full weight into the effort.

We had strength because there were so many of us, representing so many more. We had dignity because we knew our cause was just. We had no anger, but we had a passion—a passion for freedom. So we stood there, facing Mr. Lincoln and facing ourselves and our own destiny and facing the future and facing God.

I prepared my speech partially in New York City and partially in Washington, D.C. The night of the twenty-seventh I got in to Washington about ten o'clock and went to the hotel. I thought through what I would say, and that took an hour or so. Then I put the outline together, and I guess I finished it about midnight. I did not finish the complete text of my speech until 4:00 A.M. on the morning of August 28.

Along with other participant speakers, I was requested by the national March on Washington Committee to furnish the press liaison with a summary or excerpts of my intended speech by the late afternoon or evening of August 27. But, inasmuch as I had not completed my speech by the evening before the march, I did not forward any portion of my remarks which I had prepared until the morning of August 28.

"I Have a Dream"

I started out reading the speech, and read it down to a point. The audience's response was wonderful that day, and all of a sudden this thing came to me. The previous June, following a peaceful assemblage of thousands of people through the streets of downtown Detroit, Michigan, I had delivered a speech in Cobo Hall, in which I used the phrase "I have a dream." I had used it many times before, and I just felt that I wanted to use it here. I don't know why. I hadn't thought about it before the speech. I used the phrase, and at that point I just turned aside from the manuscript altogether and didn't come back to it.

I am happy to join with you today in what will go down in history as the greatest demonstration for freedom in the history of our nation.

Five score years ago, a great American, in whose symbolic shadow we stand today, signed the Emancipation Proclamation. This momentous decree came as a great beacon light of hope to millions of Negro slaves, who had been seared in the flames of withering injustice. It came as a joyous daybreak to end the long night of their captivity.

But one hundred years later, the Negro still is not free. One hundred years later, the life of the Negro is still sadly crippled by the manacles of segregation and the chains of discrimination. One hundred years later, the Negro lives on a lonely is-land of poverty in the midst of a vast ocean of material prosperity. One hundred years later, the Negro is still languished in the corners of American society and finds himself an exile in his own land.

And so we've come here today to dramatize a shameful condition. In a sense, we've come to our nation's capital to cash a check. When the architects of our republic wrote the magnificent words of the Constitution and the Declaration of Independence, they were signing a promissory note to which every American was to fall heir. This note was a promise that all men, yes, black men as well as white men, would be guaranteed the unalienable rights of "Life, Liberty and the pursuit of Happiness."

It is obvious today that America has defaulted on this promissory note insofar as her citizens of color are concerned. Instead of honoring this sacred obligation, America has given the Negro people a bad check, a check which has come back marked "insufficient funds." But we refuse to believe that the bank of justice is bankrupt. We refuse to believe that there are insufficient funds in the great vaults of opportunity of this nation. So we've come to cash this check, a check that will give us upon demand the riches of freedom and the security of justice.

We have also come to this hallowed spot to remind America of the fierce ur-gency of now. This is no time to engage in the luxury of cooling off or to take the tranquilizing drug of gradualism. Now is the time to make real the promises of democracy. Now is the time to rise from the dark and desolate valley of segrega-tion to the sunlit path of racial justice. Now is the time to lift our nation from the quicksands of racial injustice to the solid rock of brotherhood. Now is the time to make justice a reality for all of God's children.

It would be fatal for the nation to overlook the urgency of the moment. This sweltering summer of the Negro's legitimate discontent will not pass until there is an invigorating autumn of freedom and equality. Nineteen sixty-three is not an end but a beginning. Those who hope that the Negro needed to blow off steam and will now be content will have a rude awakening if the nation returns to business as usual.

There will be neither rest nor tranquility in America until the Negro is granted his citizenship rights. The whirlwinds of revolt will continue to shake the founda-tions of our nation until the bright day of justice emerges.

But there is something that I must say to my people, who stand on the warm threshold which leads into the palace of justice: in the process of gaining our right-ful place, we must not be guilty of wrongful deeds. Let us not seek to satisfy our thirst for freedom by drinking from the cup of bitterness and hatred. We must for-ever conduct our struggle on the high plane of dignity and discipline. We must not allow our creative protest to degenerate into physical violence. Again and again, we must rise to the majestic heights of meeting physical force with soul force.

The marvelous new militancy which has engulfed the Negro community must not lead us to a distrust of all white people, for many of our white brothers, as evi-

denced by their presence here today, have come to realize that their destiny is tied up with our destiny. They have come to realize that their freedom is inextricably bound to our freedom. We cannot walk alone. And as we walk, we must make the pledge that we shall always march ahead. We cannot turn back.

There are those who are asking the devotees of civil rights, "When will you be satisfied?" We can never be satisfied as long as the Negro is the victim of the unspeakable horrors of police brutality. We can never be satisfied as long as our bodies, heavy with the fatigue of travel, cannot gain lodging in the motels of the highways and the hotels of the cities. We cannot be satisfied as long as the Negro's basic mobility is from a smaller ghetto to a larger one. We can never be satisfied as long as our children are stripped of their selfhood and robbed of their dignity by signs stating "For Whites Only." We cannot be satisfied as long as a Negro in Mississippi cannot vote and a Negro in New York believes he has nothing for which to vote. No, no, we are not satisfied and we will not be satisfied until justice rolls down like waters and righteousness like a mighty stream.

I am not unmindful that some of you have come here out of great trials and tribulations. Some of you have come fresh from narrow jail cells. Some of you have come from areas where your quest for freedom left you battered by the storms of persecution and staggered by the winds of police brutality. You have been the veterans of creative suffering. Continue to work with the faith that unearned suffering is redemptive.

Go back to Mississippi, go back to Alabama, go back to South Carolina, go back to Georgia, go back to Louisiana, go back to the slums and ghettos of our northern cities, knowing that somehow this situation can and will be changed.

Let us not wallow in the valley of despair. I say to you today, my friends: so even though we face the difficulties of today and tomorrow, I still have a dream. It is a dream deeply rooted in the American dream.

I have a dream that one day this nation will rise up and live out the true meaning of its creed—we hold these truths to be self-evident that all men are created equal.

I have a dream that one day on the red hills of Georgia the sons of former slaves and the sons of former slave owners will be able to sit down together at the table of brotherhood.

I have a dream that one day even the state of Mississippi, a state sweltering with the heat of injustice, sweltering with the heat of oppression, will be transformed into an oasis of freedom and justice.

I have a dream that my four little children will one day live in a nation where they will not be judged by the color of their skin but by the content of their character.

I have a dream today!

I have a dream that one day, down in Alabama, with its vicious racists, with its governor having his lips dripping with the words of interposition and nullification; one day right there in Alabama little black boys and black girls will be able to join hands with little white boys and white girls as sisters and brothers.

I have a dream today!

I have a dream that one day every valley shall be exalted, every hill and moun-
tain shall be made low, the rough places will be made plain and the crooked places
will be made straight and the glory of the Lord shall be revealed and all flesh shall
see it together.

This is our hope. This is the faith that I will go back to the South with. With
this faith we will be able to hew out of the mountain of despair a stone of hope.

With this faith we will be able to transform the jangling discords of our nation
into a beautiful symphony of brotherhood. With this faith we will be able to work
together, to pray together, to struggle together, to go to jail together, to stand up for
freedom together, knowing that we will be free one day.

This will be the day, this will be the day when all of God's children will be
able to sing with new meaning: "My country 'tis of thee, sweet land of liberty, of
thee I sing. Land where my fathers died, land of the Pilgrim's pride, from every
mountainside, let freedom ring!" And if America is to be a great nation, this must
become true.

And so let freedom ring from the prodigious hilltops of New Hampshire.

Let freedom ring from the mighty mountains of New York.

Let freedom ring from the heightening Alleghenies of Pennsylvania.

Let freedom ring from the snow-capped Rockies of Colorado.

Let freedom ring from the curvaceous slopes of California.

But not only that.

Let freedom ring from Stone Mountain of Georgia.

Let freedom ring from Lookout Mountain of Tennessee.

Let freedom ring from every hill and molehill of Mississippi, from every moun-
tainside, let freedom ring!

And when this happens, when we allow freedom to ring, when we let it ring
from every village and every hamlet, from every state and every city, we will be
able to speed up that day when all of God's children, black men and white men,
Jews and Gentiles, Protestants and Catholics, will be able to join hands and sing
in the words of the old Negro spiritual, "Free at last, free at last. Thank God Al-
mighty, we are free at last."

If anyone had questioned how deeply the summer's activities had penetrated the consciousness of white America, the answer was evident in the
treatment accorded the March on Washington by all the media of communication. Normally Negro activities are the object of attention in the press
only when they are likely to lead to some dramatic outbreak, or possess
some bizarre quality. The march was the first organized Negro operation
that was accorded respect and coverage commensurate with its importance.
The millions who viewed it on television were seeing an event historic
not only because of the subject but because it was being brought into their
homes.

Millions of white Americans, for the first time, had a clear, long look at Negroes engaged in a serious occupation. For the first time millions listened to the informed and thoughtful words of Negro spokesmen, from all walks of life. The stereotype of the Negro suffered a heavy blow. This was evident in some of the comments, which reflected surprise at the dignity, the organization, and even the wearing apparel and friendly spirit of the participants. If the press had expected something akin to a minstrel show, or a brawl, or a comic display of odd clothes and bad manners, they were disappointed. A great deal has been said about a dialogue between Negro and white. Genuinely to achieve it requires that all the media of communications open their channels wide as they did on that radiant August day.

As television beamed the image of this extraordinary gathering across the border oceans, everyone who believed in man's capacity to better himself had a moment of inspiration and confidence in the future of the human race. And every dedicated American could be proud that a dynamic experience of democracy in the nation's capital had been made visible to the world.

The Autobiography of Martin Luther King, Jr.

115

A Journalist Reflects on President Kennedy's Assassination

The assassination of John F. Kennedy on November 22, 1963, stopped the world short. Most people could recall for years afterward where they had been and how they had reacted when they heard the news from Dallas. Over two-thirds of American adults cried that day, according to a poll, while others reported suffering loss of appetite, trouble sleeping, and lingering depression days after the attack on the youthful president. William S. White, longtime columnist for the *New York Times,* was on the job in the Capitol on the day Kennedy was shot. A native of Texas, White had been tempered as a battlefield reporter straight out of college during World War II. In 1954, his biography of the late Senator Robert Taft won a Pulitzer Prize. The fact that the book had only taken two months to write added to White's reputation as an imperturbable writer, one with an enviably smooth way of carrying himself. The Kennedy assassination broke through White's slick professional demeanor, though, disturbing him as a citizen and, even more pointedly, as a Texan.

On the night before President Kennedy was to set out upon the trip to Dallas that was to cost his life, my wife and I were among the guests at a typically spirited White House party for the Grand Duchess of Luxembourg, at which the president all but knocked himself out to be the happily untroubled host. The guests, as at any state dinner, were lined up alphabetically to march in the receiving line past the president and his guest of honor, and my wife and I, as W's, wound up in a small and pretty well isolated group including Supreme Court Justice Byron White and Mayor Robert Wagner of New York. I had not seen Wagner face to face in some years (we had, in any case, never been much more than nodding acquaintances) and as it happened I had within the preceding week written a column deploring what I felt to be the absurd cannibalism then besetting the Democratic Party in New York, for which I had heavily blamed Wagner himself. And, by coincidence, I had just a day or so before this dinner discussed the same matter briefly with Kennedy, remarking that it seemed to me that as head of the national Democratic Party he would be better off if the Republicans should win the municipal elections in New York at the first possible opportunity, and give the Democrats there something real to complain about, since in power they were so determinedly bitchy among themselves. Kennedy had grunted noncommittally, meaning that he had far bigger things to worry about.

Nevertheless, as Wagner, Byron White, and I stood together waiting to move by the president, I stood in a good deal of discomfort. Few journalists are tough enough to enjoy small talk with a politician whom they have just skewered. Then I realized that Wagner's amicability proceeded from his mistaken supposition that I was Byron White. Somehow, Kennedy sensed exactly what the situation was. For when Wagner and I reached the president in single file, Wagner being in the lead, Kennedy greeted him somewhat formally and me with a very loud "Hi, *Bill,*" and then trumpeted to Wagner: "Bob, I'm sure you know *Bill* White, the *columnist!*" Wagner gave me a chill smile; Kennedy a broad and delighted grin. This was the last time I was ever to see John Kennedy. And in the aftertime, seeking, as no doubt were so many others, some fragment of memory touched with humor rather than sorrow, I consciously nourished the recollection that I had, if unwittingly, given him some comradely amusement in the last night of his life.

Without being mawkish about it, I must say I was to need every shred of happy memory that could be dredged up. On the fatal day in Dallas I was lounging about the Senate press gallery in Washington to no special purpose, simply poking about in my mind for some satisfactory subject for a column. I did three columns a week and never, in sixteen years with the United Feature Syndicate, failed to meet a deadline. Through the desultory hum in the gallery I heard the United Press ticker ringing that series of urgent bells that means that a "flash"—a signal of some momentous news event—is coming.

I hurried to peer at the machine and read that the president had been shot in Dallas.

I have never been able to abide the sort of fellow who makes not just a parade of his grief but a majestic procession, suggesting that somehow *his* suffering is incomparably acute and must be seen by others. But the plain fact is that I *was* crushed by grief and shock and all but physically knocked down by my horror that this unspeakable thing had occurred in my home state, where not long before a handful of harpies in Dallas had spat upon Adlai Stevenson. In a rush of precognition I knew that Texas, for which I had never been any booster but which I nevertheless knew was no more hospitable a home for brutality and madness than any other state, would now be in for a long session of harsh condemnation and guilt by association. To this day, the city of Dallas has never fully recovered from its hidden trauma. Nor, I suspect, have some of the most fair-minded and decent and humane friends I have ever had, including the editor of the *Dallas Times Herald* at that time, Felix McKnight, who had steadfastly squelched every nascent lunatic element that ever showed its head in that city.

It would soon emerge in the findings of the Warren Commission that John Kennedy's assassin, Lee Harvey Oswald, had nothing whatever to do with Texas and had had, assuming that ideology had been any motivation in the first place, associations with both Cuba and the Soviet Union. Nevertheless, a trying and sorrowful and hopelessly frustrating time now opened for me, as a journalist and simply as a man, and for my wife. The circumstance that we were widely known to be old and close personal friends of the new president, Lyndon Johnson, and his wife somehow condemned us in the eyes of some of the associates of John Kennedy. The mere fact that I had been born in Texas, irrelevant in any rational context, somehow developed an ugly significance, not only to some of the Kennedy followers but even to some of my colleagues in journalism. One colleague, reviewing a book of mine, referred to me, in no relevant context discernible to me, as a "professional Texan." Walter Lippmann, whom I had known for two decades, was astonished. "*I* never knew you were from Texas," he remarked. "You don't sound like it, either." He meant, I suppose that because I had not assiduously cultivated it, my "Texas accent" had long since vanished by the natural erosion of my many years in the East.

WILLIAM S. WHITE
The Making of a Journalist

116

Lyndon Johnson's Great Society Speech

Well-known as a Texan, Lyndon Baines Johnson spent all but two years of his career in the city of Washington, working his way up in the government machine and learning it well. He was crassly effective in operating that machine. After taking office on the assassination of John Kennedy in 1963, Johnson promised to continue the late president's agenda and few people expected much more than that from a man who boasted of being a "doer," and not a "thinker." Yet in a speech at the University of Michigan in May of 1964, Johnson rebuilt a handful of Kennedy-era bills into a monument he called the Great Society. Infused with idealism, the speech revealed another side of Johnson: a man with even greater ties to his hero Franklin Roosevelt than to Jack Kennedy. Where FDR's complex of New Deal programs had sought to save the nation from a crippling depression, LBJ's Great Society was offered to save the nation from a prosperity that was proving to be equally unjust.

. . . The purpose of protecting the life of our Nation and preserving the liberty of our citizens is to pursue the happiness of our people. Our success in that pursuit is the test of our success as a Nation.

For a century we labored to settle and to subdue a continent. For half a century we called upon unbounded invention and untiring industry to create an order of plenty for all of our people.

The challenge of the next half century is whether we have the wisdom to use that wealth to enrich and elevate our national life, and to advance the quality of our American civilization.

Your imagination, your initiative, and your indignation will determine whether we build a society where progress is the servant of our needs, or a society where old values and new visions are buried under unbridled growth. For in your time we have the opportunity to move not only toward the rich society and the powerful society, but upward to the Great Society.

The Great Society rests on abundance and liberty for all. It demands an end to poverty and racial injustice, to which we are totally committed in our time. But that is just the beginning.

The Great Society is a place where every child can find knowledge to enrich his mind and to enlarge his talents. It is a place where leisure is a welcome chance to build and reflect, not a feared cause of boredom and restlessness. It is a place where the city of man serves not only the needs of the body and the demands of commerce but the desire for beauty and the hunger for community.

It is a place where man can renew contact with nature. It is a place which honors creation for its own sake and for what it adds to the understanding of the race. It is a place where men are more concerned with the quality of their goals than the quantity of their goods.

But most of all, the Great Society is not a safe harbor, a resting place, a final objective, a finished work. It is a challenge constantly renewed, beckoning us toward a destiny where the meaning of our lives matches the marvelous products of our labor.

So I want to talk to you today about three places where we begin to build the Great Society—in our cities, in our countryside, and in our classrooms.

Many of you will live to see the day, perhaps fifty years from now, when there will be 400 million Americans—four-fifths of them in urban areas. In the remainder of this century urban population will double, city land will double, and we will have to build homes, highways, and facilities equal to all those built since this country was first settled. So in the next forty years we must rebuild the entire urban United States.

Aristotle said: "Men come together in cities in order to live; but they remain together in order to live the good life." It is harder and harder to live the good life in American cities today.

The catalog of ills is long: There is the decay of the centers and the despoiling of the suburbs. There is not enough housing for our people or transportation for our traffic. Open land is vanishing and old landmarks are violated.

Worst of all, expansion is eroding the precious and time-honored values of community with neighbors and communion with nature. The loss of these values breeds loneliness and boredom and indifference.

Our society will never be great until our cities are great. Today the frontier of imagination and innovation is inside those cities and not beyond their borders.

New experiments are already going on. It will be the task of your generation to make the American city a place where future generations will come, not only to live but to live the good life. . . .

A second place where we begin to build the Great Society is in our countryside. We have always prided ourselves on being not only America the strong and America the free, but America the beautiful. Today that beauty is in danger. The water we drink, the food we eat, the very air that we breathe, are threatened with pollution. Our parks are overcrowded, our seashores overburdened. Green fields and dense forests are disappearing.

A few years ago we were greatly concerned about the "Ugly American." Today we must act to prevent an ugly America.

For once the battle is lost, once our natural splendor is destroyed, it can never be recaptured. And once man can no longer walk with beauty or wonder at nature his spirit will wither and his sustenance be wasted.

A third place to build the Great Society is in the classrooms of America.

There your children's lives will be shaped. Our society will not be great until every young mind is set free to scan the farthest reaches of thought and imagination. We are still far from that goal. . . .

In many places, classrooms are overcrowded and curricula are outdated. Most of our qualified teachers are underpaid, and many of our paid teachers are unqualified. So we must give every child a place to sit and a teacher to learn from. Poverty must not be a bar to learning, and learning must offer an escape from poverty.

But more classrooms and more teachers are not enough. We must seek an educational system which grows in excellence as it grows in size. This means better training for our teachers. It means preparing youth to enjoy their hours of leisure as well as their hours of labor. It means exploring new techniques of teaching, to find new ways to stimulate the love of learning and the capacity for creation.

These are three of the central issues of the Great Society. While our government has many programs directed at those issues, I do not pretend that we have the full answer to those problems.

But I do promise this: We are going to assemble the best thought and the broadest knowledge from all over the world to find those answers for America. . . .

The solution to these problems does not rest on a massive program in Washington, nor can it rely solely on the strained resources of local authority. They require us to create new concepts of cooperation, a creative federalism, between the national capital and the leaders of local communities.

Woodrow Wilson once wrote: "Every man sent out from his university should be a man of his nation as well as a man of his time."

Within your lifetime powerful forces, already loosed, will take us toward a way of life beyond the realm of our experience, almost beyond the bounds of our imagination.

For better or for worse, your generation has been appointed by history to deal with those problems and to lead America toward a new age. You have the chance never before afforded to any people in any age. You can help build a society where the demands of morality, and the needs of the spirit, can be realized in the life of the nation.

So, will you join in the battle to give every citizen the full equality which God enjoins and the law requires, whatever his belief, or race, or the color of his skin?

Will you join in the battle to give every citizen an escape from the crushing weight of poverty?

Will you join in the battle to make it possible for all nations to live in enduring peace—as neighbors and not as mortal enemies?

Will you join in the battle to build the Great Society, to prove that our material progress is only the foundation on which we will build a richer life of mind and spirit?

There are those timid souls who say this battle cannot be won; that we are condemned to a soulless wealth. I do not agree. We have the power to shape the civilization that we want. But we need your will, your labor, your hearts, if we are to build that kind of society.

Those who came to this land sought to build more than just a new country. They sought a new world. So I have come here today to your campus to say that you can make their vision our reality. So let us from this moment begin our work so that in the future men will look back and say: It was then, after a long and weary way, that man turned the exploits of his genius to the full enrichment of his life.

LYNDON B. JOHNSON
May 22, 1964

117

Malcolm X Finds Enlightenment in Mecca

Malcolm X was born Malcolm Little in 1925, the son of an activist Baptist minister. The Littles withstood repeated confrontations with white racists, including the burning of their home in 1929. But it was the death of Malcolm's father in 1931, in what was termed a traffic accident, that devastated the family. Malcolm, who was raised by friends of the family, was beset by frustrations, and he abandoned a promising high school career in favor of making his way on the streets. That was not where the astute young man belonged. After a prison term and conversion to Islam, he became a leading spokesman for African-American rights. Malcolm X, as he called himself, was openly racist in calling white people "blue-eyed devils," and he found little support among whites or moderate blacks. Nonetheless, he was a charismatic, often humorous, speaker, who attracted a large following, especially among the young. Many took his message of bitterness to heart, while others simply appreciated that a black man would express his anger so openly. In 1964 Malcolm visited Mecca in order to better understand his chosen religion and returned deeply affected by his journey. Afterward, he described for his followers the new feelings he embraced there, especially toward people of other races. Malcolm X was assassinated in 1965 by extremists who resented his acceptance of whites.

Never have I witnessed such sincere hospitality and the overwhelming spirit of true brotherhood as is practiced by people of all colors and races here in this Ancient Holy Land, the home of Abraham, Muhammad, and all the other prophets of the Holy Scriptures. For the past week, I have been utterly speechless and spellbound by the graciousness I see displayed all around me by people of all colors.

I have been blessed to visit the Holy City of Mecca. I have made my seven circuits around the Ka'ba, led by a young *Mutawaf* named Muhammad. I drank water from the well of Zem Zem. I ran seven times back and forth between the hills of Mt. Al-Safa and Al-Marwah. I have prayed in the ancient city of Mina, and I have prayed on Mt. Arafat.

There were tens of thousands of pilgrims, from all over the world. They were of all colors, from blue-eyed blonds to black-skinned Africans. But we were all participating in the same ritual, displaying a spirit of unity and brotherhood that my experiences in America had led me to believe never could exist between the white and the non-white.

America needs to understand Islam, because this is the one religion that erases from its society the race problem. Throughout my travels in the Muslim world, I have met, talked to, and even eaten with people who in America would have been considered "white"—but the "white" attitude was removed from their minds by the religion of Islam. I have never before seen *sincere* and *true* brotherhood practiced by all colors together, irrespective of their color.

You may be shocked by these words coming from me. But on this pilgrimage, what I have seen, and experienced, has forced me to *re-arrange* much of my thought-patterns previously held, and to *toss aside* some of my previous conclusions. This was not too difficult for me. Despite my firm convictions, I have been always a man who tries to face facts, and to accept the reality of life as new experience and new knowledge unfolds it. I have always kept an open mind, with every form of intelligent search for truth.

During the past eleven days here in the Muslim world, I have eaten from the same plate, drunk from the same glass, and slept in the same bed (or on the same rug)—while praying to the *same God*—with fellow Muslims, whose eyes were the bluest of blue, whose hair was the blondest of blond, and whose skin was the whitest of white. And in the *words* and in the *actions* and in the *deeds* of the "white" Muslims, I felt the same sincerity that I felt among the black African Muslims of Nigeria, Sudan, and Ghana.

We were *truly* all the same (brothers)—because their belief in one God had removed the "white" from their *minds,* the "white" from their *behavior,* and the "white" from their *attitude*.

I could see from this, that perhaps if white Americans could accept the Oneness of God, then perhaps, too, they could accept in *reality* the Oneness of Man—and cease to measure, and hinder, and harm others in terms of their "differences" in color.

With racism plaguing America like an incurable cancer, the so-called "Christian" white American should be more receptive to a proven solution to such a destructive problem. Perhaps it could be in time to save America from imminent disaster—the same destruction brought upon Germany by racism that eventually destroyed the Germans themselves.

Each hour here in the Holy Land enables me to have greater spiritual insights into what is happening in America between black and white. The American Negro never can be blamed for his racial animosities—he is only reacting to four hundred years of conscious racism of the American whites. But as racism leads America up the suicide path, I do believe, from the experiences I have had with them, that the whites of the younger generation, the colleges and universities, will see the handwriting on the wall and many of them will turn to the *spiritual* path of *truth*—the *only* way left to America to ward off the disaster that racism inevitably must lead to.

Never have I been so highly honored. Never have I been made to feel more humble and unworthy. Who would believe the blessings that have been heaped upon an *American Negro?* A few nights ago, a man who would be called in America a "white" man, a United Nations diplomat, ambassador, a companion of kings, gave me *his* hotel suite, *his* bed. By this man, His Excellency Prince Faisal, who rules this Holy Land, was made aware of my presence here in Jedda. The very next morning, Prince Faisal's son, in person, informed me that by the will and decree of his esteemed father, I was to be a State Guest.

The Deputy Chief of Protocol himself took me before the Hajj Court. His Holiness Sheikh Muhammad Harkon himself okayed my visit to Mecca. His Holiness gave me two books on Islam, with his personal seal and autograph, and he told me that he prayed that I would be a successful preacher of Islam in America. A car, a driver, and a guide, have been placed at my disposal, making it possible for me to travel about this Holy Land almost at will. The government provides air-conditioned quarters and servants in each city that I visit. Never would I have even thought of dreaming that I would ever be a recipient of such honors—honors that in America would be bestowed upon a King—not a Negro.

All praise is due to Allah, the Lord of all the Worlds.

Sincerely,
El-Hajj Malik El-Shabazz
(Malcolm X)
The Autobiography of Malcolm X

118

Betty Friedan Explains Writing
The Feminine Mystique

After Betty Friedan graduated summa cum laude from Smith College in 1942, she worked as a reporter for seven years, before settling down to become a housewife in the suburbs of New York. By 1958, though, she began to realize that the role didn't suit her and, moreover, that it had been forced upon her and the rest of her generation in the postwar years. Friedan studied herself and her contemporaries and found that many of the reasons behind the newly constricted role for women were crassly economic. After selling her theory to a publishing company as the basis of a book, Friedan was three years late in submitting a manuscript, in part because she had to maintain her family's home all the while. She would later term such homes "comfortable concentration camps" for women. Friedan's book, *The Feminine Mystique*, finally appeared in 1963. Sales were slow at first, but the book sparked a reaction that eventually exploded into the Women's Liberation movement. In 1966, Friedan was the founding president of the National Organization for Women. As leader of the movement, she was brash, insightful and ambitious. The very qualities she felt society had discouraged in her as a housewife became the means she employed to release the hidden qualities of the millions of women who followed her. In 1973, on the tenth anniversary of the publication of *The Feminine Mystique*, Friedan looked back on the woman she had been and the movement she began.

It seems such a precarious accident that I ever wrote the book at all—but, in another way, my whole life had prepared me to write that book. All the pieces finally came together. In 1957, getting strangely bored with writing articles about breast feeding and the like for *Redbook* and the *Ladies' Home Journal,* I put an unconscionable amount of time into a questionnaire for my fellow Smith graduates of the class of 1942, thinking I was going to disprove the current notion that education had fitted us ill for our role as women. But the questionnaire raised more questions than it answered for me—education had *not* exactly geared US to the role women were trying to play, it seemed. The suspicion arose as to whether it was the education or the role that was wrong. *McCall's* commissioned an article based on my Smith alumnae questionnaire, but the then male publisher of *McCall's,* during that great era of togetherness, turned the piece down in horror, despite underground efforts of female editors. The male *McCall's* editors said it couldn't be true.

I was next commissioned to do the article for *Ladies' Home Journal.* That time I took it back, because they rewrote it to say just the opposite of what, in fact, I was trying to say. I tried it again for *Redbook*. . . . The editor of *Redbook* told my agent, "Betty has gone off her rocker. She has always done a good job for us, but this time only the most neurotic housewife could identify." I opened my agent's letter on the subway as I was taking the kids to the pediatrician. I got off the subway to call my agent and told her, "I'll have to write a book to get this into print."

What I was writing threatened the very foundations of the women's magazine world—the feminine mystique.

. . . When *The Feminine Mystique* was at the printer's, and my last child was in school all day, I decided I would go back to school myself and get my Ph.D. Armed with my publisher's announcement, a copy of my *summa cum laude* undergraduate degree and twenty-years-back graduate record, and the New World Foundation report of the educational project I had dreamed up and run in Rockland County, I went to see the head of the social psychology department at Columbia. He was very tolerant and kind, but surely, at forty-two, after all those undisciplined years as a housewife, I must understand that I wouldn't be able to meet the rigors of full-time graduate study for a Ph.D. and the mastery of statistics that was required. "But I used statistics throughout the book," I pointed out. He looked blank. "Well, my dear," he said, "what do you want to bother your head getting a Ph.D. for, anyhow?"

I began to get letters from other women who now saw through the feminine mystique, who wanted to stop doing their children's homework and start doing their own; they were also being told they really weren't capable of doing anything else now but making homemade strawberry jam or helping their children do fourth-grade arithmetic. It wasn't enough just to take yourself seriously as a person. Society had to change, somehow, for women to make it as people. It wasn't possible to live any longer as "just a housewife." But what other way was there to live? I remember getting stuck at that point, even when I was writing *The Feminine Mystique*. I had to write a last chapter, giving a solution to "the problem that has no name," suggesting new patterns, a way out of the conflicts, whereby women could use their abilities fully in society and find their own existential human identity, sharing its action, decisions, and challenges without at the same time renouncing home, children, love, their own sexuality. My mind went blank. You do have to say "no" to the old way before you can begin to find the new "yes" you need. Giving a name to the problem that had no name was the necessary first step. But it wasn't enough.

Personally, I couldn't operate as a suburban housewife any longer, even if I had wanted to. For one thing, I became a leper in my own suburb. As long as I only wrote occasional articles most people never read, the fact that I wrote during the hours when the children were in school was no more a stigma than, for instance, solitary morning drinking. But now that I was acting like a real writer and even being interviewed on television, the sin was too public, it could not be condoned. Women in other suburbs were writing me letters as if I were Joan of Arc, but I practically had to flee my own crabgrass-overgrown yard to keep from being burned at the stake. Although we had been fairly popular, my husband and I were suddenly no longer invited to our neighbors' dinner parties. My kids were kicked out of the car pool for art and dancing classes. The other mothers had a fit when I now called a cab when it was my turn, instead of driving the children myself. We had to move back to the city, where the kids could do their own thing without my chauffeuring and where I could be with them at home during some of the hours I now spent commuting. I couldn't stand being a freak alone in the suburbs any longer.

At first, that strange hostility my book—and later the movement—seemed to elicit from some women amazed and puzzled me. Even in the beginning, there wasn't the hostility I had expected from men. Many men bought *The Feminine Mystique* for their wives and urged them to go back to school or to work. I realized soon enough that there were probably millions of women who had felt as I had, like a freak, absolutely alone, as a suburban housewife. But if you were afraid to face your real feelings about the husband and children you were presumably living for, then someone like me opening up the can of worms was a menace.

I didn't blame women for being scared. I was pretty scared myself. It isn't really possible to make a new pattern of life all by yourself. I've always dreaded being alone more than anything else. The anger I had not dared to face in myself during all the years I tried to play the helpless little housewife with my husband—and feeling more helpless the longer I played it—was beginning to erupt now, more and more violently. For fear of being alone, I almost lost my own self-respect trying to hold on to a marriage that was based no longer on love but on dependent hate. It was easier for me to start the women's movement which was needed to change society than to change my own personal life.

. . . I went to Washington because a law had been passed, Title VII of the Civil Rights Act of 1964, banning sex discrimination in employment along with race discrimination. The sex discrimination part had been tacked on as a joke and a delaying maneuver by a southern congressman, Howard Smith of Virginia. At the first press conferences after the law went into effect, the administrator in charge of enforcing it joked about the ban on sex discrimination. "It will give men equal opportunity to be *Playboy* bunnies," he said.

In Washington I found a seething underground of women in the government, the press, and the labor unions who felt powerless to stop the sabotage of this law that was supposed to break through the sex discrimination that pervaded every industry and profession, every factory, school, and office.

Some of these women felt that I, as a now known writer, could get the public's ear.

One day, a cool young woman lawyer, who worked for the agency that was not enforcing the law against sex discrimination, carefully closed the door of her office and said to me with tears in her eyes, "I never meant to be so concerned about women. I like men. But I'm getting an ulcer, the way women are being betrayed. We may never have another chance like this law again. Betty, you have to start an NAACP for women. You are the only one free enough to do it."

I wasn't an organization woman. I never even belonged to the League of Women Voters. However, there was a meeting of state commissioners on the status of women in Washington in June. I thought that, among the women there from the various states, we would get the nucleus of an organization that could at least call a press conference and raise the alarm among women throughout the country.

Pauli Murray, an eminent black lawyer, came to that meeting, and Dorothy Haener and Caroline Davis from the UAW, and Kay Clarenbach, head of the Governor's Commission in Wisconsin, and Katherine Conroy of the Communications Workers of America, and Aileen Hernandez, then a member of the Equal Employment Opportunities Commission. I asked them to come to my hotel room one night. Most didn't think women needed a movement like the blacks, but everyone was mad at the sabotage of Title VII. The consensus was that the conference could surely take respectable action to insist that the law be enforced.

I went to bed relieved that probably a movement wouldn't have to be organized. At six the next morning, I got a call from one of the top token women in the Johnson administration, urging me not to rock the boat. At eight the phone rang again; this time it was one of the reluctant sisters of the night before, angry now, really angry. "We've been told that this conference doesn't have the power to take any action at all, or even the right to offer a resolution. So we've got a table for us all to eat together at lunch, and we'll start the organization." At the luncheon we each chipped in a dollar. I wrote the word "NOW" on a paper napkin; our group should be called the National Organization *for* Women, I said, "because men should be part of it." Then I wrote down the first sentence of the NOW statement of purpose, committing ourselves to "take *action* to bring women into full participation in the mainstream of American society now, exercising all the privileges and responsibilities thereof, in truly equal partnership with men."

. . . I couldn't define "liberation" for women in terms that denied the sexual and human reality of our need to love, and even sometimes to depend upon, a man. . . . It seemed to me that men weren't really the enemy—they were fellow victims, suffering from an outmoded masculine mystique that made them feel unnecessarily inadequate when there were no bears to kill.

. . . On our first picket line at the White House fence ("Rights Not Roses") on Mother's Day in 1967, we threw away chains of aprons, flowers, and mock typewriters. We dumped bundles of newspapers onto the floor of the Equal Employment Opportunities Commission in protest against its refusal to enforce the Civil Rights law against sex-segregated "Help Wanted: Male" ads (for the good jobs) and "Help Wanted: Female" ads (for Gal Friday–type jobs). This was supposed to be just as illegal now as ads reading "Help Wanted: White" and "Help Wanted: Colored." We announced we were going to sue the federal government for not enforcing the law equally on behalf of women (and then called members of our underground in the Justice Department to see if one could do that) and we did.

. . . Our only real office in those years was my apartment. It wasn't possible to keep up with the mail. But when women like Wilma Heide from Pittsburgh, or Karen De Crow in Syracuse, Eliza Paschall in Atlanta, Jacqui Ceballos—so many others—were so determined to have NOW chapters that they called long distance when we didn't answer their letters, the only thing to do was to have them become local NOW organizers.

I remember so many way stations: Going to lunch at the for-men-only Oak Room at the Plaza Hotel with fifty NOW women and demanding to be served . . . Testifying before the Senate against the nomination to the Supreme Court of a sexist judge named Carswell who refused to hear a case of a woman who was fired because she had preschool children . . . Seeing the first sign of a women's underground in the student movement, when I was asked to lead a rap session at the National Student Congress in College Park, Maryland, in 1968 . . . After a resolution for the liberation of women from the mimeograph machines was laughed down at the SDS convention, hearing the young radical women telling me they had to have a separate women's-lib group—because if they really spoke out at SDS meetings, they might not get married . . . Helping Sheila Tobias plan the Cornell intersession on women in 1968, which started the first women's studies programs (how many universities have them now!) . . . Persuading the NOW board that we should hold a Congress to Unite Women with the young radicals despite differences in ideology and style . . . So many way stations.

I admired the flair of the young radicals when they got off the rhetoric of sex/class warfare and conducted actions like picketing the Miss America beauty contest in Atlantic City. But the media began to publicize, in more and more sensational terms, the more exhibitionist, down-with-men, down-with-marriage, down-with-childbearing rhetoric and actions. Those who preached the man-hating sex/class warfare threatened to take over the New York NOW and the national NOW and drive out the women who wanted equality but who also wanted to keep on loving their husbands and children.

. . . The man-haters were given publicity far out of proportion to their numbers in the movement because of the media's hunger for sensationalism.

Many women in the movement go through a temporary period of great hostility to men when they first become conscious of their situation; when they start acting to change their situation, they outgrow what I call pseudo-radical infantilism. But that man-hating rhetoric increasingly disturbs most women in the movement, in addition to keeping many women out of the movement.

On the plane to Chicago, preparing to bow out as president of NOW, feeling powerless to fight the man-haters openly and refusing to front for them, I suddenly knew what had to be done. A woman from Florida had written to remind me that August 26, 1970, was the fiftieth anniversary of the constitutional amendment giving women the vote. We needed to call a national action—a strike of women to call attention to the unfinished business of equality: equal opportunity for jobs and education, the right to abortion and childcare centers, the right to our own share of political power. It would unite women again in serious action—women who had never been near a "women's lib" group. (NOW, the largest such group, and the only one with a national structure, had only 3,000 members in thirty cities in 1970.)

The grass-roots strength of NOW went into organizing the August 26 strike. In New York, women filled the temporary headquarters volunteering to do anything and everything; they hardly went home at night. Mayor Lindsay wouldn't close Fifth Avenue for our march, and I remember starting that march with the hoofs of policemen's horses trying to keep us confined to the sidewalk. I remember looking back, jumping up to see over marchers' heads. I never saw so many women; they stretched back for so many blocks you couldn't see the end. I locked one arm with my beloved Judge Dorothy Kenyon (who, at eighty-two, insisted on walking with me instead of riding in the car we had provided for her), and the other arm with a young woman on the other side. I said to the others in the front ranks, "Lock arms, sidewalk to sidewalk!" We overflowed till we filled the whole of Fifth Avenue. There were so many of us they couldn't stop us; they didn't even try. It was, as they say, the first great nationwide action of women (hundreds of men also marched with us) since women won the vote itself fifty years before. Reporters who had joked about the "bra-burners" wrote that they had never seen such beautiful women as the proud, joyous marchers who joined together that day. For all women were beautiful on that day.

BETTY FRIEDAN
Introduction to *The Feminine Mystique*
1973

119

A Teenage Girl Contemplates
Feminism in Suburbia

The women's movement progressed in one great surge and many, many small jolts. The amount of actual change that could be cited varied in different fields: the military, the professions, business and labor. Overall, the movement was at its most effective when it cracked open the notion that there was any one ideal life or circumstance for all women. Self-perception was an especially keen concern for high school students, who were susceptible to the same conditioning that had affected many adult women. Connie Dvorkin was a high school student in a suburb north of New York City in 1970, when she wrote about her own struggle to think for herself—about herself.

I was born March 4, 1955, in Doctor's Hospital in New York City. All my life I have lived in an unincorporated area of the town of Greenburgh, though my mailing address is Scarsdale and the school district is Edgemont, Greenburgh Union Free District No. 6. I am in the eighth grade and have been a pacifist and a vegetarian since October 1968. I live in a Republican stronghold and the conservatism that usually goes along with that is very evident here. My prison's name is Edgemont Junior-Senior High School, grades 7–12, with approximately 850 inmates. I am the so-called secretary of Edgemont Students for Action to which all the activist radicals and more radical liberals more or less belong.

I think I first heard of the Women's Liberation Movement on WBAI (Radio Free New York), most likely on "Radio Unnameable." Like Eldridge Cleaver in *Soul On Ice,* I never realized how oppressed I was until someone brought it into the open. I wrote a letter asking for some literature on the Women's Liberation Movement that I could read. It was for a Social Studies report that never materialized. But that is irrelevant like school is. The important thing is that I read the stuff and immediately agreed with everything. Ironically the very night I was reading it I was babysitting and watching TV. The show, "I Love Lucy," was an episode where the two women were to be equal to the men for one night—no courtesies "due to a woman," no shit like that for *one* night, eating out at a restaurant—and they couldn't do it. They *had* to depend on their husbands. They couldn't face life out in front, they had to hide behind their husbands' names and souls. The kids I was sitting for laughed their asses off, and I realized that I would have, too, five months earlier.

Now, with awakened eyes, I could see all the brainwashing of my sisters that goes on at school. It starts almost the instant they are born, by their mothers, and by fathers encouraging the boys to take an interest in cars, baseball, etc., and discouraging girls. A girl I know who was always a "tomboy," now, in the compulsory intramural volley ball we have with the boys, always seems to hang back and doesn't seem as "boyish" as she always is. I feel particularly sorry for the snobs or society "chicks" of my grade. Everybody knows the type. They will probably never hear the gospel and if they do would never accept it. I once thought it was "fun" to wear miniskirts (I had a really good figure then, but no longer worry about that shit) and look good for boys and men generally. I rationalized, "Why not? It's fun and they like it." I read all the literature on women's liberation and still wore skirts. But then I heard about the momentous decision by the judge who said that principals could no longer tell girls what to wear, and I went up to my principal; he said he couldn't stop me, but he thought slacks "were in bad taste." Anyway, since that, I've worn dresses or skirts about five times—one time it was to the Passover Seder. Since I began wearing pants I have discovered two things: 1) I feel more equal with boys, and 2) I no longer have to worry as to how my legs are placed and all that bullshit as I had to when I wore skirts. I no longer feel myself fighting other girls for the attention of boys, and am generally much more at ease with the world.

In seventh and eighth grade you have the trimester along with the regular report card. The trimester consists of three subjects—Music, Art, and Home Ec "for girls" and Shop "for boys." I began thinking about a groovy idea— taking Shop instead of Home Ec. So I talked it over with my mother (whom I consider far more liberal than my father) who sent a note off to the junior high girls' guidance counselor. She said I couldn't, but she didn't really tell me why. Then my mother sent a letter off to my principal, repeating that I wished to take Shop and could he please voice his opinion on that. Three weeks later his reply came back. I thought this was a deliberate delay tactic on his part. He is a very clever conservative always having this fantasy that he's on the students' side, which of course is bullshit. Anyway, in his letter he cited several reasons why I couldn't take Shop: 1) it was traditional that a girl took Home Ec, 2) there wouldn't be enough room in Shop for one more pupil, 3) the teacher in Shop would be overworked. He knew that we would go over him to the school supervisor, Dr. Larson, so he sent Larson a copy of his letter. I obtained an appointment with Dr. Larson five days before Home Ec was supposed to start. I explained to him my reasons why I didn't want to take Home Ec. I said I thought that the school system is the mold for people in this society and that in giving a course in Home Ec just for girls and Shop just for boys they were trying to mold girls into being "homemakers" and boys into what molds people thought define "masculinity." I was very impressed by the interview because Dr. Larson, outside of one understanding teacher, was the only school official who took me seriously and listened to me while discussing school affairs. Well, Dr. Larson passed on the request to the district superintendent, Dr. Russo. Larson sent me Xerox copies of the letter to Russo and Russo's letter to an official up at Albany, so I could trust him. Word was passed along to me that nobody in Albany wanted to touch the issue, and they finally sent down an edict that I could do what I wanted to.

While this was going on Home Ec and Shop had already started and I was given a Study Hall during the period that Home Ec/Shop was in. I requested this since I am a pacifist and do not believe in confrontation politics. I wasn't trigger-happy for a confrontation like many SDSers are. (I don't mean to offend any SDS people reading this. Some of my best friends are in SDS.)

The first day I started Shop I was very apprehensive about how the boys were going to react to me being in the class. I have two very good friends in that class (including Dr. Larson's son Mark), and they congratulated me on my success. One of the boys is very condescending toward me, always speaking in the patronizing, gentle voice that really makes me angry. "Connie, let me help you," they say. "Well! I just want to tell you—fuck you, damn it, and go home and stop farting out all that chickenshit, man, just quit it!" I say furiously, but silently. But Shop is fun if the "teacher" isn't paying attention because you can goof all you want to. One thing I realized when I walked into the room the first day was that I could *never* cut, because my absence would be too noticeable.

The whole scene at a suburban school I realize is different than a city school in many ways, of which the maybe most important is that Edgemont is very isolated from other schools and the things you hear about other schools are from either the *New York Times* (who believes them?) and the lower-county paper, the *Reporter Dispatch,* based in White Plains (truthfully called the Distorter Repatch). And you can guess from their nickname what they print. The whole middle-class values, including the meek, passive, "feminine" girl and the strong, overpowering, "masculine" boy are very evident here as in any suburb but especially here since Westchester is such a wealthy suburb-county. The whole bit with the school dances where the boys ask the girls helps brainwash girls and boys into thinking that girls' places in the social caste of a social life and school and elsewhere are lower than boys. As a girl, I often find myself tongue-tied when trying to argue points with older boys, but can talk with boys my age successfully.

I am sure some people when reading this will say, "But surely there's a contradiction in Connie being a pacifist and trying to break down the old definition of feminity as passivity!" I became a pacifist simply because I do not believe that wars solve anything but only create new ones such as new hates, refugees, etc. That is also why I think that Joan Baez is correct in saying all the New Left has is anger and that anger doesn't solve anything just as war doesn't. (I assume I am misquoting her out of context and putting things in her mouth that she never said.) My belief as a vegetarian has grown out of my belief as a pacifist and a lover of life.

Connie Dvorkin
"The Suburban Scene"

120

The Frustrated Annals of a Vietnam Bomber Pilot

The United States launched its active role in Vietnam with a lie: in 1961 Robert S. McNamara, secretary of defense under Kennedy, authorized aerial combat flights by specifying that South Vietnamese airmen be seated onboard so the flights could be termed "training missions." In fact, the air force was fully engaged in bombing missions north of Saigon, using T-38 fighter planes and B-26 bombers. At the time, few Americans were aware of the shrouded war their country was waging: two years later, as the number of U.S. personnel grew from 5,000 to 25,000, the nation was still largely unaware that it was at war, or that Americans in Vietnam were anything other than "advisers." Officials in Washington vacillated in their commitment to the fighting, even as it escalated sharply at the end of 1963. In 1963 and early 1964, Capt. Jerry Shank, a pilot in the U.S. Air Force, flew over fifty missions in Vietnam in a T-28 fighter. Writing home to his wife, in letters excerpted below, he described the frustrations of waging a "training" war, one that looked real enough to those who were in it. Capt. Shank died in combat March 24, 1964.

Nov. 14, 1963.—

. . . We're using equipment and bombs from WW2 [meaning World War II] and it's not too reliable. This is an interesting place here. Everybody works together, officers and enlisted. We're out there lifting bombs and such. Every possible time, we give the men a chance to ride. On a test hop or something like that—it gives them a little motivation. We can't take them on missions, 'cause we have to have our VNAF [Vietnamese Air Force] student pilot along. . . .

We 23 Air Force run the whole T-28 war in the Mekong Delta. This will give you some idea of Uncle Sam's part in the war. . . .

Nov. 22, 1963.—

Been real busy with the armament job—really makes a day go fast. Got all kinds of problems—can't get parts or books or charts describing the different bombs and systems. The Air Force hasn't used any of this equipment since Korea, and everybody seems to have lost the books. The main problem is personnel—no good officers or NCO's over here that really know their business. Most of them are out of SAC [Strategic Air Command] and have dealt only with nuclear weapons. This doesn't apply over here; what we need is someone from World War II. Some days it's like beating your head against a brick wall. . . .

Nov. 27, 1963.—

. . . Sunday all hell broke loose with the VC [Communist Viet Cong guerrillas]. We had a big airborne operation against them—both choppers and parachutes. I woke up at 4:30 to fly my first night attack—darker than hell. . . . By 9 o'clock in the morning we had launched 12 sorties, which is a lot for our little operation. The Viet Congs got one chopper and one B-26 that day, but we (T-28s) hurt them bad. There is far more detail to this, but I don't want to put it in a letter. . . .

I'm up to 20 missions now and am real confident in myself. I do good work, I feel like a veteran and I feel like a different man. I think I am older. . . .

I have changed my opinion about the VC. They are not ornery little fellows. They are mean, vicious, well-trained veterans. They are killers and are out to win. Although this is called a "dirty little war" and it is far from the shores of old U.S.A., it's a big, mean war. We are getting beat. We are undermanned and undergunned. The U.S. may say they are in this, but they don't know we need help over here. . . .

If the U.S. would really put combat people in here we could win and win fast. It seems to be the old story of a halfhearted effort. . . .

Dec. 4, 1963.—

. . . I have debated for a week and a half now over telling you of Black Sunday—Nov. 24, 1963. I'm going to tell you and, if you don't want to hear about these things again, well, say so. You do have a right to know. . . .

. . . This was not a typical day. We flew 20 sorties. But the VC hurt us bad. All in all that day, 23 airplanes were hit, one B-26 crew lost their lives, three choppers crashed. The VC won.

What they had done was pull into the little village and commit their usual atrocities, then pull out. But all they had were small arms and rifles on them. So headquarters thought they would teach this little group of VC's a lesson and sent this operation I spoke of in after them.

But the crafty little b——s withdrew from the town into foxholes and bunkers and hiding places they had been secretly building for a week. Also, they had many friends in there plus large antiaircraft guns and all sorts of machine guns. So when the first wave of troops went in, they thought it was just a routine chase of VC's. But they soon ran against the VC wall and we pilots soon discovered that they had more weapons than pistols and homemade guns. Shrewd plan—and they won.

. . . We could have won but I could write a chapter on that. I hope you were able to follow that, Connie. A lot happened that day and it happened fast and furious. It's not a good thing to tell a wife, but she has to know—no one else will say it—no one else can or will, I guess. There are no heroes over here but there are a lot of fine men—America better not let us down. We can use help. We can win, but America must come over, for the Vietnamese will never hack it alone. We've either got to get in all the way, or get out. If we get out the VC will be in Saigon the next day.

DEC. 14, 1963.—

. . . I do get a kick out of the Vietnamese people. They're poor, dirty and unsanitary according to our standards, but they're happy and some are hardworking. . . .

DEC. 16, 1963.—

. . . The VC's [Communist guerrillas] sure gave them a rough time.

The VC are kind of a Mafia. They terrorize and then they sell "insurance" so that the people will not be harmed again. They strike especially villages where Americans have been seen. They terrorize these villages and then blame it on Americans by saying, "If Americans hadn't come to your village, we would not have plundered and killed, so if you don't want it to happen again, pay us money and don't let Americans into your village."

So you see, they gain from this. First of all, they get money or food; secondly, they instill a dislike for Americans—dirty b———s! But I do like the Vietnamese I've met and talked to. They are friendly, happy, and childlike— good people. . . .

DEC. 21, 1963.—

. . . We got a briefing today of the total result of that operation on 24 November. I'll repeat it briefly.

The air power got credit for 150 to 200 killed. No one can be sure of the amount, for the VC carry off all their dead and wounded. They never let you know for sure how bad you hurt them. . . .

Anyway, there were approximately 700 VC's dug in with three 50-caliber antiaircraft guns and three 30-caliber antiaircraft guns, plus many hundreds other machine guns. They were waiting for us, but we hurt them even though we lost. We lost because we had them trapped and they got away.

It's so mixed up over here—there are over 3,000 Air Force in Vietnam, yet there are only 50 combat crews (B-26 and T-28). What a ridiculous ratio. Also, the Army tried to show the Air Force is no good and vice versa. Ridiculous. Down at Soc Trang, Army and Air Force will die for each other, but up with the colonels and generals it's a big fight for power. And most of these idiots don't even have any idea of what it's like out in combat. . . . They're trying now to find out why we pick up so many hits. The dumb b——s. We get hit more now because the VC have very fine weapons. There are Chinese over here now. . . .

I think the next few months will tell. Either the VC will quit or this will turn into another Korea. I hope it doesn't take the U.S. too long to realize this. . . .

Dec. 22, 1963.—

. . . Flew another mission today. We escorted three trains across no-man's land and then struck some VC's. Our FAC (the guy in the L-19 who tells us where to hit) received three hits, but we got them. I'm credited with destroying a 50-caliber antiaircraft gun. Bombed him out of this world. I guess I'm a true killer. I have no sympathy and I'm good. I don't try to rationalize why I do it. No excuses. It's a target and I hit it with the best of my skill. It's a duel; only (I repeat) only the best man wins. You can't afford to be second. . . .

Dec. 30, 1963.—

. . . Well, here goes. I got shot down yesterday. We were escorting a C-123 and I picked up three slugs in my airplane. One went into my fuel strainer and I lost all my fuel. I made it to a field called Pan Tho and landed safely. Me and the airplane are both okay, not a scratch except the three bullet holes. No sweat. . . .

Jan. 3, 1964.—

Down at Soc Trang, one of the airmen came up with the idea of putting chunks of charcoal in our napalm tanks. Napalm is a gasoline which is jelled into a mass about the consistency of honey. We carry two tanks of it, each weighing 500 pounds. When you drop it, it ignites and spreads fire about 200 to 300 feet. With charcoal in it, the charcoal is thrown about another 200 feet farther, like a burning baseball, and does further damage to VC houses. We've had it at Soc Trang and it works real well.

Tomorrow three birds are going out with one half of their load of straight napalm and the other half with charcoal napalm (Madame Nhu cocktails). A photo ship is going along to take pictures. If higher headquarters thinks it's all right, then they'll buy us the charcoal. So far we've been buying it ourselves or else "borrowing" it from the kitchen.

JAN. 7, 1964.—

. . . Morale's at a big low over here, especially among the combat crews. It's the same old stuff we got in MATS. No consideration for the crew.

Lost two guys today. One was a pretty good friend of mine. The only guess is—the airplane just came apart. B-26—third or fourth that have done that now. . . . Pretty bad day—just hard to find any good news to write. Can't even talk to anybody—nobody has anything to say. Just a blue day. . . .

. . . I don't know what the U.S. is doing. They tell you people we're just in a training situation and they try to run us as a training base. But we're at war. We are doing the flying and fighting. We are losing. Morale is very bad.

We asked if we couldn't fly an American flag over here. The answer was "No." They say the VC will get pictures of it and make bad propaganda. Let them. Let them know America is in it.

If they'd only give us good American airplanes with the U.S. insignias on them and really tackle this war, we could possibly win. If we keep up like we are going, we will definitely lose. I'm not being pessimistic. It's so obvious. How our Government can lie to its own people—it's something you wouldn't think a democratic government could do. I wish I were a prominent citizen or knew someone who could bring this before the U.S. public. However, if it were brought before the average U.S. family, I'm sure all they'd do is shake their heads and say tch-tch and tune in another channel on the TV. . . .

JAN. 9, 1964.—

. . . Had a good target today finally. Felt like I really dealt a blow to the VC. On my second bomb I got a secondary explosion. This means after my bomb exploded there was another explosion. It was either an ammo dump or a fuel-storage area. Made a huge burning fireball. You really can't tell when you roll in on a pass what is in the huts and trees you are aiming at. Just lucky today, but I paid them back for shooting me down. . . .

JAN. 15, 1964.—

. . . Another B-26 went in yesterday. Nobody made it out. A couple of guys I knew pretty well "bought the farm." . . .

One of the new guys busted up a 28 (T-28) also yesterday. He thought he had napalm on but he had bombs. So at 50 feet above the ground he dropped a bomb. It almost blew him out of the sky. But he limped back to Bien Hoa and crash landed. The airplane burned up, but he got out all right. . . .

. . . That news commentary you heard is absolutely correct—if we don't get in big, we will be pushed out. I am a little ashamed of my country. We can no longer save face over here, for we have no face to save.

We are more than ever fighting this war. The Vietnamese T-28s used to come down here to Soc Trang and fly missions. But lately, since we've been getting shot so much, they moved up north. I kid you not. First they didn't want to come to Soc Trang because their families couldn't come. Second, because they didn't get enough per diem [additional pay]. Third, because they didn't want to get shot at. There were a couple of more reasons, but I can't remember them. These are the people we're supposed to be helping. I don't understand it. . . .

JAN. 20, 1964.—

. . . I have never been so lonely, unhappy, disappointed, frustrated in my whole life. None of these feelings are prevalent above the other. I guess I should say loneliness overshadows the others, but that's really not true.

I am over here to do the best job possible for my country—yet my country will do nothing for me or any of my buddies or even for itself. I love America. My country is the best, but it is soft and has no guts about it at all.

I'm sure nothing will be done over here until after the elections. Why? Because votes are more important than my life or any of my buddies' lives. What gets me the most is that they won't tell you people what we do over here. I'll bet you that anyone you talk to does not know that American pilots fight this war. We—me and my buddies—do everything. The Vietnamese "students" we have on board are airmen basics. The only reason they are on board is in case we crash there is one American "adviser" and one Vietnamese "student." They're stupid, ignorant sacrificial lambs, and I have no use for them. In fact, I have been tempted to whip them within an inch of their life a few times. They're a menace to have on board. . . .

JAN. 26, 1964.—

. . . I've done almost nothing all week. I needed the rest very badly. I actually think I was getting battle fatigue or whatever you call it. I've got 50 missions, almost all without any kind of a break, and it was telling on my nerves and temper. I feel real good today after all that sleep. I kinda hate to go to work tomorrow, for we start two weeks of combat again. But I'm rested for it now and am ready. . . .

JAN. 31, 1964.—

. . . All you read in the paper is the poor leadership of the Vietnamese, but we are just as bad. Everyone over here seems to be unqualified for his job. Like me—I'm a multi pilot, but I'm flying TAC fighters. We have no fighter pilots in our outfit. I'm not complaining, but, if the Air Force was serious, they would have sent over experienced fighter people. The same on up the line.

FEB. 2, 1964.—

. . . I'm getting to like Vietnam. Maybe I didn't say that right. I think it is a pretty country. These little villages in the Delta are about as picturesque as you'll find. Tall palm trees, fields of rice, and all kinds of flowers. The people seem happy enough, if it wasn't for the terror of VC raids. . . .

Feb. 6, 1964.—

. . . We scrambled after a fort under attack. We hit and hit good, but it got dark so we headed up here for Bien Hoa. Pretty hot target and we both were hit. Coming in here to Bien Hoa they warned us that VC were shooting at airplanes on final approach. Well, we made a tight, fast approach and held our lights (it was pitch black) until almost over the end of the runway. I forgot my landing gear and went skidding in a shower of sparks down the runway. Airplane's not hurt too bad. I'm not even scratched. My pride is terribly wounded. That was my 62nd mission. I thought I had it "wired" after that much combat experience. Then I go and goof so badly. . . .

Feb. 17, 1964.—

All B-26s are grounded, so we are the only strike force left.

. . . A B-26 crashed at Hurlburt last week. Another came with the wing just coming off. Finally the Air Force is worried about the airplanes—finally, after six of my friends have "augered in."

Feb. 21, 1964.—

. . . Tuesday evening —— —— got shot down. He fell in his airplane next to a Special Forces camp and got out without a scratch. The airplane burned completely up, though. [Another airman] was going in on his seventh strafing pass and never came out of it. Don't know what happened—whether he got shot or his controls shot out. That was two airplanes in two days. Kind of shook us up.

Not only that, the B-26s have been grounded since Monday because the wings came off one again at Hurlburt. So after the last crash the whole USAF fighter force is down to six airplanes. This should set an example of how much Uncle Sam cares. Six airplanes. Might as well be none.

. . . Rumor now is that B-26s will fly again only with greater restrictions. . . . I'm pretty well fed up. Poor B-26 jocks are really shook. That airplane is a killer.

Feb. 24, 1964.—

. . . We're down to five airplanes now, all of them at Soc Trang. We have actually got nine total, but four are out of commission because of damage. The B-26s aren't flying yet, but they've been more or less released. I don't know what U.S. is going to do, but whatever it is I'm sure it's wrong. Five airplanes can't fight the war—that's just ridiculous. Tell this to my dad. Let him know, too, how much the country is letting everyone down. . . . We fight and we die but no one cares. They've lied to my country about us.

FEB. 29, 1964.—

. . . We've got a new general in command now and he really sounds good. Sounds like a man who is out to fight and win. He's grounded the B-26s except for a few flights. But they have to level bomb, not dive bomb—no strain for the aircraft that way. He has ordered B-57s (bombers—jets) to replace them, and has asked for immediate delivery. He has also demanded they replace the T-28s with the AD-6. The AD-6 is a much more powerful single-engine dive bomber. It was designed for this type of work and has armor plating. We are pretty excited about all the new airplanes. We can really do good work with that kind of equipment. . . .

MARCH 13, 1964.—

McNamara [Secretary of Defense] was here, spent his usual line, and has gone back home to run the war with his screwed-up bunch of people. We call them "McNamara's Band." I hope and pray that somehow this man does something right pretty soon.

Just one thing right will help immensely. He did send a representative over here. All he did was make the troops sore.

One of our complaints was that we can't understand the air controller, so he suggested that we learn Vietnamese. We said we didn't have that much time, so he suggested we stay here for two years. A brilliant man. He's lucky to be alive. Some of the guys honestly had to be held back from beating this idiot up. This man McNamara and his whole idiot band will cause me not to vote for Johnson no matter how much I like his policies.

McNamara is actually second in power to Johnson. But, as a military man, he finishes a definite and decided last—all the way last. . . .

Rumors are fast and furious. Nothing yet on B-57s. Rumors that B-26s are all rigged up with extra fuel tanks for long overwater flights. B-26 should never fly again, even if rejuvenated. Also a rumor that B-26 pilots will get instruction in the A-1H—another single-engine dive bomber. All is still in the air—all rumors. . . .

MARCH 22, 1964.—

. . . Been flying pretty heavy again. We've only got 20 pilots now and 11 airplanes. It keeps us pretty busy. Also got two more airplanes they're putting together in Saigon, so we'll soon be back up to 13 airplanes again. Hope these last for a while. . . .

That was Captain Shank's last letter. He was killed in combat two days later.

CAPT. JERRY SHANK
U.S. News & World Report
May 4, 1964

121

The Democratic Convention: August 1968

The Democratic National Convention limped into Chicago in August of 1968 without two of the party's leading voices. Lyndon Johnson, the sitting president, had withdrawn his name from the race for the nomination the previous spring. Robert Kennedy had been gunned down in June. Protest groups surveyed the party that remained and decided that it was growing pale in its stand against the Vietnam War, the watershed issue of the day. Hubert Humphrey, the front-runner, had never taken a strong stance against the war; Eugene McCarthy had, but he stood little chance of affecting the convention. Students and other young activists who intended to have a say in the matter began arriving in Chi-cago during the days leading up to the convention. Some, such as Tom Hayden of the Nation Mobilization Committee, planned to make a peaceful protest. Others, including Abbie Hoffman, were undoubtedly looking for trouble (threat-ening, for example, to contaminate the city's water supply with LSD). Richard Daley, the law-and-order mayor of Chicago, amassed an outsized police force to disperse the protesters, who numbered between two and ten thousand at various times. Spurred on by Daley, the police became frenzied and the result was a two-day battle in the streets. The assault, carried live on television, seemed to bring the agonies of Vietnam home to America: a nation divided, immersed in violence and with no sense of reason to cling to, anywhere. Norman Mailer, best known as a novelist, wrote an account of the clash in his book, *Miami and the Siege of Chicago*.

They were young men who were not going to Vietnam. So they would show every lover of war in Vietnam that the reason they did not go was not for lack of the courage to fight; no, they would carry the fight over every street in Old Town and the Loop where the opportunity presented itself. If they had been gassed and beaten, their leaders arrested on fake charges (Hayden, picked up while sitting under a tree in daylight in Lincoln Park, naturally protested; the resulting charge was "resisting arrest"), they were going to demonstrate that they would not give up, that they were the stuff out of which the very best soldiers were made. Sunday, they had been driven out of the park, Monday as well, now Tuesday. The centers where they slept in bedrolls on the floor near Lincoln Park had been broken into by the police, informers and provocateurs were everywhere; tonight tear-gas trucks had been used. They were still not ready to give up. Indeed their militancy may have increased. They took care of the worst of their injured and headed for the Loop, picking up fellow demonstrators as they went. Perhaps the tear gas was a kind of catharsis for some of them, a letting of tears, a purging of old middle-class weakness. Some were turning from college boys to revolution- aries. It seemed as if the more they were beaten and tear-gassed, the more they rallied back. Now, with the facility for underground communication which seemed so instinctive a tool in their generation's equipment, they were on their way to Grant Park, en masse, a thousand of them, two thousand of them, there were conceivably as many as five thousand boys and girls massed in Grant Park at three in the morning, listening to speakers, cheering, chant- ing, calling across Michigan Avenue to the huge brooding facade of the Hil- ton, a block wide, over twenty-five stories high, with huge wings and deep courts (the better to multiply the number of windows with a view of the street and a view of Grant Park). The lights were on in hundreds of bed- rooms in the Hilton, indeed people were sleeping and dreaming all over the hotel with the sound of young orators declaiming in the night below, voices rising twenty, twenty-five stories high, the voices clear in the spell of sound which hung over the Hilton. The Humphrey headquarters were here, and the McCarthy headquarters. Half the Press was quartered here, and Mar- vin Watson as well. Postmaster General and Presidential troubleshooter, he had come to bring some of Johnson's messages to Humphrey. His suite had a view of the park. Indeed two-thirds of the principals at the convention must have had a view early this morning, two and three and four A.M. of this Tuesday night, no, this Wednesday morning, of Grant Park filled across the street with a revolutionary army of dissenters and demonstrators and college children and McCarthy workers and tourists ready to take a crack on the head, all night they could hear the demonstrators chanting, "Join us, join us," and the college bellow of utter contempt, "Dump the Hump! Dump the Hump!" all the fury of the beatings and the tear-gassings, all the bitter disappointments of that recently elapsed bright spring when the only critical problem was who would make a better President, Kennedy or McCarthy (now all the dread of a future with Humphrey or Nixon). There was also the sense that police had now entered their lives, become an element pervasive as drugs and books and sex and music and family. So they shouted up to the windows of the Hilton, to the delegates and the campaign workers who were sleeping, or shuddering by the side of their bed, or cheering by their open window; they called up through the night on a stage as vast and towering as one of Wagner's visions and the screams of police cars joined them, pulling up, gliding away, blue lights revolving, lines of police hundreds long in their sky-blue shirts and sky-blue crash helmets, penning the demonstrators back of barriers across Michigan Avenue from the Hilton, and other lines of police and police fences on the Hilton's side of the street. The police had obviously been given orders not to attack the demonstrators here, not in front of the Hilton with half the Democratic Party watching them, not now at three in the morning—would anyone ever discover for certain what was to change their mind in sixteen hours?

Now, a great cheer went up. The police were being relieved by the National Guard. The Guard was being brought in. It was like a certificate of merit for the demonstrators to see the police march off and now hundreds of Guardsmen in khaki uniforms, helmets, and rifles take up post in place, army trucks coughing and barking and filing back and forth on Michigan Avenue, and on the side streets now surrounding the Hilton, evil-looking jeeps with barbed-wire gratings in front of their bumpers drove forward in echelons, and parked behind the crowd. Portable barbed-wire fences were now riding on Jeeps.

Earlier in the week, it had been relatively simple to get into the Hilton. Mobs of McCarthy workers and excited adolescents had jammed the stairs and the main entrance room of the lobby chanting all day, singing campaign songs, mocking every Humphrey worker they could recognize, holding station for hours in the hope, or on the rumor, that McCarthy would be passing through, and the cheers had the good nature and concerted rhythmic steam of a football rally. That had been Saturday and Sunday and Monday, but the police finally had barricaded the kids out of the lobby, and now at night covered the entrances to the Hilton, and demanded press passes, and room keys, as warrants of entry. The Hilton heaved and staggered through a variety of attacks and breakdowns. Like an old fort, like the old fort of the old Democratic Party, about to fall forever beneath the ministrations of its high shaman, its excruciated warlock, derided by the young, held in contempt by its own soldiers—the very delegates who would be loyal to Humphrey in the nomination and loyal to nothing in their heart—this spiritual fort of the Democratic Party was now housed in the literal fort of the Hilton staggering in place, all boilers working, all motors vibrating, yet seeming to come apart from the pressures on the street outside, as if the old Hilton had become artifact of the party and the nation.

Nothing worked well in the hotel, and much didn't work at all. There was no laundry because of the bus strike, and the house phones usually did not function; the room phones were tapped so completely, and the devices so over-adjacent, that separate conversations lapped upon one another in the same earpiece, or went jolting by in all directions like three handballs at play at once in a four-wall handball court. Sometimes the phone was dead, sometimes it emitted hideous squawks, or squeals, or the harsh electronic displeasure of a steady well-pulsed static. Sometimes one got long distance by taking it through the operator, sometimes one got an outside line only by ringing the desk and demanding it, sometimes one could get the hotel operator only by dialing the outside line. All the while, a photograph of Mayor Daley the size of a postage stamp was pasted on the cradle of the phone. "Welcome to the

1968 National Democratic Convention," it said. Often, one could not even extract a whimper from the room phone. It had succumbed. Sometimes the phone stayed dead for hours. Success in a convention is reduced to success in communications, as the reporter was yet to learn; communications in the headquarters of the largest party in the nation most renowned for the technology of its communications was breaking apart under strikes, pressure, sabotage, security, security over-check, overdevelopment and insufficient testing of advanced technical devices: at the base of the pyramid, sheer human inefficiencies before the combined onslaught of pressure and street war.

The elevators worked abominably. On certain floors the signal did not seem to ring. One could wait a half hour for an elevator to stop on the way down. After a time everybody went up to the top in order to be able to go down. Yet one could not use the stairs, for Secret Servicemen were guarding them. It could, at worst, demand an hour to go to one's room and go down again. So it might have been better to live in a hotel across the Loop; but then there were traffic jams and police lines and demonstrators every night, demonstrators marching along with handkerchiefs to their noses.

This night with the demonstrators up and aroused in Grant Park, tear gas was blowing right into the hotel. The police had tried to gas the kids out of the park when they first arrived in numbers from Lincoln Park, but the wind blew the wrong way, blew the tears across the street into the air-conditioning of the Hilton lobby, and delegates and Press and officials walked about with smarting eyes, burning throats, and the presentiment that they were going to catch a cold. The lobby stunk. Not from the tear gas, but from stink bombs, or some advanced variety of them, for the source of the odor was either mysterious, or unremovable, or had gotten into the very entrails of the air-conditioning since it got worse from day to day and drenched the coffee shop and the bars and the lobby with a stench not easily forgettable. Standing near someone the odor of vomit always prevailed from the bombs—no, it was worse than vomit, rather like a truly atrocious body odor which spoke of the potential for sour vomit in every joint of a bad piece of psychic work. So personal relations were curious. One met attractive men or women, shook hands with them, chatted for a time, said good-bye. One's memory of the occasion was how awful it had smelled. Delegates, powerful political figures, old friends, and strangers all smelled awful.

So nothing worked well in the hotel, and everything stank, and crowds—those who could get in—milled about, and police guarded the entrance, and across the street as the reporter moved through the tight press of children sitting packed together on the grass, cheering the speakers, chanting "Join us! Join us!" and "Dump the Hump" the smell of the stink bombs was still present, but different now, equally evil and vomitous but from a faded odor of Mace. The nation divided was going to war with stinks; each side would inflict a stink upon the other. The years of sabotage were ahead—a fearful perspective: they would be giving engineering students tests in loyalty before they were done; the F.B.I. would come to question whoever took a mail order course in radio. It was possible that one was at the edge of that watershed year from which the country might never function well again, and service in American hotels would yet be reminiscent of service in Mexican motels. Whatever! the children were alive with revolutionary fire on this fine Tuesday night, this early Wednesday morning, and the National Guard policing them was wide-awake as well. Incidents occurred. Flare-ups. A small Negro soldier started pushing a demonstrator with his rifle, pushing him in sudden fury as at the wild kickoff of a wild street fight; the demonstrator—who looked to be a kindly divinity student—aghast at what he had set off; he had not comprehended the Negro wished no special conversation from him. And a National Guard officer came running up to pull the Negro back. (On the next night, there would be no Negroes in the line of National Guards.)

The kids were singing. There were two old standards which were sung all the time. An hour could not go by without both songs. So they sang "We Shall Overcome" and they sang "This Land Is Your Land," and a speaker cried up to the twenty-five stories of the Hilton, "We have the votes, you have the guns," a reference to the polls which had shown McCarthy to be more popular than Hubert Humphrey (yes, if only Rockefeller had run for the Democrats and McCarthy for the Republicans this would have been an ideal contest between a spender and a conservative) and then another speaker, referring to the projected march on the Amphitheatre next day, shouted, "We're going to march without a permit—the Russians demand a permit to have a meeting in Prague," and the crowd cheered this. They cheered with wild enthusiasm when one speaker, a delegate, had the inspiration to call out to the delegates and workers listening in the hundreds of rooms at the Hilton with a view of the park, "Turn on your lights, and blink them if you are with us. If you are with us, if you are sympathetic to us, blink your lights, blink your lights." And to the delight of the crowd, lights began to blink in the Hilton, ten, then twenty, perhaps so many as fifty lights were blinking at once, and a whole bank of lights on the fifteenth floor and the twenty-third floor went off and on at once, off and on at once. The McCarthy headquarters on the fifteenth and the twenty-third were blinking, and the crowd cheered. Now they had become an audience to watch the actors in the hotel. So two audiences regarded each other, like ships signalling across a gulf of water in the night, and delegates came down from the hotel; a mood of new beauty was in the air, there present through all the dirty bandaged kids, the sour vomit odor of the Mace, the sighing and whining of the army trucks moving in and out all the time, the adenoids, larynxes, wheezes and growls of the speakers, the blinking of lights in the Hilton, yes, there was the breath of this incredible crusade where fear was in every breath you took, and so breath was tender, it came into the lungs as a manifest of value, as a gift, and the children's faces were shining in the glow of the headlights of the National Guard trucks and the searchlights of the police in front of the Hilton across Michigan Avenue. And the Hilton, sinking in its foundations, twinkled like a birthday cake. Horrors were coming tomorrow. No, it is today. It is Wednesday already.

Meanwhile, a mass meeting was taking place about the bandshell in Grant Park, perhaps a quarter of a mile east of Michigan Avenue and the Conrad Hilton. The meeting was under the auspices of the Mobilization, and a crowd of ten or fifteen thousand appeared. The Mayor had granted a permit to assemble, but had refused to allow a march. Since the Mobilization had announced that it would attempt, no matter how, the march to the Amphitheatre that was the first purpose of their visit to Chicago, the police were out in force to surround the meeting.

An episode occurred during the speeches. Three demonstrators climbed a flag pole to cut down the American flag and put up a rebel flag. A squad of police charged to beat them up, but got into trouble themselves, for when they threw tear gas, the demonstrators lobbed the canisters back, and the police, choking on their own gas, had to fight their way clear through a barrage of rocks. Then came a much larger force of police charging the area, overturning benches, busting up members of the audience, then heading for Rennie Davis at the bullhorn. He was one of the coordinators of the Mobilization, his face was known, he had been fingered and fingered again by plainclothesmen. Now urging the crowd to sit down and be calm, he was attacked from behind by the police, his head laid open in a three-inch cut, and he was unconscious for a period. Furious at the attack, Tom Hayden, who had been in disguise these last two days to avoid any more arrests for himself, spoke to the crowd, said he was leaving to perform certain special tasks, and suggested that others break up into small groups and go out into the streets of the Loop "to do what they have to do." A few left with him; the majority remained. While it was a People's Army and therefore utterly unorganized by uniform or unity, it had a variety of special troops and regular troops; everything from a few qualified Kamikaze who were ready to charge police lines in a Japanese snake dance·and dare on the consequence, some vicious beatings, to various kinds of small saboteurs, rock-throwers, gauntlet-runners—some of the speediest of the kids were adept at taunting cops while keeping barely out of range of their clubs—not altogether alien to running the bulls at Pamplona. Many of those who remained, however, were still nominally pacifists, protesters, Gandhians—they believed in non-violence, in the mystical interposition of their body to the attack, as if the violence of the enemy might be drained by the spiritual act of passive resistance over the years, over the thousands, tens of thousands, hundreds of thousands of beatings over the years. So Allen Ginsberg was speaking now to them.

The police looking through the plexiglass face shields they had flipped down from their helmets were then obliged to watch the poet with his bald head, soft eyes magnified by horn-rimmed eyeglasses, and massive dark beard, utter his words in a croaking speech. He had been gassed Monday night and Tuesday night, and had gone to the beach at dawn to read Hindu Tantras to some of the Yippies, the combination of the chants and the gassings had all but burned out his voice, his beautiful speaking voice, one of the most powerful and hypnotic instruments of the Western world was down to the scrapings of the throat now, raw as flesh after a curettage.

"The best strategy for you," said Ginsberg, "in cases of hysteria, overexcitement or fear, is still to chant 'OM' together. It helps to quell flutterings of butterflies in the belly. Join me now as I try to lead you."

The crowd chanted with Ginsberg. They were of a generation which would try every idea, every drug, every action—it was even possible a few of them had made out with freaky kicks on tear gas these last few days—so they would chant OM. There were Hindu fanatics in the crowd, children who loved India and scorned everything in the West; there were cynics who thought the best thing to be said for a country which allowed its excess population to die by the millions in famine-ridden fields was that it would not be ready soon to try to dominate the rest of the world. There were also militants who were ready to march. And the police there to prevent them, busy now in communication with other detachments of police, by way of radios whose aerials were attached to their helmets, thereby giving them the look of giant insects.

A confused hour began. Lincoln Park was irregular in shape with curving foot walks; but Grant Park was indeed not so much a park as a set of belts of greenery cut into files by major parallel avenues between Michigan Avenue and Lake Michigan half a mile away. Since there were also cross streets cutting the belts of green perpendicularly, a variety of bridges and pedestrian overpasses gave egress to the city. The park was in this sense an alternation of lawn with superhighways. So the police were able to pen the crowd. But not completely. There were too many bridges, too many choices, in effect, for the police to anticipate. To this confusion was added the fact that every confrontation of demonstrators with police, now buttressed by the National Guard, attracted hundreds of newsmen, and hence began a set of attempted negotiations between spokesmen for the demonstrators and troops. The demonstrators finally tried to force a bridge and get back to the city. Repelled by tear gas, they went to other bridges, still other bridges, finally found a bridge lightly guarded, broke through a passage and were loose in the city at six-thirty in the evening. They milled about in the Loop for a few minutes, only to encounter the mules and three wagons of the Poor People's Campaign. City officials, afraid of provoking the Negroes on the South Side, had given a permit to the Reverend Abernathy, and he was going to march the mules and wagons down Michigan Avenue and over to the convention. An impromptu march of the demonstrators formed behind the wagons immediately on encountering them and ranks of marchers, sixty, eighty, a hundred in line across the width of Michigan Avenue began to move forward in the gray early twilight of 7 P.M.; Michigan Avenue was now suddenly jammed with people in the march, perhaps so many as four or five thousand people, including onlookers on the sidewalk who jumped in. The streets of the Loop were also reeking with tear gas—the wind had blown some of the gas west over Michigan Avenue from the drops on the bridges, some gas still was penetrated into the clothing of the marchers. In broken ranks, half a march, half a happy mob, eyes red from gas, faces excited by the tension of the afternoon, and the excitement of the escape from Grant Park, now pushing down Michigan Avenue toward the Hilton Hotel with dreams of a march on to the Amphitheatre four miles beyond, and in the full pleasure of being led by the wagons of the Poor People's March, the demonstrators shouted to everyone on the sidewalk, "Join us, join us, join us," and the sidewalk kept disgorging more people ready to march.

But at Balbo Avenue, just before Michigan Avenue reached the Hilton, the marchers were halted by the police. It was a long halt. Perhaps thirty minutes. Time for people who had been walking on the sidewalk to join the march, proceed for a few steps, halt with the others, wait, get bored, and leave. It was time for someone in command of the hundreds of police in the neighborhood to communicate with his headquarters, explain the problem, time for the dilemma to be relayed, alternatives examined, and orders conceivably sent back to attack and disperse the crowd. If so, a trap was first set. The mules were allowed to cross Balbo Avenue, then were separated by a line of police from the marchers, who now, several thousand compressed in this one place, filled the intersection of Michigan Avenue and Balbo. There, dammed by police on three sides, and cut off from the wagons of the Poor People's March, there, right beneath the windows of the Hilton which looked down on Grant Park and Michigan Avenue, the stationary march was abruptly attacked. The police attacked with tear gas, with Mace, and with clubs, they attacked like a chain saw cutting into wood, the teeth of the saw the edge of their clubs, they attacked like a scythe through grass, lines of twenty and thirty policemen striking out in an arc, their clubs beating, demonstrators fleeing. Seen from overhead, from the nineteenth floor, it was like a wind blowing dust, or the edge of waves riding foam on the shore.

The police cut through the crowd one way, then cut through them another. They chased people into the park, ran them down, beat them up; they cut through the intersection at Michigan and Balbo like a razor cutting a channel through a head of hair, and then drove columns of new police into the channel who in turn pushed out, clubs flailing, on each side, to cut new channels, and new ones again. As demonstrators ran, they re-formed in new groups only to be chased by the police again. The action went on for ten minutes, fifteen minutes, with the absolute ferocity of a tropical storm, and watching it from a window on the nineteenth floor, there was something of the detachment of studying a storm at evening through a glass, the light was a lovely gray-blue, the police had uniforms of sky-blue, even the ferocity had an abstract elemental play of forces of nature at battle with other forces, as if sheets of tropical rain were driving across the street in patterns, in curving patterns which curved upon each other again. Police cars rolled up, prisoners were beaten, shoved into wagons, driven away. The rain of police, maddened by the uncoiling of their own storm, pushed against their own barricades of tourists pressed on the street against the Hilton Hotel, then pressed them so hard—but here is a quotation from J. Anthony Lukas in *The New York Times.*

Even elderly bystanders were caught in the police onslaught. At one point, the police turned on several dozen persons standing quietly behind police barriers in front of the Conrad Hilton Hotel watching the demonstrators across the street.

For no reason that could be immediately determined, the blue-helmeted policemen charged the barriers, crushing the spectators against the windows of the Haymarket Inn, a restaurant in the hotel. Finally the window gave way, sending screaming middle-aged women and children backward through the broken shards of glass.

The police then ran into the restaurant and beat some of the victims who had fallen through the windows and arrested them.

Now another quote from Steve Lerner in *The Village Voice:*

When the charge came, there was a stampede toward the sidelines. People piled into each other, humped over each other's bodies like coupling dogs. To fall down in the crush was just as terrifying as facing the police. Suddenly I realized my feet weren't touching the ground as the crowd pushed up onto the sidewalk. I was grabbing at the army jacket of the boy in front of me; the girl behind me had a stranglehold on my neck and was screaming incoherently in my ear.

Now, a longer quotation from Jack Newfield in *The Village Voice.* (The accounts in *The Voice* of September 5 were superior to any others encountered that week.)

At the southwest entrance to the Hilton, a skinny, long-haired kid of about seventeen skidded down on the sidewalk, and four overweight cops leaped on him, chopping strokes on his head. His hair flew from the force of the blows. A dozen small rivulets of blood began to cascade down the kid's temple and onto the sidewalk. He was not crying or screaming, but crawling in a stupor toward the gutter. When he saw a photographer take a picture, he made a V sign with his fingers.

A doctor in a white uniform and Red Cross arm band began to turn toward the kid, but two other cops caught him from behind and knocked him down. One of them jammed his knee into the doctor's throat and began clubbing his rib cage. The doctor squirmed away, but the cops followed him, swinging hard, sometimes missing.

A few feet away a phalanx of police charged into a group of women reporters, and young McCarthy activists standing idly against the window of the Hilton Hotel's Haymarket Inn. The terrified people began to go down under the unexpected police charge when the plate glass window shattered, and the people tumbled backward through the glass. The police then climbed through the broken window and began to beat people, some of whom had been drinking quietly in the hotel bar.

At the side entrance of the Hilton Hotel four cops were chasing one frightened kid of about seventeen. Suddenly, Fred Dutton, a former aide to Robert Kennedy, moved out from under the marquee and interposed his body between the kid and the police.

"He's my guest in this hotel," Dutton told the cops.

The police started to club the kid.

Dutton screamed for the first cop's name and badge number. The cop grabbed Dutton and began to arrest him, until a Washington Post *reporter identified Dutton as a former RFK aide.*

Demonstrators, reporters, McCarthy workers, doctors, all began to stagger into the Hilton lobby, blood streaming from face and head wounds. The lobby smelled from tear gas, and stink bombs dropped by the Yippies. A few people began to direct the wounded to a makeshift hospital on the fifteenth floor, the McCarthy staff headquarters.

Fred Dutton was screaming at the police, and at the journalists to report all the "sadism and brutality." Richard Goodwin, the ashen nub of a cigar sticking out of his fatigued face, mumbled, "This is just the beginning. There'll be four years of this."

The defiant kids began a slow, orderly retreat back up Michigan Avenue. They did not run. They did not panic. They did not fight back. As they fell back they helped pick up fallen comrades who were beaten or gassed. Suddenly, a plainclothesman dressed as a soldier moved out of the shadows and knocked one kid down with an overhand punch. The kid squatted on the pavement of Michigan Avenue, trying to cover his face, while the Chicago plainclothesman punched him with savage accuracy. Thud, thud, thud. Blotches of blood spread over the kid's face. Two photographers moved in. Several police formed a closed circle around the beating to prevent pictures. One of the policemen then squirted Chemical Mace at the photographers, who dispersed. The plainclothesman melted into the line of police.

Let us escape to the street. The reporter, watching in safety from the nine-teenth floor, could understand now how Mussolini's son-in-law had once been able to find the bombs he dropped from his airplane beautiful as they burst, yes, children, and youths, and middle-aged men and women were be-ing pounded and clubbed and gassed and beaten, hunted and driven, sent scattering in all directions by teams of policemen who had exploded out of their restraints like the bursting of a boil, and nonetheless he felt a sense of calm and beauty, void even of the desire to be down there, as if in years to come there would be beatings enough, some chosen, some from nowhere, but it was as if the war had finally begun, and this was therefore a great and solemn moment, as if indeed even the gods of history had come together from each side to choose the very front of the Hilton Hotel before the tele-vision cameras of the world and the eyes of the campaign workers and the delegates' wives, yes, there before the eyes of half the principals at the con-vention was this drama played, as if the military spine of a great liberal party had finally separated itself from the skin, as if, no metaphor large enough to suffice, the Democratic Party had here broken in two before the eyes of a na-tion like Melville's whale charging right out of the sea.

A great stillness rose up from the street through all the small noise of clubbing and cries, small sirens, sigh of loaded arrest vans as off they pulled, shouts of police as they wheeled in larger circles, the intersection clearing fur-ther, then further, a stillness rose through the steel and stone of the hotel, con-gregating in the shocked centers of every room where delegates and wives and Press and campaign workers innocent until now of the intimate working of social force, looked down now into the murderous paradigm of Vietnam there beneath them at this huge intersection of this great city. Look—a boy was running through the park, and a cop was chasing. There he caught him on the back of the neck with his club! There! The cop is returning to his own! And the boy stumbling to his feet is helped off the ground by a girl who has come running up.

Yes, it could only have happened in a meeting of the Gods, that history for once should take place not on some back street, or some inaccessible grand room, not in some laboratory indistinguishable from others, or in the sly un-discoverable hypocrisies of a committee of experts, but rather on the center of the stage, as if each side had said, "Here we will have our battle. Here we will win."

The demonstrators were afterward delighted to have been manhandled before the public eye, delighted to have pushed and prodded, antagonized and provoked the cops over these days with rocks and bottles and cries of "Pig" to the point where police had charged in a blind rage and made a stage at the one place in the city (besides the Amphitheatre) where audience, actors, and cameras could all convene, yes, the rebels thought they had had a great victory, and perhaps they did; but the reporter wondered, even as he saw it, if the police in that half hour of waiting had not had time to receive instructions from the power of the city, perhaps the power of the land, and the power had decided, "No, do not let them march another ten blocks and there disperse them on some quiet street, no, let it happen before all the land, let everybody see that their dissent will soon be equal to their own blood; let them realize that the power is implacable, and will beat and crush and imprison and yet kill before it will ever relinquish the power. So let them see before their own eyes what it will cost to continue to mock us, defy us, and resist. There are more millions behind us than behind them, more millions who wish to weed out, poison, gas, and obliterate every flower whose power they do not comprehend than heroes for their side who will view our brute determination and still be ready to resist. There are more cowards alive than the brave. Otherwise we would not be where we are," said the Prince of Greed.

Who knew. One could thank the city of Chicago where drama was still a property of the open stage. It was quiet now, there was nothing to stare down on but the mules, and the police guarding them. The mules had not moved through the entire fray. Isolated from the battle, they had stood there in harness waiting to be told to go on. Only once in a while did they turn their heads. Their role as actors in the Poor People's March was to wait and to serve. Finally they moved on. The night had come. It was dark. The intersection was now empty. Shoes, ladies' handbags, and pieces of clothing lay on the street outside the hotel.

NORMAN MAILER
Miami and the Siege of Chicago

122

Neil Armstrong Reminisces
About His Moon Walk

In April 1961, a month before the United States launched its first manned space flight, President Kennedy wrote to Lyndon Johnson, his vice president and head of the National Space Council, demanding a progress report on moon flights. In too many ways, the Soviets seemed to be beating America to the "New Frontier," Kennedy's metaphor for space and the future. "Are we working twenty-four hours a day?" he asked Johnson, "If not, why not?" Later that spring, Kennedy announced a new American initiative to land a man on the moon before the end of the decade. At the time, it seemed a foolhardy boast, but on July 20, 1969, Neil Armstrong made good on it, spending two and a half hours walking around the surface of the moon in the company of Buzz Aldrin. The effort had involved 400,000 people over the course of the decade, according to astronaut Michael Collins, the third man in the flight crew. To Collins, orbiting overhead, the moon was "this monotonous rockpile, this withered sun-seared peach pit." That was the view from a distance of sixty miles. Neil Armstrong described his own eye-level impressions of the surface of the moon, and on the horizon of the New Frontier.

It took us somewhat longer to emerge from *Eagle* than we had anticipated but the delay was not, as my wife and perhaps some others have half jokingly suggested, to give me time to think about what to say when I actually stepped out onto the moon. I had thought about that a little before the flight, mainly because so many people had made such a big point of it. I had also thought about it a little on the way to the moon, but not much. It wasn't until after landing that I made up my mind what to say: "That's one small step for a Man, one giant leap for mankind." Beyond those words I don't recall any particular emotion or feeling other than a little caution, a desire to be sure it was safe to put my weight on that surface outside *Eagle*'s footpad.

... The most dramatic recollections I have now are the sights themselves, those magnificent visual images. They go far beyond any other visual experiences I've had in my life. Of all the spectacular views we had, the most impressive to me was on the way toward the moon when we flew through its shadow. We were still thousands of miles away but close enough so that the moon almost filled our circular window. It was eclipsing the sun, from our position, and the corona of the sun was visible around the limb of the moon as a gigantic lens-shaped or saucer-shaped light stretching out to several lunar diameters. It was magnificent, but the moon itself was even more so. We were in its shadow so there was no part of it illuminated by the sun. It was illuminated only by the earth, by earthshine. It made the moon appear blue-gray and the entire scene looked decidedly three-dimensional.

I was really aware, visually aware, that the moon was in fact a sphere, not a disk. It seemed almost as if it were showing us its roundness, its similarity in shape to our earth, in a sort of welcome. I was sure then that it would be a hospitable host. It had been awaiting its first visitors for a long time.

NEIL ARMSTRONG
First on the Moon

123

Walter Cronkite on the Virtues of Space Exploration

From 1961 to 1972, the United States launched twenty-seven manned space flights as part of the Mercury (one-man), Gemini (two-man) and Apollo (three-man) programs. All were broadcast live on television, in whole or in part. As momentous as the scientific accomplishment of each mission was the fact that viewers around the world were witnessing the new epoch in space, moment by moment. Whatever else it did, the space program made for riveting television: emotional and educational; unpredictable and unscripted. Families would gather to watch a launch and, in the early days when missions were only minutes or hours in length, they would remain by the television throughout the whole flight. Later, as missions stretched out over days, networks suspended regular programming to show at least the dramatic parts of a flight: liftoff, reentry, and the evermore daring feats of the space show, including docking, space walks, and moon walks. Walter Cronkite, who joined CBS in 1950, became initiated to the possibilities of space by covering America's early rocket programs. As the space race accelerated in the 1960s, Cronkite and other television anchors played an integral role in carrying it forth. In his memoir, *A Reporter's Life,* Cronkite described the first era of space flight, from his unique vantage between the astronauts and their audience.

Of all humankind's achievements in the twentieth century—and all our gargantuan peccadilloes as well, for that matter—the one event that will dominate the history books a half a millennium from now will be our escape from our earthly environment and landing on the moon.

The fifteenth century wasn't exactly without noteworthy events: Gutenberg's invention of the printing press, Leonardo da Vinci, Joan of Arc. But what is the one date and event we remember? October 12, 1492, when, we were told in school, Christopher Columbus discovered the New World.

In books, or on computer disks, or whatever people are using to record their past, the future residents of the universe will learn of the primitive but courageous voyage of a tiny spaceship called the *Eagle* to the surface of the moon and of men's first steps on a celestial body other than their own. They won't fully appreciate the trials and tribulations, the humor and the drama that gripped the world as humans first undertook flight in space and then extended their range to the moon itself.

I just happened to see the forerunner of all that—rocket flights of destruction rather than discovery. While the American inventor Robert Goddard was a pioneer in rocketry, the Germans, under the pressures of war, were the first to build long-range high-altitude rockets. They unleashed their so-called V-2s on London during the last days of World War II. The launch site was in Wassenaar, a suburb of The Hague in western Holland. From our airborne landing zone on the other side of the Netherlands we could watch the plumes of smoke turning into contrails that traced the rockets' pattern as they climbed to altitude before plunging, faster than the speed of sound, into London.

It would be a long time before we could watch American rockets rise into space on their fiery columns. At the war's conclusion the Russians and the Americans raced to capture the German rocket scientists based, for the most part, on the Baltic coast at Peenemünde. We got our share, including the Germans' brilliant leader Wernher von Braun.

The American test site was set up on a remote, snake-infested swamp called Cape Canaveral on the Florida coast east of Orlando. As the test site grew, so did the nearby villages of Cocoa, Cocoa Beach and Titusville, until they replicated every boomtown in every bad movie ever made—cheap hotels, bars, girlie joints, their wares proclaimed in gaudy neon.

This was the environment into which reporters lucky enough to be assigned the space beat plunged, but the background cacophony was drowned out by the melody of the great enterprise to which the area was dedicated. A spirit of high adventure permeated the place. While the eyes of the rest of our population might have been downcast as the nation dealt with a succession of problems—civil rights, assassinations, Vietnam—it seemed that everyone at the Cape was looking up, up into the skies that invited their conquering touch.

Those early days, however, were marked by battles with the military for at least a tiny modicum of information as to what was going on at the Cape. The space program was being run by the U.S. Army, whose first priority was to develop rockets as weapons. Naturally it considered that top-secret. We were not told when a launch was planned, nor were we given access to the Cape. The nearest public point from which our cameras could get at least a Telephoto look at a launch was a jetty at the Cape's southern edge on the outskirts of Cocoa Beach.

Most of the launches were at night, and the bright searchlights that illuminated the launchpad were our tip-off that a launch was imminent. We equipped ourselves with adequate food and drink and heavy coats against the night chill and fought for the most comfortable of the great granite rocks that formed the jetty.

The cameramen had it tough, as cameramen usually do. Once set up, they had to keep their eyes pretty close to their viewfinders should the rocket suddenly blast off with that spectacular burst of fire. And they had to follow it closely because, not infrequently, they went off course and exploded with apocalyptic intensity.

Our problem was that, because of the military secrecy and the fact that the searchlights usually stayed on, scrub or no, we had no way of knowing when a launch had been canceled. To our rescue rode a genial innkeeper from one of the better motels, a onetime Nazi concentration camp inmate named Henry Landwirth. When the bar at Henry's motel began filling up with the engineers back from the Cape, he sent a messenger to the jetty with the word that the mission had been postponed. He may have saved some of us from pneumonia. He saved all of us from death by boredom.

As with all trades, we had our little tricks to play on the fledglings who joined us for the first time on the jetty. Among the launching gantries on the Cape stood an ancient lighthouse. At night the lights upon it could be mistaken by the unknowing for another launchpad. It was standard initiation procedure to direct a newcomer's attention not to the real launchpad but to the lighthouse to await its launch.

When it was decided that the country should plan for manned flight as well as the perfection of ballistic missiles, it was also wisely conceded that such an expensive program was going to need public support and that this would be hard to get in an atmosphere of secrecy. Hence the National Aeronautics and Space Administration was born and the program, in most phases, opened to the press.

Now we were told when tests were planned and were provided with some primitive facilities among the snakes and mosquitoes some miles from the launchpads.

I had become particularly friendly with B. G. MacNabb, Consolidated Vultee's tough *Atlas* project engineer. *Atlas* was the rocket that would carry the first Americans into orbit. MacNabb thought more of his *Atlases* than he did of NASA's bureaucracy, and he suggested that if I'd get my crew onto the Cape before prelaunch secrecy closed the roads, he would see that we got a box seat for the launch atop the six-story *Atlas* hangar, almost overlooking the pad.

We had a little trouble getting to the roof with the camera equipment. The only access was by way of a vertical ladder that ran up the side of the building from the third floor and that terminated at the roof in a handhold that was very tricky to navigate. Finally, safely in place, we awaited nightfall and the launch.

Just before dusk there was some turmoil below, and there climbing up the ladder was the vanguard of a congressional delegation that NASA was escorting to the *Atlas* rooftop. Our floor director, David Fox, a little London Cockney with a highly developed, disrespectful and unorthodox sense of humor, stood at the top of the ladder awaiting the first congressman. As that gentleman puffed to the top rung and studied with terror how to hold the ladder and swing his legs over the parapet, Fox demanded to see his credentials.

The numerous passes required for various areas of the space complex hung on a chain around the congressman's neck. He gestured toward them with his chin. "I can't see them from here," Fox said, "and the rules say I can't touch them."

Faced with the daunting prospect of letting go of the ladder with even a single hand to present his credentials, the congressman froze. Eventually he recovered enough to tremulously begin his descent, the column of congressmen arrayed under him following suit back to the third floor and a conference with their NASA escort, who led the next ascent and exposed Fox's gambit.

The visitors finally made it up the ladder and over the parapet. We stayed, sharing an uneasy camaraderie with the congressman and suffering an embittered silence from NASA. MacNabb shrugged off his mild chastisement.

Many of us were skeptical and deeply concerned about NASA's plan to launch the Navy astronaut Alan Shepard on what would be our first space flight. We knew, as did the world, that it was a comparatively feeble attempt to begin to catch up with the Soviets, who it seemed had won the space race by sending Yuri Gagarin in orbit around the earth. The United States wasn't ready for orbital flight, but NASA considered it essential that they at least put a man into space, even if that space was only 116 miles up and the flight would be a short ballistic trajectory of just 302 miles and lasting only fifteen minutes.

Shepard would ride the tiny one-man *Mercury* capsule on top of a *Redstone* rocket, a mere firecracker compared with the rockets that would follow, and we had watched *Redstones* blow up on the pad or, tumbling wildly out of control, be destroyed shortly after launch by range safety officers. We feared that Shepard's flight was premature and that NASA was taking a terrible risk. I watched that launch with greater trepidation than any of the many space flights I would see in the years to come.

My best friend among that first class of *Mercury* astronauts was another Navy test pilot, Wally Schirra. He inherited a great wit (too frequently warped by terrible puns) from his father, a World War I Army pilot, and his mother. They had toured the air circuses popular between the wars, Pop flying an old Curtis biplane and Mom walking the wings. After Wally's first *Mercury* flight, he made all the proper public relations statements about it being just another test flight, that there had been nothing to fear thanks to NASA's constant and vigilant monitoring and the safety features built into the craft.

Over a beer one night, I promised never to tell if, off the record, he would level with me about what he had really been thinking in the last minutes before his rocket blasted off. And Wally said: "Well, I was lying there looking up at all the dials and buttons and toggle switches on the control panel and I thought to myself: 'Good God, just think, this thing was built by the lowest bidder.'"

Schirra moved into the new program after establishing himself as a hero of the preceding *Gemini-Titan* launches. He saved one of the first of the large *Titans* and the lives of his crew in a heart-stopping moment on the launchpad. The engines had just received the signal to start, a point at which there is little chance of recall, when a malfunction alarm rang through the cockpit and the control center. Within a microsecond Schirra took every action for which he had been trained. The engine shut down and the rocket, just beginning to stir toward liftoff, settled safely back on the pad.

Some of the early drama of the space program was unnecessary. There is a critical point in space travel when the vehicle plunges back into the earth's atmosphere. The friction creates a temperature of up to 5,000 degrees Fahrenheit. The spaceship is protected by a nose shield that is not effective if the craft isn't lined up perfectly for the reentry. As the heat builds, all communications are blacked out. Until the spacecraft emerges from this blackout three to five minutes later, ground control has no indication as to whether the flight has survived the reentry.

The drama of John Glenn's flight reached its pitch as, for the first time in the American space experience, we awaited that fiery return into the atmosphere. As he came out of the blackout, Mission Control piped his voice to us in the press stands and the broadcast booths and a nation cheered.

Scott Carpenter was the astronaut on the next orbiting mission after Glenn's pioneer flight. As the seconds of blackout ticked away, we heard nothing from him. What we heard was a clearly strained voice from Mission Control saying that they were trying to reestablish communication with the astronaut. All the indicators were ominous, but with no confirmation of his fate and intent upon not unduly alarming the public, in our broadcast we danced delicately around the possibilities.

This uncertainty went on for fifty-three minutes before Mission Control announced that an unharmed astronaut had been picked up by the *Atlantic* rescue craft. The delay in the announcement of his recovery, it was explained, was because he had landed several miles away from the planned point.

Only later did we learn that, right on schedule as the capsule emerged from blackout, Mission Control had all the telemetry, the digital messages, from the spacecraft indicating that everything was normal aboard. All that had failed was the voice link. But the public relations man charged with keeping the press advised neglected to give us that little detail and left us, and the world's audience, uninformed for most of an hour. It was inexcusable incompetency.

Sometimes the idiocy seemed to be on the part of the public.

After Mercury, the next phase of our space flights were the two-man trips in the larger *Gemini* capsules. On the *Gemini 8* flight the controls locked and the ship began tumbling violently. Gyrating like that, there was no hope of it returning safely to earth—of lining up that heat shield for the fiery reentry into the atmosphere. It appeared that we were about to suffer our first space tragedy. We went on the air immediately, of course, interrupting the program in progress. It was a dramatic broadcast as we listened in on the apparently doomed astronauts and Mission Control desperately fighting to solve the problem.

Meanwhile, however, telephone switchboards at CBS stations around the country lit up as angry viewers called in to complain that the program they were watching had been interrupted. The program they had been watching? A futuristic adventure serial: "Lost in Space."

Astronauts Neil Armstrong and David Scott did beat the problem and *Gemini 8* made it safely home. The first tragedy of the American space program was to be *Apollo 1,* the spacecraft designed to go to the moon. When they were running some early tests on the pad, a single spark ignited the almost explosive atmosphere of pure oxygen in the spacecraft, and within a couple of horrible last minutes, three astronauts were incinerated.

Not until the *Challenger* disaster on January 28, 1986, would we lose another astronaut, and then seven would go, including the civilian teacher from New Hampshire, Christa McAuliffe. Instead of her, it might have been a journalist. In 1983 NASA finally inaugurated a civilian-in-space program and planned for a journalist to be the first one to go. However, President Reagan, in a campaign speech attempting to lure support from a teachers' union, promised that a teacher would have that honor.

While McAuliffe underwent her extensive training, NASA began the process of selecting the journalist who would be next. There were more than a thousand applicants when the screening began. They got the list down to forty of us and were preparing to make the next cut when the *Challenger* exploded and the civilian-in-space program was canceled.

I was frequently asked if I still wanted to go into space after *Challenger*. My answer was that I did but feared that my plumbing would go before NASA fixed theirs. Actually, I would still like to go. I know, however, that I would see the glass as half empty rather than half full. An orbital flight would be the most exciting thing I can imagine—except the flight I would like above all others to make: the trip to the moon. It would be great to see Planet Earth from that vast distance, to observe as our lucky astronauts have, this great blue orb, this one spot of color in the dark expanse of space—to revel in the mystery of our existence here.

WALTER CRONKITE
A Reporter's Life

124

Fear and Loathing in Las Vegas

Hunter S. Thompson first published his account of a drug-sodden trip to Las Vegas as a series of articles in *Rolling Stone* magazine in 1971. Using the pseudonym "Raul Duke," and a freewheeling style of writing, Thompson described American values in their raw state in the high-rolling city. His articles were published in book form as *Fear and Loathing in Las Vegas* and found a large audience both within the drug culture and among those who were trying to understand it. Thompson, who had started his journalism career as a copy boy for *Time* magazine in 1958, called the trip described in the book a "gross, physical salute to the fantastic possibilities of life in this country—but only for those with true grit." The same might be said for the book itself and for much of Thompson's writing. In the excerpt from *Fear and Loathing in Las Vegas* printed below, he recalls a time of particularly fantastic possibilities: the mid-1960s in San Francisco. Bolstered by a surrounding community of universities, San Francisco and its Haight-Asbury district, in particular, became an international capital for the counterculture. Among the many nightclubs popular at the time was the Fillmore West, which is mentioned in Thompson's recollection.

Strange memories on this nervous night in Las Vegas. Five years later? Six? It seems like a lifetime, or at least a Main Era—the kind of peak that never comes again. San Francisco in the middle sixties was a very special time and place to be a part of. Maybe it *meant something*. Maybe not, in the long run . . . but no explanation, no mix of words or music or memories can touch that sense of knowing that you were there and alive in that corner of time and the world. Whatever it meant. . . .

History is hard to know, because of all the hired bullshit, but even without being sure of "history" it seems entirely reasonable to think that every now and then the energy of a whole generation comes to a head in a long fine flash, for reasons that nobody really understands at the time—and which never explain, in retrospect, what actually happened.

My central memory of that time seems to hang on one or five or maybe forty nights—or very early mornings—when I left the Fillmore half-crazy and, instead of going home, aimed the big 650 Lightning across the Bay Bridge at a hundred miles an hour wearing L. L. Bean shorts and a Butte sheepherder's jacket . . . booming through the Treasure Island tunnel at the lights of Oakland and Berkeley and Richmond, not quite sure which turn-off to take when I got to the other end (always stalling at the toll-gate, too twisted to find neutral while I fumbled for change) . . . but being absolutely certain that no matter which way I went I would come to a place where people were just as high and wild as I was: No doubt at all about that. . . .

There was madness in any direction, at any hour. If not across the Bay, then up the Golden Gate or down 101 to Los Altos or La Honda. . . . You could strike sparks anywhere. There was a fantastic universal sense that whatever we were doing was *right,* that we were winning. . . .

And that, I think, was the handle—that sense of inevitable victory over the forces of Old and Evil. Not in any mean or military sense; we didn't need that. Our energy would simply *prevail.* There was no point in fighting—on our side or theirs. We had all the momentum; we were riding the crest of a high and beautiful wave. . . .

So now, less than five years later, you can go up on a steep hill in Las Vegas and look West, and with the right kind of eyes you can almost *see* the high-water mark—that place where the wave finally broke and rolled back.

HUNTER S. THOMPSON
Fear and Loathing in Las Vegas

Richard Nixon Resigns as President

I didn't get where I am by ducking tough questions," Richard Nixon said in a speech on May 9, 1973, as he faced new allegations against his administration during the Watergate scandal. Nixon was indeed ducking tough issues at the time, trying to evade implication in the enveloping trouble in Washington. Yet, in August of 1974, when evidence finally mounted, it can be said that Nixon did not duck the toughest issue of all—his resignation. While some advisors counseled him to fight impeachment all the way through a Senate trial, Nixon calmly admitted that it was over. In his *Memoirs,* excerpted below, the dishonored president recalled the circumstances of his last day, and the details worked out with Press Secretary Ron Zeigler, Chief of Staff Alexander Haig, and Presidential Aide Stephen Bull. Nixon's most important contact that day, though, was with Gerald Ford, whom he had selected the previous autumn to replace Spiro Agnew. Nixon's first choice at that time had been former Texas governor John B. Connally, but Ford was less controversial and ultimately received the nomination. In private conversations of farewell the night before the resignation, Nixon observed that the specter of jail time for his crimes did not frighten him: all he really wanted to do was write and for that he'd only need a desk somewhere. Nixon did not go to jail—Gerald Ford pardoned him—but he would write a series of seven books before his death in 1994.

A President's power begins slipping away the moment it is known that he is going to leave: I had seen that in 1952, in 1960, in 1968. On the eve of my resignation I knew that my role was already a symbolic one, and that Gerald Ford's was now the constructive one. My telephone calls and meetings and decisions were now parts of a prescribed ritual aimed at making peace with the past; his calls, his meetings, and his decisions were already the ones that would shape America's future.

Ziegler arrived and described the technical arrangements for the resignation speech and the departure ceremony.

As we walked out of the Lincoln Sitting Room, I asked Manolo to go ahead of us and turn on all the lights. From the outside the second floor of the White House must have looked like the scene of a festive party.

Ziegler and I went into each room: the Queen's Bedroom, the Treaty Room, the Yellow Oval Room that Pat had just redecorated and which we had scarcely had a chance to enjoy.

"It's a beautiful house, Ron," I said, as we walked down the long hallway under the glow of the crystal chandeliers.

I asked Manolo to wake me at nine in the morning, and I started toward my room.

"Mr. President," Ziegler called, "it's the right decision."

I nodded. I knew.

"You've had a great presidency, sir," he said as he turned away.

Thursday, August 8, 1974, was the last full day I served as President of the United States. As on other mornings of my presidency, I walked through the colonnade that had been designed by Thomas Jefferson, through the Rose Garden, and into the Oval Office.

I called Haig in and told him that I wanted to veto the agricultural appropriations bill we had discussed in the Cabinet meeting on Tuesday, because I did not want Ford to have to do it on his first day as President. Haig brought the veto statement in, and I signed it. It was the last piece of legislation I acted on as President.

At eleven o'clock Steve Bull came in and said, "Mr. President, the Vice President is here."

I looked up as Jerry Ford came in, somber in his gray suit. His eyes never left me as he approached. He sat down at the side of the desk, and for a moment the room was filled with silence.

Then I said, "Jerry, I know you'll do a good job."

I have never thought much of the notion that the presidency makes man presidential. What has given the American presidency its vitality is that each man remains distinctive. His abilities become more obvious, and his faults become more glaring. The presidency is not a finishing school. It is a magnifying glass. I thought that Jerry Ford would measure up well under that magnification.

We talked about the problems he would face as soon as he became President in almost exactly twenty-four hours. I stressed the need to maintain our military strength and to continue the momentum of the peace initiatives in the Middle East. Above all, I said, we must not allow the leaders in Moscow or Peking to seize upon the traumatic events surrounding my resignation as an opportunity to test the United States in Vietnam or anywhere else in the world. We must not let the Communists mistakenly assume that executive authority had been so weakened by Watergate that we would no longer stand up to aggression wherever it occurred.

I said that I was planning to send messages to all the major world leaders that Jerry Ford had been one of the strongest supporters of my policies and that they could count on him to continue those policies with the same firmness and resolve.

Ford asked if I had any particular advice or recommendations for him. I said that as far as I was concerned, the only man who would be absolutely indispensable to him was Henry Kissinger. There was simply no one else who had his wisdom, his tenacity, and his experience in foreign affairs. If he were to leave after I resigned, I said, our foreign policy would soon be in disarray throughout the world. Ford said firmly that he intended to keep Kissinger on for as long as he would be willing to stay.

I also urged him to keep Haig as Chief of Staff, at least during the transition period. Haig, I assured him, was always loyal to the commander he served, and he would be an invaluable source of advice and experience in the days ahead when there would inevitably be a scramble for power within both the Cabinet and the White House staff.

I told Ford that I would always be available to give him advice at any time, but I would never interject myself in any way into his decision-making process. He expressed appreciation for this attitude and said that he would always welcome any of my suggestions, particularly in foreign affairs.

I do not think that Ford knew that he had not been my first choice for Vice President when Agnew resigned, or that he had come in fourth in the informal poll I had taken among Republican leaders. I knew that there were many who did not share my high opinion of Ford's abilities. But I had felt then that Jerry Ford was the right man, and that was why I chose him. I had no reason to regret that decision.

It was noon. It was time for him to go.

"Where will you be sworn in?" I asked as we walked to the door. He said that he had decided not to go to the Capitol because his former colleagues there might turn the occasion into some kind of celebration. I said that I planned to be gone by noon; if he liked, he could be sworn in in the White House, as Truman had been.

I told him about the call I had received from Eisenhower the night before I was inaugurated on January 20, 1969, when he had said that it would be the last time he could call me "Dick." I said, "It's the same with me. From now on, Jerry, you are Mr. President."

Ford's eyes filled with tears—and mine did as well—as we lingered for a moment at the door. I thanked him for his loyal support over the last painful weeks and months. I said that he would have my prayers in the days and years ahead.

The Memoirs of Richard Nixon

The Harrowing Evacuation of Saigon

On April 30, 1975, nineteen months after the end of the Vietnam War, the South Vietnamese capital of Saigon fell to communists from the north. By then, the end was inevitable: American interest in protecting South Vietnam any further had been completely exhausted. During the last weeks of April, looting was rampant, as South Vietnamese soldiers abandoned their posts and residents of Saigon became frantic. Vietnamese citizens with known loyalties to the United States begged for assistance in escaping the doomed country and American officials accommodated them in vast numbers. In all, 6,000 Americans and 130,000 Vietnamese left during April, in advance of the communist takeover. However, on the final day before the fall, outright hysteria gripped the city. Keyes Beech, a reporter for the *Chicago Daily News,* was in Saigon on April 30 and was part of the struggle to get out; he wrote about the deranged city in a story that he filed the next day, May 1, 1975. On that day, back in Saigon, South Vietnam's last president was trying to ameliorate the communists and save Saigon's streets by offering to surrender the city peacefully. The response ended a long, long struggle succinctly: "You have nothing left to surrender," he was told.

Aboard the USS *Hancock*—Tuesday morning I had breakfast on the ninth floor of the Caravelle Hotel in Saigon and watched a column of ugly black smoke framed by the tall, twin spires of the Catholic cathedral in Kennedy Square just up the street.

Tan Son Nhut airport was burning; the streets were bare of traffic, unnaturally but pleasantly quiet.

The waiters were nervous and the room boys said I couldn't have my laundry back until "tomorrow."

What tomorrow?

Six hours later I was fighting for my life and wishing I had never left the hotel. I nearly didn't make it out of Saigon.

My *Daily News* colleague, Bob Tamarkin, telephoned to say the embassy had ordered a full-scale evacuation—immediately. He said he hoped to see me later.

I joined others who were leaving and we went to a prearranged assembly point, a U.S. embassy building only a couple of blocks away.

Three buses were quickly filled with a mixed bag of correspondents and Vietnamese. Some of the more dignified among us held back rather than scramble for seats and waited for the fourth bus.

That was a mistake.

The first three buses made it inside Tan Son Nhut airbase and their passengers flew out. Ours never made it inside, and that accounts for one of the longest days of my life.

We heard the bad news over the driver's radio on the way out: "Security conditions are out of control at Tan Son Nhut. Do not go to Tan Son Nhut. Repeat, do not go to Tan Son Nhut."

We went on anyway, the sound of explosions and the rattle of automatic weapons growing louder by the second—incoming mixed with outgoing fire. South Vietnamese soldiers were firing wildly in the air for no apparent reason.

South Vietnamese sentries turned us back at the first checkpoint. For the thousandth time, I made mental note of the billboard legend that departing Americans see as they leave Saigon:

"The noble sacrifices of allied soldiers will never be forgotten."

We tried another approach to the airbase but were again waved back. No way, as the Vietnamese are fond of saying.

The evacuation had broken down.

It was 2 P.M. when we headed back to the city. Nobody on that bus will ever forget the next few hours. We cruised aimlessly about Saigon for at least three hours while our security escorts tried to figure out what to do with us.

We were a busload of fools piloted by a man who had never driven a bus and had to wire the ignition when it stalled because the Vietnamese driver had run away with the keys the night before.

"I'm doing the best I can," said Bill Austin of Miami, Okla., the man at the wheel, as we careened through narrow streets, knocking over sidewalk vendors, sideswiping passing vehicles and sending Vietnamese scattering like leaves in the wind.

When the back seat driving became too much, Austin, an auditor, stopped the bus and said: "If there is a bus driver aboard, I'll be glad to let him take the wheel."

There were no takers. By now we had been joined by two other buses and half a dozen cars packed with Vietnamese who figured that by staying with us they could get out of the country.

At every stop, Vietnamese beat on the doors and windows pleading to be let inside. We merely looked at them. We already had enough Vietnamese aboard. Every time we opened the door, we had to beat and kick them back.

For no reason, except that we were following another bus, we went to the Saigon port area, one of the toughest parts of the city, where the crowds were uglier than elsewhere. Police fired into the air to part the mob and let us through onto the dock.

I got off the bus and went over to John Moore, the embassy security officer who was sitting in one of those sedans with the flashy blinker on top.

"Do you know why we are here and what you are going to do with us?" I asked him.

Moore shrugged helplessly. "There are ships," he said, gesturing toward sandbagged Vietnamese vessels lying alongside the dock.

I looked around at the gathering crowd. Small boys were snatching typewriters and bags of film. This, as the Chinese would say, looked like bad joss. I didn't know how or whether I was going to get out of Saigon, but I damned well knew I wasn't going to stay here.

I got back on the bus, which was both our prison and our fortress. And other correspondents including some of my closest friends—Wendell S. (Bud) Merick of *U.S. News & World Report* and Ed White of the AP—felt the same way. White's typewriter, his most precious possession at the moment, next to his life, was gone.

Again we had to fight off the Vietnamese. Ed Bradley of CBS, a giant of a man, was pushing, kicking, shoving, his face sad. I found myself pushing a middle-aged Vietnamese woman who had been sitting beside me on the bus and asked me to look after her because she worked for the Americans and the Viet Cong would cut her throat.

That's what they all said and maybe they are right. But she fought her way back to my side. "Why did you push me?" she asked. I had no answer.

Austin didn't know what to do with us so we drove to the American embassy. There the Vietnamese woman decided to get off.

"I have worked for the United States government for 10 years," she said, "but you do not trust me and I do not trust you. Even if we do get to Tan Son Nhut, they wouldn't let me on the plane." She was right, of course.

"I am going home and poison myself," she said. I didn't say anything because there was nothing to say.

For lack of anything better to do, Austin drove us to the embassy parking lot across the street. The embassy was besieged by the Vietnamese that we were abandoning. Every gate was closed. There was no way in.

I went to the parking lot telephone and called an embassy friend. Briefly, I stated the situation: "There are about 40 of us—Americans, British and two or three Japanese. We can't get in."

"Hold it," he said. A few minutes later, he came back on the phone with the following instructions:

"Take your people to the MacDinh Chi police station next to the embassy. They know you are coming. They will help you over the wall."

An uncertain Moses, I led my flock out of the parking lot, across the street and through the police barricades to the police station. They never heard of us. When we tried to talk to them, they told us to move on and fired into the air to make their point.

We dribbled around the corner to the rear of the embassy compound, where several hundred Vietnamese were pounding at the gate or trying to scale the wall. There was only one way inside: through the crowd and over the 10-foot wall.

Once we moved into that seething mass, we ceased to be correspondents. We were only men fighting for their lives, scratching, clawing, pushing ever closer to that wall. We were like animals.

Now, I thought, I know what it's like to be a Vietnamese. I am one of them. But if I could get over that wall I would be an American again.

My attache case accidentally struck a baby in its mother's arms and its father beat at me with his fists. I tried to apologize as he kept on beating me while his wife pleaded with me to take the baby.

Somebody grabbed my sleeve and wouldn't let go. I turned my head and looked into the face of a Vietnamese youth.

"You adopt me and take me with you and I'll help you," he screamed. "If you don't, you don't go."

I said I'd adopt him. I'd have said anything. Could this be happening to me?

Suddenly my arm was free and I edged closer to the wall. There were a pair of marines on the wall. They were trying to help us up and kick the Vietnamese down. One of them looked down at me.

"Help me," I pleaded. "Please help me."

That marine helped me. He reached down with his long, muscular arm and pulled me up as if I were a helpless child.

I lay on a tin roof gasping for breath like a landed fish, then dropped to the ground. God bless the marines. I was one myself in the last of the just wars.

One American offered me a cup of water and a doctor asked me if I wanted a tranquilizer. I accepted the water and declined the tranquilizer. "Are you sure you're all right?" the doctor said anxiously.

"Sure," I croaked. "I'm just fine. But my friends?"

I looked up and saw a yellow shirt coming over the wall. That was Bud Merick of *U.S. News & World Report*. Minutes later I saw the sweaty red face of big Ed White from the Associated Press come over.

I was very happy to see him. He is not only my friend. He was carrying my typewriter.

A tall, young embassy officer in a pink shirt looked at me and said, "Aren't you Keyes Beech?"

I admitted I was. His name is Brunson McKinley and I last saw him in Peking two years ago. We made our way through the crowd of Vietnamese evacuees gathered around the embassy swimming pool and through to the main embassy building and took the elevator to the sixth floor.

Our embassy friends seemed glad to see us and expressed awe that we had come over the embassy wall. I was pretty awed too, now that I think of it.

A retired American general who has been around here a long time, Charles

Timmes, said he had been on the phone to "Big" Minh, the new president, urging him to ask the North Vietnamese for a cease-fire.

"He said he was trying but they wouldn't listen," Charlie said. "Anyway, they haven't shelled the embassy yet."

"That's nice of them," I said, slumping into a soft chair.

The man I really wanted to see was down on the third floor. His name is Graham Martin and he was our ambassador. In my view, he gambled with American lives, including mine, by dragging his heels on the evacuation.

A few minutes later I was on the embassy roof and inside a marine helicopter and on my way to the carrier *Hancock*.

It was exactly 6:30 P.M.

My last view of Saigon was through the tail door of the helicopter. Tan Son Nhut was burning. So was Bien Hoa. Then the door closed—closed on the most humiliating chapter in American history.

I looked at the man next to me. He was a Vietnamese and I moved away from him. Forty-five minutes later we put down on the *Hancock*.

The salt sea air tasted good.

> KEYES BEECH
> *Chicago Daily News*
> May 1, 1975

127

The Miracle at Camp David

Jimmy Carter received considerable criticism for his optimism: his basic belief in the potential for good in people and situations. One long-term diplomat even termed him "naive." Yet Carter's very optimism proved to be the basis for one of the finest moments in modern U.S. diplomacy: the Camp David Peace Accord, signed in March 1977. Carter had taken it upon himself to arrange a summit with Israel's Menachim Begin and Egypt's Anwar Sadat, even though he had no commitments from them in advance for an agreement. In doing so, the president risked his reputation on a positive outcome between the two perennial enemies. With high hopes and very sensitive planning, Carter played host to Begin and Sadat in the seclusion of Camp David, the presidential compound in western Maryland. Personally, the president was on excellent terms with each leader, though Begin and Sadat never allowed themselves to relax with each other: their existing animosities precluded that. Instead, over the course of the summit, Carter was very much the intermediary. He was nearly exhausted when, after thirteen days, the meeting finally broke through thirty years of war and hatred. The result was the first set of peace agreements ever signed between Israel and an Arab country. Zbigniew Brzezinski, President Carter's national security adviser, was there and recalled the signing ceremony on March 26, 1979, in his memoir, *Power and Principle*.

Toward the end of March, Carter, Begin, and Sadat assembled in Washington for the historic signing of the first peace treaty ever between Israel and an Arab state. The signing was preceded, however, by last-minute difficulties. The Israelis pressed us for tighter commitments and guarantees of U.S. support on the remaining issues in future negotiations, and there were also disagreements regarding terminology. The Israelis wanted to use Judea and Samaria and objected to the words West Bank and Gaza. Moreover, in a rather unusual move, Begin requested a private meeting with the President (to which I was invited). He told the President that he had a personal request to make, namely that Carter, as a gesture of friendship for Mrs. Begin, forgive Israel the outstanding debt on the massive $3 billion aid that the United States was extending to Israel. Begin repeated the phrase "as a gesture for Mrs. Begin" several times. Carter, who on financial matters was a bit of a miser, looked at first quite stunned, and then, turning to me, he burst out laughing.

But the dominant mood was one of profound satisfaction, and previous disagreements and bitterness were forgotten. There is no doubt that, each in his own way, both Sadat and Begin made critical decisions and undertook major political risks. Moreover, we all knew that the peace treaty marked a historic turning point and that it might usher in a period of greater hope. As I noted in my journal for Tuesday, March 27:

Last night in a huge tent in the garden of the White House we celebrated the peace treaty. It was a remarkable evening. Not only was there joy, but a sense of real reconciliation. I sat at a table with the Weizmans and the [Muhammad] Alis and Kissinger. Weizman had his son with him. Badly wounded during one of the conflicts with the Egyptians, to some extent he has been permanently scarred. Yet he was there, partaking of this event, mixing with Sadat's children. Weizman was especially moved when he told me that Sadat had embraced his son, and I could sense that the parents were deeply touched when their son and Sadat's son shook hands and embraced.

All of the participants rose to the occasion. The President was superb: moving, gentle, and yet committed. He opened with a prayer which coming from anybody else would have sounded hypocritical. From him it conveyed sincerity and genuine faith. Sadat made some references to the Palestinians, which he had omitted from the afternoon ceremony. Weizman, sitting next to me,

*groaned and said, "Now you will see the Polish character in Begin asserting itself
and he will rebut." Much to our joint surprise, Begin's response was peaceful,
warm, cordial, especially to the President, but also to Sadat, and made no reference to the Palestinian question or to the firm statement by Sadat that statehood
would be the end of the peace process. I was amazed and gratified. Peace can be
contagious.*

*Of the speakers, only Begin praised Vance publicly, and I felt that Carter should
have done it himself. After Carter, in the U.S. government Vance deserves most
credit for this achievement. I have been saying this right and left to the press and
others. The event, though it lasted for hours, was something that no one would
have wished to miss. There was electricity in the air, a sense of joy, people mixing,
shaking hands, patting [each other] on the back. And for Carter, of course, it was a
spectacular and historic triumph.*

No other U.S. President has made a comparable personal effort to obtain
peace in the Middle East. No other President has ever been as directly involved in the search for compromise. No other President has negotiated as
actively to overcome the enormous psychological and historical barriers even
to a limited peace in the Middle East. The Israeli-Egyptian treaty, though
far short of a comprehensive solution, did reduce the chances of a renewed
Arab-Israeli war, a necessary precondition to an eventual settlement, and it
created a framework for an interim arrangement for the West Bank and
Gaza. Moreover, the Israeli-Egyptian peace treaty established the important
precedents of trading territory and the dismantling of settlements for a binding peace treaty and elaborate security arrangements.

ZBIGNIEW BRZEZINSKI
Power and Principle: Memoirs of the National Security Adviser,
1977–1981

128

Ronald Reagan's Inaugural
Addresses Inspire a Nation

When Ronald Reagan was working on his first inaugural speech in January 1981, a friend in the Senate called and warned him that word was already out in the capital that he didn't intend to keep his campaign promises. Reagan immediately told his writers to insert a paragraph in his speech affirming that the president for whom people had voted was the same one being inaugurated. Indeed, most observers asserted that Ronald Reagan was always the same man, in or out of office—and Reagan himelf was among them. "Things kept happening," he said almost wistfully of his inauguration day, "and there you were making a speech and the crowd, and you still did not have that thing you thought you would, that moment of awesomeness." Reagan's first inauguration speech reflects the style he found to be his most effective: an idealized vision of Americans as a people destined for greatness. By the time of his second inauguration, the details and realities of the office had encroached. Throughout, Reagan held the same promise, though, relating the country's past, present, and future in a decoupage that he presented as hope.

1981

These United States are confronted with an economic affliction of great proportions.

We suffer from the longest and one of the worst sustained inflations in our national history. It distorts our economic decisions, penalizes thrift and crushes the struggling young and the fixed-income elderly alike. It threatens to shatter the lives of millions of our people.

Idle industries have cast workers into unemployment, human misery and personal indignity.

Those who do work are denied a fair return for their labor by a tax system which penalizes successful achievement and keeps us from maintaining full productivity.

But great as our tax burden is, it has not kept pace with public spending. For decades we have piled deficit upon deficit, mortgaging our future and our children's future for the temporary convenience of the present.

To continue this long trend is to guarantee tremendous social, cultural, political and economic upheavals.

You and I, as individuals, can, by borrowing, live beyond our means, but for only a limited period of time. Why then should we think that collectively, as a nation, we are not bound by that same limitation?

We must act today in order to preserve tomorrow. And let there be no misunderstanding—we're going to begin to act beginning today.

The economic ills we suffer have come upon us over several decades.

They will not go away in days, weeks or months, but they will go away. They will go away because we as Americans have the capacity now, as we have had in the past, to do whatever needs to be done to preserve this last and greatest bastion of freedom.

In this present crisis, government is not the solution to our problem, government is the problem.

From time to time we've been tempted to believe that society has become too complex to be managed by self-rule, that government by an elite group is superior to government for, by and of the people.

But if no one among us is capable of government himself, then who among us has the capacity to govern someone else?

All of us together—in and out of government—must bear the burden. The solutions we seek must be equitable with no one group singled out to pay a higher price.

We hear much of special interest groups. Well, our concern must be for a special interest group that has been too long neglected.

It knows no sectional boundaries, or ethnic and racial divisions and it crosses political party lines. It is made up of men and women who raise our food, patrol our streets, man our mines and factories, teach our children, keep our homes and heal us when we're sick.

Professionals, industrialists, shopkeepers, clerks, cabbies and truck drivers. They are, in short, "We the people." This breed called Americans.

Well, this Administration's objective will be a healthy, vigorous, growing economy that provides equal opportunities for all Americans with no barriers born of bigotry or discrimination.

Putting America back to work means putting all Americans back to work. Ending inflation means freeing all Americans from the terror of runaway living costs.

All must share in the productive work of this "new beginning," and all must share in the bounty of a revived economy.

With the idealism and fair play which are the core of our system and our strength, we can have a strong, prosperous America at peace with itself and the world.

So as we begin, let us take inventory.

We are a nation that has a government—not the other way around. And this makes us special among the nations of the earth.

Our Government has no power except that granted it by the people. It is time to check and reverse the growth of government which shows signs of having grown beyond the consent of the governed.

It is my intention to curb the size and influence of the Federal establishment and to demand recognition of the distinction between the powers granted to the Federal Government and those reserved to the states or to the people.

All of us—all of us need to be reminded that the Federal Government did not create the states; the states created the Federal Government.

Now, so there will be no misunderstanding, it's not my intention to do away with government.

It is rather to make it work—work with us, not over us; to stand by our side, not ride on our back. Government can and must provide opportunity, not smother it; foster productivity, not stifle it.

If we look to the answer as to why for so many years we achieved so much, prospered as no other people on earth, it was because here in this land we unleashed the energy and individual genius of man to a greater extent than has ever been done before.

Freedom and the dignity of the individual have been more available and assured here than in any other place on earth. The price for this freedom at times has been high, but we have never been unwilling to pay that price.

It is no coincidence that our present troubles parallel and are proportionate to the intervention and intrusion in our lives that result from unnecessary and excessive growth of Government.

It is time for us to realize that we are too great a nation to limit ourselves to small dreams. We're not, as some would have us believe, doomed to an inevitable decline; I do not believe in a fate that will fall on us no matter what we do. I do believe in a fate that will fall on us if we do nothing.

So, with all the creative energy at our command let us begin an era of national renewal. Let us renew our determination, our courage and our strength. And let us renew our faith and our hope. We have every right to dream heroic dreams.

Your dreams, your hopes, your goals are going to be the dreams, the hopes and the goals of this Administration, so help me God.

We shall reflect the compassion that is so much a part of your makeup.

How can we love our country and not love our countrymen? And loving them reach out a hand when they fall, heal them when they're sick and provide opportunity to make them self-sufficient so they will be equal in fact and not just in theory?

Can we solve the problems confronting us? Well the answer is an unequivocal and emphatic yes.

To paraphrase Winston Churchill, I did not take the oath I've just taken with the intention of presiding over the dissolution of the world's strongest economy.

In the days ahead I will propose removing the roadblocks that have slowed our economy and reduced productivity.

Steps will be taken aimed at restoring the balance between the various levels of government. Progress may be slow—measured in inches and feet, not miles—but we will progress.

It is time to reawaken this industrial giant, to get government back within its means and to lighten our punitive tax burden.

And these will be our first priorities, and on these principles there will be no compromise. . . .

I believe we the Americans of today are ready to act worthy of ourselves, ready to do what must be done to insure happiness and liberty for ourselves, our children and our children's children.

And as we renew ourselves here in our own land we will be seen as having greater strength throughout the world. We will again be the examplar of freedom and a beacon of hope for those who do not now have freedom.

To those neighbors and allies who share our freedom, we will strengthen our historic ties and assure them of our support and firm commitment.

We will match loyalty with loyalty. We will strive for mutually beneficial relations. We will not use our friendship to impose on their sovereignty, for our own sovereignty is not for sale.

As for the enemies of freedom, those who are potential adversaries, they will be reminded that peace is the highest aspiration of the American people. We will negotiate for it, sacrifice for it; we will not surrender for it—now or ever.

Our forbearance should never be misunderstood. Our reluctance for conflict should not be misjudged as a failure of will.

When action is required to preserve our national security, we will act. We will maintain sufficient strength to prevail if need be, knowing that if we do so we have the best chance of never having to use that strength.

Above all we must realize that no arsenal or no weapon in the arsenals of the world is so formidable as the will and moral courage of free men and women.

It is a weapon our adversaries in today's world do not have.

It is a weapon that we as Americans do have.

Let that be understood by those who practice terrorism and prey upon their neighbors.

1985

When I took this oath four years ago, I did so in a time of economic stress. Voices were raised saying that we had to look to our past for the greatness and glory. But we, the present-day Americans, are not given to looking backward. In this blessed land, there is always a better tomorrow.

Four years ago I spoke to you of a new beginning, and we have accomplished that. But in another sense, our new beginning is a continuation of that beginning created two centuries ago when, for the first time in history, government, the people said, was not our master. It is our servant; its only power that which we, the people, allow it to have.

That system has never failed us. But for a time we failed the system. We asked for things of government that government was not equipped to give. We yielded authority to the national government that properly belonged to states or to local governments or to the people themselves. We allowed taxes and inflation to rob us of our earnings and savings and watched the great industrial machines that had made us the most productive people on earth slow down and the number of unemployed increase.

By 1980 we knew it was time to renew our faith, to strive with all our strength toward the ultimate in individual freedom consistent with an orderly society.

We believed then and now there are no limits to growth and human progress when men and women are free to follow their dreams. And we were right. And we were right to believe that. Tax rates have been reduced, inflation cut dramatically and more people are employed than ever before in our history.

We are creating a nation once again vibrant, robust and alive. But there are many mountains yet to climb. We will not rest until every American enjoys the fullness of freedom, dignity and opportunity as our birthright. It is our birthright as citizens of the great republic.

And if we meet this challenge, these will be years when Americans have restored their confidence and tradition of progress; when our values of faith, family, work and neighborhood were restated for a modern age; when our economy was finally freed from government's grip; when we made sincere efforts at meaningful arms reductions by rebuilding our defenses, our economy, and developing new technologies helped preserve peace in a troubled world; when America courageously supported the struggle for individual liberty, self-government and free enterprise throughout the world and turned the tide of history away from totalitarian darkness and into the warm sunlight of human freedom.

My fellow citizens, our nation is poised for greatness. We must do what we know is right and do it with all our might. Let history say of us, these were golden years—when the American Revolution was reborn, when freedom gained new life and America reached for her best.

Our two-party system has served us well over the years, but never better than in those times of great challenge, when we came together not as Democrats or Republicans but as Americans united in the common cause.

Two of our Founding Fathers, a Boston lawyer named Adams and a Virginia planter named Jefferson, members of that remarkable group who met in Independence Hall and dared to think they could start the world over again, left us an important lesson. They had become, in the years spent in government, bitter political rivals. In the Presidential election of 1800, then years later, when both were retired and age had softened their anger, they began to speak to each other again through letters.

A bond was re-established between those two who had helped create this government of ours.

In 1826, the 50th anniversary of the Declaration of Independence, they both died. They died on the same day, within a few hours of each other. And that day was the Fourth of July.

In one of those letters exchanged in the sunset of their lives, Jefferson wrote, "It carries me back to the times when, beset with difficulties and dangers, we were fellow laborers in the same cause, struggling for what is most valuable to man, his right of self-government. Laboring always at the same oar, with some wave ever ahead threatening to overwhelm us, and yet passing harmless we rode through the storm with heart and hand."

Well, with heart and hand, let us stand as one today: one people under God determined that our future shall be worthy of our past. As we do, we must not repeat the well-intentioned errors of our past. We must never again abuse the trust of working men and women by sending their earnings on a futile chase after the spiraling demands of a bloated Federal establishment. You elected us in 1980 to end this prescription for disaster. And I don't believe you re-elected us in 1984 to reverse course.

The heart of our efforts is one idea vindicated by 25 straight months of economic growth: freedom and incentives unleash the drive and entrepreneurial genius that are the core of human progress. We have begun to increase the rewards for work, savings and investment; reduce the increase in the cost and size of government and its interference in people's lives.

We must simplify our tax system, make it more fair and bring the rates down for all who work and earn. We must think anew and move with a new boldness so every American who seeks work can find work; so the least among us shall have an equal chance to achieve the greatest things—to be heroes who heal our sick, feed the hungry, protect peace among nations and leave this world a better place.

The time has come for a new American Emancipation, a great national drive to tear down economic barriers and liberate the spirit of enterprise in the most distressed areas of our country. My friends, together we can do this, and do it we must, so help me God.

From new freedom will spring new opportunities for growth, a more productive, fulfilled and united people and a stronger America, an America that will lead the technological revolution and also open its mind and heart and soul to the treasures of literature, music and poetry, and the values of faith, courage and love.

A dynamic economy, with more citizens working and paying taxes, will be our strongest tool to bring down budget deficits. But an almost unbroken 50 years of deficit spending has finally brought us to a time of reckoning.

We've come to a turning point, a moment for hard decisions. I have asked the Cabinet and my staff a question and now I put the same question to you. If not us, who? And if not now, when? It must be done by all of us going forward with a program aimed at reaching a balanced budget. We can then begin reducing the national debt.

I will shortly submit a budget to the Congress aimed at freezing government program spending for the next year. Beyond this, we must take further steps to permanently control government's power to tax and spend.

We must act now to protect future generations from government's desire to spend its citizens' money and tax them into servitude when the bills come due. Let us make it unconstitutional for the Federal Government to spend more than the Federal Government takes in.

We have already started returning to the people and to state and local governments responsibilities better handled by them. Now, there is a place for the Federal Government in matters of social compassion. But our fundamental goals must be to reduce dependency and upgrade the dignity of those who are infirm or disadvantaged. And here a growing economy and support from family and community offer our best chance for a society where compassion is a way of life, where the old and infirm are cared for, the young and, yes, the unborn, protected, and the unfortunate looked after and made self-sufficient.

Now there is another area where the Federal Government can play a part. As an older American, I remember a time when people of different race, creed or ethnic origin in our land found hatred and prejudice installed in social custom and, yes, in law. There's no story more heartening in our history than the progress that we've made toward the brotherhood of man that God intended for us. Let us resolve: There will be no turning back or hesitation on the road to an America rich in dignity and abundant with opportunity for all our citizens.

Let us resolve that we, the people, will build an American opportunity society in which all of us—white and black, rich and poor, young and old—will go forward together, arm in arm. Again, let us remember that, though our heritage is one of blood lines from every corner of the earth, we are all Americans pledged to carry on this last best hope of man on earth.

And I have spoken of our domestic goals, and the limitations we should put on our national government. Now let me turn to a task that is the primary responsibility of national government—the safety and security of our people.

Today we utter no prayer more fervently than the ancient prayer for peace on earth. Yet history has shown that peace does not come, nor will our freedom be preserved, by good will alone. There are those in the world who scorn our vision of human dignity and freedom. One nation, the Soviet Union, has conducted the greatest military buildup in the history of man, building arsenals of awesome offensive weapons.

We've made progress in restoring our defense capability. But much remains to be done. There must be no wavering by us, nor any doubts by others, that America will meet her responsibilities to remain free, secure, and at peace.

There is only one way safely and legitimately to reduce the cost of national security, and this is to reduce the need for it. And this we're trying to do in negotiating with the Soviet Union. We're not just discussing limits on a further increase of nuclear weapons. We seek, instead, to reduce their number. We seek the total elimination, one day, of nuclear weapons from the face of the earth.

Now for decades we and the Soviets have lived under the threat of mutual assured destruction; if either resorted to the use of nuclear weapons, the other could retaliate and destroy the one who had started it. Is there either logic or morality in believing that if one side threatens to kill tens of millions of our people, our only resource is to threaten killing tens of millions of theirs?

I have approved a research program to find, if we can, a security shield that will destroy nuclear missiles before they reach their target: It wouldn't kill people, it would destroy weapons. It wouldn't militarize space, it would help demilitarize the arsenals of earth. It would render nuclear weapons obsolete. We will meet with the Soviets hoping that we can agree on a way to rid the world of the threat of nuclear destruction.

We strive for peace and security, heartened by the changes all around us. Since the turn of the century, the number of democracies in the world has grown fourfold. Human freedom is on the march, and nowhere more so than in our own hemisphere. Freedom is one of the deepest and noblest aspirations of the human spirit. People worldwide hunger for the right of self-determination, for those inalienable rights that make for human dignity and progress.

Americans must remain freedom's staunchest friend, for freedom is our best ally, and it is the world's only hope to conquer poverty and preserve peace. Every blow we inflict against poverty will be a blow against its dark allies of oppression and war. Every victory for human freedom will be a victory for world peace.

So we go forward today a nation still mighty in its youth and powerful in its purpose. With our alliances strengthened, with our economy leading the world to a new age of economic expansion, we look to a future rich in possibilities. And all of this is because we worked and acted together, not as members of political parties, but as Americans.

My friends, we, we live in a world that's lit by lightning. So much is changing and will change, but so much endures and transcends time.

History is a ribbon, always unfurling; history is a journey. And as we continue on our journey we think of those who traveled before us. We stand again at the steps of this symbol of our democracy, or we would've been standing at the steps if it hadn't gotten so cold. Now, we're standing inside this symbol of our democracy, and we see and hear again the echoes of our past.

A general falls to his knees in the hard snow of Valley Forge; a lonely President paces the darkened halls and ponders his struggle to preserve the Union; the men of the Alamo call out encouragement to each other; a settler pushes west and sings a song, and the song echoes out forever and fills the unknowing air.

It is the American sound: It is hopeful, bighearted, idealistic—daring, decent and fair. That's our heritage, that's our song. We sing it still. For all our problems, our differences, we are together as of old. We raise our voices to the God who is the author of this most tender music. And may He continue to hold us close as we fill the world with our sound—in unity, affection and love. One people under God, dedicated to the dream of freedom that He has placed in the human heart, called upon now to pass that dream on to a waiting and a hopeful world.

God bless you and may God bless America.

RONALD REAGAN
January 1981 and 1985

129

George Ball on the End of Innocence

In 1971, Dean Acheson sent a letter to George Ball: "Keep on making sense," he wrote. "You have the field to yourself." Born in 1909, George Ball was a diplomat and adviser who rose to prominence as undersecretary of state during the Kennedy administration. He continued in that post in the Johnson administration until 1966, when he dramatically resigned. Ball had been an early critic of American policy toward Vietnam, a stand which had caused a widening breech in his relationship with President Johnson, who insisted upon broadening the war. A longtime Democrat and a power broker in the party, Ball was nonetheless an elusive man to categorize. His biographer, James Bill, pointed out that he was at once a realist and idealist, a liberal and conservative, partisan and bipartisan, populist and elitist, parochial and global, isolationist and interventionist. Somewhere in between all the labels was a man who made sense, as Acheson had said. Writing in his memoir, *The Past Has Another Pattern,* Ball confronted the preeminent concern of his time: the capacity for annihilation through nuclear weapons.

Mankind's gravest danger is, of course, the nuclear bomb, which generations younger than mine have always known. I learned to live with the potential of nuclear death only late in life and cannot accept it as a normal and permanent aspect of our human existence. As a youth, I could never have imagined any hovering threat other than hellfire if I misbehaved, and my parents were too kind and rational to hold that threat over my head. During the first decade of the new century, in which I was born, the Western world was lighted by an ebullient optimism. With the popularization of Darwin's concept of evolution, prospects seemed bright indeed. Renan foresaw mankind gradually achieving a more perfect state through the growing dominance of reason. Herbert Spencer, interpreting Darwin, predicted that, with humankind's evolutionary adaptation, the "ultimate development of the ideal man is logically certain."

To be sure, confidence in man's perfectibility did not last long. When I was four years old, Europe was caught up in the first of two great civil wars that shook belief in the inevitability—even the possibility—of progress. After the carnage of Passchendaele, the Somme, gas warfare, and rotting bodies in the trenches, came dark prognoses. I well remember my first encounter with Spengler's *The Decline of the West* in the 1920s, and I was haunted by the despairing lamentations of Paul Valéry. As a student, I turned in disillusion from the cloying patriotism of Rupert Brooke to the bitter realism of Robert Graves, Wilfred Owen, and Siegfried Sassoon. Then the decade ended with a cataclysmic depression that raised festering doubts about Western institutions. Later I encountered a wholly new area of speculation when Aldous Huxley published his brilliant anti-utopian *Brave New World,* depicting a sterile bureaucracy perverting biology to create humanoid robots as mankind's slaves.

I could—and did—dismiss Spengler as a dyspeptic German theorist and shrug off Huxley's fantasy as grim satire; but Hitler and the Second World War conclusively ended my benign illusions. No one could overlook the shattering message of the Nuremburg trials that man had made small, if any, progress toward perfectibility. Hitler and his scrofulous gang had shown themselves fully as depraved and brutal as the most sadistic medieval tyrants.

Genghis Khan and Attila were not, as I had assumed, merely products of a dark satanic period; rich and powerful nations could still produce monsters as leaders.

That thought gained a new malign significance with the splitting of the atom and our destructive use of that knowledge at Hiroshima and Nagasaki. Armed with the bomb, some new power-obsessed lunatic could, as Hitler had only threatened to do, slam the world's door so hard as to bring down the whole edifice. Thus, I was dismayed though not surprised, when nuclear weapons became available to the ugly, repressive, Soviet regime of Josef Stalin. No longer could we rule out the possibility that human life might someday—even soon—perish in a pyrotechnic Armageddon.

The advent of the nuclear weapon inspired in my generation long thoughts about last things and revived the ancient anxiety that man might destroy himself if he let excessive curiosity push his exploration of nature beyond the frontiers of the forbidden. Until then, we fortunate few on this broad continent had felt protected by mighty oceans, but with the advent of nuclear weapons we faced the abhorrent reality that, though our nation was the most powerful in the world, we were now vulnerable to bombs on our cities and firesides quite as much as old Europe. That marked the end of our innocence—our exemption from the fears other men and women had always known.

Our ancestors had thought it normal to live with dragons and evil spirits, with Zeus and his thunderbolts, with Thor and his hammer. Medieval man suffered the threat of eternal damnation, and our more recent ancestors were chastened by the vision of a stern God. Though the emancipating skepticism of scientific discipline allayed the fears of divine retribution for a growing number, their respite lasted only briefly. It may be that the human psyche requires a sword of Damocles; in any event, we now used our newfound knowledge to fabricate a manmade substitute for hell—the threat of universal immolation ignited by our own willful action. We hung nuclear death like a menacing sword over mankind and we must live with the threat that it may destroy us all.

Our first reaction to our new vulnerability was irrational and demeaning. How could we have suddenly become as subject to destruction as other less favored peoples? Throughout the ugly McCarthy period, some searched for scapegoats on the vainglorious assumption that only by stealing our secrets could the Soviets have been able to build a bomb. What I found particularly repulsive in the ensuing hysteria was the realization of how little we had progressed beyond the fifteenth century; now a new form of St. Vitus' Dance afflicted even men and women I had previously regarded as intelligent. It turned friend against friend, destroying trust in human decency and producing a nation of informers.

Yet in time the fever abated; our native good sense and decency returned;

and, during the national hangover that followed the McCarthy orgy, the prospect of nuclear catastrophe became, for most people, more a figure of speech than a dour possibility. If men and women live long enough on a fault line destined to produce a major earthquake, they cease, in the years between catastrophes, to think much about it—or more important—to do much about it. History, after all, is second-guessing and only future generations know the later chapters. The Malraux quotation to which Speer alluded sums up the problem vividly: "A fish is badly placed for judging what the aquarium looks like from outside."

Our adjustment to the bomb—too easily achieved—reduced the possibility of nuclear war to a misfiled datum of day-to-day existence. Those specialized men and women who continue to think and write about it concern themselves primarily with military tactics and academic speculation expressed in a vocabulary that reduces predictions of mass human slaughter to pedantic periphrasis and dessicated statistics.

GEORGE BALL
The Past Has Another Pattern

130

Speechwriter Peggy Noonan
Reflects on Reagan's Greatness

Peggy Noonan was in her early thirties in 1984, working as a news writer for CBS anchorman Dan Rather, when she came to the conclusion that she had lost her objectivity: she was a confirmed Reaganite. As a matter of fact, one of the achievements of Ronald Reagan's presidency lay in attracting younger, more sophisticated voters to the conservative fold. "I guess everyone gets a president, one president in their adult life who's the one who moved them. For me, it's Reagan," Noonan once wrote. Using any connections she could muster, she landed a job as a speechwriter on Reagan's staff and remained there for three years, until 1987. She was considered an ace in the work, and was responsible for many of Reagan's better speeches: his words on the fortieth anniversary of D-day, for example, and those with which he consoled the nation after the *Challenger* space-shuttle disaster. Although Noonan eventually grew disillusioned with the workings of the White House, she never lost her sense of hero worship for the president. It was part of her job, however, to go further and understand exactly what qualities made Ronald Reagan seem great to so many people. She described her former boss for *Time* magazine in 1998.

He showed one kind of grit by becoming a conservative in Hollywood in the '50s and '60s. Just when everyone else was going left, particularly everyone in Hollywood who could enhance his career, he was going right. But he held to his position. It is easier to have convictions when they are shared by everyone around you; it is easier to hold to those convictions when you are surrounded by like-minded people. He almost never was.

He could take it in the face and keep on walking. Reaganites like to point to his 1976 run for the presidency, when he came within an inch of unseating Jerry Ford. When Reagan lost, he gave a valiant speech to his followers in which he spoke of the cause and signaled that he'd be back.

But I like to remember this: Reagan played Vegas. In 1954, when demand for his acting services was slowing. Reagan emceed a variety act to make money and keep his name in the air. He didn't like doing it. But it was what he had to do, so he did it. The point is he knew what it was to be through, to have people not answer your calls. When I thought about this time in his life once, I thought, All the great ones have known failure, but only the greatest of the great use it. He always used his. It deepened him and sharpened him. What was it that made him great? You can argue that great moments call forth great leaders, that the '20s brought forth a Harding, but the dramatic and demanding '30s and '80s summoned an F.D.R. and a Reagan. In Reagan's case, there was also something else. It was that he didn't become President to reach some egocentric sense of personal destiny; he didn't need the presidency, and he didn't go for it because of some strange vanity, some weird desire to be loved or a need of power to fill the empty spaces within. He didn't want the presidency in order to be a big man. He wanted the presidency so that he could do big things.

I think as we look back we will see him as the last gentleman of American politics. He was as courtly and well mannered as Bill Clinton and Newt Gingrich are not. He was a person of dignity and weight, warmth and wit. The English say a gentleman is one who never insults another by accident, but Reagan took it a step further; he wouldn't insult another on purpose.

For all that, there was of course his famous detachment. I never understood it, and neither, from what I've seen, did anyone else. It is true that when you worked for him, whether for two years or 20, he didn't care that much about your feelings. His saving grace—and it is a big one, a key one to his nature—is that he didn't care much about his feelings either. The cause was all, the effort to make the world calmer and the country freer was all.

Reagan's achievements were adult achievements, but when I think of him now I think of the reaction he got from the young. It was as if some mutual sweetness were sensed on both sides.

The man who ran speechwriting in the Reagan White House was Bently Elliott, and Ben's secretary was a woman in her early 20s named Donna. She adored Reagan. When he came back from long trips, when his helicopter landed on the White House lawn, the sound and whirr of the engine and blades would make our offices shake. We'd all stop and listen. Donna would call out, spoofing the mother in a '50s sitcom. "Daddy's home!" But you know, that's how I think a lot of people felt when Reagan was in the White House: Daddy's home. A wise and brave and responsible man is running things. And that's a good way to feel.

Another memory. Ben Elliott went with Reagan on his trip to China in 1984. Reagan spoke everywhere, as the ruling gerontocracy watched and weighed. The elders did not notice that the young of China were falling in love with the American President (that love was expressed in part in Beijing's great square during the democracy movement of 1989). One day as Reagan spoke about the history of America and the nature of democracy, a young Chinese student, standing in the back and listening to the translation, turned to the American visitor, Ben Elliott. He didn't know much English, but he turned to Ben, pointed toward Reagan and said, eyes shining, "He is great Yankeeman."

One great Yankeeman is exactly what he was, and is.

Peggy Noonan
Time
April 13, 1998

131

General Colin Powell Reflects on the Gulf War

Two hours after midnight on August 2, 1990, Iraqi tanks launched a surprise invasion of Kuwait, rolling through borders defended only by customs agents. Twelve hours later, Kuwait was no longer an independent nation; it was a possession of Iraq. Within days, the United States was preparing to send 125,000 troops to the vicinity. The impetus for the U.S. response came from the president, George H. W. Bush, whose outrage over the distant invasion surprised even his close advisers. Among them was General Colin Powell, chairman of the Joint Chiefs of Staff. Powell, sometimes called a "political general" because of his sensitivity to concerns in Washington, managed the Persian Gulf War from the capital in much the same way that his idol, General George C. Marshall, had operated during World War II. For Powell, there were many fronts in the war. While coordinating a strategy with field commanders including General Norman Schwarzkopf, he had to be equally adroit at coordinating with politicians in Washington a public-relations display for the benefit of the American people. And for the benefit of the enemy, as well, as Powell related in his memoirs, *My American Journey.* The general triumphed on all fronts, emerging as one of the heroes of a respected effort that placed America itself in the role of hero again, after a long period of uncertainty in the aftermath of Vietnam.

I was up most of the night of January 16–17, on the phone constantly, watching television out of the corner of my eye as we conducted our first war while it was being broadcast live from the enemy capital. Just after 5:00 A.M., Washington time, Schwarzkopf called me with his first summary report of the air campaign. Norm was too much the professional to be carried away by the first blush of victory, but he was hard pressed to conceal his excitement. "We got off eight hundred and fifty missions," he told me. "We clobbered most of the targets." Iraq's key biological weapons and nuclear sites had been hit hard. The Iraqis' western air defense system was knocked out. Supply dumps were in flames. Two Scud missile launching sites had been struck. "The ITT building in downtown Baghdad is glowing," he said, "and we've blown down one of Saddam's palaces."

That was the good news. I waited apprehensively. "What about losses?"

"Colin," he said, "it's incredible." It appeared so far that only two aircraft were down, while we had anticipated losing as many as seventy-five planes in this first strike. Our F-117A Stealth fighters, used in action only once before in Panama, slipped through the Iraqi air defenses like ghosts. Iraqi antiaircraft gunnery proved wild and ineffectual. And Saddam's air force barely got off the ground. That is how the war went throughout the first day, almost unopposed success.

Air traffic control alone was an astonishing feat. The first night, seven hundred coalition combat aircraft hit Iraq. Cruise missiles were launched in combat for the very first time. One hundred and sixty flying tankers circled the skies to refuel this aerial armada. The task of controlling these swarms of fighters, bombers, tankers, and missiles made Chicago's O'Hare look like a county airport.

After the initial strikes, I watched a TV reporter shove his microphone in front of a young fighter pilot just back from his first combat mission, helmet tucked under his arm, hoses dangling, face sweat-streaked, hair matted. After answering the reporter's question, the flier started walking away, then he turned back to the camera and said, "I thank God I completed my mission and got back safely. I thank God for the love of a good woman. And I thank

God I'm an American and an American fighter pilot." I sat there, melting. This was the military I wanted the country to see, not the old stereotyped dropout from nowheresville, but smart, motivated, patriotic young Americans, the best and the brightest.

The euphoria of the first day actually created a problem. Reports by CNN's Wolf Blitzer from the Pentagon made it seem as if all that remained was to organize the victory parade. I called Pete Williams, the Defense Department's spokesman. "Pete," I said, "tell Blitzer and these other press guys to cool it. This is the beginning of a war, not the end of a ballgame." In this age of instant information, people tended to expect instant results. Over the next few days, the mood shifted quickly from euphoria to a funk. Why hadn't we won yet? Was something wrong? The truth was that, in spite of heavy punishment, the Iraqis had not shown the slightest sign of caving in, despite the expectations of the most fervent airpower apostles.

On the morning of the 22nd, I went upstairs to see Secretary Cheney. "Dick, we've got to get this thing into perspective," I said. At this point, the American people had seen on television only staff briefings out of Saudi Arabia and the Pentagon. So far, no senior administration official had explained how the war was going. "Somebody should be doing that," I said.

"We'll hold a press conference tomorrow," Dick decided.

I then called my chartmakers and had them put together some graphics. Along with a detailed briefing on the operation, I also wanted a sound bite that would capture the essence of this campaign.

Late that afternoon, I was sitting at my desk jotting down phrases and running them through my mind, getting ready for the press conference. I tried out one combination that went: "We are going to cut off the Iraqi army and neutralize it." No. Cut it off and "attack" it. Maybe. Cut it off and "destroy" it. Closer, but I was still dissatisfied. I wanted something forceful, unmistakable and short. The vice chairman, Admiral Dave Jeremiah, my indispensable right-hand man, always looking out for me, stopped by the office. "Dave," I said, "I want you to hear something I've written. 'Here's our plan for the Iraqi army. First, we're going to cut it off, and then we're going to *kill* it.'"

Dave looked a little uncomfortable. "Sounds a bit stark," he said. "Are you sure that's what you want to say?"

Bill Smullen came in to discuss the press conference arrangements, and I repeated the line. Smullen's eyes widened. "Is that too strong?" I asked.

"It doesn't leave any room for misunderstanding," Bill answered.

The next day, at 2:00 P.M., Cheney and I faced the press in the briefing room on the second floor of the E-Ring. Dick led off with brief comments, and wrapped it up saying that Saddam Hussein "cannot change the basic course of the conflict. He will be defeated." He then turned the stage over to me.

I explained the battle plan. We were using our airpower first to destroy the Iraqis' air defense system and their command, control, and communications to render the enemy deaf, dumb, and blind. We then intended to tear apart the logistics supporting their army in Kuwait, including Iraqi military installations, factories, and storage depots. And then we would expand our attack to the Iraqi forces occupying Kuwait.

My presentation was deliberately understated and unemotional. And then I delivered the punch line. "Our strategy in going after this army is very simple," I said. "First we are going to cut it off, and then we are going to kill it." Those words led the press coverage on television that evening, and in the papers the next day. They achieved what I wanted. They let the world—and particularly Iraq—know our war aim unmistakably.

As I went over the charts to describe bomb damage, I said, "I've laundered them so you can't really tell what I'm talking about because I don't want the Iraqis to know what I'm talking about." And I added with a smile, "But trust me." The reporters seemed amused and did not press me further.

Colin Powell and Joseph E. Persico
My American Journey

132

An Immigrant Crosses the Border
from Mexico to America

The tide of arrivals from Mexico increased so dramatically during the post–
World War II years that it presented new issues, even within the long-running
debate in the United States on immigration. Starting with "Operation Wetback,"
the roundup of illegal immigrants in 1954, the U.S.-Mexican border was systematically militarized against the tide. Repeated initiatives attempted to curb illegal
immigration, which ran at six times the number of legal entries during the 1960s.
With Mexican Americans comprising the majority of residents in many border-
state cities, language became an impassioned issue. California and Texas
passed English-only laws pertaining to schools and other official government
activities. New Mexico, on the other hand, passed a law celebrating its bilingual
heritage. Elena Caceres was born in Mexico and came to the United States as
a child during World War II. For her, the issues bearing down around the Mexican-
American subculture were no mere abstractions. She has been finding her way
in America ever since she arrived and she learned for herself how important
language can be, when all else seems lost.

I arrived in America in 1945 as a child of five. It was a time when the
sounds of war in the Pacific reverberated on California's shores and a time
when Mexican immigrants came to the United States to fill the manpower
shortage caused by the war. My mother, who helped the war effort by working in the San Pedro shipyards as a "Rosie the Riveter," was returning to
America to marry a factory worker from Northern California. We were
properly chaperoned, mother and I, by a maiden aunt who remained until
after the civil marriage ceremony in El Paso, Texas.

My first impression of America was that it was bitterly cold. Icy winds cut
into my legs with razorlike sharpness. Outfitted for the momentous occasion,
I wore a wool coat, a knit dress, and a brand-new pair of black patent-leather
shoes specifically purchased for Mother's American marriage ceremony. We
traveled by train from the city of Chihuahua to Texas.

When we arrived at the El Paso border a cattle disease epidemic was raging, and in attempts to control it the U.S. government required every Mex-

ican immigrant crossing the border to be disinfected by stepping through troughs of a sawdust and disinfectant mixture. To my child's eyes, it looked like muddy slush. The walk through was overseen by green-uniformed INS guards.

When it was our turn, Mother instinctively reached down to carry me across the trough, but one border guard, noting her action, immediately walked over to us and told her, in perfect Spanish, to put me down, that I, too, must walk through the disinfectant. I remember feeling myself go down from my mother's protective arms into the trough. The strong smell filled my nostrils and settled into my memory forever. The sensation of stepping and sinking into the mess frightened me, but Mother held my hand steadily. We would walk across together. I looked down at my black patent-leather shoes sinking into the ugly mixture. My socks got wet and dirty; my toes hurt from the cold. I felt very frightened and confused by this new experience but did not cry. My beautiful brand-new black patent-leather shoes were ruined.

That was my prophetic entrance into the United States of America.

America is a very interesting place. Mired in contradiction, it is as beautiful as it is ugly, as objective as it is closed. Many adjectives describe the America I know. America greets its immigrants in different ways: Some are received with open arms, jobs, and appreciation; others are not. America does not always blatantly display the type of policy that requires newcomers to walk through filth to get to their goal, but it does happen. I have learned much in my fifty years in America. My once beautiful, vivacious mother, who still lives in California's lush central valley, is dead. She did not survive America.

My mother's first and lasting advice on arrival to America was to "learn English and go to school." To please her I learned English rapidly, a language that escaped her because of its difficult pronunciation. She struggled with the hard Germanic sounds, so different from her lilting Spanish. As a result, I became the family interpreter at age seven, much as I now see other children becoming interpreters for their non-English-speaking parents. Communication, English and its sounds, became an important part of my new adaptation and survival. I learned early to exist between two languages, pressed between layers of unspoken meanings.

At thirteen I began to sense that I was somehow "different." Strong messages hung in the air radiating much uncomfortable information. The messages were beyond those of common adolescent experiences of discomfort and self-discovery. It was as if there were a secret in America and that I was being perceived as undesirable and "different." The messages, imperceptible to others, weighed heavily on my thirteen-year-old self. I began to believe that *my* undesirability was related not simply to an awkward appearance but to something other.

Naively, I adopted a path to self-improvement, a true first American quest for perfection, and very fortunately experienced a great discovery at my high-insecurity phase. In the 1950s seventh-grade English class, I discovered something that was to affect me profoundly for the rest of my life. I discovered words. I discovered writing. I could write words that spellbound my restless classmates when I read to them. The ability to mesmerize with *my words* simultaneously cast an enchantment over me as the newly found word power aroused a wondrous sensation in my pubescent body. I immediately became a voracious reader who proceeded to swallow words whole like delicious little morsels. I wrote stories about gawky girls or remembered entire movies and rewrote them accurately. My sexual awakening, which occurred at about the same time as my word discovery, was less momentous. Sex on the printed page was more interesting.

As my English ability improved, my Spanish began to suffer. I symbolically pushed Spanish to the back of my brain because English was my preferred language. I began to "think" in English, which meant that Spanish words were being erased or supplanted by my English prowess. But it was wonderful. English allowed my exploration of America through the printed word, audio, and the beautiful but exaggerated images of the Hollywood screen. I developed a fascination for words. Glossy pages of print and photographs of beautiful "American" girls with perfectly straight teeth smiled at me from the pages of magazines like *Seventeen*. Oh, the agony and the ecstasy of those teeth! I flowered into puberty with pearly images of perfect American teeth and other American future perfects.

Perfect Americans. Imperfect me. How would I, a gawky misfit who had nothing of anything portrayed as American, possibly fit into America's high expectations of me? I hid my magnified adolescent imperfections, real or imagined, behind books and more words. I walked head down, shamed by my appearance and my "differentness." When I looked down at my feet, past my knobby knees and skinny legs, I saw only brown, ugly orthopedic shoes end-stopping my child-woman self like two silly commas in the middle of a sentence.

In high school I began the serious rejection of my undesirable self—that which signified my Spanish-speaking heritage. My adolescence was already being pounded by ominous forces carrying secret messages about "undesirability." I was forced to reject anything that might reveal who I *really* was, anything that might provide a clue to my undesirable "otherness." My first overt rejection was of language. I secreted my ability to speak Spanish behind my parents' doors. When anyone who visited the family did not speak English, I rejected them disdainfully, leaving the room where Spanish words might land on me and soil my English-speaking persona. I rejected the friendship of schoolmates who were not "American" (English-speaking). I also began instinctively to reject the "dark," understanding correctly that in

America, skin color determined who you were and how you were treated. All the cheerleaders were white.

So, with *Seventeen* in one hand and Revlon in the other, I decided to become American. Assisted by that strange factor, light skin color, I pored over glossy magazines to transform my appearance into something American. As a result of that metamorphosis, I was mistaken for many nationalities—but never for Mexican. My speech was distinguished only as "California" English. I was on my way to becoming assimilated, a desirable "American."

I did not have the opportunity to develop my new Americanness to any degree. Asked whether I was going to "work in the canneries" after I graduated from high school, I was shocked into my American reality. It was 1956, and the Mexican destiny was to be systematically funneled into California's central valley agricultural and industrial labor force. I had not seen myself as merely another laborer in America's work force. I did not yet know about America's bigger plans for the many.

I had bright youthful dreams. I dreamed of tulle prom dresses as voluminous as those in the movies—and I dreamed of college. I dreamed of UCLA, of studying dramatic arts and becoming a beautiful, successful actress. I would leave the central valley nothingness forever. I noticed that my dreams weren't too different from those promised to American girls. Were they? Wasn't I entitled to those same dreams also? But my high school classes, held in postwar quonset huts in one-hundred-degree weather, seemed to offer only typing classes as an escape route. I became word-perfect, though I feared a future of typing endless, monotonous words in sterile offices. The canneries provided steady work, but I did not want to become an old, sick woman in one of those places, or in a factory performing mind-numbing tasks in endless shifts. Never did I want to be like my mother, a homemaker trapped by her culture and her social displacement, and frustrated by her inability to master the English language.

Pushed by a mother who held unrealizable dreams of her own, I briefly attended junior college, an experience that became a mere repetition of high school business courses. It presented no new or challenging options. Ironically, words came to my rescue in the form of shorthand skills. They saved me from the hard labor of canneries and factories. My first job at a local private college paid 90 cents an hour, a sum smaller than the 120 wpm I recorded. In that stuffy, dusty setting of admissions records and grade point averages I stopped dreaming about UCLA and drama. Another avenue, to pay the high tuition demanded by my employer for a college education, was impossible. I stopped. Frustrated by the invisible "thing" that contained me, I turned to my very fifties option: I bolted and married a handsome Latino with no morals and a serious drinking problem.

• • •

In 1986, exactly thirty years after my high school graduation, I enrolled at the University of California, Berkeley. I was liberated by the historical events of the sixties and seventies though the *significance* of the times escaped me. I possessed the confidence that comes from true political and social naïveté and genuinely believed that a college education, a final step, would transform me into an equal and fully assimilated American. I was an unfinished product in need of final packaging.

In the 1986 climate of political correctness and under the auspices of federal guidelines, I was the perfect reentry candidate. First and foremost, regardless of my academic achievements, I was an acceptable statistic. I was also a political pawn in America's education system. As a Mexican female over the age of forty, I was one of few Hispanic females at the university and the only older Mexican female at its prestigious English department. I do not remember seeing anyone like me. I was not expected to succeed and I sensed it. Undaunted, I moved ever forward and adopted complete Berkeley standards in order to be assimilated into the academic culture. My feet were shod in politically correct Birkenstock sandals.

I was admitted to Cal Berkeley because of my own political correctness, and to its acclaimed English department because I declared an intent to study literature "relevant to my cultural background." That specific curriculum was approved for someone sanctioned by the government to be there bodily. My mind was a separate entity, to be tracked appropriately. I was unaware of "tracking" or what it meant within the American education system, and how it would restrict future educational pursuits.

In order to achieve my academic goal, I purposely reidentified as "Mexican" on my college applications, though for all intents and purposes I considered myself devoid of Mexican ethnicity. Having waited thirty years for my wonderful college education, I willingly submitted to the state's definition of me by overlooking its idiosyncratic forms and classifications. Admission to Cal Berkeley would finally correct all wrongs and any incompleteness required for Americanization.

Enamored with the idea that is Berkeley, I reverted to the role of submissive Mexican woman, grateful for any educational bit thrown to me. Something, however, alerted my recognition of glaring inequalities that particularly affected those of us classified as "minority students." I remained silent and uninvolved because I wanted my Cal college degree. I focused on books and words, and rejected the sights and sounds of painful experiences, my own and those of others. Berkeley soon began to provide more than the usual "Berkeley" experiences. Cal's illumination symbol finally proved real. I saw that Cal Berkeley was a brutal place.

Discrimination raged rampant in that most liberal of all campuses. Discriminatory practices ranged from insults hurled at minority students standing in the cafeteria lines to admitted administrative racism. "Yes," one administrator said to me informally, "we know everything about every student here, down to their eye color. This university is a microcosm of the state, where we test policy later implemented at large. If it works here, it will work statewide." In 1989, several hundred slots reserved for Hispanic applicants under supposed affirmative action guidelines were transferred to Asian applicants, who were overwhelming Cal with their high scores and demands for admission. The Hispanic contingent made no protest. The wide-sweeping action proved once again that Hispanics could be manipulated, if necessary, within the state's demographics. In 1995, California Hispanics were being summarily targeted by Governor Pete Wilson's racist Proposition 187, which denies health care and education to "illegal immigrants," meaning Hispanics who comprise the bulk of California's undocumented cheap labor force.

Cal Berkeley's unwritten discriminatory policies became more than clearly apparent. The English department's ethnic professors were not exempt, either, from a policy that paid the salary, then expected invisibility. As a group, we minority students discovered our complaints to be very similar. Teaching assistants did not "assist" us as they did other students. Ethnic slurs as embedded forms of American English were used freely both in and out of the classrooms. Everyone not ostracized as minority apparently believed they were "sacrificing" in allowing our collective stupidity within their hallowed halls. They seriously believed we could not distinguish their sometimes mildly amusing institutional terrorism.

The outrages varied. Professors literally slammed doors in our ethnic faces. I used the term "downgrading" to explain the widespread custom of lowering the grades of ethnic students. This practice was not often challenged by students, who did not dare to question the power of the institution. No one wanted to lose their "slot." Although the university's "door" opened to us symbolically, it was in fact closed.

Minority students failed, yes. In a hostile climate, defeat was part of the intended curriculum. Students who opted to transfer to other institutions were probably classified under that infamous statistic—"dropout." Most importantly, as a socioeconomic group we were not realistically *prepared* to compete on an equal level in a world-class university setting. Extensive remedial instruction blocks served as unassailable proof that minorities with their inferior brains did not belong at the university. As non-members of that privileged group who came from backgrounds of private schools and expensive tutors, we were only education's props. We satisfied statistical demands. Many left the idyllic campus because it was an American hell.

It was at Cal Berkeley that I first heard the most racist phrase in the English language directed to me: "You can pass for white." Once, I might have been elated by the culture blurring, but the myth of American equality had been clarified. I had naively existed inside an American Dream found nowhere but in my head. What my Berkeley experience taught me was that our immigrant ideas of America were only vacuous messages. In reality, mega-AMERICA with its wonderful paper-thin philosophies was only a bundle of scrap-paper promises. I was unequivocally, irrevocably, the dreaded "other." Passing for white (assimilation?) was *not* the answer.

My next metamorphosis occurred through one final Berkeley incident that left me, literally, wordless. Though my adviser counseled that I apply to "Hispanic-friendly" universities—suggesting New Mexico, Texas, or Arizona for a Ph.D. in English literature—I persisted at Cal's door. I learned survival tactics of my own and through some maneuvers changed my course of study to medieval English literature, an area of study apparently reserved for only a few, preferably non-minority students. If traditional English literature was sealed off to me, what other knowledge might also be out of my ethnic reach? I knew that I was being tracked for specific university programs designed for minority students, and I objected. My adviser continued, "Of course, you are *welcome* to apply to Berkeley, but I will tell you now, you will never be admitted here." I did not know of any student's rejection prior to application, but then, I was the department's literary thorn in the side. Burning with idealism, I rejected state-imposed tracking, demanding admission to the pristinely white ivory tower where "white" and "tower" carried dual interpretations.

The adviser who with a few cold words ended my dreams of entering the Ph.D. program at Cal then charmingly commented on my "Mexicanness" and how well I "wore" it. Her words roused a strange anger within me and a stronger sense of determination. The Germanic passion for classification surrounded me. Fortunately, I had learned my lessons well about both language and classification. Standing in the middle of the Wheeler Hall corridor, I looked down at my feet. I was not wearing the *huaraches* of a Mexican peasant tending a cornfield.

The incident that finally silenced me was not the rejection of admission to the English Ph.D. program but something more devastating. I persisted, applied to the master of arts program, and began preparing by undertaking further rigorous studies. Then, I was stunned by one of the hardest blows ever received by a much battered psyche. In a medieval history class, I became the object of derision and humiliation by yet another elitist professor, whose attack took place in the presence of an entire crowded classroom. My words, and therefore my "self," were viciously attacked to vent some deep-seated feelings about race and gender. Like printed text, I was deconstructed. I was the victim of intellectual rape. The emotional trauma is something that leaves you a sterile non-being. I was effectively silenced by a master.

• • •

I remained in total silence for several weeks. Words left my head floating out into the atmosphere as easily as they had floated in. I could not *think* of any of the thousands of English words that were the sum total of my American college education and of my assimilated self. My elderly mother nursed me, a silent object, in my sickbed. She fed my body chicken soup. She fed my fevered brain soft Spanish words. Ironically, in the midst of the volumes of silence, a letter printed with many words arrived from the university: It was my admission to the M.A. program in English literature. I saw the words and felt strangled. Unable to speak, I had been admitted to a program that required words, words, words. As in my medieval stories, I had been effectively numbed by a powerful sorcerer who laughed at my Mexican fate.

When language finally returned to me, it was in the form of Spanish words. Spanish words and comfortable images began to flood my memory with pleasant sounds and remembrances. I heard inside my head the mellifluous sounds of my childhood. Words suddenly appeared in my consciousness bright and sharp like children's color-building blocks. Words supposedly lost by my American assimilation reappeared from their secret hiding places. Words that I had disdained for their ability to define the real me reappeared to save my American self. I flailed about, reaching out for the evanescent words whirling around me and clinging to them passionately. Their forms and sounds revitalized my exhausted brain. Truth time. In America I could not shed my Mexican skin by learning a new language or by adopting an American posture. More importantly, no longer did I want to.

It has taken five years to recapture the "English" that I lost from the traumatic Berkeley experience. I have since singed the edges of American literature with some minor writing successes. My Berkeley education has meant not a thing in the America that was supposed to receive me with many equal opportunities after a rigorous college education. As a fringe spectator, I have now watched my non-minority fellow classmates, degreed or not, enter the world of publishing as editors, writers, readers, or any other occupation dear to an English major's heart. My English degree experiences have been very different. When I teach, I am inevitably placed, or offered, bilingual English positions. When I write, editors either angrily reject my work ("You will *never* be accepted by this publication") or request articles that I refer to as my "tortilla stories." My Mexicanness appears to limit my writing parameters. With one particularly crude editing experience I learned well the depth of the "power of the press." But then, my work is not easy, palatable reading. My words, once compared to those emanating from apartheid South Africa, question how it is that in free America I have something in common with millions in South African bondage.

Suppression succeeds only temporarily. Suppression contradictorily creates greater courage and determination, though that may not be immediately apparent. It takes courage to live invisible lives. While the young explode into fire and rage, the rest of us who have lived and borne outrage in measured silences simply wait. I know. I write words that are sealed away in silent boxes.

It is summer 1995. I look down now and see old, worn slippers on my tired feet. I have walked countless American miles in search of the equality and opportunity that I was told reside in America. My wanderings invariably led me to America's back doors. On my cluttered desk is a piece of crisp, white paper with printed black words. It is a letter of admission to Columbia University. Once again, expectations high, I have been admitted only through a great institution's back door. Words. Words on paper. My bane and my energy. I am words. One day America will permit my words through its front doors.

ELENA CACERES
"Fifty Years in America: Through Back Doors"

133

Bill Gates on the Birth of the Personal Computer

At a computer convention in Las Vegas in 1993, the joke making the rounds was that the only magic act people wanted was to see Bill Gates disappear. That wasn't likely to happen. Gates had vaulted into the middle of the personal-computer software business at its very inception, as he described in his book *The Road Ahead,* excerpted below. And he stayed in the burgeoning business, expanding his stake with a rapacity often compared to that of the nineteenth-century robber barons. In the span of a dozen years, Gates became the richest private citizen in the world, with a fortune estimated at over $60 billion in 1998. Bill Gates's start in the business represented a unique opportunity—as he assured his parents on leaving college behind—and yet one that has been repeated thousands of times by other young entrepreneurs since the proliferation of the personal computer.

I wrote my first software program when I was thirteen years old. It was for playing tic-tac-toe. The computer I was using was huge and cumbersome and slow and absolutely compelling.

Letting a bunch of teenagers loose on a computer was the idea of the

Mothers' Club at Lakeside, the private school I attended. The mothers decided that the proceeds from a rummage sale should be used to install a terminal and buy computer time for students. Letting students use a computer in the late 1960s was a pretty amazing choice at the time in Seattle and one I'll always be grateful for.

This computer terminal didn't have a screen. To play, we typed in our moves on a typewriter-style keyboard and then sat around until the results came chug-chugging out of a loud printing device on paper. Then we'd rush over to take a look and see who'd won or decide our next move. A game of tic-tac-toe, which would take thirty seconds with a pencil and paper, might consume most of a lunch period. But who cared? There was just something neat about the machine.

I realized later part of the appeal was that here was an enormous, expensive, grown-up machine and we, the kids, could control it. We were too young to drive or to do any of the other fun-seeming adult activities, but we could give this big machine orders and it would always obey. Computers are great because when you're working with them you get immediate results that let you know if your program works. It's feedback you don't get from many other things. That was the beginning of my fascination with software. The feedback from simple programs is particularly unambiguous. And to this day it still thrills me to know that if I can get the program right it will always work perfectly, every time, just the way I told it to.

As my friends and I gained confidence, we began to mess around with the computer, speeding things up when we could or making the games more difficult. A friend at Lakeside developed a program in BASIC that simulated the play of Monopoly. BASIC (Beginner's All-purpose Symbolic Instruction Code) is, as its name suggests, a relatively easy-to-learn programming language we used to develop increasingly complex programs. He figured out how to make the computer play hundreds of games really fast. We fed it instructions to test out various methods of play. We wanted to discover what strategies won most. And chug-a-chug, chug-a-chug—the computer told us.

Like all kids, we not only fooled around with our toys, we changed them. If you've ever watched a child with a cardboard carton and a box of crayons create a spaceship with cool control panels, or listened to their improvised rules, such as "Red cars can jump all others," then you know that this impulse to make a toy do more is at the heart of innovative childhood play. It is also the essence of creativity.

Of course, in those days we were just goofing around, or so we thought. But the toy we had—well, it turned out to be some toy. A few of us at Lakeside refused to quit playing with it. . . .

The computer we played tic-tac-toe on in 1968 and most computers at that time were mainframes: temperamental monsters that resided in climate-controlled cocoons. After we had used up the money the Mothers' Club had provided, my school friend Paul Allen, with whom I later started Microsoft, and I spent a lot of time trying to get access to computers. They performed modestly by today's standards, but seemed awesome to us because they were big and complicated and cost as much as millions of dollars each. They were connected by phone lines to tackety Teletype terminals so they could be shared by people at different locations.

We rarely got close to the actual mainframes. Computer time was very expensive. When I was in high school, it cost about $40 an hour to access a time-shared computer using a Teletype—for that $40 an hour you got a slice of the computer's precious attention. This seems odd today, when some people have more than one PC and think nothing of leaving them idle for most of the day. Actually, it was possible even then to own your own computer. If you could afford $18,000, Digital Equipment Corporation (DEC) made the PDP-8. Although it was called a "minicomputer," it was large by today's standards. It occupied a rack about two feet square and six feet high and weighed 250 pounds. We had one at our high school for a while, and I fooled around with it a bit. The PDP-8 was very limited compared to the mainframes we could reach by phone; in fact, it had less raw computing power than some wrist-watches do today. But it was programmable the same way the big, expensive ones were: by giving it software instructions. Despite its limitations, the PDP-8 inspired us to indulge in the dream that one day millions of individuals could possess their own computers.

With each passing year, I became more certain that computers and computing were destined to be cheap and ubiquitous. I'm sure that one of the reasons I was so determined to help develop the personal computer is that I wanted one for myself.

At that time software, like computer hardware, was expensive. It had to be written specifically for each kind of computer. And each time computer hardware changed, which it did regularly, the software for it pretty much had to be rewritten. Computer manufacturers provided some standard software program building blocks (for example, libraries of mathematical functions) with their machines, but most software was written specifically to solve some business's individual problems. Some software was shared, and a few companies were selling general purpose software, but there was very little packaged software that you could buy off the shelf.

My parents paid my tuition at Lakeside and gave me money for books, but I had to take care of my own computer-time bills. This is what drove me to the commercial side of the software business. A bunch of us, including Paul Allen, got entry-level software programming jobs. For high school students the pay was extraordinary—about $5,000 each summer, part in cash and the rest in computer time. We also worked out deals with a few companies whereby we could use computers for free if we'd locate problems in their software. One of the programs I wrote was the one that scheduled students in classes. I surreptitiously added a few instructions and found myself nearly the only guy in a class full of girls. As I said before, it was hard to tear myself away from a machine at which I could so unambiguously demonstrate success. I was hooked.

Paul knew a lot more than I did about computer hardware, the machines themselves. One summer day in 1972, when I was sixteen and Paul was nineteen, he showed me a ten-paragraph article buried on page 143 of *Electronics* magazine. It was announcing that a young firm named Intel had released a microprocessor chip called The 8008.

A microprocessor is a simple chip that contains the entire brain of a whole computer. Paul and I realized this first microprocessor was very limited, but he was sure that the chips would get more powerful and computers on a chip would improve very rapidly.

At the time, the computer industry had no idea of building a real computer around a microprocessor. The *Electronics* article, for example, described the 8008 as suitable for "any arithmetic, control, or decision-making system, such as a smart terminal." The writers didn't see that a microprocessor could grow up to be a general-purpose computer. Microprocessors were slow and limited in the amount of information they could handle. None of the languages programmers were familiar with was available for the 8008, which made it nearly impossible to write complex programs for it. Every application had to be programmed with the few dozen simple instructions the chip could understand. The 8008 was condemned to life as a beast of burden, carrying out uncomplicated and unchanging tasks over and over. It was quite popular in elevators and calculators.

To put it another way, a simple microprocessor in an embedded application, such as an elevator's controls, is a single instrument, a drum or a horn, in the hands of an amateur: good for basic rhythm or uncomplicated tunes. A powerful microprocessor with programming languages, however, is like an accomplished orchestra. With the right software, or sheet music, it can play anything.

Paul and I wondered what we could program the 8008 to do. He called up Intel to request a manual. We were a little surprised when they actually sent him one. We both dug into it. I had worked out a version of BASIC, which ran on the limited DEC PDP-8, and was excited at the thought of doing the same for the little Intel chip. But as I studied the 8008's manual, I realized it was futile to try. The 8008 just wasn't sophisticated enough, didn't have enough transistors.

We did, however, figure out a way to use the little chip to power a machine that could analyze the information counted by traffic monitors on city streets. Many municipalities that measured traffic flow did so by stringing a rubber hose over a selected street. When a car crossed the hose, it punched a paper tape inside a metal box at the end of the hose. We saw that we could use the 8008 to process these tapes, to print out graphs and other statistics. We baptized our first company "Traf-O-Data." At the time it sounded like poetry.

I wrote much of the software for the Traf-O-Data machine on cross-state bus trips from Seattle to Pullman, Washington, where Paul was attending college. Our prototype worked well, and we envisioned selling lots of our new machines across the country. We used it to process traffic-volume tapes for a few customers, but no one actually wanted to buy the machines, at least not from a couple of teenagers.

Despite our disappointment, we still believed our future, even if it was not to be in hardware, might have something to do with microprocessors. After I started at Harvard College in 1973, Paul somehow managed to coax his clunky old Chrysler New Yorker cross-country from Washington State and took a job in Boston, programming minicomputers at Honeywell. He drove over to Cambridge a lot so we could continue our long talks about future schemes.

In the spring of 1974, *Electronics* magazine announced Intel's new 8080 chip—ten times the power of the 8008 inside the Traf-O-Data machine. The 8080 was not much larger than the 8008, but it contained 2,700 more transistors. All at once we were looking at the heart of a real computer, and the price was under $200. We attacked the manual. "DEC can't sell any more PDP-8s now," I told Paul. It seemed obvious to us that if a tiny chip could get so much more powerful, the end of big unwieldy machines was coming.

Computer manufacturers, however, didn't see the microprocessor as a threat. They just couldn't imagine a puny chip taking on a "real" computer. Not even the scientists at Intel saw its full potential. To them, the 8080 represented nothing more than an improvement in chip technology. In the short term, the computer establishment was right. The 8080 was just another slight advance. But Paul and I looked past the limits of that new chip and saw a different kind of computer that would be perfect for us, and for everyone—personal, affordable, and adaptable. It was absolutely clear to us that because the new chips were so cheap, they soon would be everywhere.

Computer hardware, which had once been scarce, would soon be readily available, and access to computers would no longer be charged for at a high hourly rate. It seemed to us people would find all kinds of new uses for computing if it was cheap. Then software would be the key to delivering the full potential of these machines. Paul and I speculated that Japanese companies and IBM would likely produce most of the hardware. We believed we could come up with new and innovative software. And why not? The microprocessor would change the structure of the industry. Maybe there was a place for the two of us.

This kind of talk is what college is all about. You have all kinds of new experiences, and dream crazy dreams. We were young and assumed we had all the time in the world. I enrolled for another year at Harvard and kept thinking about how we could get a software company going. One plan was pretty simple. We sent letters from my dorm room to all the big computer companies, offering to write them a version of BASIC for the new Intel chip. We got no takers. By December, we were pretty discouraged. I was planning to fly home to Seattle for the holidays, and Paul was staying in Boston. On an achingly cold Massachusetts morning a few days before I left, Paul and I were hanging out at the Harvard Square newsstand, and Paul picked up the January issue of *Popular Electronics*. . . . This gave reality to our dreams about the future.

On the magazine's cover was a photograph of a very small computer, not much larger than a toaster oven. It had a name only slightly more dignified than Traf-O-Data: the Altair 8800 ("Altair" was a destination in a *Star Trek* episode). It was being sold for $397 as a kit. When it was assembled, it had no keyboard or display. It had sixteen address switches to direct commands and sixteen lights. You could get the little lights on the front pad to blink, but that was about all. Part of the problem was that the Altair 8800 lacked software. It couldn't be programmed, which made it more a novelty than a tool.

What the Altair did have was an Intel 8080 microprocessor chip as its brain. When we saw that, panic set in. "Oh no! It's happening without us! People are going to go write real software for this chip." I was sure it would happen sooner rather than later, and I wanted to be involved from the beginning. The chance to get in on the first stages of the PC revolution seemed the opportunity of a lifetime, and I seized it.

. . . There was no time to waste. Our first project was to create BASIC for the little computer.

BILL GATES
The Road Ahead

134
Educating the Generation Called "X"

Throughout the 1990s as a history professor, I regularly took college students on semester-long "road courses" to study American culture in a vehicle known as the Majic Bus. It was during this decade that the media dubbed the young people born between 1961 and 1981 as "Generation X"—a derisive term aimed at their supposed disenchantment with life and apathy toward work. In an April 1994 *Washington Post* article, I challenged the litany of assumptions being promulgated at so-called Generation Xers.   —*Douglas Brinkley*

Each year I teach a college credit course at Hofstra University called "American Odyssey: Art and Culture Across America." Thirty or so students and I spend 10 weeks traveling America by bus, studying our nation's heritage and experiencing its diversity. We read Mark Twain along the Mississippi River and Willa Cather in Nebraska, study the cold war at the Harry Truman Library in Independence, Mo., and the civil rights movement at Martin Luther King Jr.'s birthplace in Atlanta. We hold seminars on South Dakota ranches and in Chicago slums and sit around a campfire at the Gates of the Mountain park in Montana, reading from Lewis and Clark's journals on the very spot on which their expedition camped nearly 200 years ago. In this course, there is little evidence of the apathy, cynicism and general dumbness that are the supposed hallmarks of today's college students.

The intense, experiential nature of the course has enabled me to get to know my students, to share their anticipation and anxiety about the nation's future—and their place in it. If my students have taught me anything, it is their loathing of the label "Generation X," which they feel stigmatizes them. "We're not all watching MTV," a 25-year-old marketing consultant recently told *USA Today*, "we don't even consider ourselves a generation." The sentiment is echoed by nearly all of my students.

The term "Generation X" has become a derisive media catchphrase, a snide put-down for those, like me, who were born between 1961 and 1981—children of Baby Boomers. This group is, we're told, "numb and dumb," lazy underachievers, apathetic "boomerangers" who slink home to the parental nest after graduating from college, as if being born into an era of reduced economic expectations is a character defect.

Generations are, of course, labeled all the time by historians, novelists and journalists in an attempt to capture the spirit or essence of an era. But the term "Generation X" carries all the germs of propaganda and stereotype.

It is important to ask who is doing the labeling. When Gertrude Stein told Ernest Hemingway, "You're all a lost generation," she was part of it. When Jack Kerouac coined the term "the beat generation," he saw himself as a "beat." Originally, "Generation X" was the title of a 1965 British self-improvement manual for young adults by two English educators, Charles Hamblett and Jane Deverson. Its purpose was to defend the Mod culture. Billy Idol, a British rock star—a Baby Boomer himself—saw the book and named his band after it. Although "X" was meant to refer to the '60s generation, by the time the term came to the United States it began to be used by the Boomers to explain their own bewildering children.

Let's examine a recent example of the ways the stereotype is used against the young: the cover of the February 1994 anniversary issue of *The New Yorker*. There, an archtypal X-er—a young, witless, be-pimpled hip-hopper with ears pierced and baseball cap on backwards—reads a handbill for a Times Square sex show. The hormone-driven adolescent has deposed Eustace Tilley—the snooty, urbane, aristrocratic dandy who has graced every previous anniversary cover since February, 1925. The message: Seattle grunge bands, Beavis and Butthead and their friends have taken over American culture. Whether there is any truth to this assertion is irrelevant to *The New Yorker* since the aim is for a cover that will generate more sales than the necrotic Eustace ever did.

The vivid image helps us to focus on the content of the stereotype: a hapless, lower-middle-class youth whose SAT score correlates inversely with hours of MTV watched. My mention of SAT scores is not capricious. The fact is that, for myriad reasons—from differing urban idioms to an onslaught of immigration—young people as a group have not been performing well on tests. And P-SATs, SATs, LSATs, GREs and their like continue to spew from the giant computers in Princeton, serving as gatekeepers to success.

But these tests do not tell the whole story. It is important not to let ourselves become driven by test-taking as the be-all and end-all of education. It is also crucial that we not buy into the trend of pigeonholing an entire generation as underachievers. The practice is destructive in the extreme, for once teachers believe that apathy and laziness are essentially inborn generational traits, they fail to demand academic excellence and go easy on their "slacker" students who, they are led to believe, represent an inevitable historical decline in learning. This kind of stereotyping then becomes a self-fulfilling prophecy; academic performance and ambition wane, student morale sinks, and educational standards deteriorate.

The educator has an additional duty: to reach out and understand the students' points of view, and not try to force them into some procrustean bed of preconceived notions of learning, for there have always been generational differences between the teacher and the taught.

What are some of the points of view I have found to prevail among my students? They are surprisingly typical of every generation that tries to forge ahead and shed the old ways: First, they are skeptical of government and education today. We can all offer a litany of socioeconomic, political causes (with some new twists—divorce, television and the puncturing of the American Dream that promised a better life than one's parents'). They are turned off by the lies and hypocrisy in traditional history textbooks, newspapers, political campaigns and, of course, in their own parents' lives.

Young people find themselves compelled to improvise in order to survive: "Don't philosophize or preach, just deal with what comes." This street-wise instinct is grounded in disillusionment with many aspects of American life, an understandable reaction which, in kinder times, would have been praised as pragmatism. In our spinning, breathless information society, today's young people embrace deeds, not words; action, not promises. They simply don't want to repeat the mistakes of their parents, and in most circles this is called wisdom. If they appear aloof, it is because they are wary of clichés and propaganda, and because theirs is a legacy of smashed idols. If they seem inclined to take shortcuts to reach a desired result, their rationale is that old-fashioned integrity is for those who can afford it.

The young have few heroes, and are nonpolitical in the traditional two-party sense. Weaned on Watergate, on debunked and deposed political candidates, hyena scholars and yellow journalism, the students in my classes tend to admire those who live by what they preach: consumer advocate Ralph Nader, whose austere lifestyle matches his public convictions; former president Jimmy Carter, who takes up hammer and nails to build homes for the poor; Charles Barkley, who sets his own agenda on and off the basketball court; Morris Dees, who takes on bigots and hate groups in the courts. In other words, respect is granted to those elders who "walk the talk," in Twelve Step parlance. Even outspoken Arizona senator Barry Goldwater is grudgingly admired as an independent mind and a straight shooter who doesn't automatically toe the party line.

If we want to talk about generational accomplishment, consider this. Young people have effectively disposed of two of America's most enduring and time-honored myths: the rags-to-riches ethic of Horatio Alger and the soul-shrinking Puritan work ethic. Perhaps, some will argue, they had no choice, as American society copes with a rapidly changing world economy.

Let's start with the Puritans: The small, fringe cult of Massachusetts religious fanatics hell-bent on plowing from sunrise to sunset were always an oddity. Most people who migrated to America came not to become Prot-estant work beasts, but to get rich quick, without too much physical exer-tion. Institutions like slavery, indentured servitude and coolie labor attest to the importance of hard work in saving *other* people's souls. For better or for worse, young people today see the work ethic as a fraud, and, more than any other generation before them, seem to value personal happiness over mon-etary rewards.

The Horatio Alger mythology, a metaphor for America's boundless po-tential, is scoffed at. The only way to go from rags to riches in America, young people say, is to win the lottery, sue someone, screw over your neigh-bor or get lucky at one of the nation's proliferating casinos.

In the face of a deeply disappointed group of young people, what is the teacher's role? For this high-tech, visually oriented generation with a limited interest in the past (as young novelist Douglas Coupland, author of *Genera-tion X: Tales for an Accelerated Culture,* recently put it, "I'm not a wild fan of yesterday"), history teachers especially must work to develop exciting ways to make the classroom come alive, to make history relevant to today's world.

Assigning seminal books should remain the core of a history course—the basics are invaluable—but why not break up the monotony with some partic-ipatory learning? After the students read about the Lincoln-Douglas debates, have them act out the events in class. Take field trips to nearby historical sites of interest. When early-20th-century reformism is being discussed, have your class work in a soup kitchen for a day to better appreciate what conditions must have been like in that now distant era. When the civil rights movement is being studied, invite a local resident who used to work with SNCC and CORE to class to share real-life experiences.

The history teacher must move students to a broader conception of Amer-ican history. Unfortunately, the history absorbed by most of this emerging generation is composed of lessons from the 1960s and 1970s, with a cold eye focused on the bottom line: the John F. Kennedy, Bobby Kennedy, Martin Luther King and Malcolm X assassinations; numberless Americans and Vietnamese dead in a senseless war; the political crimes of Watergate; AIDS, the final chapter of "free love" and sexual liberation. They disdain anyone who sang "Give Peace a Chance" as a cheap gesture, but admire the few who devoted their lives to the cause. When someone sings "We Shall Overcome," they focus on "some day" as the seminal phrase, and find that anthem a dis-tant, wistful utopian remnant of a time deemed hopelessly naive.

But all in all, to paraphrase Gertrude Stein, a "young person is a young person is a young person." They are essentially no different from their prede-cessors; they simply want to be regarded as individuals. By 1998, those born between 1961 and 1981 will comprise the largest voting bloc ever in Ameri-can history, numbering 80 million strong. They will soon step up to the plate to try to clean up the mess. Their teachers should strive to do what education has traditionally done for the young: Bring out their best, encourage hope and nourish their imaginations.

Douglas Brinkley
Washington Post
April 3, 1994

135
Reflections on the End of the Cold War

At the beginning of 1989, the Communists had been in complete control—and seemingly permanent control—of Eastern Europe. At the end of the year, they were gone. Democratic coalitions, promising free elections in the immediate future, had taken power in East Berlin, Prague, Budapest, Warsaw, and even Bucharest (where the Romanian tyrant Nicolae Ceausescu was overthrown on December 22, then executed on Christmas Day). Most remarkable of all was the tearing down of the Berlin Wall on November 9. As a result, the Warsaw Pact had been, in effect, dismantled. Soon the Soviet Union itself collapsed. The Cold War in Europe was over. President George H. W. Bush and his National Security Advisor, Brent Scowcroft, reflect on the incredible days of 1989 and beyond when peaceful democracy swept over Europe.

BRENT SCOWCROFT

It was over. An event I had never imagined I would see in my lifetime had actually taken place. It left me feeling numb, disbelieving. It was not that I had not seen it coming. I had become accustomed, even somewhat inured, to watching a constantly embattled Gorbachev, but the signs of rapid deterioration since the attempted coup were unmistakable. No, the events themselves were creating a clear trend; it was rather the sheer incomprehensibility that such an epochal event could actually be occurring.

My initial reaction to the Soviet flag being lowered from the Kremlin for the last time was one of pride in our role in reaching this outcome. We had worked very hard to push the Soviet Union in this direction, at a pace which would not provoke an explosion in Moscow, much less a global conflagration, which was historically not an uncommon occurrence in the course of the death throes of great empires. We had done our part in crafting a beneficent outcome to this great drama, but the key actor in the final scenes was most certainly Gorbachev. He didn't plan or want it this way. He had started out to reshape the Soviet Union into a more efficient, more effective, more humane version of itself. He failed to understand that when he tried to force reform on a resistant system, his methods were pulling the threads right out of the fabric of that system. By the end, rather than reform the system, he had destroyed it.

For all his brilliance, Gorbachev appeared to have a fatal flaw. He seemed unable to make tough decisions and then stick with them. He had made a fine art of temporizing and trimming his sails. When he was personally under attack and had his back to the wall, as was more than once the case in the Supreme Soviet, he could fight back with great skill and resourcefulness. But when it came to selecting and enforcing a stern program of economic reform, Hamlet-like he shrank from the task. While I characterize his tendency to vacillate as a flaw, from our perspective it was very much a blessing. Had Gorbachev been possessed of the authoritarian and Stalin-like political will and determination of his predecessors, we might still be facing a Soviet Union. It would be one rejuvenated and reinvigorated, yet possessing at least some of the qualities which made it such a threat to the stability and security of the West.

It was a rare and great moment in history. The end of an era of enormous and unrelenting hostility had come in an instant. And, most incredible of all, without a single shot being fired.

The final collapse of Soviet power and the dissolution of its empire brought to a close the greatest transformation of the international system since World War I and concluded nearly eight decades of upheaval and conflict. The world we had encountered in January 1989 had been defined by superpower rivalry. The Cold War struggle had shaped our assumptions about international and domestic politics, our institutions and processes, our armed forces and military strategy. In a blink of an eye, these were gone. We were suddenly in a unique position, without experience, without precedent, and standing alone at the height of power. It was, it is, an unparalleled situation in history, one which presents us with the rarest opportunity to shape the world and the deepest responsibility to do so wisely for the benefit of not just the United States but all nations.

George Bush

I felt a tremendous charge as I watched the final breakup of the Soviet Union. I was pleased to watch freedom and self-determination prevail as one republic after another gained its independence. True, as Gorbachev told me in our last conversation, Russia and its neighbors still had far to go, but I had always been confident that, in the end, given the choice, the people of Central and Eastern Europe and the Soviet Union would put aside communism and opt for freedom. I remember the many uplifted bright faces in the crowds in Warsaw, Gdansk, Prague, and Budapest, sensing that freedom was near.

This was their victory. We all were winners, East and West. I think that was what made much of the process possible—that it did not come at the expense of anyone. I convinced Gorbachev that we were not trying to gain an advantage from the problems of the Soviet Union or its allies and that we sincerely wanted to see perestroika succeed. I could trust him, and I hope he knew he could trust me as we worked together to solve the international problems we confronted as our world changed. I think our relationship facilitated and smoothed matters at a critical time.

I was extraordinarily lucky to have had the privilege of serving as president during what turned out to be the closing years of the Cold War. The changes we participated in were the culmination of many years of effort by many people, both in the United States and elsewhere. We built on the careful planning and successes of Ronald Reagan and his Administration, who in turn had carried on the work of their predecessors. From those who served in our military to those who planned and implemented policy across succeeding administrations, all had a hand in bringing the Cold War to a peaceful conclusion. The special roles of Gorbachev, Shevardnadze, and the other courageous reformers around them in bringing the Soviet Union back into the international family were crucial. Without them the Cold War would have dragged on and the fear of impending nuclear war would still be with us.

While we, of course, did not (and could not) anticipate what was about to happen as we came into office, I think our accomplishment or contribution was in how we guided and shaped the final critical events we have described here as they unfolded. Some tend to see the outcome of the revolutions in Eastern Europe, German reunification, or Desert Storm as inevitable; but nothing was a foregone conclusion. We set the right tone of gentle encouragement to the reformers in Eastern Europe, keeping the pressure on the communist governments to move toward greater freedom without pushing the Soviets against a wall and into a bloody crackdown. On Germany, working closely with Helmut Kohl, we managed to unite the allies behind unification and persuade the Soviets to accept a united Germany in a new NATO— probably the most important moment in the transformation of Europe. It brought an end to the division of Europe and showed that real peace, peace without fear, was at hand. In Desert Storm I hope we set positive precedents for future responses to international crises, forging coalitions, properly using the United Nations, and carefully cultivating support at home and abroad for U.S. objectives. Above all, I hope we demonstrated that the United States will never tolerate aggression in international relations.

I am proud about what we accomplished and grateful for the wisdom, experience, and insight of the finest team I could want around me in the Administration. If there was ever a time when teamwork and camaraderie made a critical difference in policy-making, this was it. I remain convinced we had the right people in the right places at the right time. I was also fortunate to have so many wise friends among leaders elsewhere in the world—from Ottawa to Paris, Bonn, and London, and from Tokyo to Cairo, Ankara, and Riyadh—whose counsel I wanted and needed.

As I look to the future, I feel strongly about the role the United States should play in the new world before us. We have the political and economic influence and strength to pursue our own goals, but as the leading democracy and the beacon of liberty, and given our blessings of freedom, of resources, and of geography, we have a disproportionate responsibility to use that power in pursuit of a common good. We also have an obligation to lead. Yet our leadership does not rest solely on the economic strength and military muscle of a superpower; much of the world trusts and asks for our involvement. The United States is mostly perceived as benign, without territorial ambitions, uncomfortable with exercising our considerable power.

Among our most valuable contributions will be to engender predictability and stability in international relations, and we are the only power with the resources and reputation to act and be broadly accepted in this role. We need not, indeed should not, become embroiled in every upheaval, but we must help develop multilateral responses to them. We can unilaterally broker disputes, but we must act—whenever possible in concert with partners equally committed—when major aggression cannot be deterred, as in the Persian Gulf.

For these reasons, the importance of presidential leadership is probably greater now than ever. From a domestic perspective the president must take seriously his constitutional role as the chief foreign policy–maker, developing objectives and setting priorities, doing what is right for all even if it is unpopular, and then rallying the country. The challenge of presidential leadership in foreign affairs is not to listen to consensus, but to forge it at home and abroad. Nowhere is this leadership more critical than in creating a new domestic consensus for the American role in the world. There should be no question that we must face future challenges head on, without reverting to the isolationism and protectionism of the earlier part of the century. Our nation can no longer afford to retire selfishly behind its borders as soon as international conditions seemed to recede from crisis, to be brought out again only by the onrush of the next great upheaval. This was a pattern I was determined to break as we moved beyond the Cold War, and it is one we must continue to put behind us.

The present international scene, turbulent though it is, is about as much of a blank slate as history ever provides, and the importance of American engagement has never been higher. If the United States does not lead, there will be no leadership. It is our great challenge to learn from this bloodiest century in history. If we fail to live up to our responsibilities, if we shirk the role which only we can assume, if we retreat from our obligation to the world into indifference, we will, one day, pay the highest price once again for our neglect and shortsightedness.

GEORGE BUSH AND BRENT SCOWCROFT
A World Transformed

136

Militia Threats in the Wake of the Oklahoma City Bombing

Beginning in the 1980s, the white supremacy movement witnessed an unusual surge in activity. According to a watchdog group called the Center for Democratic Renewal, about 25,000 people belonged to one of the three hundred recognized white-separatist groups, while at least 150,000 considered the cause to be just. "We are proud to be white, gentile and American," said a brochure issued by the hate group White American Skinheads. "We would prefer to smash the present anti-white, Zionist (Jew) puppet-run government with a healthy, new white man's order!" The reasons for the increased fervor were hard to trace. Louis Beam, head of the Texas KKK, used his status as a decorated Vietnam War veteran to induce other embittered former soldiers to adopt a pseudo-patriotic message of terror. At the same time, the skinhead movement, with its neo-Nazi foundation, was being imported from England along with certain strains of punk-rock music. Watchdog groups track the KKK, skinheads and other white separatist organizations, but they also cite a body of "lone wolf" supremacists, acting individually or in small groups; Timothy McVeigh was probably in that category when he took a major part in the bomb attack that destroyed the Alfred P. Murrah Federal Building in Oklahoma City on April 19, 1995. Morris Dees, a lawyer from Alabama, has devoted his career to combating hate groups through his work with the Southern Poverty Law Center. The following excerpt, regarding his personal dealings with white supremacists, is from his book, *Gathering Storm*, written with James Corcoran.

I first met Louis Beam in a Texas federal court in 1981 when I forced him to stop harassing Vietnamese fishermen in Galveston Bay and to disband his 2,500-member paramilitary army. He later made the FBI's Ten Most Wanted list after being indicted, along with twelve other avowed racists, for seditious conspiracy against the United States. After his acquittal by an all-white Arkansas jury, Beam marched from the Fort Smith courthouse and saluted the Confederate memorial in the town square. "To hell with the federal government," he shouted to his supporters.

When I took Beam to court, his appeals to white supremacy and violence were the central tenets of his message. "Enough of this backing up and retreating," Louis Beam told the members of his Texas Emergency Reserve militia in 1981. "Enough of this lip service and no action. It's time to begin to train. It is time to begin to reclaim this country for white people. Now I want you to understand that they're not going to give it back to us. If you want it, you're gonna have to get it the way the founding fathers got it—Blood! Blood! Blood! The founding fathers shed their blood to give you this country, and if you want to hold on to it, you're gonna have to shed some of yours.

"Never let any race but the white race rule this country."

That racist message limited his popular appeal. Similar messages from others met with similarly limited success. Few people rallied to the likes of the Posse Comitatus, The Order, or the Aryan Nations when, during the farm crisis of the 1980s, they tried to bring embittered farmers into the fold by telling them that a Communist-Jewish-federal government conspiracy was responsible for destroying the family farm and that the only way they could protect their homes, families, and way of life was to join with the radical right in a battle for survival.

Few people rallied to the white supremacists when they echoed a similar theme to gain converts among blue-collar workers in the Northeast suffering from the decline of the steel industry. And few people rallied to them when they repeated variations on that theme during conflicts between whites and Native Americans over fishing rights in Wisconsin and between environmentalists and loggers over the spotted owl in the Northwest.

Their antigovernment theme resonated with some individuals during the 1980s, but their strident racist and anti-Semitic rhetoric kept Beam and the others at the fringes of the debate.

Nonetheless, the leader of the neo-Nazi National Alliance, William Pierce, who was never an optimist about the prospects for a white revolution, made a jarring prediction: "The wind is shifting. The 1990s are going to be different."

Today is different. Beam and his militia followers are repackaging their message. They downplay racism and focus on people's fear and anger. The fear of, and anger at, a government that overregulates, overtaxes, and, at times, murders its citizens. The fear of, and anger at, a government that is insensitive, uncaring, and callous to the needs of its people. The fear of, and anger at, a government that takes away a person's right to bear arms so that the country is vulnerable to domination by a New World Order.

Tens of thousands of people are hearing the message and thousands are joining their movement, many unaware that Beam and his fellow travelers are helping to set the agenda.

They are just the type of people racists and neo-Nazi leaders have long been after. They are mainly white and middle class. Most hold jobs, own homes, wear their hair short, don't use drugs, and, for one reason or another, they hate our government.

It is that virulent hatred of the federal government that is driving the militia movement, while at the same time masking its insidious racist underpinnings.

The racist message is never far from the surface. Timothy McVeigh condemned the federal government to anyone who would listen prior to the bombing of the Alfred P. Murrah Federal Building in Oklahoma City. His bible was *The Turner Diaries,* a fictional story of an Aryan revolt that begins with the bombing of a federal building and ends with the mass annihilation of Jews and blacks.

Hatred for the federal government is not just being preached by professional racists. Americans get a daily dose of antigovernment venom from radio talk shows, respectable lobbying organizations, and even members of Congress that competes in viciousness, mean-spiritedness, and hatefulness with anything said or written by members of the extremist movement. It has helped to create a climate and culture of hate, a climate and culture in which invective and irresponsible rhetoric is routinely used to demonize an opponent, legitimize insensitive stereotypes, and promote prejudice.

This point is not missed by the ideological thinkers behind this frightening movement. William Pierce, the author of *The Turner Diaries,* pointed out to his followers in 1994 that "most people aren't joiners, but millions of white Americans who five years ago felt so cowed by the government and [the Jewish-] controlled media that they were afraid to agree with us are becoming fed up, and their exasperation is giving them courage."

Hatred and distrust of government are running so deep that many militia members believe that federal agents exploded the Oklahoma City bomb and murdered innocent children to discredit the militia movement and to facilitate passage of an antiterrorist crime bill. They want to reclaim their America with bullets and blood, not ballots and bluster. Ammunition stockpiles are brimming full as militia groups across the country prepare for a war "to protect citizens from their government." John Trochmann, founder of the Militia of Montana, said, "We don't want bloodshed. We want to use the ballot box and the jury box. We don't want to go to the cartridge box. But we will if we have to."

I have had an all-too-close relationship with the type of fanatics who are seeking to exploit the militia movement. Because of my work against them, they have tried to kill me. In 1983, they burned the office where I work. In

1984, they came on my property to shoot me. In 1986, they plotted to blow me up with a military rocket. In 1995, they tried to build a bomb like the one that destroyed the Oklahoma City federal building to level my office. Twelve have been imprisoned for these crimes. Four await trial.

Since 1979, my associates and I at the Klanwatch Project of the Southern Poverty Law Center have been monitoring organized racists and far-right extremists through an intensive intelligence operation. Our investigative staff gathers its information from public sources, recorded speeches and publications of the leaders and groups we monitor, law enforcement sources, court depositions, Internet postings, informers, and, in some cases, carefully conducted undercover operations. Our data, computerized and cross-referenced, now contain 12,094 photographs and videos and 65,891 entries on individuals and events. We share much of this information with more than six thousand law enforcement sources through our quarterly *Intelligence Report*. Prosecutors have used information our intelligence staff has gathered to help convict more than twenty white supremacists.

In October 1994, I wrote Attorney General Janet Reno to alert her to the danger posed by the growing number of radical militia groups. I had learned that some of the country's most notorious racists and neo-Nazis were infiltrating the leadership of the so-called citizen militias.

They are men who believe that we are in the middle of a "titanic struggle" between white Aryans, God's chosen people, and Jews, the children of Satan.

Their blueprint for winning the struggle is found in *The Turner Diaries,* the story of a race war that leads to the downfall of our government.

I told the attorney general that this "mixture of armed groups and those who hate is a recipe for disaster."

Six months later, 169 people lay dead. Whether the federal government, with its vast resources, could have done something to prevent the bombing if they had taken my warning seriously is something I can't claim to know.

But I do know the Oklahoma City tragedy was not an isolated event. Similar fanatics with close ties and fueled by the same missionary zeal are at work.

MORRIS DEES
Gathering Storm: America's Militia Threat

137

Michael Kinsley on the Impeachment of Bill Clinton

In 1998, the House of Representatives voted to impeach President Bill Clinton. The case, which moved on to the Senate for trial, had been propelled for almost two years by some of the most forceful elements that can confront a country. The first of them was personal morality in an era when standards were in flux, or seemed to be. The undisputed fact of the case, as it was presented in the Senate trial, was that the president had carried on an extramarital affair with a twenty-two-year-old intern, Monica Lewinsky. Clinton's denials and his ambiguous answers in sworn testimony gave some observers cause to question his veracity, and his seeming attempts to cover up his actions became the basis for the impeachment proceedings. The element in the case that concerned many Americans most, however, was the source of the charges against Clinton. The investigation was directed by Special Prosecutor Ken Starr, whose motivation seemed at times to be partisan and whose powers, in any case, were largely unrestricted. The existence of such a powerful special prosecutor tipped the careful system of checks-and-balances delineated in the Constitution, and for many people, that was an issue that superseded the specific circumstances of Clinton's behavior. In the January 1999 impeachment President Clinton was ultimately acquitted. Before the verdict was in, though, Michael Kinsley tried to sort out the morality, the ethics, and the power struggle surrounding the scandal, in order to find out what kind of country it was that could forgive so much.

The most significant political story of 1998 is not that the President had oral sex with a 22-year-old White House intern. The most significant political story of the year is that most citizens don't seem to think it's significant that the President had oral sex with a 22-year-old *intern*. Yes, yes, and he lied about it. Under oath. Blah blah blah. They still don't care. Rarely has such an unexpected popular consensus been so clear. And rarely has such a clear consensus been so unexpected.

The press and the Washington establishment have been taking a beating for getting this one so totally wrong. But that's not fair. What about you? Suppose someone told you a year ago that the big story of 1998 would be a sex scandal involving the President and that it would reveal a great "disconnect" between Washington and the rest of the country. Then suppose you were asked to guess who was on which side. Put aside your own views on Presidents, oral sex, interns, perjury and so on. Would you have predicted

that Washington would be outraged and the rest of the country would shrug
it off? If you say yes, I don't believe you. In 1998, thanks to Bill and Monica,
we all learned something surprising about ourselves. That's what makes the
public reaction, not the events themselves, the political story of the year.

But what is that something we learned? Poor Sally Quinn had her head
chopped off for trying to explain, in the *Washington Post,* why Washington
was so outraged by the President's behavior. Her bold suggestion that Washington has moral standards offended almost everybody. An equally intrigu-
ing question is why the rest of the country hasn't been outraged. The easy
explanation—so easy that someone (me, unfortunately) raced early on to offer it in these pages—is that we've become sophisticated or decadent (take
your pick), like the French.

"What ever happened to the scarlet letter?" has become a major despairing theme of conservative political commentary. (Or, "Values, shmalues," as
America's leading value peddler, William Bennett, summarized the apparent
new culture consensus to the *New York Times* recently.) Social conservatives
used to be smug populists who tarred their critics as out-of-touch élitists.
Now they shoot furious thunderbolts at the formerly all-wise American people. Although the dismay of the sanctimony set is enjoyable to watch, their
despair may be somewhat misplaced.

Americans don't necessarily think adultery and perjury are perfectly O.K.
What they may think—what they certainly know, from personal experience—is that life is complicated and people often make a mess of it. It's complicated and messy in ways the language of politics can't describe or even
acknowledge. They may think Hillary doesn't love him, or they may think
all men have their brains in their crotch, or they may think Monica made
it too easy, or they may have no theory at all. But while Washington boils
the narrative down to issues—adultery, lies under oath—Americans who
come to the story out of human interest rather than professional obligation
are more likely to fill it out with details derived from their own life and the
lives around them.

Most people don't want to live in a society that actually tries to make life
as normal as we pretend. Or a society that stops us from pretending to more
normality than we achieve. Not that everybody is an adulterer or a perjurer.
Perhaps there are people who have nothing to be ashamed of. Even they
have messes and complications. Is there anybody with no secrets he or she
would be tempted to commit perjury for? That's not a blanket excuse for
perjury. But when the perjury was a your-secrets-or-your-life stickup staged
by a prosecutor who couldn't nail his target on anything else, anyone with
an ounce of imagination is tempted to excuse it. People who flesh out the
Bill-and-Monica story rather than stripping it down do not imagine that
Bill Clinton will go unpunished unless Congress takes him to the woodshed.
He'll suffer plenty.

This is not a morally bankrupt notion. In fact, there are obvious biblical resonances: original sin, the flesh is weak and so on. The anti-Clinton vengeance seekers claim to hate the sin while loving the sinner, but their hatred of the sinner is so obvious and so extreme that it even casts doubt on how much they actually hate the sin. Most people don't even pretend to love this particular sinner. But they see how a guy can go from succumbing to momentary temptation to lying about it to a grand jury, and they see it as a seamless human story, not as a series of discrete actions. That's why the Starr report's prurient narrative backfired so badly: by putting flesh on the bones, it made the story plausible. And that is the fatal first step toward empathy. Comic details like gifts of poetry and the semen-stained dress make it harder, not easier, for reasonable people to remain solemn enough for an impeachment.

This appreciation that life is complicated and people are funny has burst on our politics in other ways that most seers, professional and amateur, failed to predict. Tolerance of gays is an example. Despite horrible episodes like this year's torture-murder of Matthew Shepard, the general public is clearly losing patience with homophobia. Even the most obviously prejudiced politician or anti-gay political activist now feels obliged to deny any anti-gay bias, even when demonstrating one. It would be nice if this was because people concluded that gays are perfectly normal. But it's even better if people realize that nobody is perfectly normal.

Or take a small thing like flag burning. Actually, it wasn't always so small. Only a few years ago, a constitutional amendment to ban this activity— the first-ever modification of the Bill of Rights—seemed inevitable. No one dared oppose it without expressing deep horror that anyone would contemplate an act so perverse. What ever happened to all that? People didn't decide that it's O.K. to burn the flag. But maybe they decided that if some weirdo gets his rocks off by burning the flag, what's it to me? My Uncle Bernie used to stir-fry his underwear and feed it to the cat.

This sounds like straightforward libertarianism, but it's not quite the same thing. Libertarians try to persuade you that this or that form of aberrant behavior is actually harmless or beneficial. They believe that freedom from various legal or social restraints makes the individual a better person. What public response to the White House scandal demonstrates is more like the opposite: a belief that we're all weirder than we care to admit, and it's best not to get too pious about it.

Another issue of this sort coming along at year's end is assisted suicide. It is unstoppable. The medical and legal and religious establishments are against it. But people in general are increasingly for it—and for it with surprising intensity. Why? Out of empathy for someone trapped in life's messy complications. In this case empathy is enhanced by the knowledge that they not only could be that person but very likely will be. Abstract principles—even

correct ones, or ones you believe in—can't compete. No jury will convict
Dr. Kevorkian. Maybe if there were a censure option.

One thing people could be saying in their opposition to impeachment is
that we all have the right to our flaws—even the President. Or at least that
we don't want the government wringing them out of us. In that sense the new
tolerance is not a rejection of conservative values but an application of the lessons conservatives have been teaching. If you can't trust the government to
raise taxes or educate children, why on earth would you trust it to discipline
people for sexual misbehavior and the inevitable complications that follow?
Let communities, families, churches and individuals do that, just as they're
supposed to perform other formerly public functions. A pro-impeachment
commentator recently suggested that the nation would be "morally bankrupt" if we declined to punish President Clinton merely because nobody's
perfect. But maybe what America decided in 1998 was not to abandon morality. Maybe we just decided to privatize it.

MICHAEL KINSLEY
Time
December 28, 1998

138

Al Gore Concedes the Presidency

For the first time since 1888, the United States presidential election of 2000 handed the vote from the electoral college to a candidate who had lost the popular vote. By the final count, the Democratic nominee, vice president Al Gore, received 50,999,897 votes. Texas's governor George W. Bush, son of former President George H. W. Bush, won 50,456,002. But the morning after the election, the outcome was in dispute—most notably in Florida. That state's twenty-five electoral votes would decide the election. On election night some television networks declared Gore had won Florida before polls closed at precincts on the state's panhandle, which is in the central time zone. Gore requested a hand recount of votes in Florida, and for more than a month of legal wrangling it was unclear who would be the forty-third president of the United States. The Supreme Court certified Bush as the winner on December 12. Gore gave the following address the next day, striking a conciliatory tone and calling for national unity after the electoral upheaval.

Good evening.

Just moments ago, I spoke with George W. Bush and congratulated him on becoming the 43rd president of the United States. And I promised him that I wouldn't call him back this time. I offered to meet with him as soon as possible so that we can start to heal the divisions of the campaign and the contest through which we've just passed.

Almost a century and a half ago, Senator Stephen Douglas told Abraham Lincoln, who had just defeated him for the presidency, "Partisan feeling must yield to patriotism. I'm with you, Mr. President, and God bless you." Well, in that same spirit, I say to President-elect Bush that what remains of partisan rancor must now be put aside, and may God bless his stewardship of this country. Neither he nor I anticipated this long and difficult road. Certainly neither of us wanted it to happen. Yet it came, and now it has ended, resolved, as it must be resolved, through the honored institutions of our democracy.

Over the library of one of our great law schools is inscribed the motto, "Not under man but under God and law." That's the ruling principle of American freedom, the source of our democratic liberties. I've tried to make it my guide throughout this contest, as it has guided America's deliberations of all the complex issues of the past five weeks.

Now the U.S. Supreme Court has spoken. Let there be no doubt, while I strongly disagree with the court's decision, I accept it. I accept the finality of this outcome which will be ratified next Monday in the electoral college. And tonight, for the sake of our unity as a people and the strength of our democracy, I offer my concession. I also accept my responsibility, which I will discharge unconditionally, to honor the new president-elect and do everything possible to help him bring Americans together in fulfillment of the great vision that our Declaration of Independence defines and that our Constitution affirms and defends.

Let me say how grateful I am to all those who supported me and supported the cause for which we have fought. Tipper and I feel a deep gratitude to Joe and Hadassah Lieberman, who brought passion and high purpose to our partnership and opened new doors, not just for our campaign but for our country.

This has been an extraordinary election. But in one of God's unforeseen paths, this belatedly broken impasse can point us all to a new common ground, for its very closeness can serve to remind us that we are one people with a shared history and a shared destiny.

Indeed, that history gives us many examples of contests as hotly debated, as fiercely fought, with their own challenges to the popular will. Other disputes have dragged on for weeks before reaching resolution. And each time, both the victor and the vanquished have accepted the result peacefully and in a spirit of reconciliation.

So let it be with us.

I know that many of my supporters are disappointed. I am too. But our disappointment must be overcome by our love of country.

And I say to our fellow members of the world community, let no one see this contest as a sign of American weakness. The strength of American democracy is shown most clearly through the difficulties it can overcome. Some have expressed concern that the unusual nature of this election might hamper the next president in the conduct of his office. I do not believe it need be so.

President-elect Bush inherits a nation whose citizens will be ready to assist him in the conduct of his large responsibilities. I, personally, will be at his disposal, and I call on all Americans—I particularly urge all who stood with us—to unite behind our next president. This is America. Just as we fight hard when the stakes are high, we close ranks and come together when the contest is done. And while there will be time enough to debate our continuing differences, now is the time to recognize that that which unites us is greater than that which divides us. While we yet hold and do not yield our opposing beliefs, there is a higher duty than the one we owe to political party. This is America and we put country before party; we will stand together behind our new president.

As for what I'll do next, I don't know the answer to that one yet. Like many of you, I'm looking forward to spending the holidays with family and old friends. I know I'll spend time in Tennessee and mend some fences, literally and figuratively.

Some have asked whether I have any regrets, and I do have one regret: that I didn't get the chance to stay and fight for the American people over the next four years, especially for those who need burdens lifted and barriers removed, especially for those who feel their voices have not been heard. I heard you. And I will not forget.

I've seen America in this campaign, and I like what I see. It's worth fighting for and that's a fight I'll never stop. As for the battle that ends tonight, I do believe, as my father once said, that "No matter how hard the loss, defeat might serve as well as victory to shape the soul and let the glory out."

So for me this campaign ends as it began: with the love of Tipper and our family; with faith in God and in the country I have been so proud to serve, from Vietnam to the vice presidency; and with gratitude to our truly tireless campaign staff and volunteers, including all those who worked so hard in Florida for the last thirty-six days.

Now the political struggle is over, and we turn again to the unending struggle for the common good of all Americans and for those multitudes around the world who look to us for leadership in the cause of freedom.

In the words of our great hymn, "America, America": "Let us crown thy good with brotherhood, from sea to shining sea."

And now, my friends, in a phrase I once addressed to others: it's time for me to go.

Thank you, and good night, and God bless America.

ALBERT GORE
December 13, 2000

139

President Bush Comforts a Wounded Nation After 9/11

On the morning of September 11, 2001, terrorists hijacked four airplanes on the East Coast. Two were successfully crashed into the Twin Towers in downtown Manhattan. Both of those buildings toppled in a few hours, and more than 2,700 people, including all of the planes' passengers and hijackers, died. A third plane crashed near the Pentagon in Washington, D.C., and slid into the building, killing 184. A fourth plane, believed to be headed for a suicide mission at the White House or the Capitol, crashed in Pennsylvania after passengers stormed the cockpit. The attacks elicited fear, confusion, and anger across the nation along with a heightened level of patriotism. Abroad, support for the United States seemed nearly universal. In October the United States would launch a global "war on terror" and invade Afghanistan, where the attack plot had been hatched by the terrorist group al-Qaeda. For many Americans, the following address to a joint session of Congress on September 20 by President George W. Bush marked the first time they heard the name of al-Qaeda's leader, Osama bin Laden.

Mr. Speaker, Mr. President Pro Tempore, members of Congress, and fellow Americans:

In the normal course of events, presidents come to this chamber to report on the state of the Union. Tonight, no such report is needed. It has already been delivered by the American people.

We have seen it in the courage of passengers, who rushed terrorists to save others on the ground—passengers like an exceptional man named Todd Beamer. And would you please help me to welcome his wife, Lisa Beamer, here tonight. We have seen the state of our Union in the endurance of rescuers, working past exhaustion. We've seen the unfurling of flags, the lighting of candles, the giving of blood, the saying of prayers—in English, Hebrew, and Arabic. We have seen the decency of a loving and giving people who have made the grief of strangers their own. My fellow citizens, for the last nine days, the entire world has seen for itself the state of our Union—and it is strong.

Tonight we are a country awakened to danger and called to defend freedom. Our grief has turned to anger, and anger to resolution. Whether we bring our enemies to justice, or bring justice to our enemies, justice will be done. I thank the Congress for its leadership at such an important time. All of America was touched on the evening of the tragedy to see Republicans and Democrats joined together on the steps of this Capitol, singing "God Bless America." And you did more than sing; you acted, by delivering forty billion dollars to rebuild our communities and meet the needs of our military. Speaker Hastert, Minority Leader Gephardt, Majority Leader Daschle, and Senator Lott, I thank you for your friendship, for your leadership, and for your service to our country. And on behalf of the American people, I thank the world for its outpouring of support. America will never forget the sounds of our national anthem playing at Buckingham Palace, on the streets of Paris, and at Berlin's Brandenburg Gate.

We will not forget South Korean children gathering to pray outside our embassy in Seoul, or the prayers of sympathy offered at a mosque in Cairo.

We will not forget moments of silence and days of mourning in Australia and Africa and Latin America. Nor will we forget the citizens of eighty other nations who died with our own: dozens of Pakistanis; more than 130 Israelis; more than 250 citizens of India; men and women from El Salvador, Iran, Mexico, and Japan; and hundreds of British citizens. America has no truer friend than Great Britain. Once again, we are joined together in a great cause—so honored the British prime minister has crossed an ocean to show his unity with America. Thank you for coming, friend.

On September the 11, enemies of freedom committed an act of war against our country. Americans have known wars—but for the past 136 years, they have been wars on foreign soil, except for one Sunday in 1941. Americans have known the casualties of war—but not at the center of a great city on a peaceful morning. Americans have known surprise attacks—but never before on thousands of civilians. All of this was brought upon us in a single day—and night fell on a different world, a world where freedom itself is under attack. Americans have many questions tonight. Americans are asking: Who attacked our country? The evidence we have gathered all points to a collection of loosely affiliated terrorist organizations known as al-Qaeda. They are some of the murderers indicted for bombing American embassies in Tanzania and Kenya, and responsible for bombing the USS *Cole*. Al-Qaeda is to terror what the Mafia is to crime. But its goal is not making money; its goal is remaking the world—and imposing its radical beliefs on people everywhere.

The terrorists practice a fringe form of Islamic extremism that has been rejected by Muslim scholars and the vast majority of Muslim clerics, a fringe movement that perverts the peaceful teachings of Islam. The terrorists' directive commands them to kill Christians and Jews, to kill all Americans, and make no distinctions among military and civilians, including women and children. This group and its leader—a person named Osama bin Laden—are linked to many other organizations in different countries, including the Egyptian Islamic Jihad and the Islamic Movement of Uzbekistan. There are thousands of these terrorists in more than sixty countries. They are recruited from their own nations and neighborhoods and brought to camps in places like Afghanistan, where they are trained in the tactics of terror. They are sent back to their homes or sent to hide in countries around the world to plot evil and destruction.

The leadership of al-Qaeda has great influence in Afghanistan and supports the Taliban regime in controlling most of that country. In Afghanistan, we see al-Qaeda's vision for the world. Afghanistan's people have been brutalized; many are starving and many have fled. Women are not allowed to attend school. You can be jailed for owning a television. Religion can be practiced only as their leaders dictate. A man can be jailed in Afghanistan if his beard is not long enough.

The United States respects the people of Afghanistan. After all, we are currently its largest source of humanitarian aid; but we condemn the Taliban regime. It is not only repressing its own people, it is threatening people everywhere by sponsoring and sheltering and supplying terrorists. By aiding and abetting murder, the Taliban regime is committing murder.

And tonight, the United States of America makes the following demands on the Taliban: Deliver to United States authorities all the leaders of al-Qaeda who hide in your land. Release all foreign nationals, including American citizens, you have unjustly imprisoned. Protect foreign journalists, diplomats, and aid workers in your country. Close immediately and permanently every terrorist training camp in Afghanistan, and hand over every terrorist, and every person in their support structure, to appropriate authorities. Give the United States full access to terrorist training camps, so we can make sure they are no longer operating. These demands are not open to negotiation or discussion. The Taliban must act, and act immediately. They will hand over the terrorists, or they will share in their fate.

I also want to speak tonight directly to Muslims throughout the world. We respect your faith. It's practiced freely by many millions of Americans, and by millions more in countries that America counts as friends. Its teachings are good and peaceful, and those who commit evil in the name of Allah blaspheme the name of Allah. The terrorists are traitors to their own faith, trying, in effect, to hijack Islam itself. The enemy of America is not our many Muslim friends; it is not our many Arab friends. Our enemy is a radical network of terrorists, and every government that supports them. Our war on terror begins with al-Qaeda, but it does not end there. It will not end until every terrorist group of global reach has been found, stopped, and defeated.

Americans are asking: Why do they hate us? They hate what they see right here in this chamber—a democratically elected government. Their leaders are self-appointed. They hate our freedoms—our freedom of religion, our freedom of speech, our freedom to vote and assemble and disagree with each other. They want to overthrow existing governments in many Muslim countries, such as Egypt, Saudi Arabia, and Jordan. They want to drive Israel out of the Middle East. They want to drive Christians and Jews out of vast regions of Asia and Africa. These terrorists kill not merely to end lives, but to disrupt and end a way of life. With every atrocity, they hope that America grows fearful, retreating from the world and forsaking our friends. They stand against us, because we stand in their way.

We are not deceived by their pretenses to piety. We have seen their kind before. They are the heirs of all the murderous ideologies of the twentieth century. By sacrificing human life to serve their radical visions—by abandoning every value except the will to power—they follow in the path of fascism, Nazism, and totalitarianism. And they will follow that path all the way, to where it ends: in history's unmarked grave of discarded lies. Americans are asking: How will we fight and win this war? We will direct every resource at our command—every means of diplomacy, every tool of intelligence, every instrument of law enforcement, every financial influence, and every necessary weapon of war—to the disruption and to the defeat of the global terror network.

Now this war will not be like the war against Iraq a decade ago, with a decisive liberation of territory and a swift conclusion. It will not look like the air war above Kosovo two years ago, where no ground troops were used and not a single American was lost in combat. Our response involves far more than instant retaliation and isolated strikes. Americans should not expect one battle, but a lengthy campaign, unlike any other we have ever seen. It may include dramatic strikes, visible on TV, and covert operations, secret even in success. We will starve terrorists of funding, turn them one against another, drive them from place to place, until there is no refuge or no rest. And we will pursue nations that provide aid or safe haven to terrorism. Every nation, in every region, now has a decision to make. Either you are with us, or you are with the terrorists. From this day forward, any nation that continues to harbor or support terrorism will be regarded by the United States as a hostile regime.

Our nation has been put on notice: We're not immune from attack. We will take defensive measures against terrorism to protect Americans. Today, dozens of federal departments and agencies, as well as state and local governments, have responsibilities affecting homeland security. These efforts must be coordinated at the highest level. So tonight I announce the creation of a cabinet-level position reporting directly to me—the Office of Homeland Security. And tonight I also announce a distinguished American to lead this effort, to strengthen American security: a military veteran, an effective governor, a true patriot, a trusted friend—Pennsylvania's Tom Ridge. He will lead, oversee, and coordinate a comprehensive national strategy to safeguard our country against terrorism, and respond to any attacks that may come.

These measures are essential. But the only way to defeat terrorism as a threat to our way of life is to stop it, eliminate it, and destroy it where it grows. Many will be involved in this effort, from FBI agents to intelligence operatives to the reservists we have called to active duty. All deserve our thanks, and all have our prayers. And tonight, a few miles from the damaged Pentagon, I have a message for our military: Be ready. I've called the armed forces to alert, and there is a reason. The hour is coming when America will act, and you will make us proud. This is not, however, just America's fight. And what is at stake is not just America's freedom. This is the world's fight. This is civilization's fight. This is the fight of all who believe in progress and pluralism, tolerance and freedom.

We ask every nation to join us. We will ask, and we will need, the help of police forces, intelligence services, and banking systems around the world.

The United States is grateful that many nations and many international organizations have already responded with sympathy and with support— nations from Latin America to Asia to Africa to Europe to the Islamic world. Perhaps the NATO Charter reflects best the attitude of the world: An attack on one is an attack on all. The civilized world is rallying to America's side. They understand that if this terror goes unpunished, their own cities, their own citizens may be next. Terror, unanswered, can not only bring down buildings, it can threaten the stability of legitimate governments. And you know what? We're not going to allow it.

Americans are asking: What is expected of us? I ask you to live your lives, and hug your children. I know many citizens have fears tonight, and I ask you to be calm and resolute, even in the face of a continuing threat. I ask you to uphold the values of America, and remember why so many have come here. We are in a fight for our principles, and our first responsibility is to live by them. No one should be singled out for unfair treatment or unkind words because of their ethnic background or religious faith. I ask you to continue to support the victims of this tragedy with your contributions. Those who want to give can go to a central source of information, libertyunites.org, to find the names of groups providing direct help in New York, Pennsylvania, and Virginia.

The thousands of FBI agents who are now at work in this investigation may need your cooperation, and I ask you to give it. I ask for your patience, with the delays and inconveniences that may accompany tighter security; and for your patience in what will be a long struggle. I ask your continued participation and confidence in the American economy. Terrorists attacked a symbol of American prosperity. They did not touch its source. America is successful because of the hard work and creativity and enterprise of our people. These were the true strengths of our economy before September 11, and they are our strengths today. And, finally, please continue praying for the victims of terror and their families, for those in uniform, and for our great country. Prayer has comforted us in sorrow, and will help strengthen us for the journey ahead.

Tonight I thank my fellow Americans for what you have already done and for what you will do. And ladies and gentlemen of the Congress, I thank you, their representatives, for what you have already done and for what we will do together. Tonight, we face new and sudden national challenges. We will come together to improve air safety, to dramatically expand the number of air marshals on domestic flights, and take new measures to prevent hijacking. We will come together to promote stability and keep our airlines flying, with direct assistance during this emergency. We will come together to give law enforcement the additional tools it needs to track down terror here at home. We will come together to strengthen our intelligence capabilities to know the plans of terrorists before they act, and to find them before they strike.

We will come together to take active steps that strengthen America's economy, and put our people back to work. Tonight we welcome two leaders who embody the extraordinary spirit of all New Yorkers: Governor George Pataki, and Mayor Rudolph Giuliani. As a symbol of America's resolve, my administration will work with Congress, and these two leaders, to show the world that we will rebuild New York City.

After all that has just passed—all the lives taken, and all the possibilities and hopes that died with them—it is natural to wonder if America's future is one of fear.

Some speak of an age of terror. I know there are struggles ahead, and dangers to face. But this country will define our times, not be defined by them. As long as the United States of America is determined and strong, this will not be an age of terror; this will be an age of liberty, here and across the world.

Great harm has been done to us. We have suffered great loss. And in our grief and anger we have found our mission and our moment. Freedom and fear are at war. The advance of human freedom—the great achievement of our time, and the great hope of every time—now depends on us. Our nation, this generation, will lift a dark threat of violence from our people and our future. We will rally the world to this cause by our efforts, by our courage. We will not tire, we will not falter, and we will not fail.

It is my hope that in the months and years ahead, life will return almost to normal. We'll go back to our lives and routines, and that is good. Even grief recedes with time and grace. But our resolve must not pass. Each of us will remember what happened that day, and to whom it happened. We'll remember the moment the news came—where we were and what we were doing. Some will remember an image of a fire, or a story of rescue. Some will carry memories of a face and a voice gone forever.

And I will carry this: It is the police shield of a man named George Howard, who died at the World Trade Center trying to save others. It was given to me by his mom, Arlene, as a proud memorial to her son. This is my reminder of lives that ended, and a task that does not end. I will not forget this wound to our country or those who inflicted it. I will not yield; I will not rest; I will not relent in waging this struggle for freedom and security for the American people. The course of this conflict is not known, yet its outcome is certain. Freedom and fear, justice and cruelty, have always been at war, and we know that God is not neutral between them.

Fellow citizens, we'll meet violence with patient justice—assured of the rightness of our cause, and confident of the victories to come. In all that lies before us, may God grant us wisdom, and may He watch over the United States of America. Thank you.

GEORGE W. BUSH
September 20, 2001

140

Army Troops Prepare for Battle in Fallujah

The United States and its allies had spent less than a year attacking Afghan terrorist training camps and searching its caves and bunkers for al-Qaeda leaders like Osama bin Laden when President Bush began campaigning for a second front in the war on terror: Iraq. The U.S. Congress passed a resolution approving an invasion of Iraq in October 2002, after the Bush administration cited evidence that the oppressive Iraqi leader Saddam Hussein possessed weapons of mass destruction and had been in communication with al-Qaeda. The United States invaded Iraq in March 2003. Though "major combat operations" were declared over less than two months later, the war raged on largely in house-to-house urban combat against a loose-knit force of insurgent Iraqis. Hussein went into hiding after the invasion. He was captured in December 2003 and executed in 2006. The run-up to the war was met with the largest American antiwar demonstrations since the Vietnam conflict, though most Americans supported it at the outset. Public opinion turned further against the war as inspectors found no weapons of mass destruction and the veracity of Iraqi links to 9/11 dissolved. Some of the most polarizing moments came when video surfaced of soldiers and journalists being held captive and beheaded, and—in April 2004, during the battle of Fallujah—the bodies of two killed American contractors being burned and mutilated in the streets. Troops returned to Fallujah in November 2004. In the following, army Staff Sergeant David Bellavia writes of preparing himself and his men for the second battle of Fallujah.

NOVEMBER 2, 2004
DIYALA PROVINCE
OUR LAST MISSION BEFORE FALLUJAH

Seven months later, by the light of a full moon, we wade through chest-high sewage. We inch along, arms above our heads to hold our weapons out of the muck. The sludge that bathes us is exquisitely rank. Gnats swarm. Mosquitoes feast and flies crawl. If my first day in the army had been like this, I'd have gone AWOL.

Behind me, I can sense my men are pissed off. We have a mission, but some of them question it. What's beyond question is the fact that I've made them come out here in the middle of the night to wade through a trench of human excrement. I glance behind me just in time to see Piotr Sucholas nearly take a header into the filth. John Ruiz slops an arm out of the sewage and catches Sucholas before he goes under. The two of them spit funk out of their mouths, then make eye contact with me for a nanosecond.

Part of me feels guilty for their plight. Knowing they're angry with me makes it even worse. Call that my human side. At the same, the professional in me, the NCO side of my brain, gives exactly two-fifths of a fuck about how my men feel. This inner conflict doesn't usually last. The NCO in me beats the ever-loving shit out of my human side. The mission is what counts.

But tonight I just can't seem to help myself.

Voice barely a whisper, I ask, "Hey, you guys alright?"

Ruiz and Sucholas nod. So does Hugh Hall who is next to Ruiz.

"Pull your nuts out. You might just die at the end of this bitch."

They stare at me without expression, streaks of shit water running down their faces. Sucholas spits again, but does so quietly. They get the point.

The fact that my men don't say a word in response shows discipline. They are angry and miserable, but they don't display it. We both play the game, soldiers and NCOs. I'm proud of their discipline, yet at the same time I am hyperalert for the first one to break the rules.

I have pushed my squad so hard in the ten months we've been in Iraq, the men must despise me. Back at base, there is a long-standing rumor of a sock full of five-dollar bills the platoon has collected, a little wager over which of their three leading sergeants will get fragged first: Fitts, Cantrell, or me.

We push along the trench. We have almost two more kilometers to go. The moonlight leads the way; it is so bright, we don't bother with our night-vision goggles. We slop our way slowly toward a large pipe that crosses the sewer trench right at head level. It is old and rusted and looks unstable. I turn around and motion to Staff Sergeant Mike Smith. Smitty edges past me in the trench and swings a leg up onto the pipe.

A metallic groan echoes through the night. Smitty tries to shift his weight and the pipe whines in protest. It starts to buckle, and a good-sized chunk falls off, leaving a gaping hole in one side. The palm groves around us are full of chained watchdogs—the hajji version of an ADT security system. They hear the noise and bark viciously in response. The barking grows frantic. Smitty eases off the broken pipe. We can't get over it, and now we risk detection, thanks to the dogs. The whole squad freezes. I grow tense. The mission is on the line here.

We are after Ayub Ali again, the terror-for-hire arms broker who has sewn so much misery in the Diyala Province since the Shia uprising began in April. When we first arrived in-country, we had no idea who he was. Gradually, through the summer, we picked up bits of intelligence that suggested there was a network providing weapons and explosives to both the Mahdi militia and the Sunni insurgents. Ayub Ali sits atop this shadowy group.

We've tried to catch him several times already, but his luck ran strong and he evaded us at every turn. The more I learn about him, the more I want him dead. He's no ideologue or jihadist, he's just a criminal selling the tools of death to the highest bidder. He helps blow up women and children for profit. Taking Ali down will save countless innocent lives.

Tonight, we are on a sneak-and-peak mission to find his latest hideout. Intelligence reports suggest Ali has moved into a horse farm in the countryside outside Muqdadiyah. Our job is to get as close as we can, get a good look at the place, and confirm he's there. The shit trench offered the surest way to approach undetected by those vicious mutts.

Now stuck at the pipe crossing our trench, we face the possibility of blowing the op altogether. In the satellite photos I received before the mission, this pipe could not be seen. Now I have to act like I expected it. We cannot backtrack. If we do, it will be the admission of a mistake, and NCOs never make mistakes. We lie like professionals to protect that image of infallibility because that is what cements us to our men.

If they believe in you and the example you set, these men will do whatever is asked of them. This connection between soldiers is a deep bond. It is the root of what it means to be an infantryman. In this cruel here and now, it is what gives my life value and meaning. That doesn't mean my men won't despise me. The nature of soldiering brings ultra-intensity to every emotion, especially in combat. We love, hate, and respect one another all at the same time, because the alternative is the bland oblivion of death.

I look at the pipe and utter a silent curse. The men are going to have to take a bath. It is the only way to continue the mission.

I had handpicked these men for this mission. I chose Specialist Lance Ohle for his mastery of the SAW light machine gun. In a firefight, Ohle on his SAW is an artist at work. He talks like a gangsta rapper but wears cowboy hats and listens to Metallica. Neither the army nor any of those other worlds he has occupied has prepared him for this. He moans a protest about the breast stroke confronting us.

"Oh. Oohh."

"Shut the fuck up," Hugh Hall hisses.

Staff Sergeant Mike Smith stands beside me. He's our land navigation guru, though he's usually a Bradley commander, not a dismount. I nod to him and point downward, and he grimaces before taking a deep breath. An instant later, he descends into the sewage and swings around the bottom of the pipe. I hear him break the surface on the other side and exhale. Somebody hands him his weapon.

Sergeant Hall goes next. He doesn't hesitate, and I'm not surprised. I consider him one of the best soldiers in Alpha Company. He dips under the filth and pops back up on the far side of the pipe. The moonlight betrays Hall's misery. He's slick with sewage; the ochre slime drips from his Kevlar. John Ruiz sees his condition but doesn't flinch. He ducks under the pipe and breaks the surface next to Hall a second later.

I'm next. I close my eyes and hold my nose. Down into the filth I go, feeling my way under the pipe. Then I'm out the other side. Misa, Sucholas, and Sergeant Charles Knapp follow me.

We continue along the trench, more concerned about watchdogs than gunfire. Finally, we come to a stretch of palm grove that seems to be free of hajji dogs. We crawl out of the sewage and move through the grove. By now, it is 0300, and the night's chill has set in. Soaked to the bone, we start to shiver. I almost wish I was back in the shit trench. It was warmer.

We creep to a barn about 350 meters from Ali's main compound. The squad sweeps through it, hoping to find somebody to detain, but it's empty. We maneuver toward the compound. Our job is to get within view of the place, to study its layout and defenses. If possible, battalion wants us to try and flush people from the compound. If they bolt in vehicles, we can call helicopters down to follow them and others will trap them with Bradleys. Taking down these guys on the road while they're inside their cars will be easier than storming a fortified and defended compound.

On our bellies, we snake forward, bodies still shivering from the cold night air. We're just about to reach a good vantage point a hundred meters from the compound when the roar of engines shatters the stillness of the night. The cacophony grows deafening. Around us, the guard dogs howl with rage. I look over my shoulder in time to see a pair of Blackhawk helicopters thunder right over us. They hug the ground, then hover over the compound.

I hear men shouting in Arabic. A shaft of light spears the night, then another. Ali's guards are turning on searchlights. Soon the entire compound is ablaze, and the searchlights probe around us.

The birds have inadvertently compromised our mission. Cursing, we pull back to the barn, then dash into the palm grove. Behind us, the compound is fully alerted now. The guard dogs growl. The searchlights snoop. We cannot stick around. The Blackhawks dip and slide overhead. Their spinning rotors blast the buildings with mini-hurricanes of wind and dust. What was silence is now total chaos.

We hike the four kilometers back to our Brads without a word between us. This had been a perfect op until it was ruined by miscommunication with a pair of helo pilots. Stinking, frustrated, and ill-tempered, we mount up into our vehicles. We know this was our last shot at finding Ali. This mission is our swan song in the province.

Our unit is set to head out to Fallujah, a city of about 350,000 in the restive Anbar Province, along the Euphrates River. Fallujah has been under total insurgent control since April, when Operation Vigilant Resolve, a Marine offensive planned in response to the ghastly and well-publicized hanging of four U.S. contractors, was canceled for political reasons. The jarheads just loved that. All they wanted to do was finish the insurgents off once and for all. Marines. They may all be double-barreled and single-helixed. They may just be the worst historical revisionists of all time. But at their core they are fiercely proud and spoil for an unfair fight. God love 'em all.

In two days, Diyala's miseries will be behind us—the IEDs on the local highway, the Mahdi militia around Muqdadiyah, and the house-to-house firefights downtown. We can't yet know how much we'll miss them. We are leaving the good life, and heading into the mother of all city battles.

I lean back against the Bradley's bulkhead, my uniform still wet. My boys shiver violently from the cold. A few wipe their faces with rags. Piotr Sucholas, my new Bravo Team Leader, sits next me, weapon between his legs, barrel touching the Brad's floorboards. I half expect for him to start riffing on the evils of President Bush again. Sucholas is our platoon liberal. He fell in love with Michael Moore after watching a bootlegged DVD of *Fahrenheit 9/11*. Fortunately, his flaky suspicions that President Bush is out to conquer the world don't have the least effect on his willingness to do battle. When the shooting starts, he thinks only of killing the other guys and saving his men. That's why I love Piotr Sucholas.

Now he sits quietly next to me. The news that we are going to Fallujah has made everyone introspective. Sucholas has ice water for blood. In a fight, he is utterly calm, but even he is uneasy at the thought of what we will soon face.

The Brads carry us back to base. We pile out and head for our isolated three-story barracks building. From where we live, it's a twenty-five-minute walk just to reach a telephone. The battalion operations center is over a kilometer away. Even the former Iraqi army morgue that serves as our chow hall is half a kilometer from us.

Our uniforms are filthy. Cleaning them is no easy chore. We have a couple of Iraqi washing machines, but we currently don't have electricity in our building. We'll have to do our wash by hand. Fitts and I order the men to round up as many spray bottles of Simple Green cleaner as they can find. We have no running water either, so the shower room on the first floor of our barracks serves mainly as a storage area.

In the darkness, we peel off our filthy uniforms and get to work. Soon, we're all freezing cold and shaking uncontrollably as we scrub our uniforms and wash them with bottled water. When they're as clean as we can manage, we take bottled-water showers and lather up with the leftover Simple Green. The muck of the sewage trench dribbles off us as the frigid water hits our bodies. It takes us until dawn to smell semihuman again.

Once my squad is squared away, I collapse into my cot in hopes of a quick catnap. Sleep does not come easily, despite my fatigue. My mind refuses to shut off.

FALLUJAH.

When I first learned we will be redeployed to Fallujah, I pumped my fist and shouted with excitement. Finally. We'd been stuck in the backwater of the war, chasing shitheads like Ayub Ali across palm and dale without luck. We'd missed out on the Battle of Najaf in August that wiped hundreds of Mahdi militiamen and crippled al-Sadr's street army—at least for the moment. Perhaps now we'll have a chance to take part in something truly decisive. My adrenaline is already flowing.

Later that morning, we head out of the barracks to blow up our own equipment. Intelligence reports tell us that the defenders of Fallujah, who may number as many as three thousand Sunni and foreign fighters, are heavily armed—with our own weapons. Aside from the standard AK-47s, PKM machine guns, and rocket-propelled grenades, the Sunnis and foreign fighters in the city have acquired American weapons, body armor, uniforms, and Kevlar helmets. They've also used stolen Texas barriers to fortify the roads leading into Fallujah. Texas barriers are five-ton, reinforced concrete barricades that will hamper the movements of our vehicles.

We're not sure how to destroy Texas barriers, and we've never faced our own defenses and weapons before. John Ruiz, who has written the message "fuck you" on his knuckles in honor of our Fallujah vacation, wondered aloud during one meeting if our SAWs can penetrate our own body armor.

Today, we will find out. Our Brads deliver us to our firing range, just outside the wire. Usually, we shoot at pop-up targets, human silhouettes that allow us to hone our marksmanship and zero our weapons, making sure our gunsights are accurately adjusted. Not today. We pull out a couple of plates from our body armor and set them up at various intervals on the range. The plates hold up well, even against our armor-piercing rounds. This is good news and bad news. Our equipment is world-class, but some of our enemies will be wearing it.

Finally, with our SAWs, we discover a weakness. If we hit the plates with multiple concentrated bursts of fire, our rounds will penetrate the slab of armor that protects a soldier's heart and lungs. When we're done, the plates look like sieves. And this discovery, too, has a dual effect on morale—the enemy has captured our SAWs. We're in an arms race with ourselves—we know how to kill our enemy, but he can kill us in the same way.

Next, we work on ways to blow up Texas barriers. We operate with Bradleys and tanks for this exercise, and discover that a main gun round from an Abrams tank is the best option. The 120-mm shell demolishes even the thickest concrete barrier. As yet we have no reason to believe the insurgents have captured any tanks.

After lunch, our battalion command sergeant major, forty-six-year-old Steve Faulkenburg, shows up with a cache of leftover Eastern bloc goodies. He arms himself with RPGs and AK-47s and takes aim at a couple of wrecked Humvees that were dragged onto the range. He blasts the vehicles with rockets and small-arms fire, pausing every few minutes to inspect the damage. He searches for weak spots in the armor system. All afternoon, he goes about this chore and takes copious notes. Finally satisfied, Faulkenburg sets off to design extra pieces of "hillbilly armor" to cover our vulnerable spots.

We move to the vehicle range and work with the Bradleys and M1A2 Abrams tanks, practicing our breaching techniques on fortified houses. For weeks now, we have been working around the clock. Day after day, night after night, the manic routine grinds us down. We rehearse our breaching roles, refine our room-clearing fundamentals. Every mission into Muqdadiyah serves as an operational training exercise. We polish our tactics; we cross-train on different weapons systems. Every man in the platoon is now intimately familiar with everything in our arsenal. Every man can drive a Bradley and work a radio. Every man in my squad goes through combat lifesaver medical classes. I tell them they must be their own medics.

At the same time, we carry on with our twelve- to fifteen-hour combat patrols around Diyala. We're training for a fight while continuing to be in one. It leaves us brittle and bone-weary.

Toward sunset, we finally knock off. The tanks roll back across the road into the base. My platoon stays behind, tasked with guarding the sandbags and pop-up targets from marauding Iraqi thieves. The locals will steal anything.

It is easy duty, and I stretch out on the ramp of one of our Bradleys. Fitts limps over and sits down next to me. With Sergeant Cantrell on leave, Fitts is our acting platoon sergeant.

"Not to alarm you, but I am beginning to develop early stages of pretraumatic stress disorder. I want to officially go on the record to say that I am pretty sure we're all gonna die, dude," I say with as much sarcasm as I can muster.

Fitts grins. "You know, you are a difficult subordinate."

"Maybe you just can't handle me as a subordinate," I shoot back. He has already reorganized the platoon, which is sure to piss off Cantrell when he returns.

As the two of us smoke and joke, watching the Iraqi sun sinking on the horizon, Captain Sean Sims, our company commander, appears and steps past us to climb inside our Bradley. He sits down and props his feet up. He's been tense and short-tempered ever since we got the orders for Fallujah. I've also seen him head to the call center almost every night to talk with his wife. Prior to October, he rarely did that.

"Staff Sergeant Fitts and Staff Sergeant Bellavia. How are you two gentlemen doing?"

I am a little surprised by Sims's friendly tone. When Fitts returned to us over the summer, his wounds only half-healed, our captain tried to kick him out of the company. Fitts had pissed him off by bashing a hostile Muqdadiyah police officer in the face with his Kevlar helmet. Staff sergeants often piss off the higher-ups, but Fitts was particularly good at it.

"We're good, sir. You?" Fitts replies cautiously.

Captain Sims and I also have a tense relationship. In April during the house-to-house fighting in Muqdadiyah, we fought as disparate squads with little overall coordination. I later heard that Sims never left his Bradley during the fight. A commander who leads on the ground is always more desirable than one who stays in an armored vehicle. After that, I questioned his judgment on the battlefield. Later, our relationship almost fractured after I had my squad shoot three IED-laying Iraqis who turned out to be the nephews of a local good guy, an Iraqi security officer. Instead of believing my version of the events, he took sworn statements from my men and even considered opening a formal investigation. Sims dropped it at the urging of our company executive officer and other elements of our company leadership, but the incident created an uncomfortable rift between us.

Captain Sims watches the sunset in silence. Not sure he had heard us, I ask, "How are you, sir?"

"I have been better."

We can tell. He looks exhausted, and he has a quarter-sized stress zit marring his face. Since the news broke, Sims has worked relentlessly. He rarely sleeps. Instead, he pores over incoming intel reports, studying and restudying the plans the battalion staff produces. He sat for hours at night with Captain Doug Walter, our previous company commander, discussing details and working through new ideas.

Captain Sims even wanted to use Muqdadiyah for a final dress rehearsal before Fallujah. He proposed that the full task force do a cordon and search of the city, clearing every room and every house. I thought this was a brilliant idea, and it showed Sims had a lot of nuts to even pitch it. Of course, battalion command nixed the idea, afraid that such a heavy hand would stir up the locals. Nevertheless, the fact that he wanted to do it gave us newfound respect for our commander. We don't give a shit about stirring up the locals; as far as we're concerned, they're already stirred up. Using maximum force is exactly what we want to do.

Captain Sims takes his eyes off the sunset and turns to us. "What do you think about the training?"

Neither Fitts nor I hesitate. We give him some input, and he takes notes. I am astonished. He's never listened to me like this before.

We talk shop as dusk overtakes us. It is clear that Captain Sims genuinely wants our opinion. Eventually, the conversation takes another turn.

"Where are you both from?" Sims asks.

"Randolph, Mississippi," replies Fitts.

"Buffalo, New York," I answer.

"Why'd you two join the infantry?"

I reply first, "Stephen Sondheim."

"What?"

Both Fitts and Sims stare at me.

"Stephen fucking Sondheim."

"You mean the composer?" asked Sims.

"What the fuck are you talking about, bro?" says Fitts. So there's one thing about me the guy doesn't know.

"I was a theater major," I begin to explain.

"No fucking way."

"Sure. Musical theater direction and stagecraft. I ended up starting my own theater company in Buffalo. Sondheim, well, I loved his work. He was my idol, man."

"This is a very different side of you, Sergeant Bellavia."

"He wrote a musical called *Assassins*. Basically disenfranchised Americans kill presidents, except that he got his history all screwed up. John Wilkes Booth commits suicide, Leon Czolgosz kills McKinley over a girl, Lee Harvey Oswald actually shoots JFK—shit like that."

I take a drag on my cigarette. Both Fitts and Sims are just staring at me. I guess a grizzled infantryman who loves Sondheim is more shocking than one who loves Michael Moore.

"OK, so I rewrote it to make it historically accurate and show why these losers killed our presidents. When my theater company put it on, Sondheim stopped my show and threatened to sue me. I called his bluff. Only he wasn't bluffing.

"Next thing I know I'm field-dressing machine guns."

Sims and Fitts burst out laughing.

I ask Captain Sims, "What made you go infantry, sir? How'd you end up here?"

"My dad was a colonel in Vietnam. I went to Texas A&M. Married the love of my life, decided to join the army. My dad told me that I could be whatever I wanted to be, but nobody would respect me unless I started out in the infantry. And I loved it, so here I am."

He paused, then added, "I have a little boy. Sergeant Fitts, you have two children, right?"

"Three kids now, sir. Two boys and a two-year-old she-devil who runs my life."

"Are you married, Sergeant Bell?" Sims asks.

"I am. We have a four-year-old boy, Evan."

Sims looks off in the distance again. The sharing of personal details strikes me as almost unprofessional, until it dawns on me that Captain Sims is trying to do something here. He is breaking bread with us, making peace. Settling our differences.

"How are your men doing?" Sims asks.

"They're great. They're all great kids," says Fitts.

"We're lucky, sir."

"How do they feel about the intelligence reports?"

"Well," I begin, "I painted a green arrow in our living area. It points east. I figure we might as well get them used to praying six times a day now."

I know the men are ready, but they are also tense. In recent days, all the typical bitching and bickering common among infantrymen has evaporated. Those with grudges have made peace with one another. Even Cantrell did that before he left on leave earlier in the month.

One night, Cantrell was walking back to the platoon area when Sergeant Major Steve Faulkenburg spotted him and drove up in a Humvee. He told Cantrell to climb aboard. The two men seemed to detest each other. It hadn't started that way, but conflicts early in the deployment had hurt their relationship. Here was the opportunity to bury the hatchet. When Faulkenburg said good-bye to Cantrell, he looked him in the eye and remarked, "You know, we won't be able to bring them all back."

Our platoon sergeant nodded grimly. "I know, but we'll handle it head-on."

The same spirit of reconciliation drove Captain Sims to share this sunset with us. Already the past weeks have changed my view of him. Uncertain in battle, perhaps, Sims is in his element when planning and preparing for a set-piece event. He has no ego invested in his ideas, and he genuinely seeks input to make the company even more capable, even more fierce.

"You know what, sir?" I finally say, "we're gonna be all right."

Fitts looks around, spits chaw in the dust near the ramp. "The way I figure it, sir, Fallujah can't be worse than hearing Sergeant Bell bitch at me every five seconds for not having enough batteries or forty-millimeter rounds. This guy is unbelievable. What a pain in the ass."

"Sergeant Bell, are you demanding?" Sims said in mock astonishment.

"I have needs, sir," I explain. "Sergeant Cantrell met those needs. This new guy you brought in—he's such a dick. Doctrinally proficient, sure. But he's just not a people person."

Fitts scoffs, "People person."

Sims chuckles, but soon grows contemplative again. He's not finished with us. After another long pause, he asks, "Did you know Staff Sergeant Rosales well?"

Rosales was killed during an engagement on our way to Najaf in the spring. His vehicle had been targeted, and he'd been hit. Despite his wounds, he stayed in the fight, shooting his weapon until he died. He never once let anyone know he'd been wounded.

"Yeah, sir, I knew him. We all did," I explain. "He was a great guy. His wife was over in finance, so they deployed together. They had a little boy."

We had named our makeshift shooting range after Rosales, but Fitts seemed bitter about it. "And what do we give him? This piece of shit range in his honor."

I nod my head. "Yeah. When people die in the army, it isn't like the real world. They die and it's just like they went on leave or went to a new station. It isn't real till it's over, I guess."

Sims nods his head, "It sure seems that way, doesn't it."

"When you get home, sir, sit your little boy down with your dad. You tell him about us, OK? Our war. The way we fought. They can't touch us. They'll never touch us. We're gonna be all right."

"Spoken like a man who has never been shot repeatedly."

Fitts has been throwing that down a lot recently.

"Dude, I gotta hear this story again?"

Sims grinned, "It gets better every time I hear it."

"April 9, 2004. We face a company-sized element."

"Bullshit, it was a twelve-year-old with a twenty-two rifle."

Fitts shrugs, "Well, that little fucker could shoot."

Fitts hikes up his pants leg and sleeves, and we see the damage. The scars of that day in Muqdadiyah will always mark him, like bad tattoos.

The sight of them sobers Captain Sims. He slides off the bench inside the Bradley and jumps to the ground next to the ramp. Turning, he makes eye contact with us both.

"You two are the best squad leaders in the battalion. Everyone knows that. And everyone looks to you two to set the example." The compliment catches both of us off guard. "We're going to lose people."

"We know, sir."

"We're going to be tested. We will all be tested."

Silence. We wait.

"The only way we'll make it through this is to stay together."

We nod our heads. Sims is speaking from his heart.

"I am proud of the men," he manages. "I am proud to lead Alpha Company into the fight."

"Hooah, sir."

"Thank you, sir."

I needed him to say all this. As I watch Captain Sims move off into the growing darkness, my entire view of him has changed in less than twenty minutes.

I'd die for this man.

STAFF SERGEANT DAVID BELLAVIA
House to House

141

A New Orleans Musician
Mourns His Ruined City

Hurricane Katrina made landfall in Buras, Louisiana, on the morning of August 29, 2005. Its death toll would top 1,800 across coastal Louisiana, Alabama, and Mississippi. It has since been called the costliest natural disaster in American history. It put about 80 percent of New Orleans underwater in the days following the storm. Much of New Orleans sits below sea level, so the city depends on an intricate system of levees and flood walls—many of which broke or were topped when Katrina's storm surge came through the man-made canals from the Gulf of Mexico. Government relief was slow to come to New Orleans, and images of thirsty, starving, dying, and mostly African-American masses who took shelter at the Louisiana Superdome and the city's convention center shocked the country. With floodwaters up to the roofs of many homes, families spent days on roofs waiting for relief that sometimes never came—otherwise they swam or took boats to dry land. Widespread failures in emergency planning and post-storm rescue efforts became evident on the federal, state, and local level. It was weeks before the storm waters were drained from the city and longer before residents were permitted to return to the hardest-hit areas. Recovery in New Orleans, the birthplace of jazz, depended largely upon its musicians. In the following, the jazz singer John Boutté recalls his slow return to the city and the toll on his family.

I was in Brazil. I was on my way to São Paulo. I was concerned, and I was looking at the weather report in the Atlantic and what was going on. Oddly enough, I saw the wave that turned into Katrina come off the African coast. It was a powerful wave. I had an ominous feeling about it. When Katrina passed the city of New Orleans—because it didn't hit New Orleans, it hit sixty miles to the east—I was in Brazil and I couldn't get back home. I'm no holy man, but I was on my knees praying.

I can remember distinctly on the twenty-eighth calling my mother's home and speaking to my older sister. I told her, you better get out. My older sister said: I'm not going anywhere. You know, I've got a dog. I told her, I hate to be cold-blooded, but your dog is going to be dead in three months. He's old, not doing well. Do you want to die with your dog? Well, she didn't want to speak to me anymore.

She gave me my other sister, Lynette. I said, you've got to get out. She said, My shop, my shop. She's a cosmetologist. I told her, I said, Look, you've got to be crazy. You're not going to be able to cut anybody's hair. You're going to be scaling fish. She didn't want to speak to me. Then my mother got on. My mom said, I ain't going nowhere. I said, I don't want to talk to you. She gave the phone to Lolet, my other sister, I said, Leta, if you don't do anything else, I love you, but I'll never speak to you again if you don't get Mother out of New Orleans. And she did. Thank God.

My other two sisters, in their infinite wisdom, stayed. They got stuck on the I-10 for five days. Right where the cameras were showing them on CNN. They were right in that crowd. They had stayed in their house. Their house was elevated enough that they didn't get much water. Then they thought they would be able to get to higher ground. Somebody they knew passed in a boat, and they left the safety of their home and got stuck on the Interstate.

These are hardworking women. I just can't imagine . . . it broke my heart. The trauma, the terror that they went through. My older sister said that she remembered, at night, these guys were walking on the Interstate. They called them "nomads." Lots of them were smoking crack. So they couldn't sleep. They were walking up and down, just doing some horrible stuff. It was just really rough for them.

One night, they saw there was a big explosion on the river. They did have a radio. My sister's like, oh my God, we made it this long. Now we're about to die from a gas explosion. They thought there was a chemical cloud coming. They're totally traumatized over this thing, you know? Without a doubt. Without a doubt.

Fortunately, I was able to call my home. I live in the French Quarter. My roommate answered the phone. In the French Quarter, they had phone service. I couldn't believe it. Every day I checked with him. I found out what was going on. He waded through water, across dead bodies to check on my sisters and them. They said they were fine. They had food, they had water, they felt secure.

The third time he went, I said, look, I want you to go over there, and if you have to pull your gun out, and force them to come with you, get them out of that house. He went. They had already left. I didn't know where they were for a week. That really tore me apart.

Every day I called home. I called my roommate and I said, hey, do you have water? Yes. Do you have food? Yes. Do you have ammunition? Yes. I said, I hope you don't have to shoot anyone. He said the same because it would have been a tragedy. If he shot somebody, where would they get any help? You know what I'm saying? He'd have to shoot him to kill him. That would be the humane thing to do. Otherwise he would have languished there and died. He described some horrible stuff. Gangs running through, and army. It wasn't America.

One of my best friends, who I grew up with, by chance called me. Actually called the house. He was able to get my roommate. My roommate gave me his number. I was able to catch him on his cell phone. My roommate couldn't get my sisters and them, but he happened to pull out my best friend's parents, who are both in their eighties. He walked them back to the safety of our apartment. He cared for them for about four, five days, till they could get them out on a bus. To Houston, or wherever they went.

"Why" took on a whole new meaning. Annie Lennox's song "Why." Also the song that I wrote, "At the Foot of Canal Street." I wrote that about six years ago with a friend of mine, Paul Sanchez. Which predicts the flooding of New Orleans, and I never really thought of it like that.

I could hardly finish the lyrics to that. I'd get choked up, you know. I mean, still now, man, it's like nineteen months. There are times where I can't talk about it. Just thinking—the images that come back. I start thinking about how poorly we were treated. I feel like I wanna cry. I cry. I've been crying forever. Still do. I still do. Thinking about all this stuff. All the people we lost. The lifestyle we lost. The injustice of it. I feel very hurt.

I got on a plane [to come home]. We had stayed about a week. From the hotel, you could hear a pin drop. Everybody in the band was from New Orleans, musicians. Everybody realized we had no home to go to, yet we have to leave.

When we got to the airport, there must have been twenty cameras. I realized how serious it was. Global—every major network was there. It was very strange because I couldn't speak. They were putting a camera in my face. I don't speak Portuguese, so I put up my Miracle Mary necklace and I just asked them to pray for us. That was it. I cried like a baby. What can I say? Everybody did.

The day before, some lady came and gave me this beautiful silk bracelet. She said it was a good luck charm in [her] family. Evidently it worked, because, you know, everybody—they didn't come out physically unscathed, because, I mean, mentally they were really traumatized.

For me, it was like watching a car wreck on the interstate. With your family in that car and you can't get to the other side to help them.

How is that trauma ever going to be healed? I don't think it ever will. Some will stay with me until I go to my grave. You see the response that our government did. To see the politicians all posing, all of them totally incompetent. The reaction totally—can I say this? It was a clusterfuck. That's what it was. To think that they couldn't get to American people quicker with a better response. Yet they're all on TV, making like a promo or something about how great things are going? That was total bullshit. I'm still angry about it. I'm mad, I'm pissed, and guess what? Nothing's changed. And I don't mean about my attitude about it. I mean the response. Nothing's changed. So far, only 280 families have gotten money in Louisiana. Can you believe that?

What they did was they ran all the poor people out of New Orleans. Just happens to be that the poor people are the black people, huh? God bless

America. Bush's reaction. Blanco's reaction. Nagin's reaction. Brown. The only glimmer of hope was when General Honore showed up. I said, thank God. When he pulled up, the first thing I saw him do on TV was tell soldiers to stand their goddamned weapons down. They had their weapons pointed at these people like they were killing. It was bad enough that all the major networks were calling us fricking refugees. Tax-paying citizens, refugees.

I went to Miami. Then I went to Orlando with my baby sister, who's a producer with NBC. My sister from New York asked me to go to Orlando to comfort my baby sister. So I went there. Then I moved on to just south of Naples. I hooked up with my roommate, and we went to Asheville.

I spent about four weeks in Asheville with some dear friends. Thank God, man. These people were so incredible. They were just selling their house. They had an upstairs and a downstairs. They gave us the downstairs.

Those first early days in Asheville? Strange. Drunk. Depending on the kindness of strangers, you know what I'm saying? I mean, I've always been independent. To have people looking after [me], you know?

It really didn't strike me on the plane. When we were coming from Brazil, the stewardess asked us, are you from New Orleans? Yeah. She gave us handkerchiefs. I kind of like looked at her, like, what do I need this for, you know. She should have given me a two years' supply because after I got home to America and I saw what was really going on, I cried almost every goddamned day. I still have those handkerchiefs. I still cry.

I guess I was in denial. You know? It can't be that bad. But believe me. We got back to New Orleans on about the sixteenth of October. When we were coming back from Asheville the first time, we were coming through Mississippi, and I saw those pine trees broken like toothpicks. Across the lake itself, there was not a wave in the lake. You know. It was hot hot hot. We had one bird that twenty-four-mile section. Just looking for something to eat or whatever. Nothing out there. The stillness was like, I don't know, like I was about to go to a wake or a funeral. Then when I saw the city . . .

My first image was the waterline. This black line, like someone took a big marker and wrote across the whole city with a paintbrush. A line. A nasty city dirty muddy shit that they just wrote on everybody's house everywhere. That's it. Cars upside down. Trees. Shit where it wasn't supposed to be. Things where they weren't supposed to be. It was just horrible. Everything was brown. There was not a speck of green in the city. Everything was brown. The whole city was brown. It was like a bad UPS commercial.

It was almost like Calcutta, because of the flies and the bugs and the filth and the stench. There was no place to go get anything to eat. The Red Cross was there, giving out water and food rations. The military—these young boys were carrying M-16s riding around the city. The flies. Flies everywhere. Crows. All the scavengers. Some of the animals that made it through, that were emaciated. It was like a third- or a fifth-world country. And every day all these assholes are on the TV promising what they were going to do, posing, and not doing shit. And they're still not doing shit.

I was afraid to leave the city again. I was afraid that if I'd ever leave I wouldn't be able to get back again. I went straight back to work. Somehow we worked it out. We were the first musicians back on the scene.

When we had a gig, it was like church. That was the kind of reaction. People love what we do. They come like a little kid who was afraid to get away from their mom. They always begged me not to [go]. But I got to go because I got to make money. Some things didn't change. That's the financial situation of musicians in New Orleans.

The first gig I did was at Cafe Brazil on Frenchmen. A club that I first started doing music at. This was in October. It was incredible. It was absolutely incredible. The electricity was still on and off. We were doing it almost acoustically. In this little club. And it was packed. People were amazed that somebody was doing music. It was packed. They were singing along. And musicians—the ones that I knew who were there—I just invited up onstage. We started doing a weekly thing there. Not for any money. I think somebody videoed some of that stuff. I've got some video of that somewhere around.

Right after the storm. Very, very very intense.

It was like church. I got everybody—you know, it's hard to get people to participate, sometimes, to sing along, whatever. When I'd open up, the first thing I'd do is, I'd make everybody stand up and I'd say, now I want you all to do me a favor, I want everybody to scream as loud as you can. Whatever you wanted to do, just scream. It's very therapeutic. People would just get up and aaaaaahhhhhhhh! It was like this enormous roar. Get up and do it again. They'd scream again.

We'd start doing some of the old gospel tunes. New Orleans gospel tunes. It was incredible. "Just a Little While to Stay Here," "Down By the Riverside," "Over the Gloryland," "You Never Walk Alone."

What was the crowd like? The crowd was funky. Everybody was dirty, man. Nobody was dressed up. You never dressed up a lot in New Orleans anyway, but people were dirty. Nobody was like in suits, coats, ties. Nothing like that. It was kind of like a lack of a place to wash your behind. It was real funky, but it was real. It was really real. The people who have stayed throughout, they were special. They were people who had bonded together. Like never before. They really appreciated the fact that we were back and doing the music.

JOHN BOUTTÉ
"John Boutté—The Musician"
The Katrina Experience: An Oral History Project

142

"A More Perfect Union"

America elected its first African-American president in November 2008. The historic election of Barack Obama followed his meteoric rise from an obscure Illinois state senator just four years earlier. Obama delivered a stirring keynote address at the 2004 Democratic National Convention and was elected to the U.S. Senate that fall. He served in Congress for less than twenty-eight months before announcing that he was running for the highest office in the land. Obama's background was unlike any other president's. Born in Hawaii to an African father and American mother, Obama used his atypical upbringing and his keen oratorical skills to inspire Americans and eventually win their support. During a tight primary battle against Senator Hillary Clinton for the Democratic nomination in the spring of 2008, Obama delivered the following speech on American race relations after revelations that his former pastor, Reverend Jeremiah Wright, had used incendiary and anti-American rhetoric in some sermons. Delivered in Philadelphia on March 18, 2008, Obama's "A More Perfect Union" is among his most characteristic oratory—blending his campaign message of hope and unity with his own inspiring biography and the promise of what is sometimes called postracial America.

"We the people, in order to form a more perfect union."

Two hundred and twenty-one years ago, in a hall that still stands across the street, a group of men gathered and, with these simple words, launched America's improbable experiment in democracy. Farmers and scholars, statesmen and patriots who had traveled across an ocean to escape tyranny and persecution finally made real their declaration of independence at a Philadelphia convention that lasted through the spring of 1787.

The document they produced was eventually signed but ultimately unfinished. It was stained by this nation's original sin of slavery, a question that divided the colonies and brought the convention to a stalemate until the founders chose to allow the slave trade to continue for at least twenty more years, and to leave any final resolution to future generations.

Of course, the answer to the slavery question was already embedded within our Constitution—a Constitution that had at its very core the ideal of equal citizenship under the law; a Constitution that promised its people liberty, and justice, and a union that could be and should be perfected over time.

And yet words on a parchment would not be enough to deliver slaves from bondage, or provide men and women of every color and creed their full rights and obligations as citizens of the United States. What would be needed were Americans in successive generations who were willing to do their part—through protests and struggle, on the streets and in the courts, through a civil war and civil disobedience and always at great risk—to narrow that gap between the promise of our ideals and the reality of their time.

This was one of the tasks we set forth at the beginning of this campaign— to continue the long march of those who came before us, a march for a more just, more equal, more free, more caring, and more prosperous America. I chose to run for the presidency at this moment in history because I believe deeply that we cannot solve the challenges of our time unless we solve them together—unless we perfect our union by understanding that we may have different stories, but we hold common hopes; that we may not look the same and we may not have come from the same place, but we all want to move in the same direction—toward a better future for our children and our grandchildren.

This belief comes from my unyielding faith in the decency and generosity of the American people. But it also comes from my own American story.

I am the son of a black man from Kenya and a white woman from Kansas. I was raised with the help of a white grandfather who survived a Depression to serve in Patton's army during World War II and a white grandmother who worked on a bomber assembly line at Fort Leavenworth while he was overseas. I've gone to some of the best schools in America and lived in one of the world's poorest nations. I am married to a black American who carries within her the blood of slaves and slave owners—an inheritance we pass on to our two precious daughters. I have brothers, sisters, nieces, nephews, uncles, and cousins of every race and every hue, scattered across three continents, and for as long as I live, I will never forget that in no other country on Earth is my story even possible.

It's a story that hasn't made me the most conventional candidate. But it is a story that has seared into my genetic makeup the idea that this nation is more than the sum of its parts—that out of many, we are truly one.

Throughout the first year of this campaign, against all predictions to the contrary, we saw how hungry the American people were for this message of unity. Despite the temptation to view my candidacy through a purely racial lens, we won commanding victories in states with some of the whitest populations in the country. In South Carolina, where the Confederate flag still flies, we built a powerful coalition of African-Americans and white Americans.

This is not to say that race has not been an issue in the campaign. At various stages in the campaign, some commentators have deemed me either "too black" or "not black enough." We saw racial tensions bubble to the surface during the week before the South Carolina primary. The press has scoured every exit poll for the latest evidence of racial polarization, not just in terms of white and black, but black and brown as well.

And yet, it has only been in the last couple of weeks that the discussion of race in this campaign has taken a particularly divisive turn.

On one end of the spectrum, we've heard the implication that my candidacy is somehow an exercise in affirmative action; that it's based solely on the desire of wide-eyed liberals to purchase racial reconciliation on the cheap. On the other end, we've heard my former pastor, Reverend Jeremiah Wright, use incendiary language to express views that have the potential not only to widen the racial divide, but views that denigrate both the greatness and the goodness of our nation, that rightly offend white and black alike.

I have already condemned, in unequivocal terms, the statements of Reverend Wright that have caused such controversy. For some, nagging questions remain. Did I know him to be an occasionally fierce critic of American domestic and foreign policy? Of course. Did I ever hear him make remarks that could be considered controversial while I sat in church? Yes. Did I strongly disagree with many of his political views? Absolutely—just as I'm sure many of you have heard remarks from your pastors, priests, or rabbis with which you strongly disagreed.

But the remarks that have caused this recent firestorm weren't simply controversial. They weren't simply a religious leader's effort to speak out against perceived injustice. Instead, they expressed a profoundly distorted view of this country—a view that sees white racism as endemic, and that elevates what is wrong with America above all that we know is right with America; a view that sees the conflicts in the Middle East as rooted primarily in the actions of stalwart allies like Israel, instead of emanating from the perverse and hateful ideologies of radical Islam.

As such, Reverend Wright's comments were not only wrong but divisive, divisive at a time when we need unity; racially charged at a time when we need to come together to solve a set of monumental problems—two wars, a terrorist threat, a falling economy, a chronic health care crisis, and potentially devastating climate change; problems that are neither black or white or Latino or Asian, but rather problems that confront us all.

Given my background, my politics, and my professed values and ideals, there will no doubt be those for whom my statements of condemnation are not enough. Why associate myself with Reverend Wright in the first place, they may ask? Why not join another church? And I confess that if all that I knew of Reverend Wright were the snippets of those sermons that have run in an endless loop on the television and YouTube, or if Trinity United Church of Christ conformed to the caricatures being peddled by some commentators, there is no doubt that I would react in much the same way.

But the truth is, that isn't all that I know of the man. The man I met more than twenty years ago is a man who helped introduce me to my Christian faith, a man who spoke to me about our obligations to love one another; to care for the sick and lift up the poor. He is a man who served his country as a U.S. Marine; who has studied and lectured at some of the finest universities and seminaries in the country, and who for over thirty years led a church that serves the community by doing God's work here on Earth—by housing the homeless, ministering to the needy, providing day care services and scholarships and prison ministries, and reaching out to those suffering from HIV/AIDS.

In my first book, *Dreams from My Father,* I described the experience of my first service at Trinity:

"People began to shout, to rise from their seats and clap and cry out, a forceful wind carrying the reverend's voice up into the rafters. . . . And in that single note—hope!—I heard something else; at the foot of that cross, inside the thousands of churches across the city, I imagined the stories of ordinary black people merging with the stories of David and Goliath, Moses and Pharaoh, the Christians in the lion's den, Ezekiel's field of dry bones. Those stories—of survival, and freedom, and hope—became our story, my story; the blood that had spilled was our blood, the tears our tears; until this black church, on this bright day, seemed once more a vessel carrying the story of a people into future generations and into a larger world. Our trials and triumphs became at once unique and universal, black and more than black; in chronicling our journey, the stories and songs gave us a means to reclaim memories that we didn't need to feel shame about . . . memories that all people might study and cherish—and with which we could start to rebuild."

That has been my experience at Trinity. Like other predominantly black churches across the country, Trinity embodies the black community in its entirety—the doctor and the welfare mom, the model student and the former gang-banger. Like other black churches, Trinity's services are full of raucous laughter and sometimes bawdy humor. They are full of dancing, clapping, screaming, and shouting that may seem jarring to the untrained ear. The church contains in full the kindness and cruelty, the fierce intelligence and the shocking ignorance, the struggles and successes, the love and, yes, the bitterness and bias that make up the black experience in America.

And this helps explain, perhaps, my relationship with Reverend Wright. As imperfect as he may be, he has been like family to me. He strengthened my faith, officiated at my wedding, and baptized my children. Not once in my conversations with him have I heard him talk about any ethnic group in derogatory terms, or treat whites with whom he interacted with anything but courtesy and respect. He contains within him the contradictions—the good and the bad—of the community that he has served diligently for so many years.

I can no more disown him than I can disown the black community. I can no more disown him than I can my white grandmother—a woman who helped raise me, a woman who sacrificed again and again for me, a woman who loves me as much as she loves anything in this world, but a woman who once confessed her fear of black men who passed by her on the street, and who on more than one occasion has uttered racial or ethnic stereotypes that made me cringe.

These people are a part of me. And they are a part of America, this country that I love.

Some will see this as an attempt to justify or excuse comments that are simply inexcusable. I can assure you it is not. I suppose the politically safe thing would be to move on from this episode and just hope that it fades into the woodwork. We can dismiss Reverend Wright as a crank or a demagogue, just as some have dismissed Geraldine Ferraro, in the aftermath of her recent statements, as harboring some deep-seated racial bias.

But race is an issue that I believe this nation cannot afford to ignore right now. We would be making the same mistake that Reverend Wright made in his offending sermons about America—to simplify and stereotype and amplify the negative to the point that it distorts reality.

The fact is that the comments that have been made and the issues that have surfaced over the last few weeks reflect the complexities of race in this country that we've never really worked through—a part of our union that we have yet to perfect. And if we walk away now, if we simply retreat into our respective corners, we will never be able to come together and solve challenges like health care, or education, or the need to find good jobs for every American.

Understanding this reality requires a reminder of how we arrived at this point. As William Faulkner once wrote, "The past isn't dead and buried. In fact, it isn't even past." We do not need to recite here the history of racial injustice in this country. But we do need to remind ourselves that so many of the disparities that exist in the African-American community today can be directly traced to inequalities passed on from an earlier generation that suffered under the brutal legacy of slavery and Jim Crow.

Segregated schools were, and are, inferior schools; we still haven't fixed them, fifty years after *Brown v. Board of Education,* and the inferior education they provided, then and now, helps explain the pervasive achievement gap between today's black and white students.

Legalized discrimination—where blacks were prevented, often through violence, from owning property, or loans were not granted to African-American business owners, or black homeowners could not access FHA mortgages, or blacks were excluded from unions, or the police force, or fire departments—meant that black families could not amass any meaningful wealth to bequeath to future generations. That history helps explain the wealth and income gap between black and white, and the concentrated pockets of poverty that persist in so many of today's urban and rural communities.

A lack of economic opportunity among black men, and the shame and frustration that came from not being able to provide for one's family, contributed to the erosion of black families—a problem that welfare policies for many years may have worsened. And the lack of basic services in so many urban black neighborhoods—parks for kids to play in, police walking the beat, regular garbage pickup and building code enforcement—all helped create a cycle of violence, blight, and neglect that continue to haunt us.

This is the reality in which Reverend Wright and other African-Americans of his generation grew up. They came of age in the late fifties and early sixties, a time when segregation was still the law of the land and opportunity was systematically constricted. What's remarkable is not how many failed in the face of discrimination, but rather how many men and women overcame the odds; how many were able to make a way out of no way for those like me who would come after them.

But for all those who scratched and clawed their way to get a piece of the American dream, there were many who didn't make it—those who were ultimately defeated, in one way or another, by discrimination. That legacy of defeat was passed on to future generations—those young men and increasingly young women who we see standing on street corners or languishing in our prisons, without hope or prospects for the future. Even for those blacks who did make it, questions of race, and racism, continue to define their worldview in fundamental ways. For the men and women of Reverend Wright's generation, the memories of humiliation and doubt and fear have not gone away; nor has the anger, and the bitterness, of those years. That anger may not get expressed in public, in front of white coworkers or white friends. But it does find voice in the barbershop or around the kitchen table. At times, that anger is exploited by politicians, to gin up votes along racial lines, or to make up for a politician's own failings.

And occasionally it finds voice in the church on Sunday morning, in the pulpit and in the pews. The fact that so many people are surprised to hear that anger in some of Reverend Wright's sermons simply reminds us of the old truism that the most segregated hour in American life occurs on Sunday morning. That anger is not always productive; indeed, all too often it distracts attention from solving real problems; it keeps us from squarely facing our own complicity in our condition, and prevents the African-American community from forging the alliances it needs to bring about real change. But the anger is real; it is powerful; and to simply wish it away, to condemn it without understanding its roots, only serves to widen the chasm of misunderstanding that exists between the races.

In fact, a similar anger exists within segments of the white community. Most working- and middle-class white Americans don't feel that they have been particularly privileged by their race. Their experience is the immigrant experience—as far as they're concerned, no one's handed them anything, they've built it from scratch. They've worked hard all their lives, many times only to see their jobs shipped overseas or their pension dumped after a lifetime of labor. They are anxious about their futures, and feel their dreams slipping away; in an era of stagnant wages and global competition, opportunity comes to be seen as a zero-sum game, in which your dreams come at my expense. So when they are told to bus their children to a school across town; when they hear that an African-American is getting an advantage in landing a good job or a spot in a good college because of an injustice that they themselves never committed; when they're told that their fears about crime in urban neighborhoods are somehow prejudiced, resentment builds over time.

Like the anger within the black community, these resentments aren't always expressed in polite company. But they have helped shape the political landscape for at least a generation. Anger over welfare and affirmative action helped forge the Reagan coalition. Politicians routinely exploited fears of crime for their own electoral ends. Talk-show hosts and conservative commentators built entire careers unmasking bogus claims of racism while dismissing legitimate discussions of racial injustice and inequality as mere political correctness or reverse racism.

Just as black anger often proved counterproductive, so have these white resentments distracted attention from the real culprits of the middle-class squeeze—a corporate culture rife with inside dealing, questionable accounting practices, and short-term greed; a Washington dominated by lobbyists and special interests; economic policies that favor the few over the many. And yet, to wish away the resentments of white Americans, to label them as misguided or even racist, without recognizing they are grounded in legitimate concerns—this, too, widens the racial divide, and blocks the path to understanding.

This is where we are right now. It's a racial stalemate we've been stuck in for years. Contrary to the claims of some of my critics, black and white, I have never been so naive as to believe that we can get beyond our racial divisions in a single election cycle, or with a single candidacy—particularly a candidacy as imperfect as my own.

But I have asserted a firm conviction—a conviction rooted in my faith in God and my faith in the American people—that working together we can move beyond some of our old racial wounds, and that in fact we have no choice if we are to continue on the path of a more perfect union.

For the African-American community, that path means embracing the burdens of our past without becoming victims of our past. It means continuing to insist on a full measure of justice in every aspect of American life. But it also means binding our particular grievances—for better health care, and better schools, and better jobs—to the larger aspirations of all Americans: the white woman struggling to break the glass ceiling, the white man who's been laid off, the immigrant trying to feed his family. And it means taking full responsibility for own lives—by demanding more from our fathers, and spending more time with our children, and reading to them, and teaching them that while they may face challenges and discrimination in their own lives, they must never succumb to despair or cynicism; they must always believe that they can write their own destiny.

Ironically, this quintessentially American—and, yes, conservative—notion of self-help found frequent expression in Reverend Wright's sermons. But what my former pastor too often failed to understand is that embarking on a program of self-help also requires a belief that society can change.

The profound mistake of Reverend Wright's sermons is not that he spoke about racism in our society. It's that he spoke as if our society was static; as if no progress has been made; as if this country—a country that has made it possible for one of his own members to run for the highest office in the land and build a coalition of white and black, Latino and Asian, rich and poor, young and old—is still irrevocably bound to a tragic past. But what we know—what we have seen—is that America can change. That is the true genius of this nation. What we have already achieved gives us hope—the audacity to hope—for what we can and must achieve tomorrow.

In the white community, the path to a more perfect union means acknowledging that what ails the African-American community does not just exist in the minds of black people; that the legacy of discrimination and current incidents of discrimination—while less overt than in the past—are real and must be addressed. Not just with words, but with deeds—by investing in our schools and our communities; by enforcing our civil rights laws and ensuring fairness in our criminal justice system; by providing this generation with ladders of opportunity that were unavailable for previous generations. It requires all Americans to realize that your dreams do not have to come at the expense of my dreams; that investing in the health, welfare, and education of black and brown and white children will ultimately help all of America prosper.

In the end, then, what is called for is nothing more, and nothing less, than what all the world's great religions demand—that we do unto others as we would have them do unto us. Let us be our brother's keeper, scripture tells us. Let us be our sister's keeper. Let us find that common stake we all have in one another, and let our politics reflect that spirit as well.

For we have a choice in this country. We can accept a politics that breeds division, and conflict, and cynicism. We can tackle race only as spectacle, as we did in the O.J. trial; or in the wake of tragedy, as we did in the aftermath of Katrina; or as fodder for the nightly news. We can play Reverend Wright's sermons on every channel, every day and talk about them from now until the election, and make the only question in this campaign whether or not the American people think that I somehow believe or sympathize with his most offensive words. We can pounce on some gaffe by a Hillary supporter as evidence that she's playing the race card, or we can speculate on whether white men will all flock to John McCain in the general election regardless of his policies.

We can do that.

But if we do, I can tell you that in the next election, we'll be talking about some other distraction. And then another one. And then another one. And nothing will change.

That is one option. Or, at this moment, in this election, we can come together and say, "Not this time." This time we want to talk about the crumbling schools that are stealing the future of black children and white children and Asian children and Hispanic children and Native American children. This time we want to reject the cynicism that tells us that these kids can't learn; that those kids who don't look like us are somebody else's problem. The children of America are not those kids, they are our kids, and we will not let them fall behind in a twenty-first-century economy. Not this time.

This time we want to talk about how the lines in the emergency room are filled with whites and blacks and Hispanics who do not have health care; who don't have the power on their own to overcome the special interests in Washington, but who can take them on if we do it together.

This time we want to talk about the shuttered mills that once provided a decent life for men and women of every race, and the homes for sale that once belonged to Americans from every religion, every region, every walk of life. This time we want to talk about the fact that the real problem is not that someone who doesn't look like you might take your job; it's that the corporation you work for will ship it overseas for nothing more than a profit.

This time we want to talk about the men and women of every color and creed who serve together, and fight together, and bleed together under the same proud flag. We want to talk about how to bring them home from a war that never should've been authorized and never should've been waged, and we want to talk about how we'll show our patriotism by caring for them, and their families, and giving them the benefits they have earned.

I would not be running for president if I didn't believe with all my heart that this is what the vast majority of Americans want for this country. This union may never be perfect, but generation after generation has shown that it can always be perfected. And today, whenever I find myself feeling doubtful or cynical about this possibility, what gives me the most hope is the next generation—the young people whose attitudes and beliefs and openness to change have already made history in this election.

There is one story in particular that I'd like to leave you with today—a story I told when I had the great honor of speaking on Dr. King's birthday at his home church, Ebenezer Baptist, in Atlanta.

There is a young, twenty-three-year-old white woman named Ashley Baia who organized for our campaign in Florence, South Carolina. She had been working to organize a mostly African-American community since the beginning of this campaign, and one day she was at a roundtable discussion where everyone went around telling their story and why they were there.

And Ashley said that when she was nine years old, her mother got cancer. And because she had to miss days of work, she was let go and lost her health care. They had to file for bankruptcy, and that's when Ashley decided that she had to do something to help her mom.

She knew that food was one of their most expensive costs, and so Ashley convinced her mother that what she really liked and really wanted to eat more than anything else was mustard and relish sandwiches. Because that was the cheapest way to eat.

She did this for a year until her mom got better, and she told everyone at the roundtable that the reason she joined our campaign was so that she could help the millions of other children in the country who want and need to help their parents, too.

Now, Ashley might have made a different choice. Perhaps somebody told her along the way that the source of her mother's problems were blacks who were on welfare and too lazy to work, or Hispanics who were coming into the country illegally. But she didn't. She sought out allies in her fight against injustice.

Anyway, Ashley finishes her story and then goes around the room and asks everyone else why they're supporting the campaign. They all have different stories and reasons. Many bring up a specific issue. And finally they come to this elderly black man who's been sitting there quietly the entire time. And Ashley asks him why he's there. And he does not bring up a specific issue. He does not say health care or the economy. He does not say education or the war. He does not say that he was there because of Barack Obama. He simply says to everyone in the room, "I am here because of Ashley."

"I'm here because of Ashley." By itself, that single moment of recognition between that young white girl and that old black man is not enough. It is not enough to give health care to the sick, or jobs to the jobless, or education to our children.

But it is where we start. It is where our union grows stronger. And as so many generations have come to realize over the course of the two hundred and twenty-one years since a band of patriots signed that document in Philadelphia, that is where the perfection begins.

Barack Obama
March 18, 2008

Acknowledgments and Bibliography

In innumerable ways *Witness to America* has been a joint venture, and I wish to express deep appreciation to the many friends, students, colleagues, and teachers who have aided so generously in its preparation, both in its original and revised editions. Special thanks to Lou and Timmie Reda for conceiving the original project and for also helping on this updated edition. Special thanks are due to Rob Crawford at HarperCollins for bringing this new edition to life. He did a fantastic job. At HarperCollins I would also like to thank Jonathan Burnham, Kathy Schneider, Tina Andreadis, Angie Lee, Nicole Reardon, and Kyle Hansen. My former personal assistant from Tulane University, Andrew Travers, now a reporter for the *Aspen Daily News,* helped me select the more recent narratives. He was his usual ace self.

For their help on the original edition, I also wish to thank historian extraordinaire Julie Fenster, Mary Commager, and Marion Manaker. I would also like to acknowledge my former staff at the Eisenhower Center at the University of New Orleans for their superb work on the original edition, especially Kevin Willey, Matthew Ellefson, Michael Edwards, and Annie Wedekind. Naturally I also wish to acknowledge the pioneering work of my illustrious predecessors Henry Steele Commager and Allan Nevins as well as that of my friend and colleague Stephen Ambrose.

Listed below in numerical order are the sources from which the selections for *Witness to America* have been taken. Entries also include permissions information where applicable. In most, but not in all, cases, the selections have been made from the original edition of the source. Needless to say as editor I assume no responsibility for the accuracy with which these sources were originally printed. Any extended bibliographical commentary, however, would seem to be out of place in a book of this nature. This list, therefore, is neither critical nor annotated; it is included for the convenience of the reader, not for the edification of the scholar.

1. *A Retrospect of the Boston Tea-Party with a Memoir of George R.T. Hewes.* New York: 1834.
2. *The Works of John Adams.* Vol. II, *The Diary.* Edited by Charles Francis Adams. Boston: 1850.
3. William Wirt. *Sketches of the Life and Character of Patrick Henry.* Philadelphia: 1817, and many later editions.
4. *The Works of John Adams.* Vol. II, *The Diary.* Edited by Charles Francis Adams. Boston: 1850.
5. Allen French. *General Gage's Informers.* Ann Arbor, Mich.: 1932. By kind permission of Mr. French and the University of Michigan Press.

6. *The Works of John Adams.* Vol. II, *The Diary.* Edited by Charles Francis Adams. Boston: 1850.

7. *A Narrative of Colonel Ethan Allen's Captivity. . . .* Boston: 1779, and many later editions, the most accessible that by John Pell.

8. The Chevalier de Pontgibaud. *A French Volunteer of the War of Independence.* Edited by Robert B. Douglas. New York: 1898. By kind permission of the D. Appleton-Century Company.

9. James Thacher. *Military Journal During the American Revolutionary War, from 1775 to 1783.* Hartford, Conn.: 1854.

10. *Documents of American History.* Edited by Henry Steele Commager. New York: 1934.

11. *Documents Illustrative of the Formation of the Union of the United States.* Edited by C.C. Tansill. Washington: 1927. There are various other editions of Madison's notes, of which that by Max Farrand is the most comprehensive.

12. *History of the Centennial Celebration of the Inauguration of George Washington.* Edited by Clarence W. Bowen. New York: 1892.

13. *The Writings of Thomas Jefferson.* Vol. I. Edited by Albert Ellery Bergh. Washington: 1903.

14. *A Compilation of the Messages and Papers of the Presidents.* Vol. I. Edited by James D. Richardson. Various editions.

15. *The First Forty Years of Washington Society. Portrayed by Family Letters of Mrs. Samuel Harrison Smith from the Collection of Her Grandson, J. Henley Smith.* Edited by Gaillard Hunt. New York: 1906. By permission of Charles Scribner's Sons.

16. *American Eloquence.* Vol. II. Edited by Frank Moore. New York: 1864.

17. George Robert Gleig. *A Narrative of the Campaigns of the British Army at Washington and New Orleans.* London: 1826.

18. Morris Birkbeck. *Notes on a Journey in America from the Coast of Virginia to the Territory of Illinois.* London: 1818.

19. Timothy Flint. *Recollections of the Last Ten Years.* Boston: 1826, and later editions, the most accessible of which is that by C. Hartley Grattan.

20. William Cooper Howells. *Recollections of Life in Ohio from 1813 to 1840.* Cincinnati: 1895. By kind permission of John G. Kidd and Son, Inc.

21. Herman Melville. *Moby-Dick.* Innumerable editions.

22. J. H. B. Latrobe. *The First Steamboat on the Western Waters.* Maryland Historical Society Fund, Publication No. 6. Baltimore: 1871.

23. Mark Twain. *Life on the Mississippi* and "Old Times on the Mississippi." *Atlantic Monthly,* vol. 35 (February 1875). By kind permission of Harper and Brothers and the Atlantic Monthly Press.

24. Harriet Martineau. *Society in America.* 2 vols. New York: 1837, and other editions.

25. Edward Everett Hale. *A New England Boyhood.* New York: 1893. By kind permission of Little, Brown and Company.

26. *Samuel F. B. Morse, His Letters and Journals.* 2 vols. Edited by Edward Lind Morse. Boston: 1914. By kind permission of Houghton Mifflin Company.

27. *The Essays of Ralph Waldo Emerson.* Second Series. Boston: 1883, and many later editions. By kind permission of Houghton Mifflin Company.

28. Thomas Low Nichols. *Forty Years of American Life.* London: 1874. Reprinted, New York: 1937.

29. *The History of Woman Suffrage.* Vol. I. Edited by E.C. Stanton, S.B. Anthony, and M.J. Gage. Rochester, N.Y.: 1881.

30. Henry David Thoreau. *Walden, or Life in the Woods.* Boston: 1854, and innumerable later editions. By kind permission of Houghton Mifflin Company.

31. "The Correspondence of Eli Whitney." Edited by M.B. Hammond. *American Historical Review,* vol. III, 1897–98.

32. Timothy Flint. *Recollections of the Last Ten Years.* Boston: 1826.

33. Reverend R. Walsh. *Notices of Brazil.* 2 vols. London: 1830.

34. Joseph Holt Ingraham. *The South-West by a Yankee.* 2 vols. New York: 1835.

35. Thomas Low Nichols. *Forty Years of American Life.* London: 1874. Reprinted, New York: 1937.

36. James Redpath. *The Public Life of Captain John Brown.* Boston: 1860. Also in Commager's *Documents of American History.*

37. Richard Jeffry Cleveland. *A Narrative of Voyages and Commercial Enterprises.* Boston: 1842, and later editions.

38. J. C. Frémont. *The Exploring Expedition to the Rocky Mountains, Oregon and California.* Buffalo: 1849.

39. Virginia Reed Murphy. "Across the Plains in the Donner Party." *Century Magazine,* vol. XLII (New Series, vol. XX) (1891).

40. Mark Twain. *Roughing It.* 2 vols. Hartford, Conn.: 1871. By permission of Harper and Brothers.

41. Sarah Royce. Excerpts from *A Frontier Lady: Recollections of the Gold Rush and Early California,* edited by R.H. Gabriel. Copyright 1932. Reprinted with the permission of Yale University Press.

42. Nathaniel Pitt Langford. *Vigilante Days and Ways in Montana.* 2 vols. Boston: 1890. Reprinted, Chicago: 1912. By kind permission of A.C. McClurg and Company.

43. *Colonel Crockett's Exploits and Adventures in Texas....* London: 1837, and various later editions.

44. Henderson Yoakum. *History of Texas.* New York: 1856.

45. *The Memoirs of Lieutenant-General Scott.* 2 vols. New York: 1864.

46. *The First Forty Years of Washington Society. Portrayed by Family Letters of Mrs. Samuel Harrison Smith from the Collection of Her Grandson, J. Henley Smith.* Edited by Gaillard Hunt. New York: 1906. By permission of Charles Scribner's Sons.

47. *The Diary of Philip Hone.* Edited by Allan Nevins. New York: 1936. By kind permission of Dodd, Mead and Company.

48. *The Hidden Lincoln, from the Letters and Papers of William H. Herndon.* Edited by Emanuel Hertz. New York: 1938. By kind permission of the Viking Press, Inc.

49. Murat Halstead. *Caucuses of 1860: A History of the National Political Conventions of the Current Presidential Campaign.* Columbus, Ohio: 1860.

50. *Tales, Sketches, and Other Papers. The Complete Works of Nathaniel Hawthorne,* vol. XII. Edited by George Parsons Lathrop. Boston: 1883. By kind permission of Houghton Mifflin Company.

51. F. B. Carpenter. *Six Months at the White House with Abraham Lincoln.* New York: 1867.

52. *Abraham Lincoln's Complete Works.* Vol. II. Edited by John G. Nicolay and John Hay. New York: 1902.

53. *The Diary of Gideon Welles*. Vol. II. Edited by John T. Morse Jr. Boston: 1911. By kind permission of Houghton Mifflin Company.

54. *Reminiscences of Julia Ward Howe, 1819–1899.* Boston: 1899. By kind permission of Houghton Mifflin Company.

55. Anna Elizabeth Dickinson. *What Answer?* Boston: 1868.

56. Eliza Frances Andrews. *The War-Time Journal of a Georgia Girl.* New York: 1908. By kind permission of D. Appleton-Century Company.

57. Ibid.

58. Mary Boykin Chesnut. *A Diary from Dixie.* Edited by Isabella D. Martin and Myrta Lockett Avary. New York: 1905. By kind permission of D. Appleton-Century Company.

59. Abner Doubleday. *Reminiscences of Forts Sumter and Moultrie.* New York: 1876.

60. William Howard Russell. *My Diary North and South.* 2 vols. London: 1863.

61. *Soldiers' Letters from Camp, Battle-field, and Prison.* Edited by Lydia Minturn Post. New York: 1865.

62. *Port Hudson—Its History from an Interior Point of View, as Sketched from the Diary of an Officer.* St. Francisville, La.: 1938. By kind permission of Elrie Robinson.

63. *The Rebellion Record.* Vol. VII. Edited by Frank Moore. New York: 1864.

64. I. Arthur J. L. Fremantle. "The Battle of Gettysburg and the Campaign in Pennsylvania. Extract from the Diary of an English Officer Present with the Confederate Army." *Blackwood's Edinburgh Magazine* (vol. XCIV, 1863).

    II. James Longstreet. *From Manassas to Appomattox.* Philadelphia: 1896.

65. *Memoirs of General William T. Sherman. Himself.* Vol. II. New York: 1875.

66. *Personal Memoirs of U. S. Grant.* Vol. II. New York: 1885, and later editions.

67. Sidney Andrews. *The South Since the War.* Boston: 1866.

68. James Shepherd Pike. *The Prostrate State.* New York: 1874, 1935.

69. Albion Tourgée. *A Fool's Errand: One of the Fools.* New York: 1879.

70. George W. Julian. *Political Recollections, 1840 to 1872.* Chicago: 1884.

71. Walt Whitman. *Democratic Vistas.* Innumerable editions.

72. Grenville M. Dodge. "How We Built the Union Pacific Railway, and Other Railway Papers and Addresses." Pamphlet, no place, no date.

73. Robert Louis Stevenson. *Across the Plains, with Other Memories and Essays.* Numerous editions. By permission of Charles Scribner's Sons.

74. Andy Adams. *The Log of a Cowboy.* Boston: 1927. By permission of Houghton Mifflin Company.

75. Stuart Henry. "The Grasshopper Plague Hits the High Plains" (editor's title) from *Conquering Our Great American Plains.* Copyright 1930 and renewed © 1958 by Stuart Henry. Reprinted by permission of Penguin Group (USA) Inc.

76. Horace White. "The Great Chicago Fire." *Cincinnati Commercial* (October 14, 1871). Reprinted in *A Library of American Literature,* vol. IX. Compiled and edited by Edmund Clarence Stedman and Ellen Mackay Hutchinson. New York: 1889.

77. Jacob A. Riis. *How the Other Half Lives.* New York: 1890, and later editions. By permission of Charles Scribner's Sons.

78. Jane Addams. *Forty Years at Hull House* (New York: Macmillan, 1935). Reprinted with the permission of Simon & Schuster, Inc.

79. Booker T. Washington. *Up from Slavery: An Autobiography.* Copyright 1901, 1929. Reprinted by permission from Doubleday, Doran & Company, Inc.

80. Herbert Quick. Excerpts from *One Man's Life, an Autobiography*. Copyright 1925 by The Bobbs-Merrill Company, renewed 1953 by Ella Corey Quick. Reprinted with the permission of Simon & Schuster, Inc. All rights reserved.

81. Andrew Carnegie. "How I Served My Apprenticeship." *Youth's Companion* (April 23, 1896). Reprinted in *The Gospel of Wealth*. New York: 1906. By kind permission of Mrs. Andrew Carnegie.

82. Henry Ford in collaboration with Samuel Crowther. *My Life and Work*. New York: Doubleday, Doran & Company, Inc., 1922.

83. John D. Rockefeller. *Random Reminiscences of Men and Events*. New York: Doubleday, Doran & Company, Inc., 1908, 1909.

84. *America of Yesterday: The Diary of John Davis Long*. Edited by Lawrence Shaw Mayo. Boston: 1923. By kind permission of Little, Brown and Company.

85. *The Autobiography of George Dewey*. New York: 1913. By permission of Charles Scribner's Sons.

86. Frances E. Willard. *Glimpses of Fifty Years, the Autobiography of an American Woman*. New York: 1889.

87. Brand Whitlock. *Forty Years of It*. New York: 1914. By kind permission of D. Appleton-Century Company.

88. William J. Bryan. *The First Battle: A Story of the Campaign of 1896*. Chicago: 1896.

89. Irwin Hood Hoover. "The Roosevelts Take Over the White House" (editor's title) from *Forty-two Years at the White House*. Copyright 1934 by James Osborne Hoover and Mildred Hoover Stewart, renewed © 1961 by James Osborne Hoover. Reprinted by permission of Houghton Mifflin Harcourt Publishing Company. All rights reserved.

90. *Taft and Roosevelt: The Intimate Letters of Archie Butt, Military Aide*. Vol. II. New York: Doubleday, Doran & Company, Inc., 1930.

91. Brand Whitlock. "Herbert Hoover Feeds the Belgians" (editor's title) from *The Letters and Journal of Brand Whitlock* (New York: Appleton-Century, 1936). Renewed © 1964 by Allan Nevins. Reprinted with permission.

92. Robert Lansing. "Woodrow Wilson Breaks with Germany" (editor's title) from *The War Memoirs of Robert Lansing*. Copyright 1935 by The Bobbs-Merrill Company. Reprinted with the permission of Scribner, a division of Simon & Schuster, Inc.

93. Evalyn Walsh McLean with Boyden Sparkes. *Father Struck It Rich*. Boston: 1936. By kind permission of Little, Brown and Company.

94. Charles Lindbergh. Excerpts from *We*. Copyright 1927 and renewed © 1955 by Charles A. Lindbergh. Reprinted by permission of Penguin Group (USA) Inc.

95. *Documents of American History*. Edited by Henry Steele Commager. New York: 1934.

96. David Lilienthal. Excerpts from *Democracy on the March*. Copyright 1944 and renewed © 1972 by David E. Lilienthal. Twentieth-anniversary edition copyright 1953 by David E. Lilienthal, renewed © 1981 by Helen M. Lilienthal, 1982 by David E. Lilienthal, Jr. Reprinted by permission of HarperCollins Publishers.

97. Cordell Hull. "Japan Strikes at Pearl Harbor" (editor's title) from *The Memoirs of Cordell Hull* (New York: Macmillan, 1948). Reprinted with the permission of the Estate of Cordell Hull.

98. John Hersey. "The Marines Cross a River Under Fire on Guadalcanal" (editor's title) from *Into the Valley: A Skirmish of the Marines* (New York: Alfred A. Knopf, 1943). Reprinted with the permission of the Estate of John Hersey.

99. Dwight D. Eisenhower. Excerpts from *Crusade in Europe*. Copyright 1948 by Dwight D. Eisenhower. Used by permission of Doubleday, a division of Random House, Inc.

100. Ernie Pyle. *Brave Men*. New York: 1944. By permission of Henry Holt and Company, Inc.

101. William E. Laurence. "An American Plane Ushers in the Atomic Age" from *The New York Times* (September 9, 1945). Reprinted with the permission of PARS International Corp. All rights reserved.

102. Carl T. Rowan. Excerpts from *South of Freedom*. Copyright 1952 by Carl T. Rowan. Used by permission of Alfred A. Knopf, a division of Random House, Inc.

103. Roger Kahn. *The Boys of Summer*. Copyright © 1972 by Roger Kahn. Reprinted with the permission of Frankfurt, Garbus, Klein & Selz, as agents for the author.

104. Paul H. Nitze. Excerpts from *From Hiroshima to Glasnost: A Memoir*. Copyright © 1989 by Paul Nitze. Reprinted by permission of SLL/Sterling Lord Literistic, Inc.

105. George Kennan. *Memoirs 1925–1950*. Copyright © 1967 by George Kennan. Reprinted with the permission of Little, Brown and Company, Inc.

106. Merle Miller. "Harry Truman Fires Douglas MacArthur" (editor's title) from *Plain Speaking: An Oral Biography of Harry Truman*. Copyright © 1973, 1974 by Merle Miller. Used by permission of G. P. Putnam's Sons, a division of Penguin Group (USA) Inc.

107. Dean Acheson, excerpts from *Present at Creation: My Years in the State Department*. Copyright © 1969 by Dean Acheson. Used by permission of W.W. Norton & Company, Inc.

108. Rosa Parks. Excerpts from *Rosa Parks: My Story*. Copyright © 1992 by Rosa Parks. Used by permission of Dial Books for Young Readers, a division of Penguin Young Readers Group, a division of Penguin Group (USA) Inc.

109. Robert Palmer. "The Honky-Tonk Roots of Rock 'n' Roll" (editor's title) from *Rock & Roll: An Unruly History*. Copyright © 1995 by Robert Palmer. Used by permission of WGBH Educational Foundation.

110. Edward R. Murrow. "Guildhall Speech on Television and Politics" from *In Search of Light: The Broadcasts of Edward R. Murrow*. Copyright © 1967 by the Estate of Edward R. Murrow. Used by permission of Alfred A. Knopf, a division of Random House, Inc.

111. Dwight D. Eisenhower, "Farewell Address," January 17, 1961.

112. John F. Kennedy, "Inaugural Address," January 20, 1961.

113. Martin Luther King, Jr., "Letter from Birmingham Jail." Copyright © 1963 by Martin Luther King, Jr., copyright renewed 1991 by Coretta Scott King. Reprinted with the permission of The Heirs to the Estate of Martin Luther King, Jr. c/o Writer's House, LLC as agent for the proprietor.

114. Martin Luther King, Jr., "March on Washington." Copyright © 1970 by Martin Luther King, Jr., copyright renewed 1998 by Coretta Scott King. Reprinted with the permission of The Heirs to the Estate of Martin Luther King, Jr. c/o Writer's House, LLC as agent for the proprietor.

115. William S. White. "A Journalist Reflects on President Kennedy's Assassination" (editor's title) from *The Making of a Journalist* (Lexington: University Press of Kentucky, 1986). Copyright © 1986 by William S. White. Reprinted with the permission of the Estate of William S. White.

116. Lyndon Johnson, "Great Society Speech," May 22, 1964.

117. Malcolm X. Excerpts from *The Autobiography of Malcolm X*. Copyright © 1964 by

Malcolm X and Alex Haley. Copyright © 1965 by Alex Haley and Betty Shabazz. Used by permission of Random House, Inc.

118. Betty Friedan. "Introduction" from *The Feminine Mystique.* Copyright © 1983, 1974, 1973, 1963 by Betty Friedan. Used by permission of W.W. Norton & Company, Inc.

119. Connie Dvorkin. "The Suburban Scene" from *Sisterhood Is Powerful: An Anthology of Writings from the Women's Liberation Movement.* Edited by Robin Morgan. Copyright © 1970 by Robin Morgan. Reprinted with the permission of Edite Kroll Literary Agency Inc.

120. Jerry Shank. "'We Are Losing, Morale Is Bad' . . . 'If They'd Give Us Good Planes': A Pilot's Letters Home: November 1963–March 1964." Copyright © 1964 by U.S. News & World Report. Reprinted with permission.

121. Norman Mailer. *Miami and the Siege of Chicago: An Informal History of the Republican and Democratic Conventions of 1968.* Copyright © 1968 by Norman Mailer. Reprinted with the permission of Norman Mailer Licensing LLC.

122. Neil Armstrong. Excerpts from *First on the Moon.* Copyright © 1970 by Little, Brown and Company, Inc. Reprinted by permission of Little, Brown and Company.

123. Walter Cronkite. Excerpts from *A Reporter's Life.* Copyright © 1997 by Walter Cronkite. Used by permission of Alfred A. Knopf, a division of Random House, Inc.

124. Hunter S. Thompson. *Fear and Loathing in Las Vegas.* Copyright © 1971 by Hunter S. Thompson. Used by permission of Random House, Inc.

125. Richard Nixon. Excerpts from *RN: The Memoirs of Richard Nixon.* Copyright © 1978 by Richard Nixon. Reprinted with the permission of Grand Central Publishing.

126. Keyes Beech. "We Clawed for Our Lives!" from *The Chicago Sun-Times* (May 1, 1975). Copyright © 1975. Reprinted with the permission of the Chicago Sun-Times.

127. Zbigniew Brzezinski. *Power and Principle: Memoirs of the National Security Adviser, 1977–1981.* Copyright © 1983 by Zbigniew Brzezinski. Reprinted by permission of Farrar, Straus & Giroux, LLC.

128. Ronald Reagan. *Inaugural Addresses*, January 20, 1981 and January 20, 1985.

129. George W. Ball. Excerpts from *The Past Has Another Pattern.* Copyright © 1982 by George W. Ball. Used by permission of W.W. Norton & Company, Inc.

130. Peggy Noonan. "Ronald Reagan" from *Time* (April 13, 1998). Copyright © 1998 by Peggy Noonan. Reprinted with the permission of William Morris Agency, Inc.

131. Colin L. Powell. Excerpts from *My American Journey.* Copyright © 1995 by Colin L. Powell. Used by permission of Random House, Inc.

132. Elena Caceres. "Fifty Years in America: Through Back Doors" from *Multiamerica,* edited by Ishmael Reed. Copyright © 1997 by Elena Caceres. Used by permission of Viking Penguin, a division of Penguin Group (USA) Inc.

133. Bill Gates. Excerpts from *The Road Ahead.* Copyright © 1995 by William H. Gates III. Used by permission of Viking Penguin, a division of Penguin Group (USA) Inc.

134. Douglas Brinkley. "Educating the Generation Called 'X'" from *The Washington Post* (April 3, 1994). Copyright © 1994 by Douglas Brinkley. Reprinted by permission.

135. George Bush and Brent Scowcroft. "Reflections on the End of the Cold War" (editor's title) from *A World Transformed.* Copyright © 1989 by George Bush and Brent Scowcroft. Used by permission of Alfred A. Knopf, a division of Random House, Inc.

136. Morris Dees. "Militia Threats in the Wake of the Oklahoma City Bombing" (editor's

title) from *The Gathering Storm*. Copyright © 1996 by Morris Dees and James Corcoran. Reprinted by permission of HarperCollins Publishers.

137. Michael Kinsley. "Outrage That Wasn't" from *Time* (December 28, 1998). Copyright © 1998 by Time, Inc. Reprinted with permission.

138. Al Gore. "2000 Presidential Concession Speech," December 13, 2000.

139. George W. Bush. "Address to a Joint Session of Congress Following the 9/11 Attacks," September 20, 2001.

140. Staff Sergeant David Bellavia. Excerpt from *House to House: An Epic Memoir of War*. Copyright © 2007 by David Bellavia. Reprinted with the permission of The Free Press, a division of Simon & Schuster, Inc.

141. John Boutté. Excerpt from "John Boutté—The Musician" from *The Katrina Experience: An Oral History Project,* http://thekatrinaexperience.net. Reprinted with permission.

142. Barack Obama. "A More Perfect Union," speech delivered March 18, 2008, Philadelphia, Pennsylvania.

Index